Eighth International Conference on Information Systems, Logistics and Supply Chain (ILS 2020)

Interconnected Supply Chains in an Era of Innovation

Austin, Texas, USA
22 – 24 April 2020

ISBN: 978-1-7138-1065-0

Printed from e-media with permission by:

Curran Associates, Inc.
57 Morehouse Lane
Red Hook, NY 12571

Texas State University
McCoy College of Business
601 University Drive
San Marcos Texas, USA
78666-4684

Phone: (512) 245-3189

www.txst.edu

Additional copies of this publication are available from:

Curran Associates, Inc.
57 Morehouse Lane
Red Hook, NY 12571 USA
Phone: 845-758-0400
Fax: 845-758-2633
Email: curran@proceedings.com
Web: www.proceedings.com

ILS2020

INFORMATION SYSTEMS, LOGISTICS & SUPPLY CHAIN
April 22-24, 2020, Austin, TX, US

TEXAS STATE UNIVERSITY

The rising STAR of Texas

Interconnected Supply Chains in an Era of Innovation

PROCEEDINGS OF THE EIGHT INTERNATIONAL CONFERENCE ON INFORMATION SYSTEMS, LOGISTICS AND SUPPLY CHAIN (ILS 2020)

Scientific Committee Chairs

Gülgün Alpan – gulgun.alpan@grenoble-inp.fr
Tahir Ekin – tahirekin@txstate.edu
Jesus Gonzalez-Feliu – jesus.gonzalez-feli@emse.fr

April 22-24, 2020

I L S 2020

INFORMATION SYSTEMS, LOGISTICS & SUPPLY CHAIN

Interconnected Supply Chains in an Era of Innovation

Eight International Conference on Information Systems, Logistics and Supply Chain (ILS) April 22-24, 2020, Austin, Texas, US.

COMMENTS FROM ILS 2020 ORGANIZING CHAIR

Texas State University was really excited to host The Eight International Conference on Information, Logistics and Supply Chain - ILS 2020 -- April 22-24, 2020. The central theme of this edition was "**Interconnected Supply Chains in an Era of Innovation.**"

To reach competitive advantage in an era of constant innovation, organizations ought to develop infrastructure that integrates internal functions as well as relationships with suppliers, customers and all of the partners within integrated supply chains. Such theme to exchange research and practices on trends, vulnerabilities, and risks in obtaining integrated supply chains indeed became even more crucial in the unprecedent situation of the Pandemic COVID 19. Supply chain decisions provide appropriate responses to manage challenges and opportunities associated with innovative technologies, **demand uncertainty**, and deployment of all the shareholders concerned with the economic, social and environmental pillars of sustainability.

The 8th Edition of ILS 2020 conference was aligned to provide a remarkable opportunity for the academic and industrial community to discuss and share their experiences and developments under topics such as:

- Information and Decision Systems for Supply Chain Management
- E-supply Chain
- Logistics Planning and Management
- Logistics Sectors
- Supply Chain Design
- Supply Chain Management
- Supply Chain and Operations Analytics

- Capabilities in the Supply Chain

The Eight International Conference on Information, Logistics and Supply Chain - ILS 2020 to take place in Austin Texas, April 22-24, 2020 was cancelled on March 11, 2020 due to the COVID 19 pandemic. Such a difficult decision was taken after rigorous consideration and based on recent reports from the **Centers of Disease Control** (CDC) and **World Health Organization** (WHO) about the spread of coronavirus (COVID-19). Our primary concern was to protect everyone involved with the conference from contracting or spreading COVID-19.
The decision to cancel the ILS 2020 conference was not made lightly; however, given that many of our participants and attendees come from Asia, Africa, Europe, US and Latin America holding the conference would result in unnecessary risk. Consultation was done with the ILS Board of Trustees, ILS Scientific Advisory Committee, local and state institutions, etc. before arriving to this decision.

Understanding that our registrants may be feeling disappointed about missing the opportunity to share their latest research developments, the ILS 2020 organizing committee and scientific committee chairs decided that accepted manuscripts of the registered participants as of March 11, 2020 will be available in the Proceedings of the Eighth International Conference on Information, Logistics & Supply Chain – ILS 2020.

ILS 2020 recognizes and greatly appreciates the hard work and dedication many of its members put into developing the conference — especially the Scientific Committee Chairs – Gülgün Alpan, Tahir Ekin, and Jesus Gonzalez-Feliu as well as the Scientific Committee members. They took care of the peer-review process of submitted manuscripts. We are equally grateful to the Industrial Committee Chairs, especially to Ana Badell and Jesus Jimenez for working diligently in selecting the Industrial speakers and putting together panelist for forums with a variety of backgrounds in the topics of the ILS 2020 conference. Special thanks go to the Salah Elmaghraby PhD Student Competition Chairs and committee. We also appreciate the support and generosity from McCoy College of Business and our academic and industrial sponsors.

Looking forward to meeting you at future ILS conferences.

Cecilia Temponi, PhD
Chair of the ILS 2020 Organizing Committee.
Texas State University
San Marcos, TX 78666

COMMENTS FROM ILS 2020 SCIENTIFIC COMMITTEE CHAIRS

The call for papers for ILS 2020 was launched in April 2019, both for invited sessions and regular papers. Initial deadline for the submissions was September 15th, 2019, which was extended to October 15th due to numerous requests from the authors. We are grateful to the members of the scientific committee for their engagement and punctuality in the evaluation process so that we were able to notify the authors on December 15th 2019.

We received 77 papers from 24 countries for this 8th edition of the ILS conference:

23% of the articles were joint work from two or more countries: France and Morocco (4 articles), France and United States (2), Sri-Lanka and New Zealand (1), Pakistan and Hong Kong (1), France, Germany and Turkey (1), South Korea and United States (1), France and Canada (1), United States and China (1), Colombia and Spain (1), Colombia and France (1), Mexico and United States (1), Turkey and United States (1), Mexico and France (1), United Arab Emirates and Tunisia (1)

The remaining 77% are distributed as follows: Brazil (13 articles), France (13), United States (10), Canada (7), Morocco (3), Colombia (2), Italy (2), Germany (2), Chile (1), Belgium (1). India (1), Iran (1), Mexico (1), South Korea (1), United Kingdom (1).

The topic distribution of the submitted articles were as follows:

- Information and Decision Systems for Supply Chain Management (11)
- E-supply Chain (4)
- Logistics Planning and Management (6)
- Logistics Sectors (4)
- Supply Chain Design (7)
- Supply Chain Management (6)
- Supply Chain and Operations Analytics (9)
- Capabilities in the Supply Chain (3)
- Invited sessions (19)
- Student competition (8)

We are glad to have geographic and thematic diversity in the invited paper submissions which are scheduled in four sessions. The first invited session is titled "Logistics in Food Supply Chains", and is proposed by João Gilberto Mendes Dos Reis (Paulista University, Brazil). The second invited session organized by Alexandra Lagorio (University of Bergamo, Italy). It focuses oninnovative technologies for last-mile logistics and supply chains. The third session that focuses on ecommerce in urban freight and logistics is proposed by Miguel Figliozzi (Portland State

University, USA). Last invited session is proposed by Evren Sahin (Centrale Supélec, France) with a focus on supply chain analytics.

The scientific committee is composed of 65 scholars from all around the world (see http://www.ils2020conference.com/committee for the exact list). All the papers are initially screened by one of the chairs, and then reviewed by at least two other members of the scientific committee. Out of 77 submissions, 3 of them are rejected prior to review, out of remaining 74, we are glad to publish 55 papers.

After the reviews were compiled, the papers were sent back to authors with revision requests. Once the authors submitted the revisions, chairs did another round of checks ensuring the reviewers' feedback is addressed and incorporated into the revised version. We should emphasize that full responsibility for the paper rests with the author. The authors must have taken the necessary steps to obtain permission for using any material that might be protected by copyright. Papers that do not comply with the template were returned to the authors for corrections; however, the inclusion of the paper in the proceedings is subject to meeting the deadline required by the company publishing the proceedings. We are happy to emphasize that the proceedings is indexed by Scopus.

For the ILS 2020, we also programmed six exciting keynote speeches. Some of the keynote speakers were part of the Industrial Day and coordinated by the Industrial Committee Chairs;

- Ms. Ana Badell, COO of Beauty Counter, USA.
- Dr. Valerie Botta-Genoulaz, INSA, France.
- Dr. Jesus Jimenez, Texas State University, USA

The Keynote Speakers follow:

Keynote speakers

Ou Tang
Editor for the International journal of production economics
Professor of production economics
Linköping University, Sweden
Title: *Text Mining for Data Collection in Production Economics Research*

Jose Holguin-Vera
Director Of The Center For Infrastructure, Transportation, And The Environment
William H. Hart Professor

Rensselaer Polytechnic Institute, USA
Title: *Urban Logistics in Times of Rapid (and Unpredictable) Technological Change: The Good, The Bad, and The Ugly*

Leonardo Bonanni
President & CEO
Source Map - USA
Title: *Transparency in the Supply Chain: Blockchain*

Patrick Gibbons
President
Emerson Group – USA
Title: *2nd Revolution of Convenience*

Sila Çetinkaya
Department Chair & Professor
Cecil H. Green Professor Of Engineering
Southern Methodist University, USA
Title: *Reengineering the Supply Chain via Integration and Coordination*

Rafael Farromeque
Head Of Infrastructure Integration & Logistics Practice
Development Bank Of Latin America, Mexico
Title: *Promoting Logistics Development in Latin America: Logistics Corridors as a tool for improving productivity*

In these proceedings you will find all contributions (from regular and invited sessions) having submitted a final paper in the required format and having at least one author registered to the conference before the deadline related to their publishing was met. We thank all scientific and organizing committee members for their support and contribution and hope to having more exiting and interesting ILS conferences in next editions.

Gülgün Alpan, Tahir Ekin, Jesus Gonzales Feliu
Co-chairs of the Scientific Committee ILS 2020

This page intentionally left blank.

ILS Advisory and steering committees

Board of Trustees

Executive Committee

ILS 2020 Program Committee

Organization Committee

Chair

Cecilia Temponi	Texas State University (United States of America)

Members

Valérie Botta-Genoulaz	DISP - INSA-Lyon (France)
Francis A. Mendez	Texas State University (United States of America)
Diana Raulier	Permanent Secretaty of ILS Board of Trustees (Belgium)
Fouad Riane	Ecole Centrale Casablanca (Moroco)
Nikolay Tchernev	Université d'Auvergne, LIMOS UMR CNRS 6158 (France)

Scientific Committee

Co-chairs

Gülgün Alpan	Grenoble INP (France)
Tahir Ekin	Texas State University (United States of America)
Jesus Gonzalez-Feliu	Excelia Group La Rochelle Business School (France)

Members

El-Houssaine Aghezzaf	Department of Industrial Management, Ghent University (Belgium)
Madalena Araujo	University of Minho (Portugal)
Jannicke Baalsrud	Hauge Bremer Institut fur Produktion und Logistik /University of Bremen (Germany)
Hyerim Bae	Pusan National University (South Korea)
Erica Ballantyne	The University of Shefield (United Kingdom)
Eric Ballot	Mines ParisTech (France)
Lyes Benyoucef	LSIS UMR7296 (France)
Valérie Botta-Genoulaz	DISP - INSA-Lyon (France)
Miguel Gaston Cedillo Campos	Instituto Mexicano del Transporte, Mexico
Vincent Cheutet	DISP - INSA Lyon (France)
Ton de Kok	Eindhoven University of Technology (The Netherlands)
René De Koster	Erasmus University Rotterdam (The Netherlands)
Christine Di Martinelly	IESEG School of Management (France)
Alexandre Dolgui	IMT Atlantique, LS2N, CNRS (France)
Wedad Elmaghraby	University of Maryland (United States of America)
Jan Fransoo	Kuehne Logistics University (Germany)
Yannick Frein	Université de Grenoble (France)

Jonathan Gaudreault	Laval University (Canada)
Virginie Goepp	INSA Strasbourg ICube (France)
Didier Gourc	Ecole des Mines Albi (France)
Bernard Grabot	ENIT (France)
Shivam Gupta	University of Nebraska Lincoln (United States of America)
Arni Halldorsson	Chalmers University of Technology (Sweden)
Ramzi Hammami	ESC Rennes School of Business (France)
Tongdan Jin	Texas State University (United States of America)
Gulver Karamemis	University of Rhode Island (United States of America)
Walid Klibi	CIRRELT (Canada) & KEDGE Business School (France)
Dincer Konur	Texas State University (United States of America)
Matthieu Lauras	Mines Albi (France)
Jacques Lamothe	Mines Albi (France)
Manuel Mateo	Universitat Politécnica de Catalunya (Spain)
Joao Gilberto Mendes Dos Reis	Universidade Paulista, Brazil
Francis A. Mendez	Texas State University (United States of America)
Jairo R. Montoya-Torres	Universidad de La Sabana (Colombia)
Giovanni Mummolo	Politecnico di Bari (Italy)
Imen Nouira	ESC Rennes Business School (France)
Mustapha Nourelfath	Laval University (Canada)
Julio Alejandro Padilla Solis	Universidad de Lima (Peru)
Markus Rabe	TU Dortmund (Germany)
Fouad Riane	Ecole Centrale Casablanca (Moroco)
Jose Ribeiro	University of Sao Paulo (Brazil)
Ralph Riedel	TU Chemnitz (Germany)
Diane Riopel	Ecole Polytechnique de Montréal (Canada)
Mikael Ronnqvist	Laval University (Canada)
Evren Sahin	ECP (France)
Ivan Sanchez-Diaz Chalmers	University of Technology (Sweden)
Nikolay Tchernev	Université d'Auvergne, LIMOS UMR CNRS 6158 (France)
Cecilia Temponi	Texas State University (United States of America)
Laura Turrini	EBS Business School (Germany)
Bruno Vallespir	IMS, University of Bordeaux (France)
Nico Vandaele	Katholieke Universiteit Leuven (Belgium)
Marino Widmer	University of Fribourg (Germany)
Hugo Yoshizaki	University of Sao Paulo (Brazil)

Industrial Committee

Co-chairs

Ana Badell	COO of Beauty Counter University (United States of America)
Valerie Botta-Genoulaz	DISP – INSA Lyon (France)
Jesus Jimenez	Texas State University (United States of America)

Members

Valérie Botta-Genoulaz	DISP - INSA-Lyon (France)
Francis A. Mendez	Texas State University (United States of America)
Diana Raulier	Permanent Secretaty of ILS Board of Trustees (Belgium)
Fouad Riane	Ecole Centrale Casablanca (Moroco)
Nikolay Tchernev	Université d'Auvergne, LIMOS UMR CNRS 6158 (France)

PhD Student Competition

Co-chairs

Wedad Elmaghraby	University of Maryland (United States of America)
Fouad Riane	Ecole Centrale Casablanca (Moroco)

Members

El-Houssaine Aghezzaf	Department of Industrial Management, Ghent University (Belgium)
Luis Antonio De Santa Eulalia	Sherbrook University (Canada)
Ramzi Hammami	ESC Rennes School of Business (France)
Manuel Mateo	Universitat Politécnica de Catalunya (Spain)
Jairo R. Montoya-Torres	Universidad de La Sabana (Colombia)

ILS 2020 additional reviewers

Mohammed-Hichame Benbitour	CentraleSupelec (France)
Mario Chong	Universidad del Pacifico (Peru)
Miguel Angel Figliozzi	Portland State University (United States of America)
Gustavo Gatica	Universidad Andrés Bello (Chile)
Ali Khodadad Saryazdi	Mines Saint-Etienne (France)
Alexandra Lagorio	Università di Bergamo (Italy)
Mancini, Simona	Cagliari University (Italy)
Carlos Osorio Ramirez	Universidad Nacional de Colombia (Colombia)
Laura Vanessa Palacios Arguello	Université Paris Est (France)
Salomée Ruel	Excelia Group La Rochelle Business School (France)
Giovanni Zenezini	Politecnico di Torino (Italy)

8th International Conference in Information, Logistics & Supply Chain

CONFERENCE PROGRAM as set on at March 15, 2020

April 21 – Tuesday
1:30 pm- 5:00 pm -- PhD Student Competition

April 22 – Wednesday
8:00 am - Continental Breakfast
8:30 am – Welcoming & Opening of the 8th International Conference on Information, Logistics & Supply Chain.
Dean of McCoy College of Business – Denise Smart

9:00 am – 10:15 am -- Plenary Speaker: **Ou Tang -- ESC – Rennes, France**
Text Mining for Data Collection in Production Economics Research
10:15 am – Break
10:30 am – noon – Parallel Sessions for Regular Papers & Invited Sessions – There are four parallel sessions

Noon – 1:30 pm – Lunch

1:30 pm – 2:45 pm – Plenary Speaker: **Jose Holguin-Vera – RPI, NY**
Urban Logistics in Times of Rapid (and Unpredictable) Technological Change: The Good, The Bad, and The Ugly

2:45 pm – 3:00 pm – Break
3:00 pm – 5:00 pm – Parallel Sessions for Regular Papers & Invited Session - There are three parallel sessions

5:00 pm – 6:00pm -- BOT & Scientific Committee join meeting

6:15 pm – 7:15 pm – Welcoming reception.

April 23 – Thursday
8:45 am – 9:00 am – Opening of the Industrial Day
9:00 am – 10:15 am -- Plenary Speaker: **Leonardo Bonanni – SourceMap, NY**
Transparency in the Supply Chain: Blockchain

10:15 am – Break
10:30 am – noon – Industrial Forum: **Industry-Relevant Problems in Logistics 4.0**
Noon – 1:30 pm – Lunch

1:30 pm – 2:45 pm – Plenary Speaker & Panel: **Patrick Gibbons – Emerson Group**
2nd Revolution of Convenience

2:45 pm – 3:00 pm – Break

3:00 pm – 5:00 pm – Industrial Forum/Demo: **Smart Manufacturing: Opportunities and Challenges**

6:30 pm – 9:30 pm – Gala Dinner

Companies collaborating – Advanced Technology Consultants, Amazon, Emerson Group, Geodis, PlusOne Robotics, Source Map, Beauty Counter.

April 24 – Friday

9:00 am – 10:15 am -- Plenary Speaker: **Sila Cetinkaya - SMU**
Reengineering the Supply Chain via Integration and Coordination

10:15 am – Break

10:30 am – noon – Parallel Sessions for Regular Papers & Invited Sessions – There are four parallel sessions

Noon – 1:30 pm – Lunch

1:30 pm – 2:45 pm – Plenary speaker: **Rafael Farromeque – CAF, Mexico**
Promoting Logistics Development in Latin America: Logistics Corridors as a tool for improving productivity

2:45 pm- 3:00 pm – Break

3:00pm -4:45pm -- Parallel Sessions for Regular Papers – There are three parallel sessions.

5:00 pm – Closing reception.

Table of Contents

I L S 2020
INTERNATIONAL CONFERENCE ON INFORMATION SYSTEMS, LOGISTICS & SUPPLY CHAIN
Austin, Texas April 22-24, 2020

Efficient Product Representations for Automotive Demand and Capacity Management

Daniel Fruhner [1], Katja Klingebiel [1], Axel Wagenitz [2], Michael Toth [3]

[1] 1 Dortmund University of Applied Sciences and Arts, Dortmund, Germany
[2] Hamburg University of Applied Sciences, Hamburg, Germany
[3] Bochum University of Applied Sciences, Bochum, Germany
{daniel.fruhner@fh-dortmund.de, katja.klingebiel@fh-dortmund.de, axel.wagenitz@haw-hamburg.de, michael.toth@hs-bochum.de}

Abstract. Motived by the experience with a large online marketplace, we study a middle-mile network design problem in e-commerce. One novel feature in our problem is that while we decide the network configuration, the network flow and shortfall are controlled by the fulfillment policy employed by a different decision entity and are unknown. We develop a predictive model for the unknown response using observed shipment data. In particular, we apply the idea of decomposition in developing the predictive model. The predictive model is then embedded in the network design. To solve this problem, we characterize it as a c-supermodular minimization problem and propose two linear time approximation algorithms. In a numerical study, we demonstrate that these two algorithms are scalable and effective.

Keywords: E-commerce Fulfillment, Scalability, Machine Learning, Approximation Algorithm.

1. Introduction

Today, car manufacturers (original equipment manufacturers – OEMs) are offering a wide variety of models and options and are continually renewing the broad product range [1] to keep up with the strong international competition [2]. For example, the average number of possible variants of the five top-selling cars of German OEMs (Audi A4, BMW 3 Series, Mercedes C-Class, Opel Astra, Volkswagen Golf) is $4.4*10^{25}$ [3]. Customers have to deal with this diversity of variants and expect that car orders can be adapted until shortly before their production date and that a fast and precise delivery takes place [4, 5].
In production, every customer-ordered variant requires a different set of parts and modules. Today's cars are highly complex, with many rapidly evolving parts that have dependencies between each other. In consequence, the coordination of material and the related information-flow within the supply chain is a challenging and influential task in automotive logistics [6]. Especially, Demand and Capacity Management (DCM) as an integral part of logistics is responsible for the efficient allocation of demand requirements to available capacities, i.e. supplier capacities, production resources and material stocks [7]. If deviations between demands and capacities occur, it is the task of the DCM to identify, evaluate and initiate suitable countermeasures for resolving or avoiding critical situations [8]. Both, demands and capacities are regarded as variable factors and adjusted within defined restrictions [7].
Therefore, already nowadays, information technology supports increasingly successfully the complex DCM processes, but all DCM systems rely on an efficient and holistic information model covering all variants and processes – the product representation (PR). Generally, PRs are product knowledge decomposed into its elemental components (parts and options), where components are either physical or a non-physical artifact (service and software components) [9, 10]. In order to be able to translate customer orders into material demands, in the automotive PR for DCM, sales information (models and options), productions information (modules and parts), as well as logistics information (demands and capacities) have to be consolidated and connected [11]. Thus, automotive PRs are highly complex and crossfunctional. Furthermore, the requirements on these representations are continuously changing due to technological trends such as e-mobility and the digitization of cars [12]: Automotive components are getting obsolete (e.g. exhaust system in an electric vehicle), others change from physical to software components (e.g. navigation software components now running on a domain controller). Therefore, also the information to be held changes drastically. Moreover, todays PR does not document such dependencies sufficiently and these complex information is currently distributed over several systems in relational data structures [13]. In order to meet future challenges, this contribution presents an adaptable,

cross-functional and holistically integrated PR for automotive DCM, which has been validated in the German automotive industry.
The next section provides an introduction to automotive DCM. Here, all relevant terms and concepts will be described. This is followed by an introduction to automotive PRs including a respective state of the art. Information needed in an efficient graph-based PR for the automotive DCM is structured in section 4. Afterwards, section 5 describes a concept for an efficient PR for the automotive DCM as well as the validation at a German OEM. This contribution closes with a summary and a description of future work.

2. The Automotive Demand and Capacity Management

This section gives a short introduction into automotive DCM. A more in depths insight into the state of the art can be found for example in Temur et al. [14] or in Pawlikowski et al. [8].
The typical automotive DCM planning cycle is initiated by the sales department. Here, the forecasting and planning of mid-term future market demands are focused [15] covering the period from three to twelve months into the future [16]. In this first step, model volumes and option quotas (e.g. the proportion of models with xenon light or with a navigation system) are planned for all sales regions (models of a car series like the VW Golf further specify for example body type, engine and gear type). The basis for the planning is information of the automotive market (e.g. forecasts) and actual and historical orders [17–19]. In addition, the planning of sales quotas for options is influenced by strategies of each sales region, technical restrictions, strategic product decisions or anticipated customer preferences. The sales plan is then converted into a production program for all plants [17]. The consolidation of the planned demands with already existing orders, which are typically available for closer periods, is part of this step.
Due to the variety of products, the planning effort for these steps is enormous. A typical mid-range series offers about 30 to 50 different car models with up to 200 options each. As a result, several thousand different volumes and up to 10 million associated option quotas have to be planned for only one series covering all sales regions and models over a certain time period [8]. In order to ensure the integrity of the plan, the compatibility of options for a respective model is given by technical rules (TECRules) must be considered thoroughly.
Resulting plans must then be aligned with production and supply chain. In order to balance demand and resource requirements with constraints and limitations, it is necessary to close the gap between demand information (models and option quotas) and capacity information which can be given model-wise, option-wise or part-wise [13, 16, 20]. For this step, bill of material rules (BOMRules) represent the connection between the car model with its configuration, i.e. options, and the derivable part demand. The totality of rules for a mid-range series amounts for about 15,000 TECRules and 600,000 BOMRules. Figure 1 illustrates how the gap between demand- and capacity information is bridged within a state of the art DCM.

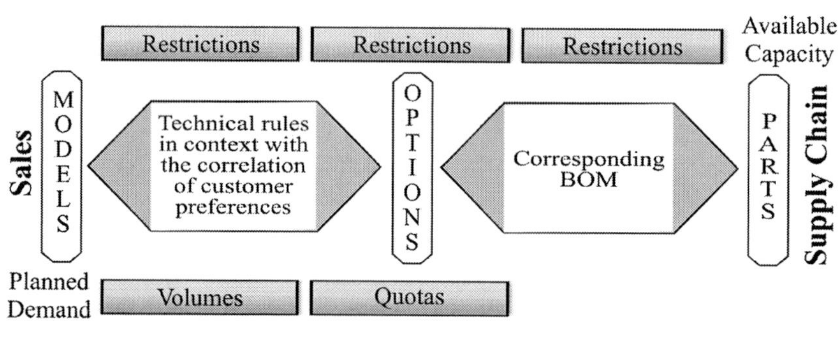

Figure 1: DCM bridges the gap between demand- and capacity information [8]

But, a large proportion of the part demand depends not only on model volumes and quotas for options but on a specific combination of model, options and sales region. When fully specified orders are available, the gap between demand and capacity can easily be closed as fully specified orders allow the derivation of part demands by BOM explosion using BOMRules. However, due to the short order-to-delivery times as opposed to long supply chain times in many cases, the DCM process has to work extensively on forecasts and plans rather than orders [15].

The planning itself is complex and challenging, due to the market dynamics, uncertainty in forecasting, the complexity of car configurations and the relationships between models, options and parts, the continuous changes of the product itself and changes in the supply chain [8, 21]. Additionally, it is characterized by conflicting goals. The sales department is under pressure to react to volatile markets, intensified global competitors and changing customer requirements. Therefore, flexibility and the ability to react to changes are required. In addition, production demands a stable production program that guarantees high capacity utilization and optimal operating results. Moreover, in order to proactively avoid bottlenecks and negotiate the optimal capacities and flexibility with suppliers, material planning aims to determine part demands as early as possible.

This conflict can be described as the dilemma of automotive DCM [22]. Numerous workshops and committee meetings between sales, program- and material planning try to solve all issues [17, 21]. There is no integrated, consistent data model here as each department uses its own data sources. Moreover, due to the long planning cycles of four to six weeks, there is a lack of flexibility in responding to market changes. In consequence, the program is manually adjusted between program releases and also after the program stop (i.e. within the so-called frozen period) [17]. Lack of program stability and lack of transparency about future part demands on the supply side are a result of these adjustments. The risk of bottlenecks increases and causes increased internal costs.

Concluding, DCM acts as an essential interface between market, production and supply chain processes [5, 23]. The ability to analyze and optimize quickly in the sense of a permanent willingness to plan is required [24] in order to handle variant diversity, process complexity and the dynamics inherent in the supply chain. One critical aspect is that the relevant product and planning information is complex, allocated to different departments and distributed across a number of systems. The various data elements such as TECRules, volumes, option quotas, BOMRules, capacity information and more are not integrated consistently. The first step to more efficiently support a proactive and fast DCM planning process is to transparently integrate all relevant information into a common information model, i.e. a cross-functional PR for DCM. The next sections gives the respective state of the art.

3. Automotive Product Representations

To ensure the alignment of demand and capacities in DCM the dependencies between components, car characteristics and planning information have to be depicted within a PR in a structured way [12]. In Fruhner et al. [13] further requirements on PRs based on upcoming challenges for the automotive industry have been defined: *New dependencies* such as the compatibility of software versions must be integrated in addition to already documented dependencies in BOMRules and TECRules. The integration of *cross-functional information* is necessary to support every phase of the product life cycle. Innovation cycles for products of new technologies are accelerating and the consistent compatibility of parts and modules must be ensured, especially as today electronic systems and their software are developed faster than car types. Consequently, a *modularity* of the PR is required. As the product car is becoming more and more complex, comprehensive and *complex information* has to be managed. And last, to identify possible bottlenecks quickly, *transparent data structures* are necessary to avoid internal expenses and a deterioration of the distribution to the customer.

Primarily, the product structure, which is a structured form of the product and its components, is an essential part of the PR [25]. But, as DCM processes synchronize market demands with capacities and restrictions of the supply chain and the production system, information on e.g. the relationship between planning information (planned model volumes, option quotas) and supply chain information (capacities and restrictions) is additionally required.

Today, the respective automotive data is typically stored in several distributed systems relying on relational data structures [13]. Relational database approaches easily lead to low transparency, contradictions and redundancy as the data is spread across multiple departments [26].

Considering the above illustrated requirements, other data structures might apply better regarding an efficient representation of the complex multi-dimensional and cross-functional information. One option is the Design Structure Matrix (DSM) [9, 26] which is already applied in automotive development. Nevertheless, a DSM merely visualizes one-dimensional relationships and does not allow to integrate additional cross-functional data, since its structure becomes easily intransparent in tabular form [10].

Semantic networks as another option can only map similar relationships between two data elements. No kind of hierarchy (as in automotive product structure prevalent) or an overall view can be integrated here. Thus, transparency and application are limited in complex data environments [26].
A promising approach is the widespread tree structure as presented for example by Kesper [27] and Schuh [25]. A disadvantage can be seen in the non-existing native modularity. Furthermore, tree structures, in general, can become very complex [27]. Nevertheless, ElMaraghy et al. [28] have introduced an approach with evolving parts/product families. Vegetti et al. [29] present a promising ontology-based approach. Relations of two or more components and more complex (partial) structures like hierarchies and sub-hierarchies can be realized within the more general graph structure [30], which support modularity better than tree structures. Both, tree structures and especially graph structures allow to integrate new dependencies in a structured way by adding new types of edges. With a little effort, by limiting the view on selected aspects, a transparent access to limited data can be realized.
Concluding, graph structures may fulfill the identified requirements on PR but need to be designed carefully. Especially, ontologies as supplement open a new perspective on the integration of cross-functional information [13]. The next section methodically structures the information that needs to be represented in a PR for automotive DCM.

4. Information Needed in an Efficient Product Representation for Automotive DCM

Based on section 3, the DCM information will be structured with the focus on a graph-based PR. A successful and holistic DCM must be shaped in the form of a process and supporting system that allows the OEM to follow market changes in production and supply chain effectively and quickly. The departments mainly involved in the DCM process are *sales*, *production planning* and *procurement/material planning.*
Today, regional and central OEM *sales* departments forecast sales *volumes* for *models* offered in the *sales regions* and corresponding proportions for selectable *options*, i.e. option *quotas*. *Options* can be aggregated by *option groups (OGroup)*. While a large number of *TECRules* describe the combinability of *options* or *OGroups* for the respective *models* (e.g. BMW 3 series), the connection between fully configured *models* and corresponding *part* demands is described via the *BOMRules*.
On the *capacity* side, there are restrictions originating from *suppliers*, the production system or distribution system [31]. Those restrictions exist at the *parts* level (e.g. *capacity* for a specific clip), *option* level (e.g. *capacity* for sunroofs) and *model* level (e.g. *capacity* for a specific car model) or a combination of these levels (*capacity* for sunroofs in a specific car model). The *model* and *sales region* define the car variant in the first place; therefore, they are important for the *sales*, *procurement* and *production planning*. *Sales* determines forecasts for future *part* demands, which *procurement* has to fulfill. Furthermore, the *production planning* plans the production for a specific *sales region.* [32] *TECRules,* which might change over time, have an effect on the *sales* department and on *procurement* as they depict the allowed combinability of *options* and *OGroups* [33].
Volumes and *quotas* are planned by the sales e.g. extract future demands in *sales regions* [15, 24]. As *capacities* have to be eventually adjusted, *procurement* and *production planning* need information about *suppliers*, *capacities* and *parts* [34]. Due to the high degree of configurability, *options* are of great importance for *procurement* and *sales.* In addition to the *parts*, the *BOMRules* are of great importance for determining *capacities* and for *procurement* (see section 2).
Concluding, resulting DCM information may be divided into the three interrelated partitions *planning information*, *resource information* and *product information*. In the *product partition* resides the automotive product with all offered *models and possible* configurations. It contains *options*, *OGroups*, *TECRule* and *BOMRules* [21, 35] and is enhanced by the concept of a *variant clusters* (*VCluster*) which is used to describe subsets of permitted variants that have common characteristic values. The *planning partition* contains planning scenarios, which describe when *models* in which quantities and with which equipment are to be produced. This typically refers to a sales and production program consisting of model *volumes* and associated option *quotas* for specific *sales regions*. The *resource* partition characterize all supplier *capacities* that are available from *supplier* side to meet the *part* requirements [20, 31] and also all relevant resource *capacities* within the production system. These information can be mapped to capacity corridors [36], which define the *resource* requirements in a certain time period (shift, day, week, month and year) which should neither exceed nor fall short of a defined or negotiated quantity.

As now the data elements have been structured, the interdependence must be discussed: *Models* consists of *VCluster*. A *VCluster* is the aggregation of several car variants. All variants in a *VCluster* are characterized by a certain set of characteristics. *Volumes* that define the planned number of respective cars to be produced for a specific *sales region* are allocated to a *VClusters*. So, *Volumes* represent demand in *sales regions*. Furthermore, *VClusters* have *options*, which are used to characterize the car configuration, whereby *options* are part of an *OGroup*. Moreover, *options* might contain one or several other *options* and therefore support a hierarchical depiction of several *options*. *Options* are restricted by *TECRules*. Furthermore, for managing demand, *options* are planned by using *quotas*. *Quotas* are planned e.g. for *models*, *options*, *options* in *sales regions* or *options* for *models* in *sales regions*. Therefore, the *quota* is allocated to the *model, option* and *sales region*. *Parts* are derived from *BOMRules*, which refer to *option* combinations and these, in turn, refer to *models*. Furthermore, *parts* have *capacities*, which are defined by the *supplier*.
The automotive industry is facing two major trends. One the one hand, e-mobility causes changes in the physical car architecture [37]. On the other hand, the digitization of the car (e.g. autonomous driving) introduces new and changed dependencies (NC-Dependencies) among components (*options* and *parts*), e.g. the compatibility of hardware (HW) and software (SW) [12]. It is important to adequately document those NC-Dependencies when developing a PR for the automotive DCM.
In Fruhner et al. [12] a three-step approach (literature research, interviews and analysis of OEM data) has been followed which has lead in identification of NC-Dependencies. In DCM, information about the component version is highly relevant. Therefore, the information of the version of the HW and SW of a component must be made available to DCM. In today's cars over 100 ECUs (electronical control units) are integrated to control various systems [38]. Less ECUs, but more domain controllers (DCs) are proposed for future car generations [39]. DCs have several advantages like the easy integration of SW modules from different partners and reduced complexity of the assembly system due to fewer part numbers [40, 41]. With the introduction of DCs, several HW components might be eliminated and replaced by SW components running on the DC. For example, a DC for connected cockpits might host SW components like a radio and a navigation application [42]. But, due to the constantly shortening life cycle of components and electronic innovations, electronic components are constantly adapted within the model's life cycle. This is already a major challenge and will continue to increase as the car becomes more and more digital. Concluding, when developing a new holistic PR, the information about the possibilities for updating HW or SW must be kept in the data.

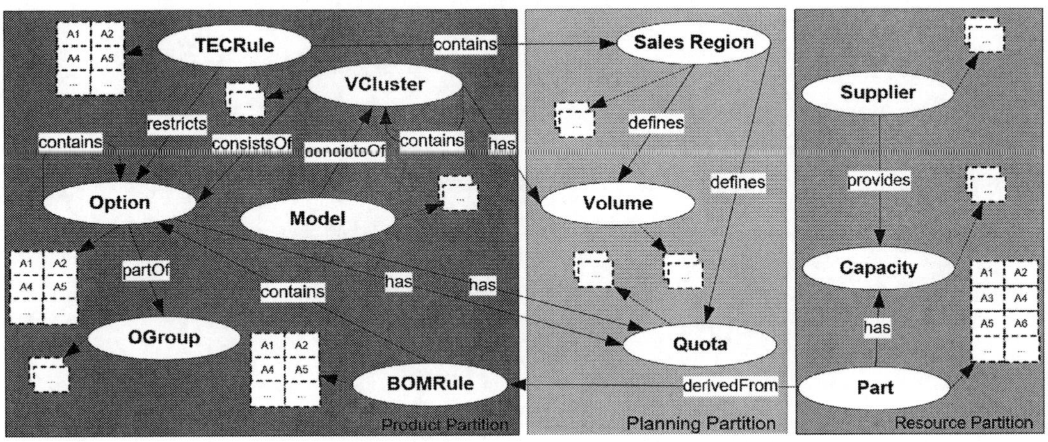

Figure 2: Excerpt of the developed ontology

As a result, six clusters of NC dependency have been identified: *SW Version* (A1), *SW Standard* (A2), *Possibility to update SW* (A3), *HW Version* (A4), *HW Standard* (A5) and *Possibility to update HW* (A6). As all of the derived NC-Dependencies regarding versions and standards relate to *options* and *parts*, which might consist of either HW, SW or both (A1, A2, A4, A5), they are assigned to the data elements *option* and *part*. Furthermore, the updateability (A3 and A6) will be integrated as well into *parts*, as components must be constantly adapted to the given structures. In *TECRules* the information of the HW and SW version needs to be integrated to ensure valid configurations among options (A1, A2, A4, A5).

Also, *BOMRules* need the same information to allow the correct derivation of *parts* within DCM. The other data elements derived in this section are not directly affected by NC-Dependencies.
For the resulting partitions, the discussed cross-functional information and the interdependencies and relations across and within are represented by a semantic network based ontology which is conglomerated in figure 2. The introduced data elements are represented by ellipses and relations by arrows. The rectangles represent simple containers for attributes. The relations connect two terms with each other and restrict them at the same time.
When integrating the relevant data from the original distributed data sources, each partition has to be structured in order to map the specific information without any loss of information. This prevents translation in the form of interpretation, so that maximum data quality is maintained when information is automatically transferred from existing IT infrastructures. Nevertheless, data optimization and cleaning are an essential process in this step to eliminate redundancies at the same time.

5. Concept and Validation of an Efficient Product Representation for Automotive Demand and Capacity Management

A modular DCM software-suite that instantiates the introduced approach for a holistic and integrated PR has been developed in a pilot project at a German OEM. The implementation uses a service-oriented architecture in order to react as flexibly as possible to new challenges. As the PR already supports the integration of the new and changed dependencies and options, unprecedented flexibility is already given in this aspect.
For the implementation, the in section 4 derived information model has been transferred into a Unified Modeling Language (UML) class diagram. Figure 3 depicts the structure of the new PR being implemented. All data elements are translated into classes. Additionally, a class option cluster (*OCluster*) has been added to allow the integration of the highly entangled hierarchical sub-structures of the automotive product structures. The interrelations between the different data elements have been designed on the basis of the findings presented in section 4.

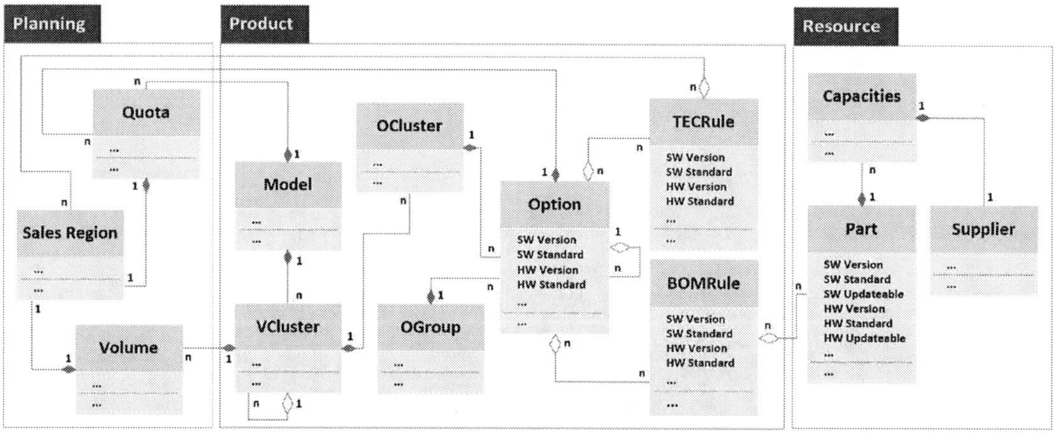

Figure 3: UML class diagram of the product representation

The integration of new dependencies has been realized by adding the NC-Dependencies as attributes in the corresponding classes. The compatibility of SW can be analyzed by the SW version of both *options* and *TECRules*. The support of cross-functional information is integrated by partitions. Modularity is supported as the *OCluster* might contain several *options*. The data structure is built upon given data structures, but by integration reduces inconsistencies and redundancies. In result, the comprehensive and complex information is more transparently managed. Given hierarchies within the data are depicted by *OCluster* and variants *VCluster*. Due to the natural partitioning of the information, a transparent data structure with responsibilities and views for the involved departments is given. The developed PR has been validated for its general use by all involved departments. First tests show that the PR supports an integrated and efficient DCM process. Part demand data from a typical production plan is derived in less than five seconds by application of the developed PR. Results of the calculation is presented in sophisticated diagrams, e.g. pivot tables and sankey diagrams.

6. Conclusion and Future Work

DCM is an integral task of automotive logistics. To ensure the availability of components, it is essential that the PR applied here provides transparent, holistic and cross-functional information and maps dependencies.
This contribution introduced an efficient PR for automotive DCM as a transparent, holistic information basis including NC-dependencies. In a first step, the dilemma of automotive DCM has been illustrated and the solution of an integrated PR has been motivated. In a next step, the relevant supply chain, product and planning information has been characterized. A following analysis of types of PRs lead to the results that graph structures are suited best as a basis for an automotive PR for DCM. Ontologies have been identified to open a new and different perspective for the integration of additional cross-functional information. Hence, the information needed in an efficient PR for the automotive DCM has been structured and transformed into an ontology as presented in section 4. Afterwards, the concept and validation of the efficient PR for the automotive DCM by an implementation at a German OEM has been described.
As a next step, KPIs shall be defined in order to compare more methodologically the benefits of the developed integrated information model with the typical DCM data structures and identify also further optimizations. An implementation at another OEMs is planned to validate the developed PR for its general applicability in automotive DCM. The applicability in other field of complex series production like the aviation or the machine building industry is also possible and shall be evaluated afterwards.

7. References

1. Schuberthan, J., Potrafke, S.: Die Anforderungen des Kunden… Logistik in der Automobilindustrie. Innovatives Supply Chain Management für wettbewerbsfähige Zulieferstrukturen. Springer, Berlin, pp. 8–18 (2007)
2. Volling, T.: Auftragsbezogene Planung bei variantenreicher Serienproduktion. Eine Untersuchung mit Fallstudien aus der Automobilindustrie. Gabler Verlag, Wiesbaden (2009)
3. Aoki, K., Stäblein, T., Tomino, T.: Monozukuri capability to address product variety. A comparison between Japanese and German automotive makers. International Journal of Production Economics (2014)
4. Alford, D., Sackett, P., Nelder, G.: Mass customisation — an automotive perspective. International Journal of Production Economics (2000)
5. Krog, E.-H., Statkevich, K.: Kundenorientierung und Integrationsfunktion der Logistik in der Supply Chain der Automobilindustrie. Das Beste der Logistik. Springer, Berlin, Heidelberg, pp. 185–195 (2008)
6. Kuhn, A., Hellingrath, B.: Supply Chain Management. Optimierte Zusammenarbeit in der Wertschöpfungskette. Springer Berlin Heidelberg, Berlin, Heidelberg, s.l. (2002)
7. Toth, M.: Eine Methodik für das kollaborative Bedarfs- und Kapazitätsmanagement in Engpasssituationen. Ein ganzheitlicher Ansatz zur Identifikation, Anwendung und Bewertung von Engpassstrategien am Beispiel der Automobilindustrie. Thesis (PhD), TU Dortmund University (2008)
8. Pawlikowski, K., Fruhner, D., Klingebiel, K., Toth, M., Wagenitz, A.: A Motivation and Evaluation of Hierarchical Data Structures for Application in Automotive Demand and Capacity Management. International Journal on Advances in Software, 155–166 (2017)
9. Deng, X., Huet, G., Tan, S., Fortin, C.: Product decomposition using design structure matrix for intellectual property protection in supply chain outsourcing. Computers in Industry (2012)
10. Kissel, M.: Mustererkennung in komplexen Produktportfolios. Thesis (PhD), Technical University of Munich (2014)
11. Rohde, J., Wagner, M.: Master Planning. Supply Chain Management and Advanced Planning. Concepts, Models, Software, and Case Studies, 4th edn. Springer, Berlin, Heidelberg, pp. 161–179 (2008)
12. Fruhner, D., Klingebiel, K., Pawlikowski, K., Toth, M.: Impacts of the digitalised car on logistics. In: Proceedings of the 25th International Annual EurOMA Conference, Budapest, Hungary (2018)
13. Fruhner, D., Pawlikowski, K., Klingebiel, K., Toth, M.: Efficient Product Representations for Automotive Logistics. In: Proceedings of the 29th European Modeling and Simulation Symposium (EMSS), Barcelona, Spain, pp. 100–109 (2017)
14. Lisanne Temur, Daniel Fruhner, Katja Klingebiel: Proactive Demand and Capacity Management for Automotive Logistics using an Efficient Information Model. In: Proceedings of the 31th European Modeling and Simulation Symposium (EMSS), Lisbon, Portugal (2019)

15.Zernechel, T.: Gestaltung und Optimierung von Unternehmensnetzwerken — Supply Chain Management in der Automobilindustrie. Die Automobilindustrie auf dem Weg zur globalen Netzwerkkompetenz. Effiziente und flexible Supply Chains erfolgreich gestalten. Springer, Berlin, Heidelberg, pp. 367–378 (2007)
16.Stäblein, T.: Integrierte Planung des Materialbedarfs bei kundenauftragsorientierter Fertigung von komplexen und variantenreichen Serienprodukten. Innovationen der Fabrikplanung und -organisation. Shaker, Aachen (2008)
17.Herold, L.: Kundenorientierte Prozesssteuerung in der Automobilindustrie. Die Rolle von Logistik und Logistikcontrolling im Prozess „vom Kunden bis zum Kunden". Deutscher Universitätsverlag, Wiesbaden (2012)
18.Scheer, A.-W.: Wirtschaftsinformatik. Referenzmodelle für industrielle Geschäftsprozesse, 7th edn. Springer, Berlin (1997)
19.Barthel, H.: Modell zur Analyse und Gestaltung des Bestellverhaltens für die variantenreiche Serienproduktion. Thesis (PhD), University of Stuttgart (2006)
20.Pfohl, H.-C.: Logistiksysteme. Betriebswirtschaftliche Grundlagen, 7th edn. Springer, Berlin (2004)
21.Meyr, H.: Supply chain planning in the German automotive industry. OR Spectrum (2004)
22.Toth, M., Wagenitz, A., Klingebiel, K.: Dynamic Supply Chain Planning with Logistic Assistance Systems. ASOR Bulletin. The Australian Society for Operations Research, vol. 2, 29th edn. (2010)
23.Arnold, D., Isermann, H., Kuhn, A., Tempelmeier, H., Furmans, K. (eds.): Handbuch Logistik, 3rd edn. VDI-Buch. Springer, Berlin (2008)
24.Wagenitz, A., Liebler, K.M., Schürrer, S.: A Holistic Approach to Demand and Capacity Management in the Automotive Industry. Innovation in product and production. Fraunhofer Verlag, Stuttgart (2011)
25.Schuh, G., Riesener, M.: Produktkomplexität managen. Strategien - Methoden - Tools. Hanser, München (2018)
26.Yang, Q., Pan, X., Wei, D., Wu, K.: Research on Individualized Product Requirement Expression Based on Semantic Network. Physics Procedia (2012)
27.Kesper, H.: Gestaltung von Produktvariantenspektren mittels matrixbasierter Methoden. Thesis (PhD), Technical University of Munich (2012)
28.ElMaraghy, H., Schuh, G., ElMaraghy, W., Piller, F.T., Schönsleben, P., Tseng, M., Bernard, A.: Product variety management. CIRP Annals - Manufacturing Technology (2013)
29.Vegetti, M., Leone, H., Henning, G.: PRONTO: An ontology for comprehensive and consistent representation of product information. Engineering Applications of Artificial Intelligence (2011)
30.Luo, Y., Peng, Q., Gu, P.: Integrated multi-layer representation and ant colony search for product selective disassembly planning. Computers in Industry (2016)
31.Wagner, H.: Kollaboratives Bedarfs- und Kapazitätsmanagement am Beispiel der Automobilindustrie. Lösungsansatz zur Sicherstellung der Wandlungsfähigkeit. Thesis (PhD), University of Stuttgart (2006)
32.Bockholt, F.: Operatives Störungsmanagement für globale Logistiknetzwerke. Ökonomie- und ökologieorientiertes Referenzmodell für den Einsatz in der Automobilindustrie. Thesis (PhD), TU Dortmund University (2012)
33.Wagenitz, A.: Modellierungsmethode zur Auftragsabwicklung in der Automobilindustrie. Thesis (PhD), TU Dortmund University (2007)
34.Liebler, K.M.: Eine prozess- und IT-gestützte Methode für die Produktionsplanung in der Automobilindustrie. Thesis (PhD), TU Dortmund University (2013)
35.Herlyn, W.J.: Zur Problematik der Abbildung variantenreicher Erzeugnisse in der Automobilindustrie. Zugl.: Braunschweig, Techn. Univ., Diss. Fortschritt-Berichte VDI Reihe 16, vol. 52. VDI-Verl., Düsseldorf (1990)
36.Hegmanns, T.: Dezentrales Planungs- und Prozesskonzept für ein kollaboratives Bedarfs- und Kapazitätsmanagement in Produktionsnetzwerken. Thesis (PhD), TU Dortmund University (2010)
37.Pawlikowski, K., Toth, M., Fruhner, D., Klingebiel, K.: How electrified car concepts effect automotive logistics. In: Proceedings of the 25th International Annual EurOMA Conference, Budapest, Hungary (2018)
38.Budaker, B.: On the way to the cyber physical car (CPC). In: 17. Internationales Stuttgarter Symposium. Automobil- und Motorentechnik, pp. 165–176 (2017)
39.Karimi, K.: Four Reasons the Next 3 Years will Determine Automakers' Fate for the Next 30 Years (Hint: IoT is One). http://blogs.blackberry.com/2016/11/four-reasons-the-next-3-years-will-determine-automakers-fate-for-the-next-30-years-hint-iot-is-one/ (2016). Accessed 6 January 2020
40.Rieth, P.E., Raste, T.: Future Integration Concepts for ADAS. Handbook of Driver Assistance Systems. Basic Information, Components and Systems for Active Safety and Comfort. Springer International Publishing, pp. 1399–1411 (2016)
41.Wendt, T.F., Bernhart, W., Behl, J., Mishoulam, D., Goldsmith, E.: Consolidation in vehicle electronic architectures. The master key to unlocking value in the next generation of "smart cars" (2015)
42.Tuzar, G.-D., Schöpp, H.: A New Approach — Connected Cockpit Multi-Domain Controller. Auto Tech Rev (2015)

I L S 2020
INTERNATIONAL CONFERENCE ON INFORMATION
SYSTEMS, LOGISTICS & SUPPLY CHAIN
Austin, Texas April 22-24, 2020

Impact of retail-platform loan programs on the SC performance under CSR dependent stochastic demand

Dinh Anh PHAN [1], Franck MORAUX[2], Thi Le Hoa VO [3], Anh Ngoc LAI [4]

[1,2,3,4] University of Rennes 1, CNRS, CREM - UMR 6211, F-35000 Rennes, France
{dinhanhdhkt@gmail.com, franck.moraux@univ-rennes1.fr, thi-le-hoa.vo@univ-rennes1.fr, anh-ngoc-lai@univ-rennes1.fr}

Abstract. We consider a supply chain in which a seller produces a finished product and sells it on the marketplace of a retail platform. The seller may invest in Corporate Social Responsibility (CSR) to increase the market demand but has limited capital and no access to bank financing due to low credit rating. To mitigate the seller's capital constraint, the retail platform offers financial loans to the seller choosing among three kinds of loan contracts: Credit limit, target rate of return, and interest rate discount based on CSR performance. We adopt a Stackelberg game to investigate the equilibrium decisions under each loan contract. The numerical examples reveal that all three contracts help improve the seller's CSR investment as long as consumer sensitivity towards CSR exists. In addition, the last one leads to the highest profitability of the overall supply chain and each member.

Keywords: CSR investment, capital constraint, retail platform, supply chain

1. Introduction

In today's global business environment, suppliers are facing increasing pressure in their business operations. Consumers, governments, and other stakeholders are pressuring companies to be more responsible for their business operations due to the severe impacts of industrial activities on our environment and society [4]. In response to this, most suppliers are increasingly interested in CSR activities such as mitigating pollutant emission, improving working conditions, philanthropic donations to ensure their business practices to be socially responsible. These CSR activities have the potential to affect the consumers' value perceptions and their intentions to purchase products [6, 7] and subsequently increase the market demand [1]. However, suppliers try to implement CSR into their business also need to incur substantial costs since the CSR programs can be costly. In addition to the external pressures to engage in socially responsible behavior, the supplier especially small and medium-sized firms are increasingly facing capital constraints that limit their ability to meet market demand as well as their sustainability performance. Consequently, suppliers often find themselves in need of short-term financing to support their operations. However, it is difficult for small suppliers to obtain financing from traditional bank because they have generally weak credit ratings and lack of sufficient assets to pledge as collateral. In efforts to manage capital constraint, some suppliers respond by cutting wages, reducing investments in working conditions and protecting the environment. This not only results in reducing SMEs' CSR performance but also influences the performance of downstream firms along the entire supply chain [8]. Recognizing the difficulty or inability of small suppliers to obtain financial support, some retail platforms (hereafter, platforms) recently have started to offer small business loans to the suppliers who sell their products via the platform (hereafter, we call these suppliers as sellers). For example,

Amazon was the world's largest e-commerce platform in terms of revenue and has launched in 2011 lending program to help sellers invest in operations (equipment, inventory, etc.). Through the lending program, Amazon offers short-term loans up to $750,000 exclusively for its sellers. In another example, Alibaba Group Holdings has adopted "Ant Micro Loan" to provide credit to small and micro-enterprises sellers in its ecosystem. Since 2011, this program has issued $64.42 billion to millions of SME sellers who are mostly in need of money. Other large retailers including eBay Inc's PayPal, JD.com, and Best Buy, which run third-party marketplaces, are also turning to credit to boost their vendor base.

Impact of the lending program on the retail platform goes on both sides: on one hand, by supporting the sellers expand their operations the platforms boost sales growth and hence increase its revenues through a referral fee for each unit sold by the seller. In addition, the platform earns a loan interest payment from a borrowing seller. On the other hand, the platform faces the default risk (the risk that the sellers cannot pay its loans). Although the platforms can evaluate a seller's credit risk more accurately than traditional banks thanks to their knowledge of historical transaction details and their past interactions with their sellers. In fact, the platforms still suffer a part of the loss when sellers are unable to pay back their loans. The default rate of the Amazon Lending program and Ant Micro Loan program are reported at 1.5% and 0.36%[1], respectively [2]. Therefore, understanding of the impacts of loan program on the platform's performance as well as the performance of entire supply chain will provide useful insights for platforms on how to offer loans to its sellers. Furthermore, in an effort to build a sustainable supply chain, we are interested in assessing the impact of loan programs on the implementation of social responsibility of sellers, and how to design a loan program for improving the profits of the supply chain members and promoting supply chain sustainability?. Hence, this paper is designed to address the following questions: (1) what is the optimal loan terms which maximize the platform profit? (2) What is the impact of platform loan on the seller's CSR decisions? (3) Can we design a lending program to achieve both increased profits and improved CSR performance? By addressing these research questions, this paper could make two following contributions: First, to the best of our knowledge, this study is the first to address issues at the interface of finance, operations, and sustainable development on Internet retailing. Second, from managerial insights, we show that the platforms can adopt the loan program as a financing mechanism to encourage the CSR performance of its capital-constrained sellers, and hence promote the supply chain sustainability.

The rest of this paper is organized as follows. Section 2 presents the problem definition and assumptions. In Section 3, we develop the mathematical models. Section 4 provides numerical examples with discussions. A summary of the findings are described in the last section.

2. Problem definition and assumptions

2.1. Supply chain structure

Consider a supply chain in which a seller ("she") produces a finished product and sells it on the marketplace of a retail platform ("he") over a single selling period at a price p which is assumed exogenous. The platform charges the seller a referral fee for each unit sold on the platform. The referral fee is an exogenously given percentage γ of the revenue. For each unit of any sold good on the platform, the platform keeps a fraction $\gamma \in (0,1)$ of the revenue for herself and returns the rest $1-\gamma$ to the seller. The seller's unit production cost is c and there are no other costs to sell the product. All unmet demand is lost and the salvage value of leftover is zero. The seller may make a CSR investment y (on each unit of product) which potentially affected the market demand X. In the subsection 2.3, we will detail the impact of the CSR investment on the market demand for the seller's product. The costs of CSR investment are borne by the seller alone. Before each season, the seller is endowed with some initial capital B which are insufficient to support her desired operations, e.g., pay for the costs of production and CSR investment. In addition, this seller has no access to bank financing due to

[1] https://www.reuters.com/article/us-amazon-com-loans-exclusive-idUSKCN0P90DW20150629

low credit rating and lack of collateral. Conversely, the platform has adequate funds to offer loans to the seller without borrowing from external channels.

2.2. Sequence of Events

At the beginning of selling period (referred to as time 0), the platform designs a general loan contract to offer to the seller. It is constructed as $\{L, r\}$ where L is the credit limit and r is the interest rate that the platform charges the seller's loan. The extreme case of L =0 represents that seller does not receive a loan offer from the platform, and the extreme case of L =+∞ represents that the platform is willing to lend the seller any amount she asks. In addition, the interest rate r may be constant or depends on the seller's production quantity and/or CSR performance level. Facing a loan contract $\{L, r\}$, the seller simultaneously decides the actual loan amount l, the production quantity Q, and CSR investment y on each unit of product such that $(c+y)Q \leq l+B$ and $l \leq L$. That is the seller must make sure that she borrows enough to cover her costs of production and CSR investment, while considering the credit limit. At the end of selling period (at time t), the demand is realized. The platform collects a portion γ of the retail revenue, $pMin\{Q,X\}$. The seller then makes the loan repayment (loan amount plus interest), $l(1+r)$ to the platform from the remainder of the retail revenue ($\gamma)$. However, if the seller's retained sales revenue is not sufficient to fully repay the loan, such that $(1-\gamma)p$), the seller then goes into default. In this case, the platform acquires the total revenue realized to recover the loan. In other words, we assume that the seller is an SME with limited liability, she commits to repay $n[(1-\gamma)p\, Min\{Q,X\}, l(1+r)]$ to the platform at the end of the selling season.

2.3. Impact of CSR investment on the market demand

In this paper, it is assumed that the CSR activities can potentially allow the sellers to enhance, e.g., their reputation, brand, and trust, which in turn attract new customers and increase the market demand [3]. Therefore, we adopt a demand function after investing in CSR as $X = \sigma[y]\xi + \mu[y]$, where ξ is a non-negative random variable that represents the market demand without CSR investment. That is, we assume the functions $\sigma[y]$ and $\mu[y]$ will take the values of one and zero at y equals to zero respectively (i.e., $\sigma[0] =$ and $\mu[0] = 0$). When the seller invests into CSR activities (i.e., y >0), different forms of $\sigma[y]$ combining with different forms of $\mu[y]$ represent the manner that the CSR investment will influence the market demand. In addition, it is supposed that the uncertain market demand without CSR investment ξ having a cumulative distribution function $F[\xi]$, a complementary cumulative distribution function $\bar{F}[\xi] = 1 - F[\xi]$, and a probability density function $f[\xi]$. Since the demand variance is non-negative, it is reasonable to assume that $\sigma[y]$ is greater than zero for any y, i.e., $\sigma[y] > 0$. Given this specification, the CSR investment affects both the demand mean and the demand variance simultaneously. As a result, it may change the CV of the demand. In the rest of this paper, we will simply denote σ as $\sigma[y]$ and μ as $\mu[y]$. We also denote the first-order derivative of σ and μ with respect to y as σ' and respectively.

3. Modeling and analysis

3.1. Non-financing benchmark

We first consider a benchmark in which the platform loan is not available and the seller does not access to capital market. In the benchmark case, the seller uses the entire initial capital to support her operations.

The expected profit of the seller at time t can be calculated as

$$E[\pi_s^0] = E[(1-\gamma)p\, Min\{Q,X\} - (c+y)Q(1+r_f)] \quad \gamma) \left(\quad \sigma \int \bar{F}(\quad d\xi \right) \tag{1}$$

and, the expected profit of the platform at time t is

$$E[\pi_r^0] = E[\gamma p Min\{Q,X\}] = \gamma p \left(\mu \quad \sigma \int \bar{F}(\quad d\xi \right) \tag{2}$$

Given $\gamma \in (0,1)$, the seller solves the following constrained optimization problem:

$$E[\pi_s^0] \quad (3)$$

$$\text{subject to} \quad (4)$$

where the inequality (4) represents the seller's capital constraint. Propositions 1 and 2 provide the optimal decisions in the benchmark case. Proofs of the Propositions in this paper are available upon request from the authors.

Proposition 1: When the seller has sufficient capital, the optimal operational decisions (Q) that maximizes the seller's expected profit are given by the following simultaneous equations.

$$)\bar{F}\left[\frac{}{}\right] - \quad \textbf{(5a)}$$

$$)\left(\mu \quad \int \bar{F}[\xi]\, d \quad \bar{F}\left[\frac{}{}\right]\frac{}{}\right) - \quad \textbf{(5b)}$$

Proposition 2: When the seller is capital-constrained, the optimal operational decisions (Q_0^*, y_0^*) that maximizes the seller's expected profit are given by the following simultaneous equations.

$$\frac{f[\frac{}{}]}{} \quad \frac{Q(1+r_f) - p(1-\gamma)(\mu' + (\int_0^{\frac{Q-\mu}{\sigma}} f[x]\, dx)\sigma' + f[\frac{Q-\mu}{\sigma}]\sigma(-\frac{\mu'}{\sigma} - \frac{(Q-\mu)\sigma'}{\sigma^2}))}{} \quad \textbf{(6a)}$$

$$\textbf{(6b)}$$

Plugging either (Q) or (Q_0^*, y_0^*) back in (3) and (4), we obtain the first-best profit of the seller and the platform respectively.

3.2. Financing with platform loans

3.2.1. The profit model under a general loan contract $\{L, r\}$

The seller's profit function at time t, π can be constructed as

$$-\gamma)p \quad Min[(1-\gamma)p\, M \quad)] \quad (7)$$

The profit function for the platform at time t, π is formulated as follows:

$$\gamma p \quad n[(1-\gamma)p \quad)] \quad \textbf{(8)}$$

To calculate the expected profit, let $\hat{X}$ —— be the seller's default threshold (i.e., the minimal demand level that the seller can fully repay her loan obligation at time t (loan amount plus interest). Then the seller's profit function at time t can be rewritten as

$$B(1 \quad) \quad \frac{\hat{X}}{} \quad \hat{X})$$

$$-\gamma)p \quad B(1 \quad) \quad \frac{\hat{X}}{} \quad \frac{}{} \quad \hat{X}$$

$$-\gamma)pQ \quad B(1 \quad) \quad \frac{}{}$$

and the platform's profit function becomes

$$\frac{\hat{X}}{}$$

$$\gamma p \quad \frac{\hat{X}}{} \quad \frac{}{}$$

$$\gamma pQ \quad \frac{}{}$$

Therefore, the expected profits the seller and the platform can be calculated as:

$$E[\pi_s^1] \qquad \gamma) \left(\sigma\int_{\hat{X}-} \bar{F}(\qquad \hat{X}\bar{F}\left[\frac{\hat{X}-\mu}{}\right]\right) \qquad \bar{F}\left[\frac{\hat{X}-\mu}{}\right] \quad \textbf{(9)}$$

$$E[\pi_r^1] = \gamma p\left(\mu \quad \sigma\int \bar{F}(\quad d\xi\right) \qquad \gamma) \left(\quad \sigma\int^{\hat{X}-} \bar{F}(\qquad \hat{X}\bar{F}\left[\frac{\hat{X}-\mu}{}\right]\right) \qquad \bar{F}\left[\frac{\hat{X}-\mu}{}\right] \quad \textbf{(10)}$$

3.2.2. Equilibrium Solutions

We model the interaction of the platform and seller as a Stackelberg game with the platform as the leader. In the first stage, the platform moves first to make his decisions on the parameters of the loan contracts (i.e., the credit limit L and the interest rate r). In the second stage, given the platform's offer $\{L, r\}$, the seller simultaneously determines the loan amount l, the production quantity, Q and CSR investment y to maximize her profit. Formally, the platform solves the following optimization problem:

$$\textbf{(P)} \qquad [\pi_r^1] \quad \textbf{(11)}$$

where the platform's objective function $E[\pi_r^1]$ as presented in Eq.(10) and $\{Q, y\}$ solves from

$$E[\pi_s^1] \quad \textbf{(12)}$$

$$\textit{subject to} \quad \Big\{$$

where the seller's objective function $E[\pi_s^1]$ as presented in Eq.(9).

Constraint (12a) is seller's capital constraint, a seller cannot spend more than what her initial capital and the loan can afford. Constraint (12b) ensures that the seller borrows within the credit limit. Problem **(P)** represents of a two-level optimization problem, where the first level problem is associated with the platform, while the second level problem, the inner problem, is associated with the seller. Problem **(P)** must be solved to find the equilibrium decisions. However, the solution for the problem **(P)** depends on how the interest rate is determined (i.e., the interest rate is constant or depend on Q and/or y), and is hard to solve in general. Next, we consider three kinds of loan contracts based on how interest rates are determined in each loan contract. The three contracts are (1) the target rate of return (TRR), (2) the credit limit (CL), and (3) the interest rate discount based on CSR performance (CSR discount).

3.2.3. The TRR contract

In the TRR contract, the platform do not limit on the loan amount. Instead, the platform charges the seller an interest rate which makes the expected payoff from offering the loan to the seller yields a TRR that we denote by $\hat{r}$. Hence, for a given $\hat{r}$ the platform's interest rate r satisfies the following equation

$$\hat{r}) = E[Min\{(1-\gamma)p\, Min\{Q, X\}, l(1+r)\}] \quad \textbf{(13)}$$

By some expanding the terms, the Eq. (13) can be rewritten as

$$\hat{r}) \qquad \bar{F}\left[\frac{\hat{X}-\mu}{}\right] \qquad \gamma) \quad \int^{\hat{X}-} \bar{F}(\qquad \hat{X}\bar{F}\left[\frac{\hat{X}-\mu}{}\right] \quad \textbf{(14)}$$

Substituting Eq. (14) into the expected profit function the seller and the platform respectively, we simplify the expected profit of the seller and the platforms as

$$E[\pi_s^1] \qquad \gamma) \left(\quad \sigma\int \bar{F}(\quad d\xi\right) - ((\qquad B)(\quad \hat{r}) \quad \textbf{(15)}$$

$$E[\pi_r^1] = \gamma p\left(\mu \quad \sigma\int \bar{F}(\quad d\xi\right) \quad ((\qquad B)(\hat{r} \quad) \quad \textbf{(16)}$$

Proposition 3: In case $\hat{r} = r_f$, the seller's optimal operational decisions under TRR contract are $\{Q_1^*, y_1^*\}=\{Q^N, y^N\}$, which are exactly the decisions in the absence of capital constraints. The loan amount *is* respectively.

Corollary 1 shows that when the platform sets the TRR equal to the risk free interest rate, the seller makes her operational decisions like when she has enough capital, and then borrows the needed amount from the platform to support her operational decisions. Hence, we find that the performance of a capital-constrained supply chain under CSR dependent stochastic demand can be enhanced to the state without capital constraints when the platform by strategically setting the TRR at the risk free interest rate. In this case, it is clear that the seller always benefits when using the platform loans. However, the platform has no obligation to set a TRR at a risk-free rate. Instead, the platform as a leader decides on the TRR to maximize his profit.

Proposition 4: In case $\mu = 0$ and 1, the platform expected profit function $E[\pi_r^1]$ in Eq. (16) is a concave function of $\hat{r}$, and there exists a unique ^ that maximizes $E[\pi_r^1]$. Moreover, the equilibrium decisions $\{\hat{r}$ $\}$ are given by the following simultaneous two equations: ^ $\frac{\gamma\bar{F}[Q_1^*]- \quad f[Q_1^*]}{}$ and $\bar{F}^{-1}[\frac{c(1+\hat{r})}{}]$.

3.2.4. Credit Limit contract

In the CL contract, the platform establishes the maximum loan amount (i.e., L) the seller can borrow. The basic decision variables of the platform under this contract are CL and fixed interest rate (which does not depend on the seller's decisions). Increasing CL allows the seller to increase the scale of her operations (production and investment in CSR). This leads to higher operation income for the platform. In the opposite effect, the platform could bear more loss in the event that the seller defaults. Therefore, we intuitively expect the existence and uniqueness of a CL that maximizes the profit of the platform for a given fixed interest rate, and the optimal CL be characterized by a balance between the platform's operation income and the expected loss on the loan amount. Mathematically, the platform's problem under the CL contract is the same as the Problem (**P**) presented in Section 3.2.2 where r does not depend on both Q and y. To solve the problem (**P**) in this case, we rely on the assumption of the concavity of seller's expected profit function with respect to Q and y. Hence, we replace the inner problem by its corresponding Karush–Kuhn–Tucker (KKT) conditions and thus reduce the problem (**P**) into a single objective function of the platform with a set of constraints (KKT conditions). This optimization problem can be solved by continuing to use the KKT approach. However, we cannot reach a closed-form solution for optimal decision in the equilibrium. Thus, we resort to numerical analysis to develop more insights.

3.2.5. CSR discount contract

In the CSR discount contract, the platform encourages the sellers invest in CSR activities by reducing the interest rate when sellers increase their CSR performance. A higher CSR performance level corresponds to a lower financing interest rate. We propose a CSR discount contract under which the platform first releases a potential maximal interest rate R and then determines a final interest rate r according to the seller's CSR performance level. That is $r = R - \beta g[y]$, where $g[y]$ represents seller's CSR performance level corresponds to her CSR investment y, and $\beta \geq 0$ represents sensitive coefficient of the seller's CSR performance level to the interest rate. The basic decision variables of the platform in the CSR discount contract are the maximal interest rate and the sensitive coefficient. Mathematically, the platform's problem under CSR discount contract as described in the Problem (**P**) where the constraint (12b) is removed, and the platform's decision on the interest rate is converted into the decisions of the maximal interest rate and the sensitive coefficient. The analytical solutions of this kind of problems are also difficult. Therefore, we leave it to be resolved by a numerical method to get the equilibrium decisions the next section.

4. Numerical analysis

In this section, we investigate numerically the SC performance under the three loan contracts discussed, and develop more insights.

4.1. The market demand for seller's product

We use a normal distribution for the demand without the CSR investment as). The demand after the CSR investment is assumed to follow a normal distribution with mean $ag[y]$) and standard deviation $bg[y]$), where a, b are non-negative parameters since the CSR investment affects the demand's mean and variance positively. The function $g[y]$ is assumed to increase in y with $g[y]$ 1 representing the relationship between the CSR investment y for each product and the CSR performance level $g[y]$. In this way, the more the CSR investment is, the higher the CSR performance level achieves [5]. The parameter a indicates the maximum increase in the demand mean due to the CSR investments while parameter b captures the effect of CSR activities on increasing demand variance. We further use a modified version of the function proposed in [4] to establish the relationship between the CSR investment and the CSR performance level through $g[y]=1-1/(1+0.5*y)$. It is also worth noting that the setting of the demand in our numerical study corresponds to a special case for the general demand function of the form $D = \sigma[y]\,\xi + \mu[y]$ with $\xi = \text{Normal}(\mu_0, \sigma_0)$, $\mu[y] = \mu_0(a - b)g[y]$ and $\sigma[y] = 1 + bg[y]$.

4.2. Impact of platform's decisions on SC performance

In order to investigate the impact of platform's decisions on the SC performance, some scenarios are investigated. Table 1 provides data for five investigated scenarios.

Table 1: Data (hypothetical) for investigated scenarios

Scenarios	Description	(μ_0, σ_0)	(a,b)	p	c	γ	B	r_f
Scenario 1	CSR has no impact on demand	100,40	(0,0)	30	18	0.15	0	0
Scenario 2	Low production cost and low demand variance	100,30	(1,0)	30	16	0.15	0	0
Scenario 3	Low production cost and high demand variance	100,50	(1,0)	30	16	0.15	0	0
Scenario 4	High production cost and low demand variance	100,30	(1,0)	30	20	0.15	0	0
Scenario 5	High production cost and high demand variance	100,50	(1,0)	30	20	0.15	0	0

Fig. 1 presents how the platform's decisions effect the seller's CSR investment. Fig. 1 also suggests that the platform can adopt different decisions in the loan contracts to encourage the CSR performance of their sellers.

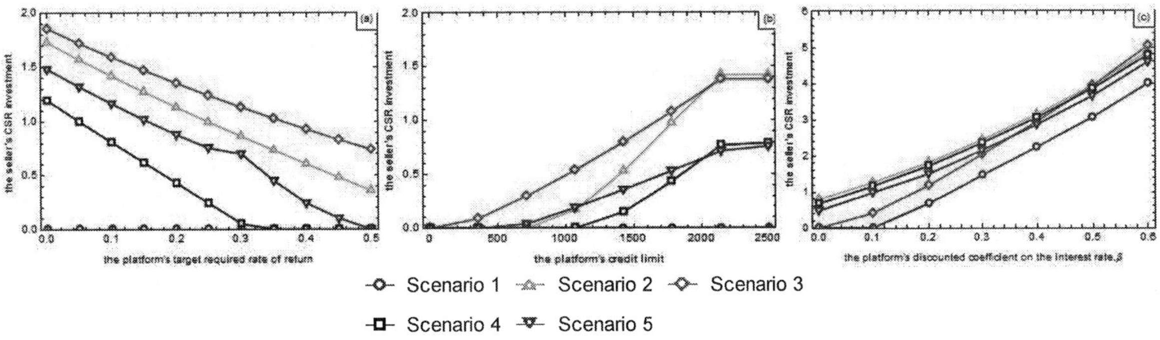

Figure 1: Impact of platform's decision on seller's CSR investment

Fig. 2 demonstrates the impact of the platform's decisions on its profit under each loan contract. As can be observed in Fig. 2 (a), the platform's profit is concave in its TRR for all scenarios. In Fig. 2 (b), we see that the shape of platform's profit under the CL contract depends on the investigated scenarios. For example, the platform's profit is a concave function in CL for scenario 5 while it is non-decreasing in CL for other scenarios. Note that both the seller's production cost and the variance of demand are high in Scenario 5. Thus, these observations reveal that the increasing in CL is not always beneficial for the platform when facing with a seller with high production cost and demand variance. Through Fig. 2 (c) we find that the platform's profit decreases with the sensitive coefficient in scenario 1 but becomes concave with the sensitive coefficient for other scenarios. Thus, the platform can improve their profit by lowering interest rate for the seller with high CSR investment but only when the CSR has positively impact on the demand

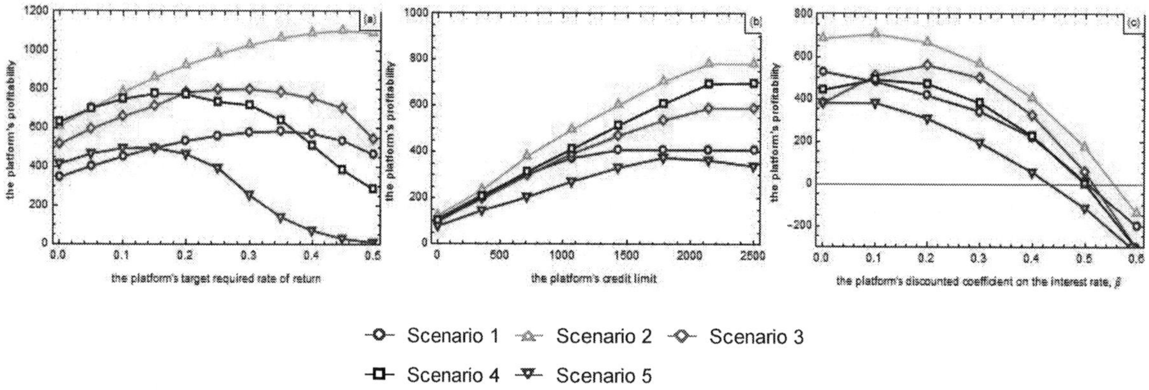

Figure 2: Platform's profit under different loan contracts

4.3. Comparisons of different loan contracts

Table 2 indicates the equilibrium results in three different loan contracts for five investigated scenarios. Comparing the CSR investment decisions across these loan contracts, we see that for all scenarios the CSR investment is the highest in the CSR discount contract, followed by the TRR contract, while it is the lowest under the credit limit contract. Having observed the profit of platform and the whole supply chain also revealed that CSR discount contract generates the highest profit for the platform and the entire supply chain for all scenarios. Hence, the CSR discount contract not only maximizes the profitability of the platform, but also motive the seller invest more in CSR activities.

Although the CSR discount contract provides the entire SC network with more profit than other two contracts, we find that this contract does not increase the economic profitability of the seller. Among the three contracts discussed, the seller earns positive profit under in the contracts of TRR and credit limit but gets zero profit under the CSR discount contract. Thus, from the perspective of the seller, she does not prefer the CSR discount contract when the contracts of credit limit and TRR are on the menu. We also would like to note that the profits of the platform and the seller are zero in the benchmark case for all five investigated scenarios since the initial capital of the seller is zero in these scenarios. Thus, CSR discount contract is the best choice for the platform in maximizing her profits while ensuring the seller's participation when the seller's initial capital is zero. In other words, facing with a zero-capital seller the platform prefers CSR discount contract and does not initiate both contracts of credit limit and TRR.

Table 2: Computational results in the equilibrium of the investigated scenarios for different contracts

	Scenario 1	Scenario 2	Scenario 3	Scenario 4	Scenario 5
TRR contract					
target rate of return	0.139	0.304	0.246	0.113	0.074
CSR investment	0.00	0.56	0.91	0.46	0.84
Seller's profit	219	295	265	183	156
Platform's profit	441	859	710	547	420
whole SC profit	661	1154	975	730	576
Credit limit contract					
Fixed interest rate	0.135	0.344	0.359	0.130	0.055
CSR investment	0	0.35	0.26	0.25	0.11
Credit limit	1582	1699	1580	1948	1291
Seller's profit	310	271	218	189	227
Platform's profit	428	890	723	564	246
whole SC profit	738	1161	941	753	473
CSR Discount contract					
The maximal interest rate	0.498	0.500	0.520	0.340	0.350
sensitive coefficient	0.180	0.330	0.340	0.358	0.380
CSR investment	0.02	1.31	1.35	1.63	1.76

Seller's profit	0	0	0	0	0
Platform's profit	795	1162	1014	911	722
whole SC profit	795	1162	1014	911	722

When the seller has some initial capitals, she can get a positive profit by using her entire fund in the benchmark case. Hence, we continue investigate whether both SC members are better off with the CSR discount contract in case the seller's initial capital is positive. Based on the scenario 3, we change the seller's initial capital from zero to 2100 (the level of capital that the seller is not capital-constrained) while fixing other parameters. We obtain the following observations: (1) When the TRR contract is unique on the menu: (i) both platform and seller earn greater profits under TRR contract than under the benchmark case for any level of initial capital in the range (0, 2100), and (ii) the CSR performance under the TRR contract is higher than those in the benchmark. (2) When the credit limit contract is unique on the menu, the platform benefits more under credit limit contract than under the benchmark, whereas the same does not hold for the seller, however, the CSR performance is always improved in the credit limit contract. (3) When all three discussed contracts are adopted, there always exist the specific parameters (R, β) in the CSR discount contract such that the SC members are better off with the CSR discount contract than the benchmark and other two different contracts. In addition, we observed that the seller's CSR investment also highest in the CSR discount contract. This reveals that the CSR discount contract will lead to highest profit not only the overall chain profit but also each member's profit. Therefore, our numerical results suggest that the CSR discount contract is the unique financing equilibrium for the SC. As a demonstration of our observations, we provide the results for the case that the seller initial capital is equal to 800, i.e., B=800 in table 3. The computational results with other values of B in the range of (0, 2100) step by 100 is available from the authors.

Table 3: Computational results in the equilibrium for different contracts when B=800

Contracts	Production quantity	CSR investment	Seller's profit	Platform's profit	whole SC profit
Benchmark	49	0.45	403.6	213.9	617.5
Credit limit ($r^*=0.212, l^*=794$)	94	0.96	268.0	556.1	824.1
TRR ($r^*=0.137$)	101	1.21	547.8	555.8	1103.6
CSR discount (R, β)					
(R, β)= (0,2, 0.2)	112	1.65	571.6	597.9	1169.5
(R, β)= (0,2, 0.3)	122	2.11	632.3	573.3	1205.6
(R, β)= (0,3, 0.4)	117	2.14	567.8	616.5	1184.4

5. Conclusion

In this paper, we investigated a supply chain where a capital-constrained seller produces a finished product and sells it on the marketplace of a retail platform. In addition, the seller may invest in CSR activities to attract new customers and increase the market demand. To tackle the seller's capital constraint, the retail platform offers financial loans to the seller choosing among three kinds of loan contracts: Credit limit, target rate of return, and CSR discount. We have adopted a Stackelberg game to analyze the equilibrium decisions under each loan contract. We obtain some observations through numerical examples. First, the seller's decisions on the CSR investment are dependent on the platform's choice of loan contract type. This suggests that the platforms can adopt the loan program as a financing mechanism to encourage the CSR performance of their capital-constrained sellers, and hence promote the sustainability of their supply chain.

Second, the profit of the platform and the seller's CSR performance in the loan program are higher than that in the absence of the loan program. Thus, by expanding their lending programs, the platforms enhance both their profit and social sustainability of their supply chain. In contrast, the seller's benefit under the loan programs depends on the type of contract adopted. Interestingly, we also find that the CSR discount contract lead to highest for both member's profit as well as the seller's CSR performance.

For future research, we will develop the model taking into account asymmetric information, moral hazard and the case with multiple sellers.

Acknowledgement

The authors wish to thank the anonymous referees for their helpful comments. The authors also thank CNRS, CREMUMR 6211, University of Rennes 1 and FILEAS FOG-ANR-17-CE10-0001-01 Project for their support. All remaining errors are ours.

References

1. Baron, D.P.: Private politics, corporate social responsibility, and integrated strategy. *J. Econ & M S.* 10(1), 7-45 (2001)
2. Dong, Lingxiu and Ren, Long and Zhang, Dennis.: Financing Small and Medium-Size Enterprises via Retail Platforms (2019), http://dx.doi.org/10.2139/ssrn.3257899
3. Flammer, C.: Does corporate social responsibility lead to superior financial performance? A regression discontinuity approach. Manag. Sci.. 61(11), 2549-2568 (2015)
4. Hsueh, C.F.:Improving corporate social responsibility in a supply chain through a new revenue sharing contract. Int. J. Prod. Econ. 151, 214-222 (2014)
5. Ni, D., Li, K.W. and Tang, X.: Social responsibility allocation in two-echelon supply chains: Insights from wholesale price contracts. Eur. J. Oper. Res. 207(3), 1269-1279 (2010).
6. Porter ME, Kramer M.R.: Strategy and society: The link between competitive advantage and corporate social responsibility. Harvard Bus. Rev. 84(12), 78–92 (2006)
7. Russo MV, Fouts P.A.: A resource-based perspective on corporate environmental performance and profitability. Acad. Management J. 40(3), 534–559(1997)
8. Zhan, J., Li, S., Chen, X.: The impact of financing mechanism on supply chain sustainability and efficiency. *J. cleaner prod*, *205*, 407-418 (2018)

I L S 2020
INTERNATIONAL CONFERENCE ON INFORMATION SYSTEMS, LOGISTICS & SUPPLY CHAIN
Austin, Texas April 22-24, 2020

Mining Serialized Data: Opportunities in the Pharmaceutical Supply Chain

Angie NGUYEN [1], Simon TAMAYO [2], Samir LAMOURI [1], David CARPENTIER [3]

[1] LAMIH CNRS, Arts et Métiers ParisTech, Paris, France
[2] CAOR Center for Robotics, Mines ParisTech PSL, Paris, France
[3] ADENTS INTERNATIONAL, Massy, France
{angie.nguyen@ensam.eu, simon.tamayo@mines-paristech.fr, samir.lamouri@ensam.eu, dcarpentier@adents.com}

Abstract. The serialization of pharmaceutical products enables the detailed monitoring of pharmaceutical flows that should lead to improvements in the performance of healthcare institutions. This article provides an analysis of the opportunities for data mining and data visualization in the pharmaceutical industry. It yields two main contributions (i) it lists the main potential usage of data mining and data visualization when applied to serialized pharmaceutical data; and (ii) it identifies the data requirements for implementation. The proposed analysis reveals that serialization analytics should help reduce the distribution of counterfeit drugs, improve demand forecasting and provide insights into improving inventory management decisions.

Keywords: data mining, data visualization, healthcare, pharmaceutical supply chain, serialization, traceability.

1. Introduction

The distribution of counterfeit medicine is a global issue that is a growing threat to public health. The World Health Organization defines counterfeit medicine (also substandard medicine) as "out of specification" products and estimates that 10% of the pharmaceuticals sold worldwide are counterfeit or substandard, killing 700,000 people each year [1]. In response, many countries, including Europe and the USA, have recently established regulatory systems that aim to secure drug distribution channels through serialization. As a result, the "Falsified Medicines Directive" (EU 2016/161) [2] and the "Drug Supply Chain Security Act" [3] require pharmaceutical companies to display a data-matrix (two-dimensional barcode) on each unit for sale that contains the product identifier, its lot number, its expiry date and its unique serial number. Unique serial numbers therefore enable the authenticity of products to be verified before they are put onto the market and used by patients.

Serialization in the pharmaceutical setting calls for data mining and data visualization techniques because it deals with massive amounts of data. According to the Healthcare Distribution Alliance (HDA) and the European Medicines Verification Organization (EMVO), by 2023, 69 billion healthcare products will be produced, serialized and traced in the USA and Europe. Beyond regulatory compliance and counterfeiting matters, the use of data mining and data visualization techniques on serialization and traceability data could lead to a real breakthrough in Pharmaceutical Supply Chain (PSC) management.

This research identifies how mining and visualizing data involved in the pharmaceutical industry, and especially serialization and traceability data, can address current issues in the PSC. The objective is to identify the issues in the PSC that data mining and visualization can address and the requirements for implementing such tools; future work would focus on analyzing and selecting relevant tools.

The contribution of this work stands at the intersection between the concepts of data mining, data visualization, Industry 4.0 and Pharmaceutical Supply Chain. Jothi [4] defines data mining as *the process of pattern discovery and extraction in which a huge amount of data is involved, in order to describe the data or predict future or unknown variables*. Data mining could be considered a sub-field of data science and artificial intelligence that overlaps with the statistical, probability, optimization, machine learning and computer science disciplines. Ilsen [5] defines data visualization (dataviz) as *the process of enhancing the understanding of massive information flows by the means of visual representations of datasets*. Newly available serialized data is completed by other massive amounts of data generated by Industry 4.0. According to Barreto [6], the notion of Industry 4.0 is related to *smart networking, mobility, flexibility of industrial operations and their inter-operability, integration with customers and suppliers and in the adoption of innovative business models*. The core elements of Industry 4.0 are Internet of Things (IoT), Internet of Services (IoS), Cyber-physical Systems (CPS), and Smart Factory [7].

The pharmaceutical industry is characterized by a complex and highly regulated supply chain; the management of this supply chain struggles to be efficient. As a matter of fact, in the results of its 2018 Survey on Medicines Shortages, the European Association of Hospital Pharmacists (EAHP) [8] reported that 91.8% of 1,666 participating hospitals consider medicine shortages to be a recurrent problem; 38% of them experience medicine shortages on a weekly basis and 35% experience this issue daily. These shortages lead to sub-optimal treatment, treatment failure and cancellation of care. In addition, companies are usually unable to provide notice of a shortage or accurate information about when stock will be available [8]. Thus, two focus areas of issues in the pharmaceutical industry can be distinguished: first, performance issues (sales forecasting, inventory management, delivery time, risk assessment); second, communication issues that prevent different actors (hospitals, manufacturers, laboratories) to efficiently collaborate.

In the past, authors have highlighted that the use of artificial intelligence and dataviz would bring significant improvements to the PSC [9], [10]. This paper builds on the hypothesis that data mining and dataviz tools, using serialized data, can help reduce costs while drastically improving drug inventory management (i.e. reduce shortages and boost service rates) both at the manufacturer and hospital levels. The rest of this paper is structured as follows: section 2 introduces the context of serialization in the pharmaceutical industry and proposes an overview of data science for decision support; section 3 presents current challenges, trends, and perspectives for the PSC; section 4 lists the opportunities identified in mining serialized data and discusses the implementation of such opportunities. Finally, section 5 concludes and lists perspectives for future research.

2. Problem Statement

2.1 Drug serialization

The question we address here is: can the smart use of serialized data related to drug manufacturing and dispensing (cf. Figure 1) improve performance in the PSC? Recording this data is part of the new European and American regulations [2], [3]. However, given the volume of data (each drug will carry a unique serial number), it is necessary to use well-adapted tools.

In the process of serialization, laboratories must transmit the information included in the production and delivery orders to authorities. On the one hand, in order to comply with these regulations, manufacturers are equipped with software solutions that generate serial numbers and print data matrices on drug packaging. Such software allows for serializing each produced drug and also collects data on manufacturing events such as manufacturing delays, supply disruptions and discontinuation. On the other hand, hospitals and pharmacies are equipped with terminals that connect to a centralized online portal in order to declare and validate the dispensing of drugs. As a result, traceability data is used to avoid the dispensing of a non-valid serial number, but it can also be aggregated in order to produce information about inventory levels at laboratories and hospitals. In an ideal world, authorities would obtain all of this information, which would allow them to work alongside manufacturers, distributors and dispensers in order to minimize shutdowns or slowdowns leading to shortages and to encourage smart distribution. Serialization regulations should make it easier to collect such data. As a matter of fact, the Electronic Product Code Information Service (EPCIS) gathers information related to each event in the life cycle of a product (production, transport, distribution, etc.) in a standard form in order to easily share it with business partners and authorities [11].

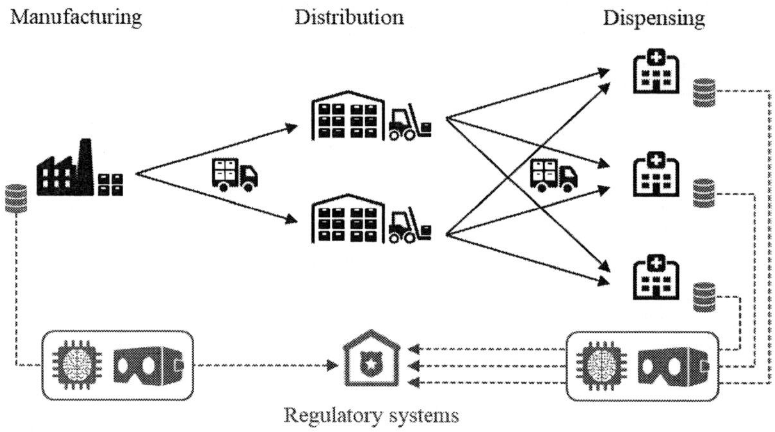

Figure 1: Data collection points in the PSC.

2.1. Data science for decision support in Supply Chain management

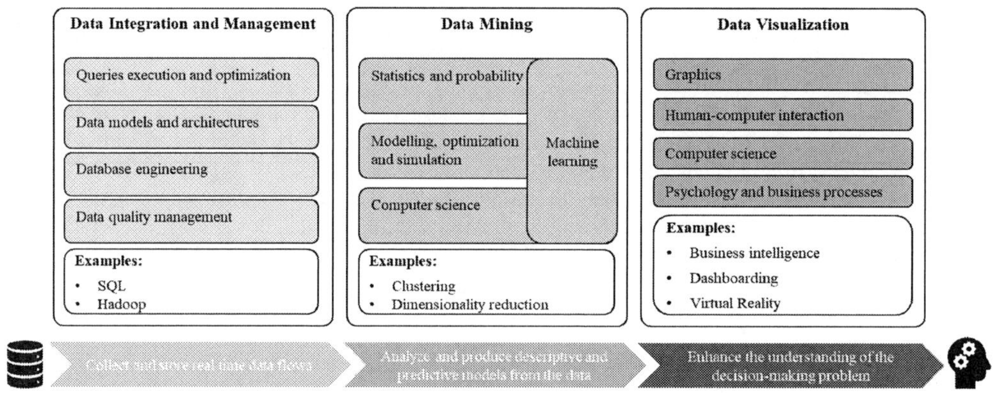

Figure 2: Overview of data science activities for decision support.

Talley [12] shows that the smart use of available data can provide an efficient decision-making support system. Figure 2 describes the process through which the three main activities of data science, namely data integration and management, data mining, and data visualization, transform raw data flows into a decision support system:

(1) Data integration and management build a global infrastructure supporting the efficient collection, storage and accessibility of massive incoming raw data flows, while ensuring security, timeliness, and data quality [12].

(2) Data mining analyzes and extracts useful information from data. It uses statistics and probability, modelling, simulation and optimization, and computer methods and tools in order to produce predictive or descriptive models [4], [13].

(3) Data visualization overlaps the research fields of graphics, computer science, human-computer interaction, psychology and business processes, in order to enhance the understanding of information flows and enable relevant decision making [5], [14].

The objective of this paper is to focus on the first two activities and investigate (i) what opportunities data mining and dataviz enable, and (ii) what the requirements are in terms of data, infrastructure and procedures in order to implement such opportunities.

3. State of the art

In order to analyze how data mining and dataviz tools can provide new insights into operational and tactical decisions of the pharmaceutical industry, this section summarizes a literature review that identifies the current main challenges in the PSC; the current applications of data mining and data visualization in healthcare; and the notion of pharmaceutical industry 4.0. This literature review was conducted by surveying the ScienceDirect database with the following strings: "pharmaceutical supply chain"; "data mining" AND "supply chain"; "visualization" AND "supply chain"; "data mining" AND "healthcare". After reviewing the abstracts, only papers dealing with the topics listed above were selected. In addition, a first analysis of these articles revealed that demand forecasting is a key challenge in the PSC, and that today, very few solutions using data mining are implemented in the pharmaceutical industry. Thus, the bibliography was supplemented with a few relevant articles that tackle the issue of "demand forecasting".

3.1. The main challenges in the PSC

Pharmaceutical supply chain management is an emerging subject of research [7], [15], with an increasing number of publications each year. Today, the PSC addresses three main challenges related to forecasting, collaboration and performance metrics.

(1) **Inaccurate forecasting:** manufacturers and dispensers rely on very simple methods such as "smoothing and averaging methods performed mainly in Excel spreadsheets", which produce considerable forecasting errors [9]. This issue affects inventory management, which is hardly efficient as well. Indeed, demand forecasting errors result in frequent medicine shortages in hospitals and at the same time, overstock in laboratories [9], [16], [17]. In addition, overstock is a source of waste, which also raises concerns about environmental sustainability [7], [15].

(2) **Inefficient collaboration between the actors in a supply chain**, which also explains inventory management issues [7], [9], [15], [17]. The various actors of the PSC do not share real-time data, which leads to poor coordination. As a matter of fact, the frequent medicine returns, accounting for 3-6% of yearly sales, are mainly due to the expiry date because manufacturers, distributors, and dispensers have different constraints and lead times [7], [16], [17].

(3) **Lack of quantitative performance criteria** in terms of PSC management [7], [17]. For instance, the lack of expertise on the part of purchasing managers in supply chain management makes it difficult to quantitatively evaluate the performance of suppliers [7].

3.2. Applications of data mining

Authors agree that the use of big data analytics, artificial intelligence, and the sharing of real-time data between all of the actors in a production and supply network are essential solutions to the previous issues, but the pharmaceutical industry is still reluctant to use them [7], [9], [15]. This explains why little is published about solutions implemented in this domain. The few works that apply artificial intelligence to the PSC deal with demand forecasting [9], [10], [18]. For instance, Merkuryeva [9] experiments with the Simple Moving Average (SMA), Linear Regression and Symbolic Regression three demand forecasting methods on a specific in-market product and concludes that symbolic regression-based forecasting provides lower error estimates.

Several studies focus on improving demand forecasting in various industries [19]. Brusset [20] analyses the correlations between demand and the weather. Agnew [21] more precisely analyses how the weather affects sales in the UK food industry. Tanizaki [22] proposes a machine learning model to predict demand in restaurants in Japan using restaurants' internal data and external data, such as the weather. Gaur experiments with the K-nearest neighbor, Bayesian networks, and Adaptative Boosting machine learning methods for demand prediction [23]. Silva [24] demonstrated that neural networks can be used as supply chain forecasting tools. The authors explored two models using historical data in order to predict the future status of a simple supply chain; their work yielded outstanding results since the neural networks reached 99.5% and 97% accuracy levels [24].

Future forecast models for PSC can draw inspiration from relevant industries such as food and cosmetics [7]. Demand for pharmaceutical products certainly depends on factors such as the location of consumers, the weather, or episodes of epidemics.

3.3. Pharma 4.0

Industry 4.0 is expected to drive higher performance in the pharmaceutical sector, mainly enabled by cyber-physical systems, which will increase the number of data sources significantly [7]. The use of cyber-physical systems should allow more accurate forecasts to be made, improve resources and processes, and reduce frequent drug shortages and overstocks [6], [7]. Additionally, track-and-trace solutions will enable the storage and distribution of products to be optimized [6], [25]. Also, new transport systems, including real-time tracking, will enable communication between pharmaceutical companies, their business partners, carriers, and customers [6], [7].

An important point to bring up is that product serialization is not only a regulatory matter, but also one of the building blocks of Industry 4.0 [7]. Indeed, serialization devices enable the collection and sharing production and track-and-trace information among the different actors in a PSC. Indeed, data sharing between the different actors of a PSC significantly reduces the logistical costs of manufacturers, which is quantified by Lee [26]. Today, the fact that companies are reluctant to share real-time sales and production information with their partners is the main inhibitor to the implementation of efficient demand forecasting models [20]. Hence, serialization should be a real catalyst for such data sharing, and it should foster supply chain visibility, collaboration and communication between stakeholders.

4. Results and discussion

This section presents the opportunities identified that would make use of serialized pharmaceutical data through data mining and dataviz. In particular, it highlights the enablers and requirements in terms of the data from such opportunities, as summarized in Table 1, and the prerequisites in terms of infrastructure and procedures for the implementation of such opportunities.

Table 1: Main opportunities for serialized data mining of pharmaceuticals.

Opportunity	Value for hospitals	Value for laboratories	Data requirements
Forecast demand	Predicting demand accurately should significantly reduce uncertainty at the hospital level, reducing stock-outs and overstocks.	Predicting demand accurately should streamline the pharmaceutical supply chain, reducing stock-outs and overstocks and improving overall service rates.	• Consumption by product. • Orders and receipt of orders at hospitals. • Manufacturing logs. • Inventories (manufacturers and hospitals). • External data (weather, holidays, news, social media …).
Predict inventories behavior (stock-outs and/or overstock.)	Predicting inventory levels should allow hospitals to anticipate upcoming stock-outs and deploy backup plans to reduce impacts on final consumers (i.e. avoid medicine shortages and sub-optimal treatment).	Predicting inventory levels should allow manufacturers to consistently adjust their short-term plans and communicate with hospitals in order to increase overall resilience.	• Consumption by product. • Orders and reception of hospitals. • Shipments of manufacturers. • Manufacturing and transportation logs. • Inventories (manufacturers and hospitals). • External data (weather, holidays, news, social media, …).
Cluster customers, suppliers and/or products	Clustering drugs and suppliers according to different parameters (consumption, delivery times, availability) should provide hospitals with decision support for improving planning.	Clustering clients (hospitals) according to different parameters should provide laboratories with decision support for planning production, inventories and distribution.	• Consumption by product. • Orders and reception of hospitals. • Orders and shipments of manufacturers. • Master data of customers, products and suppliers.
Identify seasonal behaviors of customers, suppliers and/or products	Identifying seasonal peaks of consumption for each product should provide hospitals with decision support for managing inventories and improve tactical decision-making (medium-term planning).	Identifying seasonal peaks of consumption for each product and client should allow manufacturers to improve planning in manufacturing and distribution.	• Consumption by product. • Orders and reception of hospitals. • Orders and shipments of manufacturers. • Lead-times of manufacturers (by product). • Master data of customers, products and suppliers. • External data (weather, holidays, news, social media, …).

4.1. Opportunities and enablers

Four main opportunities are identified, namely: (1) demand forecast; (2) inventory prediction; (3) client, supplier, and product clustering; and (4) identification of seasonal behavior.

Authors have shown that performing statistical analysis and machine learning on historical data of consumption, production, inventory, and distribution, provides more accurate predictions of demand [9], [23], [19]. Such methods should therefore enable a better understanding and more accurate estimate of the demand and inventory of medicine. So far, the lack of sharing data has been a major obstacle in implementing such tools. The context of serialization should help overcome this issue. In addition, mining algorithms can use exogenous data such as the weather, the calendar, or news articles warning about epidemic episodes. Thus, data mining techniques should provide more accurate forecasts and enable higher service levels, reduced stock-outs and overstocks, enhanced communication between stakeholders, and better anticipation of disruptive events.

In addition, deeper analyses of this data and its correlation should provide better insight into the dynamics of the pharmaceutical industry. In particular, clustering clients, manufacturers and products according to relevant parameters should provide support for identifying segments and applying different management policies. Likewise, identifying the seasonal behaviors of consumers and products should help decision makers point out sensitive periods in the year when special actions must be taken.

4.2. Prerequisites for implementation

Implementing these opportunities implies having a given infrastructure for collecting data. Table 1 specifies the required data for each opportunity. Although companies are often reluctant to share such data [7], it is noteworthy that most of this information is already available and furthermore, some of it is collected in the context of drug serialization. In Table 1, the symbol 💻 relates to the data of internal information systems such as enterprise resource planning (ERP), transport management systems (TMS), warehouse management systems (WMS), manufacturing execution systems (MES); ▦ relates to data collected to comply with serialization regulations; and ✓ relates to data that mining systems already collect and exploit mainly for marketing purposes and for which proficient algorithms exist.

Accurate predictions for demand and inventory cannot replace human expertise, which is necessary to adjust the forecasts to factors that are not considered by the models, such as competition, advertising and disruptive events (breakdowns, errors, or delays) [27]. Therefore, to fully exploit these opportunities, it is necessary to develop visualization interfaces in which decision makers find deeper insights into tactical and operational issues. It should be noted that in the context of multiple sources of highly heterogeneous data with dynamic behaviors, it would be very important to build user-friendly visualization tools so that all of this data could truly embody a decision support system.

Last, it would be necessary to tackle technical issues concerning how to collect and process these real-time data streams securely, how to collect and integrate exogenous data, which methods and tools for data mining and dataviz should be adapted and implemented, and how to integrate these models with the information systems in place.

5. Conclusion

With new regulations on serialized traceability and Industry 4.0, pharmaceutical flows will generate massive volumes of data, which can no longer be managed with the tools used so far, such as spreadsheet software. As a result, the use of data science (cf. Figure 2) will not only be necessary to handle these flows in the era of Pharma 4.0, but also represent an opportunity to substantially enhance the PSC. In particular, data integration and management will be necessary for the collection, storage and access to serialized pharmaceutical data, while ensuring security, timeliness, and quality. Once this infrastructure is set up, data mining and dataviz should transform this data into useful and clearly understandable information, thus improving upon the decision making in supply chain management.

This paper has focused on the opportunities for using data mining and dataviz to improve tactical and operational decisions in PSC management. Four main opportunities were identified: (1) demand forecasts; (2) inventory prediction; (3) client, supplier, and product clustering; and (4) seasonal behavior identification.

Data mining tools will provide more accurate predictions on the PSC, while dataviz will be essential in better understanding the data involved in the PSC and the correlation between that data. Thus, such solutions would help the PSC take on the current major challenges related to inaccurate forecasts and poor communication and collaboration between actors in a production and distribution network. Both manufacturers and hospitals would gain similar benefits from such opportunities, mostly related to demand forecasts, which are a major issue since they are the starting point of all PSC planning decisions [9].

So far, a major inhibitor for implementing such solutions was the fact that companies are reluctant to share their manufacturing and sales data. In this context, serialization regulations should foster data sharing and open a way for the pharmaceutical industry to take more interest in these opportunities to use data mining and dataviz techniques to enhance the PSC. Also, future research will focus on how to collect and process real-time serialized pharmaceutical flows, which techniques in data mining and dataviz best address the identified PSC challenges, and how to integrate such solutions into different information systems.

6. References

1. World Health Organization: A Study on the public health and socioeconomic impact of substandard and falsified medical products. (2017)
2. European Commission: 2016/161 Supplement to Directive 2001/83/EC. (2015)
3. United States Congress: Drug Supply Chain Security Act. (2013)
4. Jothi, N., Rashid, N. A., Husain, W.: Data Mining in Healthcare - A Review. Procedia Comput. Sci. vol. 72, pp. 306–313 (2015)
5. Ilsen, R., Rupprecht, F., Mert, G., Yi, L., Ebert, A., Aurich, J. C.: Impact-visualization to evaluate resource efficiency of technical Product-Service Systems. Procedia CIRP vol. 79, pp. 215–220 (2019)
6. Barreto, L., Amaral, A., Pereira, T.: Industry 4.0 implications in logistics: an overview. Procedia Manuf. vol. 13, pp. 1245–1252 (2017)
7. Ding, B.: Pharma Industry 4.0: Literature review and research opportunities in sustainable pharmaceutical supply chains. Process Saf. Environ. Prot. vol. 119, pp. 115–130 (2018)
8. European Association of Hospital Pharmacists: Medicines Shortages in European Hospitals. (2018)
9. Merkuryeva, G., Valberga, A., Smirnov, A.: Demand forecasting in pharmaceutical supply chains: A case study. Procedia Comput. Sci. vol. 149, pp. 3–10 (2019)
10. Fruggiero, F., Iannone, R., Martino, G., Miranda, S., Riemma, S.: A forecast model for pharmaceutical requirements based on an artificial neural network. In: Proceedings of 2012 IEEE International Conference on Service Operations and Logistics, and Informatics pp. 263–268 (2012)
11. GS1: https://www.gs1.org/standards/epcis
12. Talley, T. M., Talburt, J. R., Chan, Y.: Introduction., In: Data Engineering: Mining, Information and Intelligence, Yupo Chan and John R. Talburt, Springer, Boston, MA, pp. 1–16 (2001)
13. Jure, L., Anand, R., Ullman, J.: Data Mining., In: Mining of Massive Datasets, 2014th ed., (2014)
14. B. Bederson, B., Shneiderman, B.: The Craft of Information Visualization: Readings and Reflections. Morgan Kaufmann, (2003)
15. Narayana, S. A., Kumar Pati, R., Vrat, P.: Managerial research on the pharmaceutical supply chain - A critical review and some insights for future directions. J. Purch. Supply Manag. vol. 20 no. 1, pp. 18–40 (2014)
16. Nematollahi, M., Hosseini-Motlagh, S. M., Ignatius, J., Goh, M., Saghafi Nia, M.: Coordinating a socially responsible pharmaceutical supply chain under periodic review replenishment policies. J. Clean. Prod. vol. 172, pp. 2876–2891 (2018)
17. Kapoor, D., Vyas, R., Dadarwal, D.: An Overview on Pharmaceutical Supply Chain: A Next Step towards Good Manufacturing Practice. Drug Des. Intellect. Prop. Int. J. vol. 1 no. 2, pp. 49–54 (2018)
18. Candan, G., Taskin, M. F., Yazgan, H. R.: Demand Forecasting In Pharmaceutical Industry Using Neuro-Fuzzy Approach. J. Mil. Inf. Sci. vol. 2 no. 2, p. 41 (2014)
19. Usuga Cadavid, J. P., Lamouri, S., Grabot, B.: Trends in Machine Learning Applied to Demand & Sales Forecasting : A Review. (2018)
20. Brusset, X., Bertrand, J. L.: Hedging weather risk and coordinating supply chains. J. Oper. Manag. vol. 64 no. December, pp. 41–52 (2018)
21. Agnew, M. D., Thornes, J. E.: The weather sensitivity of the UK food retail and distribution industry. Meteorol. Appl. vol. 2 no. 2, pp. 137–147 (1995)
22. Tanizaki, T., Hoshino, T., Shimmura, T., Takenaka, T.: Demand forecasting in restaurants using machine learning and statistical analysis. Procedia CIRP vol. 79 no. ii, pp. 679–683 (2019)
23. Gaur, M., Goel, S., Jain, E.: Comparison between nearest Neighbours and Bayesian network for demand forecasting in supply chain management. In: 2nd International Conference on Computing for Sustainable Global Development, INDIACom 2015 pp. 1433–1436 no. July (2015)
24. Silva, N., Ferreira, L. M. D. F., Silva, C., Magalhães, V., Neto, P.: Improving Supply Chain Visibility With Artificial Neural Networks. Procedia Manuf. vol. 11 no. June, pp. 2083–2090 (2017)
25. Da Silva, R. B., de Mattos, C. A.: Critical success factors of a drug traceability system for creating value in a pharmaceutical supply chain (PSC). Int. J. Environ. Res. Public Health vol. 16 no. 11, (2019)
26. Lee, H. L., So, K. C., Tang, C. S.: The Value of Information Sharing in a Two-Level Supply Chain. Manage. Sci. vol. 46 no. 5, pp. 626–643 (2000)
27. Perera, H. N., Hurley, J., Fahimnia, B., Reisi, M.: The human factor in supply chain forecasting: A systematic review. Eur. J. Oper. Res. vol. 274 no. 2, pp. 574–600 (2019)

A Systematic Literature Review of Ecosystems: An Approach to Introduce Logistics Ecosystems into Academia

Marvin Lamberjohann [1], Boris Otto [2]

[1] Technical University Dortmund, Dortmund, Germany
[2] Fraunhofer Institute for Software and Systems Engineering ISST, Dortmund, Germany
{marvin.lamberjohann@tu-dortmund.de, boris.otto@tu-dortmund.de}

Abstract. The term *ecosystem* experiences a peak in academic attention, however, its usage varies as well as its application in certain industries. In the world of logistics, the usage of the term ecosystem is not common within academia. Hence, a systematic literature review has been performed by scanning 146 studies out of an original dataset of 2264 results. This systematic literature review has got the goal to create a methodological overview of the term ecosystem, create types of ecosystems, and merge them with similar studies out of the supply chain management research area. Finally, this paper identifies a commonality that justifies a merge of supply chain management collaboration approaches and the general research of ecosystems and sets a foundation for future research.

Keywords: logistics ecosystem, supply chain management, collaborative networks, platform, systematic literature review

1 Introduction

In academia [1] but as well in practice [2] *ecosystems* and *platforms* are two of the most discussed topics. Ecosystems are in the focus of these disciplines because once established in the right way, these kinds of platform-based business models represent the most value-creating and highest valuated companies in the world [3]. Moreover, their relevance increased in academia since the design and setup represent a complex challenge. Mainly since its advent by Moore's [4] published article about business ecosystems, academia concentrates more on this topic with tangible case studies and further examinations with regards to multiple industries.

The intention and idea for this paper originate from the question of how logistics or supply chain ecosystems can be actually understood from an Information Systems (IS) perspective. Logistics ecosystem represents a wording that rather stems from managerial studies, but these studies already create a link from the pure supply chain management (SCM) view to the ecosystem research [5]. Since logistics or SCM represents an interdisciplinary area of research with multiple participants along the value chain [6], it embodies a perfect breeding ground for the discussion around ecosystems [7]. Especially in the SCM studies, supply chain networks and collaborative networks are vivid terms that can be compared to ecosystems. For analyzing this hypothesis, a proper analysis of the term ecosystem and its synonyms has to be conducted, including its clustering and classifications for finally bringing it together with relevant studies out of the area of SCM. For having a proper overview and understanding of the idea of an ecosystem, it is necessary to identify the different definitions proposed by the scholars. That is done by listing the stated definitions out of the ecosystem versus SCM research community and showing differences and similarities. Thus, the first research question reads as follows:

RQ1: How is the term ecosystem defined in literature?

The outcome of *RQ1* is used in order to group the identified literature and derive ecosystem types. Hereby, the outcome of Benedict [8] is used and critically reviewed. The clustering is performed according to the given definitions and how the scholars are sorting in their research outcome, which leads to *RQ2*:

RQ2: What types of ecosystems can be derived according to literature?

As outlined in the introduction, the purpose of this paper is to examine if there is an overlap or connection between research in the area of SCM and ecosystems. According to the derivation of ecosystem types, an excerpt of common SCM studies is compared to that for identifying commonalities, which is pointed out in *RQ3*:

RQ3: How can the outcomes of research in the area of supply chain management contribute to the ecosystem undertakings or vice versa?

The remaining parts of the article are structured as follows: in chapter 2, the design of the systematic literature review (SLR), its review protocol, and the collection of the literature body are described. In the following chapter 3, the research questions get answered by analyzing the retrieved literature. Chapter 4, opens a discussion with regards to the focal study's validity and specific risks, respectively, inaccuracies according to the given review protocol and dataset. Lastly, chapter 5 summarizes the outcome and concludes the article.

2 Research Design

2.1 Design of Literature Review and Review Protocol

The authors chose to carry out a SLR as a rigorous approach to answer the research questions outlined above [9,10]. Its purpose is to summarize the existing evidence in the focal research area, to identify research gaps, and to address future research avenues [9,11]. For ensuring an auditable literature review, it is necessary to define a review protocol considering its research questions and review method [9]. The applied parameters can be reviewed for allowing repetition of the literature retrieval process. Since the focal paper tries to merge different research areas, the epistemological model of literature reviews by Schryen *et al.* [12] is applied, too. In this particular case, the review strategy is twofold by (a) executing a database search and (b) conducting a manual retrieval process. The manual process has been used to avoid biases in the automated keyword research [9,11].

Regarding (a) the search takes into consideration the years from January 1993 to June 2019 where 1993 has been chosen due to the set nucleus of business ecosystems by Moore [4]. For each database the search terms *ecosystem* and *platform* have been used in order to have a broad coverage. These search terms have been scanned for titles, abstracts, and keywords. Initially, only the term *ecosystem* should have been used but due to the application of forward and backward research *platform* has been identified as a comparable term [13]. The databases of choice have been picked according to Manikas and Hansen [14] as well as Schreieck *et al.* [15]. Moreover, options to apply filters have been used to narrow down the amount of results since ecosystems and platforms are widely used terms across different scientific disciplines. For executing the search, the following scientific libraries have been used:

- The ACM Digital Library[1]
- Thomson Reuters' Web of Science[2]
- EBSCO[3]

According to the results, all the sources have been merged into one document for eliminating duplicates and having a proper overview. With regards to (b) the manual search, a forward and backward search have been conducted by taking Moore [4] as the nucleus and searching for further links [13]. By comparing the references across the different articles, one could derive relevant articles and cluster them into specific research areas. Furthermore, comparisons of keywords helped to find other adjacent papers of interest.

[1] Source: https://dl.acm.org; filters: PDF format; results: 541.
[2] Source: https://apps.webofknowledge.com; filters: Economics, Computer Science Information Systems, Computer Science Theory Methods, Computer Science Interdisciplinary Applications, Management, Computer Science Software Engineering; Social Science Citation Index; Highly cited in field; results: 219 (from 2009 – 2019).
[3] Source: http://web.a.ebscohost.com; filters: academic journals; communication systems, computer science, information and communication, management & management theory, systems theory; control, applications; English; results: 1544 (whereby only 1504 exportable and therefore analyzable).

2.2 Collecting the Literature Body

For conducting the SLR properly, the review protocol of chapter 2.1 has been applied in six steps as you can see below (see Figure 1).

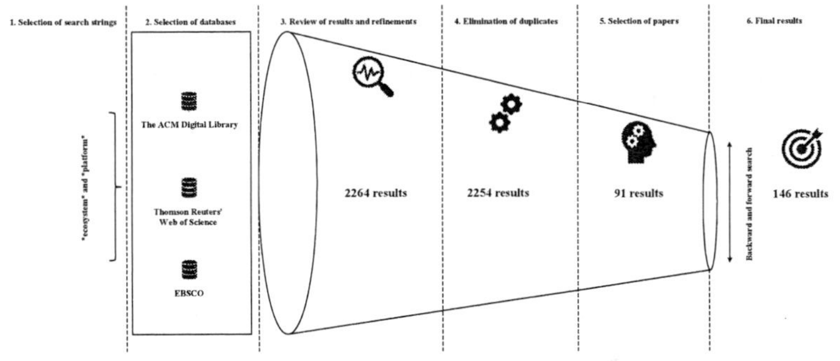

Figure 1: Six step process for the systematic literature review.

The extraction date of all three database retrieval processes is June 23rd, 2019. Hence, an initial dataset covering the search terms *ecosystem* and *platform* has been collected which ended up in 2264 results. Ten duplicates could be eliminated that resulted in 2254 entries. The remaining results have been manually checked according to expected content in the area of management and information systems. This covered mainly checking the titles, abstracts, and areas of research [10]. Due to the already mentioned broad usage of the terms *ecosystem* and *platform* many results came out of adjacent research fields. Moreover, additional filtering for narrowing down the results was not possible via the chosen databases. Many others were not covering the core of a definition of these terms and were therefore excluded, too. Thus, afterwards, 91 results remained that have been studied in detail, which have been further enriched with manually re-trieved research papers through backward and forward searches, which resulted in 146 papers total. These articles have been mainly identified through citation paths going further from the nucleus of Moore [4].

3 Literature Analysis

3.1 Ecosystem Definition

This chapter covers the analysis of the research questions by taking into consideration the literature results of chapter 2.2. Generally, it is observable that after the year 2009, an increasing number of articles have been published in the area of ecosystems. Within the given dataset it peaked in 2016 with 19 published papers. Referencing to the outcomes of research question one, most of the groundwork has been done in the years between 2000 and 2006. Afterwards, the research topics and ecosystems types spread steadily, which resulted in more published papers with the general topic of ecosystems. The year 2019 only covers published papers until the beginning of June, which might be one reason for its comparatively low figure of only two published papers. Details about the publishing years can be found in the following exhibit (see Figure 2):

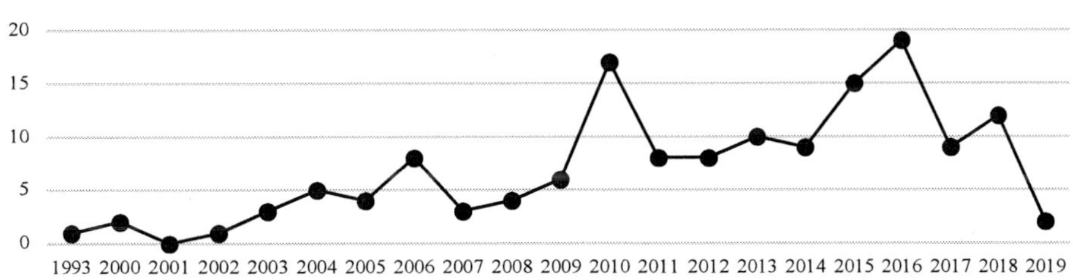

Figure 2: Papers published per year.

RQ1: How is the term ecosystem defined in literature?

The ecosystem term has steadily evolved over time. The nucleus of business ecosystems has been set by Moore [4]. From that point onward, the term was developed further and later broadened and used in other contexts. Initially, Moore [4] defines a *business ecosystem* as a conglomerate of companies that "[...] co-evolve capabilities around a new innovation: they work cooperatively and competitively to support new products, satisfy customer needs, and eventually incorporate the next round of innovations [...]". This definition has been further developed by Iansiti and Levien [16,17] by focusing on the success or health factors and thereby coining the term *keystone*. Keystones can be described as companies that bring balance into the ecosystem because they "[...] aim to improve the overall health of their ecosystems by providing a stable and predictable set of common assets [...]" [16]. Still, their focus is on business ecosystems where it is about creating value by sharing values with other participants.

In parallel, a further ecosystem definition can be found that has been named *two-sided platforms*. They evolved during the same time but are rather inspired by Moore's [4] business ecosystem idea. Rochet and Tirole [18,19] used the ideas of Baxter [20] and Wright [21] related to the pricing and card payment systems. The concept can be described as "[...] one or several platforms [that] enable interactions between end-users and try to get the two (or multiple) sides "on board" [...]"[19]. The separation from the earlier mentioned business ecosystems can be seen in the way in which terms are emphasized. A business ecosystem concentrates on a co-evolutionary work and on new capabilities for maximizing value, a two- or multi-sided platform rather takes care of the problematic of onboarding the distinct sides in a proper way and charging respectively incentivizing them accordingly, which can be as well-referenced as the *chicken and egg problematic* [22].

A branch that appeared during the same time is the one coined by Cusumano and Gawer [23]. It focuses on the term *platforms* with respect of driving innovation around the technological platform across diverse participants [23]. Hence, it is closely related to the idea of a business ecosystem. However, it emphasizes the need for a common scope and product or platform technology across the different complementors [23]. The idea of supply chain, industry or cross-industry platforms has been further pursued by Gawer [24], Cusumano [25,26], and Tiwana [27], which focus on the idea of the platform with a defined scope and standard technology to maximize value.

In the meantime, a further path can be noted, which is the area of *alliances*. From a plain definition, alliances can be seen as "[...] complex organizational forms that are usefully viewed as incomplete contracts [...]" [28], which ultimately implies that unforeseen changes can quickly disrupt their existence or at least affect them drastically. Alliances try to create value in an accumulated fashion by summing up the individual experience for a common goal [28]. Due to its intention of pursuing a common goal in an interfirm relationship, alliances appear to belong as well to the ecosystem environment.

Another endeavor that arose is the idea of *collaborative networks*. They represent, similar to alliances, heterogeneous and autonomous organizations that collaborate in "[...] networks with larger numbers of indirect ties [to create] an effective way for actors to enjoy the benefits of network size without paying the costs of network maintenance [...]" [29]. Camarinha-Matos [30] further elaborates that "[...] collaborative networks shall focus on the structure, behavior, and evolving dynamics of networks of autonomous entities that collaborate to better achieve common or compatible goals [...]".

Based on the ideas of Chesbrough [31–33], *innovation ecosystems* represent a different form of ecosystems. It merges the idea of open innovation with business ecosystems which "[...] embed the focal firm within an ecosystem of interdependent innovation [...]" [34] and where "[...] firms combine their individual offerings into a coherent, customer-facing solution [...]" [35].

Knowledge platforms hook into this idea of innovation ecosystems since they lay the foundation to exchange knowledge. Knowledge platforms allow interaction across multiple companies to create transparency and synergies across the value chain [36,37]. Thus, there is a close relation to the concept of innovation ecosystems to share openly information about a dedicated topic, respectively, processes.

A separate stream that appeared that relates to the concept of ecosystems are *software ecosystems*. According to Manikas and Hansen [14], the original definition of a software ecosystem stems from Messerschmitt and Szyperski's book [38] where they claim that software ecosystems are a collection of software products with a certain relationship. This definition has been further enhanced by adding characteristics like business functions, enabling services, collaboration, developer community that work within the same environment or ecosystem [39–43]. From an overall idea, it points back to the origins of business ecosystems where entities are openly collaborating for driving innovation and creating value.

In a similar area, the term *digital ecosystem* is used. It is based upon business ecosystems and represents "[...] a software infrastructure for supporting large numbers of interacting business users and services [...]" [44,45]. Moreover, digital ecosystems adapt according to economic forces by sharing knowledge and foster distributed and cooperative work [45]. So, in contrast to the software ecosystem that rather represents a purely technical system, digital ecosystem still can be seen as part of the socio-technical system area [8,45].

Lastly, the term of *service ecosystem* can be observed. Vargo and Lusch [46] coined this term by introducing the service-dominant logic, which emphasizes that value is co-created by and with the consumers and not in a pure output fashion. Liu *et al.* [47] put it further and define service ecosystems as "[...] a value-propagating system, [which] incorporates the mechanism of self-organization and co-evolution of ecosystem into service system to construct a capability infrastructure that synergizes and improves organizations' collective intelligence continuously to adapt to new business vision and chances [...]" [48].

In summary, the difference between the presented definitions is in most of the cases minor, which allows to merge them under the subsuming headline of ecosystems. However, by comparing all the diverse definitions of the specific derivations of ecosystems, ecosystems are still understood in different ways. Nevertheless, a commonality can be seen which allows a possible overarching ecosystem definition accordingly:

> *An ecosystem represents typically loosely coupled or self-organized entities collaborating in a symbiotic relationship in order to co-evolve capabilities, co-create innovative services or solutions, share knowledge, foster transactions, and leverage network synergies in a typically technology-enabled environment for offering optimized or novel customer- or partner-facing solutions.*

3.2 Ecosystem Types

As shown in the previous chapter, ecosystem definitions evolved over time and tackled various areas of interest. However, the identified definitions already cluster themselves according to given references, which ultimately leads to ecosystem types and therefore to *RQ2*.

RQ2: What types of ecosystems can be derived according to literature?

Benedict [8] already worked on a comprehensive overview of ecosystems that shall be used as a basis but as well be challenged by putting it into a broader context and later to compare it to supply chain research. By analyzing the given definitions and comparing it to Benedict's [8] seven types of ecosystems, the technology ecosystem has not been identified in the given data set and could therefore not be approved. It is far away from the classical ecosystem goal of creating or maximizing value. Normally, the idea of ecosystems is driven by the actors, however, the technology ecosystems skips this perspective [8]. Thereby, three new ones have been identified and introduced: alliances, collaborative networks, and knowledge platforms. According to the definition of these two types of alliances and collaborative networks and the derived ecosystem definition, they fit into concepts like business ecosystems or platforms with the common target to achieve a common target and create value together with the involved entities. Hence, it is proposed to add them to the overarching family of ecosystems. The knowledge platforms are closely related to the innovation ecosystem but rather concentrated on pure exchange without a common goal. Most of the analyzed ecosystems are software ecosystems with 49 entries that especially became more important after 2010. The second mostly classified ecosystem type is the platform with 23 entries. According to the applied review protocol, the least entries can be indicated in the area of alliances and collaborative networks with two and three results, which seems reasonable since they are normally not linked with ecosystem or platform terms. Clustering the ecosystem types into the system types of (a) socio-economic, (b) socio-technical, and (c) technical systems according to Benedict [8], it results into (a) 42, (b) 87, and (c) 49[4] entries. That already shows that the clear majority is preferably in a mixture of social-technical, which emphasizes the move to technical ecosystem environments. So irrelated from an industry focus the pure ecosystem analysis shows a tendency to more software-related ecosystems (see Figure 3).

---

[4] The software ecosystem type has been counted twice into socio-technical and technical systems due to reasons of simplicity.

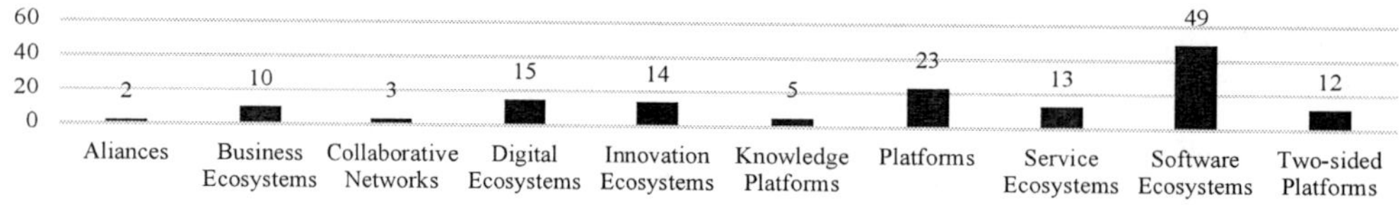

Figure 3: Papers published by ecosystem types.

3.3 Merge of Ecosystems with Supply Chain Management

RQ3: How can the outcomes of research in the area of supply chain management contribute to the ecosystem undertakings or vice versa?

Especially the collaboration between multiple entities to achieve a common goal is something that plays a vital role in the supply chain, too. For example, Adams *et al.* [49] already made references to Vargo and Lusch [46,50] and mentioned the need to develop "[...] collaborative, relational capabilities that support supply chain integration [...]" [49]. Moreover, challenges in the world of ecosystems like, for instance, the *chicken and egg problematic* is readopted in the SCM literature. Barratt [51], for instance, lists the different challenges with regards to the collaboration in the supply chain as follows: "[...] supply chain collaboration has proved difficult to implement [52]; there has been an over-reliance on technology trying to implement it [53]; a failure of differentiate between whom to collaborate, i.e. segmentation of customers and or suppliers [52]; and fundamentally a lack of trust between trading partners [54][...]" [51]. These overlaps come along with the fragmented supply network that somehow needs to be orchestrated [55]. Furthermore, trends like the general mechanization foster the need to find common ways of interaction [6,56,57]. In the past, the focus was mainly on physical transportation and the conversion from raw materials into products [58] but today, the focus has shifted to create transparency, share knowledge, and maximize value [59]. This is supported by the trend of increasing software ecosystem related studies. Since the SCM already represents an interdisciplinary function, its merge with ecosystem research seems to be reasonable [59]. This should be done by re-using for instance the first drafts of tackling the *chicken and egg problematic*, co-creating services in the right way, organizing partners, and applying these on issues identified in the area of SCM.

4 Discussion

The purpose and intention of the focal study is to lay a foundation for a closer interlinkage between the research of ecosystem and SCM based on the analysis of the review protocol. As elaborated in chapter 2, the ecosystem literature and especially the usage of the keywords are broad. Hence, the literature review has been conducted to the best of the author's knowledge by applying the right filters in order to drill the issues down to the critical studies relevant to the focal work. The same applies to the addition of relevant scientific works on a manual basis. Certain overlaps and similarities could be identified across the different usage of the term ecosystem. Still, the commonality shows that these studies definitely belong to the same area of research. Apart from the commonalities, the differences across the analyzed studies were sufficient to allow creating ecosystem types with the general ecosystem approach. Although the outcome seems reasonable with the given dataset, it cannot be ruled out that further literature might have been added for getting further insights. Furthermore, a bigger dataset than 146 sources might have a varying impact and maturity as well. Nevertheless, the given dataset and its analysis could show a clear tendency which allows making the derivations and statements that have been presented in chapter 3. Moreover, the connection with common literature out of the SCM area showed clear tendencies that similar challenges are described in comparison to the ecosystem literature.

5 Conclusion

In this study, the term ecosystem has been examined with the goal to show the differences in meaning. That has been done by analyzing 146 scientific papers published between 1993 and 2019 with corresponding keywords. The result shows that there are overlaps and comparable challenges faced in the research areas of ecosystems and SCM, which supports the argumentation of an interlinkage of both areas and that should help to solve unanswered questions in both scientific disciplines. However, future research is necessary to bring these two disciplines closer. Generally, this paper contributes to the existing literature by extending it with a comprehensive SLR and defining a common understanding of ecosystems. Furthermore, this article sketches a first move to bring two separated research disciplines closer together. From a managerial perspective, it delivers a proper concept overview of ecosystem types and their differences. Since the conclusions are based upon a pure literature review without practical insights, they bear certain limitations. Thus, further reviews should enhance this foundational study by conducting empirical and qualitative studies that uses outcomes of the ecosystem research applied in SCM practice and vice versa.

6 Bibliography

1. How Digital Platforms Have Become Double-Edged Swords, https://sloanreview.mit.edu/article/how-digital-platforms-have-become-double-edged-swords/.
2. The Right Digital-Platform Strategy, https://www.mckinsey.com/business-functions/digital-mckinsey/our-insights/the-right-digital-platform-strategy.
3. Plattform-Index 15, https://www.plattform-index.com.
4. Moore, J.F., Predators and Prey: A New Ecology of Competition, Harvard Business Review (1993).
5. It Takes An Ecosystem: Transportation-Focused Executives Turn To Outside Providers, Customers, Suppliers And Competitors, https://www.forbes.com/sites/insights-penske/2018/09/25/it-takes-an-ecosystem-transportation-focused-executives-turn-to-outside-providers-customers-suppliers-and-competitors/#581ef3b61de6.
6. Sanders, N.R., Premus, R., Modeling the Relationship Between Firm IT Capability, Collaboration, and Performance, Journal of Business Logistics. 26 (2005).
7. Jacobides, M.G., Cennamo, C., Gawer, A., Towards a Theory of Ecosystems, Strat Mgmt J. 39, 2255–2276 (2018).
8. Benedict, M. (Ed.), Modelling Ecosystems in Information Systems - A Typology Approach, 2018.
9. Kitchenham, B., Charters, S., Guidelines for Performing Systematic Literature Reviews in Software Engineering, 2007.
10. Vom Brocke, J., Simons, A., Niehaves, B., Reimer, K. (Eds.), Reconstructing the Giant: On the Importance of Rigour in Documenting the Literature Search Process, 2009.
11. Kitchenham, B., Pearl Brereton, O., Budgen, D., Turner, M., Bailey, J., Linkman, S., Systematic Literature Reviews in Software Engineering – A Systematic Literature Review, Information and Software Technology. 51, 7–15 (2009).
12. Schryen, G., Wagner, G., Benlian, A. (Eds.), Theory of Knowledge for Literature Reviews: An Epistemological Model, Taxonomy and Empirical Analysis of IS Literature, 2015.
13. Webster, J., Watson, R.T., Analyzing the Past to Prepare for the Future: Writing a Literature Review, MIS Quarterly. 26, xiii–xxiii (2002).
14. Manikas, K., Hansen, K.M., Software Ecosystems – A Systematic Literature Review, Journal of Systems and Software. 86, 1294–1306 (2013).
15. Schreieck, M., Wiesche, M., Krcmar, H., Design and Governance of Platform Ecosystems: Key Concepts and Issues for Future Research, European Conference of Information Systems. 24 (2016).
16. Iansiti, M., Levien, R., Strategy as Ecology, Harvard Business Review (2004).
17. Iansiti, M., Levien, R., The Keystone Advantage: What the New Dynamics of Business Ecosystems Mean for Strategy, Innovation, and Sustainability, Harvard Business School Pub, Boston, 2004.
18. Rochet, J.-C., Tirole, J., Platform Competition in Two-Sided Markets, Journal of the European Economic Association. 1 (2003).
19. Rochet, J.-C., Tirole, J., Two-Sided Markets: A Progress Report, RAND Journal of Economics. 37, 645–667 (2006).
20. Baxter, W.F., Bank Interchange of Transactional Paper: Legal and Economic Perspectives, The Journal of Law And Economics. 26, 541–588 (1983).
21. Wright, J., Optimal Card Payment Systems, European Economic Review. 47, 587–612 (2003).
22. Caillaud, B., Jullien, B., Chicken & Egg: Competition among Intermediation Service Providers, The RAND Journal of Economics. 34, 309–328 (2003).
23. Cusumano, M.A., Gawer, A., The Elements of Platform Leadership, MIT Sloan Management Review. 43 (2002).
24. Gawer, A., Towards a General Theory of Technological Platforms, Opening Up Innovation: Strategy, Organization and Technology (2010).
25. Cusumano, M.A., The Platform Leader's Dilemma, Communications of the ACM. 54, 21 (2011).
26. Cusumano, M.A., Yoffie, D.B., Hopkins, S.P., Gawer, A., The Business of Platforms: Strategy in the Age of Digital Competition, Innovation, and Power, Unabridged., HarperAudio, New York, 2019.

27. Tiwana, A., Evolutionary Competition in Platform Ecosystems, Information Systems Research. 26, 266–281 (2015).
28. Anand, B.N., Khanna, T., Do Firms Learn to Create Value? The Case of Alliances, Strategic Management Journal. 21, 295–315 (2000).
29. Ahuja, G., Collaboration Networks, Structural Holes, and Innovation: A Longitudinal Study, Administrative Science Quarterly. 45, 425–455 (2000).
30. Camarinha-Matos, L., Virtual enterprises and collaborative networks: IFIP 18th World Computer Congress TC5/WG5.5 - 5th Working Conference on Virtual Enterprises, 22-27 August 2004, Toulouse, France, Kluwer Academic Publishers, Boston, London, 2004.
31. Chesbrough, H., Open Platform Innovation: Creating Value from Internal and External Innovation, Intel Technology Journal. 7 (2003).
32. Chesbrough, H., Open Business Models: How to Thrive in the New Innovation Landscape, Harvard Business School, Boston, Mass., 2006.
33. Chesbrough, H., Why Companies Should Have Open Business Models, MIT Sloan Management Review. 48 (2007).
34. Adner, R., Kapoor, R., Value Creation in Innovation Ecosystems: How the Structure of Technological Interdependence Affects Firm Performance in New Technology Generations, Strat. Mgmt. J. 31, 306–333 (2010).
35. Adner, R., Match Your Innovation Strategy to Your Innovation Ecosystem, Harvard Business Review. April (2006).
36. Danskin, P., Englis, B.G., Solomon, M.R., Goldsmith, M., Davey, J., Knowledge Management as Competitive Advantage: Lessons from the Textile and Apparel Value Chain, J of Knowledge Management. 9, 91–102 (2005).
37. García-Holgado, A., García-Peñalvo, F.J., Knowledge management ecosystem based on drupal platform for promoting the collaboration between public administrations, in: Proceedings of the Second International Conference on Technological Ecosystems for Enhancing Multiculturality - TEEM '14, Salamanca, Spain, pp. 619–624, 2014.
38. Messerschmitt, D.G., Szyperski, C., Software ecosystem: Understanding an indispensable technology and industry, The MIT Press, Cambridge, Mass., London, 2003.
39. Jansen, S., Brinkkemper, S., Finkelstein, A. (Eds.), Business Network Management as a Survival Strategy: A Tale of Two Software Ecosystems, 2009.
40. Bosch, J. (Ed.), From Software Product Lines to Software Ecosystems, 2009.
41. Bosch, J., Architecture Challenges for Software Ecosystems, in: Proceedings of the Fourth European Conference on Software Architecture Companion Volume - ECSA '10, Copenhagen, Denmark, p. 93, 2010.
42. Lungu, M., Lanza, M., Gîrba, T., Robbes, R., The Small Project Observatory: Visualizing software ecosystems, Science of Computer Programming. 75, 264–275 (2010).
43. den Hartigh, E., Tol, M., Visscher, W. (Eds.), The Health Measurement of a Business Ecosystem, 2006.
44. Briscoe, G. (Ed.), Complex Adaptive Digital EcoSystems, 2010.
45. Nachira, F., Nicolai, A., Dinim Paolo, Le Louarn, M., Rivera Leon, L., Digital Business Ecosystems (2007).
46. Vargo, S.L., Lusch, R.F., Evolving to a New Dominant Logic for Marketing, Journal of Marketing. 68, 1–17 (2004).
47. Liu, P., Zhang, P., Nie, G., Business Modeling for Service Ecosystems, in: Proceedings of the International Conference on Management of Emergent Digital EcoSystems - MEDES '10, Bangkok, Thailand, p. 102, 2010.
48. Sawatani, Y. (Ed.), Research in Service Ecosystems, Portland, 2007.
49. Adams, F.G., Richey, R.G., Autry, C.W., Morgan, T.R., Gabler, C.B., Supply Chain Collaboration, Integration, and Relational Technology: How Complex Operant Resources Increase Performance Outcomes, Journal of Business Logistics. 35, 299–317 (2014).
50. Vargo, S.L., Lusch, R.F., Service-Dominant Logic: Continuing the Evolution, Journal of the Academy of Marketing Science. 36, 1–10 (2008).
51. Barratt, M., Understanding the Meaning of Collaboration in the Supply Chain, Supply Chain Management: An International Journal. 9, 30–42 (2004).
52. Sabath, R., Fontanella, J., The Unfulfilled Promise of Supply Chain Collaboration., Supply Chain Management Review. July/August, 24–29 (2002).
53. McCarthy, S., Golocic, S., Implementing Collaborative Planning to Improve Supply Chain Performance, International Journal of Physical Distribution & Logistics Management. 32, 431–454 (2002).
54. Ireland, R., Bruce, R., CPFR: Only the Beginning of Collaboration, Supply Chain Management Review. September/October, 80–88 (2000).
55. Bitran, G.R., Gurumurthi, S., Sam Lin, S., Emerging Trends in Supply Chain Governance, 2006.
56. Mentzer, J.T., Foggin, J.H., Golicic, S.L., Collaboration: The Enablers, Impediments, and Benefits, Supply Chain Management Review. 52–58 (2000).
57. Mentzer, J.T., Min, S., Zacharia, Z., The Nature of Interfirm Partnering in Supply Chain Management., Journal of Retailing. 76, 549–568 (2000).
58. Stank, T., Daugherty, P.J., Supply Chain Collaboration and Logistical Service Performance, Journal of Business Logistics. 22, 29–48 (2001).
59. Sanders, N.R., Zacharia, Z., The Interdisciplinary Future of Supply Chain Management Research, Decision Sciences. 44 (2013).

I L S 2020
INTERNATIONAL CONFERENCE ON INFORMATION SYSTEMS, LOGISTICS & SUPPLY CHAIN
Austin, Texas April 22-24, 2020

Sustainable and collaborative local productive arrangement strategies to guarantee an eco-market concept: A case study of the Alto Tietê community

Lais da Silva Oliveira [1], Alexander Georges Meytre Junior [1], Luiz Teruo Kawamoto Junior, Sivanilza Teixeira Machado [1]

[1] NAPOLE, Group of Research of Federal Insitute of São Paulo, Suzano, Brazil
{lais.dan@outlook.com, alexandergmjunior@gmail.com, teruo@ifsp.edu.br, sivanilzamachado@ifsp.edu.br}

Abstract. Over the years, the Alto Tietê community is a source of many sustainable development projects. However, most of the projects are related to the production system and not emphasizes the structure of the local market. Thus, this paper aims to discuss the current food local productive arrangements (LPA) and suggest a sustainable and collaborative food supply chain framework to drive the future market. A literature review was carried out and local visits to understand the current situation of LPA. The results showed the framework proposed based on the literature review and the current situation and suggest some market strategies to promoting the native fruits from Alto Tietê LPA. To increase the integration and communication networking, and a must establish the Alto Tietê Council involving all stakeholders and politics integration.

Keywords: Atlantic Forest, Eco-market, Local productive arrangement, Framework.

1. Introduction

The engagement for developing worldwide partnership among countries promoted the global market and became the production and commercializing zones more distant. Many studies improved the strategies and process to resources flows connecting global supply chain [1][2][3]. However, in this development process, the sustainable principles were not considered in the production and operation system. More recently, the customers questioned the traditional production process and required new practices more aware [4][5]. The sustainable practical applied in the production process was required to maintain the balance among human being life, exploration economic from industry process and nature recover process.

Nowadays, many companies have sought to organize arrangements to jointly compete in the increasingly competitive marketplace. Thus, local productive arrangement are agglomerations of companies located in the same territory that have productive specialization, governance and maintain links of interaction and cooperation to learning among themselves to compete in marketplace [6]. This kind alliances are emerging in many countries with their characteristics and specificities that may differ between countries and localities so this concept intends to be clearer what kind of supply they are [1]. The sustainable local productive arrangement (SLPA) is a market incentive due to expectation to reduce the environmental impact and guarantee the future of the planet. Furthermore, the SLPA concepts are relating the balance among ecological, social, and economic aspect of the production system installed in some region. According to Seuring and Muller, the production process incurred in different supply chain stages impact in environmental and social condition, hence burden are included the value of the products [2]. The Wang and Ran perspective, the sustainable concepts do not encompass the triple-bottom-line but extend to internal supply chain capability to develop itself sustainably [7]. So, the local productive arrangement isolated or

undeveloped, without understanding the market perspective, its weakness for the food sector due to the market new demand to minimally processed food [4].
This SLPA concept applied in the food production system to human being requires the exchange learning among supply chain actors and a partnership in a collaborative way. Thus, in a competitive global market, collaborative supply chain is important to consolidate the concepts of sustainable and innovative. In this view changing the perspective of customer to the innovative production process. Supply chain collaborative is related to the sharing the supply chain governance, based on gains from the collaborative working [7]. This implies that two or more independent members of supply chain work jointly to improve their performance [8]. However, the main problem indicated from previous research about supply chain collaborative was the supply chain governance that does not show effective strategies to develop management considering the whole supply chain perspective, due to the collaborative chain concept involving the local productive arrangement with a perspective the supply chain governance to a management contract, conflict, power, and trust among actors [7].
The main issues to the governance supply chain are related to complexity and dynamic process business and the structure of decision-making. Thus, create the flexible structure and engagement the decision-making process to quickly response is a better way to deal with a dynamic market. Despite the Preiss et al. not agree with local food systems concepts because tends to obfuscate the diversity of market practices and could be a prejudice to small farmers and defend the market direct between producer and consumers [1], the Alto Tietê community had been practiced the open gate farms, gastronomic fairs, however without active action from consumers, as proposed by Preiss et al. Furthermore, the consumption rate from native fruits is shallow due to the lack of knowledge of consumers, and it is not a stimulation to protecting the Forest. So, to boost the native fruits market, we understand that it is necessary for the community union and work for everyone's gain. Thus, this paper aims to discuss the current Alto Tietê food local productive arrangement and suggest a sustainable and collaborative food supply chain framework to drive the future market.

1.1. Alto Tietê community and Local Productive Arrangement

The competitive market scenario is growing, and the supply chain should be learning to work with several companies and make the partnership to become active in the market and support the market variation mainly during economic crises. Financial crises affect directly the productive sector, particularly rural small and medium farms, thus it necessary to adopt the financing rate of the production system [9][10]. Furthermore, the constant problem involving food industries, e.g., disease, food processed adulteration, increase the consumer's distrust, concerning food safety and contribute to the level of marginalization and vulnerability of the small farmers [1]. The food supply chain is composing mainly by big or median companies and family farming. The family farming is working without facilities, and it is using the rudimentary way, due to the lack of access to appropriate technology applied in the food production system. Despite the importance of family farming to food sector economy, it is necessary a consolidate politic that developing the sector. For instance, Brazil has been carried out the PNAE – Programa Nacional de Alimentação Escolar (National School Feeding Program), and it determined that 30% of the school food should be a buyer from family farming. However, the PNAE do not clear neither how agricultural food procurement will have occurred, or the communication between school and farmers will be happened to meet the PNAE requirements.
More than 140 million people that living in Atlantic Forest have ecosystem services, such as food production, wood production, fibers, oils e medicines, water supply, climatic balance, so on [11]. Composed of 11 cities and more than 3,0 million people [12], the Alto Tiete community shows a potential market to Native Fruits of Atlantic Forest. Part of the areas from the Alto Tietê community stay under protective law to preserve the natural environment, and almost 21% of its territory is of the Atlantic Forest [13]. The Atlantic Forest provides employment and income to the local population, allowing the harmonious life with the natural environment. Among all possibilities, we can introduce the production of the native fruits, like the cambuci, pitanga, jabuticaba, uvaia, juçara, jerivá e araçá [14]. Among the cities of Alto Tiete, we can highlight Guarulhos, Mogi das Cruzes, and Suzano that are among the 100 largest economies in the country [15]. However, these situation is not the reality of others cities in Alto Tiete, for instance, Salesópolis city has almost of the 98% of its territory into Water Protection Areas and 1/3 of the county is part of Atlantic Forest [16][17], consequently, the population can not expand industries, commercialization or services activities in Salesópolis community. The government strategies to Salesópolis is to invest in the tourism sector and sustainable agriculture.

The investment in the agriculture sector, the exploration of resources must have to observe the concept of agroecology (environmental awareness), that means to provide the sustenance for the community without to attack the natural environment [18]. This production system transition from traditional to awareness had as the main drive to the sustainable local productive arrangement in Alto Tietê community. The main problem to the agricultural sector is the practices fractional production adopted by small farmers that do know how to become more productive without impact on the environment process. On the other hand, the solution could be easy, teaching these small farmers to apply the agroecology concepts and become a bio-economy farmer. In 2017, the 'Pomares Mata Atlantica' (Atlantic Forest Orchard) project started by local Social and Environmental Entrepreneurship company (SEEC), with a proposal to recover the environmental aspect and develop a sustainable local network, creating the protection of hydric resources and Forest Atlantic located in Alto Tiete community [14]. However, the project became a new perspective to develop the local market and contribute to promoting the production with origin Alto Tiete and created a shared sense of sustainable market share to local farmers, as was called the "Eco-market". The project put the Alto Tiete farmers and SEEC in evidence and others project emerged, like Emporium Atlantic Forest, Cambuci Route, and the Cambuci Geographic Identify.
The project Emporium Atlantic Forest is an open channel to promote the main products to consumers with a Cooking Guide and several recipes on how to include the native fruits in alimentation family habits, like juice, ice cream, jelly, cakes [19]. To proposal a retrieve the local tradition and the same time to structure to the sustainable local productive arrangement, the SEEC supply local farmers and families with training and technical assistance. To maintain the network-connected, the SEEC develop a partner program with Association, Cooperative, Educational organizations, Governmental, private companies.
Despite de success of the project implemented by SEEC in Alto Tiete community, the local productive arrangement is facing commercialization problems, due to the missing information of the Brazilians consumers about the benefits of products and the food family's habits that do not include native fruits, for instance. As well, the lack of structured and consolidated market to sell the products. As an example, natives' fruits from Atlantic Forest was not found in common retails, like supermarkets or convenience stores. Retails are not engaging in products with low sale index.

2. Methodology

To develop this paper, we use the case study about the Alto Tietê community, located Southeast region, Brazil. The objective of this paper is to discuss the current local productive arrangement and suggest a sustainable and collaborative food supply chain framework to become the SLPA stronger and competitive. Eleven cities composed the Alto Tietê community that it is characterized by extensive vegetable area and the primary water source, it is responsible for vegetable supply. Furthermore, the region is the leader in national fruits production [15], Table 1.

Table 1: General Information about Alto Tietê community (Population, area, WPA, GDP, HDI, NEBE, and NC)

Community	Population (2018)	Area (km²)	WPA (%)	GDP ($)* (2016)	HDI (2010)	NEBE (2018)	NSC (2016)
Arujá	88,455	96,167	51	13,593.62	0.784	21,047	2,040
Biritiba Mirim	32,251	317,406	89	5,743.79	0.712	5,987	509
Ferraz de Vasconcelos	191,993	29,564	40	3,747.07	0.738	37,095	2,167
Guararema	29,451	270,816	w.i	12,189.15	0.731	7,003	1,040
Guarulhos	1,365,899	318,675	30	9,883.35	0.763	304,337	30,022
Itaquaquecetuba	366,519	82,622	w.i	4,465.86	0.714	80,935	4,557
Mogi das Cruzes	440,769	712,541	49	8,227.05	0.783	98,592	11,433
Poá	116,530	17,264	6	9,275.69	0.771	26,994	3,482
Salesópolis	17,022	424,997	98	2,857.20	0.732	3,552	335
Santa Isabel	56,792	363,332	82	5,466.89	0.738	11,561	1,247
Suzano	294,638	206,236	72	8,048.11	0.765	72,347	6,271
Amount Alto Tietê	**2,517,270**	**2,839.62**				**669,450**	**63,103**

WPA = water protection area; GDP = Gross domestic products; HDI = Human development Index; NEBE = numbers of students enrolled in basic education; NSC = number of schools that offer basic education; * Exchange rate R$ 4.0844 (date may, 17/2019); w.i = without information. Source: Adapted from [12], [17]; [20].

2.1. Research Local and Technical Applied

The present study is a qualitative approach applying the Convenience Technique to explore the current structure of LPA and it suggests a market strategy to grow sustainably and collaboratively. We conducted the research following the steps:

- First, we started with a literature review using the Web of Science database. We used the terms "sustainable", "sustainable AND supply chain", "collaborative supply chain" and sustainable and collaborative" AND "supply chain". The term "sustainable" appeared 63,000 times. The term "sustainable" together "supply chain" appeared 2,000 times. The term "collaborative supply chain" returned 900 papers. It is important to highlight that this concept was started in the late' 90s. More newer terms, the "sustainable and collaborative" AND "supply chain" retrieved 15 researches [21].
- Second, we conducted a visit to an event promoted by Alto Tiete community. The event was proposed to discuss the main problems that LPA was facing, and it was attended by farmers, leaders of private companies, and from education and government sectors. Thus, it was possible to collect the information from different perspectives about the LPA.
- Third, based on the event discuss, we applied the open interview with the leader of SEEC in Alto Tiete community (LDR). The open interview revolves around questions about the effective action of SEEC in current LPA (project developed together with community), the main problem facing by SEEC, the main results obtained by SEEC with projects, the real situation of LPA, the conflicts involve actors of LPA, rate of consumption, market and logistics strategies.
- Four, we analyzed the documents of SEEC project involving LPA Alto Tiete to understand the current situation.
- Five, we visited Poa city Department of Education to understand the National School Feeding Program and strategies integration among Government, Local Farmers, and School.
- Finally, we visit two schools in different communities of Poa and Suzano to verify the supply system.

To analyze all information collected we created a mind map to structure and synthesize information to obtain a better comprehension of the real situation of current LPA Alto Tietê.

2.2. Framework propose based on literature review and mind map created

Supported by the literature review, we adapted the Lockamy and McCormack model [3] and drawing the framework as a suggestion driving the future market in Alto Tiete community. Based on the sustainable concept and collaborative supply chain with integration in both sides of the supply chain, the Alto Tiete food supply chain resulted in Eco-market Alto Tietê, propose by Auá Institute [14], Figure 1.

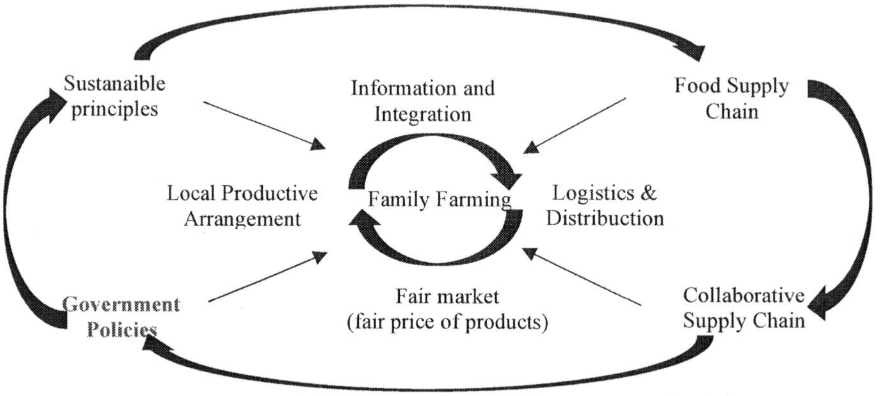

Figure 1: Sustainable Local Productive Arrangement toward Eco-market

To develop the framework, we consider the three broad topics: Current Government Policies and Food Supply Chain research, Productive Strategies integration with social and environmental aspects; and Market Strategies applied to community social and economic collaborative.

3. Results

First of all, the framework idea is not only to deepen the awareness about ecosystem service [22] but also to recover the local social tradition [19], and the same time to structure to SLPA, using the current situation and to explore the new market possibilities, through the creation of Alto Tiete Community Council with propose to integration SLPA and politics strategies to promote the employment and income to prevent the social vulnerability (Figure 2), as well as offer the new fruits applying the market competitive by differentiation [23] and including the implications of an economic demand, compare attributes between SLPA and conventional production, preferences and values to consumers [24], price and how much consumers' willingness-to-pay (adapted from [4]).

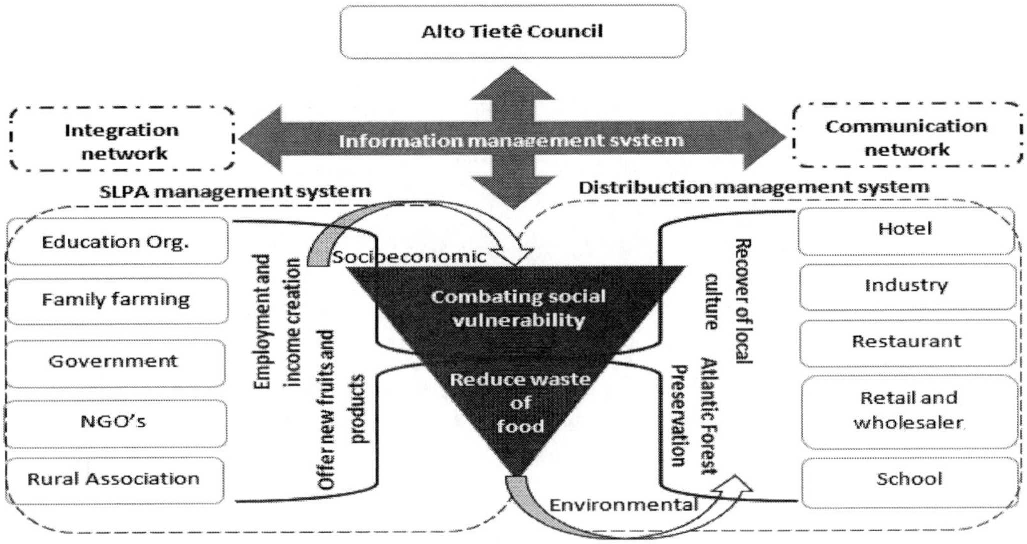

Figure 2: The framework of the Alto Tiete Council to ensure the SPLA's competitiveness

According to Lockamy and McCormack to supply chain management planning decision is essential to observe the operation strategies, demand, production, procurement, delivery, balancing change, and distribution management [3]. Thus, we adapted this point of view, follow:

Alto Tiete Council: general plan management of source, make, delivery, information, communication and integration; values and ethical, environmental, and politics involve all cities in Alto Tiete that are working on a project. The Alto Tiete Council are responsible for creating a political project involving the 11 communities and structure a flexible decision-making system to governance the supply chain of the native fruits from Atlantic Forest. LDR: "we applied the solidarity economy concept in social projects to develop a sustainable community based on cooperative working and it not competition working".

Information management system: plan the information products (label, production system, origin, ethical system, legal, safety, and human health benefits) and market (consumers preferences, market profile, consumption frequency, relevant places, consumers demand) – the information system input the integration and communication networks.

Integration network: integration planning involves variables from internal and external relationships SLPA (supplier), environmental, social requirements, and market shoppers. During the interview was possible identify that Eco-market was a concept that involves more than production resources (the land usage, labor, and capital), but included ethical concepts to develop a fair market that respects the limit of environmental, contribute to community, products with health awareness and based on reasonable price of goods sharing along the supply chain. LDR: "We produced a product that no one knows to a market that does not exist". "We do not want to see our principles the eco-market, to develop a social and environment market, on the hands of the big companies." (…) "We wish to become a big market, generate value for the community and carry on working to prevent the environment".

Communication network: communication strategies plan, local social media, radio and television programs, events, fairs, communication performance indicators. LDR: "we have one person responsible for

marketing that creates our slogan, campaign and keeps the information on our page". Market communication is essential to success to SLPA, as well as to provide support and complete information to consumers about everything of the native fruits production systems.
SLPA management system: plan source and make (product life-cycle management, natural resources management, technical performance indicators, demand and risk management, and return of investment. LDR: "when we start the project Pomares Mata Atlântica in community, we face some problems, because farmers do not want forest in their territory. The forest was unproductive land, (...) to convince farmers that it is possible to use the forest to produce and applying agroecology concepts to prevent the environment, to create harmony between the human production system and nature. One question was put in action: how to make the forest standing has more value to the farmer than the aggressive agricultural system or other urban occupation areas?". Nowadays, the production system has consolidated into sustainable concepts. Indeed, what is missing is an integration among farmers and understand that they need to work in a collaborative way to develop together with the local productive arrangement, sharing the knowledge, technology, and market earnings. To develop a knowledge bank about technical of the sustainable production system that could be accessed by all stakeholders involved in Alto Tiete Council and contribute to farmers, professionals from education institute exchange the experience and help each other. LDR: "A better way to forest preservation, after the public politics that forbidden the forest areas accessed, it would be precisely the economic aspects, because the farmers called the preservation laws of the 'environmental restriction' or 'environmental passive'. Thus, the forest should be a better economic option for local development".
Distribution management system: plan delivery (transport, warehouse, package, routes, logistics performance indicator). Rural logistics is a challenge for farming farmers because they are working without production and logistics infrastructure. The logistics management is complex, and it is responsible for available goods to market on time without manage mistakes. Faria recommends applying the central distribution to the products flow more efficient, manage the flow of the reception of products from many suppliers, and distributing for several clients [25]. Develop a confidence market it is necessary to have excellent logistics service that involves the customer satisfaction level.

4. Discuss

Alto Tiete community has 63,103 schools that assist children since the pre-stage until high-school, and also it has installed almost 63 thousand private companies [12]. The future of the Alto Tietê bio-economy depends on the construction of a dynamic and strong network to face the competitive market in a perspective of the sustainable and collaborative supply chain. The native fruits supply chain engagement to create awareness into society to preserve the Atlantic Forest and, at the same time, living from a productive economic process in balance. This supply chain maturity reflects the degree of trust and strength of ties between each member, acting in a collective and shared way. As presented previously in literature, the supply chain collaborative is a complex model that requires independents members to work jointly in planning and executing supply chain operations, and they shared the profits; however, one of the main problems is the difficulty in performing a fair assessment of their benefits [8]. This is another critical point that was observed in Alto Tietê SLPA, the lack of confidence among the members. Some members discussed the price of supply, delivery and the financial return to them. This perspective is a weakness of supply chain governance that should work to find a balance among the actors and fair contribution. According to Preiss et al., the governance it is responsible to manage tasks and decision-making process, division of working as ordering, delivering, accountability and payments as well as promoting social and political activities [1].

4.1. Strategies to developing the distribution management system

To develop a partnership program with all stakeholders to open the Alto Tiete market (families farming, rural association, cooperative, Educational organizations, Governmental, SEEC). The council can explore some strategies, Table 2. Firstly, the SLPA should focus on Market Alto Tietê offering the products to School; after expanding the Market to the hotel, restaurants, and industry. Finally, available products to consumers in alternative shopping. Gradually, include the native fruits into culinary to School and creating consumption habits. Develop the food preference towards children and teens is a strategy to expand from

School to Family changing the eating habits of Brazilian families. Thus, the Schools located in Alto Tiete cities have been buying processed foods to student consumption (school lunch), such as juice in boxes, kits of snacks, crackers due to facilities in distribution and storage of foods. Therefore, the SLPA should be investing in meets the school market demand.

Table 2: Strategies proposed to develop and strengthen the Eco-market in Alto Tietê community

Strategies	Description
1: Meets the school demand	1.1: To understand the school new demands (the governmental program to schools lunch distribution: the law 11.947/2009 provides that 30% of food shopping to school have to be from family farming) 1.2: Developing products to children nutrition (Heath snacks) 1.3: Developing the suppliers to process the *in nature* products (Products semi-processed or processed) 1.4: Training employees to public sales (Bidding, designate a person responsible for following the food demand of the school) 1.5: Developing logistics distribution 1.6: Training employees to guarantee the quality products and service
2: To become a supplier of juice and dessert to hotels, restaurants, and industries	2.1: To understand the market characteristics (General market research) 2.2: Make sales meetings and product display (The regional characteristics of the population and tourists) 2.3: Offer product sample for customers appreciation (Create demand and focus on product benefits for health, diversify the menu (typical drinks and food)) 2.4: To understand the client expectation (Specific market research) 2.5: Offer goods and service customized (Consultative sales and offer sales solution for each customer demand) 2.6: Developing relationships (Make and maintain suppliers contracts with hotels, restaurants, and industries) 2.7: After-sales service (Improve the sales and supply solution)
3: Offer products in the alternative shopping facilities or other sales strategies	3.1: Display products in nature store (Franchises food systems) 3.2: Expose products in gastronomy fairs, grocery store (fruits in nature, and processed products). 3.3: Buying direct from the farmer (a virtual market using 'App')

Source: Author (2019)

Nowadays, the School lunch are bought from other regions like Rio Grande do Sul. This reality occurred due to a lack of communication development among the Education Department of the Alto Tiete community with rural associations to develop the school lunch supplier from its community. It is necessary to reach the children to change their eating habits. LDR: "the sustainable market will grow fast if each other, at the time of purchase, we asked by a product free from an aggressive agricultural system. If the seller tries sales us a traditional product, we learned to answer thank you, but I do not want food or drink from an agricultural system that used pesticides, that it does not respect the nature system. We will buy food and drink from a sustainable process." Moreover, the SLPA should introduce yourself like a supplier of typical products from Alto Tiete local and the eco-market to try to rescue the local identity and Offer Sustanaible products as an opportunity to culture valorization.

5. Conclusion

We can conclude that despite currents projects working to develop local productive arrangements, it is impossible to create a market without appropriate collaborative strategies and a food supply chain framework to emphasizes the regional characteristics. The governance of SLPA should be aligned with the interests of the members, and the SLPA strengthen based on the partnership among members of the food supply chain could boost the Alto Tiete market.

6. References

1. J. S. C. Preiss, Potira; Charão-Marques, Flávia ; Wiskerke, "Fostering Sustainable Urban-Rural Linkages through Local Food Supply: A Transnational Analysis of Collaborative Food Alliances," *sustainability*, vol. 9, no. 1155, pp. 1–30, 2017, doi: doi:10.3390/su9071155.
2. S. Seuring and M. Mü Ller, "From a literature review to a conceptual framework for sustainable supply chain management," *J. Clean. Prod. J.*, vol. 16, pp. 1699–1710, 2008, doi: 10.1016/j.jclepro.2008.04.020.
3. A. Lockamy and K. McCormack, "Linking SCOR planning practices to supply chain performance: An exploratory study," *Int. J. Oper. Prod. Manag.*, vol. 24, no. 12, pp. 1192–1218, 2004, doi: 10.1108/01443570410569010.
4. E. K. Yiridoe, S. Bonti-Ankomah, R. C. Martin, and C. Ottawa, "Comparison of consumer perceptions and preference toward organic versus conventionally produced foods: A review and update of the literature," *Renew. Agric. Food Syst.*, vol. 20, no. 4, pp. 193–205, 2005, doi: 10.1079/RAF2005113.
5. C. R. Carter and D. S. Rogers, "A framework of sustainable supply chain management: moving toward new theory," doi: 10.1108/09600030810882816.
6. Ministerio da Economia, "APL - Arranjos Produtivos Locais." 2018.
7. B. Wang, Jiguang; Ran, "Sustainable Collaborative Governance in Supply Chain," *sustainability*, vol. 10, no. 171, pp. 1–17, 2018, doi: doi:10.3390/su10010171.
8. M. Dorigatti, A. Guarnaschelli, O. Chiotti, and H. E. Salomone, "A service-oriented framework for agent-based simulations of collaborative supply chains," *Comput. Ind.*, vol. 83, pp. 92–107, Dec. 2016, doi: 10.1016/J.COMPIND.2016.09.005.
9. M. Gazolla and S. Schneider, "Qual 'fortalecimento' da agricultura familiar? Uma análise do Pronaf crédito de custeio e investimento no Rio Grande do Sul," *Rev. Econ. e Sociol. Rural*, vol. 51, no. 1, pp. 45–68, Mar. 2013, doi: 10.1590/S0103-20032013000100003.
10. BANCO CENTRAL DO BRASIL, "Anuário estatístico do crédito rural – 2012," 2012.
11. M. AMBIENTE, "Mata Atlântica." 18AD.
12. IBGE - Instituto Brasileiro de Geografia e Estatística, "Panorama: Cidades." 2018.
13. M. HIROTA, M.; RIBEIRO, "Bacia do Tietê tem apenas 7% de Mata Atlântica preservada." 2016.
14. I. AUÁ, "Instituto AUÁ lança projeto Pomares da Mata Atlântica para recuperação do Alto Tietê com agroflorestas," 2017.
15. C. de D. dos M. do A. Tietê, "Perfil do Alto Tietê," *CONDEMAT*, 2019. [Online]. Available: https://condemat.sp.gov.br/perfil-alto-tiete/. [Accessed: 25-Sep-2019].
16. SALESÓPOLIS, "A estanca turística de Salesópólis," 2018. [Online]. Available: http://www.salesopolis.sp.gov.br/site/index.php?option=com_content&view=article&id=115&Itemid=1282. [Accessed: 20-Sep-2019].
17. F. FIA, "Salesópolis," 2018. [Online]. Available: http://www.fundacaofia.com.br/gdusm/salesopolis.htm. [Accessed: 20-Sep-2019].
18. L. Azevedo, L. F. de Azevedo, and T. A. Netto, "AGROECOLOGIA: O 'CAMINHO' PARA O DESENVOLVIMENTO RURAL SUSTENTÁVEL," *Rev. Eletrônica em Gestão, Educ. e Tecnol. Ambient.*, vol. 19, no. 3, pp. 639–645, May 2015, doi: 10.5902/2236117017031.
19. I. AUÁ, "Pomares Mata Atlântica avança com formação de mulheres e beneficiamento de nativas," São Paulo, 2018.
20. BANCO CENTRAL DO BRASIL, "Exchange rate," 2019. [Online]. Available: https://www.bcb.gov.br/acessoinformacao. [Accessed: 17-May-2019].
21. Clarivate Analytics, "Web of Science: Core collection." Thomson Reuters, Philadelphia, 2019.
22. R. B. Norgaard, "Ecosystem services: From eye-opening metaphor to complexity blinder," *Ecol. Econ.*, vol. 69, pp. 1219–1227, 2010, doi: 10.1016/j.ecolecon.2009.11.009.
23. P. KOTLER, *Administração de Marketing: análise, planejamento, implementação e controle*, 5th ed. São Paulo, 2009.
24. R. MACHADO, ST; REIS, JGM; SILVA, AM; BUENO, RC; TANAKA, WY; ZAMPINI, EF; TOLOI, "Brazilian consumer's preference towards fruits: the drivers of banana, orange, lemon and apple supply chain," in *ILS - Information Systems, Logistics and Supply Chain*, 2018.
25. F. A. D. FARIA, "Estudo da Centralização de Estoques em um Sistema de Distribuição de Medicamentos," Universidade de Brasília, 2016.

I L S 2020
INTERNATIONAL CONFERENCE ON INFORMATION
SYSTEMS, LOGISTICS & SUPPLY CHAIN
Austin, Texas April 22-24, 2020

A Digital Twin Framework of a Material Handling Operator in Industry 4.0 Environments

Abhimanyu Sharotry [1], Jesus Jimenez, Ph.D.[1], David Wierschem, Ph.D. [2], Francis Mendez, Ph.D. [2], George Koutitas, Ph.D. [1], Damian Valles, Ph.D. [1], Semih Aslan, Ph.D. [1], Koldenhoven RM, Ph.D. [3]

[1] Ingram School of Engineering, Texas State University, San Marcos TX 78666, U.S.A.
[2] CIS & QM Department, McCoy College of Business, San Marcos TX 78666, U.S.A.
[3] Department of Health and Human Performance, Texas State University, San Marcos TX 78666, U.S.A.
{jj30@txstate.edu, a_s1241@txstate.edu}

Abstract. This paper presents framework of a manual material handling operator to enhance worker performance using digital twin approach. We explore the successful transition of operators in Industry 4.0 including physical implementation of demonstrators and execution of experiments in a realistic environment. Since the changing factory ecosystem requires models which adapt over time, we justify the use of the digital twin for this industrial transformation. The framework has three modules: Data Collection Module, Digital Twin Application Module & Operator Analysis/Feedback Module. The contributions of researchers in the context of operator fatigue models and operator 4.0 are discussed with future research opportunities.

Keywords: Digital Twin, Operator 4.0, Manual Material Handling, Literature review

1. Introduction

Industry 4.0, a manufacturing movement, is considered a critical component of the "Fourth Industrial Revolution," and has the potential to affect entire industries by transforming the methods in which companies design, manufacture, and deliver their products [1]. Originally initiated in Germany, Industry 4.0 (I4.0) has attracted significant worldwide attention in recent years. It is closely related with the internet of things (IoT), cyber-physical systems (CPS), information & communication technology (ICT), enterprise architecture (EA) and services [1]. The goals of Industry 4.0 are to achieve a higher level of operational efficiency & productivity along with a higher level of automatization; yet these highly advanced and automated manufacturing environments should remain human-centered to enable technology to coexist with humans. The major features of this fourth industrial revolution, as discussed by J. Posada et al. [2] and V. Roblek et al. [3] are digitization, optimization, customization of production, automation & adaptation, human machine interaction (HMI), value added services & businesses, automatic data exchange & communication.

The futuristic I4.0 manufacturing environment focuses on shorter delivery times, increased levels of customization, product variety, quality, as well as demand variability. With the transition in manufacturing to more technologically advanced and automated systems, it is important to understand the role of the human operators who work in these environments. The development of I4.0 is accompanied by a change in the range of worker tasks and demands in the factory context [4], the operators now are multi-skilled and perform jobs at several workstations capable of responding to mass-customized products, processing large amounts of information [5]. D. Romero et al. [6] has defined this smart generation of operators as Operator 4.0, i.e. humans who are assisted by machines and technology to enhance their physical, cognitive and sensorial capabilities to perform their manufacturing tasks.

Statistics from U.S. Department of Labor, Bureau of Labor Statistics [7] show that in manufacturing industries, Musculoskeletal disorders (MSD) accounted for 34% of the "Days Away From Work" (DAFW) cases in 2017. Sprains, strains, and tears were accounted as the leading type of injury in manufacturing with 34,110 cases. Due to a boom in warehousing and storage business, the trends have shown an increase from 662.2 employees (thousands) in January 2009 to 1180.9 in January 2019, a 78% increase in the number of workplace injuries and illnesses. Overexertion and bodily reaction rose from 1,350 cases to 8,310 in 2017, along with an increase of 3,120 cases in transportation and material moving workers leading to DAFW [7]. Therefore, our research attempts to identify opportunities to track and reduce the basis of MSD, sprains, strains, overexertion activities that are caused by traditional repetitive tasks, such as lifting, picking, pushing, pulling, carrying, moving, manipulating, holding or restraining objects, often defined as Manual Material Handling (MMH) activities. This research has also identified the lack of research literature, which would help quantify the amount of mental and physical workload operators experience in working with Industry 4.0 technology.

The main objective of this research is to conceptualize a digital twin of a human operator and propose a framework that enables the understanding and analysis of the factors that influence human variability and error, while performing their manufacturing tasks with the aid of digital twin (DT) technology. The proposed framework (Figure 1) has the following main components: 1) Data Collection Module, 2) Digital Twin Application Module, and 3) Operator Analysis/Feedback Module. These modules and their applications will be explained below.

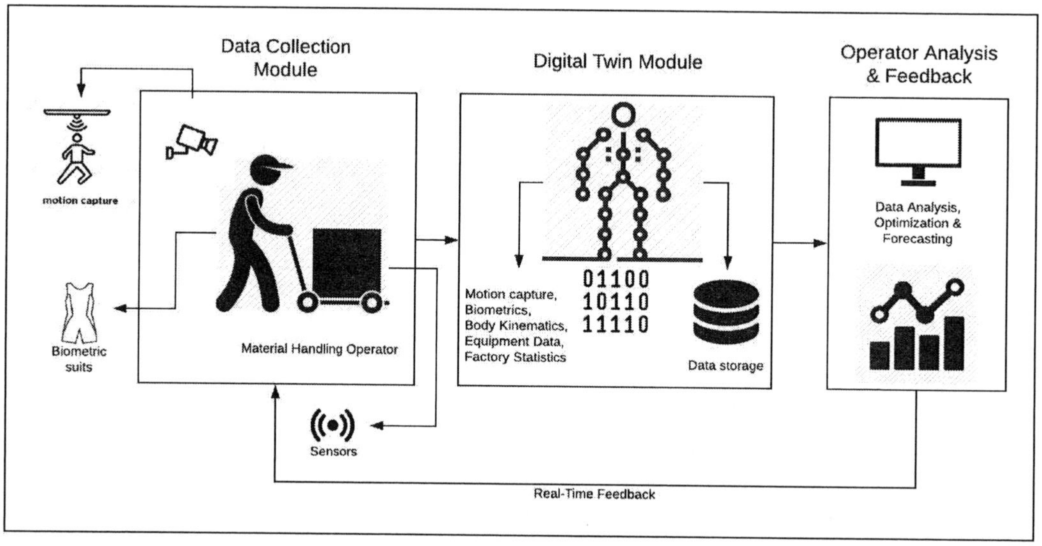

Figure 1: Framework of proposed operator centric Industry 4.0 environment.

The article is structured as follows. Section 2 describes the proposed digital twin framework and provides a literature review focused on past work motivating each of the modules. Section 3 provides conclusions and future work.

2. Modules of Proposed Framework

2.1. Module I: Data Collection Module

Manual Materials Handling (MMH) operations are carried out in most workplaces, demanding a unique skill from the operator [8]. During these activities, operators are subjected to both mental and physical fatigue, discomfort, injury and a performance reduction, all of which have a cost to an organization. The costs related to discomfort and fatigue are more difficult to quantify than those costs caused by injuries, primarily because the worker remains at the workplace with reduced work capabilities [9]. Healthy worker performance, work quality, and system output can be compromised via poor design of human factors (workstation layout), cumulatively hazardous and excessively fatiguing worker motions. Physical fatigue is the only one that can be evaluated objectively as it involves movement of the whole body and can be generalized as general body fatigue [10]. With more accurate predictions of the levels of fatigue in the operators, the hazards of MMH can be assessed by the nature of load, task, environment & the operator's biometrical characteristics [8]. Hence, there is an increasing interest by researchers and practitioners to develop methods to quantify and monitor fatigue.

Multiple tools have been proposed over time to measure and reduce the fatigue among the workforce. Preexisting ergonomic assessment tools such as RULA [11], REBA [12], the NIOSH lifting equations [13] can be categorized as observational. Virtual human factor (VHF) tools, such as digital human models (DHM), discrete event simulation (DES), virtual reality (VR), etc., allow the user to perform ergonomic assessment on the systems not yet constructed [9]. Predictive tools proposed by M. A. Greig et al. [9] can be used during the design stages to assist in layout planning and task balancing, followed by the suggested additive model based on VR experimentation environment by G. Chryssolouris et al. [14], estimating an interactive process performance but missing the tools to support an exact representation of specialized process characteristics [14]. The strain index methodology of J. S. Moore et al. [15] is another way of calculating the distal upper extremity disorder, which is derived from physiological, biomechanical and epidemiological principles; though some of the subjective estimates in the study act as limitations of this approach [15].

Other methods of assessing fatigue rates by subjective ratings include the Likert scale and the commonly used Borg scale, using the rate of perceived exertion which solely depends on the subjective feedback and variance in the perceived effort of completion of different exercises, acting as a weakness of this process. Another possible way of monitoring fatigue is via the energy expenditure rate, which differs from the conventional ways as it is considered the only method that can be evaluated objectively, involving the movement of whole body rather than focusing on a specific part of it [10]. Adding to which, parameters such as rest time, recovery time estimation, and rest allowance can also be measured as the result of models concluded by V. Valentina et al [10].

One limitation of the models discussed above is their lack of including weight as a decision variable, which is a major component of MMH tasks. Another limitation is their requiring post experiment evaluation, resulting in an inability to provide real-time feedback. To address these limitations, objective measures are preferable.

Since we know that fatigue has a protective function against irreversible muscle damage [16], it plays an important role in the redistribution and reorganization mechanisms of the human body, which optimizes the coordination of active muscle fibers and multi-joint coordination [16]. Objective measures for muscle fatigue include surface electromyography (sMEG), mechanomyography (MMG) and ultrasound strain imaging. A limitation of using sMEG is that it can only provide measures for the muscles the sensor is attached to.

Research shows that fatigue influences postural control and movement coordination, leading to observable changes in movement kinematics such as range-of-motion (ROM) and angle velocities with accumulation of muscle fatigue [16]. Hence, optical motion capture methodology with infrared cameras can be used to compute joint angles via inverse kinematics from recorded marker positions, providing an accurate measurement as compared to computer vision and inertial measurement units (IMUs), making it the preferred method for determining physical fatigue. As concluded by M. Golan et al. [17] and M. Peruzzini, et al. [18] the lack of standard datasets makes it difficult to validate standard human behavior and the real-time mapping of operator movements. Using motion capture methodology would make it possible to determine, evaluate and create the required datasets for operator movement analysis.

The current components of this data collection module are briefly summarized in Table 1.

Table 1: Components of Data Collection Module.

No.	Components	Brief Description
1	Participants	Healthy adults recruited from the university population.
2	Nature of Task	Seven fundamental moves {Back Lifting, Leg Lifting, Pulling (Shoulder), Pulling (Elbow), Pushing (Shoulder), Pushing (Elbow), Walking, Walking with weights} were determined and the data shall be collected for the specific movements in controlled conditions.
3	Biometrics	Use of wearable biometric system via cardiac, movement & breathing sensors to collect biometric data during experiment.
4	Biomechanical Model	Dynamic biomechanical model of the body segments for analysis.
5	Data Analysis	Statistical analysis of multiple data collected.

2.2. Module II: Digital Twin Application Module

Mathematical models have been used since the 1700s to evaluate a system's performance. The availability of I4.0 tools such as the internet of things (IoT), big data, cloud computing, artificial intelligence and digital reality have made the interaction of such physical and digital systems possible. Creating interactive and identical cyber physical models of real-world systems are the definition of Digital Twin (DT) technology [19]. Such smart, connected product systems (SCPs) are driven by their type, granularity and the amount of information enclosed. Emerging as a tool for Product Lifecycle Management (PLM), the concept of DT technology has evolved over time. An example of a DT developed by GE is that of an airplane engine where the engine is being manufactured in physical space and the data is sent to a virtual space, creating a DT environment [20]. With characteristics like scalability, interoperability, expansibility and fidelity, cyber twins can provide value to an organization via visualization, analysis, prediction and optimization tools [21].

Frameworks for DTs have been developed by researchers in the field of ergonomics [22], hybrid production systems [23] and Body-in-White production systems [24]. A hybrid network outline was proposed by A. K. R. Venkatapathy et al. [25] with the use of digital twin concepts, aiming to develop a decentralized logistics system. Application of DT technology within the field of MMH is scarce.

MMH work contributes to over half a million cases of musculoskeletal disorders annually. Tools have been developed to access operator wellbeing as mentioned in the previous module. The goal of such ergonomic assessment tools is to provide an optimal fit between work requirements and operator capabilities, but fail to provide a benefit in safety and productivity when applied [26]. Most ergonomic analysis techniques have a limited task application. For instance, RULA targets the risk of upper limb musculoskeletal injury and NIOSH analysis targets only lifting and lowering tasks. Also, such assessment methods do not consider dynamic biomechanical analysis. These characteristics can be combined to develop a multi-scale, multi-physical and probabilistic simulation model of the operator, with the measurement of fatigue and other performance metrics under dynamic conditions. Dynamic fatigue models, including array inputs such as maximum forces, torque loads, varying levels of forces at different time intervals and joint movements for the measurement of operator performance have been created, but are limited to specific instances only [22] [24]. A DT framework for the operator will act as a platform to bridge the gap between current workplace scenarios and future factories with more advanced workplace operators. Such frameworks will allow for more proactive decisions to be made for the MMH industry. Assessing the factory environments with respect to I4.0, our proposed framework provides a digital platform to evaluate the various factors leading to MMH hazards (Figure 1).

As concluded by B. Schleich et at. [21], the DT model must have specific characteristics such as: scalability, interoperability, expansibility and fidelity. Our digital framework concentrates on determining the basic attributes of a smart operator. Scalability can be defined as the ability of a model to analyze varying information fed into the system. This makes it possible to analyze the operator behavior in future workspaces for smart operators as defined by D. Romero et al. [27] using tools such as exoskeleton, AR, VR, wearable tracker, robots and data analytics. The interoperability feature of DT allows the analyst to track operator performance characteristics along with factory statistics. Analyzing parameters such as worker scheduling and rest time allows the system to work in tandem with other systems. The components of this DT module are listed in Table 2.

Table 2: Components of Digital Twin Module.

No.	Components	Brief Description
1	Data Collection	The necessary data shall be collected as per the specific instance of DT.
2	Communication	Use of cloud based cyber-physical systems for communication within factory environment.
3	Data Analysis	Real-time statistical analytics via inverse dynamics for joint reaction forces, moments and other ergonomic analysis.
4	Feedback	Personalized feedback to operators and floor manager via improved data analytics to improve operational performance.

We can summarize the attributes of our digital framework as:

- It is the virtual model of a human operator.
- Continuously collects data such as biometrics, joint movement & factory statistics.
- Connects with the operator, updating in real-time.
- Provides data and feedback through visualization, analysis & optimization techniques.

DT technology is being used in the manufacturing industry, achieving real-time interconnection between physical products and virtual models, enhancing the flexibility and competitiveness of the system [28]. The use of this technology in product service has been of use in the manufacturing and construction industries, allowing real-time dynamic monitoring and precise prediction of product performance [29]. In recent years, the automotive manufacturer TESLA has been planning to develop a DT for every manufactured vehicle enabling data sharing & analysis between the vehicle and the company [21]. Another instance can be seen in DHL's first digital twin warehouse which enables the use of this technology to reduce congestion, optimize space usage, real-time data assessment and improve safety in the warehouse [30]. Since the key factor in all the mentioned industries is their human eccentricity, we represent our digital twin of the human operator in Industry 4.0 environment, with the ability to analyze the characteristics of workers in real-time scenarios. The human integration in cyber physical systems is still considered a societal challenge. [31]. As the human involvement plays an important role in productivity of the system, risks related to MMH tasks associated with the nature of load, type of task, work environment & the operator [8] (Figure 2), allow the use of technology to analyze the ergonomics of the work environment with the aim of reducing worker fatigue.

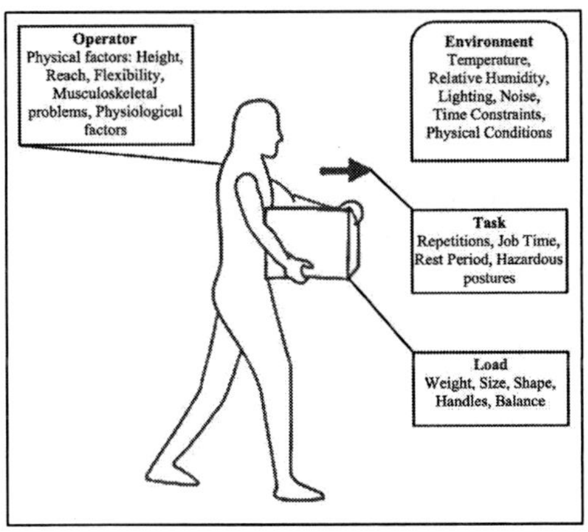

Figure 2: Operator environment with factors leading to MMH hazards.

The implementation of a successful DT, with its need for large amounts of data and a suitable development environment, can be successfully overcome by the proposed framework [32].

2.3. Module III: Operator Analysis/ Feedback Module

The interaction of human operators with various industrial and digital production technologies, can be summarized as: Operator 1.0 – humans conducting manual and dexterous work with minimal support from mechanical and manually operated tools; Operator 2.0 – humans performing assisted work with the support of computer assisted tools; Operator 3.0 – humans involved in cooperative work with robots, also defined as human-robot collaboration; Operator 4.0 –humans who are assisted by machines and technology to enhance their physical, cognitive and sensorial capabilities to perform the manufacturing tasks. [6]. This philosophy focuses on treating automation as a further enhancement of the human's physical, sensorial and cognitive capabilities by means of cyber physical system integration. Strategies aiming at the cognitive capabilities of an operator, playing an important role in the mental workload, decision making, human-computer interaction & skilled performance have been presented by S. Mattsson, et al. [33] and D. Romero et al. [6].

Human characteristics such as age, gender, cultural background and personality are often neglected in traditional decision-making models and the DES approach used in design and management of production and logistic systems resulting in a need for a 'system of systems' that considers the increasing number of human factors [34] [35]. A procedure for a pragmatic assessment of the relation between physical and cognitive measurable human factors and workplace design by using virtual and mixed reality set-ups was proposed by M. Peruzzini, et al. [18]. However, the lack of assessment of the emotional response, applicability and data holds it back from being used in the industrial environment.

The proposed digital twin framework allows for taking into consideration current operator scenarios, analysing them in real-time and providing feedback to the experts. As concluded by the systematic literature review by E. Rauch, et al. [36] there is a lack of data and practical experience resulting from implementation of I4.0 technologies. The proposed DT framework will allow the user to analyse outcomes of industrial revolution in the early stages of adaptation as a result of its real-time capabilities.

M. Golan et al. [17] provided a framework of the future human operator based on cognitive and behavioural theories regarding workstation interaction in the current I4.0 era. Despite studies available on the use of machine learning and technology to transform the production floor, the author concluded that none of the studies explored human-machine interaction. The proposed DT is aimed at the development of techniques for understanding the implications of the entire scene unfolding at the workstation (Figure 2).

3. Discussion and Conclusion

This paper presents a framework for a digital twin of an operator in the industry 4.0 environment. Material handling tasks, being highly repetitive, are considered as the leading contributors to injuries with 1,180,900 workplace injuries and illnesses in January 2019.

The Data Collection Module summarized the various fatigue detection methods. It concluded that the use of an integration of motion capture and biometrics technologies to detect worker fatigue via methods like strain index, energy expenditure and Borg's scale, creates a platform of fatigue detection more objectively and accurate. The use of digital twin technology was recommended to provide real-time feedback, enhancing operator well-being.

With characteristics like scalability, interoperability, expansibility and fidelity, the use of this technology will enhance the role of operators in the factory. This ideology was presented in the Digital Twin Application Module, demonstrating that the use of a DT would enable real-time insight, forecasting and decision support for live operations.

The Operator Analysis / Feedback Module presented the role of operators with insight on various levels of research being done for human centric industrial developments. It was identified that the proposed DT framework would address the various challenges faced by researchers in analysing human characteristics. Future stages of research are anticipated to include collection of additional datasets covering a variety of human characteristics, body movements and other factory prevalent MMH motions. The analysis of these datasets will act as the basis for recognizing the hazardous motions leading to higher fatigue rates. This study will allow us to determine the optimal motion required for a specified task. Using machine learning algorithms, the simulation model can be trained to assist the smart operator 4.0 with task recommendations resulting in lower fatigue rates. Also, the integration of these fatigue models with real-time factory statistics will allow the simulation engineers to predict the job time more efficiently.

4. References

1. E. Hofmann and M. Rusch, "Industry 4.0 and the current status as well as future prospects on logistics," Computers in Industry, no. 89, pp. 23-34, (2017)
2. J. Posada, C. Toro, I. Barandiaran and D. Oyarzun, "Visual Computing as a Key Enabling Technology for Industrie 4.0 and Industrial Internet," IEEE Computer Graphics and Applications, vol. 35, no. 2, pp. 26-40, Mar.-Apr. (2015)
3. V. Roblek, M. Meško and A. Krapež, "A Complex View of Industry 4.0," SAGE Open, vol. 6, no. 2, (2016)
4. D. Gorecky, M. Schmitt, M. Loskyll and D. Zühlke, "Human-Machine-Interaction in the Industry 4.0 Era," in 12th IEEE International Conference on Industrial Informatics (INDIN), (2014)
5. L. Lu, F. M. Megahed, R. F. Sesek and L. A. Cavuoto, "A survey of the prevalence of fatigue, its precursors and individual coping mechanisms among U.S. manufacturing workers," Applied Ergonomics, vol. 65, pp. 139-151, (2017)
6. D. Romero, P. Bernus, O. Noran, J. Stahre and Å. Fast-Berglund, "The Operator 4.0: Human Cyber-Physical Systems & Adaptive Automation Towards Human-Automation Symbiosis Work Systems," in IFIP International Conference on Advances in Production Management Systems, (2016)
7. "United States Department of Labor, Bureau of Labor Statistics," 2017. [Online]. Available: https://www.bls.gov/home.htm
8. "Workplace Safety & Prevention Services," 2011. [Online]. Available: https://www.wsps.ca/Home.aspx.
9. M. A. Greig, J. Village, F. A. Salustri, S. Zolfaghari and W. P. Neumann, "A tool to predict physical workload and task times from workstation layout design data," International Journal of Production Research , vol. 56, no. 16, pp. 5306-5323, (2018)
10. V. Valentina, S. Fabio, C. Martina and P. Alessandro, "Fatigue accumulation in the assignment of manual material handling activities to operators," IFAC-PapersOnLine, vol. 51, no. 11, pp. 826-831, (2018)
11. L. McAtamney and E. Corlett, "RULA: a survey method for the investigation of work-related upper limb disorders," Applied Ergonomics, vol. 24, no. 2, pp. 91-99, (1993)
12. S. Hignett and L. McAtamney, "Rapid Entire Body Assessment (REBA)," Applied Ergonomics, vol. 31, no. 2, pp. 201-205, (2000)
13. T. R. Waters, V. Putz-Anderson, A. Garg and L. J. Fine, "Revised NIOSH equation for the design and evaluation of manual lifting tasks," Ergonomics, vol. 36, no. 7, pp. 749-776, (1993)
14. G. Chryssolouris, D. Mavrikios, D. Fragos and V. Karabatsou, "A virtual reality-based experimentation environment for the verifcation of human-related factors in assembly processes," Robotics and Computer-Integrated Manufacturing, vol. 16, no. 4, pp. 267-276, (2000)
15. J. S. Moore and A. Garg, "The Strain Index: A Proposed Method to Analyze Jobs For Risk of Distal Upper Extremity Disorders," American Industrial Hygiene Association Journal, vol. 56, no. 5, pp. 443-458, (1995)
16. M. Karg, G. Venture, J. Hoey and D. Kulić, "Human Movement Analysis as a Measure for Fatigue: A Hidden Markov-Based Approach," IEEE Transactions on Neural Systems and Rehabilitation Engineering , vol. 22, no. 3, pp. 470-481, (2014)
17. M. Golan, Y. Cohen and G. Singer, "A framework for operator – workstation interaction in Industry 4.0," International Journal of Production Research, (2019)
18. M. Peruzzini, F. Grandi and M. Pellicciari, "Exploring the potential of Operator 4.0 interface and monitoring," Computers & Industrial Engineering, (2018)
19. K. Masudul Alam and A. El Saddik, "C2PS: A Digital Twin Architecture Reference Model for the Cloud-Based Cyber-Physical Systems," IEEE Access, vol. 5, pp. 2050-2062, (2017)

20. "GE Research," GE, 2019. [Online]. Available: https://www.ge.com/research/offering/digital-twin-creation
21. B. Schleich, N. Anwer, L. Mathieu and S. Wartzack, "Shaping the digital twin for design and production engineering," CIRP Annals - Manufacturing Technology, vol. 66, pp. 141-144, (2017)
22. F. Caputo, A. Greco, M. Fera and R. Macchiaroli, "Digital twins to enhance the integration of ergonomics in the workplace design," International Journal of Industrial Ergonomics, vol. 71, pp. 20-31, (2019)
23. N. Kousia, C. Gkournelos, S. Aivaliotis, C. Giannoulis, G. Michalos and S. Makris, "Digital twin for adaptation of robots' behavior in flexible robotic assembly lines," Procedia Manufacturing, vol. 28, pp. 121-126, (2019)
24. F. Biesinger, D. Meike, B. Kraß and M. Weyrich, "A Case Study for a Digital Twin of Body-in-White Production Systems," in IEEE 23rd International Conference on Emerging Technologies and Factory Automation (ETFA), (2018)
25. A. K. Ramachandran Venkatapathy, H. Bayhan, F. Zeidler and M. t. Hompel, "Human Machine Synergies in Intra-Logistics: Creating a Hybrid Network for Research and Technologies," in Federated Conference on Computer Science and Information Systems, (2017)
26. J. (Christy) Du and V. G. Duffy, "A methodology for assessing industrialworkstations using optical motion captureintegrated with digital human models," Occupational Ergonomics , vol. 7, pp. 11-25, (2007)
27. D. Romero Díaz, J. Stahre, T. Wuest, O. Noran, P. Bernus, Å. Fast-Berglund and D. Gorecky, "Towards An Operator 4.0 Typology: A Human-Centric Perspective On The Fourth Industrial Revolution Technologies," in 46th International Conference on Computers & Industrial Engineering 2016, (2016)
28. F. Tao, Q. Qi, L. Wang and A. Nee, "Digital Twins and Cyber–Physical Systems toward Smart Manufacturingand Industry 4.0: Correlation and Comparison," Engineering, vol. 5, no. 4, pp. 653-661, (2019)
29. X. Yusen, V. Kovalev, N. Bondaletova and A. Komrakov, "Digital Twin Concept in Managing Industrial Capital Construction Projects Life Cycle," in Eleventh International Conference "Management of large-scale system development" (MLSD), (2018)
30. "DHL Press releases," DHL , July 2019. [Online]. Available: https://www.dpdhl.com/en/media-relations/press-releases/2019/dhl-supply-chain-partners-tetra-pak-implement-first-digital-twin-warehouse-asia-pacific.html
31. T. Borangiu, D. Trentesaux, A. Thomas, P. Leitao and J. Barata, "Digital transformation of manufacturing through cloud services and resource virtualization," Computers in Industry, vol. 108, pp. 150-162, (2019)
32. "An Introduction to Digital Twin Development," [Online]. Available: https://www.anylogic.com/resources/white-papers/
33. S. Mattsson, Å. Fast-Berglund, D. Li and P. Thorvald, "Forming a cognitive automation strategy for Operator 4.0 in complex assembly," Computers & Industrial Engineering, (2018)
34. J. Perez, M. de Looze, T. Bosch and W. Neumann, "Discrete event simulation as an ergonomic tool to predict workload exposures during systems design," International Journal of Industrial Ergonomics, vol. 44, no. 2, pp. 298-306, (2014)
35. H. Panetto, B. Iung, D. Ivanov, G. Weichhart and X. Wang, "Challenges for the cyber-physical manufacturing enterprises of the future," Annual Reviews in Control, vol. 47, pp. 200-213, (2019)
36. E. Rauch, C. Linder and P. Dallasega, "Anthropocentric perspective of production before and within Industry 4.0," Computers & Industrial Engineering, (2019)

I L S 2020
INTERNATIONAL CONFERENCE ON INFORMATION
SYSTEMS, LOGISTICS & SUPPLY CHAIN
Austin, Texas April 22-24, 2020

Brazilian Import Transport Network of Fertilizer (NPK): An Analysis using SNA

João Gilberto Mendes dos Reis[1,2], Sivanilza Teixeira Machado[3], Fernando Gorni Neto[1], Aguinaldo Eduardo de Souza[1], and Irenilza de Alencar Naas[1]

[1] RESUP – Supply Network Research Group, Post-graduate in Production Engineering, Universidade Paulista - UNIP, São Paulo, Brazil
[2] Post-Graduation Program in Agribusiness – Universidade Federal da Grande Dourados - UFGD, Dourados, Brazil
[3] Federal Institute of Sao Paulo, Campus Suzano
{betomendesreis@msn.com, sivanilza.machado@ifsp.edu.br, fernando.gorni@gmail.com, souza.eduaguinaldo@gmail.com, irenilza@gmail.com}

Abstract. The world population is expected to increase to 9.8 billion by 2050, increasing food demand. Fertilizer is one of the key factors that can increase food production in the world. This article aims to investigate the flow of fertilizers among country origin, main ports of entry in Brazil, and international suppliers. For this purpose, data were collected from the Brazilian Ministry of Industry and Foreign Trade, and we analyzed these data using the Ucinet 6.0 ® and Netdraw ® software. The results showed that imports of fertilizing products to Brazil are concentrated in Santos and Paranagua ports.

Keywords: Logistics, Fertilizers Imports, International market, Agricultural Supply Chain.

1. Introduction

The world population is expected to reach 9.8 billion in 2050 and 11.2 billion in 2100, according to the United Nations, Department of Economics, and Social Affairs [1] that will affect the global demand for food production. Brazil is one of the most important players in Food Production being responsible for 101,482,104 cereal tons in 2014 [2]. However, despite this importance, two problems need to be highlighted: poor and concentrated logistics infrastructure, and the dependence of imported agriculture inputs.

Poor and concentrated logistics imply bottlenecks to import and export goods [3, 4] while imported agriculture inputs cause international dependence and reduce revenue margins in the Brazilian agriculture supply chain [5]. Souza et al. [3] argue that the flow of commodities exports depends on a few routes and ports that entail logistics bottlenecks. Brazilian agricultural products were on average 36.27% higher than the price of an equivalent from Germany or the United States [6].

It is important to note that these issues are not only correlated to Brazilian agriculture, Latin America, in general, faces challenges on logistics and production, planning and control. Pérez – Pérez et al. [7] argue that limited visibility of demand, the seasonality of productive supply of raw materials and restricted planning, put at risk agricultural production. Coba et al. [8] affirm that the agricultural supply chains in Peru, for instance, are mainly related not to organized agroindustry groups but too small producers, with a low level of integration in supply chain practices.

Given that, we can infer that agricultural inputs have an essential role in the agriculture supply chains. Seeds, for example, are crucial because of the impacts on the prices of final products [9]. The same occurs with fertilizers that are essential to help the soil to produce efficiently. Therefore, it is vital to find out ways to improve internal logistics to facilitate the inland flow of agriculture products to export and receive these essential agriculture inputs

Particularly in this paper, we investigate imports of fertilizers (NPK - Nitrogen, Phosphorus and Potassium) in Brazil and its logistics framework to access production areas of the country. This study will provide an overview of how fertilizers enter into Brazil that can help decision-makers evaluate alternatives to improve hinterland logistics.

To this end, we used government data from Brazilian fertilizer imports identifying the origin and Port/Airport of entered. Our proposal is to analyze this network, identify the flow of fertilizer and the role of stakeholders, and using Social Network Analysis (SNA) measures.

The novelty of this article relies on to establish an overview of Brazilian Import Fertilizer related to origins, logistics flows, and bottlenecks. Currently, there aren't studies focus on understanding this vital flow of raw material to Brazilian Agriculture cultures.

2. Fertilizer Industry

Among the agriculture inputs fertilizers essential to Food Production the most important is composed of three primary macronutrients: nitrogen (N), phosphorus (P) and potassium (K); which are mixed according to the needs of each soil and crop. Currently, Brazil is the world's second-largest importer of phosphate fertilizers after India and the fourth largest potash-importing country after the United States, China, and India [10]. Projections showed that the country imported an average of 24.4 M per year.

The world fertilizer production is composed of a couple of countries that directly affect the entire supply chain such as Canada, China, the Russian Federation, and Norway.

According to Rappel and Loiola [11], the primary components in fertilizers are nutrients, which are vital for plant growth. Primary fertilizers include substances derived from nitrogen, phosphorus, and potassium. Several raw materials are used to produce these compounds. When ammonia is used as the nitrogen source in a fertilizer, one method of synthetic production requires the use of natural gas and air. The phosphorus component is made using sulfur, coal, and phosphate rock. The potassium source comes from potassium chloride, a primary component of potash.

The Brazilian market, specifically, is the fourth largest importer market in the world of nutrients, with imports in the order of 11.9 million tons of NPK in 2014, surpassed only by China, India, and the USA [12].

Fertilizers are products of seasonal demand; being in Brazil, the peak demand is during the second half of each year. This seasonality has a decisive impact on the performance of companies that, in the first half of the year, have poor economic and financial performance, with rising levels of short-term debt and inventories, resulting in negative operating results. This situation improves in the second half of the year, when sales grow significantly and, as a result, performance indicators improve.

3. Methodology

This work is part of an exploratory study as presented by Kothari [13] that aims to understand the flow of imported fertilizers (NPK) to Brazil and its logistical procedures. The idea was to identify the players, the volume of cargo, the origins and destinies, and ports of access inside the country. Once we defined this objective we seek a feasible method for our analysis. Thus, we find out that the Social Network Analysis (SNA) has been used to study logistics flows and relationships. According to Ta-Wei et al. the potential of Social Network Analysis to characterize supply network structures is growing interest in supply chain management [14]. This interest occurs because SNA allows identifying the flows of goods among actors in supply networks, and also the main players involved. Moreover, it allows transforming a qualitative idea about these flows and leadership in quantitative analysis.

To develop this research the following methodological procedures were adopted:

- A bibliographic research was conducted to identify the global fertilizer chain, specifically focused on fertilizers (NPK), the main world fertilizer using information from International Institute of Plant Nutrition (IPNI) [15], National Fertilizer Diffusion Association (ANDA) [10], and the Food and Agriculture Organization of the United Nations (FAO/UN) [2].

- The volumes of Brazilian import fertilizers, including their origin and logistic hub of the location they entered in Brazil, were collected using the Aliceweb system of the Ministry of Industry, Foreign Trade and Services (MDIC) [16]. The data reflects the imports of fertilizer of NPK between 2012 and 2016. Data were organized in tables to analyze using Microsoft Excel® 2016 software.
- Social Network Analysis was performed using Ucinet 6.0 © and Netdraw © software[17]. They enabled the graphics analysis of trade and understand the behavior of actors in the network.

The SNA is a technique used to study relationships between different actors in a network. According to Can and Alatas [18] a social network is made up of structures that are comprised of actors and their relationships with each other. Among main metrics of SNA the centrality is the most important that consist in the indices of the power, prestige, influence, prominence and importance in a network, in general, it is associated with instrumental outcomes, such as an individual's access to network resources and social capital [19]. The centrality is divided into three-fold: degree, betweenness, and closeness [20]. Moreover, the SNA studies involved the visual analysis of the network, where we can measure and analysis the same metrics using a graphical model. Notably, we conducted it to evaluate the fertilizer flows from international suppliers and Brazilian areas.

Regarding SNA centrality measures, we adopted the centrality degree where the in-degree is associate to the number of countries that send fertilizer to Brazilian cargo receive areas, and the closeness where the inclose refers to the ability of a node to connect to all the actors of a Network [20], that in this case is associated to network involving Brazilian cargo areas and importer countries.

4. Results

As previously mentioned, the data collected on the Aliceweb platform of the Ministry of Industry, Foreign Trade and Services allowed the analysis of the fertilizer import network (NPK). Using Netdraw® software, the network of countries that export to Brazil and their respective volumes between 2012 and 2016 were plotted (Figure 1).

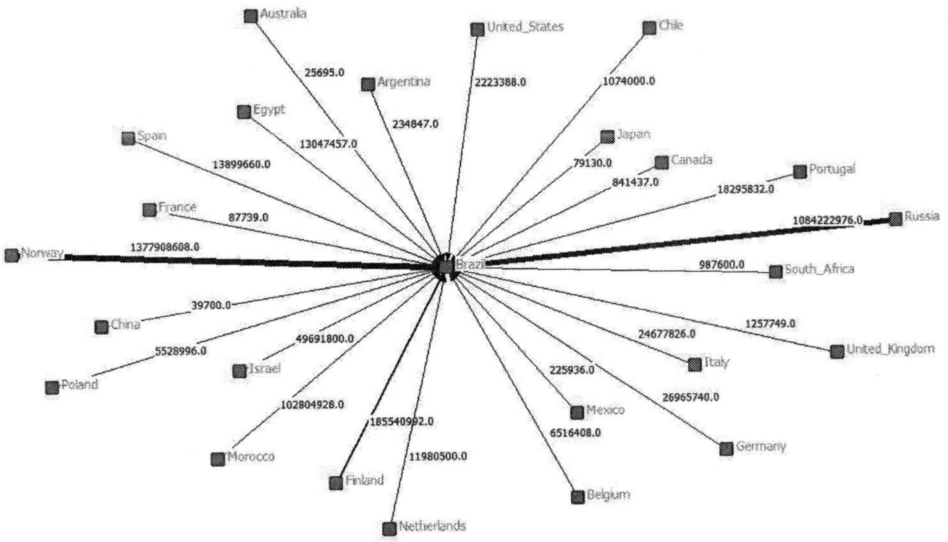

Fig. 1. Brazilian Fertilizer (NPK) Import Network

The purpose of Figure 1 was to identify the flow of import fertilizers to Brazil. From 2012 to 2016, the major countries to send fertilizer to Brazil were Norway and Russia. Norway is responsible for 47% of the exports and Russia by 37%. Yara International is the world's largest producer of ammonia, nitrates and NPK fertilizers and operates 26 production plants in 16 countries [21]. It is the leading trading company in this sector operating in Brazil, and Russia is among the world's four largest producers of NPK in the world, with 25% of the Brazilian domestic market [10].

In order to identify the ports of entry and the modalities involved in this fertilizer input, data were collected as the country of origin of these cargos, port, airport, or customs of the entry road, which consequently allows relating to the transport system used. Figure 2 also produced using Netdraw® allowed to identify the network and its subgroups (Figure 2).

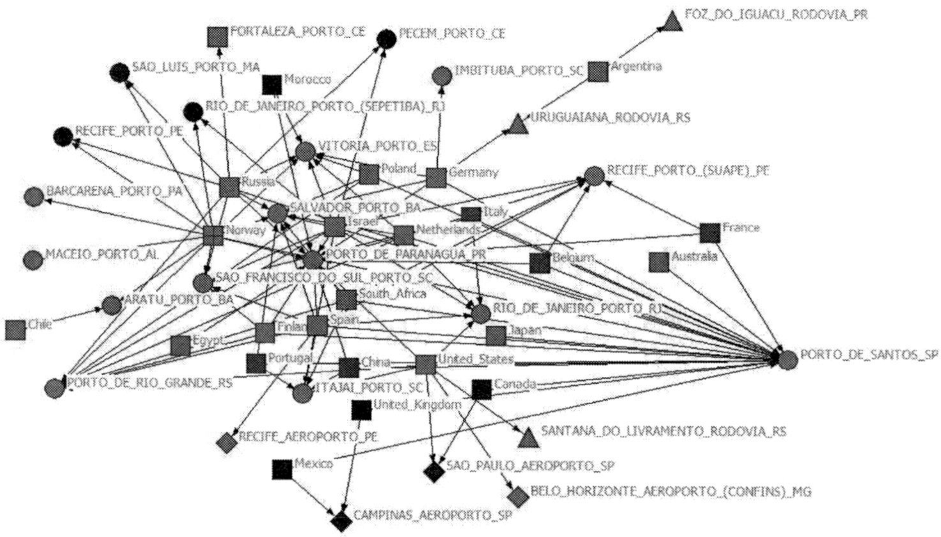

Fig. 2. Ports and the modes involved in this fertilizer input

The circle nodes represent Seaports, square nodes Exporting Countries, diamond nodes Airports, and triangle nodes road customs. Our results showed that most of the cargo is carried out by 18 Seaports in a volume corresponding to 99.88% of volume imported. The largest volume of imports occurs by Santos, Paranagua, and Rio Grande ports, as can be seen in Figure 3. Santos is the major port of access to Fertilizer (NPK) with 35% of this total volume.

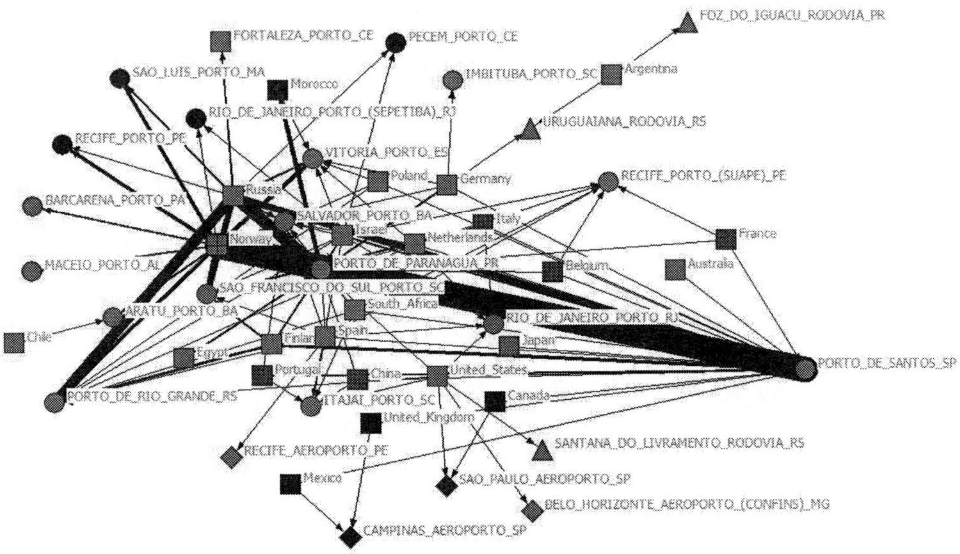

Fig 3. Volume of imports-fertilizers

Santos and Parangua are the major port of access to Fertilizer (NPK) and both respond for 36% each of total volume and Rio Grande 15%. The analysis of networks allowed us to identify the volumes and main access ports in Brazil.

Afterwards, we seek to comprehend if the volumes were related to the main actors in the network. To do so, we used some SNA measures using Ucinet® 6.0 software.

Our previous result showed the Santos was the major access port to fertilizer. Thus, to verify its degree of centrality, we established a relationship between the nodes of the network, where 1 represented the relationship and 0 was not. The degree centrality is the number of actors to which an actor is directly connected. This is divided into Input Degree and Output Level depending on the direction of the flows of fertilizers [9]. In this study imports are Input Degree (indegree) and Exports are Output Degree. The results are shown in Table 1. They represent the five main logistics hubs in Brazil.

Table 1. Main Logistics Hubs of Fertilizer in Brazil

ID	Indeg	nIndeg
PORTO_DE_SANTOS_SP	20	0.4167
PORTO_DE_PARANAGUA_PR	14	0.2917
PORTO_DE_RIO_GRANDE_RS	9	0.1875
SALVADOR_PORTO_BA	9	0.1875
VITORIA_PORTO_ES	7	0.1458

The results showed that the Port of Santos has a greater centrality of degree, interacting with 20 countries and representing approximately 42% of the centrality of this network. Paranagua (PR) is the second with 16.02%, and in third the port of Rio Grande (RS) with 15.66% (nIndeg). Comparing the degree of centrality with volumes, it is possible to conclude that despite Santos having more relationships in the network than Paranagua, this is not reflected in a higher volume of fertilizer importation for this cargo port.

The same analysis in SNA allows checking the index of network centralization that consists of a special condition in which an actor plays a clearly central role in being connected to all the nodes, which will move him to the central point in order to connect to each other [20]. The results indicate that Outdegree Network Centralization is 21% (exports), and Indegree Network Centralization is 38% (imports). This network is clearly not centralized in both ways. However, it confirms that more numbers of relationships between actors do not mean there is more volume of trade.

Finally, it was calculated the degree of closeness that consists of the ability of a node to connect to all the actors of a Network [16]. This measure is also obtained in degrees of output and degrees of input. In Table 2 can be seen the ten major fertilizer imports selected by the degree of closeness of fertilizer input.

Table 2. Closeness Measures

ID	InClose
PORTO_DE_SANTOS_SP	0.63158
PORTO_DE_PARANAGUA_PR	0.58537
PORTO_DE_RIO_GRANDE_RS	0.55172
SALVADOR_PORTO_BA	0.55172
VITORIA_PORTO_ES	0.53933
ITAJAI_PORTO_SC	0.53333
RECIFE_PORTO_(SUAPE)_PE	0.53333
SAO_FRANCISCO_DO_SUL_PORTO_SC	0.53333
RIO_DE_JANEIRO_PORTO_RJ	0.52747
ARATU_PORTO_BA	0.51064

As can be seen in Figure 2 Santos can be connected to 0.63158 of the network. Paranagua, second place, connects 0.58537 of the network. Despite the analysis does not show a considerable difference between Santos and Aratu, the results help to confirm the degree results where Ports of Santos are the Paranagua are the main players in the network reflected in the volume of cargo. In other words, to send fertilizer to Brazil, companies probably use Santos or Paranagua where the leading trading companies find important terminals to receive agricultural inputs.

5. Conclusion

Despite this article to be exploratory analysis, it identified Santos and Paranaguá as the main routes of import for fertilizers and constitutes a bottleneck of logistics operations.

Finally, the concentration in only two routes creates logistics bottlenecks in both ports and allows the creation of traffic jams and excessive use of capacity. Therefore, the subsequent studies will focus on the study of the flow of these raw materials from these ports to the production.

6. References

1. United Nations, Department of Economics and Social Affairs, "World Population Projected to Reach 9.8 Billion In 2050 and 11.2 Billion in 2100" https://www.un.org/development/desa/en/news/population/world-population-prospects-2017.html.
2. Food and Agriculture Organization of the United Nations, "FAOSTAT: Brazil," http://www.fao.org/faostat/en/#country/21.
3. de Souza, A.E., dos Reis, J.G.M., Abraham, E.R., Machado, S.T.: Brazilian Corn Exports: An Analysis of Cargo Flow in Santos and Paranagua Port," in Advances in Production Management Systems. The Path to Intelligent, Collaborative and Sustainable Manufacturing, Lödding, H., Riedel, R., Thoben, K.-D., von Cieminski, G., and Kiritsis, D., Eds., 2017, pp. 105–112.
4. Amann, E., Baer, W., Trebat, T., Lora, J.V., "Infrastructure and its role in Brazil's development process," Q. Rev. Econ. Finance. 62, pp. 66–73, 2016.

5. Brainard, L., Martinez-Diaz, L., Brazil as an Economic Superpower?: Understanding Brazil's Changing Role in the Global Economy, Washington: Brookings Institution Press, 2009.
6. Camargo, F.A.O., Silva, L.S., Merten, G.H., Carlos, F.S., Baveye, P.C., Triplett, E.W., "Chapter Two - Brazilian Agriculture in Perspective: Great Expectations vs Reality," in Advances in Agronomy, Sparks, D.L. Ed., 2017, pp. 53–114.
7. Arribasplata, L.C., Pérez-Franco, R., González-Feliu, J., Chong, M.: Improved planning of imported corn seeds demand of Hortus s.c (Peru) using a supply chain strategy assessment methodology. In: Sustainable impacts of digitalised supply chains. pp. 367–374. INSA-Lyon, Lyon (2018).
8. Coba, L., Shimabuku, C., González-Feliu, J.: Improvement of the Demand Planning of Imported Seeds in the Company Agro Perú SA. In: García Alcaraz, J.L., Rivera Cadavid, L., González-Ramírez, R.G., Leal Jamil, G., and Chong Chong, M.G. (eds.) Best Practices in Manufacturing Processes. pp. 261–281. Springer International Publishing, Cham (2019).
9. Pérez-Pérez, A., Villamonte-Cornejo, J.C., López-Rosas, C., Pérez-Franco, R., Chong, M.G.: Demand Management to Optimize the Supply Chain of an Agribusiness Company. In: García Alcaraz, J.L., Rivera Cadavid, L., González-Ramírez, R.G., Leal Jamil, G., and Chong Chong, M.G. (eds.) Best Practices in Manufacturing Processes. pp. 137–157. Springer International Publishing, Cham (2019).
10. National Fertilizer Diffusion Association, Anuário Estatístico, São Paulo: ANDA, 2016.
11. Rappel, E., Loiola, E., Study of the competitiveness of the Brazilian Industry, competitiveness of the fertilizer industry, Campinas: IE/UNICAMP - IEI/UFRJ - FDC - FUNCEX, 1993.
12. National Fertilizer Diffusion Association, http://www.anda.org.br/index.php?ver=por.
13. Kothari, C., Research Methodology, Methods and Techniques, New Delhi: New Age International, 2004.
14. Kao, T.-W., Simpson, N.C., Shao, B.B.M., Lin, W.T., "Relating Supply Network Structure to Productive Efficiency: A Multi-Stage Empirical Investigation, Eur. J. Oper. Res. 259, pp. 469–485, 2017.
15. International Plant Nutrition Institute: Consumo de fertilizantes por região, nutrientes e natureza física, http://brasil.ipni.net/article/BRS-3132#consumo.
16. Ministry of Industry, Foreign Trade and Services, Séries Históricas, http://www.mdic.gov.br/comercio-exterior/estatisticas-de-comercio-exterior/series-historicas.
17. Borgatti, S.P., Netdraw Software for Network Visualization, Nicholasville, Analytic Technologies, 2002.
18. Can, U., Alatas, B.: A new direction in social network analysis: Online social network analysis problems and applications. Physica A: Statistical Mechanics and its Applications. 535, 122372, 2019.
19. Kurt, Y., Kurt, M.: Social network analysis in international business research: An assessment of the current state of play and future research directions. International Business Review. 101633, 2019.
20. Alejandro, V.A., Norman, A.G., Manual Introdutório à Análise de Redes Sociais, Universidad Autonoma Del Estado de Mexico, 2005.
21. Haugen, H.A., Eldrup, N.H., Fatnes, A.M., Leren, E.: Commercial Capture and Transport of CO2 from Production of Ammonia. Energy Procedia. 114, pp. 6133–6140, 2017.

I L S 2020
INTERNATIONAL CONFERENCE ON INFORMATION SYSTEMS, LOGISTICS & SUPPLY CHAIN
Austin, Texas April 22-24, 2020

An Evolutionary Algorithm based on Multidimensional Multiple-Choice Knapsack Model for Resource Allocation Problem in a Construction Equipment Manufacturer

Alejandra Duenas [1], Christine Di Martinelly [2], Joaquin Aguado[3], Yazgi Tütüncü[4]

[1] *ICN Business School, CEREFIGE, Nancy, France*
[2] *IESEG School of Management, LEM-CNRS (UMR 9221), Lille, France*
[3] *University of Bamberg, Germany*
[4] *İzmir University of Economics, Department of Mathematics, Turkey*
{alejandra.duenas@icn-artem.com, c.dimartinelly@ieseg.fr, joaquin.aguado@uni-bamberg.de, yazgi.tutuncu@ieu.edu.tr }

Abstract: This paper presents an approach to production resource allocation applied to a real-world problem within the construction equipment manufacturing industry. It shows an original way of determining the outcome manufacturing production problems using existing mathematical modeling techniques combined with evolutionary heuristics. A multidimensional knapsack problem was formulated, the proposed model being based on an evolutionary algorithm using a three-dimensional binary-coded chromosome. Three different selection strategies were applied to evaluate the algorithm's performance and tests were carried out to show the appropriateness of the solutions. The results obtained were of a high quality from the company's perspective.

Keywords: Multidimensional multiple-choice knapsack problem, evolutionary algorithm, combinatorial optimization, resource allocation, heuristics

1. Introduction

This paper presents an approach to a real-world assembly line problem. Complex products are produced on a high-variety, sequentially operated assembly line; components are added as the products being assembled move from station to station. Component assembly occurs on-site on dedicated machines that require specific manpower competencies; therefore, the component assembly department requires workers with different skills. Components are assembled the day before they are needed for the main production line to avoid storage difficulties. Assembly workers are assigned to both machines and components and can be reassigned during the day depending on need. The skills of a worker to work on a machine directly impacts on the processing time of the component on that particular machine. The throughput on the main production line is generally stable over a period of time and generates the demand for components from the component assembly department. The number of components required for each excavator is identical. However, component specifications are dependent upon the product being assembled and this influences the processing time. As a result, the workload of the component assembly department is unstable and subject to variability which causes dissatisfaction among the personnel, increases overtime work and results in delays on the main production line.

The present paper addresses the optimization of the assignment of personnel to different machines and components, considering personnel competencies, so as to level the workload and minimize operational disturbances on the main assembly lines. An evolutionary algorithm is proposed to solve this problem.

The paper presents an extended version of a past paper [1]. In the earlier version, the assignment to machines was not considered explicitly and the problem was modelled as a generalized assignment problem (GAP). By considering the job assignment to machines and to personnel, a multi-dimensional assignment problem is now presented, more precisely a three-dimensional assignment problem. The proposed solution algorithm has therefore been adapted.

The multi-dimensional assignment problem (MAP) is found in the literature under 2 main variants. The first considers the generalization to k dimensions of the classical assignment problem, for which the problem is to find the optimal matching between n elements of 2 sets (one-to-one matching). This problem was first defined by Pierskalla [2] and is shown to be NP-hard [3]. Researchers are interested in finding, in an efficient way, feasible and near optimal solutions. Pasiliao, Pardalos [4] studied the performance of branch and bound algorithms based on different tree representations of the MAP. Problem instance structures, based on costs, weights, and capacity, have been studied and were proven to influence the solution time. Grundel, Krokhmal [5] studied the number of local minima in the case of instances with independent cost structure. The number of local minima increases with the number of dimensions and has a negative impact on local neighborhood search heuristics. Huang and Lim [6] used a local search heuristic hybridized with a genetic algorithm. The general idea of their method was to solve a problem of smaller dimensions by considering the original problem as fixed. Karapetyan and Gutin [7] showed that heuristic methods performed differently on problems with independent weights vs decomposable weights and adjusted the local search algorithms.

The second variant is a generalization to k dimensions of the generalized assignment problem, for which one has to find the best one-to-many assignment, recognizing capacity limits. This problem has been presented by Ross and Zoltners [8] under the name weighted assignment model. Gilbert and Hofstra [9] and Pentico [10] presented the applications and variants of this version of the MAP. Geetha and Vartak [11] reviewed how to balance problems with 3 dimensions so that known heuristics can be applied. Park, Byung Ha [12] used a Lagrangian dual-based branch-and-bound algorithm to the lower bounding scheme, and accelerated the search process. This later variant is mostly encountered in the literature under the name "multidimensional multiple-choice knapsack problem" (MMKP). Indeed, the multiple knapsack problem (MKP) is a GAP [13]; its generalization to k dimensions can thus be considered as a MMKP. The MMKP is a variant of the 0-1 knapsack problem which is a NP-complete problem [14]. As in the case of the AP generalized to k dimensions, the structure of the problem has an influence on the efficiency of the method used to solve it. Han, Leblet [15] studied known algorithms to solve the MMKP and showed that when there is correlation between the parameters, the instances are harder to solve. Ghasemi and Razzazi [16] developed a branch-and-bound approach for instances with non-correlated cost problems.

The specific emphasis of this paper is to propose an evolutionary algorithm to solve an assignment problem of jobs to machines and personnel, taking into account the workers' skills and capacity constraints – workers can be assigned to different machines. The model is developed in order to benefit from the characteristics of the problem and to apply an evolutionary algorithm (EA). The EA is tested with different selection strategies.

Section 2 contains the definition of the (real-world) problem. The evolutionary algorithm proposed to solve the resource allocation problem is presented in Section 3. The results analysis is presented and discussed in Section 4. Finally, conclusions and directions for future work are outlined in Section 5.

2. Multi-dimensional multiple-choice knapsack problem

The objective of the proposed model, elaborated in partnership with a construction equipment manufacturer, is to minimize the total completion time. A final product is composed of c types of components; the component assembly department is composed of m machines ($m = 1,..,M$); each machine is dedicated to the assembly of one type of component. The number of components of each excavator is identical and equal to the number of machine. Every day, the main assembly line produces E construction equipment (excavators). As a result, the demand for the component assembly department on the previous day is $E * M = J$ jobs. For instance, if 6 excavators are being produced on day d+1 on the main assembly line and the component assembly department is composed of 7 machines, the component assembly department must have assembled 6*7 jobs on day d. The number of jobs constitutes the items to schedule. The assembly time of component c of excavator e on machine m is denoted as $a_{c_e m}$; which can then be further simplified as the processing time of excavator e on machine m, a_{em} (the component c of excavator e can only be produced on machine m).

The number of employees available in the component assembly department is fixed to O. Each operator o $(o = 1,..,O)$ possesses different competencies on each machine m, which depends on his level of training, k_{om}. The processing time of job j of excavator e on machine m by operator o is denoted p_{oem} and is equal to $k_{om} * a_{em}$. Each operator o can be reallocated and transferred from machine to machine in order to fulfil assembly activities according to his competencies, as long as it does not exceed a maximum number of working hours, W_o, which can differ based on their contracts.
Table 1 presents the MMKP notation used in this model.

Table 1. MMKP Notation

Sets		**Indices**	
O	Set of operators in the component assembly department	o	An operator
M	Set of machines	m	A machine
C	Set of components	c	A component
J	Set of jobs	j	A job
E	Set of excavators	e	An excavator
Parameters			
a_{em}	Assembly time of (component c of) excavator e on machine m		
k_{om}	Competencies of operator o to work on machine m		
p_{oem}	Processing time for (component c of) excavator e being produced on machine m by operator o		
W_o	Maximum number of working hours of operator o		
Variable			
	$x_{oem} \begin{cases} 1 & \text{if operator } o \text{ is selected to produce excavator } e \text{ on machine } m \\ 0 & \text{otherwise} \end{cases}$		

The mathematical formulation of the MMKP with the objective of minimizing the total completion time is as follows:

$$MIN \sum_{m=1}^{M} \sum_{o=1}^{O} \sum_{e=1}^{E} p_{oem} * x_{oem} \quad (1)$$

Subject to

$$\sum_{m=1}^{M} \sum_{e=1}^{E} p_{oem} * x_{oem} \leq W_o, \forall o = 1,..,O \quad (2)$$

$$\sum_{o=1}^{O} x_{oem} = 1, \forall m = 1,..,M, \forall e = 1,..,E \quad (3)$$

$$x_{oem} \in \{0,1\} \quad (4)$$

Equation (2) represents the constraint that operators cannot work longer than W_o hours per day. Equation (3) represents the constraint that each component of excavator e should be produced once and only once on each machine m. Equation (4) defines the domain of the variables.

3. Methodology

Due to the complexity of the MMKP, it was decided to use an evolutionary heuristic to search the optimal solution of the given multidimentional knapsack problem. Therefore, the encoding of the solution to the problem was a binary-coded chromosome. Figure 1 presents a schematic representation of the chromosome, considering o different operators, m different machines and e different excavators. This representation is similar to the representation proposed in Tavana, Khalili-Damghani [17].

3.1 Evolutionary Algorithm

Evolutionary algorithms (EAs) are instances of algorithms that work with evolutionary principles. An EA is a search algorithm, inspired by natural selection and genetics that uses a population of possible solutions (candidate solutions) instead of a single solution. The candidate solutions are usually represented as strings (chromosomes) and they are evaluated by an objective (fitness) function. The search is iterative, where better solutions are generated in each iteration after applying certain genetic operators (selection, recombination, mutation etc.) [18].

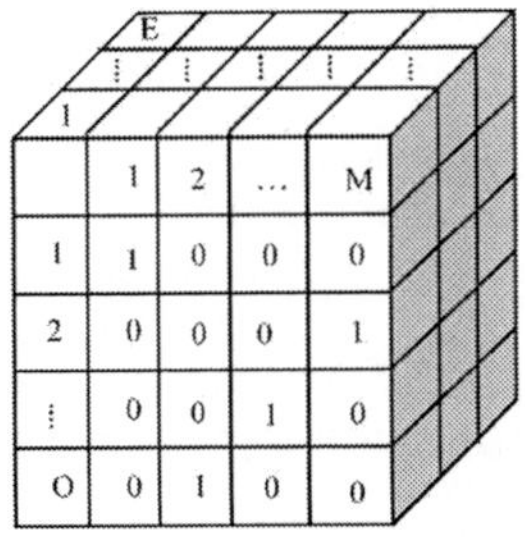

Figure 1. Binary-coded chromosome for the MMKP

Due to the problem formulation and especially due to constraints (3), it was decided to propose an EA where only a mutation operator is applied without using recombination in order to keep constraint violations to a minimum. As demonstrated by Hesser and Manner [19] the mutation operator can be considered as a search operator in itself. Hence, Figure 2 shows the EA's pseudocode with selection and mutation operators:

```
begin
t ← 0
initialise P(t)
evaluate P(t)
while (not termination-condition) do
begin
        t ← t + 1
        select P(t) from P(t - 1)
        mutate P(t)
        evaluate P(t)
end
end
```

Figure 2. EA's pseudocode

The EA's initial population is generated making sure that all individuals are feasible. Each individual represents an initial assignment that satisfies constraint (3) and constraint (4).

To determine the position of undergoing mutation a uniform random choice is used, so each position has the same probability of mutation p_m; where, p_m is defined as the probability of independently inverting the value assigned to operator o from 0 to 1 or from 1 to 0. Once the inversion is performed, a repair algorithm is applied to make sure that only one operator is allocated a value of 1 as shown in Figure 3.

In this way, the mutated offspring meets the constraint that only one operator can be assigned to one machine at a time (equation (3)) but might generate infeasible solutions with respect to the constraint that operators cannot work longer than W_o hours per day (equation (2)). This later issue is dealt with using a repair algorithm according to the different selection strategies.

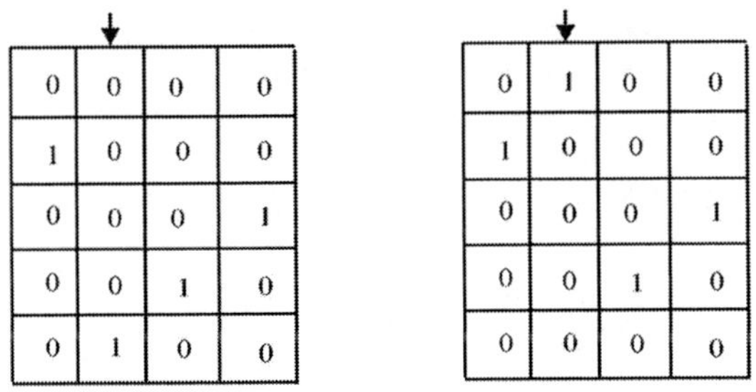

Figure 3. Mutation operator for the MMKP

3.2 Evolutionary algorithm selection strategies

Selection strategies drive the search of the EA and have an impact on its performance. Therefore, based on the characteristics of the problem, three selection strategies are proposed and described in the following subsections.

3.2.1 Strategy 1: Non-overlapping selection model
In this type of selection algorithms, a selection pool is defined for both reproduction selection and deletion selection. In a non-overlapping model the selection pool is determined by the entire current population which is also selected for deletion. In other words, the parent population (μ) is replaced by the offspring population (λ) [20]. This kind of strategy is similar to a generational model in genetic algorithms in which the whole population is replaced at each run. It converges faster but may take time to finish off [21]. Also, it keeps diversity at each generation.

3.2.2 Strategy 2: Overlapping selection model (Elitist strategy)
This type of selection strategy was chosen to ensure that the offspring with the best fitness values survive into the next generation. In the selected evolution strategy $(\mu + \lambda)$ parents and offspring compete and the best μ are selected. This kind of strategy is similar to an incremental model in genetic algorithms that can benefit from exploiting any new individual [22]. In this way, the best individuals are kept longer in the next generation.

3.2.3 Strategy 3: Constraint handling approach with tournament selection
In most applications of population-based search methods (such as EA) the penalty function approach of handling constraints is used. In this way comparisons between two feasible solutions, one feasible and one infeasible solution, and two infeasible solutions are possible. In this paper, it was decided to use the constraint handling approach presented by Deb [23]. Therefore, a tournament selection operator is used where two solutions (mutated offspring) are compared enforcing the following criteria: any feasible solution is preferred to any infeasible solution; from two feasible solutions the one with the better objective function value is preferred; and from two infeasible solutions the one with the smaller constraint violation is preferred. Consequently, in the comparison of two infeasible solutions only the constraint violation is used without having to compute the objective function value [23].

$$F(\bar{x}) = \begin{cases} f(\bar{x}) & \text{if } \bar{x} \text{ is feasible} \\ f_{max} + g(\bar{x}) & otherwise \end{cases} \quad (5)$$

where $f(\bar{x})$ represents the objective function value given by equation (1), f_{max} is the objective function value of the worst feasible solution in the population and $g(\bar{x})$ represents the constraint violation defined as follows:

$$g(\bar{x}) = \sum_{o=1}^{O}(W_o - \sum_{m=1}^{M}\sum_{e=1}^{E} p_{oem} * x_{oem}) \quad (6)$$

4. Experimental results and analysis

The problem under consideration is a real-world production resource allocation problem defined in collaboration with a construction equipment manufacturer. In this problem, 18 operators with different skills are to be allocated to 7 machines in order to produce 7 different excavators per day. The 7 excavators are made of 7 components, each one produced on a specific machine. All the algorithms were implemented in Visual Basic for Applications using Excel as user interface. This was decided in order that the developed software is easy to implement and use by the manufacturing company. The tests were executed on a personal computer with Intel Core i7 3770S Processor 3.1 GHz, 16GB RAM, running on Windows 7.
Table 2 presents the results found when running the EA with different seeds for different initial populations for the different strategies.

4.1 Results of Strategy 1: Non-overlapping selection

The initial parameter specifications of the EA are as follows; population size $\mu = 50$, $W_o = 7.24$ hours a day, and a selection size $\lambda = 50$. Once the mutation operator is applied, it is possible to find infeasible solutions. Therefore, a repair algorithm is applied to make sure that only one operator is allocated a value of 1.
In order to test the performance of the algorithm different measurements were determined such as the best, worst and average solution for each time the algorithm was run. Two ratios 'best/average' and 'worst/average' were calculated to see the convergence of the algorithm. The mean and the deviation were also calculated to measure the differences between the different simulations.

From Table 2, 'non-overlapping selection', it can be observed that (as expected) according to the results of strategy 1 (non-overlapping selection), the values of best, worst and average solutions of each set of experiments was decreased as the size of the population increased. This trend was observed for each of the different initial populations. Moreover, an increase was observed for the difference between the best results and worst results for each of the different initial populations which is entirely consistent with the diversity of the algorithm throughout different parts of the solution space. Even though it is not possible to point out a stable trend for the ratios, in general it can be said that the results support the conclusion regarding the convergence of the algorithm to the optimal solution.

4.2 Results of Strategy 2: Elitist Strategy

In this section, the test results for the elitist strategy are presented. The initial parameter specifications of the EA are as follows; population size $\mu = 50$, $W_o = 7.24$ hours a day, and offspring size $\lambda = 25$. In order to test the performance of the algorithm the same measurements used in strategy 1 are assumed; best and worst solutions, 'best/average' and 'worst/average', mean and deviation.

From Table 2, 'elitist strategy', it can be observed that for all of the initial populations the elitist strategy does not provide any trend with regard to improving the quality of the solutions, even if the number of the solutions is increased. The diversification is pretty low due to the fact that in each iteration the algorithm considers the elite solution space. Furthermore, the results are supported by the ratios.

4.3 Results of Strategy 3: Tournament selection

The initial parameter specifications of the EA are a population size $\mu = 50$, $W_o = 7.24$ hours a day, and a tournament size $q = 2$. This tournament size was selected to avoid having a high loss of diversity θ as introduced by Blickle [24] $(q) = q^{-1/(q-1)} - q^{q/(q-1)} = 0.25$. In other words having a tournament size q of 2 will lead to the smallest loss of diversity possible which is 25%.

From Table 2, 'tournament selection', it can be observed that tournament selection provides the best solution for all seeded initial populations. After analysis of the three different strategies, it can be seen that the better values were obtained after 4000 runs, being mindful that the progression is non-linear.

Also, it can be noted that the standard deviations of the solutions are higher than in the previous strategy, which is due to the diversification introduced at each run. The ratio "best/average" follows a decreasing trend and provides lower values than strategy 1, demonstrating a better convergence.
Strategy 3 deals with constraint 2 explicitly by keeping either the solutions with no violation of that constraint or with the smallest violation. Based on the results collected, it is however impossible to know if the violation is due to a number of operators who work slightly more that W_o or to some operators working a lot more. As a result, it was decided to run fewer simulations to completely understand how the constraint violation behaves.

npletion time (hours) on the 7 machines found using a non-overlapping selection strategy, an elitist strategy and tourna

non-overlapping selection strategy					**elitist stratety**						
500	**1000**	**2000**	**3000**	**4000**	**100**	**500**	**1000**	**2000**	**3000**	**4000**	**100**
23.9	32.9	33.6	29.7	26.7	34.8	32.9	34.7	26.5	39.3	28.5	26.10
75.2	77.7	70.8	75.5	70.2	77.3	77.1	61.9	64.1	83.7	74.0	73.98
52.7	51.8	50.4	51.2	48.8	51.7	50.2	48.6	50.0	54.1	50.1	41.70
12.4	10.3	9.0	10.6	11.2	9.5	11.3	7.6	10.1	11.9	11.7	12.69
0.453	0.634	0.666	0.580	0.547	0.672	0.655	0.714	0.531	0.726	0.570	0.626
1.429	1.498	1.405	1.475	1.439	1.495	1.536	1.273	1.281	1.548	1.478	1.774
500	**1000**	**2000**	**3000**	**4000**	**100**	**500**	**1000**	**2000**	**3000**	**4000**	**100**
32.3	23.4	26.2	20.8	26.6	32.40	33.68	18.83	27.00	34.13	29.08	22.26
75.0	67.5	78.0	71.3	72.3	70.41	74.84	69.43	68.91	72.81	71.41	86.56
50.3	49.2	48.7	48.2	48.3	46.40	51.55	48.63	46.32	49.15	50.86	40.51
9.8	11.2	11.2	11.3	9.9	10.09	9.77	12.44	11.46	9.06	10.90	12.91
0.641	0.477	0.538	0.431	0.551	0.698	0.653	0.387	0.583	0.694	0.572	0.550
1.492	1.373	1.600	1.480	1.495	1.518	1.452	1.428	1.487	1.481	1.404	2.137
500	**1000**	**2000**	**3000**	**4000**	**100**	**500**	**1000**	**2000**	**3000**	**4000**	**100**
25.3	26.5	25.4	27.6	29.4	36.9	30.3	30.3	23.4	29.2	32.6	22.47
78.1	84.8	80.7	72.3	78.2	72.1	77.5	59.3	72.0	78.0	71.1	82.81
52.2	51.9	51.9	52.0	52.2	49.6	50.2	48.5	50.4	49.4	48.7	41.93
11.8	12.3	11.7	9.7	9.6	8.4	11.3	8.9	10.4	12.9	10.4	14.63
0.484	0.510	0.489	0.531	0.564	0.743	0.603	0.626	0.464	0.591	0.670	0.536
1.497	1.634	1.555	1.390	1.497	1.453	1.545	1.224	1.429	1.580	1.460	1.975
500	**1000**	**2000**	**3000**	**4000**	**100**	**500**	**1000**	**2000**	**3000**	**4000**	**100**
26.23	19.95	31.28	24.49	32.07	29.3	30.2	40.7	34.0	35.7	31.8	20.40
74.68	72.68	82.79	78.35	69.31	75.4	78.9	72.0	74.3	67.2	68.8	70.28
49.23	51.34	48.45	48.25	49.83	51.2	52.7	55.4	50.7	51.7	52.3	43.68
10.85	10.60	10.91	11.55	10.20	11.3	12.9	8.0	10.4	9.2	9.5	11.74
0.533	0.389	0.646	0.508	0.644	0.573	0.573	0.735	0.670	0.691	0.608	0.467
1.517	1.416	1.709	1.624	1.391	1.473	1.497	1.300	1.465	1.301	1.315	1.609

Table 3 presents the results obtained when running the EA using the approach presented.

Table 3. Results found by the EA

Number of simulation runs	Number of operators with constraint violations (Constraint (2))	Violation constraint value
100	9	8.4714
300	6	7.4206
500	6	4.296
800	4	3.1923
1000	3	1.63205
1500	3	1.50405

From Table 3, it can be observed (as expected) that the violation constraint value decreases as the number of simulations increases. It is also shown that the number of operators which have a constraint violation may decrease, because the constraint violation is related to the fact that operators cannot work longer than W_o hours per day. This, in economic terms, means that the company has to pay overtime to those operators with a constraint violation, having a direct impact on the company profits.
Furthermore, when comparing the algorithm run 300 to 500 simulations, it is possible to see that the number of operators with a constraint violation remains the same. However, the violation constraint value for 500 simulations is almost 50% lower than the value found for 300 simulations. This shows that the EA has not been defined to decrease the number of operators with a constraint violation but to decrease the violation constraint value. Finally, when comparing the violation constraint values between 1000 and 1500, it can be seen that the difference between them is not as big as in other instances. This suggests that it may not be advisable to run the EA for a bigger number of simulations since the results might not improve after a certain number of iterations.

5. Conclusions

In this paper, an approach to solve the MMKP is presented. The approach is applied to a real-world problem in the construction equipment manufacturing industry with the aim of allocating different operators to different components to be processed on different machines. The main characteristic of the problem is that the operators' different skills and competences need to be considered in the operators' processing times. The problem can be considered as an MMKP, which is NP-complete.
This paper proposes an EA which is suited to the characteristics of the problem and keeps the solution process fast. The MMKP coding considered is a 3D binary-coded chromosome; however, a 2D mutation operator is also applied together with a repair algorithm to model the constraints. Three selection strategies are proposed: non-overlapping selection, elitist strategy and tournament; the non-overlapping selection strategy is defined as $\mu = \lambda = 50$; the elitist strategy is type $(\mu + \lambda)$; and finally, for the tournament selection strategy the EA's fitness function is represented by the sum of the objective function and a penalty term.
The application of the EA with different strategies using the data of the construction company not only confirms the findings in the literature but also demonstrates that this well-known MKKP can be used in real applications to yield high quality solutions in a fast and effective way. Although the time to converge takes longer the solutions in the non-overlapping strategy decrease the completion time. Based on the characteristics of the problem, it can be said that the EA, in strategy 2, is trapped in a local optimum and the lack of diversity in the population prevents the algorithm from finding a better solution. On the other hand, strategy 3 provides the better solutions in terms of total completion time and converges faster than the other 2 strategies. Those better solutions in terms of total completion time are obtained by relaxing the constraint on the maximum amount of working time. The constraint violation is however minimized and decreases over the runs.
The model is quick and easy to use and can be utilized by the company on a daily basis or if and when required without delaying production.
Future work could include the variant where two or more operators can be allocated to the same component and the problem solution when more than one objective is simultaneously considered (e.g., minimizing the overtime costs). Another aspect to analyze is the uncertainty related to the processing time definition since

no historical data is available. The use of fuzzy sets for modeling this uncertainty would also be interesting for future research.

6. References

1. Duenas, A., C. Di Martinelly, and Y. Tutuncu, *A Multidimensional Multiple-Choice Knapsack Model for Resource Allocation in a Construction Equipment Manufacturer Setting Using an Evolutionary Algorithm*, in *APMS 2014, IFIP AICT 438*, B.G.e. al., Editor. 2014, Springer-Verlag Berlin Heidelberg p. pp. 539–546.
2. Pierskalla, W.P., *The multidimensional assignment problem.* Operations Research, 1968. **16**(2): p. 422-454.
3. Crama, Y. and F.C.R. Spieksma, *Approximation algorithms for three-dimensional assignment problems with triangle inequalities.* European Journal of Operational Research, 1992. **60**(3): p. 273-279.
4. Pasiliao, E.L., P.M. Pardalos, and L.S. Pitsoulis, *Branch and bound algorithms for the multidimensional assignment problem.* Optimization Methods and Software, 2005. **20**(1): p. 127-143.
5. Grundel, D., et al., *On the number of local minima for the multidimensional assignment problem.* Journal of Combinatorial Optimization, 2007. **13**(1): p. 1-18.
6. Huang, G. and A. Lim, *A hybrid genetic algorithm for the Three-Index Assignment Problem.* European Journal of Operational Research, 2006. **172**(1): p. 249-257.
7. Karapetyan, D. and G. Gutin, *Local search heuristics for the multidimensional assignment problem.* Journal of Heuristics, 2011. **17**(3): p. 201-249.
8. Ross, G.T. and A.A. Zoltners, *Weighted Assignment Models and Their Application.* Management Science, 1979. **25**(7): p. 683-696.
9. Gilbert, K.C. and R.B. Hofstra, *multidimensional assignment problems.* Decision Sciences, 1988. **19**(2): p. 306-321.
10. Pentico, D.W., *Assignment problems: A golden anniversary survey.* European Journal of Operational Research, 2007. **176**(2): p. 774-793.
11. Geetha, S. and M.N. Vartak, *The three-dimensional bottleneck assignment problem with capacity constraints.* European Journal of Operational Research, 1994. **73**(3): p. 562-568.
12. Park, J.S., L. Byung Ha, and L. Youngho, *A Lagrangian Dual-Based Branch-and-Bound Algorithm for the Generalized Multi-Assignment Problem.* Management Science, 1998. **44**(12): p. S271-S282.
13. Martello, S. and P. Toth, *Knapsack problems.* 1990: Wiley New York.
14. Hifi, M., M. Michrafy, and A. Sbihi, *Heuristic algorithms for the multiple-choice multidimensional knapsack problem.* Journal of the Operational Research Society, 2004. **55**(12): p. 1323-1332.
15. Han, B., J. Leblet, and G. Simon, *Hard multidimensional multiple choice knapsack problems, an empirical study.* Computers & Operations Research, 2010. **37**(1): p. 172-181.
16. Ghasemi, T. and M. Razzazi, *Development of core to solve the multidimensional multiple-choice knapsack problem.* Computers & Industrial Engineering, 2011. **60**(2): p. 349-360.
17. Tavana, M., K. Khalili-Damghani, and A.-R. Abtahi, *A fuzzy multidimensional multiple-choice knapsack model for project portfolio selection using an evolutionary algorithm.* Annals of Operations Research, 2013. **206**(1): p. 449-483.
18. Bäck, T., ed. *Introduction to evolutionary algorithms, Chapter 7*. Evolutionary Computation 1, ed. T. Bäck, Fogel, D.B. and Michalewicz, Z. 2000, Institute of Physics Publishing.
19. Hesser, J. and R. Manner, *TOWARDS AN OPTIMAL MUTATION PROBABILITY FOR GENETIC ALGORITHMS.* Lecture Notes in Computer Science, 1991. **496**: p. 23-32.
20. Sarma, J., & De Jong, K., *Generation Gap Methods*, in *Evolutionary Computation 1*, T. Bäck, Fogel, D. and Michalewicz, Z. , Editor. 2000, Institute of Physics Publishing: Bristol & Philadelphia.
21. Hancock, P.B., *An empirical comparison of selection methods in evolutionary algorithms*, in *Evolutionary Computing*, T. Fogarty, Editor. 1994, Springer Berlin Heidelberg. p. 80-94.
22. Goldberg, D.E. and K. Deb, *A comparative analysis of selection schemes used in genetic algorithms.* Foundations of genetic algorithms, 1991. **1**: p. 69-93.
23. Deb, K., *An efficient constraint handling method for genetic algorithms.* Computer Methods in Applied Mechanics and Engineering, 2000. **186**(2-4): p. 311-338.
24. Blickle, T., & Thiele, L. *A mathematical analysis of tournament selection.* in *6th International Conference on Genetic Algorithms*. 1995. Pittsburg, PA: Morgan Kaufmann.

A New S&OP Maturity Assessment Model for Mass Customization Production Systems: A Case Study of an Automotive OEM

Yahya GHRAB [1], Mustapha SALI [2]

[1] DRM UMR 7088, PSL-Paris-Dauphine University, Paris, France
[2] DRM UMR 7088, PSL-Paris-Dauphine University, Paris, France
{yahya.ghrab@dauphine.eu, mustapha.sali@dauphine.psl.eu}

Abstract. Sales and Operations Planning (S&OP) is a critical business alignment process for industries with large product portfolio. Indeed, high variety is a driver of complexity and results in a poor planning efficiency. Diagnosing the root causes of the process failure starts by assessing the maturity of its actual technical and organizational performance. The existing body of research lacks context-related maturity assessment frameworks that measure the maturity regarding activity-related dimensions. In this paper, we intend to propose a new S&OP maturity assessment model that considers the critical attributes linked to the context of mass customization production systems. Our review of existing contributions on maturity assessment combined with the results of workshops organized in a major automotive company ended-up on a suitable context-related design. The new framework has been tested within the automotive company by interviewing major decision makers and operational teams involved in the S&OP process.

Keywords: Sales and operations planning, Context-related maturity assessment, Performance, Automotive industry, Product variety, Mass customization production systems

1. Introduction

New consumption paradigms are shaping today's markets. Customers nowadays seek unique on-size products and are more sensitive to delivery speed [2],[3]. Consequently, manufacturers are pushed to offer a large panel of choices in their catalogues to avoid the chance of missing a selling opportunity and to stand out among competitors. This trend has exploded product variety [5],[7]. As a result, manufacturers deal with a lot of data which weighs heavily on their planning processes. In a previous paper [6], we outlined the importance of S&OP as a business process, the critical alignment role it plays in mass customization production systems and the challenges it faces. Our findings show that S&OP struggles to deliver the intended outcomes despite the relevant number of academic and practitioner contributions on the subject. We hypothesized that the observed weak performance is linked to the poor management of product variety and to the absence of clear aggregation rules. Undeniably, choosing which product to produce among billions of alternatives is challenging, especially if such decision must be taken long before the order date to anticipate the long delivery lead time for some parts. Regarding these challenges, considering the product high variety impact on S&OP performance seems promising.

To test our hypothesis, we needed a tool that diagnose the current situation and measure performance. Maturity models fill exactly that requirement. Indeed, assessing the maturity represents a common practice for performance measurement and serves as a valuable tool to assist decision-makers [7]. Our review of existing S&OP maturity assessment contributions presented in the next section outlines the absence of context-related models that measure S&OP performance regarding contextual critical attributes. Motivated by the recommendation of several authors to design more context-fitted assessments [8, 9], we contribute to fill this gap by designing a new context-related S&OP assessment jointly with professionals. More specifically, based on the existing literature, on our observation made within an automotive company (OEM) and on expert opinion gathered during workshops, we identified maturity dimensions linked to the high product diversity and integrated them in the assessment. The evaluation grid was submitted to a panel of actors involved in the S&OP process of a large automotive company. Each dimension has been assessed during the assessment whose results are discussed in this paper.

This paper is organized as follow: The second section will be dedicated to a literature review of existing maturity models and their limits. The third section will cover the construction and design of the new framework. Section four will cover the case study of a major car manufacturer, its results and analysis. The last section will be dedicated for a conclusion and future research.

2. Literature review

In this section, we present the maturity models, then we focus on those dedicated to S&OP and finally we try to explain why context-related frameworks are beneficial.

2.1. Maturity models

A maturity assessment is designed according to a maturity model. It consists on evaluating the performance of a process over a set of performance criteria in order to be positioned at a certain level called 'maturity level'. The practice is a derivation from Capability Maturity Models (CMM) [10] originally developed for the quality management of software development. The use of maturity models has been since then generalized to reach the supply chain operations research applications and related areas [11, 12].
Maturity models have been proven useful through their benefits [13] and can be deployed for three purposes [12]. They can be used as descriptive and serve to give insights related to actual situation of the process with no intention for improvement or relationship to performance. A maturity model can be also used for prescriptive purposes and indicates how to improve the maturity and business performance. The last purpose is comparative and aims to provide a benchmark across industries or regions. Furthermore, maturity models develop a standard roadmap to follow while seeking improvements[14], they serve as educative tools by generating awareness toward the assessed aspects [15]. For more details, an interesting systematic review on business process maturity models has been performed by [16].

2.2. S&OP maturity models

Sales and Operations Planning (S&OP) is a collaborative tactical planning business process that aligns the demand to production capacities. The process can be evaluated using S&OP maturity models which represent a sub-family of maturity models as their focus is limited to the evaluation of S&OP performance. There have been a countable number of contributions on maturity assessment for S&OP evaluation. They differ mainly by the number of maturity levels and the choice of performance criteria as shown in ***Table 1***.

Table 1: Existing S&OP maturity models.

Contribution	Dimensions	Maturity levels
[17]	Information Technology	1.Integrated 2.Collaborative 3.Fully connected
[13]	Meetings Alignment Integration of IT	1.Marginal 2.Rudimentary 3.Classic 4.Ideal
[18]	Meetings and Collaboration Organization Measurements Information Technology Integration	1.No S&OP 2.Reactive 3.Standard 4.Advanced 5.Proactive
[19]	Process Goal Focus of the demand model Focus of the replenishment model Focus of the process model	1.Feasible 2.Balanced 3.Integrated 4.Demand driven 5.Market driven
[20]	Process effectiveness Process efficiency People and organization Information Technology	0.Undeveloped 1.Rudimentary 2.Reactive 3.Consistent 4.Integrated

		5.Proactive
[21]	Outcome Process focus Organization Metrics Time horizon Technology	1.No shared goals 2.Functional 3.Integrated 4.Collaborative 5.Value-driven
[22]	DATA Forecast accuracy Resource and Plan adherence Gap Measurements Process Organization People	1.No S&OP 2.Reactive 3.Standard 4.Advanced 5.Proactive
[23]	Tools : - Metrics - Technology Process : - Integrated Planning - People organization - Process organization	1.Very low 2.Low 3.Medium 4.High 5.Very high
[7]	People and organization Process and methodologies Information technology Performance measurement	1.No S&OP 2.Reactive 3.Standard 4.Advanced 5.Proactive
[11]	Data Method System Performance Organization People	Score from [0,5]

2.3. Context related maturity models

Following an established 'one-size-fits-all' S&OP maturity model have been proven to be inefficient for most cases[8], [9]. Therefore, designing context-related models could help getting accurate assessments. Among the ten reviewed models, only the contribution of [17] was successful in establishing a context-related S&OP assessment that evaluates S&OP considering the requirements of a pharmaceutical industry. Being a critical practice for the automotive industry, we believe that developing a S&OP context-related assessment would yield a better diagnosis for the process and would contribute to the existent literature. Even if there are few known contributions that assess process maturity by considering critical context attributes [17, 24, 25], the remaining models can serve as a basis to design a framework for maturity assessment in a context of mass customization.

3. S&OP maturity assessment model for mass customization production systems

This paper proposes a new context-related model to assess the maturity of the S&OP for companies operating under a mass customization production system. The model, inspired from the template proposed by [21], has been developed jointly with practitioners and consists of five maturity levels scaling six dimensions. The following sub-sections detail the development phases and the content of the model.

3.1. Research methodology: The model building process

The development of our assessment instrument followed a five-phase approach (***Table 3***). It relies mainly on academic contributions, on workshops organized with the process practitioners and on the project team recommendations. The latter joined two academics, a project manager and a S&OP expert.

Table 2: Assessment development phases

Phase	Actors	Mean	Input	Output
1.Initiation and planning	Project team	Workshops	Business objectives	Assessment objectives List of interviewees Assessment planning
2.Literature review	Project team	Research Databases	Keywords	State of the art
3.Expert opinion	Project team Practitioners	Workshops	State of the art performance criteria	Context-related performance criteria
4.Template formatting	Project team Practitioners	Excel workbooks Workshops	Chosen criteria/levels Assessment in English	Assessment instrument Assessment in French
5.Test iterations	Project team Practitioners	Excel assessment	Original assessment	Improved versions

3.2. Maturity levels:

A maturity level can be defined in practice as the stage at which a company is situated for a given dimension and serves to qualify the actual performance. Conventionally, the higher the stage is, the more performant the process is. The models presented in ***Table 1*** range from three levels [17] to six levels[20]. The most used ranking method is the Likert five-point scale[26]. Consequently, we used it for our model. A clear benefit of our choice resides in the possibility of comparing our results to most of the existing models. ***Table 3*** summarizes the design of our maturity ranking scale:

Table 3: Maturity ranking scale

Level	Description
Level 1 Marginal	S&OP is a marginal process that requires more involvement and development to add significant value to the planning.
Level 2 Functional	S&OP is a functional process limited to basic data and aims for balancing volumes and mix while firefighting short-term issues. The process is very manual and consumes a lot of resources and time.
Level 3 Flexible	S&OP process is satisfying in terms of functioning. The key added value at this level is the integration of financial data that assist decision making and enable effective scenario comparison. The process is more fluid due to the use of more mature and sophisticated IT tools and the focus is on flexibility.
Level 4 Integrated	The process is an efficient stable process that integrates various stakeholders and capable of delivering high quality scenarios to guarantee a robust plan. At this level, the focus switches toward profitability. Decision making is supported by BI analysis and demand forecast relies on strong data management.
Level 5 Strategic	At this level, the process is very sophisticated. An end-to-end integration is enabled, and the process satisfy the company orientations. The focus is thus on strategic development of the company.

3.3. Maturity dimensions:

Maturity dimensions constitute the axes upon which a process is assessed. We have identified six dimensions to constitute our model relying on literature and workshops. ***Table 4*** provides their description.

Table 4: Maturity dimensions and sub-dimensions

Dimension	Description	Sub-dimensions	Description
Outcome	The outcome reflects the extent to which a S&OP is oriented toward achieving good results.	Time horizon for decision making	Mature S&OP focuses more on long and mid-term than on short term. Less mature S&OP is harassed by the short-term issues and operates on a firefighting mode which gives no room for practitioners to think and decide about important tactical subjects.
		Degree of alignment	Alignment is one of the most important criterions for S&OP performance. The process should bring together people from different Business units in order to establish a plan that satisfies the demand and ensure green KPI's (bigger market share, less costs…).

		Components of the plan	The S&OP is about establishing a plan for sales and production. The plan can be limited to volumes, include mix and integrate financial data and flexibilities at higher stages.
Process	This dimension is intended to assess the process design performance.	Level of integration	Integration refers to the participation of internal and external actors. It questions the ability of the process to integrate the stakeholders.
		Meetings	Assesses the efficiency and organization of meetings.
		Transparency	S&OP is a multi-stakeholder process, transparency can be key to alignment and yield high benefits for the process.
		Synchronization	A mature process should be able to synchronize the plans of major actors and put them in-line to get correct and synchronous data.
Organization	Organizational dimension assesses the position of each stakeholder in the process and the level of collaboration.	Ownership	Alignment is crucial for S&OP, thus, clarifying "who owns what" is an important aspect and helps avoid misunderstanding and conflicts.
		Sponsorship	S&OP is a major process that impacts the whole company, top management sponsorship is key to solve issues and facilitate decision making.
		KPI's	A strong S&OP is a process that links all functions together toward shared KPI's and objectives.
Data	A strong S&OP relies highly on the quality of data shared between stakeholders.	Data standardization	This performance criteria measures the level of standardization of data which could be crucial since the process is transversal and data are going to be handled by many departments, so it might be crucial to have a clear communication and common understanding of data by all stakeholders.
		Data quality and sources	Mastering data quality and sources in term of stability, exhaustivity and consistency is an advantage for a forecast-based process.
		Data management	Data are precious assets and should be well managed to boost the performance of the process. Regular updates and historization are important for traceability and for actions follow-up.
Product portfolio management	This dimension was identified by the practitioners as one of the most critical context-related S&OP performance criteria since the composition of the product mix heavily impacts the procurement and production plans.	Aggregation level	This criterion measures the suitability of the aggregation level in product definition. In fact, from one side, it is impossible to discuss and build S&OP at SKU level in the automotive industry since we have billions of SKU's for one model. From the other side, planning with high granular level hides a lot of information since one model can be declined to billions of varieties that are totally different. Therefore, aggregate families at arbitrary levels are constituted, and we aim to measure the satisfaction of stakeholders with the proposed aggregation levels.
		Product definition	Each stakeholder has his own product definition. Salespeople speak the customer language and define a product as options and features while Operations teams speak the suppliers/plants language and define a product as a set of parts. Having an unambiguous link between the two world and a common ground is crucial for S&OP success and alignment.
Information Technology	This dimension assesses the maturity of IT tools.	Level of assistance	This criterion evaluates the use of IT tools to assist elaboration of scenarios and process. The use of IT tools is critical in the case of mass customization since they have to deal with a huge load of data.
		Performance and Ergonomics	IT tools should be performant, intelligent and user-oriented to yield better results and reduce process execution time.

4. Case study

To test the applicability of our model, we conducted a case study within an automotive company. Many authors have affirmed the benefits of conducting real life applications as they help to test the robustness and applicability of developed models [15]. The next sub-sections will define the environment in which our model was tested as well as the results of the study and our analysis.

4.1. Context

The assessed company is a major automotive OEM who owns several brands and have numerous joint ventures with other manufacturers. The group has more than 30 plants, operates in 5 continents, offers 18 different models and produces more than 3 million cars per year. The supply chain department is centralized in the operations headquarter and disposes of two supply chain planning teams: one for engines and powertrains and one for vehicles. Each planning team has his own S&OP. In this study, we focus on the vehicle S&OP for all brands and consider the powertrain and engines team as a stakeholder and a major

supplier. In total, five departments negotiate to establish a valid plan: Sales Planning (SP), Supply Chain Planning (SCP), Power Train (PWT), Part Supply (PS) and Cost Controlling and Finance (CCF).
The assessment had two goals: identify the current maturity level of the process and educate about what a better S&OP can be, and what a worst S&OP is.

4.2. Interview process

At the start of the assessment, we briefly mention who we are, why we conduct this study and we present some instructions about the confidentiality and anonymity of the answers. For each one of the six performance dimensions, we intended not to order the five possible choices corresponding to five different maturity levels (i.e. first choice is neither the best nor the worst) to avoid possible bias of choosing intentionally answers that reflect a good or a bad image. Therefore, the interviewees had to read carefully all five choices of each maturity dimension and choose the most appropriate one. For example, the 'Information technology' performance dimension comprises five choices ordered as follow:

A. Strong reliance on IT tools for automatic data collection and consolidation. Ready-to-use configurable scenarios are provided and artificial intelligence is used for clean demand data (Level4)
B. No or very poor use of IT tools to support planning and data consolidation. (Level 1)
C. IT tools are used for What-if simple scenarios construction and integrate financial data. Business intelligence analysis tools are deployed. (Level 3)
D. IT tools enable better alignment, automated shorter cycles and compliance of operational decisions with strategic objectives. (Level 5)
E. Elementary use of IT tools for data collection and consolidation with primary analysis. No scenario simulation is done (Level 2)

Moreover, the interview instrument presented in the previous section was not distributed to guarantee spontaneous answers. At the end, we review in the last sheet of the assessment instrument the answers and we present the results as a dimension-score radar. In total, the average assessment time was around 30min. Seeking the highest possible rate of answers, we followed a hierarchical top-down approach. We started by interviewing the top managers who served as ambassadors for the assessment in their teams and provided us with a list of subordinates capable of filling the assessment. One author assisted all interviewees to answer their questions. He also recorded comments that were not directly related to the questionnaire items. This opening, combined with previous interviews performed with the practitioners, supported the analysis resulting from the quantitative formatting of the answers.
All interviews took place at the company operations headquarters and were face-to-face. The total number of interviewees was twenty-eight. Twenty-seven persons belong to the five up-mentioned departments where twelve of them held top-managerial positions and fifteen held operational positions. One interviewee was an external expert hired by the company.

4.3. Results and Analysis:

The results were compiled by calculating the average score per dimension either by business unit or by hierarchical level. This section focusses on the difference of perceptions between departments and hierarchical levels. It provides insights on global trends for each dimension for each actor. In fact, we believe that alignment is a major requirement for S&OP. Therefore, disparities in perceptions represents an interesting and original lever for analysis. Additionally, due to confidentiality restrictions, we cannot publish the results scores.

4.3.1. Department results:

In general, the aggregated results of all dimensions show that the SP department detains the highest S&OP maturity score, while the PS department detains the lowest score. This can be explained by the position of the SP teams as clients of the whole process while the PS teams represent the major supplying unit and deal with a huge product diversity derived in thousands of parts and suppliers. As a result, they carry the burden of shortages and are accountable for volume gaps. Additional interviews with their managers reveal that they have to deal with short term issues and are always under the pressure of 'fire-fighting' shortages.

For the Outcome dimension, all S&OP stakeholders, except for the SP teams, agreed on the same score. The SP teams tend to be more optimistic about the achievements of the S&OP while the remaining departments provided a poorer evaluation. We believe that the higher perception of the outcome given by the SP is correlated to the design of S&OP process that position them as clients 'to be satisfied'.
The Process dimension results are distributed between departments. SP and SCP teams are aligned on the same score. These two departments work very closely which explains their alignment on process maturity. However, Part Supply dept. is the least satisfied while the CCF dept. is the most satisfied. This can be explained, as for the general results, by the complexity of product variety and the burden carried by the PS teams versus relatively far position of the CCF teams whose involvement is limited to financials.
The results of the IT dimension show that the main S&OP stakeholders seem to be aligned on the same level of satisfaction toward the quality of IT tools except for the CCF teams. They seem to be less satisfied. The lack of S&OP financial data and the limited contribution of CCF teams to the process can explain this.
The Data dimension shows an interesting pattern characterized by the clear disparity between department's perception to data quality. Remarkably, we can clearly observe that the more a department is involved in the S&OP process and close to data sources, the better it evaluates the data quality. The given score gets worse in the same direction of the information flow. SP teams, detainer of the first demand data signals, have the best perception. The demand is then amended and sent to SCP teams, which express lower satisfaction regarding data quality, and so on, until reaching the PS teams, who gave the lowest evaluation. This pattern can refer to a lack of transparency or a poor data transfer tools between departments.
The Product portfolio results show that the Powertrain teams are the most satisfied while the supply chain planning teams represent the least satisfied entity. To understand the root causes behind these results, one should know that in terms of diversity, PWT teams deal with a limited number of references (less than 10^4 different SKU) while the SCP teams deal with a product diversity that goes up to 10^{20} for some car models. On the other hand, SP teams score higher than SCP teams. To understand this behavior, we need to consider the fact that a major task of SCP teams consists on disaggregating the high granular sales demand into the SKU level to get accurate procurement needs. Thus, they must decide the exact mix of the plan among 10^{20} varieties. ***Fig. 1 (left)*** illustrates the dept. radar results. Graduations are removed to preserve confidentiality.

4.3.2. Hierarchical results

The aggregated hierarchical results show that the top managers see the process differently compared to their subordinates. Top managers tend to be more optimistic for all the dimensions except for the outcome where they appear to be more pessimistic about the intended results of the process. We believe that such disparity is natural and can be explained by two things: the relatively high-level distant position of managers compared to daily practitioners and by a managerial attitude supposing they provided what's needed to do the job but wanting teams to perform better. ***Fig. 1 (right)*** summarizes the hierarchical results.

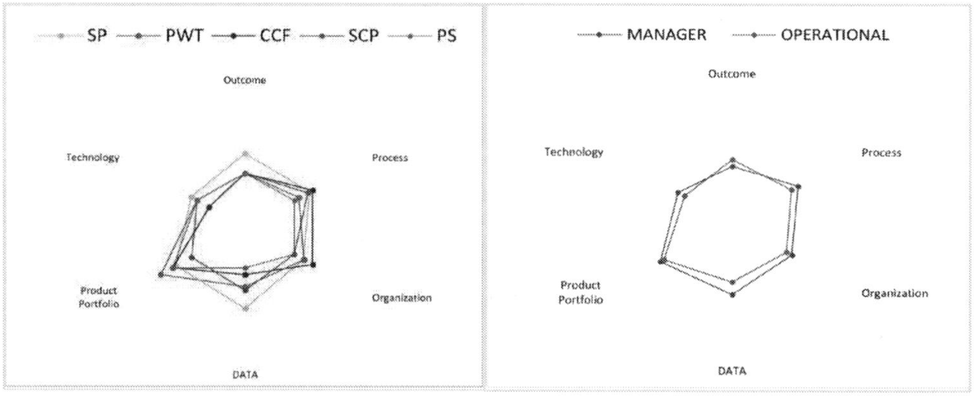

Figure 1: Dimensions results radar by department (left) and by hierarchical level (right).

5. Conclusion

Assessing the performance of a business process using maturity models is a common practice in both academic and professional environments. Motivated by the lack of context-related frameworks in a sufficiently mature body of literature full of generic models, our paper aimed to provide a new S&OP

maturity model that considers context-related attributes. We believe that maturity assessments should target the process main pain points related to the industry particularities. The developed model is fit for industries that deal with a high level of product diversity and relies on both academic and professional literature since it was designed considering practitioner opinion. The study output was tested and implemented in a major automotive OEM. The results presented in the previous section show how the different process stakeholders evaluate each dimension. Through the assessment, we shed the light on two main aspects: the impact of diversity as a critical context-related attribute and the interactions between different actors of the process, more precisely, how the position and the tasks of each actor affect the evaluation score. These results gave us a better understanding of the S&OP process by picturing it through the eyes of its actors.
The next steps of our work will focus on diversity management and organizational transformations to benefit the process and enable better alignments. We are preparing and testing a model that reconnect Operations to Sales and complete the loop of S&OP interactions. We do so by equally dividing the diversity management tasks and by defining an appropriate aggregation level that suits different stakeholders and handles diversity. Our solution is intended to benefit the organizational aspects of S&OP since it provides a decision support tool and enhances collaboration and communication between actors of the process.
At the end, there is no doubt that this study would suffer from several limits. First, the number of interviewees was limited because we only had the chance to interview the corporate head operations site employees. Second, our case study was limited to one OEM, yet for a model to be used comparatively it must be applied to many other industries characterized by high diversity. Such generalization would enhance the robustness of the model. Finally, the evaluations are highly subjective and depends on personal opinions. The study could benefit from other techniques like fuzzy set theory to recalculate the scores.

6. References

1. Marino G., Zotteri G., Montagna F.: Consumer sensitivity to delivery lead time: a furniture retail case Int. J. Phys. Distrib. Logist. Manag., 48, pp. 610–629 (2018)
2. Xia S., Wang L.: Customer requirements mapping method based on association rule mining for mass customization J. Shanghai Jiaotong Univ., 13, pp. 291–296 (2008)
3. ElMaraghy H., Schuh G., Elmaraghy W., Piller F., Schönsleben P., Tseng M., Bernard A.: Product variety management CIRP Ann. - Manuf. Technol., 62, pp. 629–652 (2013)
4. Staeblein T., Aoki K.: Planning and scheduling in the automotive industry: A comparison of industrial practice at German and Japanese makers Int. J. Prod. Econ., 162, pp. 258–272 (2015)
5. Pil F.K., Holweg M.: Linking product variety to order-fulfillment strategies Interfaces (Providence)., 34, pp. 394–403 (2004)
6. Ghrab Y., Sali M.: Sales and Operations Planning (S&OP) Performance Under Highly Diversified Mass Production Systems Proceedings of the 2019 International Conference on Management Science and Industrial Engineering. pp. 42–47. ACM Press, New York, New York, USA (2019)
7. Danese P., Molinaro M., Romano P.: Managing evolutionary paths in Sales and Operations Planning: key dimensions and sequences of implementation Int. J. Prod. Res., 56, pp. 2036–2053 (2018)
8. Bower P.: 12 Most Common Threats To Sales and Operations Planning Process J. Bus. Forecast., pp. 4–14 (2005)
9. Kristensen J., Jonsson P.: Context-based sales and operations planning (S&OP) research Int. J. Phys. Distrib. Logist. Manag., 48, pp. 19–46 (2018)
10. Paulk M.C.: The capability maturity model: Guidelines for improving the software process. Addison-Wesley Prof., (1995)
11. Vereecke A., Vanderheyden K., Baecke P., Van Steendam T.: Mind the gap – Assessing maturity of demand planning, a cornerstone of S&OP Int. J. Oper. Prod. Manag., 38, pp. 1618–1639 (2018)
12. de Bruin T., Freeze R., Kulkarni U., Rosemann M.: Understanding the Main Phases of Developing a Maturity Assessment Model 16th Australas. Conf. Inf. Syst., (2005)
13. Lapide Larry: AN S&OP MATURITY MODEL J. Bus. Forecast., 24, pp. 15–19 (2005)
14. Fraser P., Moultrie J., Gregory M.: The use of maturity models/grids as a tool in assessing product development capability IEEE International Engineering Management Conference. vol. 1. pp. 244–249. IEEE (2002)
15. Wendler R.: The maturity of maturity model research: A systematic mapping study Inf. Softw. Technol., 54, pp. 1317–1339 (2012)
16. Tarhan A., Turetken O., Reijers H.A.: Business process maturity models: A systematic literature review Inf. Softw. Technol., 75, pp. 122–134 (2016)
17. Wing L., Perry G.: Toward twenty-first-century pharmaceutical sales and operations planning Pharm. Technol., pp. 20–26 (2001)
18. Grimson J.A., Pyke D.F.: Sales and operations planning: An exploratory study and framework Int. J. Logist.

Manag., 18, pp. 322–346 (2007)

19. Cecere L.: Market-driven S&OP A Guidebook on How to Build a Market-driven S&OP Process, (2012)
20. Wagner S.M., Ullrich K.K.R., Transchel S.: The game plan for aligning the organization Bus. Horiz., 57, pp. 189–201 (2014)
21. Kohler J., Pukkila M., Tarafdar D.: Toolkit : S & OP Maturity Self-Assessment for Supply Chain Leaders Gartner, pp. 1–5 (2016)
22. Hulthén H., Näslund D., Norrman A.: Framework for measuring performance of the sales and operations planning process Int. J. Phys. Distrib. Logist. Manag., 46, pp. 809–835 (2016)
23. Pedroso C.B., Calache L.D.D.R., Lima Junior F.R., Silva A.L. da, Carpinetti L.C.R.: Proposal of a model for sales and operations planning (S&OP) maturity evaluation Production, 27, (2017)
24. Bagni G., Marçola J.A.: Evaluation of the maturity of the S & OP process for a written materials company : a case study Gest. Prod., (2019)
25. Carvalho J.V., Rocha Á., Wetering R. Van De, Abreu A.: A Maturity model for hospital information systems J. Bus. Res., 94, pp. 388–399 (2019)
26. Likert R.: A technique for the measurement of attitudes. Arch. Psychol., 22 140, pp. 55 (1932)

I L S 2020
INTERNATIONAL CONFERENCE ON INFORMATION SYSTEMS, LOGISTICS & SUPPLY CHAIN
Austin, Texas April 22-24, 2020

Toward Automated Qualitative Supply Chain Diagnoses in Engineering-to-Order Environment

Anthony FOUQUE [1,2], Matthieu LAURAS [2], Hamideh AFSARMANESH [3], Frédérick BENABEN [2]

[1] AGILEA Conseil, Toulouse, France
[2] University of Toulouse - IMT Mines Albi, Albi, France
[3] University of Amsterdam, Amsterdam, Netherlands
{anthony.fouque@agilea.fr, matthieu.lauras@mines-albi.fr, h.afsarmanesh@uva.nl, frederick.benaben@mines-albi.fr}

Abstract. Engineer-To-Order (ETO) environments are more and more numerous in Supply Chains. Most of the concerned companies use continuous improvement methods such as Lean Engineering, Agile Management or Thinking Processes from the Theory of Constraints to stay competitive. All these methods start with a diagnosis step and their relevance is highly depending of the quality of this step. However, literature analysis shows that they are often time-consuming and inconsistent. One of the key issues of these weaknesses is that they do not consider enough the qualitative dimension of the ETO context. Consequently, we suggest in this paper a decision support system able to manage a rapid and relevant qualitative ETO diagnosis based on the Thinking Processes paradigm. This system is designed around a generic reality tree knowledge base and a set of dedicated inference rules. A real industrial application case is described and discussed. In this case study of an ETO oil&gas company, the diagnosis process has been reduced from 15 days to 1 day using this tool with the same starting conditions of the classical diagnosis.

Keywords: Engineer-To-Order, Diagnosis, Thinking Processes, Supply Chain, Decision Support System.

1. Introduction

Supply Chains (SCs) are now evolving in a VUCA (Volatile, Uncertain, Complex, Ambiguous) world. This is a consequence of several factors such as variabilities on demand, supply or operation. But it is also the consequence of an increasing demand in new products and customization of existing products portfolio. This is what Gosling and Naim [1] call the product proliferation paradigm. Whatever the sector is, a SC must be able to manage efficiently these new challenges of customization and new product development. This often implies that the SC moves from a Make-To-Order (MTO) or a Make-To-Stock (MTS) strategy [2] to an Engineering-To-Order (ETO) strategy where high customization and low volumes are key features [3]. Whether the strategy, the global challenge consists generally in ensuring the performance level of the SC organization. To reach this goal in MTO or MTS environments, SC stakeholders usually apply continuous improvement methods such as Lean Manufacturing or 6 Sigma [4]. In ETO environment, similar methods might also be used such as Critical Chain from Theory of Constraints or Lean Engineering. Basically, all these methods recommend diagnosing the system as a starting point, setting up the solutions to the identified issues and implementing them [5], [6]. In all cases, the quality of the initial diagnosis is fundamental [7]. If the diagnosis is not well executed, there should be a misalignment between the suggested solutions and the core problem. Considering this, the quality of the diagnosis must be protected. However, literature review on that topic indicates that very few papers exist on this specific aspect [8], particularly in ETO environment. Moreover, most of the existing literature on that topic are based on quantitative data [9]. If such a quantitative approach can be valid for MTS or MTO environments, it is much more questionable in ETO context where behavior, communication and management are key qualitative factors of the organization as mentioned by [10], [11], [12]. These authors also mention that such data collection and analysis is very time-consuming. They especially recommend not to base ETO environment diagnosis on quantitative data and to add qualitative information to the process to be more relevant and consistent. This has also been confirmed by [7] and [8] who suggest getting numerous additional qualitative data to make good diagnosis in ETO environment and to support the necessary associated change management process. Based on the previous elements and even though it is a critical subject, we notice that no satisfactory solution exists regarding the manner to make a rapid, consistent and relevant diagnosis in ETO environment. Particularly, no solution considering qualitative data has been developed. Consequently, in this paper we address the following research question: *How to support a qualitative diagnosis in an ETO environment which is rapid, consistent and relevant?* To answer this question, the paper will first develop a quick background about existing methodologies dedicated to ETO environment. Secondly, the paper will describe the proposal by explaining both the suggested functional process and its associated decision support system. Thirdly, some feedbacks and discussions about a real industrial application case are given to highlight potential benefits and limits of the proposal.

2. Background and Research Statement

In this paper, we focus on qualitative aspects of diagnoses in ETO environments in order to reduce or avoid the previously mentioned difficulties. In the coming paragraphs, a brief description and analysis of the most popular diagnosis methods regarding ETO context is provided: Lean Engineering, Agile Management [6] and Theory of Constraints. Then, the Thinking Process based on the Theory of Constraints is highlighted as it may help to improve the diagnosis approach in ETO environment.

2.1. Continuous Improvement Projects' Approaches

Lean Engineering approach has been developed in the following of the Lean Manufacturing trend. Despite this sequence, both get the same objective: improving the customer satisfaction and the value for the company. In an ETO environment, Lean Engineering practitioners are looking for wastes [13], called *muda* [14] in order to withdraw them. The way to proceed consists in starting through a project plan based on a Value Stream Mapping tool. Basically, the process is the following: (i) setting a team, (ii) creating the value stream map, (iii) identifying and closing a maximum of identified *muda*. In order to support this process, Lean Engineering uses a set of tools mainly based on the Lean Manufacturing former approach. For instance, the change management process is driven through the Plan-Do-Check-Act (PDCA) technique [15]. The main idea of using PDCA in this context is to develop a recurrent process which will help the team to drive step-by-step changes across the system [16]. Regarding the diagnosis phase itself, the Lean Engineering approach is mainly focusing on quantitative information to build the changes inside the project organization despite the first information required is about quality of the situation of the project [17]. Finally, we retain that Lean Engineering process is a mix of qualitative and quantitative information as the process begins with a qualitative analysis and then jumps into a quantitative one. Another approach dedicated to the improvement of project management and ETO environments has been developed since the 2000s [18]. This the Agile Management approach [19]. The concept has been initially developed for project management and more specifically for software development projects [20]. The principle is to create a list of features which are executed through a series of sprints [21]. Once the first sprint is finished, the team is delivering what they have to the customers who made comments about the deliverables. These comments will be taken into consideration for the next sprint. Agile Management is not necessarily using diagnosis approach to introduce its approach [22]. It assumes that there are lots of variabilities in the ETO environment (or project environment) but not mention any solution to detect them [23]. Moreover, the data used to follow the project execution are also only focusing on quantitative dimension [24]. Very few things are documented about change management process in Agile Management except the fact that team building is fundamental [25]. Theory of Constraints (TOC) methodology is very counter intuitive compared to the previous ones. It only focuses on qualitative information which are considered as negative for the system. The problem-solving process is called Thinking Processes and proposes to connect all the negative information together in order to describe the current reality of the system. Quantitative information is very limited in this method and used only to clarify a qualitative information [26]. Another aspect in the TOC approach is about the change management process which is clearly defined through 3 steps: (i) get a common sharing on the problem, (ii) define and agree on the solution, (iii) be aligned on the way to implement it. This approach will be detailed in the following. Because our objective is to build a diagnosis according to qualitative information, there is only one method (TOC) which provides such clear basic statement. This method is also the only one which assumes a clear opinion about resistance to change and change management process. However, this approach has been regularly considered as very hard to implement and is not generally used today [27].

2.2. The Thinking Processes

2.2.1. The Approach

Let's now go deeper in the TOC. It has been created by Eli Goldratt through the novel entitled "The Goal" [28]. Behind this famous book, there is a specific method called Thinking Processes which has been defined and structured. This method is described in full details in [29]. Logic is the key word of this approach. It affirms that for every undesirable effect (called symptom in the methodology) of the system, there is a core conflict which can summarize all of them. A conflict is recognized as two opposite actions which cannot instantiate at a same time despite the system is pushing to take both.
According to that, the Thinking Processes method develops an approach around four major phases [30]:

- Create a current reality tree which describes the logical connection between all symptoms of the systems. At the base of that tree, you find a conflict, a Policy, a Measurement and a Behaviour (PMB) which may reinforce negatively the current situation.
- Then people create a solution which is called injection in order to check if the solution is good enough to solve the current situation.
- The third step is a simulation process. One tests that the solution is solving all the negative identified statements. If it is not the case, new injection must be added to complete the first idea.
- Once the simulation is effective, a project plan is set up through a Prerequisite Tree. The way to proceed consists in using the first injection and collect obstacles avoiding achieving it. Once the collection is done, the obstacles are converted in a positive way to create actions that might be added to the project plan.

2.2.2. The Limits

Today implementing a Thinking Process in an ETO environment is very long [31] because it is a complex process and it is essentially manual. The record of the symptoms is hard to do, and the interviewer needs specific abilities and knowledge. Then, usually, companies are not autonomous to build the Current Reality Tree by themselves. They consequently need to have an expert to support that process. Due to the difficulty to build it, the solution step is also very hard to accomplish. For example, there is an obligation to keep the same team during the whole process because the way to build the trees is so specific that having new comers during the process will slow it down [32]. To finish, the project plan design can also be intensive because it needs different competencies to do it [33], but you cannot add new people at that stage because it will increase the complexity for them to recover since the beginning of the process. Usually the process is done in two full weeks if you want to do it correctly [34]. This can be justified by the bias that can be generated by accelerating the current reality tree phase. To protect the team against that bias, the TOC community developed a set of control check tool named Category of Legitimate Reservation. The aim of that tool is to check the veracity of job done but not to accelerate the process.

3. Proposal

3.1. Research Framework and Methodology

Therefore, the main objective of this research work is to develop a decision support system able to automatically support a Current Reality Tree generation in an ETO environment. This approach is directly inspired from [26] that used a similar way to manage diagnosis in MTO/MTS environment. Basically, as mentioned in Figure 1, the proposal consists in building a decision support system which will automatically connect symptoms of the ETO system with the associated core conflicts. From a pragmatic standpoint, this decision support system must embed a knowledge base able to make concrete links with the noticed symptoms (i.e. concrete things that practitioners observe). Once feeding with concrete symptoms, it should be able to build automatically the Current Reality Tree of the studied ETO system through execution of dedicated inference rules (logical connections between symptoms).

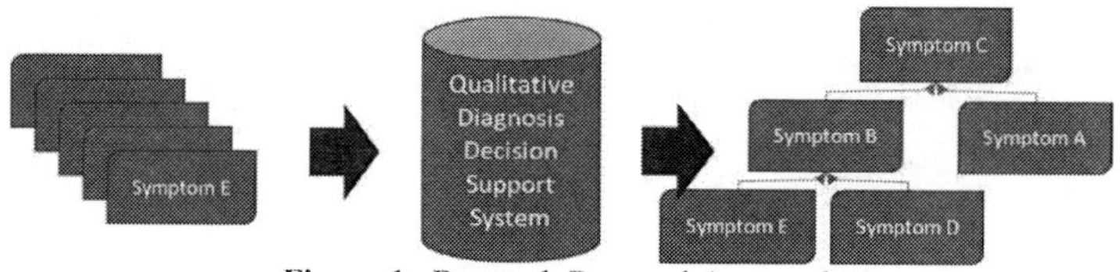

Figure 1 : Research Proposal Approach

In terms of methodology, the research proposal implies first to structure the knowledge about SCs' symptoms by defining a generic ETO reality tree and a set of generic associated conflicts. Once the knowledge base created and the inference rules implemented, a test-run phase must be instantiated to assess benefits and limits of the proposal (regarding the speed of the diagnosis process notably) and validate its relevance for business practitioners.

3.2. Thinking-Process oriented Diagnosis Step

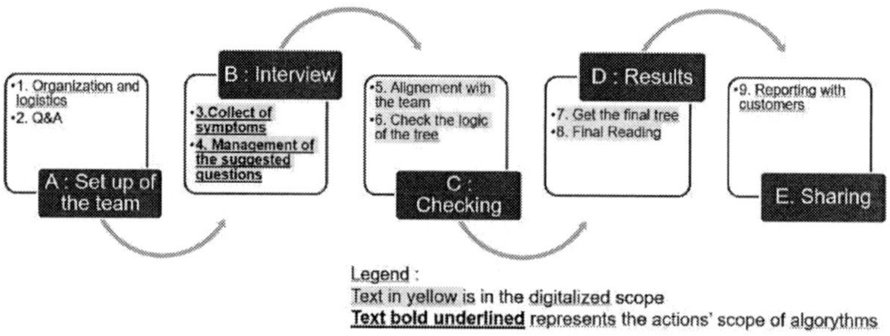

Figure 2 : Thinking-Process Oriented Diagnosis Step

In order to support a rapid, consistent and relevant diagnosis, we suggest the following thinking-process oriented diagnosis step (see Figure 2):

A. A diagnosis team is set up. This team must be composed of key practitioners of the ETO system under-study (field-operators, intermediate employees, managers and to top-managers) and a Thinking-Processes facilitator.
B. The team makes interviews to company business experts to identify the symptoms they have currently to cope with. Continuously, these symptoms are recorded in the decision support system to be compared with the generic ETO reality tree in order to identify the missing information. In practice, during the interviews, the decision support system makes suggestion of additional questions to the team in order to prevent forgetting something that put a stop to diagnosis.
C. The tool will display the tree and let the users check the logic.
D. Then the team will check the obtained Current Reality Tree in order to make sure that it is fully aligned with their reality. They can influence the semantic and/or improve the clarity of the current situation picture.
E. The next step consists in sharing the Current Reality Tree with the customers (internal/external).

3.3. Thinking-Process oriented Decision Support System

3.3.1. Decision Support System Architecture and Behavioural Description

Figure 3 shows the developed decision support system architecture and its behavioural description.

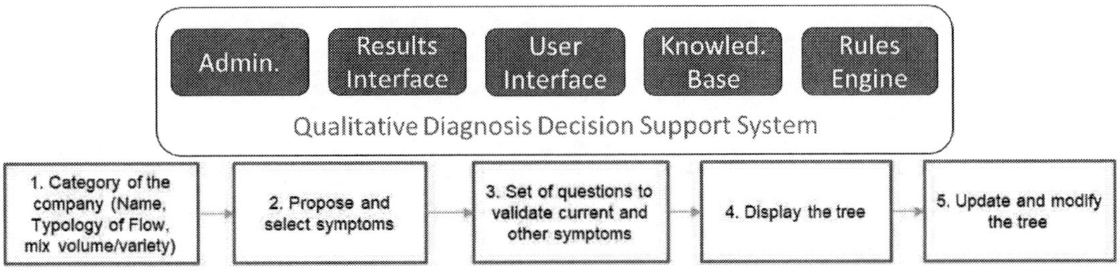

Figure 3 : Decision Support System Architecture and Behavioral Description

The top of the Figure 3 represents the architecture of the tools. It is composed of 5 main pillars: The first one regarding administration helps to set up the team and the organization associated which the Phase A of the figure 2. Then, the user interface helps to collect the symptoms. Once the symptoms are collected there is a knowledge database which will analysis these symptoms through the defined rules of execution. Finally, the tool will generate a specific interface of results to display the tree. The bottom of the figure 3 represents the behavior of the tools regarding the architecture. The user will first to select the profile of the company in order to select the symptoms right after. Then, the tool will generate a set of questions in order to fine tune the tree and display it to the users.

3.3.2. Decision Support System Knowledge Base

The core of the decision support system is a generic "Current Reality Tree" knowledge base dedicated to ETO environment. In this tree, boxes represent symptoms given by the customers during the interview phase. Each symptoms of the tree are linked together by a cause and effect relationship. For example, there is a conflict root cause which is release or not new projects in the work in progress. Symptoms can be connected from different ways:

- The link between them can be unique
- The link between two of them can relate to a "And" and a third symptom. For example, if I have Symptom A and Symptom B then I have symptom C
- A symptom can be connected to two symptoms, but these two symptoms are independent.

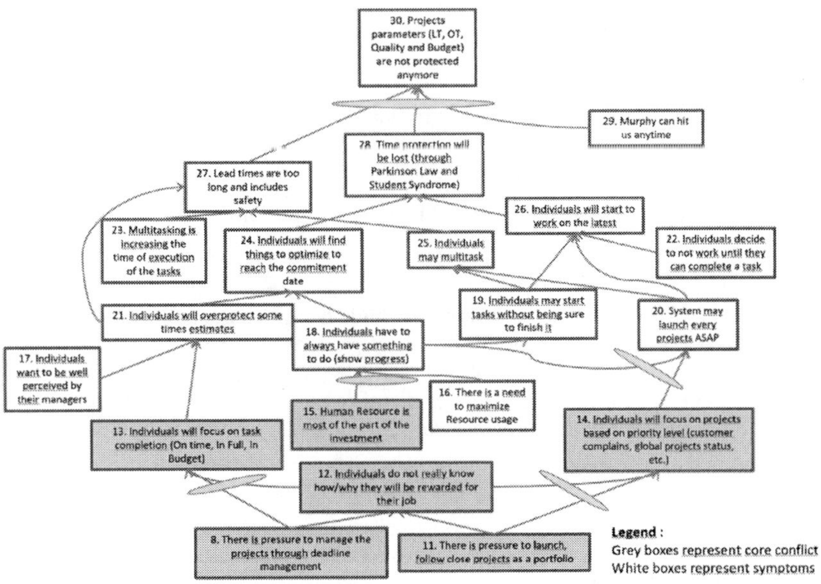

Figure 4: ETO diagnosis generic tree extraction.

3.3.3. Decision Support System Inference Rules

In order to speed up the process of diagnosis and point out the right questions, there are some rules which have been settled to achieve that:

- Rules #1: At the beginning, the selection of the industrial environment (MTO, MTS, ETO) is selecting the generic tree associated.
- Rules #2: When a symptom is selected, the tool is going to ask the next symptoms upstream and downstream to the tree where the symptom is. It is a way to validate the negative impact of it.
- Rules #3: If two symptoms belong to same sequence of cause and effect and that historical diagnosis show a 70% recurrence, then the tool will validate the whole sequences. If not, the tool is going to suggestion question to validate the right level.
- Rules #4: When a symptom is connected to different intermediate cause, then the tool is going to check and ask each different cause.
- Rules #5: When answers to questions are Yes, and the percentage of Yes is up to 70%, then the tool did not ask question anymore.
- Rules #6: When answers to questions are No, symptoms are deleted from the trees. If the percentage of No is up to 70%, then the tool does not ask any question in the sequence associated to the symptoms.

4. Illustrative Application and Discussion

4.1. The use-case

Let's now consider a real application case. The studied system is an oil & gas company which produces pumps for nuclear and petroleum customers. This sector can be defined as a pure ETO environment as for each customer order, the company is going through a continuous process from design to delivery including purchasing, production, quality control, etc. The company studied is building oil & gas pump which represents a project of 750 tasks associated to a portfolio of 270 projects. A typical project from this company contains engineering tasks which are done by employees. When, this step is done, there is a phase of validation from quality in order to validate the routine. Then, there is a long step of purchasing which includes also engineering of the suppliers but also sub-contractors. When, it is done, the flow of tasks continues to assemble, test and delivery where customers are involved. The company is a SME (Small and Medium size Enterprise) of 250 people spread in 3 countries (France, Italy, India).

4.2. Thinking-Processes oriented Diagnosis Step and Decision Support System application

4.2.1. Step A: Set up the teams

The team was composed of 10 people included field-operators and top-managers.

4.2.2. Step B: Interviews

During the interview process the following symptoms have been shared by the team: (i) Leadtime of our projects are increasing; (ii) Projects are late; (iii) Priorities are changing a lot; (iv) No visibility of the project status; (v) No visibility of the project portfolio. Practically, our decision support system identified 85 symptoms. During the interviews phase, the auditor identified 5 critical symptoms which were in common with our generic tree. It means that the auditor started to use the tool with only 5% of the total possible symptoms.

4.2.3. Step C: Checking

With such few symptoms compared to the generic tree, the auditor expected a large list of questions to ask to team. However, only 42 questions have been generated. This can be explained by the fact that the symptoms given are quite far away from each other except for the two last ones. The auditor may feel a connection between "Leadtime of our projects are increasing" and "Priorities are changing a lot" but there is a much more obvious connection between "No visibility of the project status" and "No visibility of the project portfolio". Answering these questions was fast and help to clarify some issues which may appeared very local to someone but has huge impact on the system. The next step is the results of the tree. The other reason why there are less questions than expected is about the algorithm. According to the code, the system considers the symptoms and pop up directly the core conflict. Due to the fact that the database contains already other diagnosis, the algorithm is able to check, validate and display the relevancy of the questions.

4.2.4. Step D: Results

In this stage, the tool generated the following Current Reality Tree (The full view is available at http://static.agilea.fr/anthony-fouque-phd.pdf). At this stage, the team went through the tree and check if they can recognize themselves in the results. In most of the case, they agreed on it but had to make some changes which were mainly focusing on the vocabulary used.

4.2.5. Step E: Sharing

In the last stage, the team focused mainly on vocabulary. Despite the tree was right in terms of meaning, they made changes according to their company vocabulary. The positive aspect of this phase is that each time they were adapting the vocabulary it was like they were becoming more and more trustful with the results of the tools. During that stage, they never challenge any conclusion of the diagnosis established by the decision support system.

4.3. Discussion and perspectives

It took 1 day to do the interviews, then we fulfilled the results in the decision support system and 1 hour later we had the diagnosis. During the next phase, the team quickly realized that the tree was roughly good (up to 70%) but needed some vocabulary alignment to be fully shared in their company. At the end, the feedbacks from the company were very good. People found it fast and very relevant compared to the previous diagnosis they used to do. It is also the first time they saw a clear picture of the company shared between each member of the team. Regarding the algorithm, there are some misalignment between cause and effect analysis. Regarding the display of the tree, team found difficult to navigate into the tree and make comments. During the next phase, numerous research developments will be done, notably:

- To set up a new functionality in the decision support system to update automatically the generic tree according to what is observed in the field (automatic learning algorithm);
- To develop an algorithm to speed up the emergence of questions during the interview phase;
- To formally demonstrate the benefits of this system comparing to manual approaches.

5. References

1. Gosling, Jonathan, et Mohamed M. Naim. « Engineer-to-order supply chain management: A literature review and research agenda ». *International Journal of Production Economics* 122, nº 2 (1 décembre 2009): 741-54.

2. Bonner, Joseph M., Robert W. Ruekert, et Orville C. Walker. « Upper Management Control of New Product Development Projects and Project Performance ». *Journal of Product Innovation Management* 19, nº 3 (2002): 233-45.

3. « Systems engineering effective supply chain innovations: International Journal of Production Research: Vol 52, No 21, Tillmann Böhme,Eric Deakins,Matthew Pepper &Denis Towill

4. Huan, Samuel H., Sunil K. Sheoran, et Ge Wang. « A Review and Analysis of Supply Chain Operations Reference (SCOR) Model ». *Supply Chain Management: An International Journal*, 1 février 2004.

5. Chen, Sheu Hua, et Hong Tau Lee. « Performance evaluation model for project managers using managerial practices ». *International Journal of Project Management* 25, nº 6 (1 août 2007): 543-51.

6. Karagiannis, Dimitris. « Agile Modeling Method Engineering ». In *Proceedings of the 19th Panhellenic Conference on Informatics*, 5–10. PCI '15. New York, NY, USA: ACM, 2015.

7. Naim, M. M., P. Childerhouse, S. M. Disney, et D. R. Towill. « A supply chain diagnostic methodology: determining the vector of change ». *Computers & Industrial Engineering* 43, nº 1 (1 juillet 2002): 135-57..

8. Crawford, Paul, et Paul Bryce. « Project monitoring and evaluation: a method for enhancing the efficiency and effectiveness of aid project implementation ». *International Journal of Project Management* 21, nº 5 (1 juillet 2003): 363-73.

9. Denton, Paul D., David Little, Richard H. Weston, et Alex Guerrero. « An enterprise engineering approach for supply chain systems design and implementation ». *International Journal of Services and Operations Management* 3, nº 2 (1 janvier 2007): 131-51.

10. Pandit, Aarti, et Yimin Zhu. « An ontology-based approach to support decision-making for the design of ETO (Engineer-To-Order) products ». *Automation in Construction* 16, nº 6 (1 septembre 2007): 759-70.
11. Sen, Wang, Shaligram Pokharel, et Wang YuLei. « Supply chain positioning strategy integration, evaluation, simulation, and optimization ». *Computers & Industrial Engineering*, Computers and Industrial EngineeringSpecial Issue on Selected papers form the 29th.International Conference on Computers and Industrial Engineering, 46, nº 4 (1 juillet 2004): 781-92.
12. Sou-Sen Leu and You-Che Lin,« Project Performance Evaluation Based on Statistical Process Control Techniques | Journal of Construction Engineering and Management | Vol 134, No 10 ».
13. McManus, H. L., A. Haggerty, et E. Murman. « Lean Engineering: A Framework for Doing the Right Thing Right ». The Aeronautical Journal 111, no 1116 (février 2007): 105-14. https://doi.org/10.1017/S0001924000001809.
14. Svetoslav Novkov, Ivan Dakov, « Assessment of the Lean Production Effect on the Sustainable Industrial Enterprise Development ». Verslas: Teorija Ir Praktika, no 4 (2007): 183-88.
15.McManus, Hugh, Al Haggerty, et Earll Murman. « Lean Engineering: Doing the Right Thing Right », 4 août 2005. https://dspace.mit.edu/handle/1721.1/84165.
16. Matsuo, Makoto, et Jun Nakahara. « The effects of the PDCA cycle and OJT on workplace learning ». *The International Journal of Human Resource Management* 24, nº 1 (1 janvier 2013): 195-207.
17. Amin, Md Al, et M. A. Karim. « A time-based quantitative approach for selecting lean strategies for manufacturing organisations ». *International Journal of Production Research* 51, nº 4 (15 février 2013): 1146-67.
18. Chen, Sheu Hua, et Hong Tau Lee. « Performance evaluation model for project managers using managerial practices ». International Journal of Project Management 25, no 6 (1 août 2007): 543-51. https://doi.org/10.1016/j.ijproman.2007.03.004.
19. Costa, Janaina M. H., Monica Rossi, Eric Rebentisch, Sergio Terzi, Marco Taisch, et Deborah Nightingale. « What to Measure for Success in Lean System Engineering Programs? » Procedia Computer Science, 2014 Conference on Systems Engineering Research, 28 (1 janvier 2014): 789-98. https://doi.org/10.1016/j.procs.2014.03.094.
20. Fernandez, Daniel J., et John D. Fernandez. « Agile Project Management —Agilism versus Traditional Approaches ». *Journal of Computer Information Systems* 49, nº 2 (1 décembre 2008): 10-17.
21.Kettunen, Petri. « Adopting Key Lessons from Agile Manufacturing to Agile Software Product Development—A Comparative Study ». Technovation 29, no 6 (1 juin 2009): 408-22. https://doi.org/10.1016/j.technovation.2008.10.003.
22.Paige, Richard F., Ramon Charalambous, Xiaocheng Ge, et Phillip J. Brooke. « Towards Agile Engineering of High-Integrity Systems ». In Computer Safety, Reliability, and Security, édité par Michael D. Harrison et Mark-Alexander Sujan, 30-43. Lecture Notes in Computer Science. Berlin, Heidelberg: Springer, 2008. https://doi.org/10.1007/978-3-540-87698-4_6.
23.« Agile concurrent engineering | Emerald Insight ». Consulté le 6 janvier 2020. https://www.emerald.com/insight/content/doi/10.1108/09576069910257572/full/html.
24.Klein, Thorsten P., et Gunther Reinhart. « Towards Agile Engineering of Mechatronic Systems in Machinery and Plant Construction ». Procedia CIRP, The Sixth International Conference on Changeable, Agile, Reconfigurable and Virtual Production (CARV2016), 52 (1 janvier 2016): 68-73. https://doi.org/10.1016/j.procir.2016.07.077.
25. Kinoshita, F. « Practices of an Agile Team ». In *Agile 2008 Conference*, 373-77, 2008.
26. « The theory of constraints thinking processes: retrospect and prospect | Emerald Insight ». Consulté le 9 septembre 2019. https://www.emerald.com/insight/content/doi/10.1108/01443570810846883/full/html.
« Root Cause Analysis: A Framework for Tool Selection: Quality Management Journal: Vol 12, No 4 ». Consulté le 9 septembre 2019. https://www.tandfonline.com/doi/abs/10.1080/10686967.2005.11919269.
27. Goldratt, Eliyahu M., et Jeff Cox. The goal: a process of ongoing improvement. Routledge, 2016.
28. Goldratt, Eliyahu M. It's not luck. Routledge, 2017.
29. Cox, III, James F. | Mabin, Victoria J. | Davies, John« A case of personal productivity: Illustrating methodological developments in TOC - IOS Press ». Consulté le 9 septembre 2019. https://content.iospress.com/articles/human-systems-management/hsm574.
30. Rahman, Shams-ur. « The Theory of Constraints' Thinking Process Approach to Developing Strategies in Supply Chains ». *International Journal of Physical Distribution & Logistics Management*, 1 décembre 2002.
31. Smith, Debra. *The measurement nightmare: How the theory of constraints can resolve conflicting strategies, policies, and measures*. CRC press, 1999.
32. Doggett, Dr Anthony Mark. « A Statistical Comparison of Three Root Cause Analysis Tools ». *Journal of Industrial Technology* 2019, nº 2 (2004): 10.
33. Doggett, A. Mark. « Root Cause Analysis: A Framework for Tool Selection ». *Quality Management Journal* 12, nº 4 (1 janvier 2005): 34-45.
34. Fouque, Anthony, Matthieu Lauras, Hamideh Afsarmanesh, et Frederick Benaben. « Toward Automated Qualitative Supply Chain Diagnoses », 8 juin 2018. https://hal-mines-albi.archives-ouvertes.fr/hal-01886041.

I L S 2020
INTERNATIONAL CONFERENCE ON INFORMATION SYSTEMS, LOGISTICS & SUPPLY CHAIN
Austin, Texas April 22-24, 2020

Transportation Lot Sizing Problem: An Airbus Case Study

David Arturo Pardo Melo [1,2], Vincent Bernier[1], Yannick Frein[2], Bernard Penz[2]

[1] Airbus Helicopters, Marseille, France
[2] Univ. Grenoble Alpes, CNRS, Grenoble INP, G-SCOP, 38000 Grenoble, France
{david-arturo.pardo-melo@grenoble-inp.fr, vincent.bernier@airbus.com, yannick.frein@grenoble-inp.fr, bernard.penz@grenoble-inp.fr}

Abstract. Defining transportation responsibility is a critical decision in inbound logistics management. This paper analyses two scenarios at Airbus Helicopters from a transportation lot sizing point of view. In the first one, suppliers manage transportation, each one acting on his own. In this scenario, Airbus does not have any visibility over transportation costs and hence, it defines transportation lot sizes based only in inventory costs. In the second scenario, Airbus masters transportation for inbound flow in a way that it is possible to define optimal transportation lot sizes per supplier based on transportation and storage costs. To this end, we develop an economic transportation quantity model based on Parcel and Courier Services (PCS), Less than Truck Load (LTL) and Full Truck Load (FTL) transportation costs. Results show that by controlling transportation and optimizing transportation lot sizes, we can significantly reduce logistics costs compared to the first scenario.

Keywords: Transportation Lot Size, Supply Chain, Transportation Management, Economic Order Quantity

1. Introduction

Defining transportation responsibility is a critical decision in Supply Chain Management, particularly in inbound logistics management. In one hand, by giving suppliers the responsibility of managing transport operations, a company could release transportation tasks resources for the company core activity. However, in some cases, this could mean losing control over transportation and procurement policies because of the lack of transparency and visibility in transportation management and costs. In the other hand, by internalizing transportation management, a company has total control over its transportation system, and hence, it could optimize transportation and procurement policies by defining optimal transportation lot sizes in function of transportation and storage costs. This study evaluates these two scenarios based on a case study conducted at Airbus Helicopters (AH), a division of Airbus, a worldwide leader in the aerospace industry.

A common approach used for defining optimal transportation lot sizes in literature, is the classic economic lot size model introduced at first by Harris in 1913 (reprint 1990 [1]) and after developed by Wilson in 1934. This model allows estimating optimal order quantities in function of order and storage costs. We have adapted this approach to the Airbus case in order to evaluate the second scenario and compare it to the first scenario.

In the next section we present a state of the art for the transportation lot sizing problem. After we present the Airbus case study and we develop a transportation lot sizing model based on literature and in Airbus transportation system. Finally, we present the main results obtained for both scenarios defined and the main conclusions.

2. State of the Art of the Transportation Lot Sizing Problem

The classic Economic Lot Size model is a framework that allows obtaining orders quantities that minimize ordering and storage costs. Let us assume that there is a retailer, which faces a constant demand per unit of time **D** for a determined item. This retailer must place orders for the same item to another facility. It fixes order quantities at **Q** units per order. The retailer must pay a fixed ordering cost **K** every time he places an order and storage cost per unit held in inventory per unit of time is **h.** Given these assumptions we can define the economic order quantity or the **Q*** that minimizes ordering and storage costs as [2]:

$$Q^* = \sqrt{\frac{2KD}{h}}. \tag{1}$$

There are many variants of the EOQ model; Meyer [3] provides a literature review of main variants and extensions of this model. In our case, we will focus on models that include transportation costs. Blumenfeld *et al.* [4] were one of the first who extended the EOQ formula to the case of the point-to-point transportation. In this case, they calculate the EOQ taking into account the inventory at the origin and the destination and the in-transit inventory. Instead of defining a fixed ordering cost, they define a fixed freight charge per shipment. After they define the optimal shipment size as the minimum between the optimal given by the EOQ formula and the capacity of the transportation mean. Later Lee [5] extends the EOQ model in order to include freight costs quantity discounts. In this case, he defines a set up cost function S(Q) per shipment as follows:

$$S(Q) = F_i + A, \text{ if } N_{i-1} < Q \leq N_i \ i = 1,2,\ldots, I. \tag{2}$$

Where Q is the amount of each order, F_i is the freight cost for shipment sizes Q between N_{i-1} and N_i and A is a fixed cost. In this case, the author uses the EOQ formula to estimate a Q_i per interval. After he develops an algorithm to find the optimal Q that yields the minimum cost over all the intervals. Swenseth and Godfrey [6] define a model for FTL (Full Truck Load) and LTL (Less than Truck Load) shipment methods for transportation costs with quantity discounts. Concerning the LTL tariffs, they assume a variable cost per pound with quantity discounts. The model proposed allows obtaining the optimal Q* taking into account both shipment methods. Arcelus and Rowcroft [7] propose a model that allows defining inventory policies for problems with freight-rate structures and incremental quantity discounts. They evaluate three different freight structures. There is a lot at variants and extensions for the transportation lot-sizing problem. For example, Abad and Aggarwal [8] propose a model that allows defining the optimal reselling price and transportation lot size for a reseller. Jaruphongsa *et al.* [9] consider a two stage lot-sizing model, this model provides an optimal replenishment plan for a warehouse (first stage) and an optimal delivery plan from the warehouse to a distribution center (second stage). These extensions are not in the scope of this study. For a further literature in transportation lot sizing problem the author can refer to Meyer [3] or Rieksts and Ventura [10].

Nowadays the EOQ model is a tool very often used to solve industrial transportation lot sizing problems or in general order lot-sizing problems, especially in the automotive industry. Blumenfeld *et al.* [11] develop an EOQ tool for point-to-point transportation for General Motors: TRANSPART. They apply it at first at General Motors' Delco Electronics Division showing a 26% logistics costs saving opportunity. The automotive industry has a fast increasing demand and very important productions rates (Ex. Approximately 13000 cars per day at Toyota). Therefore, in this industry the EOQ model is a very convenient tool to optimize inventory management policies. In this paper, we will evaluate the implementation of this method in the Aeronautic Industry, which in contrast has small demand and low production rates (Ex: <500 units per year).

3. Airbus Case Study

As we mentioned it before, we evaluate two transportation management scenarios at Airbus Helicopters:

1. **First scenario:** In this scenario, each supplier manages transportation on his own, and Airbus does not have visibility over transportation costs; they are included in the part prices. In other words, total transportation cost paid by Airbus does not depend on delivery frequencies in appearance. Hence Airbus define replenishment policies that minimize only inventory costs, without taking into account transportation costs which leads to big delivery frequencies and small shipment sizes.
2. **Second scenario:** Airbus manage transportation and has full visibility over transportation costs. It optimizes transportation lot sizes based on transportation and storage costs.

Before evaluating these scenarios, it is necessary to define the three transportation modes used at Airbus Helicopters. We define different hypothesis for transportation costs based on available information and in cooperation with Airbus concerned departments:

1. **Full Truck Load** (FTL): All the transportation mean capacity is used (truck, container). Concerning FTL costs, we assume that FTL transportation mean capacity is equal to 24000 kg and that transportation cost per FTL shipment is linear. In other words, the cost of two FTL shipments (ex. two truck shuttles) is equal to two times the cost of one FTL shipment. We estimated FTL cost based on quotation demands made for different transportation providers.
2. **Less than Truck Load** (LTL): Transportation mode used when volume is not significant enough to use all the transportation capacity. In this case, we define transportation costs per pallet and we assume that they are linear, in other words, the cost of shipping two pallets is equal to two times the cost of shipping one pallet. We define a capacity of 1000 kg per pallet. We estimate transportation cost per pallet using a DHL quotation tool [12].
3. **Parcel and Courier Services** (PCS): Door to door small parcel method of delivery. In this case, we use Multi-parcel (Multi-product shipments) UPS tariffs presented in Table 1 [13] to estimate PCS costs. In this table, each column represents a geographic zone and each row represents a shipment weight. The geographic zones classify shipments according to the distance between the source and the destination. The longer is the distance between a source and a destination the bigger is the number of the geographic zone (1 to 8).

Table 1: Multi-parcel UPS tariffs.

Tarif des envois multi-colis										
zone	1	2	3	4	5	6	61	7	71	8
Poids										
5 kg	24,70	27,35	30,15	33,15	55,80	76,30	85,25	94,30	103,00	157,95
10 kg	26,80	30,30	33,55	37,15	109,85	133,75	169,45	180,80	194,75	201,60
15 kg	28,90	33,20	37,15	41,50	132,65	162,60	206,15	228,45	239,00	249,95
20 kg	31,10	36,15	41,00	45,65	145,55	178,30	230,30	256,95	268,45	288,85
25 kg	33,30	39,00	44,75	50,25	159,10	195,05	246,50	273,95	291,50	334,05
30 kg	35,55	41,85	48,30	54,30	172,05	210,90	261,75	289,60	313,00	378,10
40 kg	39,40	47,35	55,45	62,00	180,55	224,50	272,80	305,20	328,60	388,75
50 kg	42,75	52,80	62,15	69,60	189,05	238,05	283,90	320,90	343,90	399,40
60 kg	46,55	58,20	69,10	77,20	197,55	251,65	295,00	336,60	359,50	409,75
70 kg	50,25	63,80	76,00	84,95	205,95	265,10	306,10	352,25	374,85	420,45
80 kg	53,85	69,05	82,90	92,40	214,30	278,60	323,70	367,85	390,25	430,90
90 kg	57,45	74,65	89,75	100,10	222,95	292,25	341,40	383,45	405,75	441,50
100 kg	61,00	80,10	96,65	107,65	231,35	305,80	359,10	399,10	421,00	452,15
120 kg	68,65	91,55	110,25	124,60	240,20	323,05	376,80	414,80	453,60	538,65
140 kg	76,30	103,05	123,80	141,45	248,95	340,30	394,40	430,45	486,25	625,35
160 kg	84,15	114,70	137,50	158,30	257,70	357,55	439,20	491,05	555,70	711,85
180 kg	91,65	126,20	150,95	175,25	266,60	374,70	483,75	551,75	625,15	798,25
200 kg	99,40	137,75	164,70	192,15	275,40	392,00	528,60	612,35	694,60	885,00
Plus de 200 kg										
Prix par kg	0,49	0,68	0,82	0,96	1,37	1,96	2,64	3,06	3,47	4,42
Prix min	99,40	137,75	164,70	192,15	275,40	392,00	528,60	612,35	694,60	885,00

Transportation cost is given for multiples of 5 until 25 kg, for multiples of 10 between 30 and 100 kg and for multiples of 20 between 100 and 200 kg. In order to estimate transportation cost in-between each interval (0-5kg, 5 -10kg, etc.), we linearize it. We take this decision based on UPS mono-parcel tariffs (see Table 2 [13]), in this case costs are presented for weights between 1 and 5 kg and between 5 and 10 kg. We make a linear regression for each interval and we find that it is a good approximation for costs in-between these intervals (Determination coefficient > 0.98 for all the geographic zones).

Table 2: Mono-parcel UPS tariffs.

Tarif des envois mono-colis										
zone	1	2	3	4	5	6	61	7	71	8
EUR										
Poids										
1 kg	15,20	18,10	19,70	20,00	33,20	46,50	63,55	73,75	84,90	105,25
2 kg	16,00	19,05	21,20	21,60	37,35	52,35	67,75	76,15	90,80	122,15
3 kg	16,90	20,20	22,75	23,10	41,70	57,95	72,05	78,70	94,75	133,15
4 kg	17,65	21,25	24,20	24,55	46,00	63,90	76,40	81,10	98,75	143,95
5 kg	18,60	22,30	25,85	26,10	50,10	69,70	80,70	84,00	102,45	154,70
6 kg	19,35	23,70	27,15	27,55	59,95	80,75	93,25	105,00	119,50	163,35
7 kg	20,35	25,20	28,45	29,05	69,70	91,90	105,55	126,35	136,55	171,95
8 kg	21,25	26,60	29,80	30,55	79,60	103,10	117,90	144,15	153,50	180,60
9 kg	22,10	28,10	31,05	32,05	89,20	114,20	130,40	161,85	170,55	189,25
10 kg	22,95	29,55	32,30	33,50	99,05	125,40	142,95	179,55	187,55	197,95

3.1. First Scenario Transportation Cost Estimation

In order to estimate transportation cost for the first scenario we use two methods:

1) **First method:** As we mentioned it before, in the first scenario we assume that transportation cost is included in part cost. In other words, transportation cost for a supplier j is X_j% of the product cost. At Airbus, in cases where Supplier manages transportation, even if the value of X_j is not known for almost all suppliers, we know that it varies between A% and B% for all suppliers ($A \leq X_j \leq B$ for all j). In this case, in order to estimate transportation costs for the first scenario, we assume that transportation cost is equal to A% of the product cost for all the suppliers. In that way, we ensure that transportation cost is not overestimated. This method allows estimating a realistic transportation cost for the first scenario. We do not specify values of A and B in this study because of Airbus privacy policies.
2) **Second method:** In this method, we assume that Airbus places orders taking into account only inventory cost. Transportation costs are calculated using PCS, LTL and FTL tariffs. In other words, supplier transportation costs are subject to the same PCS, LTL and FTL tariffs than Airbus for the second scenario. Using this method allows estimating total cost reduction purely due to transportation lot sizes optimization, and hence evaluating the application of an economic transportation quantity model in the aeronautic industry.

3.2. Second Scenario: FTL, LTL and PCS Transportation Lot Sizing Model

We develop a method based on transportation lot sizing literature to estimate optimal transportation lot sizes for FTL, LTL and PCS transportation cost structures defined before. To this end, we assume that time horizon is infinite, due to products range renewal small frequency (less than once each ten years per product), and that demand is constant, given that the objective of implementing such a replenishment policy would be to smooth orders quantities according to production rates. We don't include order costs, we consider they are fixed (procurement staff fixed). We calculate optimal transportation lot sizes in kilograms (multi-products) using an approach per interval similar to the one used by Lee [5]. Quantity discounts are taken into account for PCS costs implicitly, based on UPS tariffs table presented previously (Table 1).
As we mentioned it before, we assume that UPS (PCS) costs are described by a linear function per interval for each geographic zone:

$$\text{UPS cost}_i(Q) = Cv_i Q + Cc_i \qquad \text{if } L_i < Q \leq U_i. \tag{3}$$

Where Q is the shipment weight, Cc_i represents the intercept (constant cost), Cv_i represents the slope (variable cost per kg), L_i is the lower bound of the interval and U_i is the upper bound of the interval. If we assume that Cs is the storage cost per kg per year, D is volume delivered in kg per year and T is the time interval between deliveries (in years) in which we consume Q, total cost TC_i per shipment for a given interval is:

$$TC_i(Q) = Cv_i Q + Cc_i + Cs\frac{Q}{2}T \qquad \text{if } L_i < Q \leq U_i. \tag{4}$$

Given that T is equal to $\frac{Q}{D}$, total cost per shipment can be written as:

$$TC_i(Q) = Cv_iQ + Cc_i + Cs\frac{Q^2}{2D} \qquad \text{if } L_i < Q \leq U_i. \tag{5}$$

If we divide TC by Q, we obtain the total cost per kilogram TC per kg_i:

$$TC \text{ per } kg_i(Q) = Cv_i + \frac{Cc_i}{Q} + Cs\frac{Q}{2D} \qquad \text{if } L_i < Q \leq U_i. \tag{5}$$

TC per kg_i is a convex function, hence we can find the Q^* that minimizes the total cost TC_i for the interval i which corresponds to the EOQ:

$$Q^* = \sqrt{\frac{2DCc_i}{Cs}} \qquad \text{if } L_i < Q \leq U_i \tag{6}$$

Concerning the LTL costs, given that it is assumed that cost per pallet is linear and that a pallet has a capacity of 1000 kg, transportation cost is constant for weights between 0 and 1000 kg (Cost of one pallet), 1000 kg and 2000 kg (Cost of 2 pallets), and so on. Consequently, we calculate the Q^* per interval using the EOQ formula too, by replacing Cc_i with the corresponding LTL cost C_{LTLi} of the interval; in other words, C_{LTLi} is the cost of shipping one pallet if 0 kg $< Q \leq$ 1000 kg, C_{LTLi} is the cost shipping two pallets if 1000 kg $< Q \leq$ 2000 kg and so on.

$$Q^* = \sqrt{\frac{2DC_{LTLi}}{Cs}} \qquad \text{if } L_i < Q \leq U_i \tag{7}$$

Concerning FTL costs, assuming that the truck/container capacity is equal to 24000 kg, transportation cost is constant for weights between 0 and 24000 kg (Cost of one FTL shipment), 24000 kg and 48000 kg (Cost of two FTL shipments) and so on. As for LTL costs, we calculate the Q^* per interval using the EOQ formula replacing Cc_i with the corresponding FTL cost C_{FTLi}.

$$Q^* = \sqrt{\frac{2DC_{FTLi}}{Cs}} \qquad \text{if } L_i < Q \leq U_i \tag{8}$$

When calculating the EOQ for each interval i for the PCS, LTL and FTL cases, it is necessary to take into account the interval bounds. If the EOQ is less or equal than the lower bound L_i of the interval, the EOQ for the interval must be equal to the lower bound L_i. Similarly, if the EOQ is more or equal than the upper bound U_i of the interval, the EOQ for the interval must be equal to the upper bound U_i. To illustrate this situation, let us see Figure 1. There are two total cost curves: the first one (blue) for a transportation cost of 100 and the second one for a transportation cost of 300 (red). The first curve corresponds to the total cost function for weights between 0 and 40 kg (dotted over the second interval) and the second curve corresponds to the total cost function for weights between 40 and 80 kg (dotted over the first interval). The Q^* optimal for the first interval, corresponds to the optimal (EOQ) of the first curve (blue), which is in the first interval, then it is not necessary to modify it. In contrast, the Q^* optimal for the second interval is 40 kg (lower bound of the interval), given that the optimal (EOQ) of the second curve (red) is less than 40 kg.

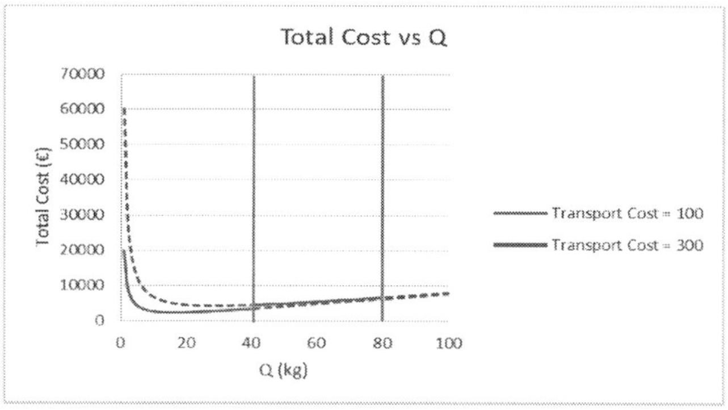

Figure 1: Total cost curves per interval - Example

We calculate the Q^* for all the intervals for each transportation mode. After we select the Q^* and the transportation mode that minimize the total cost per supplier. These Q^* are traduced after into optimal delivery frequencies. In order to obtain realistic results we approximate these delivery frequencies to industrial delivery frequencies defined in Table 3. After we use industrial delivery frequencies obtained to calculate transportation cost and storage cost for the second scenario.

Table 3: Multi-parcel UPS tariffs.

Industrial delivery frequencies
Once each 6 months
Once each 3 months
Once each 2 months
Once per month
Twice per month
Once per week
Twice per week
Three times per week
Every day

4. Analysis of the Case Study

The scenarios described before were evaluated for a panel of 153 suppliers located in North America and Europe and two destinations (Airbus Sites). Suppliers selected in this panel are representative of suppliers' product variety. Only suppliers providing expensive and bulky/heavy products (Ex. Engines) were excluded in order to avoid unrealistic results (Ex. ½ engine).
Because of Airbus privacy policies, results obtained in the study have been normalized to present total cost comparison between the two scenarios presented before. Table 4 presents results obtained using the first method defined previously for calculating transportation costs for the first scenario and Table 5 presents results obtained using the second method.

Table 4: Airbus Case Study Results – 1st method used for the first scenario

Scenario	Storage Cost	Transportation Cost	Total Cost	Cost Reduction
1st Scenario	9	95	104	-
2nd Scenario	20	54	74	**- 29%**

Table 5: Airbus Case Study Results – 2nd method used for the first scenario

Scenario	Storage Cost	Transportation Cost	Total Cost	Cost Reduction
1st Scenario	9	91	100	-
2nd Scenario	20	54	74	**- 26%**

Table 4 shows that by defining optimal transportation lot sizes and managing transportation, we can potentially reduce logistics cost by at least 29% compared to the first scenario when we assume that transportation cost correspond to A% of part costs. In other words, in the second scenario, if after internalizing transportation, suppliers reduce parts cost by A%, total cost (transportation and storage costs) could be potentially reduced by 29% by optimizing transportation lot sizes.
Table 5 shows that if we assume that in both scenarios transportation costs are subject to the same PCS, LTL and FTL tariffs, by optimizing transportation lot sizes, we can potentially reduce logistics costs by 26%. In this case cost reduction is purely due to transportation lot sizes optimization.
Logistics cost reduction is due mainly to orders consolidation. In the second scenario for 84% of couples supplier-site, delivery frequency per year is reduced compared to the first scenario (storage cost increase and transportation cost decrease) and for 5% of couples delivery frequency is not modified (expensive parts). For the remaining 11%, delivery frequency increase. These cases must be studied in detail: delivery frequency increase could be a consequence of suppliers minimum lot sizes constraints in the first scenario.
Comparing Table 4 and Table 5, total cost reduction shown in Table 4 is more realistic. It estimates transportation cost based on Airbus suppliers information. While total cost reduction shown in Table 5 allows evaluating potential cost reduction purely due to the application of the transportation lot sizing model proposed in section 3.2. In this case both scenarios are subject to the same transportation tariffs.
Finally, the second scenario assume that transportation management is internalized. Logistics cost gains due to transportation lot sizes optimization in this scenario are reduced by transportation internalization costs (transportation management costs). It is necessary to study transportation internalization cost in detail. However the magnitude of the economic gain achieved in the second scenario suggests that transportation internalization cost may be smaller than logistics cost reduction.

5. Conclusion

The present study analyses two suppliers' transportation management scenarios at Airbus Helicopters from a transportation lot sizing point of view. In the first one, Airbus defines transportation lot sizes based only on inventory costs because suppliers manage transportation on their own and there is no visibility over transportation costs (they are included in part costs). In the second one, Airbus manages transportation costs, hence, it optimizes transportation lot sizes in function of transportation and storage costs. Results show that by managing transportation and optimizing transportation lot sizes logistics costs could be significantly reduced compared to the first scenario. Consequently, implementing a transportation organization that allows having visibility over transportation costs and operations could enhance logistics cost reduction facilitating the optimization of transportation lot sizes. Logistics cost reduction should be evaluated in parallel with transportation management costs associated to the transportation organization defined.
In the other hand, this study suggests that the use of the EOQ model in order to optimize transportation lot sizes could lead to logistics costs reduction in the aeronautic industry despite low production rates compared to the automotive industry.
Finally, to go further in the analysis, transportation lot sizes optimization could be studied in parallel with other logistics optimization axes. Particularly the location of cross-docking facilities and the implementation of milk runs. These optimization axes allow consolidating logistics flows and could enhance supplementary logistics cost reduction in the second scenario.

6. References

1. Harris, F.W.: How many parts to make at once. Operations Research 38(6), pp. 947—950 (1990)

2. Simchi-Levi, D., Chen, X., Bramel, J.: Economic lot size models with constant demands. In: The Logic of Logistics, pp. 137-150. Springer Series in Operations Research and Financial Engineering, New York (2014)
3. Meyer, A.: Milk Run Design, Definitions, Concepts and Solution Approaches. Karlsruher Institut für Technologie, 10.5445/IR/1000051064 (2015)
4. Blumenfeld, D.E., Burns, L.D., Diltz, J.D., Daganzo, C.F.: Analyzing trade-offs between transportation, inventory and production costs on freight networks. Transportation Research Part B: Methodological 19 (5), 361-380 (1985)
5. Lee, C.Y.: The economic order quantity for freight discount costs. IIE Transactions 18, pp 318-320 (1986)
6. Swenseth, S.R., Godfrey, M.R.: Incorporating transportation costs into replenishment decisions. International Journal of Production Economics 77(2), pp. 113 – 190 (2002)
7. Arcelus, F., Rowcroft, J.: Inventory policies with freight and incremental quantity discounts. International Journal of System Science 22, pp. 2025-2037 (1991)
8. Abad, P., Aggarwal, V.: Incorporating transportation cost in the lot sizing and pricing decisions with downward sloping demand. International Journal of Production Economics 95, pp. 297-305 (2005)
9. Jaruphongsa, W., Çetinkaya, S., Lee, C.Y.: Outbond shipment mode considerations for integrated inventory and delivery lot-sizing decisions. Operations Research Letters 35(6), pp. 813-822 (2007)
10. Rieksts, B.Q., Ventura, J.A. : Optimal inventory policies with two modes of freight transportation. European Journal of Operational Research 192(2), pp. 429-411 (2008)
11. Blumenfeld, D. E., Burns, L.D., Daganzo, C. F., Frick, M. C., Wall, R. W.: Reducing logistics costs at General Motors. Interfaces 17(1), pp. 26-47 (1987)
12. DHL. Freight Quote Tool. https://www.logistics.dhl/fr-en/home/our-divisions/freight/road-freight/road-freight-quote-tool.html. Accessed on 10-09-2018
13. UPS. https://www.ups.com/fr/fr/shipping/zones-and-rates.page. Accessed on 10-09-2018

I L S 2020
INTERNATIONAL CONFERENCE ON INFORMATION SYSTEMS, LOGISTICS & SUPPLY CHAIN
Austin, Texas April 22-24, 2020

A Bibliographic Review and Qualitative Comparison of Scenarios for Returnable Transport Items Distribution Planning in the Automotive Industry

Najoua Lakhmi [1], Evren Sahin [2], Yves Dallery [3]

[1 2 3] LGI, CentraleSupelec, Gif-sur-Yvette, France

{najoua.lakhmi@centralesupelec.fr, evren.sahin@centralesupelec.fr, yves.dallery@centralesupelec.fr}

Abstract. Returnable transport items (RTIs) are used for the handling and transportation of products between supply chain entities. Once they are emptied at receivers, they are returned to senders to be reused again for the forward flows. RTIs distribution planning problem consists in defining the timing and the quantity of RTIs to be delivered to each consumption point (i.e. the point where empty RTIs are needed). The key issue is to ensure the best service level at consumption points at minimum cost. Our research is motivated by the practical case of an OEM in the automotive industry, where RTIs are shared among the suppliers of the OEM, and where RTIs distribution planning is a critical issue. The objective of this paper is to present RTIs distribution planning models that are available in the literature. Furthermore, a discussion on possible scenarios to optimize RTIs distribution planning in the automotive industry is conducted.

Keywords: closed-loop supply chain, reverse logistics, returnable transport item, operations management, distribution planning, decision making

1. Introduction

Supply chain (SC) was defined by [1] as a "network of organizations that are involved, through upstream and downstream linkages, in the different processes and activities that produce value in the form of products and services in the hands of the ultimate consumer". More recently, the notion of reverse supply chain (RSC) was introduced to integrate value that can be recovered from products return [2]. Reverse logistics (RL), consists in planning, implementing and controlling, the efficient flows of products at different processing stages (raw materials, intermediate products, finished goods), originating from various supply chain entities (manufacturing, distribution or consumer), and moving towards a point of recovery or disposal (Council of Logistics Management).
In the context of RSC and RL, returned products are very diverse, as well as the reasons behind their return. [3] distinguishes three types of returns: manufacturing returns (raw materials surplus, quality control returns, ...), distribution returns (product recalls, packaging returns, ...) and customer returns (warranty returns, end-of-life returns, ...). Problems raised by each type of return, from an operations management point of view, can be very different. A substantial part of research in RL falls within manufacturing and customer returns, as stated by [4]. The focus of our paper is on packaging returns. More specifically, we study secondary and tertiary packaging (e.g. plastic boxes, metallic stillages, plastic pallets, etc.) which are used in industry to facilitate semi-finished and finished products handling and transportation between facilities.
Indeed, industrial packaging can be either disposable (one-way), or reusable (returnable). Reusable packaging allows for waste reduction and offers better cube utilization and significant savings on packaging

purchasing and disposal cost [5]. For instance, Canada's CAMI Automotive, the Canadian joint venture between General Motors of Canada Ltd. and Suzuki Motors Corp., increased cube utilization on inbound trucks to about 85 to 90% by using RTIs [6]. On the other hand, using reusable packaging implies the existence of a return (reverse) flow of empty packaging, generating additional transportation, storage and management costs. Despite this, companies are increasingly investing in reusable packaging, because of legislation pressure, the raise of societal and environmental awareness, and economic performance improvement [7].
In our paper, we designate reusable packaging by the term 'returnable transport items' (RTIs) and we consider the following definition derived from [8]: "all means to assemble goods for transportation, storage, handling and product protection in the supply chain which are returned for further usage". One of the main challenges for a company using RTIs is to balance RTIs demand and supply by returning enough empty RTIs to meet consumption points' needs [9]. This can be achieved through an effective distribution plan that determines the quantity and timing of empty RTIs deliveries, so as to provide a high service level (i.e. the percentage of consumption points whose RTIs stock level is above minimum stock target) at minimum cost. The case that motivated this research deals with the RTIs reverse network of an automotive carmaker, in which RTIs distribution planning problem is a real challenge. In fact, despite the millions of euros invested each year in the RTIs fleet by the carmaker, the service level average doesn't exceed 70%, which generates over costs to ensure the availability of RTIs for the forward flows. The objective of this paper is to clarify RTIs distribution planning problem and its stakes, to give a state-of-the-art overview on this problem and to discuss possible optimization scenarios in the automotive industry.
The remainder of the paper is structured as follows. Section 2 introduces the RTIs supply chain with a particular focus on the RTIs distribution planning. Section 3 presents a review of the relevant literature on the distribution planning problem in the context of RTIs RSC. Section 4 discusses possible scenarios to optimize RTIs distribution planning in the automotive industry.

2. RTIs Distribution Planning Problem in Reverse Supply chains

RTIs distribution planning problem deals with the planning of the return flow of empty RTIs. We consider a logistics network with a fixed RTIs fleet size, made of a set of consumption points (a consumption point is the receiving point of empty RTIs and the shipping point of loaded ones) that deliver products loaded in different types of RTIs to a set of release points (a release point is the shipping point of empty RTIs and the receiving point of loaded ones). In the automotive industry, consumption points are parts suppliers and engine plants, while release points are assembly plants. Each consumption point consumes an inventory of empty RTIs and generates an inventory of loaded ones. Thus, consumption points have a demand for empty RTIs that is related to the demand for loaded RTIs. Similarly, each release point consumes an inventory of loaded RTIs and generates an inventory of empty ones. Consequently, release points provide a supply with empty RTIs according to their consumption rate of products contained in RTIs.
In order to satisfy the demand for forward flows (loaded RTIs containing products), consumption points must be delivered with empty RTIs from release points in different time periods. RTIs distribution planning (**Figure 1**) refers to the problem of defining for each type of RTI (r) and in each period of the planning horizon (t): which release point (j) delivers which consumption point (i) and in what quantity (Z_{ijrt}). In supply chains involving distribution centres (k), in addition to consumption and release points, RTIs can be distributed directly from release points or indirectly through distribution centres. This case adds another dimension to RTIs distribution planning related to flows allocation and shipments sizes upstream (X_{ikrt}) and downstream distribution centres (Y_{kjrt}).
The problem of RTIs distribution planning is critical for different reasons. First, the fleet of RTIs represent a substantial investment for the supply chain, thus RTIs distribution planning must ensure a high rotation rate in order to amortize RTIs investments. Secondly, RTIs distribution planning must ensure empty RTIs availability at consumption points, because it has a major impact on loaded RTIs deliveries for the forward supply chain. When consumption points are short of RTIs, one option is to delay loaded RTIs shipments until RTIs are available, which can possibly cause shortages for receivers of forward flows. Another option is to use express shipping to deliver RTIs, which generates high transportation costs. In certain cases, RTIs can be replaced by substitution packaging, which can be reusable or disposable (one-way). Using disposable packaging as a substitution is not possible for all products, for among other reasons, quality issues. Also, disposable packaging generates additional costs related to waste management. Using reusable substitution packaging is possible if it is available in the inventory of the consumption point in question (used for another

product for instance) or if it can be delivered from another entity of the system. From a distribution point of view, the use of substitution packaging can cause imbalances in terms of RTIs needs, that are not considered in RTIs capacity planning. Moreover, it can generate inventory inconsistencies if substitution packaging flows are not well controlled and tracked in information systems. From a transportation point of view, substitution packaging can decrease transportation efficiency. In other words, the number of products loaded in substitution packaging can be lower than that of initial RTI, as well as transportation stacking conditions.

RTIs distribution planning is strongly connected to RTIs transport planning. Indeed, RTIs transport planning consists in defining the optimal set of routes to be performed by a fleet of vehicles in order to deliver empty RTIs from release points to consumption points. The main issue raised by RTIs transport planning is the minimization of transport costs to deliver empty RTIs, which translates into a minimization of the number of trucks used and the total travelled distance. As such, RTIs transport planning pushes RTIs distribution planning toward infrequent and short-distance deliveries. For instance, if RTIs are available in multiple release points, they must be delivered from the closest release point. Additionally, in order to decrease the frequency of deliveries, RTIs are returned in batches, optimally including the different types of RTIs needed by a consumption point for a given period of time. On the other hand, depending on RTIs availability at release points and demand at consumption points, RTIs distribution planning seeks a high service level even if it generates high transport costs. This means that in the case where not enough RTIs are available or only at distant release points, RTIs transport planning must allow for frequent and long-distance deliveries.

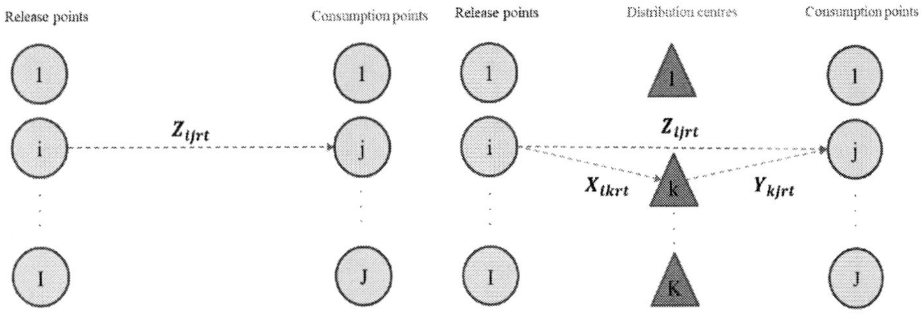

Figure 1 : RTIs distribution planning problem

3. Literature review

In the following, our purpose is to survey existing research about quantitative models for RTIs distribution planning. Reviewed papers are classified according to demand stability (i.e. demand for loaded RTIs containing products). In fact, two types of RTIs distribution planning models can be distinguished in the literature: models that consider a constant demand (i.e. deterministic constant rate over time) and models that consider a variable demand of RTIs (i.e. deterministic variable rate over time or stochastic).

3.1. RTIs distribution planning models with constant demand

When constant demand is assumed, RTIs distribution planning models (**Table *1***) adopt an EOQ (Economic Order Quantity) approach, which consists in defining the optimal quantity of empty RTIs to be returned by release points to consumption points, that minimizes RTIs holding and order costs. These models usually consider a tactical planning horizon and optimize jointly other decisions such as production lot size, loaded RTIs shipment size and RTIs capacity planning.

One example is the work of [10], who suggest a model to coordinate a supply chain of a vendor that uses RTIs to transport finished products to a buyer. The authors define jointly optimal production lot size and shipment frequencies for both finished products and RTIs, that minimize the total costs of the system. They also give insights on the definition of optimal RTI sizes, as well as interdependencies between downstream and upstream flows. [11] extend the previous work to model a single-vendor multi-buyer supply chain. Two

cases are considered: late finished products shipments after the end of production lot and early shipments while production lot is still in progress. [12] develop an integrated model for network design and inventory management in a three-level supply chain made up of factories, distribution centers and customers. The main contribution of the paper is to address location, allocation and shipment sizes decisions jointly, in the case of large logistics networks with capacitated transportation, multiple sourcing, direct and indirect shipments. The proposed model considers the trade-off between transport and inventory costs under EOQ policy and perfect coordination assumptions and is solved using an iterative heuristic.
In practice, RTIs returns are frequently subject to uncertainties. [13] study the case where RTIs return times are stochastic, consequently if RTIs are returned late, they generate delays in products shipments and shortages at the retailer. They develop mathematical models to investigate the impacts of different safety measures on the system, specifically a safety return time, a safety stock and a combination of both measures. The objective is to derive optimal operational policies while minimizing the total costs of the supply chain. The results of the paper show that implementing a safety stock or a combination of a safety stock and a safety return time give better results than that of no safety measure is in place or only a safety return time is applied. [14] present a similar problem to the one of [13]. They study a supply chain where RTIs return times are stochastic, and where the vendor can rent RTIs at a service provider to ensure products shipments for the retailer in case RTIs are returned late. Their approach suggests that renting option is especially interesting when the risk of late returns and shortages costs are high, and when finished products inventory costs at the vendor are important. [15] propose an inventory model in a supply chain with deteriorating products and stochastic return times for RTIs. In this paper, it was shown that increasing RTIs return lot size allows to decrease the probability of late RTIs returns and large back orders of finished products. [16] study an RTIs system subject to RTIs loss. They develop two models comparing the case where the retailer invests in staff training to reduce RTIs loss and the case where he does not. The authors demonstrate that the retailer investment has a positive impact on the system efficiency and supply chain total cost. Authors suggest side payments contracts with the manufacturer as an incentive to encourage the retailer investment. A related work is the one of [17], which generalizes the previous inventory model to a supply chain consisting of a vendor and multiple buyers, with investment in RTIs loss reduction. The results show, similarly to the first model, that when the buyers invest, the total cost of the supply chain decreases.

Table 1 : RTIs distribution planning models with constant demand

Reference	**Supply chain configuration**	**RTIs diversity**	**Costs structure**
[12]	multiple factories multiple distribution centers multiple customers	single	fixed costs for locating a distribution center, handling costs, transport costs, inventory costs
[15]	single supplier single buyer	single	order costs, inventory costs, setup costs, shortage costs
[11]	single vendor multiple retailers	single	inventory costs, setup costs, ordering costs, management costs
[18]	single vendor single buyer	single	inventory costs, setup costs, ordering costs, handling costs, transport costs, purchasing costs
[13]	single vendor single retailer	single	inventory costs, setup costs, ordering costs, shortage costs, transport costs
[14]	single vendor single buyer	single	rental cost, order costs, setup costs, inventory costs, transport costs
[16]	single manufacturer single retailer	single	inspection costs, purchasing costs, inventory costs, retailer investment
[17]	single vendor multiple buyer	single	inspection costs, order costs, inventory costs, purchasing costs

3.2. RTIs distribution planning with variable demand

In operational planning, constant demand assumption is no longer valid. Several models (**Table** *2*) were developed in the literature to optimize RTIs distribution planning while taking into consideration a variable demand. [19] develop an integrated model to address the day-to-day operational issues of production and distribution in a supply chain with RTIs. The formulation proposed includes two subsystems: a pair of optimization models that provides daily aggregated and disaggregated production, washing and distribution plans for products and RTIs, and a simulation model that helps decision makers to evaluate the impacts of modifications on the initial master plan, on a shift-by-shift-basis. The model does not consider explicit costs. The objective is to increase the number of clean containers at the plants and the quantity of products at the depots. [20] investigate the problem of coordinating the flows of perishable food products and RTIs considering food quality and variable customer demand. The objective of the proposed model is to optimize production quantities, outsourcing quantities, transported quantities of finished products, returned quantities of empty RTIs and purchased quantities of new RTIs, while maximizing the total supply chain profit. The authors develop an improved kernel search-based heuristic to solve the problem and demonstrate that it is more efficient than the direct use of CPLEX. [21] study the distribution planning problem of RTIs for the Canada Post, the problem is modeled as a minimum-cost flow problem and aims at defining the optimal return quantities of RTIs between Canada Post plants and its customers. The authors show, for the case studied, that a reduction of 40% of the travelled distance by RTIs can be achieved. [22] study an RTIs system of several customers, suppliers and depots, with both direct returns from customers to suppliers and indirect returns through depots. The purpose of the proposed model is to optimize loaded and empty containers movements and inventory. They model the problem as a network flow problem minimizing transport and storage costs and propose a resolution approach for a network of one supplier, one customer and one depot. The results of the paper show that a simple recurring formula solves the model under certain costs configuration. [23] propose a generic model to optimize RTIs distribution planning and capacity planning, while considering both economic and environmental indicators. The authors also conduct a case study at a luxury goods company to compare the use of RTIs and disposable packaging. The results show that because of high transport costs, RTIs use is more expensive than disposable packaging use. [24] consider the pallets dispatching problem in an express freight network with multiple demand and supply points. The specificity of the proposed model is to optimize the quantity of pallets transported between supply points and demand points and the quantity of leased pallets at demand points, while taking into consideration some predefined transport routes. The costs structure includes, consequently, transport costs, leasing costs, inventory costs and penalty costs related to early and late deliveries. The authors conduct computational experiments comparing the performance of genetic algorithm and improved cloud clonal selection operation and demonstrate that this latter is better in terms of run time and convergence.
As explained before, RTIs distribution and transport planning are closely linked. Some authors propose integrated models to optimize RTIs distribution and transport decisions. [25] study the problem of inventory routing in a CLSC of one depot and several retailers with multiple products and demand uncertainty. A probabilistic mixed-integer linear program is proposed to optimize both product deliveries and reverse flows of RTIs. The solutions obtained were evaluated using a simulation model that considers total fuel, wage, inventory holding and shortage costs. The results show that significant savings can be achieved by optimizing simultaneously inventory and routing decisions for forward and reverse operations. [7] address a similar problem to the one of [25] in the case of a single product with deterministic demand and time windows constraints. The objective function of the mixed-integer linear model developed includes production costs, transport costs, loaded and empty RTIs inventory costs and purchasing costs of new RTIs. The authors suggest a combination of clustering heuristic and branch-and-cut algorithm to solve realistic instances.

4. Comparison of RTIs distribution planning scenarios in the automotive industry

The automotive industry is one of the industries where the use of RTIs is widespread. This section proposes some possible optimization scenarios for RTIs distribution planning from an operational point of view with a specific focus on its link with RTIs transport planning. For this purpose, we rely on the reviewed literature as well as discussions with practitioners from an OEM dealing with the RTIs distribution planning issue. Two main approaches can be distinguished when optimizing RTIs distribution and transport planning: integrated approach and sequential approach (**Figure** *2*).

Table 2 : RTIs distribution planning models with variable demand

Reference	Supply chain configuration	RTIs diversity	RTIs distribution planning	RTIs transport planning	Costs structure
[19]	multiple plants multiple depots	multiple	X		NA
[21]	multiple plants multiple customers	single	X		transport costs
[22]	multiple suppliers multiple depots	single	X		transport costs, storage costs
[23]	multiple warehouses multiple stores	multiple	X		transport costs, CO2 emissions, purchasing costs
[25]	single depot multiple retailers	single	X	X	transport costs, inventory costs
[7]	single depot multiple customers	single	X	X	inventory costs, transport costs, production costs, purchasing costs
[24]	multiple supply points multiple demand points	multiple	X		transport costs, inventory costs, leasing costs, loss costs
[20]	single manufacturer single retailer	single	X		inventory costs, transport costs, production costs

In the integrated approach, RTIs distribution and transport daily planning are optimized jointly. This means that decisions about which release point delivers which consumption point, in what quantity and through which detailed route are taken simultaneously, while maximizing service level at consumption points and minimizing inventory and transport costs. From a theoretical point of view, this approach would give a global optimum in terms of distribution and transport costs. However, in large supply chains involving multiple release and consumption points and several types of RTIs (as is the case in the automotive industry), this problem is complex to solve from a computational point of view. In addition, from an organizational point of view, RTIs distribution planning and RTIs transport planning usually fall under the scope and responsibility of different supply chain functions. Consequently, adopting a sequential approach in optimizing RTIs distribution and transport planning is more realistic. The sequential approach would certainly give less optimal solutions in terms of costs optimization, however it is computationally and organizationally more tractable.

In the sequential approach, Scenario 1 would consist in optimizing RTIs distribution planning before optimizing RTIs transport planning. In this case, the first step is to determine a daily RTIs distribution plan that optimizes distribution costs, based on RTIs demand, supply and inventory levels at consumption and release points. The second step is to define a daily transport plan that minimizes transport costs, based on the predefined distribution plan. Under Scenario 1, in order to allow transport optimization, RTIs distribution planning must either include some criteria enabling the pre-optimization of transport costs (e.g. criteria related to the distance and frequency of delivery of empty RTIs) or integrate a temporal flexibility (e.g. by proposing flexible departure and arrival dates). In this scenario, RTIs distribution planning is less constrained, because it is optimized prior to transport planning. Indeed, daily RTIs distribution plan is completely dependent on RTIs demand and supply variability. This means, for instance, that in the case of insufficient supply of empty RTIs at close release points at a given period of time, RTIs distribution planning will generate the necessary flows, probably from distant release points, to deliver consumption points whose forecasted stock is below stock target, regardless of the impact on the efficiency of the resulting transport plan (i.e. number of trucks, trucks filling rate, travelled distance). As a result, transport planning is more complex and costlier, since RTIs transport plan must be re-optimized each day depending on RTIs distribution plan. This leaves limited possibilities for transport function to establish long term contracts with haulers, with negotiated transport costs. Moreover, internal flow organization at consumption and release points in terms of receiving and shipping operations is difficult to plan, because RTIs transport plan can be different from one period to another depending on RTIs distribution requirements.

Scenario 2 considers two sub-processes to plan RTIs distribution and transport: a short-term planning process and a very short-term planning process. In the short-term planning process, a forecasted distribution plan, that maximizes service level and minimizes inventory and transport costs, is optimized periodically (e.g. on a weekly basis), based on forecasted demand and supply at consumption and release points. The obtained distribution plan must be stable in terms of flows allocation (i.e. which release point delivers which consumption point) and delivered quantities, from one period to another. This must translate first into smoothed deliveries over the planning horizon on each link (i.e. given release point and consumption point), to ensure a stable transport capacity to execute the RTIs distribution plan. In addition, this must also translate into a robust sourcing to deliver empty RTIs (i.e. the number of distinct release points that deliver each consumption point) over the planning horizon, to ensure a stable transport plan in terms of routing. The next step is to optimize the short-term transport plan in accordance with the predefined short-term distribution plan, which results in a set of regular routes that will be used to deliver empty RTIs for a given period of time. Subsequently, the very short-term distribution planning process would consist in defining a daily distribution plan while maximizing the use of the predefined regular routes (those defined in the short-term transport plan). Occasionally, some additional transport orders can be added to the initial transport plan in order to satisfy intermittent RTIs needs. This scenario results in a stable transport plan to distribute empty RTIs, which allows for a better organization at release points and consumption points. Moreover, keeping a stable transport plan for empty RTIs distribution provides better negotiated costs with haulers and ensures the availability of transport capacity to fulfill RTIs distribution needs. Nevertheless, this scenario implies that the RTIs transport plan must be updated periodically in order to adjust it to the variation of RTIs needs and releases.

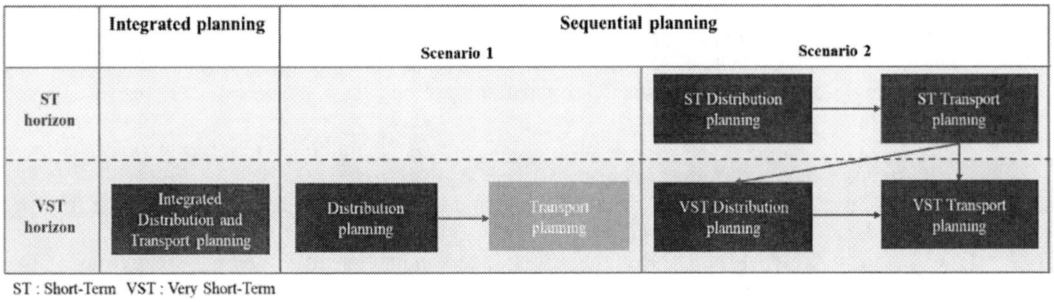

Figure 2 : RTIs distribution planning scenarios

5. Conclusions and Perspectives

In supply chains where RTIs are used, distribution planning is a critical issue. It aims at ensuring a high service level at consumption points while minimizing inventory and transport costs. In this paper, we have presented the decisions raised by RTIs distribution planning and the different issues behind. We have also reviewed existing research about quantitative models for RTIs distribution planning and classified them according to RTIs demand stability. Finally, we discussed the advantages and drawbacks of some possible scenarios to optimize RTIs distribution planning in the automotive industry, with a specific focus on its interdependency with RTIs transport planning. In the future, it would be interesting to develop optimization models to support the proposed scenarios and to compare them from a quantitative point of view. In addition, the proposed scenarios could be extended to the case where parts and RTIs flows are considered jointly in order to optimize the overall costs.

6. References

1. Christopher M.: Logistics and supply chain management : strategies for reducing cost and improving service, Financial Times/Pitman, (1998)
2. Rogers D.S., Tibben-Lembke R.: An Examination Of Reverse Logistics Practices J. Bus. Logist., 22, pp. 129–148 (2001)
3. de Brito M.P., Dekker R.: A Framework for Reverse Logistics Reverse Logistics. pp. 3–27. Springer Berlin Heidelberg, Berlin, Heidelberg (2004)
4. Glock C.H., Kim T.: Safety measures in the joint economic lot size model with returnable transport items Int. J. Prod. Econ., 181, pp. 24–33 (2016)
5. Rosenau W. V, Twede D., Mazzeo M.A., Singh S.P.: Returnable-Reusable Logistical Packaging: A Capital Budgeting Investment Decision Framework J. Bus. Logist., 17, pp. 139–165 (1996)
6. Orbis Corporation: Why Reusables? Using Plastic Reusable Packaging to Optimize Your Supply Chain, (2004)
7. Iassinovskaia G., Limbourg S., Riane F.: The inventory-routing problem of returnable transport items with time windows and simultaneous pickup and delivery in closed-loop supply chains Int. J. Prod. Econ., 183, pp. 570–582 (2017)
8. ISO: Information technology — Unique identifiers — Part 5: Unique identifier for returnable transport items (RTIs), (2005)
9. Carrasco-Gallego R., Ponce-Cueto E., Dekker R.: A framework for closed-loop supply chains of reusable articles Econom. Inst. Rep. EI 2009-21, pp. 1–40 (2009)
10. Glock C.H., Kim T.: A joint economic lot size model with returnable transport items Int. J. Integr. Supply Manag., 9, pp. 202–224 (2015)
11. Glock C.H., Kim T.: Container management in a single-vendor-multiple-buyer supply chain Logist. Res., 7, pp. 112 (2014)
12. Tancrez J.-S., Lange J.-C., Semal P.: A location-inventory model for large three-level supply chains Transp. Res. Part E Logist. Transp. Rev., 48, pp. 485–502 (2012)
13. Glock C.H., Kim T.: Safety measures in the joint economic lot size model with returnable transport items Int. J. Prod. Econ., 181, pp. 24–33 (2016)
14. Hariga M., Glock C.H., Kim T.: Integrated product and container inventory model for a single-vendor single-buyer supply chain with owned and rented returnable transport items Int. J. Prod. Res., 54, pp. 1964–1979 (2016)
15. Kim T., Glock C.H., Kwon Y.: A closed-loop supply chain for deteriorating products under stochastic container return times Omega, 43, pp. 30–40 (2014)
16. Fan X., Gong Y., Xu X., Zou B.: Optimal decisions in reducing loss rate of returnable transport items J. Clean. Prod., 214, pp. 1050–1060 (2019)
17. Fan X., Xu X., Zou B., Bai Q.: Returnable containers management in a single-vendor multi-buyer supply chain with investment in reducing the loss fraction Measurement, 143, pp. 93–102 (2019)
18. Glock C.H., Kim T.: A joint economic lot size model with returnable transport items Int. J. Integr. Supply Manag., 9, pp. 202 (2015)
19. Castillo E. Del, Cochran J.K.: Optimal Short Horizon Distribution Operations in Reusable Container Systems J. Oper. Res. Soc., 47, pp. 48 (1996)
20. Zhang Y., Chu F., Che A., Yu Y., Feng X.: Novel model and kernel search heuristic for multi-period closed-loop food supply chain planning with returnable transport items Int. J. Prod. Res., pp. 1–18 (2019)
21. Duhaime R., Riopel D., Langevin A.: Value Analysis and Optimization of Reusable Containers at Canada Post Interfaces (Providence)., 31, pp. 3–15 (2001)
22. Chandoul A., Cung V.-D., Mangione F.: Optimal repositioning and purchasing policies in returnable container management 2009 IEEE International Conference on Industrial Engineering and Engineering Management. pp. 1439–1443. IEEE (2009)
23. Goudenege G., Chu C., Jemai Z.: Reusable Containers Management: From a Generic Model to an Industrial Case Study Supply Chain Forum An Int. J., 14, pp. 26–38 (2013)
24. Zhou K., He S., Song R., Guo X., Li K.: Optimization Model and Algorithm of Empty Pallets Dispatching under the Time-Space Network of Express Shipment J. Adv. Transp., 2018, pp. 1–9 (2018)
25. Soysal M.: Closed-loop Inventory Routing Problem for returnable transport items Transp. Res. Part D Transp. Environ., 48, pp. 31–45 (2016)

I L S 2020
INTERNATIONAL CONFERENCE ON INFORMATION SYSTEMS, LOGISTICS & SUPPLY CHAIN
Austin, Texas April 22-24, 2020

Implementing e-Health Interoperability with KBE. Building a Universal Medical Record in Brazil

1st Neusa Andrade [1], 2nd Henrique Ribeiro [2], 3rd Jair G. M. Torres [1], 4th Pedro Luiz de Oliveira Costa Neto [1], 5th Irapuan Glória Júnior[1], 6th Welleson Gazel[4]

[1] Postgraduate Studies Program in Production Engineering, Paulista University, São Paulo, Brazil
[2] National School of Public Health Sérgio Arouca -ENSP FIOCRUZ. Rio de Janeiro Brazil,
[3] Faculdade Metropolitanas Unidas (FMU), São Paulo, Brazil São Paulo, Brazil

{ neusa@agenciaweb.com.br, henrique.ribeiro9@hotmail.com, jair_gustavo@yahoo.com.br, politeleia@uol.com.br, ijunior@ndsgn.com.br, w.gazel@gmail.com}

Abstract. Health Sector is depending on interoperability between systems. Health systems are fragmented and even so need to produce valuable outcomes including social engagement and a better government-citizen relationship aiming to improve the quality of access, patient care, and transparency generating accurate indicators for managers and health professionals and also for patients. This paper aims to describe a phase of development of a pilot in a public health system realized through an Action Research using combined quality tools in a Multidisciplinary Design Optimization (MBO) and Knowledge-Based Engineering (KBE) methodology, aiming to reach a strategy and model to spread best practices used in this EHR interoperability experience applied into a Brazilian small-town.

Keywords: Universal Medical Record, Universal Electronic Record, Healthcare Process Management, Healthcare Enterprise Integration, Healthcare Enterprise Interoperability, KBE

1. Introduction

The implementation of a Universal Electronic Medical Record (UEMR) is at the same time an interesting and also challenging quest for the Healthcare Sector for any country.[1]Recent research suggests that critical knowledge to improve interoperability studies is yet a gap that could be fulfilled on collecting data obtained through primary care patient´s experiences as a key able to offer valuable indicators for implementation of Web-based repositories including also transparency access to patients controlling their own history medical records [2-3]
Released on July 2, OECD Health Statistics 2019 provides a comparative database that offers an overview of the healthcare sector in measuring health systems performance, but opportunities for cross-country comparative analysis of outcomes are also very limited especially regarding exploring capabilities, policies, and standards related to exchange data and interoperability [4].
As a fully successfully already implemented example of interoperability, we can quote Estonia. The country implemented an interconnected national Electronic Health Record, as a pillar for a computerized health base that reduced costs, facilitating future care and makes it possible to share efforts between a chain of patients, doctors, clinics or hospitals, where a UEMR is an electronic system realized through an authenticated, unique and individual access, according to professional or patient profile comprising the registration, agenda, clinical history, and evaluation modules The government regulates demands and managing performance and at this moment continue improving the system joining all suppliers and their roles. [5,6]

Best practices, standards of interoperability, ontologies, and for developing systems to deliver Electronic Health Records, as an efficient solution and a cost-effective platform are suggested as patterns by the American Hospital Association (AHA), especially regarding how to share responsibilities with stakeholders aiming to attend a new society demand [7]. The best worldwide practices suggest also an ideal framework that should include standards of secure single access with dual authentication key (password usage, digital certificate and or biometrics) aiming to attend to interoperability requirements and also requirements for citizen engagement, government transparency, and social responsibility. [8,9]
This paper is part of a series of one Action Research, their design practices, and tools to reach one strategy to be followed. [10] This phase aimed to applied at an interoperability experience for the first time in a Brazilian little town aiming to exchanging data between health units and patients, using Knowledge-based engineering (KBE) methodology as tool to design and implement complex systems that have the goal to set the steps for management implementation of a health system [11]. The final project intends to offer a framework model to implement interoperability extending the model for other cities but in this paper, the research will only show which combined tools were used to implement the system to reach interoperable Information. The final goal of Action Research will be to present standards that were chosen to build a proposal of a Web-based repository cost-effective platform to reach interoperability and data integration between entities, using a single key of patient's records.

2. Context and Background

The Brazilian Government offers a kind of health system covered by Brazilian taxes, but uses of public taxes in health care are subjects of a polarized debate that is not a subject of this research, but must be presented as illustration since their requiring coordination between services organized in networks, and according to best practices, the design principles of systems to attend this kind of healthcare must also consider as an issue claims of participation and trade-offs with society. [12]
In European countries, universality in health generally refers to the public coverage of national systems for each country. Some programs are paid for entirely out of tax revenues, others using a mix of funds insurance. In some cases such as the UK, government involvement also includes directly managing the health care system, and many countries use mixed public-private systems. In most European countries, healthcare entails a government-regulated network and also private companies. [13] The US health system, for instance, uses a restriction for the right to health in a model based on different types of insurance, with a strong emphasis on the private sector. In developing countries, the term universal health coverage (UHC) is used to refer to a basic range of services coverage or public or private health insurance. In several ways, Latin American countries have followed different paths from Brazil towards universal health coverage to address social determinants of health.[14]
Brazil is a country with continental dimensions composed of 5563 municipalities that present widespread regional and social inequalities. Their health system has decentralized management, composed of three levels of autonomy forming a Unified Health System (SUS) that is financed by taxpayers, aiming to provide healthcare, as a right of citizenship offered for the major population-based on principles of right for citizens and duty of the state. [15]
Even if logistic and the financial role of universal healthcare vary by country, places such as the United States and England, Australia, Canada is reviewing the scope at primary Health Care and health roles, trying to optimizing the workforce, reducing costs, providing greater equity and quality. These countries are also concerned about exchange data between professionals and to offer better services for a society that is claiming transparency and requires systems able to exchange data with citizens. [16]
That is a reason why to reach interoperability is a global trend and the reason for this study. The best practices say that health systems need to acquire, generate and exchange information data aiming to generate indicators to be filled critical knowledge gaps, and many researchers are pointing pathways using EHR and obtained metrics like Patient-Reported Experience Measure (PREM) and Patient-Reported Outcome Measure. (PROM) [17].

2.1. Health Sector Interoperability Experiences

The 2018 edition of Health at a Glance Europe show general rules to improve the health of citizens and an effective performance for build health systems reducing wasteful based on 4 pillars: 1) Improve more access to health care, 2) Offering more people-centered health systems, 3) Build more resilient health systems, 4) Promote more protection and prevention. [8]
The American Hospital Association (AHA) model remarks seven pathways aiming to implement interoperability: 1) Security and Privacy, 2) Efficient and usable solutions, 3) Cost-Effective, enhanced infrastructure, 4) Standards developments, 5) Connecting beyond Electronic Health Records, 6) Share of Best Practices. [7] Health care information exchange and interoperability (HIEI) and their regards about inter-organizational relationships are properly addressed at literature, comprehending aspects of clinical, financial, and organizational value, electronic data workflow, exchange data through stakeholders and providers, like hospitals, medical groups, laboratories, radiology centers, pharmacies, payers, public health departments, etc. [17]
About EHR best practices we can highlight a solution 99% already implemented in Estonian for all e-health solutions. In 2005 the Estonian Ministry of Social Affairs released a strategic sector information system in which the core project was based in Electronic Health Record (EHR) providing a basic integrated information technology system as a comprehensive central register aiming to exchange health information data from birth to death. [5,6]. The e-Health information is a centralized Electronic Health Record (EHR) complemented by three systems: 1) Digital images, 2) Digital Registration, and 3) Digital Prescription which creates a unified national health information system. This system attends 1.35 million Estonian residents [2, 29].
To complement the requirements of the development of this Action research, we also used the standards offered by the "*Trusted Exchange Framework and Common Agreement*" (TEFCA) released in January 2018. This document brought light to specifications and standards for interoperability that will be used in the web-based platform that will be developed at the end of this research.
The suggested pattern indicates that we will need 1) To establish patterns for HIEs enabling providers, hospitals and other health care stakeholders using EHRs, aiming to join any health information network, as well as automatically connect and participate in a nationwide HIE, 2) To create a "Qualified Health Information Networks" (QHINs) to help facilitate a standardized methodology for HIE inter-connectivity, 3) To create a new administrative organization to administer and to put the network in operation, as suggest in Trusted Exchange Framework showed at figure 1. [19]

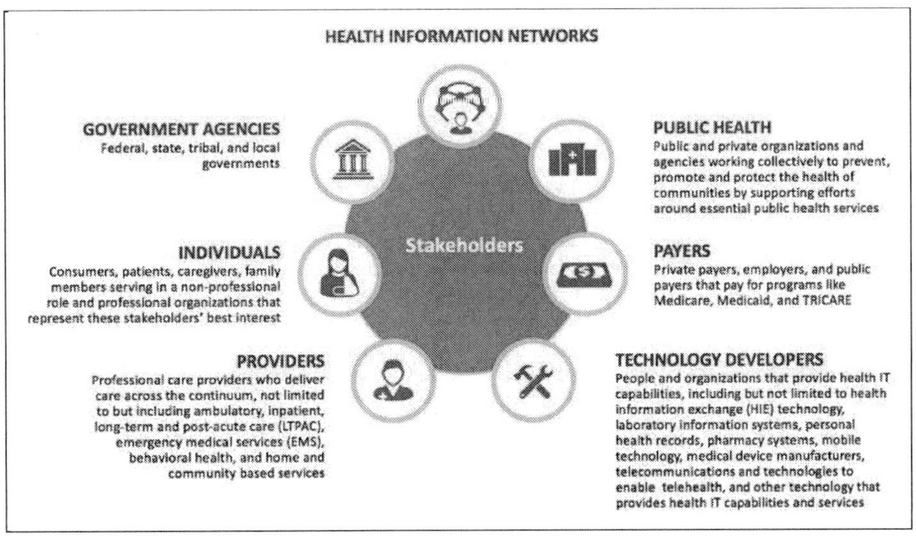

Figure 1: Trusted Exchange Framework and Common Agreement Stakeholders [19]

3. Methodology

Action Research was the chosen method to conduct this project aiming to affect and change the social reality using observations. Action Research also allows the combined use of techniques, diagnostic tools, and several instruments to support tasks. [10] To support the conceptual background was did a benchmarking of major experiences in implementing systems that reach interoperability exploring their capabilities, policies, and standards to exchange data. [9] The best practices to implement these solutions in health care suggested using data from Patient-Reported Experience Measures (PREM) and Patient-Reported Outcome Measures (PROM) [17]
About the best models of implementation for Universal Electronic Record, we select the experience implemented in the United Nations University from Estonian [5,6]. American Hospital Association (AHA) standards are used for interoperability ontologies and medical record exchange data [7]. Regarding quality impacts and transparency, we chose The Lancet Global Health Commission on High-Quality Health Systems. [8]
To design this project was necessary to acquire a lot of knowledge about how acquiring the data routine of stakeholders. [27] The solution for task management that satisfied many competing requirements demanding multidisciplinary was to use design optimization (MDO) that also provide support and consistency for automation of repetitive tasks the schematic proposal is shown in figure 2 [21]. The chosen quality tools were Kanban, World Cafe, Communities of Practice, PDCA used in a combined way to build interconnection and to solve daily problems reducing time and costs of development. Table 1 describes Knowledge-based engineering (KBE) acquired through used tools to implement the project. [20, 21, 27]

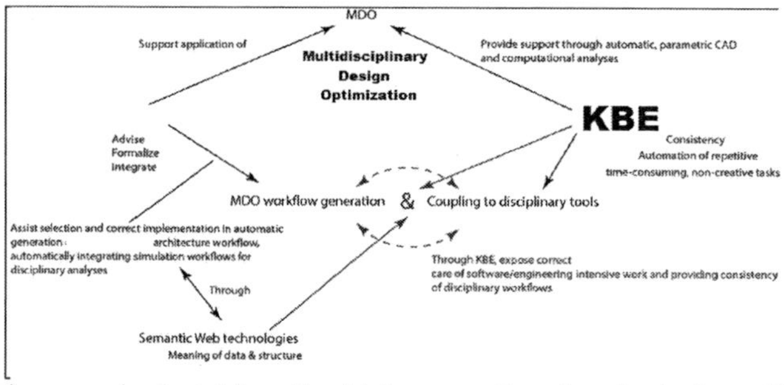

Figure 2: KBE schematic proposal adapted from Combining semantic web technologies and KBE to solve industrial MDO problems [20, 21]

Table 1: Adapted MDO chosen quality tools

Goal	Tool	Description	Contributions
Unit Resource management	Kanban	A Kanban is placed in a specific place at the entrance. The tool allows us to indicate by color and with easy visualization the distribution of the agents' daily in the time and places to be attended.	Speed the production in the health service.
To hear Patient Voice	World Café	World Café is a group conversation widely used to explore topics relevant to the group and create space for collective intelligence to emerge.	It is an instrument that facilitates to answer questions and implement the methodology.
Community Engagement	Communities of Practice	A Community of Practice is a superior resulted by World Café ideas and can also be understood as an informal gathering of people who have common interests, especially a subject or theme, and whose main purpose is the practical application of learning	Promotion knowledge in the group, promoting responsibilities in the process.
Check Tasks	PDCA	PDCA as a management tool aiming used to promote continuous process improvement through a circuit of four actions: plan, do check and act.	Correctly act on process standard deviations, document and maintain the standardization established in the resource management and implementation plan

4. Results

In this case study, we present to address used solutions to design an interoperability solution that could be applied in healthcare systems, collected through an example in an universal health coverage, as a broad concept aiming to extend access to health care to major populations, that could be implemented in several ways but always with local governments following best practices. [27]

4.1. Implementing Interoperability Brazilian Case

Region of Vale do Paraíba with 10,775 inhabitants [25]. To offer healthcare for their population the town owns only one Joint Health Unit, four spread facilities that offer family health strategy, and a single facility for primary care. To register patient's data they only use paper and not exchange information among themselves, also causing many duplicates records, and other unnecessary costs. As the final goal of this Action Research, we intend, in three months, to acquire all patients data in the city and using a single key of patient data inputted in a Web-Based platform, convert all paper medical records into electronic versions, generating a huge of savings resources, reducing uses of space and material, enabling to deliver better and faster service to city, healthcare professionals and patients, that will care their own data on their mobile phones and also communicate with local government. [27, 28, 29, 30]

4.2. Exchange Purposes and Benefits

Exchange purposes and best practices are suggested in *Trusted Exchange Framework and Common Agreement* (TEFCA) are detailed in figure 3 and will be present in a final framework that intends to be easily replicated. The project will also include how all details about infrastructure, policies, and technologies were acquired enabling the exchange of health information between units, cities, doctors, and patients, establishing interoperability and data compatibility between various systems, adopting standardized terminologies. [19]

Figure 3: Exchange Purposes at Trusted Exchange Framework and Common Agreement (TEFCA) [19]

The work expects to reach some benefits as listed below: [5, 6, 19, 24, 25, 27]

- •Practical and traceable scheduling
- •Reduced paper flow and faster service
- •Confidentiality according to access profile
- •An economy with printing and storage
- •Mobility through Smartphone, web portal and records and can be viewed from
- •Easy sharing between professionals, clinical staff with structured data and readability
- •Easy learning system
- •Individual longitudinal health data
- •An individual's complete health record on palm

• Access to provider-generated (e.g., medical visit records) and person-generated
• Data from medical devices, labs
• EHRs and quality reporting
• Specialty field-complete custom sign-ups and flags

4.3. Pilot prototype

After the pilot conclusion, the forecast is to implement the same project to exchange data between the neighboring cities Silveiras (5,792 habs), Areias (3,693 habs), São José do Barreiro (4,097 habs), and Cruzeiro (81,082 habs) totalizing of population of 105, 449 as showed in figure 4 [25].

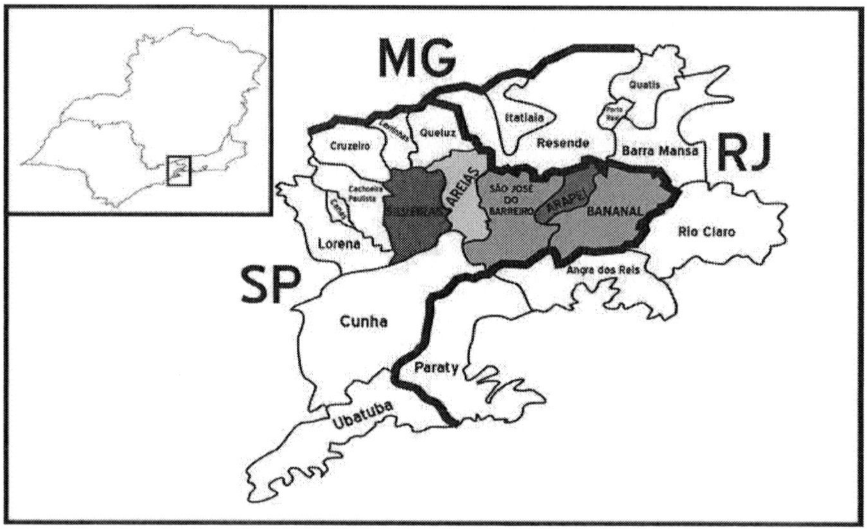

Figure 4: Figure captions should always be positioned below the figures. [25]

The implementation at Bananal town will generate a prototype, an important stage in any implementing of technology, easy to replicate in a scalable way to reach an interoperability system and a workbook using Multidisciplinary Design Optimization (MBO) as a KBE Methodology. [20, 21, 27]
Sponsored by a consortium between local private initiative and the Brazilian Government the cities would receive the same model to be implemented to exchange patient data and the same standards to be replicated on a large scale for attending interoperability at most of the Brazilian municipalities. [27].

5. Conclusion

Health Sector has an important role in society that need to improve access to the population in an affordable way [1,3,4]. Since the patients are the core in health business, and the data patient-centric is a trend, there are many regards about this question and some countries are exploring ways of embedding into Electronic Patient Records metrics requirements like Patient-Reported Experience Measure (PREM) and the Patient-Reported Outcome Measure (PROM) aiming to generate more accurate indicators for health professionals, managers, society and also for patients. [17, 27, 29]
The reason for the Healthcare Sector is be depending on interoperability, also considered a complex and recurring issue, is that Health systems are fragmented and even so need to produce valuable outcomes, including social engagement and a better government-citizen relationship aiming to improve the quality of access, patient-care, and transparency. [23, 27] Healthcare systems need to be designed to require a lot of integration across different platforms and applications, artefacts and processes, sharing data in a way that can save lives, but the World Health Statistics series says that usually health systems are not developed from patient's perspectives and also are not prepared to deliver own health data. [3-8]

A new society demand is rising regulations worldwide to solve the Action Research was chosen to this work that used combined techniques for diagnostic tools, and several instruments to support tasks aiming to develop a pilot, as a small scale or preliminary study. [1-8]
A Proof of Concept, or a pilot, was built to confirm the idea and evaluate feasibility using the KBE methodology, that showed as an assertive method for setting and addresses the steps for management implementation of this phase of implementation to connect healthcare facilities to exchange patient data in a little Brazilian town. [25, 27] The data were acquired through the combined use of tools like Kanban (resources), World Café (customer's voice) and Communities of Practice (stakeholders engagement) and PDCA to check and measure implement continuous improvement. [20, 21, 27].
As future work will be implemented a website as a portal for receive and exchange data at one Unified Medical Record Center offering high security according to permissions and rules of access and data protection. Both portal and APP visualization can be customized according to the availability of local resources using geolocation and also blockchain [27-30]. An APP will reunite records and keeps health information permanently updated in a single environment integrating health histories by the patient on palm [5].
The final purpose is to improve patient engagement in the rational and intelligent use of resources and also help patients to engage in their health trajectory and evaluating all city health services, collaborating to improve it. [27]. Also, in a long run, a new trend in Health Sector is to use the concept of Applied Intelligence Platform (AIP) to embark AI with data, analytics, and automation embracing functions, processes, and new technologies especially to solve the regards, demands, and principles of Society 5.0 [27-30]

Acknowledgments
The authors thank Coordenação de Aperfeiçoamento de Pessoal de Nível Superior (CAPES) for their support and University Paulista (UNIP), and the Ministry of Health Brazilian Government.

6. References

1. World Health Organization (WHO) - Monitoring Health for the SDGs (Sustainable Development Goals) - World Health Statistics (2019)
2. Moll J, Rexhepi H, Cajander Å, Grünloh C, Huvila I, Hägglund M, Myreteg G, Scandurra I, Åhlfeldt RM Patients' Experiences of Accessing Their Electronic Health Records: National Patient Survey in Sweden J Med Internet Res 2018;20(11):e278 DOI: 10.2196/jmir.9492
3. World Health Organization (WHO) Library - Recommendations to OECD Ministers of Health from the high-level reflection group on the future of health statistics- Strengthening the international comparison of health system performance through patient-reported indicators January (2017)
4. The Organisation for Economic Co-operation and Development (OECD) Health at a Glance: Europe 2018: State of Health in the EU Cycle, OECD Publishing, Paris. https://doi.org/10.1787/health_glance_eur-2018-en (2018)
5. Janek Metsallik, Peeter Ross, Dirk Draheim, and Gunnar Piho - Ten Years of the e-Health System in Estonia - available at http://ceur-ws.org/Vol-2336/MMHS2018_invited.pdf, accessed 01/29/2019
6. Estonian eHealth Strategic Development Plan 2020 - The Strategic Development Plan was developed by the Task Force operating within the Government Office from July 2014 to November 2015- 5. available at http://etervis2025.sm.ee/ - accessed in accessed 01/29/2019
7. American Hospital Association (AHA) Sharing Data, Saving Lives: The Hospital Agenda for Interoperability - January (2019)
8. Kruk, M. E. et al.: High-quality health systems in the Sustainable Development Goals era: time for a revolution. The Lancet Global Health Commission. Lancet Glob Health 2018; 6: pp. 1196–252. Published Online September 5. Doi: http://dx.doi.org/10.1016/S2214-109X(18)30386-3 (2018).
9. Spyrou, S., Berler, A. A., Bamidis, P.D.: Information System Interoperability in a Regional Health Care System Infrastructure: a pilot study using Health Care Information Standards. Studies in health technology and informatics, 95, pp. 364-9 Research Support, Non-U.S. Gov't, Journal Article - PMID:14664014 (2003)
10. Mello, C. H. P., Turrioni, J. B., Xavier, A. F., Campos, D. F.: Pesquisa-ação na engenharia de produção: proposta de estruturação para sua condução. Production, 22(1), pp. 1-13. November 08. Doi: https://dx.doi.org/10.1590/S0103-65132011005000056 (2012).
11. Wim J.C. Verhagen, Pablo Bermell-Garcia b, Reinier E.C. van Dijk , R. Curran - A critical review of Knowledge-Based Engineering: An identification of research challenges - Advanced Engineering Informatics 26 (2012)
12. Massuda A, Hone T, Leles FAG, et al. The Brazilian health system at crossroads: progress, crisis, and resilience. BMJ Glob Health 2018;3:e000829. DOI:10.1136/ bmjgh-2018-000829T. (2018).

13.Barnes, Marian and Vera Schattan Coelho - Social participation in health in Brazil and England: inclusion, representation, and authority - 2009 The Authors. Journal compilation - 2009 Blackwell Publishing Ltd Health Expectations, 12, pp.226–236doi: 10.1111/j.1369-7625.2009.00563.x. (2009).
14.Paim , J et al- Health in Brazil 1-The Brazilian health system: history, advances, and challenges - Lancet 2011; 377: 1778–97 Published Online May 9, 2011, DOI:10.1016/S0140-6736(11)60054-8 (2011).
15.Girardi, Sabado Nicolau et al. Scope of practice in Primary Care: physicians and nurses in five health regions in Brazil. Rev. Bras. Saude Mater. Infant., Recife, v. 17, supl. 1, p. S171-S184, 2017. Available from <http://www.scielo.br/scielo.php?script=sci_arttext&pid=S1519-38292017000600008&lng=en&nrm=iso>. access on 12 Oct. 2019. http://dx.doi.org/10.1590/1806-9304201700s100008. (2017)
16.Greer, S. L., Hervey T. K., Mackenbach, J. P, McKee, M.: Health law and policy in the European Union. Doi: http://dx.doi.org/10.1016/S0140-6736(12) 62083-2 (2013).
17.Kupcík Michal, Šír Michal Bradác Zdenek - Interoperability through ontologies - Grant Agency of the Czech Republic (102/09/H081 SYNERGY – Mobile Sensoric Systems and Network) - IFAC Proceedings Volumes-Volume 45, Issue 7, 2012, Pages 196-200 https://doi.org/10.3182/20120523-3-CZ-3015.00039. (2012).
18.D. Miller C. S. Gray K. Kuluski -Patient-Centered Care and Patient-Reported Measures: Let's Look Before We Leap - Health System Performance Research Network. Toronto, 2014- DOI 10.1007/s40271-014-0095-7. (2014).
19.The Office of National Coordinator for Health Information Technology- Trusted Exchange Framework and Common Agreement (TEFCA) - Draft 2 - https://www.healthit.gov/sites/default/files/page/2019-04/finaltefcaqtf41719508version.pdf - April (2019)
20.Olivier Kuhn. Methodology for knowledge-based engineering template update: focus on decision support and instances update. Computers and Society [cs.CY]. Université Claude Bernard - Lyon I,2010. English. NNT: 2010LYO10223. (2010)
21.Raju Kulkarni, Akshay & Hoogreef, Maurice & La Rocca, Gianfranco. (2017). Combining semantic web technologies and KBE to solve industrial MDO problems. 10.2514/6.2017-3823. (2017).
22.Brasil: Ministério da Saúde. Available at http://portalms.saude.gov.br, last accessed 2019/02/25
23.González, C., Blobel, B.G., López, D.M.: Ontology-based framework for electronic health records interoperability. Stud Health Technol Inform. Vol. 169, pp. 694-698 (2011).
24.Liang, X., Zhao, J., Shetty, S., Liu, J., Li, D.: Integrating blockchain for data sharing and collaboration in mobile healthcare applications. IEEE 28th Annual International Symposium on Personal, Indoor, and Mobile Radio Communications (PIMRC), Montreal, pp. 1-5 (2017).
25.Instituto Brasileiro de Geografia e Estatística (IBGE) Pesquisa Nacional 2013. Rio de Janeiro: IBGE. Available at https://ww2.ibge.gov.br/geociencias/ geografia/geografia_urbana/arranjos_populacionais/default.shtm?c=9 (2013).
26.O'Leary, Danielle A., & Kiel, Joan M.. (2019). Understanding The Organizational Barriers of Promoting Electronic Delivery Options in The United States Healthcare System: An Insurer's Perspective. JISTEM - Journal of Information Systems and Technology Management, 16, e201916003. Epub May 23, 2019.https://dx.doi.org/10.4301/s1807-1775201916003 (2019)
27.Andrade N, Costa Neto PLO, Torres JGM, Glória Júnior I, Scheidt CG, Gazel W. E-Health: A framework proposal for interoperability and health data sharing. A Brazilian Case. IFIP International Conference on Advances in Production Management Systems, vol. 1, Austin: Springer; 2019, p. 544–551.
28.Carvalho, Antônio Ivo, Bodstein, Regina Cele, Hartz, Zulmira, & Matida, Álvaro Hideyoshi. (2004). Concepts and approaches in the evaluation of health promotion. Ciência & Saúde Coletiva, 9(3), 521-529. https://dx.doi.org/10.1590/S1413-81232004000300002 (2004)
29.CSPH-AI. Council for Social Principles of Human-centric AI: Social Principles of Human-Centric AI 2019
30.Koornneef E, Robben P, Blair I. Progress and outcomes of health systems reform in the United Arab Emirates: a systematic review. BMC Health Serv Res. 2017;17(1):672. Published 2017 Sep 20. DOI:10.1186/s12913-017-2597-1 (2017)

I L S 2020
INTERNATIONAL CONFERENCE ON INFORMATION SYSTEMS, LOGISTICS & SUPPLY CHAIN
Austin, Texas April 22-24, 2020

Inter-firm Relationships in the Construction Industry: A Systematic Literature Review

Ahmed Khouja [1], Nadia Lehoux [1], Yan Cimon [2]

[1] Department of Mechanical Engineering, Faculty of Science and Engineering, Laval University, Quebec, Canada
[2] CIRRELT, Faculty of Business Administration, Laval University, Quebec, Canada
{ahmed.khouja.1@ulaval.ca, nadia.lehoux@gmc.ulaval.ca, yan.cimon@fsa.ulaval.ca}

Abstract. Supply chains in the construction field are very different from other industries such as manufacturing. One of the peculiarities is the lack of collaboration between its members, which affects the performance of construction projects. This paper aims at identifying the organizational forms and relational practices established between companies working in the construction field. A systematic literature review was conducted to uncover the various elements and aspects of inter-firm relationships relevant to construction. It was observed that it is possible to distinguish between various types of relationships by the outlining characteristics that describe them. Furthermore, lists of drivers, facilitators, barriers and outcomes were drawn from the review. The observations led to the creation of a conceptual framework bound to help construction companies establish partnerships.

Keywords: inter-firm relationships, partnerships, collaboration, construction, supply chain.

1. Introduction

Supply chains in the construction industry typically consist of many stakeholders i.e. clients, general contractors, subcontractors, designers, suppliers, service providers [1], [2]. This causes highly fragmented supply chains, which in turn increase the adversity between supply chain members [3]. Another particularity of such supply chains is that they are based on projects rather than processes [2], [4]. This temporary nature induces the continuous reconfiguration of the organization and the supply chain relationships for each project [2], [5]. This results in a short-term orientation of the different participants, which creates opportunistic behavior among them [2]. The temporality also leads to an abstention of project participants in sharing information [6]. In this context of project-based supply chains, a construction company can be placed at different levels from one project to another, e.g. being a focal point between the supply and demand sides in one project while playing the role of a supplier in a different project [7]. Furthermore, relationships in the construction supply chain tend to be merely transactional, affected by mistrust and conflicts. In such relationships, the focus is put on the tendering price as a selection criterion. It was also found that construction companies are not resilient to change due to project risks [2]. Traditionally, construction projects are run in a sequential process [2]. In most cases, the construction supply chain is convergent i.e. material flows join with each other at the construction site [5]. The lack of integration in the construction supply chain does not only lead to a limited efficiency but also affects relationships between its members [8]. The implementation of Supply Chain Management (SCM) principles in the construction field has brought some limited improvements [9]. One suggested idea to remedy the issues of fragmentation and adversity are better inter-firm relations through collaboration, partnering and alliances [3], [10]. However, collaboration and integration did not receive much attention in the construction industry [11]. To the best of our knowledge, no previous literature review has proposed an extensive study on the collaborative forms and practices in the construction industry. Therefore, this research aims to investigate how construction companies organize their inter-firm interactions and which elements define and affect these relationships. To reach these objectives, a Systematic Literature Review (SLR) was conducted. In the SLR, keyword combinations were searched is specific fields. 101 articles were selected and analyzed thoroughly to identify forms and practices of inter-firm relationships as well as the elements surrounding them. Results indicated that partnering, alliancing and supply chain integration are the concepts typically considered for the building construction field. To overcome issues not addressed by the reviewed literature, a conceptual framework was developed. This framework is intended as a tool to help construction companies determine the type of relationship they could establish to ensure greater coordination and productivity. It also gives a first evaluation of the success of such relationship. This paper is structured as follows: the next section presents the research methodology and analytical results. The inter-firm forms or practices of organization retrieved from the literature review as well as the elements surrounding them are then addressed. Based on these thematic findings, a conceptual framework was developed and is explained in section 4 before this paper's conclusion.

2. Research Methodology and Analytical Results

A systematic literature review was carried out between February and May 2019 based on the following research questions: Q1: What organizational forms were defined between companies working in the construction field? Q2: What are the drivers, facilitators, barriers and outcomes identified in such relationships? After a series of search trials, certain keywords were selected and 16 combinations were elaborated using a specific syntax (e.g. AND, OR). The review was conducted using the Engineering Village database (Compendex and Inspec). This database provided so-called controlled terms that helped to narrow down the search field, for example: *(((organisation OR organization*) AND (form* OR type*)) OR (relation* OR strateg*)) AND (building* AND construction)*, with the controlled terms : *construction industry AND project management AND organisational aspects*. Then, the title, abstract, and keywords of the resulting articles were examined. Afterwards, a deeper analysis of the content was performed. It is noteworthy that for Q1, selected articles do not just mention the forms or practices behind inter-firm relationships but describe them in detail. Another selection criterion was that the forms or practices mentioned should be related to the building construction sector.
From the 101 papers selected for the review, 80 included forms or practices specified in Q1 while 65 contained elements to answer Q2. It seems that the interest in inter-firm relationships in the construction industry awoke in the late 90s, about at the same time as the Egan report [4] was published (1998). This report analyzed the shortcomings of the construction industry in the UK and suggested some improvements. The UK published most of the studies (16%) included in this review, followed by the USA and Sweden (11%), as well as China (9%).

3. Thematic Findings

Q1: What organizational forms were defined between companies working in the construction field?
One of the organizational solutions used to face challenges arising in the construction industry is alliancing between stakeholders of that field. This can be seen as two organizations tied together by common objectives and interests working to benefit each other and the end customer as well. Two types of alliancing are suggested: project alliancing and strategic alliancing. Whatever the type may be, the components of an alliance are classified into contractual components and relationship-based factors. They encompass the formal contract, a mechanism to share benefits and losses, trust, a long-term commitment, shared objectives, an agreement on standardized techniques, continuously improving the performance, communication, equity in sharing and a win-win behavior [12]. For their part, Gottlieb and Storgaard [13] described a continuum of contracting relationships where they place strategic alliances in the middle between two extremes: arm's length transactions characterized by contract-related trust, absence of personal relations and low degree of integration; and in-house performing of activities that reflects a goodwill-based trust, cooperation and high level of integration and personal relations. This conceptualization presents strategic alliances as a hybrid governance structure located between these two types of organization. Therefore, two important aspects of strategic alliances are identified here: long-term formal commitment and vertical integration. Davis and Love [14] used the terms alliancing and partnering interchangeably. For them, alliancing and partnering prompt collaborations between members and enhance project performance. They considered alliancing as a contractual procurement agreement.

Likewise, in a context of partnering, researchers identified two types of partnering: project partnering and strategic partnering [15]. In the same perspective, Sundquist *et al.* [16] elaborated a framework to support the transition from a project-based partnering to a strategic one. They suggested that enterprises should invest more in long-term relationships and better exploit their partners' networks. Ellison and Miller [17] believed that partnering goes through four levels: arm's length relations; collaboration; integration; and synergistic strategic partnership. Anvuur and Kumaraswamy [18] saw partnering as a "transformative mechanism" that helps in creating cooperation in project situations that lack trust, thus changing a "workgroup into a high-performance team". Other authors [19] referred to partnering and alliancing as a high degree of collaborative work, which designates the joint work of clients with contractors to achieve more benefits than would be achieved while operating individually. Ngowi [20] considered partnering as a form of alliancing where partners do not share equity and do not establish a control hierarchy, rather they form an informal relationship to foster open interaction and joint performance. According to the author, partnering is opposed to joint ventures in terms of equity and control.

Another form of organization in construction projects similar to partnering is the quasi-fixed network where the client integrates project participants on two levels: one level with strong formal commitment and another level with less dependency. To ensure the success of partnerships on the first level, shared workspaces are implemented to foster collaboration, information sharing and activity coordination [21].

Albino and Berardi [22] included a typology of supplier integration consisting of four types: incidental sourcing that focuses on pricing; sourcing that emphasizes the quality; integral sourcing based on collaboration; and sourcing based on integration that implies the participation of suppliers at early stages. The fourth type of supplier integration contributes to the creation of a "comakership" relationship that promotes trust and openness and where partners solve problems collectively while benefiting from the supplier's experiences and knowledge in developing innovative solutions. Supply chain integration is viewed as a concept that improves the performance of the construction industry. From a client perspective, this integration is supported by the choice of a long-term relationship-oriented procurement strategy. From a supplier perspective, partners extend their collaboration beyond the project span and incorporate similar activities together. The researchers think that a change towards a connected supply chain with more aligned and centralized functions (as an extended enterprise) constitutes a high potential to deal with shortcomings of the construction industry [23]. In this context of supply chain integration, Dey *et al.* [3] proposed a framework to assign the appropriate form of relationship between the main contractor and members of the supply chain. Two dimensions were used to generate six forms of relationships. The first dimension, commitment to long-term relationship, refers to the frequency of repeated transactions with the same member. The second dimension, ways of working, consists of three classes: authority, where members of the supply chain are subordinates to the general contractor; collaboration, meaning joint efforts in planning and controlling; and arm's length, where the main contractor delegates responsibilities to the other members. In a context of prefabricated construction supply chains, Xuejian and Shusheng [24] proposed a model based on a "supply-hub", supported by Building Information Modeling (BIM) technologies. The supply-hub (third-party or contractor) is in charge of organizing and coordinating the information and logistics flows horizontally and vertically using a BIM-based information platform. Furthermore, the supply-hub promotes the collaboration between suppliers in different stages and helps in managing material changes triggered by on-site contractors.

Walker and Johannes [25] discussed another collaborative form: Joint Ventures (JVs). The authors considered an alliance model where types of relationships are described according to two scales: a scale for risk and a scale referring to human resources and cost. Mergers and acquisitions represent the highest risk. Joint Ventures are just one level below. They are new organizations resulting from the joint investment of so-called parent companies to achieve shared objectives. The challenge here is to set the right portion of dependency and contribution of each partner. A relatively riskier form is the Joint Venture with equity investment. Beneath the JVs are R&D relationships. Yu *et al.* [26] referred to Construction Joint Ventures (CJVs), where initially independent partners join their resources and skills to achieve a large scope of construction services (e.g. furnishing, procurement). Partners have responsibilities towards each other (JV contract) and towards the client (construction contract). This double contract regulation distinguishes CJVs from other joint ventures types. Lin and Ho [27] studied the governance structures of construction joint ventures. This collaboration form is very common in multinational or mega projects, where contractors share competences, funds and assets for the accomplishment of one project. The number of parties involved in joint ventures makes projects run by CJVs a managerial challenge. In this regard, researchers [26], [27] have identified organizational structures to govern these strategic relationships: Jointly Managed Joint Ventures (JMJs); Separately Managed Joint Ventures (SMJs).

A specific form of collaboration takes place during the design phase of a construction project. Participants establish a contractual relationship in the form of groups with different disciplines aiming at a common goal. Collaborative design can take many forms depending on the design stage: when defining the concept, the collaboration is seen as a Participatory Design (PD) where the focus is put on the involvement of the user in the process. The Integrative Design (ID), which is set during the development of technical aspects, has recourse to BIM tools. Finally, when designers work with contractors/builders in the implementation phase in order to optimize the construction costs, it is called Concurrent Engineering (CE). It is noticeable that PD and CE are more oriented towards an external integration whereas ID concerns the internal integration of the design unit [28].
Haugen *et al.* [29] provided an overview of organizational forms, known as project delivery methods, that serve to assign roles for each participant in a construction project. These forms are actually contractual arrangements that delimit responsibilities between the client, the contractor and/or other parties. In a Design-Build (DB) methodology, the contractor not only operates the construction but is also in charge of the design activity. This relationship is framed by one client-contractor contract. In a traditional case, a Design-Bid-Build (DBB) methodology is followed, which implies a separation between design and construction. This creates barriers in communication and knowledge exchange. The idea of distinction between design and construction is also found in the Construction Management (CM) method. In this case, the so-called construction manager ensures the effectiveness of the designers and the efficiency of project implementation by the contractor. The collaborative behavior encountered in the CM limits conflicts in a construction project. Contractors can also participate in the development phase. This is called Early Contractor Involvement (ECI), which is similar to the Dutch Building Team (BT) [30].
Some researchers [31] took an interest in assessing the impact of team integration on the project outcomes. They noticed that team integration is considered either as a form of Integrated Project Delivery (IPD) or managerial guidelines to enhance the delivery of projects. IPD is a project organization structure where only one arrangement contractually binds the project participants. Hence, communication is more direct, and the client fosters the creation of a team-oriented culture [32]. It was observed that the integrated project delivery is a more relational arrangement than DBB, DB or CM.
Another relational practice found in construction is the collaborative planning, which concerns the sharing of decision-making between project stakeholders. According to Daniel *et al.* [33], this joint planning involves all stakeholders in order to develop an ideal construction program. Moreover, collaborative planning practices entail regular meetings and joint project progress assessment.
Participants of construction projects could collaborate in assessing and dealing with project risks, be it unpredictable or dynamic risks. This joint risk management requires a special team with certain attributes to be formed. Examples of such attributes are trust between partners and in collaborative efforts, clear communication, mutual understanding, etc. It is important to consider the dynamic aspect of these risks as they change through the project span, which triggers the necessity of flexible contract conditions [34].
Collaborative relationships can be restricted to just sharing resources. It is the case of contractors working in the same construction project but in different sections. This kind of collaboration is triggered by an urgent need of a contractor due to insufficient allocated equipment. This shortage is covered by extra materials coming from another contractor in return for a compensation. Such cooperative behavior is stimulated by a reward-penalty system set by the project owner [35]. Inter-organizational collaborations can grow to such an extent that some partners benefit other parties by a non-contractual action bearing the potential risk of a non-reciprocal profit or even negatively affecting their own interests. This concept is designated as contingent collaboration [36].

Q2: What are the drivers, facilitators, barriers and outcomes identified in such relationships?
In this section, the reasons that motivate companies to work together are highlighted. Moreover, elements that support the creation and enhancement of such inter-firm relationships (the facilitators) as well as their counterparts (the barriers) are presented. Possible outcomes of these relationships are also included.
As far as drivers are concerned, economic motivations were the most cited. These include: sharing risks and rewards between partners [14]; resource pooling [26]. Cognitive reasons were found to be the second mentioned drivers. This category encompassed: gaining access to innovation and technology [37]; and creating knowledge [25]. Social drivers came in third place. Companies are motivated to work together in order to solve conflicts and decrease the risk of an opportunistic behavior [38].
A large number of facilitators were identified in this review. They were classified into several categories. Behavioral facilitators came first as for the number of citations. (Mutual) trust was the most important one [8]. Less cited but still important is an equitable allocation of risks and rewards [8]. It was observed that the use of technology plays a considerable role in facilitating inter-organizational relationships. Such

technologies can be the BIM [11] or the information and communication technology [7]. Collaborative tools were the third most cited facilitators. These tools cover for example workshops and surveys [39]; and space proximity [28]. Elements referring to the relationship contract were also deemed to be facilitators. In this regard, the literature suggested for example clearly defined incentives [18]. The organizational category was the next on the list with facilitators like early involvement (of designer, subcontractors) [7]. Some facilitators are related to the partners like long-term orientation [37] and compatibility of partners [37]. Besides, effective communication can contribute to the development of inter-firm partnerships [7]. Other facilitators concern the resources as a supportive leadership [40]. Some facilitating elements relate to the processes of the companies as the use of indicators [28]. Like for the drivers, a social category is also noticeable for the facilitators. It includes: conflict resolution [15]; and team working [8]. Furthermore, elements reflecting the culture of the involved enterprises can be considered as facilitators: no-blame culture [8]; and cultural compatibility [37]. Another category of facilitators refers to activities that should be performed jointly by the partners as joint technical specifications [34]. A last category of facilitators concerns the environment of the involved companies. Here, it is found that a limited bid invitation could help the establishment of inter-firm partnering [34].

Barriers, seen as obstacles that discourage potential partners from establishing a relationship or hinder the development of such practice, are classed into four categories. Researchers mentioned mostly barriers belonging to the cultural category [15]. The list comprises e.g. traditional adversarial approach [7]; communication [28]; exploitation (i.e. opportunism) [14]; lack of trust development [14]; short-term orientation [7]; and cultural fit [39]. Organizational barriers [15] occupied the second place. Reviewed publications refer to: traditional procurement procedures [34]; disagreements over management and operational strategies [37]. Obstacles related to the construction industry and its practices were ranked third. Such barriers [15] can be: competitive tendering [16]; and public procurement law (e.g. stringent public regulations, and laws) [39]. The final category is resources (e.g. financial security [39]).

The last elements reported in this section are the outcomes. It seems that the economic outcomes are the most mentioned among authors. Reduced costs [35] have the greatest number of citations, followed by improvements in project performance [38]. Outcomes related to project schedules such as completion on time [27] were also high ranking. The social category is also present in the case of outcomes. Included elements are: stimulating collaborative relations, e.g. fostering and maintaining a collaborative spirit among project actors [14]; and conflict resolution [39]. The third category of outcomes is the cognitive one. It encompasses the following aspects: joint organizational learning [16]; and holistic creativity [28].

Table 1 sums up the forms/practices identified in Q1 alongside the top 3 (per category) of the elements found in Q2. The numbers represent the frequency of citation.

Table 1: Summary of the SLR-results

Forms/practices found in Q1		Elements found in Q2		
Partnering	34	Drivers	Economic	53
Alliancing	18		Cognitive	6
Supply Chain Integration	11		Social	2
Project Delivery Methods	10	Facilitators	Behavioral	31
Joint Ventures	8		Use of technology	24
Integrated Project Delivery	6		Collaborative tools	21
Joint Risk Management	3	Barriers	Cultural	44
Collaborative design	3		Organizational	32
Quasi-fixed network	1		Industrial	10
Equipment sharing	1	Outcomes	Economic	74
Collaborative planning	1		Social	17
Contingent collaboration	1		Cognitive	11

4. A Conceptual Framework

After analyzing the review results, two main observations were deduced. When examined separately, the forms presented in the answer to Q1 do not cover several characteristics of an inter-firm relationship. This led to the need to develop a comprehensive descriptive framework of interorganizational interactions. The comparison of the forms with each other revealed some features that exist in more than one form with different degrees while some others appeared to be more specific. As a result, all these characteristics could be employed to distinguish inter-firm relationships. It was also observed that none of the reviewed articles provided a mechanism that depicts the interaction between elements retrieved from the response to Q2 while linking those with the success of the relationship. Therefore, a conceptual framework comprised of two tools was elaborated. The first one serves to identify the relationship profile. It consists of defining the suitable organizational form based on 8 dimensions with two opposite attributes. The idea here is to place a cursor on the dimension scale according to the desired degree (cf. Figure 1). The second tool brings facilitators (Fs) and barriers (Bs) into play. Once the lists of such elements are drawn up, each facilitator is assigned to a barrier where F helps overcome the corresponding B (cf. Figure 2). Considering facilitators as plus points (+) and barriers as minus (-), three scenarios are possible: zero-sum, i.e. a neutral situation; positive sum means the relationship presents an opportunity; and negative sum indicates a risk when venturing in a partnership.

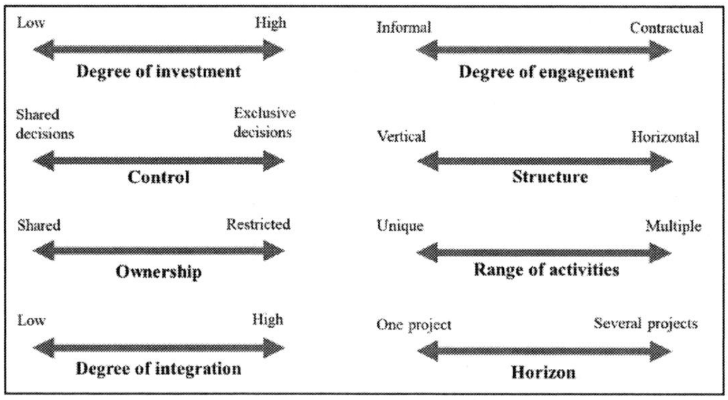

Figure 1: Multidimensional profile of the relationship

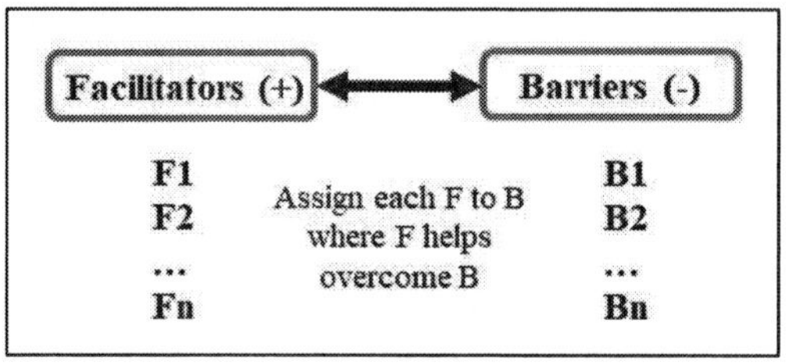

Figure 2: Success potential of the relationship

5. Conclusion

Considering the potential of inter-firm collaboration as a means to enhance the performance of the construction supply chain, a systematic literature review was carried out. The goal was to investigate existing forms and practices of inter-firm relationships and to identify elements surrounding them. The observations resulting from the review led to the elaboration of a conceptual framework. The multidimensional profile provides an extensive and detailed description of the relationship as well as a clearer distinction between the forms. Additionally, evaluating the success of the relationship based on facilitators and barriers gives potential partners a prognosis about possible future opportunities or risks. When it comes to the research on collaboration in the construction field, the literature tends to prioritize certain topics such as developing tools or methods to foster the collaborative design (e.g. BIM, user integration) or the concept of the IPD [28]. Therefore, more studies should be undertaken to cover other areas of the collaboration phenomenon in the construction context, in particular the supply chain aspects. There is also a need to develop quantitative models that assess the financial risks of the forms found in this review. Since the lack of trust is a major issue in the construction industry, organizational behavior investigations in multi-actor construction projects should be carried out.

6. Acknowledgments

The authors are grateful to Natural Sciences and Engineering Research Council of Canada for the financial support through its IRC and CRD programs (IRCPJ 461745- 18 and RDCPJ 524504-18) as well as the industrial partners of the NSERC industrial chair on eco-responsible wood construction (CIRCERB).

7. References

[1] A. R. J. Dainty, S. J. Millett, and G. H. Briscoe, "New perspectives on construction supply chain integration," *Supply Chain Manag. Int. J.*, vol. 6, no. 4, pp. 163–173, Oct. 2001.

[2] P. Behera, R. P. Mohanty, and A. Prakash, "Understanding Construction Supply Chain Management," *Prod. Plan. Control*, vol. 26, no. 16, pp. 1332–1350, Dec. 2015, doi: 10.1080/09537287.2015.1045953.

[3] P. K. Dey, W. Ho, C. Charoenngam, and W. Deewong, "Relationship characteristics within the supply chain of Small and Medium-Sized Construction Enterprises in Thailand," *Int. J. Manuf. Technol. Manag.*, vol. 15, no. 1, p. 102, 2008, doi: 10.1504/IJMTM.2008.018242.

[4] J. Egan, "Rethinking construction," Department of the Environment, Transport and the Regions, London, UK, 1998.

[5] R. Vrijhoef and L. Koskela, "The four roles of supply chain management in construction," *Eur. J. Purch. Supply Manag.*, vol. 6, no. 3–4, pp. 169–178, Dec. 2000.

[6] J. C. P. Cheng, K. H. Law, H. Bjornsson, A. Jones, and R. Sriram, "A service oriented framework for construction supply chain integration," *Autom. Constr.*, vol. 19, no. 2, pp. 245–260, Mar. 2010, doi: 10.1016/j.autcon.2009.10.003.

[7] A. Segerstedt and T. Olofsson, "Supply chains in the construction industry," *Supply Chain Manag. Int. J.*, vol. 15, no. 5, pp. 347–353, Aug. 2010, doi: 10.1108/13598541011068260.

[8] X. Meng, "The effect of relationship management on project performance in construction," *Int. J. Proj. Manag.*, vol. 30, no. 2, pp. 188–198, Feb. 2012, doi: 10.1016/j.ijproman.2011.04.002.

[9] M. Saad, M. Jones, and P. James, "A review of the progress towards the adoption of supply chain management (SCM) relationships in construction," *Eur. J. Purch. Supply Manag.*, vol. 8, no. 3, pp. 173–183, Sep. 2002, doi: 10.1016/S0969-7012(02)00007-2.

[10] A. Gosselin, P. Blanchet, N. Lehoux, and Y. Cimon, "Collaboration Enables Innovative Timber Structure Adoption in Construction," *Buildings*, vol. 8, no. 12, p. 183, Dec. 2018, doi: 10.3390/buildings8120183.

[11] T. Karrbom Gustavsson, O. Samuelson, and Ö. Wikforss, "Organizing IT in construction: Present state and future challenges in Sweden," *J. Inf. Technol. Constr. ITcon*, vol. 17, pp. 520–534, 2012.

[12] J. F. Y. Yeung, A. P. C. Chan, and D. W. M. Chan, "The definition of alliancing in construction as a Wittgenstein family-resemblance concept," *Int. J. Proj. Manag.*, vol. 25, no. 3, pp. 219–231, Apr. 2007, doi: 10.1016/j.ijproman.2006.10.003.

[13] S. C. Gottlieb and K. Storgaard, "Flexible strategic partnerships in Danish construction," in *Proceedings 22nd Annual ARCOM Conference*, Birmingham, UK, 2006, pp. 415–424.

[14] P. Davis and P. Love, "Alliance contracting: adding value through relationship development," *Eng. Constr. Archit. Manag.*, vol. 18, no. 5, pp. 444–461, Sep. 2011, doi: 10.1108/09699981111165167.

[15] T. Singleton and K. Cormican, "The influence of technology on the development of partnership relationships in the Irish construction industry," *Int. J. Comput. Integr. Manuf.*, vol. 26, no. 1–2, pp. 19–28, Jan. 2013, doi: 10.1080/0951192X.2012.681907.

[16] V. Sundquist, K. Hulthén, and L. E. Gadde, "From project partnering towards strategic supplier partnering," *Eng. Constr. Archit. Manag.*, vol. 25, no. 3, pp. 358–373, Apr. 2018, doi: 10.1108/ECAM-08-2016-0177.

[17] S. D. Ellison and D. W. Miller, "Beyond ADR: Working Toward Synergistic Strategic Partnership," *J. Manag. Eng.*, vol. 11, no. 6, pp. 44–54, Nov. 1995, doi: 10.1061/(ASCE)0742-597X(1995)11:6(44).

[18] A. M. Anvuur and M. M. Kumaraswamy, "Conceptual Model of Partnering and Alliancing," *J. Constr. Eng. Manag.*, vol. 133, no. 3, pp. 225–234, Mar. 2007.

[19] S. Wu, G. Steel, and D. Greenwood, "Measuring the associations between collaborative working and project performance," in *Proceedings 25th Annual ARCOM Conference*, Nottingham, UK, 2009, pp. 939–48.

[20] A. B. Ngowi, "The role of trustworthiness in the formation and governance of construction alliances," *Build. Environ.*, vol. 42, no. 4, pp. 1828–1835, Apr. 2007, doi: 10.1016/j.buildenv.2006.02.013.

[21] R. Shields and K. West, "Innovation in clean-room construction: a case study of co-operation between firms," *Constr. Manag. Econ.*, vol. 21, no. 4, pp. 337–344, Jun. 2003.

[22] V. Albino and U. Berardi, "Green Buildings and Organizational Changes in Italian Case Studies: Green buildings and organizational changes," *Bus. Strategy Environ.*, vol. 21, no. 6, pp. 387–400, Sep. 2012, doi: 10.1002/bse.1728.

[23] R. Vrijhoef and H. de Ridder, "A systems approach to construction supply chain integration," in *Performance Improvement in Construction Management*, B. Atkin and J. Borgbrant, Eds. London: Routledge, 2009.

[24] W. Xuejian and S. Shusheng, "Research on Collaborative Mode of Prefabricated Construction Supply Chain Based on Supply-hub," *IOP Conf. Ser. Earth Environ. Sci.*, vol. 242, p. 062005, Mar. 2019, doi: 10.1088/1755-1315/242/6/062005.

[25] D. H. T. Walker and D. S. Johannes, "Construction industry joint venture behaviour in Hong Kong—designed for collaborative results?," *Int. J. Proj. Manag.*, vol. 21, no. 1, pp. 39–49, Jan. 2003.

[26] Z. Yu, C. Lu, and D. W. M. Chan, "Review of Joint Venture Studies in Construction," in *ICCREM 2017*, Guangzhou, China, 2017, pp. 139–149, doi: 10.1061/9780784481080.017.

[27] Y.-H. Lin and S. P. Ho, "Impacts of Governance Structure Strategies on the Performance of Construction Joint Ventures," *J. Constr. Eng. Manag.*, vol. 139, no. 3, pp. 304–311, Mar. 2013.

[28] J. M. Savolainen, A. Saari, A. Männistö, and K. Kähkonen, "Indicators of collaborative design management in construction projects," *J. Eng. Des. Technol.*, Aug. 2018.

[29] A. Haugen, P. A. Wondimu, J. Lohne, and O. Lædre, "Project Delivery Methods in Large Public Road Projects – A Case Study of E6 Jaktøyen - Sentervegen," *Procedia Eng.*, vol. 196, pp. 391–398, 2017, doi: 10.1016/j.proeng.2017.07.215.

[30] J. S. J. Koolwijk, C. J. van Oel, J. W. F. Wamelink, and R. Vrijhoef, "Collaboration and Integration in Project-Based Supply Chains in the Construction Industry," *J. Manag. Eng.*, vol. 34, no. 3, p. 04018001, May 2018, doi: 10.1061/(ASCE)ME.1943-5479.0000592.

[31] S. Mollaoglu-Korkmaz, L. Swarup, and D. Riley, "Delivering Sustainable, High-Performance Buildings: Influence of Project Delivery Methods on Integration and Project Outcomes," *J. Manag. Eng.*, vol. 29, no. 1, pp. 71–78, Jan. 2013, doi: 10.1061/(ASCE)ME.1943-5479.0000114.

[32] H. A. Mesa, K. R. Molenaar, and L. F. Alarcón, "Exploring performance of the integrated project delivery process on complex building projects," *Int. J. Proj. Manag.*, vol. 34, no. 7, pp. 1089–1101, Oct. 2016, doi: 10.1016/j.ijproman.2016.05.007.

[33] E. I. Daniel, C. Pasquire, G. Dickens, and H. G. Ballard, "The relationship between the last planner® system and collaborative planning practice in UK construction," *Eng. Constr. Archit. Manag.*, vol. 24, no. 3, pp. 407–425, May 2017, doi: 10.1108/ECAM-07-2015-0109.

[34] E. Osipova and P. E. Eriksson, "The effects of procurement procedures on joint risk management," in *Proceedings 25th Annual ARCOM Conference*, Nottingham, UK, 2009, pp. 1305–14.

[35] Z. Liu, H. Wang, and H. Li, "Model of Equipment Sharing between Contractors on Construction Projects," *J. Constr. Eng. Manag.*, vol. 144, no. 6, Jun. 2018.

[36] D. Yang, Q. He, Q. Cui, and S.-C. Hsu, "Organizational Citizenship Behavior in Construction Megaprojects," *J. Manag. Eng.*, vol. 34, no. 4, p. 04018017, Jul. 2018.

[37] A. Gale and J. Luo, "Factors affecting construction joint ventures in China," *Int. J. Proj. Manag.*, vol. 22, no. 1, pp. 33–42, Jan. 2004, doi: 10.1016/S0263-7863(03)00012-7.

[38] P. Löfgren and P. E. Eriksson, "Effects of collaboration in projects on construction project performance," in *Proceedings 25th Annual ARCOM Conference*, Nottingham, UK, 2009, pp. 595–604.

[39] A. E. Sparkling, S. Mollaoglu, and A. Kirca, "Research Synthesis Connecting Trends in Architecture, Engineering, and Construction Project Partnering," *J. Manag. Eng.*, vol. 33, no. 1, p. 04016033, Jan. 2017, doi: 10.1061/(ASCE)ME.1943-5479.0000481.

[40] M. E. J. Rutten, A. G. Dorée, and J. I. M. Halman, "How companies without the benefit of authority create innovation through collaboration," in *Proceedings 24th ARCOM conference*, Cardiff, United Kingdom, 2008, pp. 557–566.

I L S 2020
INTERNATIONAL CONFERENCE ON INFORMATION SYSTEMS, LOGISTICS & SUPPLY CHAIN
Austin, Texas April 22-24, 2020

Using Quality Function Deployment (QFD) Combined with the World Café Method in a Smart Cities Application

Jair Gustavo de Mello Torres [1,2], Neusa Maria de Andrade [1], Pedro Luiz de Oliveira Costa Neto [1]

[1] Paulista University (UNIP), São Paulo, Brazil
[2] SENAC, Professor, São José dos Campos, Brazil
{jair_gustavo@yahoo.com.br, neusa@agenciaweb.com.br, pedroluiz@plocn.com}

Abstract. Smart mobility is one of the dimensions of Smart City implementation and affects other dimensions of the city, such as aspects of citizens' quality of life. The purpose of this paper is to investigate the use of data generated in the diagnostic workshops of the new public transport model of the city of São José dos Campos - SP, through the World Café method, as QFD Voice of the Customer (VOC) to obtain the characteristics quality of the municipality's mobility. We conducted a case study of the eight diagnostic workshops held for the new public transport model.

Keywords: QFD; World Café; Smart Cities; Mobility as a Service.

1. Introduction

According to the United Nations, in 2018, it is estimated that 55.3% of the world's population lived in urban settlements. By 2030, urban areas are designed to house 60% of the world's people and one in three people will live in cities with at least half a million inhabitants. Understanding the key urbanization trends that are expected to develop in the coming years is crucial for the implementation of the 2030 Agenda for Sustainable Development, including the Sustainable Development Goal 11, to make cities and human settlements inclusive, safe, resilient and sustainable [1]. Although they represent only 2% of the world's surface area, urban areas consume more than 70% of the world's total resources [2]. Concern about “intelligence” in city management is particularly obvious in Latin America because it is one of the most urbanized regions in the world. By 2050, urbanization rates are expected to reach 90% in this region [3].

Smart Cities are defined by applying smart methods to build livable and sustainable cities [4]. In this context, smart urban mobility is a major topic because it integrates social capital, traditional transport, and modern information and communication technology (ICT) infrastructure to provide sustainable economic development and high quality of life [5]. The concept of smart mobility is based on reducing the inefficient use of private vehicles and increasing environmentally sustainable transport [6].

Advances have also transformed public participation in city planning and design, as citizens have greater access to information about what is happening in their communities and can play a more active role in urban management [7].

Federal Law no. 12,587 instituted the National Urban Mobility Policy (PNMU) in January 2012. The PNMU is based on principles such as the sustainable development of cities, equity in citizens' access to public transportation and the use of public circulation space. The law states that social participation is indispensable throughout the process. In this scenario the process of elaboration of the new urban mobility model of São José dos Campos [8].

The aim of this paper is to investigate the results of the use of data generated in the diagnostic workshops of the new public transport model of the city of São José dos Campos - SP, through the World Café method, as Voice of the Customer (VOC) of the QFD method for obtaining the quality characteristics of the municipality's mobility, within the concept of Smart Cities.

Thus, while this work has social implications, demonstrating the feasibility of using the QFD method to improve the quality of public services, it also contributes to a better understanding of the particularities of employing the method in a new context: Smart Cities. Therefore, this study suggests the use of citizen-centered procedures, such as World Café and Quality Function Deployment (QFD) methods, in municipal management processes and Smart Cities projects, in search of innovation in existing management processes in the municipal governments, integrating and interacting the intellectual capital, local culture and existing new technologies, as well as those that will come into existence, providing the full development of a Smart City. The use of the QFD method is a means of ensuring that citizens' needs expressed in diagnostic workshops will be considered in the new mobility model of the municipality.
This paper is divided into six sections. The introduction is the first section, which provides an overview of the article's theme. The second section reviews the literature on Smart Cities, Quality Function Deployment and the World Café method. The third section presents the methodological procedures. In the fourth section, the results are presented and discussed. The fifth section presents the final considerations of this paper. Finally, in the sixth section are the thanks.

2. Background

2.1. Smart Cities

The Smart City is a place that combines the real digital environment and community, has a high level of knowledge, belongs to a geographical area that shares knowledge; it relies on an information and communication technology (ICT) -based framework and optimizes knowledge management [9]. There are six dimensions in a smart city: economy, mobility, governance, environment, socializing and people [10].
Many challenges in the urban area put enormous pressure on the city and the transportation system. The urban logistics, in the context of a Smart City, is a very complex issue not only for its effects in the structure of the city but also as a main factor for the development of businesses in city area. To solve this problem, one solution is to change the way you organize a system that is dealing with mobility in the city. This new approach should start from the new Smart City concept and target all those coming from the Smart City goals. Mobility as a service is changing the way urban transportation is organized [11].
Mobility as a Service (MaaS) is a user-centric service that embraces advances in technology and ICT to offer customers multiple mobility solutions, conceptualizing travel differently. In this new context, people will have a wide list of options to choose from, based on public and private modes of transport, multiple needs and preferences, and a service that allows them to pursue more activities on the same schedule (multitasking) [12]. For a society that enjoys efficient urban mobility, it is necessary to create conditions that make it possible to move around, be it cars, people or cargo. In other words, urban mobility planning has an impact on urban cargo logistics and vice versa.

2.2. Quality Function Deployment (QFD)

Quality Function Deployment (QFD) is an input and output matrix-based system that enables you to transform customer desires into the design, process, and product requirements [13].
Although QFD is a recognized methodology for increasing customer satisfaction, the method has some limitations, such as difficulties in identifying needs, as "Voice of the Customer" may contain different ambiguities and meanings and not all have the same meaning, same perception of linguistic description. QFD can be combined with other methodologies and tools in a complementary way to gain flexibility [14].
The starting point for carrying out systematic deployments is the Voice of the Customer (needs and wants). Selecting QFD's assistive technique to obtain the most appropriate Voice of the Customer depends on the desired information and available budget. Qualitative techniques are most appropriate at this stage because they allow the generation of ideas and deepening from the product user [15].

2.3. World Café

The World Café method is conceptualized as a simple but powerful process of conversation to promote constructive dialogue, access to collective intelligence and create innovative possibilities for action, particularly in groups that are larger than those for which most traditional approaches to dialog is designed to accommodate [16].
The World Café format offers a way for the creative process to emerge and deepen participants' responses, while a structured methodology for participant dialogue and conversation, which includes one important assumption: that participants already have the experiences and knowledge [17].
The methodology has seven fundamental principles, namely:

1. Set the context;
2. Create a welcoming space;
3. Explore significant issues;
4. Stimulate the contribution of all;
5. Promote cross-pollination and connect different points of view;
6. Listen together to discover deeper patterns, perceptions, and issues;
7. Collect and share collective discoveries.

The World Café methodology is very useful for generating creative ideas or for building consensus. However, concerning solving problems of a technical nature, they have been less successful and stress that implementing the World Café method results can be difficult [18].

3. Methodology

In this section, we will describe the methodological procedures that guided the development of this work. As for the approach, the present research is qualitative. As for nature, it is applied research, since it aims to generate knowledge for practical application, directed to the solution of specific problems [19].
The research can be classified according to its general objectives. In this regard, current research is exploratory. Exploratory research aims to provide greater familiarity with the problem in order to make it more explicit or to make hypotheses [20].
As for the technical procedures used, the research is classified as a case study, which consists of a deep and exhaustive study of one or a few objects, to allow their broad and detailed knowledge. The research can also be classified as technical procedures as a documentary because it is analyzed the reports of the diagnostic workshops to elaborate on the new model of public transportation of São José dos Campos.
It is presented in Figure 1 as the World Café method is used in a combined way to QFD method.

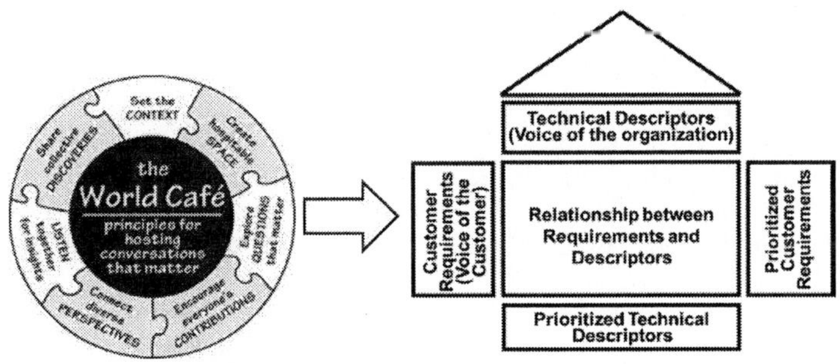

Figure 1: World Café as Voice of the Customer in Quality Matrix. Source: Prepared by the authors.

4. Results and Discussions

4.1. São José dos Campos

Located in Brazil, at a distance of about 100 km from the state capital of São Paulo, São José dos Campos is a medium-sized municipality with an estimated 702,866 inhabitants in 2019 and a total area of 1,099.41

km2 [20]. It is part of the metropolitan region of Vale do Paraíba and the North Coast. The municipality connects to the capital São Paulo by the highways BR 116 (Rodovia Presidente Dutra) and SP 070 (Ayrton Senna Highway / Governador Carvalho Pinto) and is also cut by SP 099 (Rodovia dos Tamoios), one of the main accesses to the North coast of São Paulo. It is also cut by a rail section, a variant of the former Central Railway of Brazil, which is currently operated for the transportation of cargo, under the concession system by the company MRS Logística [21].

4.2. Diagnostic Workshops of the New Public Transport Model

From May 3 to June 1, 2019, eight workshops were held open to the population, to listen to the population about how technological changes and the advent of transport by applications influence urban mobility and public transport systems and include it in the collective construction of the city's new public transport model. The methodology used in the workshops was the World Café [16]. Workshop responses are used in this paper as input data for the QFD application [21].

To allow the inclusion of greater diversity of segments of society, the São José dos Campos City Hall sent an invitation addressed to representatives of municipal, class, environmental, representative of organized civil society, universities, foundations and research institutes, supervisory and control bodies, transportation sector, large companies in the city and citizens in general interested in the subject, as well as a large publicity campaign in the municipal media [21].

In the first part of the event, there was a lecture by invited speakers with a presentation about the new concepts involving urban mobility, especially public transport, as well as the new technologies and operating models that are available. After the first lecture, the technicians from the Secretariat of Urban Mobility - SEMOB presented the data related to the city's Urban Mobility system, with emphasis on public transportation. The events took place in different regions of the city - south (two workshops), central (one workshop), east (one workshop), southeast (one workshop), north (two workshops) and west (one workshop) - presenting the same schedule on all four opportunities [21].

After the informative and didactic exhibitions, the workshop participants were invited to a café, part of the methodology adopted for the participatory dynamics, the “Café com Prosa”. Participatory dynamics occurred to obtain answers to two questions:

1) **“What are the facilities and difficulties encountered by those using the public transport system operating in the city?”,** The first question launched to be debated in two rounds of 10 (ten) minutes per table. The objective was to reach a consensus on three facilities and three most relevant difficulties raised in the discussion of each table.
2) **“What would make public transport more attractive? What are the main features that the new transport system should have?”,** was the second question worked out in two 10 (ten) minute discussion rounds by the groups, which consolidated the answers in features for the new system identified by a table.

At the end of the discussions, everyone was presented with the collection of the main topics raised by each group, consensus fruits, organized by thematic groups.

In addition to the table discussions, a panel called the "Parking Lot of Ideas" was created, in which people were able to post comments, ideas, and suggestions that they considered relevant and that were not addressed in the dynamic. This panel was available at all four workshops throughout the event. At the end of the four workshops, these ideas were collected, photographed and incorporated into the final report [21].

After completion of the eight workshops, all the files were photographed and systematized. The result of this systematization was made available in a report that was made available to the population on a website created specifically for the process of building the new public transport model of the municipality [21].

4.3. Data processing and results

In this section, we present how the results obtained by the World Café application are used as input data for the QFD application, as in a way they represent what, in circumstances more linked to a consumer market, would represent the Voice of the Customer (VOC) [22].

The data obtained from the World Café conversations, available in the report of the participatory workshops of the new São José dos Campos public transport model, were analyzed by the authors, who grouped them by their affinities and then named each group with a title that represented that set. For the

present work, as an illustration, we present only the data resulting from the first question asked at the World Café workshops regarding the difficulties in using the public transportation system operating in the city. In total, twenty-three needs were identified, which would compose the table of demanded qualities of the quality matrix.
The importance of the items that make up the quality demanded (IDi) was obtained by the number of times the item was mentioned during the dynamics of the World Café, in order to establish a prioritization of the needs presented by the citizens. The degrees of importance attributed by customers to the quality demanded items should be transformed into percentage weights. This procedure ensures that each block will have its weight correctly assigned and must be calculated by dividing the value of the amounts of each item by the sum of the amounts of all items [22].
Table 1 shows the result of applying the World Café as a tool to assist QFD to obtain Customer Voice (VOC), the importance of quality demanded items (IDi), and the relative weight of each importance.
Table 1 lists the 23 difficulties that, according to participants in the participatory workshops of the new public transport model, make it difficult to use the public transit system operating in São José dos Campos. The difficulties were obtained by applying the World Café and affinity analysis of the answers to question 1: "What are the facilities and difficulties encountered by those using the public transit system operating in the city"?

TABLE 1 - Calculation of the prioritization of demanded quality items (IDi).

			Degree of Importance (IDi)	Relative Weight
Public transportation	Bus capacity	Bus overcrowding at peak times	33	16,26
	Bus lines	Travel time	9	4,43
		Few bus lines compared to passenger demand	25	12,32
		Routes	11	5,42
		Alternative transport	13	6,40
		Shared transport expansion	1	0,49
	Transportation vouchers	Ticket value	16	7,88
		Few single tickets reload points	5	2,46
		Payment options	2	0,99
		Alternative single ticket	7	3,45
		School pass restrictions	2	0,99
	Quality	Punctuality	2	0,99
		Supervision and audit in companies	7	3,45
		Bus corridor surveillance	1	0,49
		Transportation quality (employee training)	4	1,97
	Infrastructure	Lack of integration of different modes	23	11,33
		Bus lanes	5	2,46
		Accessibility	9	4,43
		App	7	3,45
		Street maintenance	6	2,96
		Bike paths linking downtown neighborhood	1	0,49
		Bus comfort	4	1,97
	Bus stop	Bus Stop Infrastructure	10	4,93
		Total	203	

The importance of the demanded quality items (IDi) demonstrates that the greatest difficulty of travel, in the opinion of the participants, is "There are a lack of education and awareness campaigns regarding mobility in the city", with IDi = 12.78, followed by "Overcrowding in the buses at peak times ", with IDi = 9.02," Peak hour vehicle congestion ", with IDi = 7.00," Missing connection between existing bike paths ", with IDi = 7.00 and" Little amount in terms of passenger demand on available lines ", with IDi = 7.00.

Then, the quality characteristics were established through the unfolding of each of the difficulties mentioned in the workshops. The quality characteristics, presented in Table 2, are measurable aspects that evaluate the quality of the product or service. The quality relationship stage demanded with the quality characteristics complements the completion of the typical QFD Quality Matrix. The intensity of the relationship between the demanded quality items and the quality characteristics (DQij) was made using the scale from 1 to 9 (1 - weak; 3 - average; 9 - strong).

If most matrix relationships are weak, then the matrix should be reviewed, as the quality characteristics are not adequately translating to the quality demanded by customers. And if there are any items of quality demanded that do not relate to any item of quality characteristics, special attention should be given to identifying other quality characteristics that relate to them [22].

Note that the relationship between quality demanded and quality characteristics are good, as detailed in Figure 2. Most research relationships are correlated, with 134 strong correlations, 53 medium correlations, and 10 weak correlations.

From the definition of the relationship between the demanded quality items and the quality characteristics, the importance of each quality characteristic (IQj) was determined, considering, in addition to these relationships, the relative importance of the demanded qualities (IDi). The importance of each quality characteristic (IQj) allows us to identify which characteristics if developed, will have the greatest impact on customer satisfaction. Equation 1 was used to calculate (IQj):

$$IQj = \sum_{i=1}^{n} \frac{IDi.DQij}{100} \quad (1)$$

Table 2 details the quality characteristics raised for the São José dos Campos Mobility Plan and their respective IQj importance. The table was organized in decreasing order, highlighting the most important characteristics.

TABLE 2 - Calculation of the prioritization of quality characteristics IQj.

Quality Characteristics	IQj
Complaints Rate (Total Complaints / Total Passengers Transported)	18,21
Average travel time of users (number of passengers carried / travel time of each line)	17,79
The ratio of total passengers carried by some lines available	17,27
Number of connection points between different modes	17,13
Percentage of exclusive bus lanes by total lanes available	15,21
Ticket Value	14,60
Total number of buses running at peak times	11,47
Number of payment options	10,56
Number of transport voucher recharge points	8,90

Table 2, which details the importance of the characteristics of the quality demanded (IQj), shows that the "Complaints Rate (Total Complaints / Total Passengers Transported)", with IQj = 18.21, followed by "Average travel time of users (number of passengers carried / travel time of each line) ", with IQj = 17.79," Ratio of total passengers carried by number of lines available", with IQj = 17.27, are the most important quality characteristics.

The importance of each quality characteristic (IQj) allows us to identify which characteristics if developed, will have the greatest impact on customer satisfaction. That is if these characteristics are prioritized in the implementation of the new model of public transportation of the municipality will bring greater results to the demands of residents raised in the diagnostic workshops using the methodology of World Café.

Figure 2 shows the QFD Quality Matrix for the case in question.

			Total number of buses running at peak times	Ratio of total passengers carried by number of lines available	Average travel time of users (number of passengers carried / travel time of each line)	Number of payment options	Number of transport voucher recharge points	Ticket Value	Complaints Rate (Total Complaints / Total Passengers Transported)	Number of connection points between different modes	Percentage of exclusive bus lanes by total lanes available	Degree of Importance (IDi)	Relative Weight
Public transportation	Bus capacity	Bus overcrowding at peak times	9	9	9	1	3	9	9	9	9	33	16,26
	Bus lines	Travel time	9	9	9	3	3	9	9	9	9	9	4,43
		Few bus lines compared to passenger demand	9	9	9	3	3	9	9	9	9	25	12,32
		Routes	9	9	9	3	1	9	9	9	9	11	5,42
		Alternative transport	9	9	9	3	3	9	9	3	3	13	6,40
		Shared transport expansion	3	9	9	3	1	9	3	9	3	1	0,49
	Transportation vouchers	Ticket value	3	9	9	9	9	9	9	9	9	16	7,88
		Few single ticket reload points		9	3	9	9	3	9	9	3	5	2,46
		Payment options	1	9	9	9	9	9	9	9	9	2	0,99
		Alternative single ticket	1	9	9	9	9	9	9	9	3	7	3,45
		School pass restrictions		1				3	9	3	1	2	0,99
	Quality	Punctuality	9	9	9	9	3	3	9	9	9	2	0,99
		Supervision and audit in companies		3	9	9	9	9	9	9	3	7	3,45
		Bus corridor surveillance	1	9	9			3	9	9	3	1	0,49
		Transportation quality (employee training)	3	9	9	9		3	9	3	3	4	1,97
	Infrastructure	Lack of integration of different modes	3	9	9	9	3	3	9	9	9	23	11,33
		Bus lanes	3	9	9	9	3	3	9	9	9	5	2,46
		Accessibility	9	9	9	9	3	3	9	9	9	9	4,43
		App		3	9	9	9	9	9	9	1	7	3,45
		Street maintenance	1	9	9	3	3	3	9	9	9	6	2,96
		Bike paths linking downtown neighborhood		9	9	3	3	3	9	9	3	1	0,49
		Bus comfort	9	9	9	3	3	3	9	9	9	4	1,97
	Bus stop	Bus Stop Infrastructure	3	9	9	3	9	9	9	9	9	10	4,93
											Total	203	
		IQj	11,47	17,27	17,79	10,6	8,9	14,6	18,21	17,13	15,21		

Figure 2: Quality Matrix. Source: Prepared by the authors.

5. Conclusion

From the results obtained, it can be concluded that the combined use of the World Café and QFD methods proved to be effective for generating and prioritizing project client needs. It is clear that the QFD allows the solution of a limitation of the World Café method, which is the implementation of the results found. The World Café method, on the other hand, assists QFD in the difficulty of identifying needs, since the "Voice of the Client" may contain different ambiguities and meanings and not everyone has the same perception of linguistic description.

The application of QFD resulted in the prioritization of the 23 quality demands generated in the diagnostic workshops and 9 quality characteristics to evaluate the current public transport model of the municipality. These are measurable indicators that have a direct correlation with the needs reported by workshop participants.

The correlation analysis of the QFD method allowed the authors to analyze which needs raising by the residents in the workshops have the highest correlation with the unfolded characteristics. It also made it possible to verify which ones have a weak or nonexistent correlation. The need " School pass restrictions" should be analyzed with greater criteria by managers, as it presented the lowest correlation indexes.

By calculating the prioritization of quality characteristics (IQj), it is concluded that municipal managers should use mobility strategies that prioritize: "Complaint rate", "Average travel time of users" and "Ratio of total passengers carried by a number of lines available". It will be these indicators that, if developed by the municipal management, will provide greater satisfaction to users of municipal mobility.

The use of World Café combined with the QFD method, which seeks to listen to customer needs, enhances the view that Mobility as a Service - MaaS provides mobility solutions that reflect user needs. This conclusion reinforces that the method enables the citizen to be nailed within the context of Smart Cities.

As it was not found in the literature application of the World Café method integrated with QFD in a Mobility as a Service - MaaS context for Smart City applications, it can be concluded that the present study showed an innovation. Besides, the study shows a major contribution of World Café and QFD methods to the development of Smart Cities, as well as contributing to the strategic planning of the new mobility model of São José dos Campos-SP.

6. Acknowledgment

The authors would like to thank the Secretariat of Urban Mobility of São José dos Campos – SEMOB, São José dos Campos City Council for Urban Mobility - COMOB and SENAC São José dos Campos.

7. References

1. ONU. United Nations - Population Division of the Department of Economic and Social Affairs, https://population.un.org/wup/, Accessed in October (2019)
2. Buhrkal, K.; Larsen, A.; Ropke, S.: The Waste Collection Vehicle Routing Problem with Time Windows in a City Logistics Context. Procedia - Social And Behavioral Sciences. 39, 241-254. (2012)
3. De Halleux, M.; Estache, A.: How "smart" are Latin American cities?. ECARES Working Papers, 2018 (2018)
4. Chourabi, H., Nam, T., Walker, S., Gil-Garcia, J. R., Mellouli, S., Nahon, K., Pardo, T. A., Scholl, H. J.: Understanding Smart City Initiatives: An Integrative and Comprehensive Theoretical Framework. In: Proceedings of the 45th Hawaii International Conference on System Sciences, 2289-2297.
5. Cerutti, P. S., Martins, R. D., Macke, J., & Sarate, J. A. R.: "Green, but not as green as that": An analysis of a Brazilian bike-sharing system. Journal of Cleaner Production. 217, 185-193. (2019).
6. Zhang, L., Zhang, J., Duan, Z., Bryde, D.:Sustainable bike-sharing systems: Characteristics and commonalities across cases in urban China. Journal of Cleaner Production. 97, 124–133. (2015)
7. Batty, M.; Axhausen, K. W.; Giannotti, F.; Pozdnoukhov, A.; Bazzani, A.; Wachowicz, M.; Ouzounis, G.; e Portugali, Y.: Smart cities of the future. The European Physical Journal Special Topics. 214, 481-518. (2012)
8. Embarq Brasil: Sete Passos: Como construir um Plano de Mobilidade Urbana. Porto Alegre (2015)
9. Komninos, N., Intelligent Cities: Innovation, Knowledge Systems and Digital Spaces. London, Routledge, (2013)
10. Giffinger, R.; Fertner, C.; Kramar, H.; Meijers, E.: City-ranking of European medium-sized cities. Cent. Reg. Sci. Vienna UT. 1-12 (2007)
11. Nemtanu, F.; Schlingensiepen, J.; Buretea, D. Iordache, V.: Mobility as a service in smart cities. In: 9th International Conference for Entrepreneurship, Innovation and Regional Development, p.425-435, Comunicare.ro (2016)
12. Jittrapirom, P.; Caiat, V.; Feneri, A. M.; Ebrahim, S.; González, M. J. A.; Narayan, J.: Mobility as a Service: A Critical Review of Definitions, Assessments of Schemes, and Key Challenges. Urban Planning. 2, 13-25. (2017)
13. Costa Neto, P. L. O.; Canuto, S. A. Administração com Qualidade: Conhecimentos necessários para a gestão moderna. Blucher, São Paulo (2010)
14. Souza, V. H. A.; Miguel, P. A. Cauchick.: Aplicação do desdobramento da função qualidade em serviços: uma análise da literatura. Revista Produção Online. 17, 268-294 (2017)
15. Cheng, L. C.; Melo filho, L. R.: QFD: Desdobramento da Função Qualidade na Gestão de Desenvolvimento de Produtos. Blucher, São Paulo (2007)
16. Brown, J. ; Isaacs, D.: The World Café: dando forma ao nosso futuro por meio de conversações significativas e estratégicas. Cutrix, São Paulo (2007)
17. Kempnich, J.; Costanzo, C.: World Café for Leadership Development. Nurse Leader. 12, 98-101 (2014)
18. Lefika, P. T.; Mearns, M. A.: Adding knowledge cafés to the repertoire of knowledge sharing techniques. International Journal Of Information Management. 35, 26-32 (2015)
19. Gerhardt, T. E.; Silveira, D.T. Métodos de pesquisa. Plageder, (2009)
20. Gil, A. C. Como elaborar projetos de pesquisa. São Paulo, (2002)
21. Secretariat for Urban Mobility - SEMOB São José dos Campos, http://www.sjc.sp.gov.br/servicos/mobilidade-urbana/novo-transporte-publico/, Accessed in October (2019)
22. Ribeiro, J. L. D.; Echeveste, M. E.; Danilevicz, A. M. F. A Utilização do QFD na Otimização de Produtos, Processos e Serviços. FEENG/PPGEP/EE/UFRGS, Porto Alegre (2001)

I L S 2020

INTERNATIONAL CONFERENCE ON INFORMATION SYSTEMS, LOGISTICS & SUPPLY CHAIN
Austin, Texas April 22-24, 2020

Indoor Positioning based Data Management System for Smart Factory

Park Jin Sung[1], Lee Sung Jin[1], Jesus Jimenez[2], Kim Jun Woo[1]

[1] Dong-A University, Busan, South Korea
[2] Texas State Univeresity, San Marcos, United States
{jinsung0958@gmail.com, kairence@naver.com, Jesus.Jimenez@txstate.edu, kjunwoo@dau.ac.kr}

Abstract. The ultimate goal of smart factory is to utilize manufacturing resources more effectively by analyzing data collected from shop floor. However, many manufacturing companies still have significant trouble in collecting data relevant for operations management. Especially, movement of mobile resources such as human operators and material handling equipment have been not appropriately recorded within conventional ICT infrastructures. In this context, this paper aims to develop a novel data management system for collecting and managing the mobile resource movement data by applying modern indoor positioning technology.

Keywords: Indoor positioning, Smart factory, Mobile resource, Data collection, Structured data

1. Introduction

With the advent of the Industry 4.0 era, much attention is being paid to smart factory, which is obtained by integrating traditional manufacturing facilities with modern information and communication technology (ICT) infrastructures [1][2][3]. The ultimate goal of smart factory is to utilize manufacturing resources more effectively, and this can be achieved by using ICT capabilities for data collection and analysis [4]. For example, wireless sensor networks and internet of things (IoT) can be used for real-time data gathering [3][5], however, many manufacturing companies still have significant trouble in utilizing the raw data provided by such technologies. What is important is that many modern ICT infrastructures for real-time data gathering generate too much data that is not suitable for practical use. In this context, ICT infrastructures should be integrated with appropriate user interfaces and data processing capabilities.

This paper focuses on indoor positioning technology, which can be used to track the positions of mobile resources such as human operators and material handling equipments [6]. Inherently, indoor positioning equipment generates number streams of 3 dimensional coordinates of the tracked tags, which can be used to visualize the positions of human operators or objects in real-time. However, it is difficult for the managers of manufacturing companies to interpret and utilize the raw data. To overcome this limitation, this paper aims to propose an indoor positioning based data management system (IP-DMS) that enables the users to extract meaningful data from the raw data collected by indoor positioning equipment. To this end the indoor positioning equipment of IP-DMS is integrated with a user application which enables the users to define event to track and collect the event-related data, in more structured form than the raw data. For example, the user application of IP-DMS can be used to collect simple descriptive statistics or log data. Therefore, it is expected that the indoor positioning equipment can be utilized more effectively for operations management in manufacturing environment. The remainder of this paper is organized as follows. Section 2 provides a brief literature review on indoor positioning technologies and Section 3 outlines the overall concepts and structures of IP-DMS. Section 4 illustrates the prototype of IP-DMS, and Section 5 concludes this paper and suggests some future research topics.

2. Indoor Positioning Technology for Tracking Mobile Resources

In recent, many manufacturing companies utilizes POP (point of production) system to track the position of materials. Typically, POP systems identify the position of material by applying tag and reader based technologies, such as barcode and RFID (radio frequency identification) [7]. In order to recognize position of material, tag attached to material must be detected by reader. Moreover, the information about position of materials can be used to monitor and control manufacturing processes. Similarly, information about position of mobile resources such as human operator can be useful for operations management in shop floor, however, this was not appropriately considered in existing information systems.

What is important is that tag and reader based technologies are not suitable for tracking mobile resources. First, they can identify position of physical objects only at discrete times. In other words, it is difficult to continuously track the position of mobile resources by using barcode or RFID. Second, recognition procedure can cause significant inconveniences of human operator, since it requires additional motions that do not contribute to perform manufacturing processes. In this context, this paper aims to apply indoor positioning technology to develop IP-DMS.

The objective of indoor positioning is to locate the position of a physical object inside buildings by applying wireless communication technology. Indoor positioning technologies can be categorized into 2 main types, active and passive. In active technologies, the position of target object is determined by using electronic devices that can recognize the signals generated from the object. In contrast, target object in passive technologies must be equipped with capabilities for determining its own location. Examples of active indoor positioning technology include Active Badge [8] and Active Bat [9] of AT&T that utilize ultrasonic waves, RADAR [10] of MicroSoft that utilizes propagation delay of radio signals, and PAL (Precision Asset Location) system of Multispectral Solutions, Inc., which is based on ultra wide-band (UWB) communications [11][12], etc. On the contrary, Cricket Location System [13] of MIT is an example of passive indoor positioning technology.

UWB communication is a kind of wireless communication technology, which uses a bandwidth of higher than 500Mhz or has non-bandwidth (bandwidth corresponding to the center frequency) of more than 20% [14]. Wider bandwidth can increase the resolution of indoor positioning and makes it possible to recognize multipath signals. Moreover, UWB technology can be used for precise indoor positioning, since it is less affected by channel fading. IEEE 802.15.4a is a technological standard for UWB communication, and its main objective is to overcome the problems related with accuracy of distance measurement, stability of communication range, recognition of multipath effect, interference with other wireless communications, and mobility, etc [15][16]. According to the technological standards for UWB communication established by Task Group 4h, there are 2 physical layers (PHYs), Chirp Spread Spectrum UWB (CSS-UWB) and Impulse Radio UWB (IR-UWB) [16][17]. Among them, IR-UWB, which emits signals at -41dBm/MHz in 3-10 GHz bandwidth, is more suitable for low powered wideband communications [18]. In this paper, we use UWB based indoor positioning devices to develop IP-DMS.

3. Indoor Positioning based Data Management System

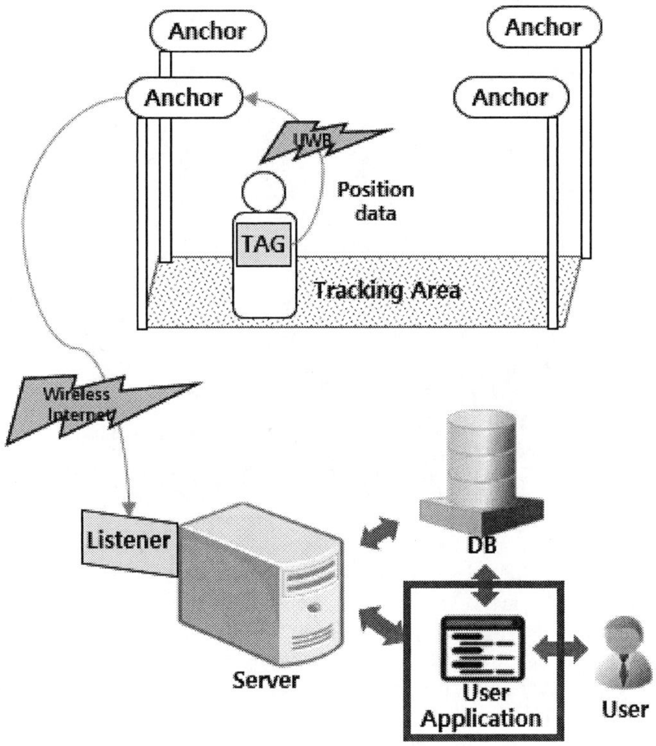

Figure 1: Main components of IP-DMS

Figure 1 shows the overall structures of IP-DMS proposed in this paper. Firstly, anchor, tag and listener in Figure 1 are physical devices used to recognize and collect raw real-time position data. In IP-DMS environment, human operators or physical objects that need to be tracked are provided with tags, small objects for identification. Anchor is an electronic device used to recognize the positions of tags in real-time. That is, the anchors can locate the 3 dimensional coordinate values of tacking objects, human operators or physical object, during tacking phase. In order to obtain precise position data, we deploy 4 anchors and the area created by them is called tracking area in this paper. In other words, the anchors are used to collect the position data for tags inside the tracking area in real-time. Moreover, the position data of tag is transferred to the anchors via UWB communication.

The anchors transfer the recognized position data to the listener connected to server computer as shown in the lower part of Figure 1, where listener is also an electronic device used for communication between anchors and server computer. After the listener processes the input signal from anchors and transfers the position data to server computer, the raw data can be used for visualization or data accumulation. In addition, the user application and DB are used for visualization and data accumulation, respectively.

Figure 2 illustrates the example of indoor positioning devices manufactured by DecaWave company, and they are used to develop IP-DMS in this paper. Note that these devices can communicate with each other via UWB communication and they can be used to implement active type indoor positioning. We can see 12 devices in Figure 2 and all of them can be used as tag, anchor and listener. For example, in order to track a single human operator, at least 6 devices including 1 tag, 4 anchors and 1 listener are required.

Figure 2: Example of indoor positioning devices

Figure 3 depicts the entire workflow of IP-DMS proposed in this paper. The first 3 steps, including installation and setting, tag and anchor registration, and tracking area detection, are required for initial configuration of the system. When these steps are completed, the position data of tags are transferred to the server computer and it can be visualized in user application.

In order to collect structured data via indoor positing devices, user has to define the events to track. An event to track is a pre-defined movement of the tracking object, human operator or physical objects in manufacturing facility. For example, entrance into a zone, exit from a zone and stay in a zone can be defined as event to tracks. The information on the events to track are stored in DB, and event-related data can be collected after those events are registered to the system. The event-related data is data in structured form, which is extracted from raw real-time position data by using user application. In more detail, user application collects event-related data whenever an individual event to track occurs. For example, the user application can be used to collect simple statistics such as time stamp, frequencies and durations for the registered events to track. Moreover, the occurrence records of events to track can be used to generate event log data. Furthermore, the user application of IP-DMS provides functionalities for reporting and analysis of event-related data and log data, which enables the users to make operational decisions in an effective manner.

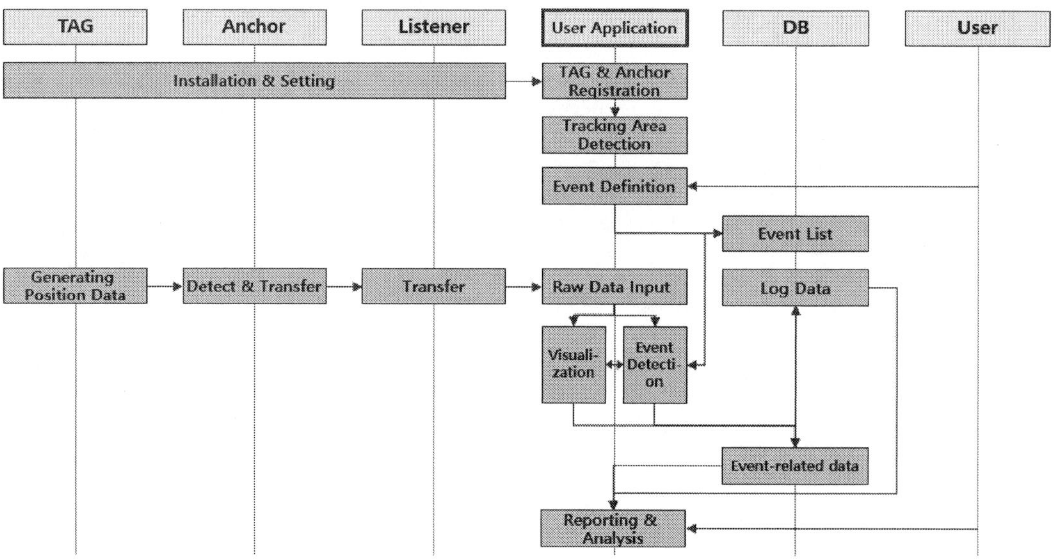

Figure 3: Workflow of IP-DMS

The details of event to track can be found in Figure 4. As explained earlier, tracking area is a physical area created by 4 anchors, and it is visualized in the user application after initial system configuration. Moreover, a tracking object is displayed as a point or simple icon, and its movement can be monitored in the tracking area of the user application in real-time.

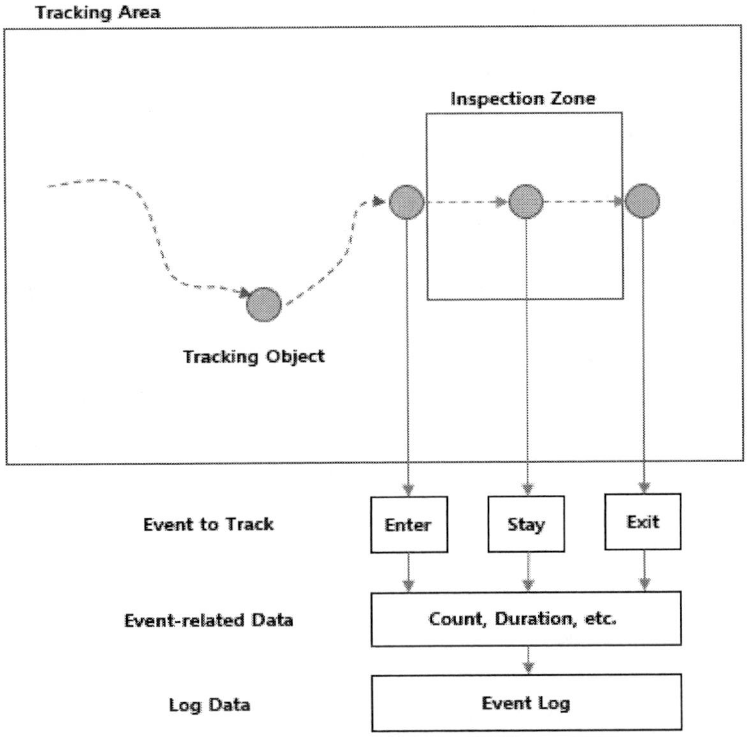

Figure 4: Event-based data processing and collection

In order to collect structured data, user has to define appropriate events to track by using the user application, and an event to track in this paper is based on the concept of inspection zone. As shown in Figure 4, an inspection zone is a user-defined sub area within the tracking area. Moreover, each event to track has to be associated with an inspection zone, which means that inspection zone should be created before defining event to track. Therefore, inspection zone should be a meaningful sub area within tracking area. For example, working area for a specific operation or storage area for materials can be defined as inspection zone.

For an individual inspection zone, movements such as entrance, exit and stay can be defined as event to track. Similarly, users can choose relevant event-related data such as time stamp, frequency and duration for each event to track. Note that the event to track and types of event-related data for an inspection zone can be defined by user flexibly.

During tacking phase, the movement of tracking object is displayed within the user application in real-time. Moreover, the user application continuously determines if any registered event to track occurs. Whenever an event occurs, one instance of event-related data is created and stored in DB. The event-related data can be used not only to extract simple statistics such as frequency and average duration, but also to create event log data for advanced use.

4. Prototype Implementation

Figure 5 depicts the design of user application for IP-DMS, developed in C# language. We can see the virtual tracking area under Tacking Area tab of main pane, where green circle and incarnadine rectangle indicate tracking object and inspection zone, respectively. After the indoor positioning equipment is set up, user can initiate the tracking task of user application by clicking the start button under the menu. Then, the tracking object automatically appears if the associated mobile resource is inside the real tracking area. On the contrary, inspection zone should be created by user. To this end, user has to click the inspection zone button in the right side and draw a rectangle within the virtual tracking area in a click and drag manner. Moreover, user can move a created inspection zone from its original place to another by dragging it. The icon in the upper left side of the inspection zone indicate that this inspection zone is associated with a stay type simple event. Moreover, user can create such events by clicking a button for appropriate type of event in the right side and choosing an inspection zone which the event will be assigned to. Note that events and inspection zones must be created before initiating the tracking task.

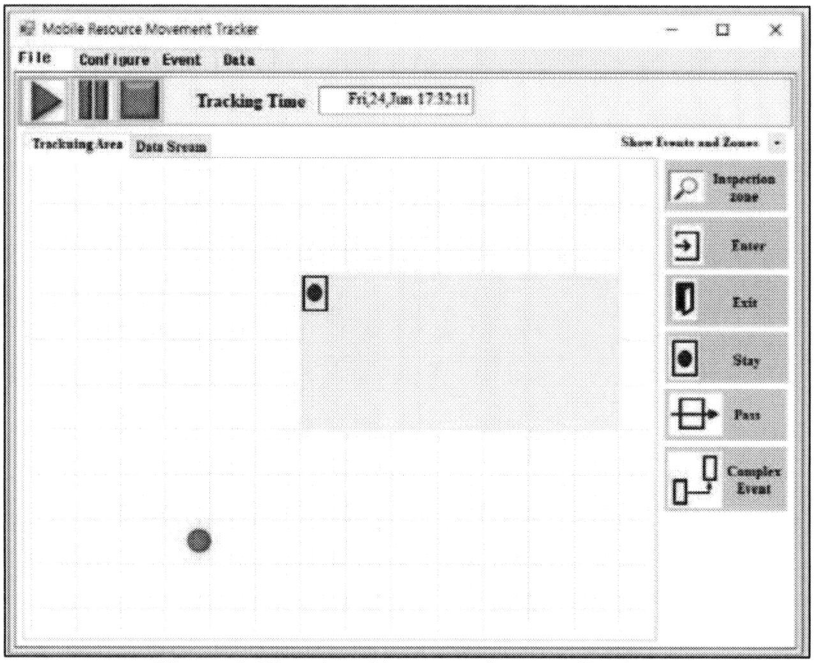

Figure 5: Virtual tracking area of user application

In this paper, we apply the prototype of IP-DMS to measure processing time of a simple manual task. It is well-known that processing time of a task or a process is an important input parameter for performance evaluation or further analysis. Especially, variation of processing times can significantly affect the performance measure of manufacturing systems. Nevertheless, processing times are often assumed to be constant in many shop floors. Similarly, the standard processing time of the manual task was known to be 210 seconds. The manual task is performed at a workbench by a single human operator, and raw materials for this task is stored at storage box apart from the workbench. Hence, the human operator has to bring the materials to the workbench before performing the task. The human operator stays in front of workbench during he performs the task. When the task is finished, the human operator leaves from workbench to transport the processed materials to another place.

In order to measure processing time of aforementioned task, we installed 4 anchors around the workbench and chose the working place as inspection zone by using user application. After the components of IP-DMS are configured, we observed the human operator's stay time for the inspection zone. In other words, we assumed that processing time is equivalent to the stay time for the workbench. Hence, the human operator was provided with a tag, and we tracked the position of the operator during he performs the manual task 10 times. Especially, this paper focuses on the human operator's stay time for the inspection zone and Table 1 summarizes the observation result. We can see that the processing time has a certain degree of variation in that standard deviation is 17.13, though its average, 222.53, is similar with the standard processing time, 210. This means that assumption of constant processing time is not appropriate for this manual task. Furthermore, such observation data can be used to determine the type of statistical distribution that the processing time follows. The descriptive statistics and statistical distribution can be used as input for further analysis such as performance evaluation. Consequently, the proposed system will contribute to perform a wide range of analysis for operations management in more effective manner.

Table 1. Observed processing times

Repetition	Stay Time(s)
1	242.5350
2	233.5331
3	213.5088
4	198.5256
5	215.9537
6	237.5412
7	231.3251
8	243.1452
9	209.4711
10	199.7230
Average	222.53
Standard deviation	17.13
Max	243.15
Min	198.53

5. Conclusions and Future Research Topics

Recently, we can collect a wide range of digital data by applying modern ICT technologies, and indoor positioning is one of them. However, such technologies often generate a huge amount of raw data continuously, and it is difficult for the practitioners to interpret and utilize it effectively. In this context, the modern ICT technologies for digital data collection should be integrated with appropriate capabilities for data manipulation and processing. Especially, this paper proposes an indoor positioning based application, IP-DMS, which supports to collect structured data flexibly. Consequently, it is expected that the proposed system will help the managers in manufacturing companies to make decisions on operational management in more effective manner.

Nevertheless, development of IP-DMS is currently in conceptual design phase, and the details of IP-DMS should be further refined in future. Firstly, intuitive user interfaces for defining inspection zone, event to track and event-related data are required for practical use. Secondly, data models for IP-DMS should be carefully designed so that various entities and data can be utilized effectively. Especially, IP-DMS should provide various types of event to track and event-related data that can be applied to a wide range of manufacturing companies. Moreover, this paper considers only simple event, which contains only one event to track. On the contrary, tracking complex event, a series of two or more events to track, can be more useful in many practical manufacturing environments. Thus, we plan to further refine and extend the concepts of event to track and event-related data in future. Finally, the reporting and analysis functionalities of IP-DMS also should be better organized. Currently, only simple descriptive statistics are considered in prototype of IP-DMS, however, it is expected that more systematic data can be collected if the concepts of event to track are extended appropriately. For example, let's assume that an inspection condition is given to an event to track, such as "duration time is longer than 30 seconds" for stay event. Then, the user application collect data for this stay event if and only if the condition is met. Analysis for log data created by the user application is another valuable research topic in that it can be utilized to extract frequent sequence of events or diagnose the desirability of operations of manufacturing resources. The analysis techniques for log data such as sequence mining and process mining can be promising approaches for handling the log data in IP-DMS. The authors will apply the prototype of IP-DMS to real manufacturing environments and continue to enhance the concepts and functionalities of IP-DMS.

6. Acknowledgements

This research was supported by the KIAT(Korea Institute for Advancement of Technology) grant funded by the Korea Government(MOTIE: Ministry of Trade Industry and Energy). (No. N0002429).

7. References

1. Radiziwon, A., Bilberg, A., Bogers, M., Madsen E.S.: The Smart Factory: Exploring Adaptive and Flexible Manufacturing Solutions. Procedia Engineering, 69, 1184--1190 (2014)
2. Longo, F., Nicolettie, L., Padovano, A.: Smart Operations in Industry 4.0: A Human-centered Approach to Enhance Operators' Capabilities and Competencies within the New Smart Factory Context. Computers and Industrial Engineering, 113, 144--159 (2017)
3. Kim, J. W., Park, J. S., Kim, S. K.: Application of FlexSim Software for Developing Cyber Learning Factory for Smart Factory Education. Multimedia Tools and Applications, forthcoming.
4. Kusiak, A.: Smart Manufacturing. International Journal of Production Research, 56, 508--517 (2018)
5. Lee J.: Smart Factory Systems. Informatik-Spektrum, 38, 230--235 (2015)
6. Du, P., Zhang, S., Zhong, W. D., Chen, C., Yang, H., Alphones, A., Zhang, R.: Real-time Indoor Positioning System for a Smart Workshop using White LEDs and a Phase-difference-of-arrival Approach. Optical Engineering, 58, 084112 (2019)
7. Want, R., Hopper, A., Falcao, V., Gibbons, J.: The Active Badge Location System. ACM Transaction on Information System, 10, 91--102 (1992)
8. Lee, S., Nam, S. J., Lee, J. K.: Real-time Data Acquisition System and HMI for MES. Journal of Mechanical Science and Technology, 26, 2381—2388 (2012)
9. Harter, A., Hopper, A., Steggles, P., Ward, A., Webster, P.: The Anatomy of a Context-Aware Applications. Proceedings of 5th Annual ACM/IEEE International Conference on Mobile Computing and Networking, 59--68 (1999)
10. Bahl, P., Padmanabhan, V. N.: RADAR: An Inbuilding RF-based User Location and Tracking System. Proceedings of IEEE Infocom, 775--784 (2000)
11. http://www.multispectral.com
12. Fontana, R. J., Richley, E., Barney, J.: Commercialization of an Ultra Wideband Precision Asset Location System. Proceedings of IEEE Conference on Ultra Wideband System and Technologies, 369--373 (2003)
13. Priyantha, N. B., Chakraborty, A., Balakrishnan, H.: The Cricket Location-Support System. Proceedings of the 6th Annual International Conference on Mobile Computing and Networking, 32--43 (2000)
14. http://www.fcc.gov/oet/info/rules
15. Sahinoglu, Z., Gezici, S., Guvenc, I.: Ultra-Widebank Positioning Systems. Cambridge, New York (2008)
16. IEEE Standard 802.15.4a-2007
17. IEEE Standard 802.15.4-2011
18. Joshi, M.: Ultra Wide Bandwidth. Proceedings of 2nd International Conference on Education Technology and Computer, 374--378 (2010)

I L S 2020
INTERNATIONAL CONFERENCE ON INFORMATION SYSTEMS, LOGISTICS & SUPPLY CHAIN
Austin, Texas April 22-24, 2020

Decision-Making in Coffee Supply Chains: An AHP application Considering Minas Gerais Case, Brazil

Paula Ferreira da Cruz Correia[1], João Gilberto Mendes do Reis [2]

[1] Universidade Paulista – RESUP/PPGEP, São Paulo, Brazil
[2] Universidade Paulista – RESUP/PPGEP, São Paulo, Brazil; UFGD, PPGA, Dourados, Brazil
{paulafecruz@gmail.com, betomendesreis@msn.com}

Abstract. The growing demand for food has led agribusiness to become one of the main focuses of the economy. In Brazil, this market has a great impact due to the fact that the country is one of the largest producers of food and agricultural products. Moreover, the country is the largest producer and exporter of coffee worldwide. With this scenario mind, this study aims to determine which decision factors influence the quality and production of Brazilian coffee. To this end, a Multicriteria Decision-Making was conducted using the Analytical Hierarchy Process. This method adopts paritarian comparisons of several criteria based in a priority scale establish considering data analysis and expert judgments. As the result of this work, it can be emphasized that the most prominent criterion was marketing and the best alternative of the Brazilian Coffee is selling to premium market (organic/gourmet).

Keywords: AHP, Coffee Production, Logistics, Coffee Quality, Multicriteria Method.

1. Introduction

The increase in global demand for food transforms the agribusiness in one of the main sectors of the economy. In Brazil, for instance, agribusiness responds for 21.1% of total GDP [1, 2] and the country has expressive global participation in the production of food and agricultural products [3]. Moreover, Brazil is one of the largest exporters of products such as grains, cereals, fruits and so on and is the largest producer and exporter of coffee worldwide [4, 5]. Only coffee production reached 82,355 thousand bags (60 Kg) in 2018 [6].

The supply chains of products marketed were abundantly explored and studied by entities which mediate these businesses, presenting several models about their use. On the other hand, the producers of these negotiated goods did not take part in those studies and their production chain is still little explored [7] .Based on the lack of studies on the subject, the development of research to highlight the processes and analyze, within the producers, how the coffee production chain behaves in the national and international market in relation to marketing, is of great interest.

There is information associated with the production and logistics of coffee grain, but they are generic. A study related to the largest producing state in Brazil, Minas Gerais, is relevant and the participation of specialists in this geographic region makes the results as close as possible to reality.

The results of Brazilian agribusiness are related to abundant rainfall, which offers an ideal environment for the cultivation of many products. However, many of these food supply chains suffer from infrastructure problems, low added value and absence of agroindustries. Sometimes agribusiness can suffer from the lack

of government incentives or too much help from it, what, on the other hand, do not encourage sustainable activity practices and only collaborate with fostering to remedy any problems [8].
Brazilian coffee is a typical case since it is exported as green coffee, which has low added value [9, 10]. Furthermore, some obstacles are interposed along with the processes involving the production and sale of it. These are factors that directly or indirectly interfere in the way the grain will be produced or in the way it will be marketed. However, there are some factors that favor the form of production or means of commercialization.
In an attempt to draw a scenario with the obstacles and opportunities which are part of this environment, research was undertaken in order to point to this situation. To do so, the present study aims to determine which decision factors influence the quality and production of Brazilian coffee in a specific region, the state of Minas Gerais.
To outline the profile of the obstacles faced, a multicriteria analysis was used as methodology, making paritarian comparisons and establishing a priority scale. This method is based on data analysis and expert judgments on the subject, making it possible to make decisions when there are several criteria involved.
This work is divided into sections. Shortly after this introduction is presented the section about material and methods, which is subdivided into site characterization and data collection, using the multicriteria decision method of the Analytic Hierarchy Process (AHP), problem definition and decision tree. Then it presents results and discussion and is finished with conclusions and outlooks.

2. Materials and Methods

2.1. Analytic Hierarchy Process (AHP)

Analytic Hierarchy Process (AHP) is a method developed by Thomas L. Saaty in the 1970's to deal with multicriterial analysis. It conducts comparisons and establishes weights based on a priority scale. The comparisons are made through judgments of specialists on the topic [11]. It allows decision making when there are several criteria involved. Reis et al (2016) [12] suggest that AHP can be used to solve problems associated with logistics and strategies. In order to use the AHP method, it is necessary to divide a problem in different parts [13]:

- (1) the problem is defined and what competencies would be necessary to elucidate it are established;
- (2) the decision tree is constructed considering the objective to be achieved and the valuation criteria are constructed hierarchically;
- (3) a matrix is constructed for pairison comparison, in which the upper level should be analyzed with their respective lower levels;
- (4) the priority scale of the comparisons is used to indicate the weights and priorities of the immediate lower level.

The specialists who participate in the study with the AHP methodology assign weights to each criterion established by the available bibliography. Such specialists are people directly involved in the production processes and by acquired experiences are able to assign a greater or lesser weight to the criteria that will be presented in the study.

2.2. Problem definition and Decision Tree

In this article, the purpose of using the AHP method is to determine which decision factors influence the decisions in coffee supply chains. Based on literature and interviews, Table 1, we established the criteria which affect the decision-making process: Marketing (M) - negotiation, price and reliability; Logistics/Distribution (L/D) - storage, transportation and handling; Rural Production (RP) - cost of inputs, climate, soil quality and mechanization; Type (T) - standard, organic, specialty and premium.

Table 1: Description of the literature used to assist in the assignment of criteria weights in parity comparisons

Source	Marketing	Logistics / Distribution	Rural Production	Type
Caldeira et al (2017)	X			X
CECAFE (2019)	X		X	X
CEPEA-ESALQ/USP (2019)			X	X
CONAB (2019)			X	X
Correa and Ramos (2010)		X		
Da Cruz Correia (2019)	X	X	X	X
FAO (2019)			X	X
Gelaw et al (2016)	X			X
IBGE (2016)		X	X	X
ICO (2019)	X		X	X
Läderach et al (2011)				
Levy et al (2016)	X		X	X
Machado Filho et al. (2019)	X			
MAPA (2019)		X	X	X
Minter et al (2018)	X			X
Patino et al (2013)		X		
Producers	X	X	X	X
Santos et al (2019)	X			
Weber (2011)	X		X	
WIPO (2017)			X	X

After the problem was defined, a decision tree was built, Figure 1. The decision tree presents the objective, criteria and subcriteria and indicates the alternatives. The variables of the decision model were established, and the Expert Choice software was used to analyze the data.

2.3. Place of Research, Judgments and Calculations

The study was conducted considering the coffee supply chains of Minas Gerais, a major Brazilian production state which accounts for about 82% of the exported volume of the country [14].

To establish the weights was considered the literature and information from representatives of two exporter companies and one big farmer. Those are people directly linked to grain production and their opinion reinforces the information found in the literature. Furthermore, the material provided by the International Coffee Organization-ICO (2019) [6], Council of exporters of coffee of Brazil – CECAFE (2019) [5], Brazilian Institute of Geography and Statistics-IBGE (2019) [2]and Ministry of Agriculture, Livestock and Supply-MAPA (2019) [4] were used. The AHP was calculated using the Expert Choice software v.11®.

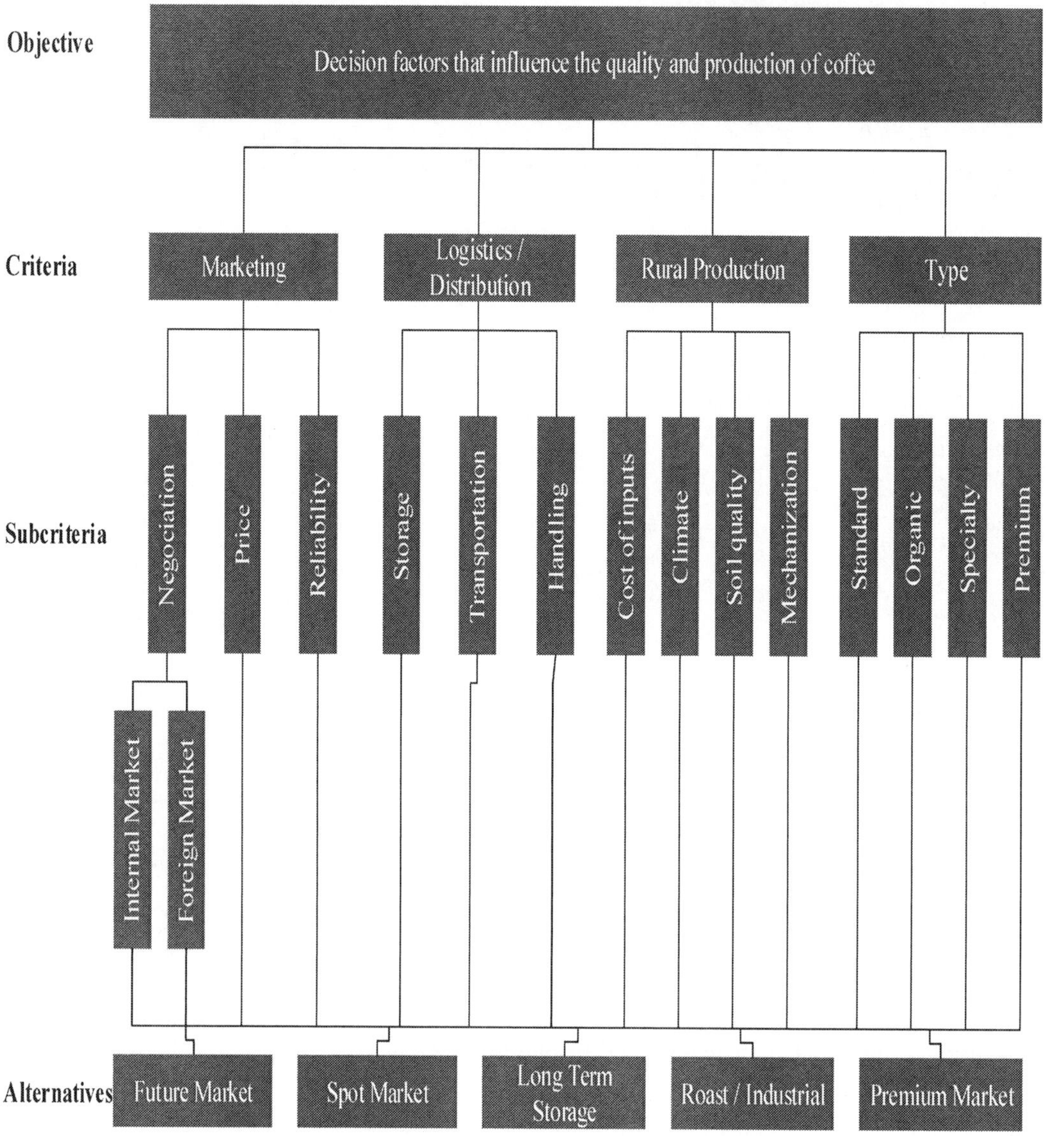

Figure 1: Hierarchical decision model for coffee quality and production.

3. Results and Discussion

3.1. Overall Result

In order to answer to the objective of this work, Table 2 summarizes the main results obtained using the AHP method.

Table 2: Main results versus criteria and alternatives with respective weight

Criteria	Weight	Alternative	Weight
Marketing	0.403	Future Market	0.171
Logistics / Distribution	0.235	Long Term Storage	0.201
Rural Production	0.201	Spot Market	0.144
Type	0.161	Roast / Industrialization	0.189
		Premium Market (organic/gourmet)	0.294

The criterion with the highest weight in the decision model was Marketing (0.403), followed by Logistics/Distribution (0.235), Rural Production (0.201) and Type (0.161). Given that, the results show that the best option for producers is to sell coffee in the Premium Market (Organic/Gourmet) (0.294).
The premium market is based on product quality and plantation location. Such factors directly interfere with the marketing work carried out, which labels the product as something different and with a superior quality among the various options available in the market [15].
The quality certifications are offered in a limited way, giving the coffee an even higher status, not counting the predicates that make it a premium coffee [16]. This type of premium / organic niche is taking a bigger share of the market as consumers become more demanding [17].

3.2 Criteria, Subcriteria and alternatives

Regarding the whole results of the AHP approach, Table 2 presents the values of the comparisons of each criterion, subcriteria and alternatives and the results.

Table 3: Criteria, subcriteria and alternatives weights

Criteria	Subcriteria		Alternatives				
			Future Market	Long Term Storage	Spot Market	Roast / Industrial	Premium Market
Marketing (0.403)	Negociation (0.540)		0,070	0,272	0,165	0,099	0,395
	Price (0.163)	Internal Market (0.125)	0,083	0,166	0,083	0,260	0,408
		Foreign Market (0.875)	0,118	0,246	0,118	0,064	0,453
	Reliability (0.297)		0,407	0,071	0,186	0,119	0,218
Logistics / Distribution (0.235)	Storage (0.333)		0,262	0,416	0,123	0,105	0,093
	Transportation (0.140)		0,167	0,167	0,167	0,333	0,167
	Handling (0.528)		0,143	0,230	0,121	0,286	0,220
Rural Production (0.201)	Cost of Inputs (0.215)		0,127	0,190	0,165	0,190	0,329
	Climate (0.490)		0,167	0,167	0,167	0,167	0,333
	Soil Quality (0.106)		0,167	0,167	0,167	0,167	0,333
	Mechanization (0.189)		0,231	0,231	0,231	0,231	0,077

Type (0.161)	Standard (0.068)	0,130	0,260	0,130	0,408	0,071
	Organic (0 .529)	0,099	0,105	0,102	0,301	0,393
	Specialty (0.268)	0,09	0,127	0,130	0,283	0,370
	Premium (0.134)	0,083	0,166	0,083	0,260	0,408

3.2.1 Marketing

Marketing (0.403) was the criterion which most stood out in the decision-making model. Hence, it is possible to infer that coffee is a commodity that suffers the influence of subcriteria such as negotiation, price and reliability. Marketing revolves around the way coffee production is seen by its potential buyers and how this impression impacts consumers [18].
A classic case that can be used as an example refers to Colombian coffee. The Government of that country makes a strong campaign in order to establish a brand of its coffee worldwide. The quality of the grain is really very good since the country is favored by climate and relief. But the divulgation of the production process leads its buyers to believe that the fact of using water in the process of preparing the grain for drying makes it of better quality[19].
It also occurs in some productive properties in Brazil, where they make use of water to pulper the grain and still continue this process to expedite the fermentation by advancing the drying stage.
Looking at the background of the sub-criteria associated with Marketing, it can be noted that, with the exception of reliability, which is higher for future markets, all other sub-criteria are higher for the premium market.

3.2.2 Logistics and Distribution

The second criterion influencing the quality and coffee production was logistics and distribution (0.235). Brazil has a poor logistics system where transportation is carried out by the road modal and most of the roads are not suitable to withstand the heavy traffic of vehicles, offering a precarious quality [20].
Most of the coffee, mostly, is produced in the region of Minas Gerais, a state which has no communication with the sea, increasing the difficulty and distance to drain this production as export. Long distances associated with the deterioration of the pavement of the roads can influence the quality of the grain, which needs some care to remain intact and, in the conditions, suitable for consumption. Inadequate storage conditions also strongly influence the quality of the coffee. The grain must remain without contact with moisture, sheltered from the weather in order to keep its properties until the final consumer. This is the subcriterion of greatest impact [21].

3.2.3 Rural Production

The third most relevant criterion is Rural production (0.201). This criterion is associated with the costs of input, climate, soil quality and mechanization of the process. Among the sub-criteria presented, the most prominent is the climate. Brazil is a country that benefited by its reliefs and rainfall.
These factors give the coffee a higher quality. The higher the altitude and the higher the rainfall index, the better the quality of the grain produced [2, 22].
The climate, undoubtedly, has a very strong influence on grain production. This fact can be reaffirmed if a comparison of Brazilian coffee with the Colombian is performed. Colombia is a small country in extension, but very strong in coffee production, having a considerable volume in relation to its territory.

3.2.4 Type

Eventually, the production Type (0.161), kind of coffee is the fourth and less important criterion. It is related to the possible ways in which coffee can be produced. Currently, Minas Gerais produces standard coffee, organic, specialty and premium. With the exception of standard coffee in the roast process, all other types of coffee are more viable in relation to quality and production for the Premium Market alternative. The

Premium Market is a niche that is presenting significant growth in the marketplace. The sales in this type of market are something lucrative, with demanding consumers willing to pay a higher price for a higher quality product[15, 17].

4. Conclusions and Outlooks

This article covered in its objective the determination of decision-factors which influence coffee commercialization. To do so, it was traced to a scenario, through research, with obstacles and opportunities. The tracing profile was analyzed with the support of the AHP methodology, which made joint analyses through the establishment of a priority scale, based on data observation and expert opinion for the purpose of decision making with Multicriteria.

The criteria studied were Marketing, Logistics/Distribution, Rural Production and Type of coffee. The most evident was Marketing, which is supported by price, negotiation and reliability.

The alternatives analyzed were Future Market, Long Term Storage, Spot Market, Roast/Industrialization and Premium Market. Among them, the most distinguished alternative was the sale of coffee to the Premium Market (organic/gourmet).

This type of market is demanding and grows every day. The consumption of premium coffees is a new segment for grain production and offers its connoisseurs differentiated coffees. In the coffee business, good negotiation and price reliability is essential for Marketing to be effective and to customer loyalty. As a suggestion of further studies, a deeper analysis of the factors influencing the production, quality and exportation of coffee, focusing on external markets, would be useful.

5. Acknowledgment

This study was financed in part by the Coordenação de Aperfeiçoamento de Pessoal de Nível Superior Brasil (CAPES) Finance Code 001.

References

1. CEPEA - Esalq/USP, I.T.: Centro de Estudos Avançados em Economia Aplicada - CEPEA-Esalq/USP, https://www.cepea.esalq.usp.br/br/indicador/cafe.aspx, last accessed 2019/08/16.
2. IBGE ed: A geografia do café: dinâmica territorial da produção agropecuária. IBGE, Instituto Brasileiro de Geografia e Estatística, Rio de Janeiro (2016).
3. FAO: Food and Agriculture Organization of the United Nations, http://www.fao.org/home/en/, last accessed 2019/08/16.
4. MAPA: Café no Brasil, http://www.agricultura.gov.br/assuntos/politica-agricola/cafe/cafeicultura-brasileira, last accessed 2019/03/07.
5. CECAFÉ, C.: Fatia do Brasil nas exportações globais de café deve aumentar, https://www.cecafe.com.br/publicacoes/fatia-do-brasil-nas-exportacoes-globais-de-cafe-deve-aumentar-20190116/, last accessed 2019/03/07.
6. ICO: International Coffee Organization - Notícias, http://www.ico.org/, last accessed 2019/02/19.
7. Solís, J.P., de Lima, U.: Inserción de las empresas peruanas en las cadenas globales de suministro. Universidad de Lima. 267–273 (2016).
8. Gonzalez-Feliu, J., Chong, M., Vargas Florez, J., Padilla Solis, J. eds: Handbook of Research on Urban and Humanitarian Logistics: IGI Global (2019). https://doi.org/10.4018/978-1-5225-8160-4.
9. WIPO: World Intellectual Property Report 2017: intangible capital in global value chains. World Intellectual Property Report, Place of publication not identified (2017).
10. Läderach, P., Oberthür, T., Cook, S., Estrada Iza, M., Pohlan, J.A., Fisher, M., Rosales Lechuga, R.: Systematic agronomic farm management for improved coffee quality. Field Crops Research. 120, 321–329 (2011). https://doi.org/10.1016/j.fcr.2010.10.006.

11. Saaty, T.L., Shang, J.S.: An innovative orders-of-magnitude approach to AHP-based multi-criteria decision making: Prioritizing divergent intangible humane acts., (2011).
12. Reis, J.G.M. dos, Vendrametto, O., Naas, I. de A., Costabile, L.T., Machado, S.T.: Avaliação das Estratégias de Comercialização do Milho em MS Aplicando o Analytic Hierarchy Process (AHP). Rev. Econ. Sociol. Rural. 54, 131–146 (2016). https://doi.org/10.1590/1234-56781806-9479005401007.
13. Saaty, T.L.: Decision making with the analytic hierarchy process., (2008).
14. da Cruz Correia, P.F., dos Reis, J.G.M., de Souza, A.E., Cardoso, A.P.: Brazilian Coffee Export Network: An Analysis Using SNA. In: Ameri, F., Stecke, K.E., von Cieminski, G., and Kiritsis, D. (eds.) Advances in Production Management Systems. Production Management for the Factory of the Future. pp. 142–147. Springer International Publishing, Cham (2019). https://doi.org/10.1007/978-3-030-30000-5_19.
15. Weber, J.G.: How much more do growers receive for Fair Trade-organic coffee? Food Policy. 36, 678–685 (2011). https://doi.org/10.1016/j.foodpol.2011.05.007.
16. Minten, B., Dereje, M., Engida, E., Tamru, S.: Tracking the Quality Premium of Certified Coffee: Evidence from Ethiopia. World Development. 101, 119–132 (2018). https://doi.org/10.1016/j.worlddev.2017.08.010.
17. Levy, D., Reinecke, J., Manning, S.: The Political Dynamics of Sustainable Coffee: Contested Value Regimes and the Transformation of Sustainability: The Political Dynamics of Sustainable Coffee. Journal of Management Studies. 53, 364–401 (2016). https://doi.org/10.1111/joms.12144.
18. Gelaw, F., Speelman, S., Van Huylenbroeck, G.: Farmers' marketing preferences in local coffee markets: Evidence from a choice experiment in Ethiopia. Food Policy. 61, 92–102 (2016). https://doi.org/10.1016/j.foodpol.2016.02.006.
19. Caldeira, L.G., Sette, R. de S., Portugal, N. dos S., Fonseca, A.S. da, Garcia, G.F.R.: CAFÉ ARÁBICA DO BRASIL: o problema da imagem e a consequência no preço DOI: http://dx.doi.org/10.5892/ruvrd.v15i1.3598. Revista da Universidade Vale do Rio Verde. 15, 717–726 (2017). https://doi.org/10.5892/ruvrd.v15i1.3598.
20. Patino, M.T.O., et al: Analysis and forecast of the storage needs of soybean in Brazil., (2013).
21. Correa, V.H., Ramos, P.A.: A precariedade do transporte rodoviário brasileiro para o escoamento da produção de soja do Centro-Oeste: situação e perspectivas., (2010).
22. Conab - Comercialização, https://www.conab.gov.br/comercializacao, last accessed 2019/03/12.

I L S 2020
INTERNATIONAL CONFERENCE ON INFORMATION SYSTEMS, LOGISTICS & SUPPLY CHAIN
Austin, Texas April 22-24, 2020

Brazilian Soybean Logistics Bottleneck: A Proposal for Allocation and Dimensioning of Intermodal Terminals in the State of Mato Grosso

Gabriel Faria de Oliveira [1], Gustavo Rodrigues de Morais [2,4], Rodney Rezende Saldanha [3]

[1,2,3] Graduate Program in Electrical Engineering – Universidade Federal de Minas Gerais, Av. Antônio Carlos 6627, 31270-901, Belo Horizonte, MG, Brazil.
[4] Institute of Integrated Engineering – Federal University of Itajubá – Itabira *Campus*, MG, Brazil.

{ gfaria.134@gmail.com, gustavomorais@unifei.edu.br, rodney@cpdee.ufmg.br }

Abstract. Currently, Brazil is the second-largest soybean producer in the world. However, logistic planning of the transportation for this cash crop is a problem - which impacts its final price. The inefficiencies of the transport network combined with the reduced number of integrator terminals outweigh the merits of having a large international market for export. This paper proposes a strategic case study for the allocation and sizing of soybean integrator terminals in the state of Mato Grosso. In this paper, we use integer linear programming model, with primary focus on optimizing the whole process of logistic movement of soybeans to the terminals, indicating its candidate position and storage capacity. The results of the operation flow and adjustments of the sizing of the intermodal terminals were obtained by process simulation. The post-optimization treatment proved to be efficient and innovative, by allowing a reduction in the projection of the implantation costs, thereby yielding satisfactory results.

Keywords: Facility Location Problems, Intermodal Terminal, Soybean Production, Integer Linear Programming, Simulation.

1. Introduction

Soybean is one of the major crops produced in the world. According to [7] during the 2017/2018 harvest, the world production of this grain was 336.699 million tons, with a planted area of 124.580 million hectares. Brazil, using the 2017/2018 crop as a reference, is the world's second-largest producer of this grain with a production of 116.996 million tons and a planted area of 35.100 million hectares, behind only the United States, which has a production of 119.518 million tons with a planted area of 36.228 million hectares for the same period. In Brazil, soybean production is most prominent in the state of Mato Grosso, which corresponds to approximately 28% of national production [9].
However, according to a report released by the United States Department of Agriculture [12] for the 2019/2020 crop, the forecast is that Brazil will have a harvest of 123 million tons, while the forecast for the United States would be 100.16 million tons.
Despite being considered one of the main soybean producers, the Brazilian soybean producers face a major challenge with regards to the logistics planning of the grain produced. The high logistics cost impacts the pricing of the final product value and hinders the country's competitiveness in the world market. According to the National Association of Agricultural and Veterinary Input Distributors [1] the grain transportation in Brazil is four times more expensive than their international competitors such as the United States and Argentina.

Currently, large producers have to transport their products over long distances using road transport as their only means of transport, given the inefficiency of multimodal transport in Brazil. In addition, the number of intermodal terminals is another factor that hinders the producers' competitiveness in the world market. According to [9] the Midwest region, the largest grain producer in the country, is the one with the largest gap in storage capacity.
Given the above problem, this paper presents an innovative and strategic study for the allocation and sizing of intermodal terminals, through integer linear programming and simulation, for Mato Grosso state region. Also, this work presents the opportunity to explore the potential of the soybean production and its storage in the region, a subject rarely addressed in the literature.
One of the objectives of the study is to identify the location of soybean production centers in Mato Grosso and then to determine the best position for the implementation of intermodal terminals. For the same, the proposed work begins with the premise of delimiting the distance, such that 400 km is the longest distance between sectors involved in grain processing, thus ensuring a better production flow. For this initial study, the differences in relief found near the state were disregarded. Additionally, the study is focused on analyzing these facilities and the operation flow of soybeans for export.

2. Literature Review

Brazil's position in the world soybean export scenario has a direct impact on internal logistics planning issues, where it is essential to analyze the structure of this grain processing, from its planting to its departure from the territory, as well as the storage and flow sectors. According to [12] in the 2019/2020 crop Brazil will rise to the level of leading soybean producer and exporter globally - which reinforces the need to shed light on the biggest challenges faced by this sector, as explained in [9] – the high cost of transporting soybean to ports and the deficit in the product's storage capacity.
According to [11] and [5], 61% of cargoes in Brazil are transported by road transport, which puts leaves behind other networks – railways (21%) and waterways (14%), which have a relatively lower cost, but do not provide the appropriate structure for cargo transportation. Therefore, we can see the drawbacks of the current transportation situation, which is inefficient. Several factors, such as limited modes of transport, interfere with the entire logistics plan and compromise the exportation of soybeans through the desired means. One of these factors is illustrated by [4] due to the high fuel consumption in the road mode, with 15.4 liters to transport 1 ton of inputs per 1000 km. Besides the high cost for the fuel, [6] to further shed light on other factors that affect the final pricing of cargo, we observe that the price is influenced intrinsically by transport-related conditions, such as poor road structure, cargo vulnerability - subject to loss and theft on the route - and the delay in the path, relevant issues to be considered. In this context, it is necessary to analyze which mode of transport suits each load, with cost-benefit analysis for road, rail, waterway or transport intermodality.
The issue related to soybeans is very recurrent as in [16] and [17] from the economic and productive point of view. However, the use of optimization as a strategic planning tool for soybean storage is a subject little addressed in the literature.
Also, according to [9] over the last few years, more precisely from 2007 there was a significant increase in soybean production, exceeding the limits dedicated to storage. In this study, it is possible to see that the number of intermodal terminals remained practically constant, not following the evolution in production capacity and generating a lag in the amount of soybean in the market. This situation creates a major problem, since such structures are fundamental to prevent the loss of the product, and ensure the maintenance of its quality, even for long periods after harvest.
Another important point that the production storage implies is the increase in the bargaining power of the producer. By using such terminals, it is possible to escape the seasonality of the crops and obtain some flexibility concerning the yield period. Thus, it is possible to maximize profits by disposing of production at times out of the crop when the freight price is lower and the price of the product tends to be higher [2] and [9]. In [14] and [15] the review of the state of the art and several applications for the facility allocation problem are presented, but without a joint approach with simulation. It is in this matter that the present study is relevant and innovative, in the sense of using scientific techniques in seeking strategic solutions to aid in decision making.
Given an ideal scenario of soybean production, soybean storage and flow, it can be found in the literature [10] and [3] that a good limiting factor for the maximum distance to be traveled by road, between the producing center and the intermodal terminal would be 400 km. Thus, by reducing the distance, proper

storage of the product would be allowed, which would result in economies of scale throughout the logistic plan involved in this process.
According to the United States Department of Agricultural [11] in 2018, the volume of soybean exported was from 68.2 to 83.6 million tons, which reinforces the country's position in the scenario of competitiveness in the international market. This report explains that due to the tariff tension between the United States and China, China's demand for Brazilian soybeans has increased. This situation contributes to the evidence that Brazil is increasingly moving towards the consolidation of its position as the largest producer and exporter of soybeans in the world.

3. Methodology

3.1. Representation of the Problem

In order to achieve the proposed objectives, a real data survey was initially carried out to perform the simulations and present a terminal allocation model. The state of Mato Grosso has a total area of approximately 904,000 km^2 - with consolidated production of 30.5 million tons for 2017 [8]. After analysis of the IBGE Automatic Recovery System - SIDRA, it was seen that the state of Mato Grosso has 141 registered cities that, among its agricultural activities, focuses on planting and harvesting soybean. From these cities, for 2017, a total of 22 cities had no production. The remaining 119 cities, which presented some production, can be seen in Figure 1.

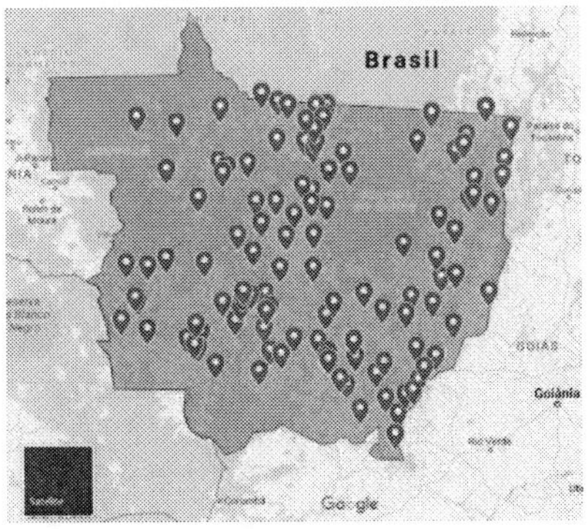

Figure 1: Soybean producing cities of Mato Grosso. Adapted from Google My Maps.

In order to facilitate the resolution of the problem and find the candidate terminal locations, a simplified representation was made in the shape of a square – 1040 km East-West direction and 960 km North-South direction covering the 119 soybean-producing cities of the state. Also, it was proposed to divide this quadrilateral into 40 grain-producing poles with equal rectangle-shaped dimensions - each of the 40 poles 208 km East-West direction and 120 km North-South direction.
In addition to addressing the minimization of intermodal terminal deployment costs, another important goal of this paper was to identify the location of producers and determine an ideal candidate position for the deployment of these terminals in the state. Thus, it is considered that the producers do not have to move the load for more than 400 km, the limited distance restriction is supported by [10] and [3], thus ensuring a better production flow.
In addition, a 10% refusal rate was considered due to possible excess soybean stored at the terminals, i.e., each terminal may refuse up to 10% of the annual demand requests.
Another factor to be considered is the storage capacity of the possible terminals deployed in the state, which will be given in tons. For the present study, a cargo handling demand of approximately one-third of the total production of the period was used, this value represents the percentage of state production destined for export, around 10 million tons. Data already separated by regions are highlighted in Table 1.

Table 1: Soybean production in tons divided into 40 poles.

Region	Demand	Region	Demand	Region	Demand	Region	Demand
R1	1,376	R11	504,144	R21	620,086	R31	303,754
R2	5,738	R12	890,753	R22	355,951	R32	258,889
R3	0	R13	570,249	R23	247,535	R33	51,815
R4	429,934	R14	40,728	R24	0	R34	338,381
R5	224,282	R15	17,990	R25	27,048	R35	551,579
R6	38,108	R16	0	R26	70,882	R36	359,831
R7	0	R17	132,038	R27	0	R37	178,685
R8	0	R18	361,421	R28	178,938	R38	37,395
R9	3,395	R19	1,486,235	R29	421,685	R39	0
R10	224,190	R20	651,626	R30	415,339	R40	0

The terminal sizes will be proportional to the output of the region to be inserted. Table 2 shows the cost of deploying the terminal according to its size, such that the larger the terminal, the lower the cost of deployment – clearly indicating an economy of scale [13].

Table 2: Types of Intermodal Terminals.

Terminal	Cost (Mill. R$)	Capacity (ton)	Terminal	Cost (Mill. R$)	Capacity (ton)
T1	11	10,000	T18	175	200,000
T2	17	15,000	T19	190	250,000
T3	23	20,000	T20	205	300,000
T4	28	25,000	T21	220	350,000
T5	35	30,000	T22	235	400,000
T6	40	35,000	T23	242	450,000
T7	44	40,000	T24	250	500,000
T8	50	45,000	T25	265	550,000
T9	57	50,000	T26	275	600,000
T10	70	60,000	T27	285	650,000
T11	83	70,000	T28	296	700,000
T12	90	80,000	T29	310	750,000
T13	100	90,000	T30	320	800,000
T14	115	100,000	T31	332	850,000
T15	130	125,000	T32	343	900,000
T16	145	150,000	T33	360	950,000
T17	160	175,000	T34	378	1,000,000

The average permanence time of 6 days of the product and the costs of deployment of the terminals was considered based on information obtained from the operational research of a logistics company that operates with intermodal terminals. This value was used as a standard in all units to analyze, together with the cargo arrival and flow rate, the soybean flow in the study region. This paper considered the same storage cost for all intermodal terminals.

Finally, the modeling of the integer linear programming problem was performed to handle the candidate positions for the installation of intermodal terminals. These facilities and the operation flow were also analyzed with the strategic bias of the flow of this soybean production destined for export. After all data were consolidated, the model, the objective function and the constraints were defined, as presented in the next section.

3.2. Optimization Model

Below is the model used together with the meaning of the variables that compose it.

$$minTotalCost = \sum_{k}\sum_{s} Y_{ks} * Cost_{s}. \tag{1}$$

Subject to:

$$\sum_{s} Y_{ks} \leq 1, \forall k. \tag{2}$$

$$\sum_{k} X_{ik} \leq 1, \forall k. \tag{3}$$

$$X_{ik} * Distance_{ik} \leq 400, \forall k, \forall i. \tag{4}$$

$$X_{ik} \leq \sum_{s} Y_{k}, \forall k, \forall i. \tag{5}$$

$$X_{kk} = \sum_{s} Y_{ks}, \forall k. \tag{6}$$

$$\sum_{i}\sum_{k} X_{ik} * Demand_i = TotalDemand. \tag{7}$$

$$\sum_{s} capacity_s * Y_{ks} * \rho \geq \sum_{i} \frac{X_{ik} * Demand_i * AvTimePerm}{120}, \forall k. \tag{8}$$

$$\sum_{i}\sum_{k} X_{ik} * Demand_i \leq \sum_{k}\sum_{s} \frac{120 * \rho * Capacity_s * Y_{ks}}{AvTimePerm}. \tag{9}$$

Indexes and parameters representation:

- i – region i;
- k – candidate position k (which may receive an intermodal terminal);
- s – s-type intermodal terminal (according to the storage capacity);
- ρ – occupancy rate (depending on the size of the terminal);
- $Cost_s$ – cost of deploying each s-type terminal;
- $Capacity_s$ – storage capacity in tons of each s-type terminal;
- $Demand_i$ – load demand from region i;
- $Distance_{ik}$ – distance in kilometers from region i to candidate position k;
- $AvTimePerm$ – Average time of permanence at intermodal terminals.

The variables x and y are binary, i.e.:

- $x_{ik} \in [0, 1]$ – This value will be 1 if the load demand from region i is directed to the terminal at candidate position k.
- $y_{ks} \in [0, 1]$ – This value will be 1 if candidate position k receives an s-type terminal.

The objective function (1) focuses on minimizing the cost of deploying all terminals. Equation (2) defines that each region k can have at most 1 s-type terminal. Equation (3) indicates that each region directs its demand to 1 single terminal. Equation (4) restricts the maximum distance to the terminal to be up to 400 km. Equation (5) indicates that there is only grain flow to a region if there is a terminal installed in that region. Equation (6) defines that every region that has a terminal installed will direct its demand to it. Equation (7) determines that the sum of the storage demands must be equal to the total runoff/dispatch demand. Equation (8) indicates that each intermodal terminal must have sufficient capacity to meet the load demand addressed to it. Equation (9) indicates that the sum of the demands must be less than or equal to the sum of the storage capacities of the installed terminals.

3.3. Computational Resources

The software Microsoft Excel, LINGO (v. 18.0) and Arena (v. 14) were used to solve the proposed problem. The LINGO and Excel software were used in the proposed model of the previous section in order to find the candidate positions for the installation of the intermodal terminals, and also to propose a size of these structures to meet the stipulated refusal rate of 10%. The Arena software focused on testing and adjusting the size of the proposed terminals in the previous modeling result, analyzing the flow of cargo movement and verifying if it meets the configured refusal rate. The solution was performed on a laptop with the following configurations: Processor: Intel i7, CPU 2.40Ghz - 64 bits, 12.0 GB memory, Windows 8.1.

4. Results and Discussions

After performing the procedure described in the previous sections, the representative mathematical model was implemented in LINGO. The software handled the modeling of the Linear Programming problem with the objective of pointing out which would be the candidate positions for the installation of the intermodal terminals, according to the demand of loads throughout the state.
The second focus of the study was to better size the capacity of these terminals to find what would be their "optimal" size to meet the refusal rate. The results achieved are described in Table 3. Eight candidate positions (regions) were allocated to hold terminals of 6 different models.

Table 3: Comparative table of the results.

Terminal	Quantity	Cost (Mill. R$)	Installation Region	Assisted Region	Demand (ton)
T1	1	11	R37	R37	178,685
T2	2	17	R5	R3	0
				R5	224,282
				R6	38,108
				R7	0
				R8	0
		17	R40	R32	258,889
				R39	0
				R40	0
T3	1	23	R24	R15	17,990
				R16	0
				R24	0
				R31	303,754
T4	1	28	R2	R1	1,376
				R2	5,738
				R4	429,934
				R9	3,395
T7	2	44	R34	R34	338,381
				R36	359,831
				R25	27,048
		44	R35	R33	51,815
				R35	551,579
				R38	37,395
T22	1	235	R20	R10	224,190
				R11	504,144
				R12	890,753
				R13	570,249
				R14	40,728
				R17	132,038
				R18	361,421
				R19	1,486,235
				R20	651,626
				R21	620,086
				R22	355,951
				R23	247,535
				R26	70,882
				R27	0
				R28	178,938
				R29	421,685
				R30	415,339
Final Cost		419	Total demand		10,000,000

After the results of the mathematical model, Arena software was used to generate the load flow in the analyzed terminals. An average residence time of 6 days was used, with a variation according to an exponential distribution to generate the flow of this terminal.

For each of the terminals suggested by LINGO, a simulation of the incoming and outgoing soybean cargo flow was performed. After the simulation, some regions where a terminal was installed were updated. The new values found are represented in Table 4.

Table 4: New terminals configuration.

Installation Region	Previous Terminal	New terminal size	Previous Refusal Rate	Current Refusal Rate	Previous Capacity (ton)	Current Capacity (ton)
R2	T4	T3	0%	7.66%	25,000	20,000
R5	T2	T2	0%	0%	15,000	15,000
R20	T22	T22	0%	0%	400,000	400,000
R24	T3	T2	0%	5.75%	20,000	15,000
R34	T7	T6	0%	0.16%	40,000	35,000
R35	T7	T5	0%	8.57%	40,000	30,000
R37	T1	T1	0%	0%	10,000	10,000
R40	T2	T2	0%	0%	15,000	15,000

As an example of analysis, LINGO software was used to size a terminal to 25,000 tons. However, its refusal rate was 0%. As the objective of this work is to reduce the cost of deploying the intermodal terminals, ensuring a refusal rate of up to 10%, the flow simulation for each terminal was analyzed case by case, in order to reduce its size and the value of the objective function. The new results are described in Table 5.

Table 5: Objective Function after the Arena simulation.

Installation Region	New terminal size	Cost (Mill. R$)
R2	T3	23
R5	T2	17
R20	T22	235
R24	T2	17
R34	T6	40
R35	T5	35
R37	T1	11
R40	T2	17
Total		395

In this way, after analyzing Table 5, a new cost value for the proposed problem can be verified. Thus, it was noted that the value of the objective function changed (from 419 to 395 million Reais – R$395,000,000.00) due to the new configuration of the terminals, which reduced the cost of deployment by reducing their storage capacity and still meeting a refusal rate of up to 10% of cargo demand.

5. Conclusion and Future Steps

In this paper, a strategic proposal for the allocation and sizing of intermodal terminals for soybean production in the Mato Grosso region was addressed. After conducting a real data survey and problem formulation, a linear programming technique was applied to solve the mathematical model and a load flow simulation was built to adjust the size of the intermodal terminal to meet a specified refusal rate.

The results presented demonstrate value savings in the cost of implementing intermodal terminals by choosing the optimal allocation position and the type of terminal to be deployed in the 40 suggested producing regions. With the help of the simulation, we were able to ascertain that with the reduction of the distance between the producing center and the storage sector there is a significant impact on the reduction of logistics costs.

The Arena simulation of the mathematical model results proved to be efficient in allowing a reduction in the proposed implementation costs, since it can create an operating flow condition of this system.

The presented analysis has great flexibility and scalability for application in different scenarios, since the mathematical model allows for modification of the input parameters and new results can be generated and analyzed to adapt to new situations.
The present paper covered the entire logistic process from soybean farm to the intermodal terminals. As possible future contributions, it would be interesting to add the whole post-routing process by building a new model with the rail modal of cargo displacement through the multimodal project from the Mato Grosso terminals to the ports. Other possible improvements are the insertion of new crops, such as corn and rice, in the current model and instead of considering cities, consider the exact location of producing farms, giving greater accuracy to the results. Other candidate position allocation techniques may also be addressed. Finally, the inclusion of the few existing terminals is indicated, thus giving more assertiveness to strategic decision making regarding the terminal optimization of the state of Mato Grosso.

6. Acknowledgment

The Brazilian agencies CAPES, CNPq and FAPEMIG for providing financial support to conduct this research.

7. References

1. National Association of Agricultural and Veterinary Input Distributors (ANDAV), http://www.andav.com.br/artigo/o-transporte-de-graos-no-brasil/
2. Andrade, L. E. C.: Um estudo sobre terminais intermodais para granéis sólidos. Departamento de Engenharia Naval e Oceânica, Universidade de São Paulo – USP (2002).
3. ANTT (2016) Agência Nacional de Transportes Terrestres. Caderno de demanda, http://www.antt.gov.br/backend/galeria/arquivos/caderno_de_demanda.pdf
4. Confederação Nacional do Transporte. Pesquisa CNT da Navegação Interior 2013, http://cms.cnt.org.br/Imagens%20CNT/PDFs%20CNT/Pesquisa%20CNT%20Navegacao%20Interior/Principais_Dados_Pesquisa_Navegacao_Interior_2013_CNT.pdf
5. Confederação Nacional do Transporte. Transporte Rodoviário: Desempenho do setor, infraestrutura e investimentos, http://cms.cnt.org.br/Imagens%20CNT/PDFs%20CNT/Estudos%20CNT/estudo_transporte_rodoviario_infraestrutura.pdf
6. CORRÊA-JUNIOR, G.; et al. Oferta de Transportes: fatores determinantes do frete e o caso das centrais de cargas. In: CAIXETA-FILHO, J. V.; MARTINS, R. S. Gestão logística do transporte de cargas. 1ª ed. 12ª reimpressão. Atlas, São Paulo (2015)
7. Embrapa (2019) Empresa Brasileira de Pesquisa Agropecuária - Soja em números para safra 2017/2018, https://www.embrapa.br/soja/cultivos/soja1/dados-economicos
8. IBGE – Instituto Brasileiro de Geografia e Estatística SIDRA – Produção Agrícola Municipal, https://sidra.ibge.gov.br/Tabela/1612
9. Resende, L. M. S.: Modelo logístico de soja e milho no estado de mato grosso: minimização de custos de transporte por meio do ideal dimensionamento e localização de armazéns de grãos. Universidade Federal de Mato Grosso – UFMT (2016)
10. TCU (2012) Tribunal de Contas da União - Áreas Temáticas – Infraestrutura – Transportes: Ferrovias, https://portal.tcu.gov.br/tcu/paginas/contas_governo/contas_2012/fichas/9.8-Infraestrutura-TransportesFerrovia.pdf
11. USDA (2019). United States Department of Agriculture - Soybean Transportation Guide: Brazil 2018, https://www.ams.usda.gov/sites/default/files/media/BrazilSoybeanTransportationGuide2018.pdf
12. USDA (2019). United States Department of Agriculture – World Agricultural Production, https://downloads.usda.library.cornell.edu/usda-esmis/files/5q47rn72z/n583z624w/n583z6255/production.pdf
13. Cullinane, K., Khanna, M.: Economies of scale in large containerships: optimal size and geographical implications. Journal of Transport Geography. Vol. 8, 181-195 (2000).
14. Farahani, R. Z., Asgari, N., Heidari, N., Hosseininia, M., & Goh, M., Covering problems in facility location: A review. Computers & Industrial Engineering, 62(1), 368–407 (2012).
15. Ortiz-Astorquiza, C., Contreras, I., & Laporte, G., Multi-level facility location problems. European Journal of Operational Research, 267(3), 791–805. (2018).
16. Morales, V., Vendrametto, O., Reis, J.G.M., Toloi, R.C., Canuto, S.A. Information Systems in the Soybean Brazilian Supply Chain: an Analysis from the Trading Companies Perspective. Proceedings of ILS Conference 2016 Bordeaux, France. (2016).
17. Toloi, R.T., Reis, J.G.M., Vendrametto, O., Machado, S.T., Rodrigues, E.F., How to improve the logistics issues during crop soybean in Mato Grosso state Brazil? Proceedings of ILS Conference 2016, Bordeaux, France. (2016).

I L S 2020
INTERNATIONAL CONFERENCE ON INFORMATION SYSTEMS, LOGISTICS & SUPPLY CHAIN
Austin, Texas April 22-24, 2020

Food Security: A Case Study in the Guarani Rio Branco and Aguapeú Indigenous Villages

Aguinaldo Eduardo de Souza [1], João Gilberto Mendes dos Reis [2], Luciana Melo Costa [3], Emerson Rodolfo Abraham [4], Oduvaldo Vendrametto [5]

[1] Paulista University - UNIP, RESUP/PPGEP, São Paulo, Brazil
[2] Paulista University - UNIP, PPGEP, São Paulo, Brazil
[3] Itanhaém City Hall, São Paulo, Brazil
[4] Paulista University - UNIP, RESUP/PPGEP, São Paulo, Brazil
[5] Paulista University - UNIP, PPGEP, São Paulo, Brazil
{souza.eduaguinaldo@gmail.com, betomendesreis@msn.com, lueducita@yahoo.com.br, emerson_abraham@yahoo.com, broduvaldov@gmail.com}

Abstract. The Brazil has articulated intersectoral actions to ensure nutritional food and promote hunger eradication, especially among indigenous and communities descended from slaves. This research analyzed the project implemented in the Guarani Villages of Rio Branco and Aguapeú, located in the state of São Paulo. This project seeks to revitalize indigenous family agricultural production as well as include indigenous producers as citizens of rights. Data were collected through interviews with the professionals who participated in the project design and execution and beneficiaries (Guarani Indigenous Farmers). After three years of negotiations, building a relationship of trust with indigenous communities, in 2017, two farmers were registered as suppliers. In 2018, an increase of 80% in farmers' income compared to 2017 was pointed out. Also, in 2019/2020, four new farmers were included.

Keywords: Family Farming, Local Food, Indigenous Farmer

1. Introduction

Eliminating poverty in all its dimensions, including extreme poverty, is the greatest challenge facing global society and an indispensable requirement for sustainable development. In 2015 world leaders established a global action plan with the 2030 Agenda for Sustainable Development, having as one of its main axes the total eradication of hunger, guaranteeing the dignity and equality of people [1] [2].

However, the Food and Agriculture Organization of the United Nations [3] points out that one in nine people currently suffer from hunger, about 820 million of the world's population. The distribution of food-insecure people on the globe reaches a total of 2 billion people suffering from food insecurity, with 1.04 billion (52%) being in Asia; 676 million (34%) in Africa; and 188 million (9%) in Latin America. This underscores the immense challenge facing world leaders regarding the global Zero Hunger target by 2030 [3].

In this context, Brazil has articulated intersectoral actions to ensure nutritional food security and promote hunger eradication. In 2006, the National Food and Nutrition Security System (SISAN) was established in Brazil through the Organic Food and Nutrition Security Law (LOSAN) nº 11,346/06 [4].

SISAN aims to develop and implement policies and plans for food and nutrition security, to stimulate participatory management through the integration of efforts between government and civil society at the federal, state, and municipal levels, also monitoring and evaluating food and nutrition security in the country [5].

LOSAN is based on the right of all people to a healthy, affordable, quality, sufficient, and permanent diet. Adequate and healthy eating should be based on health-promoting eating practices without compromising access to other essential needs. Also, it must be produced sustainably, ensuring environmental protection, social justice, and the right to land and territory, therefore, ensuring the Brazilian population the Human Right to Adequate Food (DHAA) [4].

Continuing on LOSAN, the law aims to promote the health, nutrition, and food of the population, including socially vulnerable population groups, and traditional communities of all food identities and cultures, respecting the socio-cultural and regional dimensions.

In Brazil, social inequality is even more noticeable between black and indigenous communities [6] [7] [8] [9] [10] [11] [12]. However, this is most evident among indigenous peoples, when one observes the inexpressive articulation of civil society and practically the nonexistent social movements, compared to other communities, making them even more vulnerable and invisible in the Brazilian social context.

This reality justifies the initiative of the project to seek the integration and rescue of indigenous cultivars, in the environment of building a new macro vision of local public policies of National Food Security (SNA). Studies have pointed to the strategic importance of supply chains in local agri-food networks in developing countries [13] [14] [15]. Agricultural supply chains are related to small local producers and low integration of supply chain practices [13]. Thus, the implementation of integrated supply chain management is fundamental for the efficiency of food distribution aiming at food security for communities in situations of nutritional vulnerability and, therefore, a source of social welfare [14]. Moreover, efficient chains allow loss reduction in all links in the chain [15].

Considering that the SNA is a social and humanitarian project, and should be built by governmental and civil society actors, this research aims to demonstrate a case study on public policy of inclusion of traditional cultivars in the food of indigenous schools, besides allowing the insertion of family farmer from traditional communities (Guarani Indians) in the network of government program providers.

The project resulted from the socioeconomic demands in search of food security of the Guarani Indigenous community and the networked efforts of the Municipal Department of Education and the Department of Agriculture of the city of Itanhaém [16] with the National Indian Fund (FUNAI) [17]. The study was conducted at Guarani Village of Rio Branco and Aguapeú located in the Brazilian city of Itanhaém and Mongaguá respectively, in the southern coast of the State of São Paulo.

2 Methodology

The methodological procedures adopted in this research had an exploratory and descriptive approach. Data collection is one of the main characteristics of descriptive research, as it observes, records, and analyzes facts and phenomena [18]. Thus, the present study was built in three main stages:

Step 1: Data collection from governmental sources such as Brazilian Institute of Geography and Statistics, Ministry of Social Development, National Indian Foundation, Ministry of Education, Itanhaém City Hall, as well as the main bases for scientific work consultations (Science Direct, Scopus, IEEE, Scielo, CAPES Journal Portal).

Step 2: Field research. Three structured interviews were conducted in July and August 2019 to collect quantitative and qualitative: a) with Guaranis indigenous farmers in the Rio Branco and Aguapeú villages located in the cities of Itanhaém and Mongaguá (Fig. 34); b) with the manager of the Itanhaém Food Bank; and c) with Indian technician from FUNAI.

Step 3: Discussion of the results sought to present the results that could qualify the project.

3. Literature Review

3.1 Family Farming in Brazil

Family Farming in Brazil is composed of a heterogeneous population, ranging from farmers descending from European immigrants, quilombolas descended from slaves, native Brazilian Indians, and migrant peasants from the regions of Brazil [19] [20].

Many family farmers were settled on small plots of land through the settlement program of the National Institute of Colonization and Agrarian Reform (INCRA). Since the 1970s, 9,437 settlement projects have been created throughout Brazil, and the distribution of 87.9 million hectares of land has benefited 973,471 families [22].

The profile of the Brazilian family producer is contrasting, varying from families with subsistence agriculture with low purchasing power and manual production, to farmers with access to technology and mechanized production [22].

Law 11,326 [23] defines the prerequisites for framing rural farmers in FF national policy to qualify family rural enterprises.

3.2 Indigenous Population in Brazil

The National Indian Foundation is the official Brazilian indigenous body, created in 1967 and linked to the Ministry of Justice. Its main assignment is to execute the indigenous policy in Brazil. The agency promotes studies of delimitation, demarcation, land regularization, and registration of lands traditionally occupied by indigenous peoples [27].

Also, it monitors and inspects indigenous lands and implements policies to protect isolated and newly contacted peoples, to protect the rights of indigenous peoples in Brazil. Within its responsibilities, the agency accounts for interinstitutional articulation that guarantees social and citizenship rights to indigenous peoples, through policies aimed at social security and indigenous school education [17].

The 2010 Indigenous Census, according to the Brazilian Institute of Geography and Statistics (IBGE) [24], indicates that indigenous people in Brazil represent 0.4% of the Brazilian population.

Also, the data revealed that of the 896,000 people who claimed or considered themselves to be indigenous, 572,000 (63.8%) lived in rural areas, and 517,000 (57.7%) lived in officially recognized indigenous lands (Tab.1). Indigenous lands, with limits already defined in Brazil, total 12.9% of the national territory (851 million ha) [17].

Table 1 – Indigenous poputaions

Indigenous poputaions, by household status, by household locations – Brazil - 2010

Location domicilio	Indigenous population by household situation		
	Total	Urban	Rural
Total	896,917	324,834	572,083
Indigenous lands	517,383	25,693	491,420
Out of indigenous lands	379,534	298,871	80,633

Source: [24]

Regarding spatial distribution (Tab. 2), 38.2% of the indigenous people are concentrated in the Northern Region, which is predominant in the Legal Amazon. Then the Northeast Region 25.9%, Midwest 16.0%, Southeast 11.1%, and South 8.8%.

Table 2 – Indigenous population by regions

Spacial distribution indigenous population by regions Brazil - 2010

Region	Indigenous lands	Out of indigenous lands	Total
North	251,891	90,945	342,836
Northeast	106,142	126,597	232,739
Midwest	15,904	83,233	99,137
Southeast	39,427	39,346	78,773
South	104,019	39,413	143,432
Brazil	**517,383**	**379,534**	**896,917**

Source: [24]

The North, Northeast and Midwest Regions, as can be seen in Table 2, showed an increase in the population volume of indigenous self-declarations. In the Southeast and South Regions, in both urban and rural areas, there was a reduction in the indigenous population, 39.2%, and 11.6%, respectively.
The survey pointed out that indigenous people in Brazil are made up of 305 ethnic groups and speak 274 languages. Moreover, while 84.4% of the national population lives in urban centers, in the case of indigenous people, only 36.2%, making their link with the land evident [24].

3.3 Guarani Indians in Brazil

In South America, there's an estimated Guarani Indigenous population of 225,000 is located in Argentina, Brazil, Paraguay, Uruguay, and Bolivia. [25] In Brazil, the contingent is 67,523, 7% of the Brazilian indigenous, distributed mainly in the South (the Rio Grande do Sul, Santa Catarina, Paraná), Southeast (São Paulo, Rio de Janeiro, Espírito Santo) and Midwest (Mato Grosso do Sul) [24]. In São Paulo, the Guarani population is 4,138 people.
Guarani people living in Brazil is divided into three subgroups: Guarani-Ñandeva, Guarani-Kaiowa, and Guarani-Mbya [25]. This large group speaks Guarani dialects that are included in the Tupi-Guarani language family, from the Tupi language trunk [26].
The Guarani mainly inhabit territories near the coast, in the South and Southeast of Brazil. The Atlantic Forest is of special importance to these people, especially to those of the Mbya subgroup (Fig. 3), as they believe it is a privileged place for the search for sacred living spaces [28].

3.4 Itanhaem Food bank

Created in 2007 through the agreement of the Federal Government and the Itanhaém City Hall, the Itanhaém Food Bank (BAI), in addition to fighting hunger, is responsible for operationalizing Nutrition Food Security programs in the Municipality through the Food Acquisition Program. (PAA) [28].
In Itanhaém, the PAA guarantees nutritional quality food assistance to ten social entities registered with the Municipal Social Assistance Council (CMAS), covering about 2,500 families in a condition of food insecurity. The PAA was established in Brazil in 2003 and aims at the development of Family Farming, the economic and social inclusion in rural areas, and to meet the needs of people in situations of food and nutrition insecurity [30].
In 2018, the country allocated 64.9 million reais of PAA resources to acquire 23,611t of food produced by 9,675 family farmers [30].
Another activity no less relevant is the Bank's intersectoral articulation with the National School Feeding Program (PNAE). Although PNAE resources are managed by the Municipal Secretariat of Education, the Bank is an interlocutor between civil society and the public authorities and has promoted actions to encourage indigenous agricultural production and its inclusion as a local supplier to PNAE to the PAA.
Federal Law 11,947/09 [31] was instrumental in strengthening Family Farming, as it mandates that PNAE use 30% of its resources to buy food directly from family producers, prioritizing land reform settlers [21], traditional communities indigenous and quilombolas [32].
Also, the Bank promotes training programs such as the agroecological production system and agribusiness management to develop the business autonomy of local farmers.

4 Case study

The project was implemented in the Guarani Villages of Rio Branco and Aguapeu (Fig. 3), located in the Serra do Mar State Park-Conservation Unit - Curucutu Nucleus [34], cities of Itanhaém and Mongaguá, State of São Paulo.

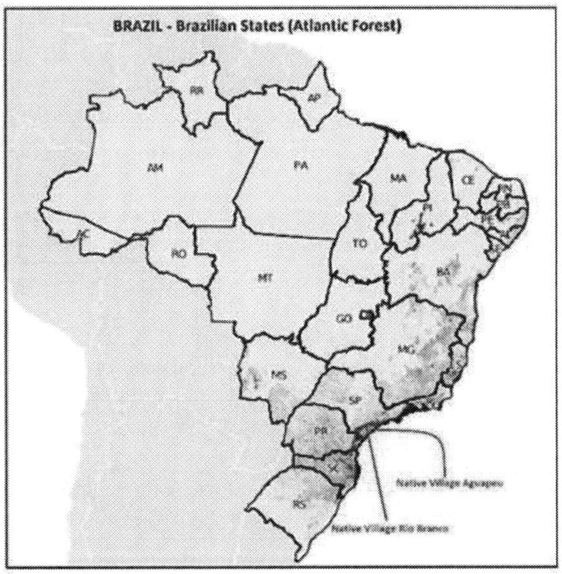

Figure 3 – Location Guarani Indian Villages. **Source**: [33]

Since its inauguration in 2007, the Food Bank, in conjunction with CORLIS, has undertaken actions to identify and mitigate food insecurity in Indigenous communities. However, the Bank's coordination "needed to provide answers beyond palliative actions".

Based on this assumption, in 2017, traditional cultivars were included in the food menu of the indigenous school of Native Village Rio Branco, through guarani corn (avaxi ete'i). Thus, two indigenous farmers (Fig. 5) were registered as PNAE suppliers for Itanhaém.

The PNAE resource operational guidelines require that its resources be allocated only to schools in the beneficiary municipality. However, the program makes it easier for farmers from other locations as a source of purchase, thus allowing the insertion of the farmer of Native Village Aguapeu in the registration of the program.

Guarani avaxi ete'i corn cultivation (Fig. 4) is carried out by the indigenous themselves in agroecological management, respecting the millenary spiritual traditions of the Guarani culture [35].

Figure 4 – Guarani corn drying. **Source:** [17]

Figure 5 - Indigenous farmers. **Source:** [16]

For these people, keeping seeds of their traditional cultivars has to do with preserving their cultural and ethnic identity, a way of perpetuating life.

Guarani corn, in indigenous schools, is consumed fresh or turned into flour for the production of cakes, mush, and beiju. For them, being considered a sacred food with healing power and strengthening body and spirit, avaxi ete'i should only be consumed by the Guarani themselves. [35] Therefore, the purchase of Guarani corn by the city has the sole purpose of supplying indigenous communities and schools [28].

5 Results and discussion

The volume purchased was 163.87 kg, according to per capita calculation by students, resulting from the insertion in the PNAE supplier register of two indigenous producers (Indigenous 1 - Native Village Aguapeu, and Indigenous 2 - Native Village Rio Branco), which together had an income of 1,802.57 reais in 2017.
After 2017, the project gained ground, and other products of indigenous cultivars were inserted in the public call for school food, increasing the scope of action of indigenous producers.
In 2018 there was a significant advance in the project. In addition to guarani corn (140 kg), Guarani sweet potato (300 kg) was added, generating an increase in revenue of the two producers of about 50% compared to the previous year, which together had a gain of 2,725.00 reais.
For 2019, the highlight is the insertion of another Guarani traditional product in the purchase call (PNAE) by the municipality. Guarani cassava is provisioned at 260 kg, in addition to sweet potato 300 kg and avaxi ete'i corn with 146 kg. The supply of these products should generate revenue of 3,315.10 reais, about 21% growth over 2018.
Another major advance of the project was the inclusion of four more indigenous producers in the supplier register, from the second semester of 2019. In addition to the two initial producers, all will be part of the call for the acquisition of the municipality in the PAA program (Tab. 3).

Table 3 – Proposed PAA Supply

INDIGENOUS FARMERS	PRODUCT	KG	R$	R$ TOTAL
Indigenous 1	Silver Banana	208.32	2,40	499.97
Indigenous 2	Silver Banana	833.33	2,40	2,000.00
	Palm Heart	270.27	3,70	1,000.00
Indigenous 3	Sweet Potato	869.56	2,30	2,000.00
	Mandioca	909.09	1,10	1,000.00
Indigenous 4	Silver Banana	833.33	2,40	2,000.00
	Palm Heart	270.27	3,70	1,000.00
Indigenous 5	Banana Prata	1,666.66	2,40	4,000.00
	Palm Heart	675.67	3,70	2,500.00
Indigenous 5	Lettuce	454.54	2,20	1,000.00
	Kale	800.00	2,50	2,000.00
	Sweet Potato	1,304.34	2,30	3,000.00

Source: [16]

Table 3 shows the 2019/2020 proposal, with the six indigenous farmers inserted in the SISPAA - PAA Computerized Management System [5] approved by the Federal Government operational plan.

6 Conclusion

The project to revitalize indigenous family agricultural production, as well as to include indigenous producers as citizens of rights, constituted the need to comply with the Resolution of the National School Feeding Program, which sets priorities for the purchase from indigenous farmers and respect for food sovereignty from traditional communities.
With the purpose of evolving the discussions and putting into practice, the Food Bank, together with the local Government and CORLIS-FUNAI, incorporated the project aiming at internalizing a public policy with dimensions of social justice, not just about guaranteeing healthy food for an ethnic community, but the recovery of the productive memory of the planet from the perspective of global food systems.
As evidenced in this study, the achieved results were quite significant. After three years of negotiations, building a relationship of trust between BAI and indigenous communities, in 2017, two farmers were registered as suppliers. The following year saw an 80% increase in farmer income, compared to 2017. Also, for the 2019/2020 (PAA) public food call, four new farmers were included, and together, the six producers will bring to their communities about 22 thousand reais in the period.

Given the potential for replicability in new communities and traditional families, for future work, we intend to develop a supply network model through the management of the agricultural supply chain as proposed by the studies of [13] [14] [15], aiming to guarantee the food security of local communities and the socioeconomic sustainability of family farmers in Itanhaém.

7 Acknowledgement

Itanhaém Food Bank and Department of Education and the Department of Agriculture of the city of Itanhaém. This study was financed in part by the Coordenacão de Aperfeicoamento de Pessoal de Nível Superior - Brasil (CAPES) - Finance Code 001.

8 References

1. Weber H. Politics of 'Leaving No One Behind': Contesting the 2030 Sustainable Development Goals Agenda. Globalizations. 16 de abril de 2017;14(3):399–414. doi10.1080/14747731.2016.1275404
2. UN-United Nations Organization. Transforming our world: the 2030 Agenda for Sustainable Development. Sustainable Development Knowledge Platform. 2019. Disponível em: https://sustainabledevelopment.un.org/post2015/transformingourworld
3. FAO-Food and Agriculture Organization of the United Nations - UN. SOFI 2019 - The State of Food Security and Nutrition in the World [Internet]. www.fao.org. 2019. Disponível em: http://www.fao.org/state-of-food-security-nutrition/en/
4. Federal Government. Lei nº 11.346. Federal Government Plateau - Civil House. 2006. Disponível em: http://www.planalto.gov.br/ccivil_03/_Ato2004-2006/2006/Lei/L11346.htm
5. MDS-Ministry of Citizenship - Special Secretariat for Social Development. O Direito Humano à Alimentação Adequada e o Sistema Nacional de Segurança Alimentar e Nutricional. Brasilia, DF: ABRANDH; 2013. 263 p. Disponível em: http://www.mds.gov.br/webarquivos/publicacao/seguranca_alimentar/DHAA_SAN.pdf
6. Rocha C, Liberato RS. Food Sovereignty for Cultural Food Security: The case of an Indigenous Community in Brazil. Food, Culture & Society. dezembro de 2013;16(4):589–602. doi10.2752/175174413X13673466712047
7. Domingues P. Ações afirmativas para negros no Brasil: o início de uma reparação histórica. Revista Brasileira de Educação. agosto de 2005;(29):164–76. doi10.1590/S1413-24782005000200013
8. Soares Filho MM, Bueno PMMG. Demografia, vulnerabilidades e direito à saúde da população prisional brasileira. Ciência & Saúde Coletiva. julho de 2016;21(7):1999–2010. doi10.1590/1413-81232015217.24102015
9. Batista MQ, Zanello V. Saúde mental em contextos indígenas: Escassez de pesquisas brasileiras, invisibilidade das diferenças. Estudos de Psicologia. 2016 ;21(4). Disponível em: http://www.gnresearch.org/doi/10.5935/1678-4669.20160039
10. Borges MC, Buffarini R, Santos RV, Cardoso AM, Welch JR, Garnelo L, et al. Anemia among indigenous women in Brazil: findings from the First National Survey of Indigenous People's Health and Nutrition. BMC Women's Health. 2016. 16(1). Disponível em: https://bmcwomenshealth.biomedcentral.com/articles/10.1186/s12905-016-0287-5
11. Madeira Z, Gomes DD de O. Persistentes desigualdades raciais e resistências negras no Brasil contemporâneo. Serviço Social & Sociedade. dezembro de 2018;(133):463–79. doi10.1590/0101-6628.154
12. Cardoso CS, De Melo LO, Freitas DA. Condições de saúde nas comunidades quilombolas. Revista de Enfermagem UFPE on line. 4 de abril de 2018;12(4):1037. doi10.5205/1981-8963-v12i4a110258p1037-1045-2018
13. Coba, L., Shimabuku, C., & González-Feliu, J. (2019). Improvement of the demand planning of imported seeds in the company Agro Peru SA. In Best Practices in Manufacturing Processes (pp. 261-281). Springer, Cham
14. Gonzalez-Feliu, J., Osorio-Ramirez, C., Palacios-Arguello, L., & Talamantes, C. A. (2018). Local production-based dietary supplement distribution in emerging countries: Bienestarina Distribution in Colombia. In Establishing Food Security and Alternatives to International Trade in Emerging Economies (pp. 297-315). IGI Global.
15. Orjuela-Castro, J. A., Sanabria-Coronado, L. A., & Peralta-Lozano, A. M. (2017). Coupling facility location models in the supply chain of perishable fruits. Research in transportation business & management, 24, 73-80.
16. PMI-Itanhaém Food Bank. 2019. Disponível em: http://www.itanhaem.sp.gov.br/noticias/2011/novembro/banco_alimentos_completa_quatro_anos_referencia_nacional_programa_social.html
17. FUNAI-National Indian Foundation. 2019. Disponível em: http://www.funai.gov.br/
18. Cervo AL, Bervian PA, Silva R da. Metodologia científica. São Paulo: Pearson Prentice Hall; 2009.
19. Buainain, A. M., Romeiro, A. R., & Guanziroli, C. (2003). Agricultura familiar e o novo mundo rural, (pp. 312–347).URL: http://www.scielo.br/scielo.php?script=sci_arttext&pid=S1517-45222003000200011&lng=pt&tlng=pt. doi:10.1590/S1517-45222003000200011.

20. Medina, G., Almeida, C., Novaes, E., Godar, J., & Pokorny, B. (2015). Development conditions for family farming: Lessons from brazil, 74, 386–396. URL: https://linkinghub.elsevier.com/retrieve/pii/S0305750X15001412. doi:10.1016/j.worlddev.2015.05.023
21. INCRA-National Institute of Colonization and Agrarian Reform. Colonization and Agrarian Reform. 2019. Disponível em: http://www.incra.gov.br/
22. Sabbato, A. d., Souza, A. C. d., Buainain, A. M., Guanziroli, C. E., & Filho, H. M.d. S. (2007). Agricultura familiar e inovação tecnológica no Brasil: características,desafios e obstáculos. UNICAMP
23. Federal Government. Lei nº 11.326. Federal Government Plateau - Civil House. 2006. Disponível em: http://www.planalto.gov.br/ccivil_03/_Ato2004-2006/2006/Lei/L11346.htm
24. IBGE-Brazilian Institute of Geography and Statistics - Indigenous People in the 2010 Population Census. Disponível em: https://censo2010.ibge.gov.br/noticias-censo?busca=1&id=3&idnoticia=2194&t=censo-2010-poblacao-indigena-896-9-mil-tem-305-etnias-fala-274&view=noticia
25. CPISP-São Paulo Pro-Indian Commission. Guarani and Tupi. 2019. Disponível em: http://cpisp.org.br/indios-em-sao-paulo/povos-indigenas/guarani-e-tupi/
26. PIB-Indigenous Peoples in Brazil. Guarani Ñandeva 2019. Disponível em: https://pib.socioambiental.org/pt/Povo:Guarani_%C3%91andeva
27. Federal Government. Lei nº 5.371. Federal Government Plateau - Civil House. 1967. Disponível em: http://www.planalto.gov.br/ccivil_03/Leis/1950-1969/L5371.htm
28. PMI-School Feeding Council. Prefeitura de Itanhaém. 2019. Disponível em: http://www2.itanhaem.sp.gov.br/educacao/conselho-de-alimentacao-escolar/
29. MDA-Ministry of Agrarian Development. Secretariat of Family Farming and Cooperatives. 2019. Disponível em: http://www.mda.gov.br/sitemda/secretaria/saf-paa/sobre-o-programa
30. CONAB-National Supply Company. Food Acquisition Program - PAA. 2019. Disponível em: https://www.conab.gov.br/agricultura-familiar/execucao-do-paa
31. Federal Government. Lei nº 11.947. Federal Government Plateau - Civil House. 2009. Disponível em: http://www.planalto.gov.br/ccivil_03/_ato2007-2010/2009/lei/l11947.htm
32. FNDE-National School Feeding Program - PNAE. 2019. Disponível em: https://www.fnde.gov.br/programas/pnae
33. PESM-Parque Estadual Serra do Mar. Unidades de Conservação Núcleo Curucutu. 2019. Disponível em: https://www.infraestruturameioambiente.sp.gov.br/pesm/nucleos/curucutu/
34. INPE-National Institute for Space Research. Maps SOS Mata Atlântica. 2019. Disponível em: http://mapas.sosma.org.br/
35. Felipim AP, Queda O. The guarani mbyá agricultural system and its maize varieties: a case study. Interciencia - Revista de Ciencia y Tecnología de las Américas. 2005;30(3):143–50. Disponivel https://www.interciencia.net/

I L S 2020
INTERNATIONAL CONFERENCE ON INFORMATION SYSTEMS, LOGISTICS & SUPPLY CHAIN
Austin, Texas April 22-24, 2020

PRONAF Rural Financing Distribution Study in Brazilian States

Aguinaldo Eduardo de Souza [1], João Gilberto Mendes dos Reis [2], Paula Ferreira da Cruz Correia [3], João José Giardulli Junior [4], Oduvaldo Vendrametto [5]

[1] Paulista University - UNIP, RESUP/PPGEP, São Paulo, Brazil
[2] Paulista University - UNIP, PPGEP, São Paulo, Brazil; UFGD, PPGA, Dourados, Brazil
[3] Paulista University - UNIP, RESUP/PPGEP, São Paulo, Brazil
[4] Paulista University - UNIP, RESUP/PPGEP, São Paulo, Brazil
[5] Paulista University - UNIP, PPGEP, São Paulo, Brazil
{souza.eduaguinaldo@gmail.com, betomendesreis@msn.com, paulafecruz@gmail.com, jjgiardulli@hotmail.com, oduvaldov@gmail.com}

Abstract. As the world's population grows, the food security chain gets endangered. As declared by the United Nations Organization in 2014, Family Farming has an important place in this scenario. Regarding this situation, since 2006, Brazil has been adopting several family farming funding policies (e.g. PRONAF) aiming to strengthen this kind of familiar production, generate jobs and enhance the income of those farmers. This text intends to demonstrate how this funding works, especially PRONAF, and the main weaknesses of this governmental policy, highlighting the inequality of the resources' distribution among the Brazilian regions, as the Southern region holds 88.79% of all the resources. One of the several causes aggravating this situation is the fact that the family farmers' organization and the Southern region's infrastructure is much better than the other Brazilian regions.

Keywords: PRONAF, Farming Funding, Family Farming.

1. Introduction

The challenges of nations in providing food for their inhabitants cause much discussion. World population growth, estimated at 9.8 billion by 2050, and the global demand for food has drastically increased the pressure on global agriculture [1]. Given these challenges, Family Farming (FF) stands out as a solution to the global food chain, due to the abundant volume of food it generates to sustain the world's population. FAO data [2] indicate that out of 570 million rural establishments, about 90% are of family origin.
In 2011, the United Nations Organization declared 2014 as the "International Year of Family Farming" highlighting the importance of socio-environmental policies in national agendas towards sustainable development for the "Zero Hunger Challenge", recognizing the role that FF plays in reach of food security on the planet [3]. Other studies have reflected on the importance of family-based agriculture as a source of viability for environmental and socioeconomic solutions [4] [5] [6] [7] [8] [9] [10].
In Europe e.g., 70% of farms are family-owned [11]. In Brazil, according to the IBGE Agricultural Census [12], of the more than five million existing rural establishments, 86% (4.3 million) is Family Farming.
[13] [14] [15] emphasize the leading role of family farmers and their social and economic influence on Brazilian agriculture. About 70% of the food consumed in Brazil originates from family farming [16] [17] [18], which reveals the need for specific government policies to promote sustainable development of FF.
Given this reality, it is clear that credit policy is a fundamental instrument for the development of family rural establishments. Over the past 50 years, the Brazilian government has implemented improvements in its rural credit policy, notably with the creation of the National Program for Strengthening Family Farming (PRONAF), specifically targeting small farmers [19] [20] [21] [22].

PRONAF is the main agricultural financing line in Brazil. Since its inception in 1999, it has made more than R$ 21.5 billion available for its subprogram credit lines; In 2018 alone, R$ 3.6 billion were allocated [12].
Nevertheless, the decapitalization of rural producers and limited access to equipment and new technologies are a reality, having, as their primary cause, the difficulty of access to rural credit lines. This is most often observed among low-income farmers in small plots of land in lower-potential productive chains [23] [24] [21] [25].
In this context, this paper aims to contribute to the understanding of the challenges faced by the government in the distribution of credit financing. Considering that the Federative Units of Brazil have specific and antagonistic socioeconomic characteristics, the study aims to analyze PRONAF's resource allocation distribution network.
For this, a social network analysis (SNA) was performed using UCINET 6.0© and NETDRAW 2.166©, to quantify the monetary resources allocated to the states through the PRONAF credit lines.

2. Family Farming in Brazil

A Family Farming in Brazil is composed of a heterogeneous population. From farmers descending from European immigrants, quilombo communities descended from slaves, native Brazilian Indians, and migrant peasants from the Brazilian regions [23] [26].
The settlement program of the National Institute of Colonization and Agrarian Reform (INCRA) has settled many family farmers on small plots of land. Since the 1970s, 9,437 settlement projects have been created throughout Brazil. The distribution of 87.9 million hectares of land benefited 973,471 families [27].
The profile of the Brazilian family producer is contrasting, ranging from households with low-income subsistence agriculture and manual production to farmers with access to technology and mechanized production [28].
Law nº 11,326 [29] defines the prerequisites for framing rural farmers in FF's national policy to qualify family rural enterprises [26]. To be considered family farmers, in addition to the activities being developed in rural areas, the law states that: i) they must have less than four fiscal modules, whose area varies according to the municipality; ii) the workforce must belong to the family; iii) income must come from rural economic activities only; and iv) the establishment must be family managed.

2.1 Government actions in support of Family Farming

Family Farming is an instrument of socio-economic development and promotes wealth and job generation in rural locations [13] [18]. Also, it has been a source of environmental solutions with management models for the conservation of environmental areas [16] [15].
Over the last decades, governments around the globe have put an effort to execute actions aimed at increasing world FF. The United Nations (UN) declared 2014 the International Year of Family Farming, aiming to discuss with the world community the impacts of family farmers on food security, distributive economic development, and sustainability [8].
Academic research has focused on the topic, highlighting the importance of rural farmers as a tool for income distribution and combating social inequality. However, there is a long way to go to implement a system of public policies that meets the demands of world food security, ensuring livelihoods and sustainable development [9] [31]. In this sense, logistical efficiency in agri-food networks is a prime factor for sustainable production in search of food sovereignty and social welfare of local communities [10].
Actions for the development of Family Farming should have a global, not an isolated vision. It is necessary to create a national development strategy [23]. Therefore, strengthening Family Farming in Brazil must be an ongoing state policy process.
In addition to PRONAF, section 3 approaches another important public policy instrument to support family farming. In recent years Brazil has been formulating actions to strengthen Family Farming.
In 2003, the Family Farming Food Acquisition Program (PAA) is instituted [31]. With PAA, the federal government created an institutional market for the acquisition of family agricultural production. This tool aims to ensure food security and support for small farmers [32]. In 2018, 9,675 family farmers submitted 575 projects and received R$ 64.9 million through PAA acquisition instruments [31].
In 2009, another public policy supporting FF was implemented. A law stipulated that 30% of the funds from the National School Meals Program (PNAE) be invested in the direct purchase of FF products, aiming at stimulating the economic and sustainable development of local communities [33].

3. National Program for Strengthening Family Farming (PRONAF)

Regarding social policy, the Family Farming Law (11,326/06) was fundamental to establish concepts and principles, enabling Brazil to develop specific actions aimed at small farmers [34]. Although the Family Farming concept was institutionalized only in 2006, it is noteworthy that the main governmental action related to family farmers was the creation of PRONAF.

Rural credit in Brazil gained importance with the creation of the National Rural Credit System (SNCR) in 1967 [22], becoming at the time one of the main public policy instruments to boost the modernization of agricultural production in Brazil [25].

According to [35], SNCR policy favored the Center-South region of the country, especially the most developed products and users of more advanced technologies, to the detriment of the North-Northeast, traditionally a subsistence monoculture region and with a low incidence of equipment used for agricultural production. In the analysis of [19], the structure of the SNCR focused on capitalized farmers with more economically profitable production chains.

Since the function of credit policy is to promote economic development, it configures a contradiction. Such was the distortion that in the first decade of the program, 1% of producers, i.e. about 10,000 farmers, received 40% of SNCR resources [20]. Rural credit was a catalyst for wealth in favor of the richer: only farmers who could offer greater guarantees received the benefit [22].

In 1994, meeting the demands of social movements linked to family farmers, led by the National Confederation of Agricultural Workers (CONTAG), the Brazilian government institutionalized the Small Rural Production Appreciation Program (PROVAP) [18].

The historical claims of rural producers proposed instruments that could mitigate the deleterious actions of the selective character of the SNCR [25]. However, their results were insignificant as most family farmers had difficulty to access them.

Nevertheless, PROVAP was the structural basis for the creation in 1996 of the first and most important public policy for the rural sector, PRONAF [18]. The program was established to solve the difficulty of access to rural credit by small producers [21] and represented the state's recognition of a new social category, "family farmers", so far classified as small producers, family producers, low-income producers or subsistence farmers [24].

PRONAF's general guideline is to strengthen the productive capacity of family farms, create jobs and income in rural areas, and improve the quality of life of family farmers [36]. Specifically, the authors highlight: a) to adjust public policies according to the reality of family farmers; b) to provide adequate infrastructure to improve the productive performance of family farmers; c) promote the professionalization of family farmers through access to new technologies and social management; and d) insert farmers into input and output markets.

The mechanism of access to PRONAF is the Declaration of Aptitude (DAP), a supporting instrument for framing the farmer as a small producer [37]. Also, the DAP provides smallholder farmers with access to other public policies such as marketing, rural housing programs, and documenting the farmer's agricultural activities for retirement [18].

In the 20-year historical series (Fig. 1), since its existence, the program has financed about R$ 21.5 billion in rural credit, divided into seventeen credit subprograms.

Figure 1: Pronaf rural credit evolution in Brazil

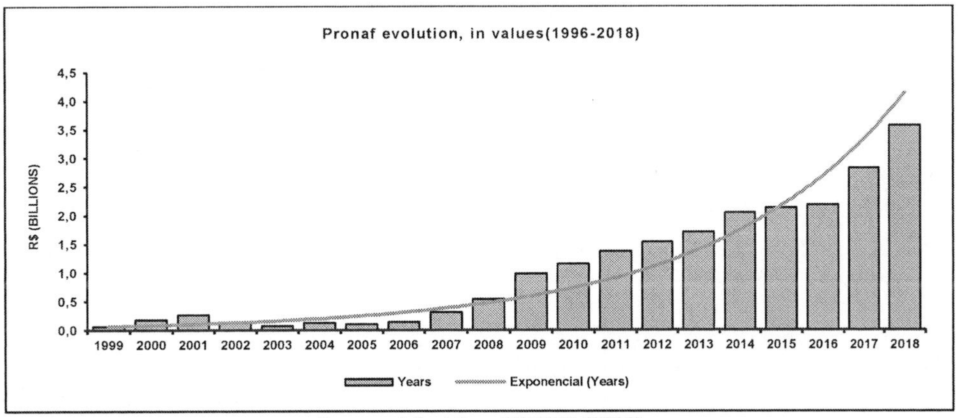

Source: Adapt from BNDES (2019).

As illustrated in Figure 1, the analysis of the 20-year historical series saw a growth of approximately 6,000 percent compared to 1999 (R$ 58.7 million) and 2018 (R$ 3.57 billion). However, 87% of the resources were allocated only in southern Brazil.

Figura 2: Evolution Pronaf subprograms in Brazil

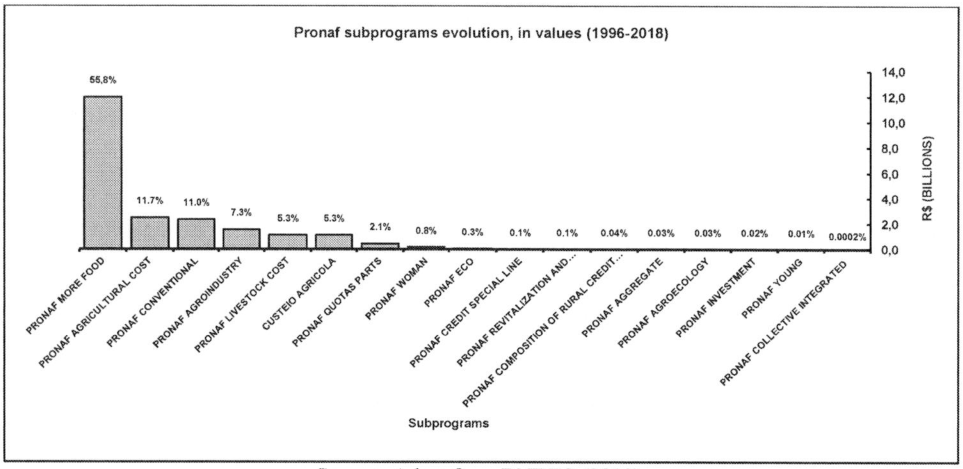

Source: Adapt from BNDES (2019).

Pronaf Agricultural Costing represented 11.7%, which aims to finance the payment of expenses with soil preparation, planting, fertilization, crop treatment, and harvest, especially for the family farmer to achieve higher productivity and higher income.

The third main credit line was the Pronaf Conventional (11%), created initially to combat poverty in the Northeast Region, the credit line aims to serve family members with income up to R$ 23,000 a year, and who invest in productive systems with water and feed reserve; recovery and strengthening of regional food crops; recovery and strengthening of livestock and small farms and irrigated semiarid agriculture.

4. Materials and Methods

To analyze the allocations of PRONAF credit line resources to the Brazilian states, exploratory quantitative research was chosen. The study was conducted in the following steps:

First: Data on financial flow to the Brazilian states were collected through the PRONAF subprogram credit lines in 2018 from the National Development Bank database [37].

Second: The data were structured and compiled using Microsoft Excel in a relational matrix, considering 17 PRONAF credit lines and 27 Brazilian beneficiary states. It was established in two-fold: (i) considering the number of credit lines and the states that receive each benefit; and (ii) demonstrating the number 1 when a connection was produced and 0 otherwise. This arrangement is fundamental to Software UCINET 6.0 ©and Netdraw 2,166 © perform the analysis [38]

Third: Considering the relationships between credit line values and resource receiving states, we create a graphical network with the matrix of credit lines and Brazilian beneficiary states and a degree centrality with matrix 1 and 0. The results are discussed in the next section.

5. Results and Discussions

The analysis performed by the UCINET software translates into numbers the scenario of the destination of 17 PRONAF credit lines (Table 2) concerning the 27 Brazilian states. However, it was decided to list only the seven most prominent states. This representation characterizes the actors involved in the processes and their importance in the interaction network.

The first aspect measured was the degree of centrality that indicates how many actors the study agent is related to, and the normalized degree indicates the percentage of the actors involved [38].

Table 1 shows the degree of entry for the Brazilian states, that is, it translates into numbers the lines of credit each state has received.

Table 1: Degree of entry

Estados	Indegree	nInDegree
Paraná	15	0.349
Rio Grande do Sul	15	0.349
Santa Catariana	15	0.349
Minas Gerais	13	0.302
Espírito Santo	11	0.256
Rondônia	10	0.233
Bahia	9	0.209
Goiás	9	0.209
São Paulo	8	0.186
Ceará	7	0.163
Mato Grosso	7	0.163
Pernambuco	7	0.163
Mato Grosso do Sul	6	0.14
Rio de Janeiro	6	0.14
Para	5	0.116
Paraíba	5	0.116
Piauí	4	0.093
Rio Grande do Norte	4	0.093
Alagoas	3	0.07
Maranhão	3	0.07
Sergipe	3	0.7
Tocantins	2	0.047
Acre	1	0.023
Amazonas	1	0.023
Distrito Federal	1	0.023
Roraima	1	0.023
Amapá	0	0

Source: Adapt from BNDES (2019).

According to Table 1, it is observed that Southern Brazil was responsible for the largest concentration of credit lines. The three southern states, Parana, Rio Grande do Sul, and Santa Catarina obtained fifteen of the seventeen credit lines from the PRONAF program (credit lines such as PRONAF Mais Alimentos and PRONAF Conventional) representing 34%. Then comes the Southeast Region, with the state of Minas Gerais (30%) with twelve and Espírito Santo (25%) with eleven credit lines. The state of Rondônia appears with ten credit lines (23%). It is noteworthy that, of the 27 Brazilian states, the state of Amapá was the only state to have no credit facility for the year 2018.

In Table 2, we chose to analyze the degree of exit, that is, how many interactions credit lines have with the states. These are the types of PRONAF programs studied and the number of times a particular program has been used among Brazilian states.

It is possible to highlight the main programs most used PRONAF Mais Alimentos with 25 interactions, PRONAF Conventional with 22 interactions. The third and fourth-placed PRONAF Aggregate and Livestock Costing have less significant participation with 14 interactions.

Table 2: Degrees of output

Programa	OutDegree	nOutDegree
PRONAF More foods	25	0.581
PRONAF Conventional	22	0.512
PRONAF Aggregate	14	0.326
PRONAF Livestock Costing	14	0.326
PRONAF Agricultural Costing	13	0.302
Agricultural Costing	12	0.279
PRONAF Eco	11	0.256
PRONAF Investment	11	0.256
PRONAF Agroindustria	10	0.233
PRONAF Woman	10	0.233
PRONAF Young	7	0.163
PRONAF LEC- BACEN	7	0.163
PRONAF Agroecology	6	0.14
PRONAF CDCR	4	0.093
PRONAF Quotas Shares	3	0.07
PRONAF Collective Integrated	1	0.023
PRONAF Revitalization and Construction	1	0.023

Source: Adapt from BNDES (2019).

As can be seen in Table 2, it is possible to observe which programs are most used within the country and each doctrine and to draw a profile of the states that use them. The states in the southern region are more developed for agriculture and their members concentrate much of the PRONAF resources, as can be confirmed in Table 1.

Tables 3 and 4 show how close an actor can connect with other actors in the network. This is the calculation of distances so that actors can connect and interact [38].

In this case of Table 3, it is evident that the states that have the largest number of relationships, Paraná, Santa Catarina, and Rio Grande do Sul are those that also have a greater ability to interact with other stakeholders, receive credit lines from many programs.

Table 3: Input proximity degree

Estados	inFarness	inCloseness
Paraná	1247	3.448
Santa Catarina	1247	3.448
Rio Grande do Sul	1247	3.448
Minas Gerais	1333	3.226
Espírito Santo	1419	3.030
Rondônia	1462	2.941
Goiás	1505	2.857
Bahia	1505	2.778
São Paulo	1548	2.778
Pernambuco	1591	2.703
Ceara	1591	2.703
Mato Grosso	1591	2.703
Rio de Janeiro	1634	2.632
Mato Grosso do Sul	1634	2.632
Pará	1677	2.564
Paraíba	1677	2.564
Rio Grande do Norte	1720	2.564
Piauí	1720	2.500
Sergipe	1763	2.439
Alagoas	1763	2.439
Maranhão	1763	2.439
Tocantins	1806	2.439
Roraima	1849	2.381
Distrito Federal	1849	2.326
Acre	1849	2.326
Amazonas	1849	2.326
Amapá	1982	2.273

Source: Adapt from BNDES (2019).

Table 4 shows the PRONAF programs that have the greatest ability to interact with each state. The programs that stood out are the same as those mentioned in Table 2, reinforcing what has already been said. These are programs that have better acceptance among the states.

Table 4: Output proximity degree

Programas	outFarness	outCloseness
PRONAF More foods	817	5.263
PRONAF Conventional	946	4.545
PRONAF Aggregate	1290	3.333
PRONAF Livestock Costing	1290	3.333
PRONAF Agricultural Costing	1333	3.226
Agricultural Costing	1376	3.125
PRONAF Eco	1419	3.030
PRONAF Investment	1419	3.030
PRONAF Agroindustria	1462	2.941
PRONAF Woman	1462	2.941
PRONAF Young	1591	2.703
PRONAF LEC- BACEN	1591	2.703
PRONAF Agroecology	1634	2.632

PRONAF CDCR	1720	2.500
PRONAF Quotas Shares	1763	2.439
PRONAF Collective Integrated	1849	2.326
PRONAF Revitalization and Construction	1849	2.326

Source: Adapt from BNDES (2019).

6. Conclusion

This research aimed to analyze the distribution of PRONAF financing lines between Brazilian regions and their respective states in 2018. Despite the history of actions focused on public policies in the last 50 years (SNCR-1967, PROPAV-1994 and PRONAF-1996), aiming at facilitating access to rural credit, especially for small farmers, and thus equalizing agricultural financing between lower and upper income farmers, the results of the interaction network analysis highlighted the Southern Region. for presenting a higher concentration of use of these resources.

Resource concentration in southern states has been the subject of discussion for some time through studies [19] [23] [20] [21] [22]. Among the factors observed by the authors and responsible for the greater flow of credit in the South Region, are credit lines directed to projects with broad technological development, farmers holding larger areas of production, inserted in the production of economically more profitable chains.

The survey also highlighted the lowest inflow of rural credit financing in the Northeast and North regions. The regions have opposite characteristics of the Southern Region, subsistence agriculture-based production, manual production, low access to technology, and dispersed on small plots of land.

Although in the first three years of PRONAF (1999-2001) the contribution of resources in the North and Northeast Regions has improved, since 2002, resources are scarce for these regions, especially the Northeast. This scenario is slightly modified from 2017. However, by analyzing the distribution of resources in 2018, the Southern Region maintained its role as the program's main borrower with 88.79%. Therefore, when the data show only 11.21% of the resources distributed among other regions (Southeast 4.88%, Midwest 4.77%, North 1.34%, and Northeast 0.22%), it is concluded that PRONAF has not met one of its main objectives: socioeconomic development and the reduction of social inequalities.

7. Acknowledgement

This study was financed in part by the Coordenacao de Aperfeicoamento de Pessoal de Nivel Superior - Brasil (CAPES) - Finance Code 001

8. References

1. UN, U. N. (2017). World population to hit 9.8 billion by 2050, despite nearly universal lower fertility rates. URL: https://news.un.org/en/story/2017/06/560022-world-population-hit-98-billion-2050-despite-nearly-universal-lower-fertility.
2. FAO, F. a. A. O. o. t. U. N. (2019). "smallholders and family farming". family farming knowledge platform. URL: http://www.fao.org/family-farming/themes/small-family-farmers/en/.
3. Swaminathan, M. S., & Kesavan, P. C. (2017). 2014 International Year of Family Farming: a boost to evergreen revolution. World Scientific. URL: http://www.worldscientific.com/worldscibooks/10.1142/10279. doi:10.1142/10279.
4. Hill, B. (1993). The 'myth' of the family farm: Defining the family farm and assessing its importance in the european community. 9, 359–370. URL: https://linkinghub.elsevier.com/retrieve/pii/074301679390048O. doi:10.1016/0743-0167(93)90048-O.
5. USDA, D. d. A. d. E. U. (2012). Census of agriculture - 2012. URL: https://www.nass.usda.gov/AgCensus/.
6. USDA, N. A. S. S. (2015). Fazendas familiares s o foco de novos dados do censo agropecuio | USDA. URL: https://www.usda.gov/media/press-releases/2015/03/17/family-farms-are-focus-new-agriculture-census-data
7. Toader, M., & Roman, G. V. (2015). Family farming – examples for rural communities development, . 6, 89–94. URL: https://linkinghub.elsevier.com/retrieve/pii/S221078431500176X. doi:10.1016/j.aaspro.2015.08.043.
8. Graeub, B. E., Chappell, M. J., Wittman, H., Ledermann, S., Kerr, R. B., & Gemmill-Herren, B. (2016). The state of family farms in the world,. 87, 1–15. URL: https:12//linkinghub.elsevier.com/retrieve/pii/S0305750X15001217. doi:10.1016/j.worlddev.2015.05.012.
9. Maldonado, M., Moya, S. (2013). The Challenge of Implementing Reverse Logistics in Social Improvement: The Possibility of Expanding Sovereignty Food in Developing Communities. In Cheung, J., & Song, H. (eds.) Logistics: Perspectives, Approaches and Challenges (pp. 1-34). Nova Science Publishers, New York), por favor, consulte essas duas obras seminais no assunto.

10. Gonzalez-Feliu, J., Osorio-Ramirez, C., Palacios-Arguello, L., & Talamantes, C. A. (2018). Local production-based dietary supplement distribution in emerging countries: Bienestarina Distribution in Colombia. In Establishing Food Security and Alternatives to International Trade in Emerging Economies (pp. 297-315). IGI Global.
11. Joosse, S., & Grubbström, A. (2017). Continuity in farming - not just family business, 50, 198–208. URL:https://linkinghub.elsevier.com/retrieve/pii/S0743016716306520. doi:10.1016/j.jrurstud.2016.11.018.
12. IBGE, B. I. o. G. a. S. (2017). Agricultural census 2017 – preliminar results. URL: https://sidra.ibge.gov.br/pesquisa/censo-agropecuario/censo-agropecuario-2017.
13. Veiga, J. E. d. (1996). Agricultura familiar e sustentabilidade 13, 383–404.
14. IPEA, I. d. P. E. A. (2010). A agricultura brasileira: desempenho, desafios e perspectivas.
15. EMBRAPA, B. A. R. C. (2011). Environmental economics and environmental services: a study applied to family agriculture, traditional populations and indigenous peoples. URL: https://www.embrapa.br/busca-de-publicacoes/-/publicacao/579891/economia-do-meio-ambiente.
16. Guilhoto, J., Ichihara, S. M., Silveira, F. G., Diniz, B. P. C., Azzoni, C. R., & Moreira,
17. Hoffmann, R. (2015). A agricultura familiar produz 70% dos alimentos consumidos no brasil? 13, 417. URL: https://periodicos.sbu.unicamp.br/ojs/index.php/san/article/view/1386. doi:10.20396/san.v21i1.1386.
18. MDA, M. o. A. D. (2019). Secretariat of family agriculture and cooperativism. URL: http://www.mda.gov.br/sitemda/o-impacto-da-agricultura-familiar-na-economia-brasileira.
19. Schneider, S., Mattei, L., & Cazella, A. A. (2004a). Histórico, caracterização e dinâmica recente do Pronaf – Programa Nacional de Fortalecimento da Agricultura Familiar. SCHNEIDER.
20. Búrigo, F. L. (2010). Sistema Nacional de Crédito Rural: uma trajetória de privilégios, crises e oportunidades. Midiograf.
21. Souza, P. M. d., Ponciano, N. J., Ney, M. G., & Fornazier, A. (2013). Análise da evolução do valor dos financiamentos do pronaf-crédito (1999 a 2010): nero, valor mio e localização14geográfica dos contratos, 51, 237–254. URL: http://www.scielo.br/scielo.php?script=sci_arttext&pid=S0103-20032013000200002&lng=pt&tlng=pt.doi:10.1590/S0103-20032013000200002.
22. Souza, P. M. d., Ney, M. G., & Ponciano, N. J. (2015). Análise da distribuição dos financiamentos rurais entre os estabelecimentos agropecuários brasileiros, 53, 251–270. URL: http://www.scielo.br/scielo.php?script=sci_arttext&pid=S0103-20032015000200251&lng=pt&tlng=pt.doi:10.1590/1234-56781806-9479005302004.
23. Buainain, A. M., Romeiro, A. R., & Guanziroli, C. (2003). Agricultura familiar eo novo mundo rural, . (pp. 312–347). URL: http://www.scielo.br/scielo.php?script=sci_arttext&pid=S1517-45222003000200011&lng=pt&tlng=pt.doi:10.1590/S1517-45222003000200011.
24. Schneider, S., Silva, M. K., & Marques, P. E. M. (2004b). Políticas Públicas e Participação Social no Brasil Rural. (2nd ed.). UFRGS.
25. Godoi, T. G., Burigo, F. L., & Cazella, A. A. (2016). A sustentabilidade dos financiamentos do PRONAF para a agricultura familiar, . 38. URL: http://revistas.ufpr.br/made/article/view/42657. doi:10.5380/dma.v38i0.42657.
26. Medina, G., Almeida, C., Novaes, E., Godar, J., & Pokorny, B. (2015). Development conditions for family farming: Lessons from brazil, 74, 386–396. URL: https://linkinghub.elsevier.com/retrieve/pii/S0305750X15001412. doi:10.1016/j.worlddev.2015.05.023.13
27. INCRA, N. I. o. C. a. A. R. (2019). Colonization and agrarian reform. URL: http://www.incra.gov.br/.
28. Sabbato, A. d., Souza, A. C. d., Buainain, A. M., Guanziroli, C. E., & Filho, H. M.d. S. (2007). Agricultura familiar e inovação tecnológica no Brasil: características, desafios e obstáculos. UNICAMP
29. Federal, G. (2006). Lei 11.326. URL: http://www.planalto.gov.br/ccivil_03/_Ato2004-2006/2006/Lei/L11326.htm.
30. Smith, L. C., & Haddad, L. (2015). Reducing child undernutrition: Past drivers and priorities for the post MDG era, 68, 180–204. URL: https://linkinghub.elsevier.com/retrieve/pii/S0305750X14003726. doi: 10.1016/j.worlddev.2014.11.014.
31. CONAB, C. N. d. A. (2019). Programa de aquisio de alimentos - PAA. URL: https://www.conab.gov.br/agricultura-familiar/execucao-do-paa.
32. Ueno, V. A., Neves, M. C., Queiroga, J. L. d., Filho, L. O. R., & Oliveira, L. P. d. (2016). Estratias de comercialização da agricultura familiar: estudos de caso em assentamentos rurais do estado de s paulo. In 30 anos de assentamentos na Nova República: qual agricultura e qual sociedade queremos?
33. Federal, G. (2009). Lei 11.947. URL: http://www.planalto.gov.br/ccivil_03/_ato2007-2010/2009/lei/l11947.htm.
34. Rockenmeyer, A. C., & Vieira, E. T. (2014). A assimetria informacional e os impactos na política plica de crédito do PRONAF, 3, 198–213. URL: https://doaj.org/article/7c51e9cfde2547b692f41c231aa961ba.
35. Silva, J. G. d., Kageyama, A. A., Romão, D. A., Neto, J. A. W., & Pinto, L. C. G. (1983).
36. Spanevello, R. M., Matte, A., & Boscardin, M. (2016). Crédito rural na perspectiva das mulheres trabalhadoras rurais da agricultura familiar: uma análise do programa nacional de fortalecimento da agricultura familiar (PRONAF), 15, 393–414. URL: http://www.scielo.cl/scielo.php?script=sci_arttext&pid=S0718-65682016000200018&lng=en&nrm=iso&tlng=en. doi:10.4067/S0718-65682016000200018.
37. BNDES, N. D. B. (2019). PRONAF - national program for strengthening family agriculture. URL: http://www.bndes.gov.br/wps/portal/site/home/financiamento/produto/pronaf.
38. Alejandro, V., Norman, A.: Manual Introdutrio Anlise de Redes Sociais. Universidad Autonoma Del Estado de Mexico (2005).

I L S 2020
INTERNATIONAL CONFERENCE ON INFORMATION
SYSTEMS, LOGISTICS & SUPPLY CHAIN
Austin, Texas April 22-24, 2020

Reduction of Number of Empty-Truck Trips in Inter-Terminal Transportation using Multi-agent Q-Learning

Taufik Nur Adi, Yelita Anggiane Iskandar, Hyerim Bae, Yulim Choi

Industrial Engineering Department, Pusan National University, Busan, South Korea
{taufiknuradi@pusan.ac.kr, yelita_iskandar@pusan.ac.kr, hrbae@pusan.ac.kr, flamethrower@pusan.ac.kr}

Abstract. In a port consisting of multiple container terminals, the demand for transportation of containers and cargo among port facilities is high. Almost all transshipment containers bound for a vessel generally are transported from one terminal to another within a short period, which process is known as inter-terminal transportation (ITT). Adequate ITT planning is required in order to reduce ITT-related costs. Minimization of the number of Empty-Truck trips has gained attention, as the ITT problem incurs ITT-related costs. A single Q-Learning-based technique developed in a previous study for minimization of the number of empty-truck trips required high computational time while learning from a considerable amount of orders data. This paper proposes multi-agent Q-Learning to improve the performance offered by the previous single-agent-based model. Our results show that multi-agent Q-Learning performs better than the single-agent alternative in terms of computation time and, therefore too, the quality of its results.

Keywords: Inter-Terminal Transportation, Empty-Truck Trips, Multi-agent Q-Learning

1. Introduction

The immense growth of global trade has greatly increased the numbers of containerized shipments, which fact obliges most major ports to develop more terminals to satisfy the swelling container transport demand. Adding more terminals, however, increases the demand for transportation of containers between different terminals in a port, which process is known as inter-terminal transportation (ITT). A shipping liner has an exclusive contract with a trucking company to transport a container from one terminal to another. This container transportation process might produce empty-truck trips if the trucking company does not perform adequate planning. According to [1], [2], one of the efficient-ITT objectives is the minimization of Empty-Truck trips. Appropriate planning is crucial in achieving such objectives in support of a port's competitiveness. [3] states that Empty-Truck trips at container terminals remain a critical problem, since trucks are still the primary mode of freight transportation in most terminals, and the trucking company has to pay the costs incurred whether the truck's cargo space is filled or empty. Busan New Port is the new port of Busan developed by the South Korean government to alleviate cargo congestion. It operates five container terminals with 23 berths (of 45 planned). According to data collected in 2013, approximately 2600 containers are moved between the terminals each day [4]. The ITT evaluation project conducted by Busan Port Authority (BPA) in 2014 [5] indicated how critical efficient ITT operations are to the competitiveness of many large seaports. In our previous study, [6], we attempted to alleviate Empty-Truck trips using single-agent Q-Learning. Q-Learning is one of the Reinforcement Learning (RL) methods that can be applied to solve a broad spectrum of complex real-world problems such as robotics, manufacturing, and others. Despite its interesting properties, Q-Learning is a prolonged method that requires a long training time to learn an acceptable policy. Based on our previous study, the performance of single-agent Q-Learning is acceptable when learning from a small amount of data, but the performance drops as the data significantly expands in size. In order to solve or at least minimize this problem, [8] and [9] propose multi-agent models to speed up the learning process and to gain better results. Thus too, in the present study, multi-agent Q-learning was employed to overcome the performance problem of the previous single-agent Q-learning.

This paper is organized as follows. Section 2 discusses the related work, section 3 provides the problem description, section 4 outlines the proposed multi-agent Q-Learning, and section 5 presents the experimental results. Finally, section 6 draws conclusions and looks forward to future work.

2. Related Work

In the literature, several studies on the reduction of the number of Empty-Truck trips can be found. [10] conducted a comprehensive review of the Empty-Truck problem at container terminals. The author identified the causes, benefits, and constraints, and proposed two collaborative approaches, namely collaborative logistics network (CLN) and shared transportation, to overcome the problem. [11] proposed a collaborative Truck Appointment System (TAS) to reduce Empty-Truck trips and evaluated that approach with a simulation model based on a case study with real-world data from Santo Antonio, Chile. The result showed that collaborative TAS might be a useful tool to reduce Empty-Truck-trip numbers. [12] proposed a mathematical approach that combines multiple trips, such as import, export, and inland trips, in a specific port environment. This study considered a scheme to reduce the number of total Empty-Truck trips, whereby two 20 ft containers are carried simultaneously on the same truck and according to the same load unit. [13] used modified Q-Learning to find a more optimal travel plan for an on-demand bus system. Most of the previous studies mentioned above, tackled problems with similar characteristics to those of ITT-related problems, such as the transportation mode used, the transportation demand, the transportation capacity, the order time-window, and transportation trip plans. Utilization of the RL approaches to solve ITT-related problems, meanwhile, remains limited. But certainly, as emphasized in [9], performance improvement of single-agent RL remains an interesting topic of discussion as well as an opportunity for further research.

3. Problem Description

ITT refers to container transportation between separated port facilities such as container terminals, empty container depots, repair stations, logistics facilities, dedicated transport terminals, and administrative facilities. Essential information needing to be provided in ITT operations includes ITT demand, origin, destination, delivery time-windows, available modes, and available connections [14]. In our present case, all of the essential information was known in advance. A solution to the ITT problem had to satisfy the following feasibility restrictions: each transport task has to be performed, and it must be performed by only one truck; the transport task has to be performed within its given time window. In the beginning, the starting location of the truck is terminal 1. After the truck has served a task, its ending location will be the destination of the task it has performed. TABLE 1 shows an example of a task table, which consists of task id, origin, destination, start, and end of the time window. In our case, only five terminals (T1, T2, T3, T4, and T5) involved as origin and destination. The objective of our case is to produce a trip plan that entails the minimum number of Empty-Truck trips for a given task list. Utilization of RL helped to determine which task was to be served next under certain conditions in order to minimize the number of Empty-Truck trips.

Table 1. Example of the task

Task Id	Origin	Destination	Start TW	End TW
1	T1	T3	0	15
2	T3	T1	0	60
3	T2	T5	20	80
4	...	...	...	...

In our previous study [6], single-agent Q-learning was utilized to learn from different numbers of container transportation tasks (10, 20, 40, 80, 180) consisting of task id, origin, destination, start, and end of time window. Q-learning required 59 seconds for learning from the 180 tasks, and which time duration increased drastically for more than 180 tasks. This performance issue became a significant problem when Q-learning had to learn from real ITT data that might contain thousands of tasks.

4. Proposed Multi-agent Q-learning

This section presents single-agent Q-learning along with the proposed multi-agent Q-learning. Fig. 1 provides an overview of the RL component, which consists of state (s), action (a), and reward (r). An agent interacts with the environment by executing an action in the current state; the agent receives a reward from the environment and moves to the next state. The reward acts as feedback that indicates how good the actions chosen by the agent from a state were.

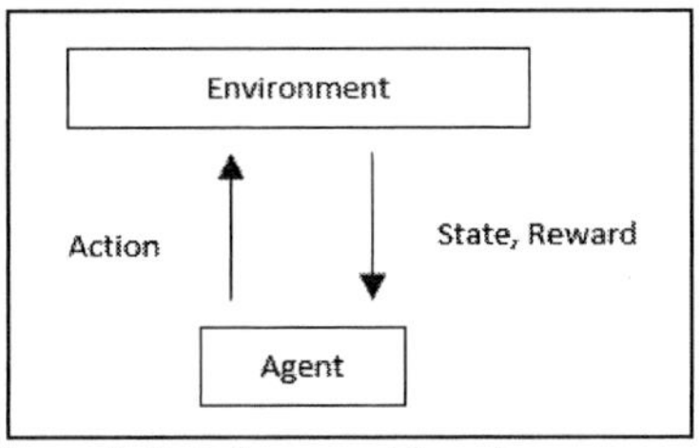

Figure 1. Reinforcement learning component

4.1. Single-agent Q-learning

Q-learning, the most popular among the RL algorithms, is categorized as a model-free algorithm since it does not require any knowledge of the agent's environment. In single-agent Q-learning, the environment is mapped into a finite number of states. In any state, an agent can choose an action according to a given policy. The agent learns the optimal state-action value for each state-action pair based on the principle of Dynamic Programming (DP) and realizes it with the Bellman Equation (BE) [15]. The agent attempts to determine the optimal policy in order to maximize the sum of discounted expected rewards [16]. Single-agent Q-learning is updated using the following equation (1)[17]:

$$Q(s,a) \leftarrow (1-\alpha)Q(s,a) + \alpha[r(s,a) + \gamma \sum_{s'} P[s' \mid (s,a)] \underset{a'}{Max} Q(s',a')] \quad (1)$$

where $Q(s,a)$ is the Q-value and $r(s,a)$ is the immediate reward in state s corresponding to action a, $a' \in \{a\}$ is the action in the next state $s' \in \{s\}$, $\gamma \in [0,1]$ denotes the discounting factor, and $\alpha \in [0,1]$ is the learning rate. Q-learning estimates the Q-value based on both the current state and its expected values in the future, where $r(s,a) + \gamma \sum_{s'} P[s' \mid (s,a)] \underset{a'}{Max} Q(s',a')$.

The Q-function updates the Q-values continuously and stores them in a table called Q-table. Based on [6], our Q-table structure is a matrix of size n x m, where n is the number of possible actions of an agent, and m is the number of states in the environment. The state and action space of our Q-learning is 240 states and five actions, respectively.

4.2. Proposed Multi-agent Q-learning

Fig. 2 shows the learning architecture of multi-agent Q-learning. The design of the proposed multi-agent Q-learning was adopted from [9], which implemented one of the partitioning techniques known as domain decomposition. This technique will divide the whole data, which is learned by RL, into several groups. And, each group of data will be assigned to an identical agent. In other words, the learning process of each agent operating over a different portion of the Q-table will focus on one subgroup of states. An agent maintains its own Q-table while learning. At the same time, at every end of the learning episode, an agent must store its Q-value to the global Q-table by considering the specific updating rule. The structures of global and local Q-tables are the same. The local Q-table is used by an agent for storage of Q-values as learning results from a segment of the data. The global Q-table is used to save the optimal learning results from all of the agents.

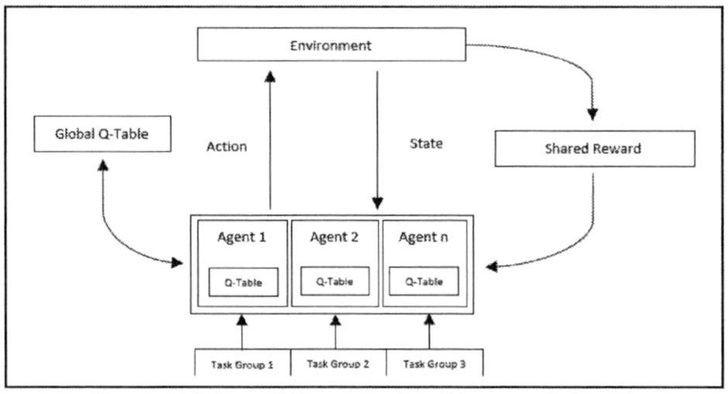

Figure 2. The architecture of multi-agent Q-learning

With the architecture shown in Fig. 2, synchronization between the global and local Q-tables becomes a challenging issue. A specific rule must be applied to prevent the race condition and unexpected overwriting value in the global Q-table. The following rule is applied when updating the Q-value in the global Q-table:

$$Q^{global}(s,a) = \begin{cases} Q^{local}(s,a), \text{ if } Q^{global}(s,a) < Q^{local}(s,a) \\ Q^{global}(s,a), \text{ otherwise} \end{cases} \quad (2)$$

The agent performs the process of updating the global Q-table after finishing one episode of learning, and notably, this process runs only one way, from local Q-table to global Q-table.

5. Experimental Results

The algorithm was implemented in Python and run on a PC equipped with an Intel® Xeon® CPU E3-1230 v5 of 3.40 GHz and 16GB memory. To assess the proposed method, we considered three scenarios for the numbers of tasks (250, 500, and 1000 tasks, respectively) and three scenarios for the numbers of agents (1, 2, and 4 agents). Each task is characterized by origin, a destination, start and end time-window, as shown in TABLE 1, and a task can be assigned to one truck only. A truck will serve tasks for 8 hours (one shift standard period) as a constraint. For the Q-learning configurations, the γ value was set to 0.9, and α was set to 0.01; the algorithm ran for 100 episodes.

Table 2. Computational time and Empty-Truck-trips comparison for each scenario

		Fastest Computational Time and Lowest Empty-Truck Trips (LETT) Found					
No	**Tasks**	**1 Agent**	**LETT**	**2 Agents**	**LETT**	**4 Agents**	**LETT**
1	250	564.976 s	124	562.137 s	121	564.027 s	124
2	500	955.672 s	172	953.385 s	180	954.154 s	178
3	1000	1404.323 s	236	1401.285 s	230	1403.836 s	232

TABLE 2 compares the computational time and Empty-Truck trips for each scenario. The single-agent here was used as a baseline for the comparison in order to determine whether the multi-agents obtain a better result of not. In terms of computational time, all of the scenarios showed a slight decrement within the range of 1 to 3 seconds when the number of agents was increased. On the contrary, the increasing number of agents did not always lead to a minimal number of Empty-Truck trips. In both respects, scenario 3 obtained better results than did scenarios 1 or 2.

Table 3. Computational time speedup comparison for each scenario

Num. of the agent(s)	Number of tasks					
	250 Tasks		500 Tasks		1000 Tasks	
	Time	Speedup	Time	Speedup	Time	Speedup
1	564.976 s	---	955.672 s	---	1404.323 s	---
2	562.137 s	2.839 s	953.385 s	2.287 s	1401.285 s	3.038 s
4	564.027 s	0.949 s	954.154 s	1.518 s	1403.836 s	0.487 s

TABLE 3 shows the speedup improvement of the computational time for each scenario. Overall, the increasing number of agents decreased the computational time by up to 3 seconds. The use of two agents in all of the task scenarios obtained a better speedup (2.7213 seconds of average decrement) in computational time than did the use of four agents, which obtained 0.984 seconds of average decrement.

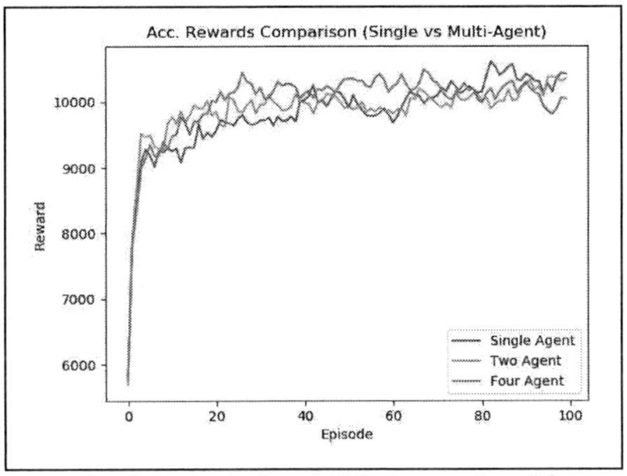

Figure 3. Rewards comparison between single-agent RL, two agents, and four agents for scenario 3

Fig. 3 shows the rewards comparison between the single-agent and multi-agents for scenario 3. At the end of the episode, single-agent RL obtains better rewards than did multi-agent RL. Nonetheless, overall, multi-agent RL outperformed single-agent RL, since, in most episodes, such as 20 to 75, it gained better rewards than did single-agent RL.

6. Conclusion

In this paper, we have presented a multi-agent Q-learning implementation. The multi-agent architecture adopts the concept of domain decomposition, which divides the data into several groups, and assigns each group to identical RL agents to be learned. The results obtained show that, overall, multi-agent RL has the potential to speed up the computational time by increasing the proper number of agents, and, thereby, to achieve a better result. However, the expected significant improvement was not achieved. Based on our investigation, the strategy on how the agents synchronize its local and global Q-table becomes one of the bottlenecks for the computational time. Therefore, the critical challenge when dealing with multi-agents is the cost of synchronization between the global Q-table and the agent's local Q-table, which might affect the overall computational time. This notwithstanding, domain decomposition will enable the multi-agents to handle the larger problem. The alternative architecture and strategy are needed in the future works to solve the cause of computational time bottlenecks. The applicability of the proposed approach, however, remains limited by the following factors: the number of container terminals is fixed (i.e., five), the number of tasks is static (i.e., known in advance), the number of available trucks is manually determined in advance (i.e., 40 trucks for scenario 1 and 2, 100 trucks for scenario 3) and the capacity of the truck is only one container. The study of ITT is drawing more attention these days, simply because container port competitiveness is so critical. Designing RL methods to solve more complex and more realistic ITT problems, such as multi-objective inter-terminal truck routing, collaborative inter-terminal transportation, and dynamic trip planning, is the goal and the opportunity of future research.

Acknowledgement.
This research was a part of the project titled 'Development of IoT Infrastructure Technology for Smart Port', funded by the Ministry of Oceans and Fisheries, Korea.

7. References

1. Duinkerken, M., Dekker, R., Kurstjens, S., Ottjes, J. and Dellaert, N.: Comparing transportation systems for inter-terminal transport at the Maasvlakte container terminals, OR Spectrum. vol. 28. no. 4. pp. 469-493 (2006)
2. Tierney, K., Voß, S., and Stahlbock, R.: A mathematical model of inter-terminal transportation. European Journal Operation Research 235(2). pp.448–460 (2014)
3. Islam, S.: Empty truck trips problem at container terminals. Business Process Management Journal. vol. 23. no. 2. pp. 248-274 (2017)
4. Jin, X., and Kim, K.: Collaborative Inter-Terminal Transportation of Containers. Industrial Engineering & Management Systems. vol. 17. no. 3. pp. 407-416 (2018)
5. Kopfer, H., Jang, D., and Vornhusen, B.: Scenarios for Collaborative Planning of Inter-Terminal Transportation. Lecture Notes in Computer Science. pp. 116-130 (2016)
6. Adi, T., Iskandar, Y., Bae, H.: Q-Learning-based Technique for Reduction of Number of Empty-Truck Trips in Inter-Terminal Transportation, 14th International Conference on innovative Computing, Information and Control (ICICIC2019), August 26-29, 2019, Seoul, South Korea.
7. Zhou, T., Hong, B., Shi, C. H. Z.: Cooperative behaviour acquisition based modular Q-Learning in multi-agent system. Proceeding of the fourth international conference on machine learning and cybernetics. Guangzhou. 18-21 August (2005)
8. Busoniu, L., Babuska, R., and De Schutter, B.: A Comprehensive Survey of Multiagent Reinforcement Learning. IEEE Transactions on Systems, Man, and Cybernetics, Part C (Applications and Reviews). vol. 38. no. 2. pp. 156-172 (2008)
9. Printista, A., Errecalde, M., and Montoya, C.: A parallel implementation of Q-learning based on communication with cache. Journal of Computer Science & Technology. vol. 1, no. 6 (2002)
10. Islam, S.: Empty truck trips problem at container terminals. Business Process Management Journal. vol. 23, no. 2. pp. 248-274 (2017)
11. Schulte, F., González, R. and Voß, S.: Reducing Port-Related Truck Emissions: Coordinated Truck Appointments to Reduce Empty Truck Trips. Lecture Notes in Computer Science. pp. 495-509 (2015)
12. Caballini, C., Rebecchi, I. and Sacone, S.: Combining Multiple Trips in a Port Environment for Empty Movements Minimization. Transportation Research Procedia. vol. 10. pp. 694-703 (2015)
13. Mukai, N., Watanabe, T. and Feng, J.: Route Optimization Using Q-Learning for On-Demand Bus Systems. Lecture Notes in Computer Science. pp. 567-574 (2008)
14. Heilig, L., Lalla-Ruiz, E. and Voß, S.: port-IO: an integrative mobile cloud platform for real-time inter-terminal truck routing optimization. Flexible Services and Manufacturing Journal. vol. 29, no. 3-4, pp. 504-534, (2017)
15. Bellman, R.E.: Dynamic programming, Proc. Natl. Acad. Sci. USA 42 (10) (1957)
16. Pashenkova, E., Rish, I., Dechter, R.: Value iteration and policy iteration algorithms for Markov decision problem. AAAI 96: in: Workshop on Structural Issues in Planning and Temporal Reasoning. (1996)
17. Watkins, C.J., Dayan, P., Technical note: Q-learning, Mach. Learn. 8 (3–4) (1992)

I L S 2020
INTERNATIONAL CONFERENCE ON INFORMATION
SYSTEMS, LOGISTICS & SUPPLY CHAIN
Austin, Texas April 22-24, 2020

Costs of Soybean Transportation in Piaui State, Brazil: A Case Study

José Alberto Alencar Luz[1,2], João Gilberto Mendes dos Reis[1,2]

[1] RESUP/PPGEP - Universidade Paulista, São Paulo, Brazil
[2] Dinter PPGEP – UNIP/FSA
{josealberto@socimol.com, joao.reis@docente.unip.br}

Abstract. Soybean plays an important role in world agribusiness. Nowadays, Brazil is the largest global exporter and the main impact for the country is transportation costs. These costs are influenced by the mode of transport used, distance to the cargo ports and infrastructure. The Piauí state, for instance, is the new frontier of soybean production in Brazil with a low cost of land and excellent productivity rates. However, the logistics infrastructure affects the profitability of growers and transporters. In this sense, this article analysis the transportation costs of soybean movements among Piaui regions and cargo ports and explore different scenarios considering the future implementation of the railway service. The results showed that despite efforts to improve the movement of soybean exports from Piaui state, with the building a new railway and two new routes, the current route remains the best option for growers and transporters.
Keywords: Soybean, Piaui state, Transportation costs, Competitiveness, Growers profitability.

1. Introduction

Soybean is one of the leading world commodities, being consumed in nature, as bioproducts and as the main protein source of animal feed. The major producers of this grain are Argentina, Brazil, and the United States, with China as the world-leading importer [1]. Due to the need for large planting areas and adequate climate, soybean needs to be transported over large distances domestically and abroad to be processing and consumed. Therefore, the costs and investments in the supply chain and logistics play an essential role in the competitiveness of this product.

The transportation costs in Brazil, for example, are extremely high while the land cost is very low. Hyland [2] emphasizes that soybean production costs in the United States are higher compared to South American countries; however domestic transportation costs are significantly lower. Brazil, for example, has higher grain yields at lower production costs [3], but transportation costs may reach 146% higher during the harvest [4].

The primary consumer market for soybean is China. The Chinese government has been increasing grain imports in recent years due to the growing demand determined by improved population quality of life and changes in consumption structure [5]. The imports of Chinese grain increased from 84.64 Mt in 2013 to 130.62 Mt in 2017, an increase of 54% [6].

In this scenario, Brazil appears as one of the leading global soybean exporters but faces bottlenecks relate to the lack of transport infrastructure with limited rail availability and high dependence on roadway modal [3]. The problem is increasing due to the migration of production to regions with lower land costs but with a more deficient logistics infrastructure. One of these new production centers in the state of Piaui.

The main logistical problem of the state is the lack of a port of discharge. The closest port to the Piauiense Savanna vegetation is the Port of Itaqui which operates Mato Grosso grain production and handled 8.5 million tons in 2018. The route between Piaui Savanna and Itaqui only can be made by truck. Piaui production is accounting for 9% of total Brazilian soybean exports and almost 8% of exports to China,

Currently, the road transport alternative from production to the port is the most used in the Piauiense Savanna [7] and is ongoing a railway constructing linking the city of Eliseu Martins to the ports of Pecem and Suape, in Ceara and Pernambuco state respectively.

Based on this new future opportunity to move grains from the state to the ports that the present article analyzes whether the current characteristics of logistic flow such as cost, transport time and distance impact will be improved with these new routes. For this purpose, a cost comparison was made between the current route and the projected routes, considering the distances and costs per route between the soybean-producing municipalities and the destinations.

This article is structured as follows; After the Introduction, Methodology session 2 presents different scenarios considering origin and destinations, in addition to the use of available and designed modes. This method has been used in other countries with different results. In session 3 the results of the research are presented, and the discussion was held.

2. Methodology

This paper aims to analyze the routes available for the Soybean Transport from the Piauiense Savanna to the available cargo ports and to project future situations using other modes of transport for the soybean flow to the port. The railroad used in the analyzes it is still under construction. In the near future, this railway will enable producers to make strategic decisions involving time and cost. This study also seeks to offer guidelines for new projects and to improve the logistics infrastructure of Brazilian exports of soybean, as well as grain exports in general.

Based on the research developed by Ndembe [8] on transport logistics in Australia, with the analysis of different scenarios on rail sections from origin and destination to compose transport costs and time, and studies from Ghaderi [9] who verified the system of logistics transport Vietnamese, discussing the logistics infrastructure based on strategic dimensions that involve aspects of the infrastructure, we decided to verify the case of the state of Piaui.

In addition, this study also adopted the work of Banomyong [10] who explored the various transport route alternatives and methods available for exporters from Laos, Asian countries to make it easier to sell their products to the European Union. The authors used a multimodal transport model to verify route alternatives, using the following variables: cost, time, distance, mode of transport and transshipment.

Specifically, the present study adopted the following procedures:

- First, the values of road freight were established using the values of freight provided by the Brazilian National Land Transportation Agency - ANTT [11]. The value of road freight was considered according to Resolution No. 5820/2018 of the entity defining the minimum road freight. The road distances were consulted on Google Maps®. The routes envisaged considered road displacements from municipalities to the Ports. The size of the trucks considered in the analysis for bulk cargo was 7-axle, two-axle profile, carrying 38 tons of soybean per trip [12]. The Freight cost is considered per kilometer.
- Second, the rail freight was performed regarding the spreadsheet of the West SA stretch concessionaire Latin America logistics - ALL controlled by ANTT Resolution No. 3730/2011 [13] corresponding to the transportation of soybeans that operates in the Midwest region of Brazil, as a reference, once Transnordestina railway mentioned is not running yet.
- Third, a formation of the routes and the determination of the values follow steps presented in Figure 1. Eleven cities were chosen, which represent [14] 96% of the soybean production of the state.

To calculate the cost of the routes we used equations 1, 2 and 3.

$$FRA = DItq \times Cfr \tag{1}$$

Where:

FRA = Current Freight Cost in Dollar / Ton
DItq = Road distance from the municipality to Porto Itaqui-MA in KM
* Cfr = Freight cost Dollar / ton / KM:

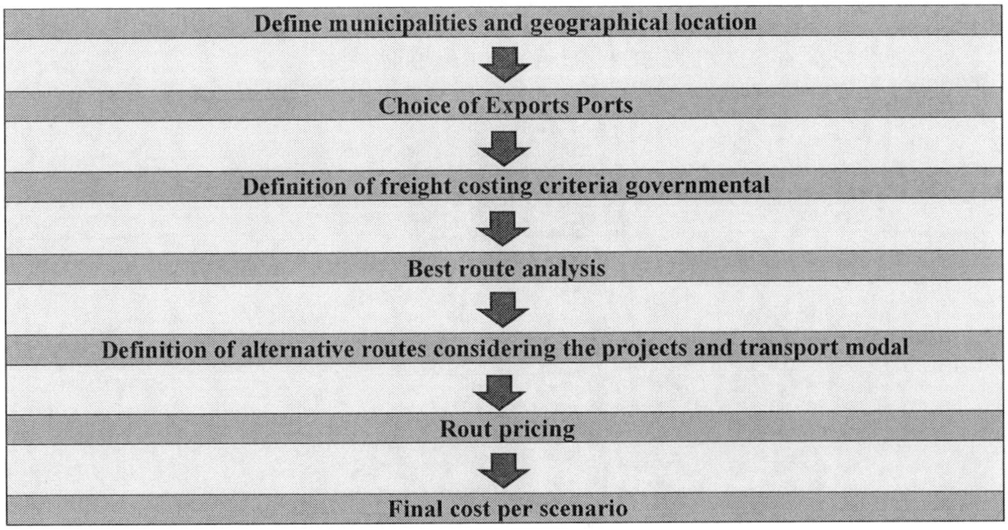

Figure 1: Data preparation steps for method application

$$\text{TFR} = (\text{DistEM x CRdFr}) + \text{Tcost} + (\text{DistFP x RlFr}) \tag{2}$$

Where:

TRF = Total freight cost Dollar / ton
DistEM = Road distance from the municipality to the city of Elizeu Martins, intermodal point for the KM rail
CRdFr = Road Freight Cost Dollar / ton / KM[1]
Tcost = Transfer cost Dollars / ton
DistFP = Railway Distance to destination cargo port KM
CRlFr = Rail Freight Cost Dollar / ton / KM[2]

$$\text{CFR} = \text{Dist x CkamE x NA} \tag{3}$$

Where:

CFR = Freight Cot road
Dist = Distance
CkmE = kilometer cost per axle
NA = number of axes

3. Results

3.1 Soybean Logistics in Piauí State

Piauí is in the third position at the soybean exporter ranking in northeastern Brazil according to the United States Department of Agriculture - USDA [3]. It has a great potential for expansion due to the availability of areas. According to Gibbs [15] the area of MATOPIBA - Soybean production area that encompasses

[1] Road Freight = Distance Distance by Track x Standard cost per kilometer related to the number of axles of the truck according to the stretch.

[2] Rail Freight = freight cost per ton / km between 810 and 1,600 km for soybean.

the states of Maranhão, Tocantins, Piaui and Bahia, that also includes Piauí, is one of the most recent areas of expansion of soy production.

The state current logistics are operationalized as shown in Figure 2.

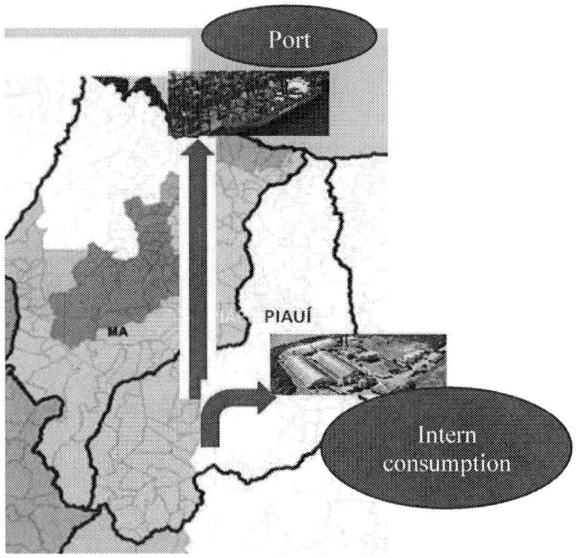

Figure 2: Current soybean runoff situation

The smallest portion of the soybean production of the Piaui is destined for domestic consumption and the majority (around 90%) is exported [16]. Currently, the production is all transported to Ports by trucks. Soybeans destined for domestic consumption are usually purchased by trades such as the company Bunge Food Company, headquartered in the municipality of Uruçuí / PI. The company crushes to produce bran and oil to supply nearby markets mainly for animal feed, as well as other human consumption products. Regarding the external market, Brazilian Federal Government are building a new railway among the city of Eliseu Martins in Piaui connecting the Ports of Pecem, Ceara state and Suape, Pernambuco state [17], Figure 3.

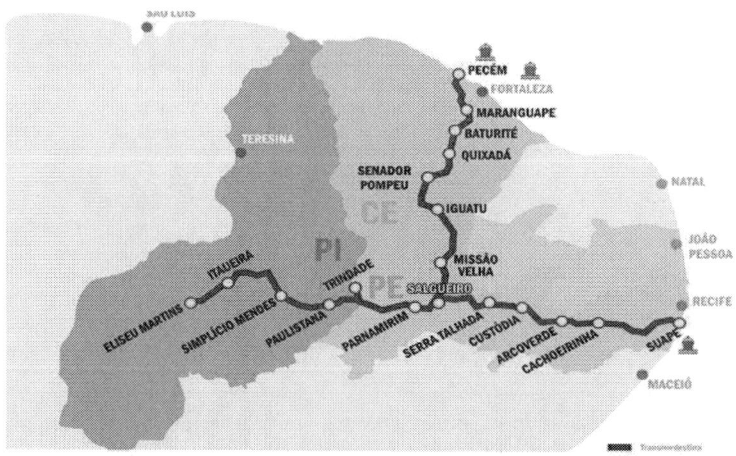

Figure 3: Transnordestina Railway Project Map. Retrieved from [17]

3.2 Cost Statement of Freight and Rout Projections

The soybean outflow to the foreign market should consider the distances traveled from farms to ports or farms to rail terminals. This article used the distance between the downtown of the municipalities and cargo ports. In addition to the mentioned aspects, the value of freight did not consider the period of high demand or harvest, as freight usually gets higher due to the increased demand for transportation.

As mentioned early, three situations are compared. First, the production areas to Port of Itaqui, Table 1. Second, production areas to Port of Pecem using intermodal system (road + rail), Table 2. Third, production areas to Port of Suape using intermodal system (road + rail), Table 3. Soybean reference values were surveyed on 6/18/2019 from $ 312.82 [18] a ton and the exchange rate in one dollar to $ 4,1734 [19] quote at the Brazilian central bank in 09/23/2019.

Regarding Tables 1, 2 and 3, the representation of the reference values of soybean transportation costs considered acceptable in the literature represents 30% of the total value [20]. Tables 2 and 3 consider the cost of transhipment between the modes. When comparing the hypothesis of road freight, theoretically, the highest result of flow I cause a percentage of 14.05%, shown in the current scenario.

A study from USDA [3] presented a table with the freight costs of the municipality of Bom Jesus-PI to Porto worth U$ 0.0358, however, two years ago, when compared to the survey data, represents an increase of 28,49%, in addition to the rising cost of fuel in recent years. It is believed that the new pricing policy established by the Brazilian government following the strike movements in 2018, among other things, influenced this variation.

Table 1: Current flow to Itaqui Port

Municipalities Origin - Soybean producers	Road distance (KM)	freight cost / ton U$	Total Freight Cost U$	Transit time day
Baixa Grande do Ribeiro	970	0,042	40,674	1
Uruçuí	749	0,051	38,387	1
Ribeiro Gonçalves	796	0,047	37,087	1
Bom Jesus	941	0,046	43,404	1
Santa Filomena	1045	0,046	47,714	1
Currais	954	0,046	44,004	1
Gilbués	1106	0,046	50,499	1
Sebastião Leal	760	0,047	35,764	1
Monte Alegre do Piauí	1096	0,046	50,043	1
Corrente	1183	0,046	54,015	1
Palmeira do Piauí	914	0,046	42,159	1

[a] Lowest value [b] Highest value

Table 2: Flow from Eliseu Martins to PECÉM / CE Port via Transnordestina Railway

Municipalities Origin - Soybean producers	Road distance (km)	Road freight cost / ton (U$)	Railway distance (km)	Cost freight/ ton Railway (U$)	Transshipment cost (U$)	Total Freight Cost (U$)	Transit time (days)
Baixa Grande do Ribeiro	291	0,055	1112	0,037	0,4	57,182	3
Uruçuí	174	0,062	1112	0,037	0,4	52,101	3
Ribeiro Gonçalves	280	0,055	1112	0,037	0,4	56,582	3
Bom Jesus	142	0,062	1112	0,037	0,4	50,118	3
Santa Filomena	412	0,075	1112	0,037	0,4	72,032	3
Currais	153	0,062	1112	0,037	0,4	50,800	3
Gilbués	305	0,051	1112	0,037	0,4	56,950	3
Sebastião Leal	100	0,010	1112	0,037	0,4	51,290	3
Monte Alegre do Piauí	295	0,055	1112	0,037	0,4	57,400	3
Corrente	382	0,051	1112	0,037	0,4	60,897	3
Palmeira do Piauí	113	0,062	1112	0,037	0,4	48,321	2

[a] Lowest value [b] Highest value

Table 3: Flow from Eliseu Martins to SUAPE / PE Port via Transnordestina Railway

Municipalities Origin - Soybean producers	Road distance (km)	Road freight cost / ton (U$)	Railway distance (km)	Cost freight/ ton Railway (U$)	Transshipment cost (U$)	Total Freight Cost (U$)	Transit time (days)
Baixa Grande do Ribeiro	291	0,055	1130	0,037	0,4	57,633	3
Uruçuí	174	0,062	1130	0,037	0,4	52,552	3
Ribeiro Gonçalves	280	0,055	1130	0,037	0,4	57,031	3
Bom Jesus	142	0,062	1130	0,037	0,4	50,570	3
Santa Filomena	412	0,075	1130	0,037	0,4	72,485	3
Currais	153	0,062	1130	0,037	0,4	51,250	3
Gilbués	305	0,051	1130	0,037	0,4	57,405	3
Sebastião Leal	100	0,010	1130	0,037	0,4	51,742	3
Monte Alegre do Piauí	295	0,055	1130	0,037	0,4	57,857	3
Corrente	382	0,051	1130	0,037	0,4	61,354	3
Palmeira do Piauí	113	0,062	1130	0,037	0,4	48,777	3

[a] Lowest value [b] Highest value

3.3 Freight costs and routes remakes

Table 4 shows the cost of freight in the current stretches and hypotheses of the Transnordestina railway to the ports of Pecém and Suape.

Tabela 4: Scenario Comparison

Scenario	Highest reight costs found (US$)	Lowest freight costs found (US$)	Average freight costs (US$)	Soybean Ton (US$)	Percentage
Current scenario	$43,97	$38,387	$54,015	$312,82	14,05%
Scenario Simulation I Pecém Transnordestina	$55,78	$48,321	$72,032	$312,82	17,83%
Scenario Simulation II Suape Transnordestina	$56,24	$48,777	$72,485	$312,82	17,97%

Table 4 presents the percentage of cargo freight on soybean prices. The value differences between flows are relatively small. In the two scenarios projected with the railway, costs are bigger compared to the current situation. One of the factors that increase intermodal freight costs is the long road distance from producing cities to the rail terminal, south as the case of Santa Filomena- PI whose distance is 512 km from the terminal.

The transit times when using rail is higher in both simulations involving the scenarios II and III. The differences found presented a percentage of approximately 3% higher than in the current scenario. The use of rail transport was expected to reduce the value of freight.

4. Conclusions

The study identified the unfeasibility of investment in Transnordestina railway considering the soybean movement of Piaui. Comparing the higher freight of the simulations with the current section, a cost growth of 33.35% is expected. Moreover, the port of São Luis has been more competitive, taking third place in 2017, with 8% of soybean exports to China [21]. Therefore, it comes the advantage of continuing to distributing soybeans through the port in ITAQUI-Northeast Brazil is the largest soybean exporter to China. The results allow concluding that railway projected need to be modified or improved to better meet the logistic needs for soybean production in Piauí.

5. References

1. Lopes, H., Lima, R. Ferreira, R.: A Cost Optimization Model of Transportation Routes to Export the Brazilian Soybean. Costs and agribusiness on-line 12, 90 - 109 (2016)
2. Hyland, M. F., MhamassaniHani S.M., Lama B.: Analytical Models of Rail Transportation Service in the Grain Supply Chain: Deconstructing the Operational and Economic Advantages of Shuttle Train Service. Transportation Research Part E: Logistics and Transportation Review 93, 294-315 (2016)
3. Lopes, J. C. R.: Rail Transport in Northeastern Brazil and the Development Potential of Southwestern Piauí State. Universidade de Campinas (2016)
4. Embrapa, https://www.embrapa.br/gite/projetos/matopiba/matopiba.html
5. Reis, J. G. M. dos et al.: Evaluation of Maize Commercialization Strategies Applying the Analytic Hierarchy Process (AHP). Journal of Economics and Rural Sociology 54, 131-146 (2016)
6. Lin, Y.P., Deng, Z., Lin, K., Xu, Y.L. The Research of Fujian Imported Grain Designated Port Standardized Supervision and Management Mode. China's Sci. Technol. Overview 264, 237–240 (in Chinese) (2017)
7. Salin, D.: Soybean Transportation Guide: Brazil 2017. U.S. Dept. Of Agriculture, Agricultural Marketing Service (2018)
8. Ndembe, E. M.: Derived Demand for Grain Freight Transportation, Rail-Truck Competition, and Mode Choice and Allocative Efficiency. North Dakota State University (2016)
9. Ghaderi, H., Cahoon, S., Nguyen, H.: An Investigation into the Non-Bulk Rail Freight Transport In Australia. The Asian Journal of Shipping and Logistics 31, 59-83 (2015)
10. Banomyong, R., Thai, V., Yuen, Kum F.: Assessing The National Logistics System Of Vietnam. The Asian Journal of Shipping and Logistics 31, 21 - 58 (2015)
11. Brazilian National Land Transportation Agency, https://anttlegis.datalegis.inf.br/action/UrlPublicasAction.php?acao=abrirAtoPublico&sgl_tipo=RES&num_ato=00005820&seq_ato=000&vlr_ano=2018&sgl_orgao=DG/ANTT/MTPA&cod_modulo=161&cod_menu=5412
12. TRC, http://www.guiadotrc.com.br/lei/bitrem.asp.
13. Brazilian National Land Transportation Agency, http://www.antt.gov.br/ferrovias/arquivos/America_Latina_Logistica_Malha_Oeste_SA.html
14. Brazilian Institute of Statistical Geography, https://sidra.ibge.gov.br/tabela/1612#resultado
15. Gibbs, H. K. et al.: Brazil's Soy Moratorium. Science 347, 377-378 (2015)
16. Brazilian Integrated Foreign Trade, https //comexstat.mdic.gov.br/pt/geralexportation
17. Noticias Mineração Brasil, https://www.noticiasdemineracao.com/geral/news/1132484/ferrovia-transnordestina-poderia-dobrar-produ%C3%A7%C3%A3o-gesso-em-pernambuco
18. IFAG, http://ifag.org.br/cotacao-soja
19. Brazilian Central Bank, https://www.bcb.gov.br/acessoinformacao/legado?url=https:%2F%2Fwww4.bcb.gov.br%2Fpec%2Ftaxas%2Fbatch%2Ftaxas.asp%3Fid%3Dtxdola
20. Pera, T. G. et al.: Evaluation of Green Transport Corridors of Brazilian Soybean Exports to China. Brazilian Journal of Operations & Production Management 16, 398-412 (2019)
21. Ministry of Development, Industry and Foreign Trade, http://comexstat.mdic.gov.br/pt/home

I L S 2020
INTERNATIONAL CONFERENCE ON INFORMATION SYSTEMS, LOGISTICS & SUPPLY CHAIN
Austin, Texas April 22-24, 2020

Considering quasi-real time delivery information in product recommendation

Dadouchi, Camélia[1], Agard, Bruno[2,3],

[1], [2] Polytechnique Montreal, Laboratory of Ddata Iintelligence, CIRRELT
[3] IVADO
{camelia.dadouchi@gmail.com, bruno.agard@polymtl.ca}

Abstract. Recommender systems are used in a wide range of applications, such as news, e-learning and travel recommendations. In e-commerce, they have become necessary because of the high diversity of products. Current recommender systems do not consider supply chain constraints in product recommendations. This paper presents a first approach to the consideration of delivery constraints, such as scheduled deliveries, remaining capacity and the physical constraints of items in product recommendations. A methodology and individual case study are presented in this paper.

Keywords: Recommender systems, delivery scheduling, context-aware recommendation, supply chain.

1. Introduction

In the past decade, recommender systems have been largely used by retail companies to promote their products and to increase sales. Studies have shown that recommender systems can be responsible for up to 35% of online sales [22]. Research in the domain of recommendation in general has attracted a lot of interest, especially regarding the accuracy of recommendations. However, very little work has been done concerning the consideration of supply chain constraints in product recommendations [1]. In today's global markets, customers have heightened expectations about companies' services, expecting shorter lead-times and cheaper delivery costs [2]. In order for companies to be able to meet customers' requirements, recommendations that are made should consider the capacity of the network to deliver products to the customer during a defined time window. This paper presents a first approach into the consideration of delivery constraints such as scheduled deliveries, remaining capacities and delivery constraints in product recommendations. The remainder of this paper is structured as follows: Section 2 presents the state of the art regarding recommender systems and delivery constraints in a supply chain. Section 3 presents the problem definition, followed by section 4 with a proposed method depicted in six stages. Section 5 presents a case study. A conclusion is presented in section 5.

2. State of the art

2.1. Recommender systems

Recommender systems are tools that help users receive personalised content to address the problem of information overload. They have been defined as programs that predict a user's interest in an item based on related information about the items, the users and the interactions between items and users [3]. Many approaches and techniques have been presented in classical literature, the most widely used and accepted ones divide them into (a) collaborative filtering, (b) content-based filtering and, (c) hybrid filtering [4], [5], [6].

Collaborative filtering (CF) is a literature choice for e-commerce recommendations [7] and is based on the assumption that a person is more likely to have preferences that are similar to those of people that are considered similar to the active user. CF is usually categorised into memory-based collaborative filtering and model based collaborative filtering, and requires data on the users [3].

Content-based recommender systems (CBF) are based on the characteristics of the products or services consumed by the user [8]; these use data about item descriptions and characteristics and do not require information about the user.

Hybrid recommender systems commonly use both content-based filtering and collaborative filtering, [9] presents seven classes of hybrid recommendation techniques.

Other recommendation techniques have also been developed and are presented in a survey from [3], the methods usually consider social, demographic or contextual data. [3] also presents a hierarchy of data used for the computation of product recommendations. Although a variety of data has been used to compute recommendations, to the best of our knowledge no previous work has considered quasi-real time information about the network state and delivery constraints in product recommendations.

2.2. Delivery constraints in the supply chain

Using e-commerce as a channel for distribution has increased complexity with regards to delivery services. Clients have a variety of options for buying products and can easily switch from one retailer to another, which makes client retention complex. A recent report [10] states that the speed of delivery as well as the rapid availability of products are the main expectations of more than one in two consumers. The efficiency of delivery has become a necessity to be competitive and survive in market conditions [11].

Delivering products to a customer in a time frame that is considered acceptable to the customer is not a new problem; a lot of research is being conducted to minimize both costs and lead-time, whether that is by using traditional pick-up and delivery problems by considering a dedicated fleet [12] or more recent approaches, such as considering crowdsourced and real-time deliveries [13].

Many constraints need to be considered to evaluate the cost of delivering to a customer [14]. Some of the constraints are: the availability and the number of vehicles, the number and locations of pick-up and delivery points, the time windows for delivery, the precision of the time of delivery, physical constraints of products, the capacity of the vehicles, travel distance, vehicle-supported physical constraints, and more.

The delivery problem in e-commerce is usually presented as the dynamic routing problem (DVRP) with pick-up delivery and capacity constraints in a given time. A variety of solutions to this problem have been presented in the literature; depending on the size of the problem, the solution can be optimal or can be found using meta heuristics and heuristics. Solutions obtained through the Dantzig-Wolfe decomposition are leading the field [15]. Near-optimal solutions have also been found using [16],[17],[18],[19],[20].

Results vary in terms of accuracy and computational time and cost [21]. Many techniques are available to compute recommendations and vehicle routing problems with regards to computational time, cost and accuracy. However, a literature review shows that, although recommender systems and delivery problems are well known fields in the literature, these two fields do not intercept.

3. Problem definition

This paper addresses the problem of considering delivery constraints in product recommendations for online retail. The objective is to present recommendation lists that take into consideration the time frame and costs in which the product can be delivered without using additional resources.

In order for the delivery constraints to be considered in recommendations, an evaluation of potential profits from vehicle routing problems need to be performed in a hidden time during the computation of recommendations.

We define the parties involved in the problem as follows:

Customers: clients that made previous purchases or that are known by the company.

Transporters: parties responsible for freight transport (vehicles).

Warehouses: Pick-up points for the retrieval of items.

Delivery points: addresses for deliveries of items.

Delivery list: time and location for picking up and delivering items with required quantities.
Distribution tours: Scheduled paths for pick-ups and deliveries.
For the purpose of this paper, we will consider that pick-ups and deliveries are made by trucks and that the recommendations are performed using collaborative filtering.

4. Methodology

The proposed method is presented in figure 1 and follows four phases. The process starts when a user logs into the system. Recommendation scores are computed for the active user in phase 1. From the ranked recommended items, a list of the top X items with their scores are to be used in the remainder of the phases. Phase 2 considers a user's location and evaluates, from a list of vehicles that have been scheduled, which ones are within a given radius of a user's location. For the active trucks, those that cannot be used to ship the items from the recommendation are removed from the list of active trucks. Phase 3 evaluates potential profits that may result from the pick-up and deliveries of each of the X items of the recommendation list. Phase 4 adjusts the recommendation list scores for the items that can be delivered to the active user with a positive profit. The phases are detailed in the remainder of this section.

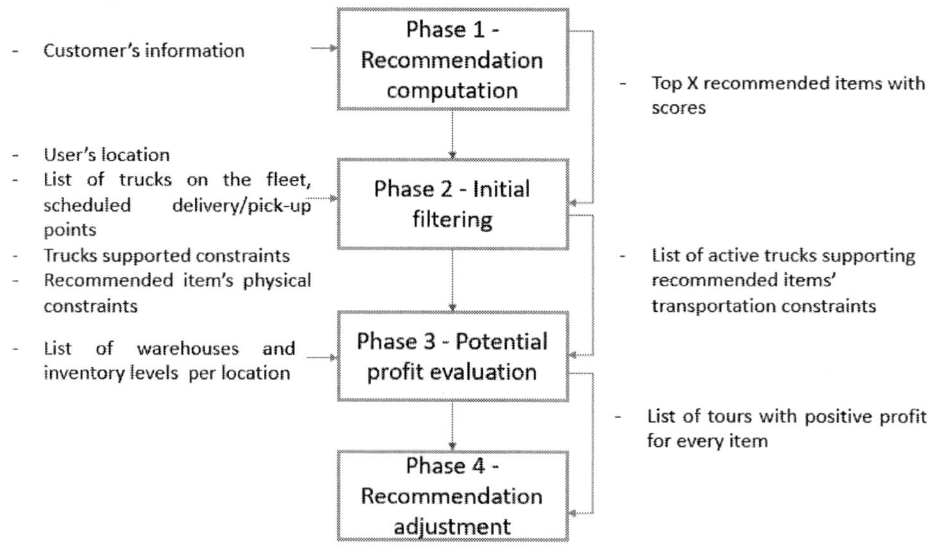

Figure 1 : Methodology for recommendation adjustment based on scheduled tours

4.1. Phase 1: Recommendation computation

In this step, the traditional recommendation process applies. Information about the active user is retrieved and used to compute the utilities of each item in the catalogue.

Input data:
User's information
Input parameter:
Number of items X: top X items (i) to consider for recommendation adjustments.

A user profile is created based on all available data about the active user (historical purchases, location, demographic information, social media, clickstream.) Afterwards, recommendations are computed using any recommendation technique that results in a score for each item.
As stated in section 2, collaborative filtering is a state-of-the-art approach for product recommendations in e-commerce, thus, they are used to evaluate the utility of each item for the active user.

Collaborative filtering generates a list of items with the utility of each item for the active user. From the ranked list of the item's utilities, we select the top X items to consider in the remaining phases.

4.2. Phase 2: Initial filtering

In this step, we evaluate which of the products could be delivered within a given time window and radius to the active user, considering the available resources and transportation constraints. If a user's location is unknown and cannot be retrieved, initial recommendation scores are kept unchanged and the remainder of the method does not apply.

Input parameters:

- *Maximum radius (P):* The maximum radius from which a product can be picked-up or from which a truck can be assigned to the delivery,
- *Time window (TW):* The period of time in which the scheduled tour is considered.

Input data:

A user's location, scheduled pick-up/delivery points, the support constraints of trucks, the physical constraints of recommended items.

Considering the input data, a first filter is applied to pick out the trucks that are considered to be close enough to the active user with regards to P and TW. P and TW are defined based on the business environment of the company by implementing the proposed method.

Once the active trucks are selected, a matrix is computed to evaluate the compatibility between the physical constraints of X items from the recommendation list and the vehicles' supported constraints.

There are various physical constraints considered for **items** (*i*), such as: an item's weight, volume, shape, fragility, perishability, need to be placed in a specific orientation, environmental requirements, and more. **Vehicles** (*t*) can be characterized by their capacity, configuration of the loading space and unloading possibilities, temperatures, humidity, and more.

This phase is computed to avoid considering all of the constraints in the routing problem for profit evaluation, making it easier and faster to compute. Items that cannot be delivered are not considered in the following phases.

4.3. Phase 3: Potential profit evaluation

Once the X recommended items that could be transported using the active trucks are filtered, we evaluate the availability of the items in the inventory and the location of the warehouses in which each item is available.

Input data: List of warehouses (*e*) and inventory level per item.

The vehicle routing problem (VRP) is considered for profit evaluation. Since the problem has constraints related to pick-ups and deliveries, capacity and time windows with consideration of fixed and variable costs, we propose using a dynamic routing problem (DVRP).

For each item *i* from the filtered recommendation list, we evaluate the marginal profit of adding that item to the already scheduled tour by evaluating the cost of the new tour and subtracting the initial cost of the tour. We consider a pessimistic scenario, in which the user potentially buys one item at a time to evaluate the potential profit and the marginal profit. The marginal profit of adding item *i* from the warehouse *e* in the active truck *t* is evaluated using formula (1).

$$P_{Marginal} = P_{i;e;t} - P_{init} \quad (1)$$

P_{init} is the profit from the previously scheduled tour for the active truck.

$P_{i;e;t}$ is is the profit generated by picking item *i* from the warehouse *e* in a truck *t*.

If the new request cannot be incorporated into the solution due to delivery constraints, it is automatically rejected while evaluating the route at phase 2.

4.4. Phase 4: Recommendation adjustment

Once all marginal profits for each item have been calculated, the recommendations are adjusted considering the best potential profit per item. In order to adjust the scores, a threshold P_{min} representing the minimum acceptable profit for a company to update its scheduled tour should be set. The adjusted recommendation score is computed using equation (2)

$$\textit{Adjusted Recommendation score} = \beta.\ \textit{Initial Recommendation score} \quad (2)$$

with $\beta = P_{Marginal}/P_{min}$

β always being superior to 1, if not, the recommendation score remains unchanged since the profit is considered low when considering a company's strategy. The higher that β is, the stronger the priority of the item in the recommendation list and the higher its visibility to the customer. β is correlated to the minimum profit for which a company would accept changing its delivery schedule. If the company requires high profits, adjustments of the scores may be low.

Once the scores are adjusted, Y items with the best scores are selected and recommended to the active user. The proposed method never deteriorates the current situation and the effect on logistics and sales is either an improvement or none. If the recommendation is followed by the user, the method will help improve truckload utilization, which could lower operation costs and lessen the number of vehicles used for delivery. If not, the recommendation will remain unchanged.

5. Individual case study

The presented case study is a simulation, considering 20 different locations, 3 warehouses, 100 different items and 5 vehicles. Each item and vehicle is characterised by features retrieved from their description. An individual case study is presented, because personalised recommendations are always computed for one user at a time. The same approach would be implemented each time a new user logs into the web site.

Phase 1: Recommendation computation

We consider that the recommendation scores are computed using collaborative filtering and customers' information.

In the phase, parameters for the number of items to consider for recommendation adjustments and the number of items for the final recommendation need to be set.

Input parameters:

X =5 items, Y =3.

Table 1 presents the pair of item/scores for the Top X recommendations.

Table 1: Pair of items/scores for the active user

Items	I1	I2	I3	I4	I5
Recommendation score	0.92	0.68	0.49	0.47	0.6

In a traditional recommendation, the final recommended items would be the Y items with the highest scores (I1, I2 and I5).

Phase 2: Initial filtering

In this step, a time window and radius are set around an active user. Available resources and transportation constraints are considered to filter items that cannot be shipped using the scheduled vehicles in a given time window.

Input parameters:

- *Maximum radius (P):* 200km,
- *Time window (TW):* 8hours

Input data: A user's location, scheduled pick-up/delivery points, the trucks' supported constraints, the recommended items' physical constraints.

Once a user's location is known, the vehicles for which a pick-up point or delivery is scheduled within the active radius are selected, the two active vehicles with their physical characteristics are presented in table 2. Table 3 represents the 5 items selected at phase 1 with their physical constraints and characteristics.

Table 2: Vehicles' capacities and supported constraints.

Vehicles	Capacity (units)	Capacity (kg)	Supported constraints	Remaining capacity (kg)	Remaining units
Vehicle 1	1 000	24 000	fragile, fixed orientation, isolation	10 710	242
Vehicle 2	1 000	24 000	refrigerated, fragile,fixed orientation, isolation	6 000	442

Table 3: Items' physical characteristics.

Item	Unit price ($)	Loading units	Weight (kg)	Constraint
I1	75	1 or less	5	Fragile
I2	150	1 or less	1	Refrigerated
I3	300	1 or less	0.5	Refrigerated
I4	175	1 or less	5	Extreme value
I5	700	1 or less	8	Fixed orientation

Data about physical characteristics of the vehicles are crossed with an item's physical constraints to create a compatibility matrix between the vehicles and items, as presented in table 4.

Table 4: Matrix of supported physical constraints.

Items	I1	I2	I3	I4	I5
Vehicle 1	Supported	-	-	-	Supported
Vehicle 3	Supported	Supported	Supported	-	Supported

Item I4 cannot be delivered by active trucks, thus item 4 is not considered for recommendation adjustments.

Phase 3: Potential profit evaluation
For each item that can be shipped with one of the active vehicles, we evaluate the profit associated with adding the item to the tour, if a sale was to be completed. The software used is presented in [23].
Input data: List of warehouses (e) and inventory level per item.
For each item, the location of the warehouse in which the product needs to be retrieved is evaluated along with the availability of the product. **Table 5** presents which of the warehouses has each item in stock.

Table 5: The item's locations.

Items	Warehouse A	Warehouse B	Warehouse C
I1	e1,1	e1,2	e1,3
I2	-	-	-
I3	e2,1	e2,1	e2,1
I5	-	e5,3	-

Considering the active radius, only warehouse A and warehouse C are considered for the remainder of the phases. Since warehouse B is out of the active parameters, items I2 and I5 are not evaluated.
The VRP is launched to evaluate the profit associated with the initial tour and the profit associated with the addition of the selected items in the delivery list.
We used the following tour scheduling parameters: (1) geographical information was retrieved from Microsoft Bing maps, (2) average speed was set to 70km/h, (3) the selected algorithm was VRP with a return to the warehouse using the fastest route. (4) Driving parameters are set to: a maximum capacity (loading units) of 1000, a fixed cost per trip of $200.00, variable costs per unit of distance of $0.95, a distance limit of 1000.00km, a driving time limit of 8 hours and a working time limit of 8 hours.

In order to illustrate the results, we present the initial tour and the tour associated with adding Item I3 to the delivery tour. Item I3 is selected because it shows a positive profit. The tour for vehicle 1 is presented in Table 6, while the tour for vehicle 2 is presented in Table 7. Both tables present the initial tour and the adjusted tour. Table 8 presents the total profits for the initial and adjusted tour.

Table 6: Initial and adjusted tour for vehicle 1.

	Initial tour	Adjusted tour
Distance travelled	952.53 km	968.25 km
Driving time	11:09 hours	11:45 hours
End of tour time	19:09	19:45
Duration of tour	11:09 hours	11:45 hours
Profit collected	$18,075	$18,075

Table 7: Initial and adjusted tour for vehicle 3.

	Initial tour	Adjusted tour
Distance travelled	190.87 km	343.93 km
Driving time	2:44 hours	4:28 hours
End of tour time	10:44	12:28
Duration of tour	2:44 hours	4:28 hours
Profit collected	$28,118.68	$28,800

Table 8: Total for initial and adjusted tour.

	Initial tour	Adjusted tour
Total profit	$45,088.78	$45,228
Total distance travelled	1 143.39 km	1 312.18 km

Considering the total profit of the initial and adjusted tour, the marginal profit related to picking up and delivering product I3 is calculated using equation 1.

$$P_{Marginal} = \$45{,}228 - \$45{,}088.78 \quad (21)$$

$$P_{Marginal} = \$139.22$$

The same have been applied to item I1 resulting in a $P_{Marginal}$ = -\$85.35. Since the profit is negative, no adjustment will be made for the score of item I1.

Phase 4: Recommendation adjustment

P_{min} represents the minimum acceptable profit for a company to update its scheduled tour, which is set to \$100.00 for this case study. The recommendation score is adjusted for item I3 using equation (2)

$$\textit{Adjusted Recommendation score} = (139.22/100) \times 0.49 = 0.682$$

Table 8 presents the top three recommendation list with the adjusted score for item I3.

Table 8: Final recommendation list with adjusted scores.

Items	I1	I3	I2
Recommendation score	0.92	**0.682**	0.68

We can observe that the final Y recommendations have changed, and Item 3 was favoured over Item 5, which no longer appears in the recommendations. Item 3 was also ranked ahead of Item 2, changing the overall ranking of the recommendation.

6. Conclusion

The proposed approach consists of an adaptation of recommender systems using the vehicle routing problem to evaluate tour costs related to adding items to the delivery tour. The proposed solution dynamically adjusts to the network state by considering quasi-real time information from the information systems and including it in the recommendation systems. The objective is to improve recommendations by allowing it to shift demand toward products that will be delivered in a short time frame with an acceptable profit.

Possible outcomes of this method are: an improvement in truck-load utilization, resulting in customer satisfaction, competitiveness of the seller and a reduction in traffic congestion and pollution in communities. The results of such a method could present a significant opportunity for increased customer satisfaction and profits for the seller. However, the results of the method depend on the accuracy of the recommendation and the efficiency of the VRP. The recommendation technique selected for this paper is collaborative filtering, which implies that a strong base of information about customers also needs to be available.

7. References

1. Dadouchi, C & Agard, B.: Lowering penalties related to stock-outs by shifting demand in product recommendation systems. Decision Support Systems, 114, 61–69, 2018.
2. Simchi-Levi, D, Kaminsky, P, Simchi-Levi, E & Shankar, R.: Designing and managing the supply chain: concepts, strategies and case studies. McGraw-Hill Education, 2008. Introduction to Supply Chain Management, 99.
3. Bobadilla,J, Ortega, F, Hernando, A & Gutiérrez, A.: Recommender systems survey. Knowledge-Based Systems, vol. 46, 109–132, 2013.
4. Adomavicius, G & Tuzhilin, A.: Toward the next generation of recommender systems: A survey of the state-of-the-art and possible extensions, IEEE transactions on knowledge and data engineering, vol. 17, no. 6,734–749, 2005.
5. Candillier, L, Meyer,F, & Boullé,M.: Comparing state-of-the-art collaborative filtering systems, International Workshop on Machine Learning and Data Mining in Pattern Recognition. Springer, 2007, 548–562.
6. Schafer, J-B, Frankowski, D, Herlocker, J, & Sen, S.:Collaborative Filtering Recommender Systems. Berlin, Heidelberg: Springer Berlin Heidelberg, 2007, 291–324.
7. Yang, Z, Wu, B Zheng, K, Wang, X, & Lei, L.: A survey of collaborative filtering-based recommender systems for mobile internet applications, IEEE (2016), 3273-3287.
8. Wu, M-L, Chang, C-H & Liu, R-Z.: Integrating content-based filtering with collaborative filtering using co-clustering with augmented matrices, Expert Systems with Applications, 41, 6, 2754–2761, 2014.
9. Burke, R.: Hybrid recommender systems: Survey and experiments, User modeling and Customer-Adapted Interaction, 12, 4, 331–370, 2002.
10. Beaudoin, J, Bourget, C, Normand, M, & Skerlj, A.: Portrait de la logistique en commerce éléctronique au québec, Centre Francophone d'Informatisation des Organisations (CEFRIO), tech. report, 2018.
11. Anand, N, Grover, N,: Measuring retail supply chain performance: Theoretical model using key performance indicators (kpis). Benchmarking: An International Journal, 22, 1, 135–166, 2015.
12. Berbeglia, G., Cordeau, J. F., Gribkovskaia, I., & Laporte, G. (2007). Static pickup and delivery problems: a classification scheme and survey. Top, 15(1), 1-31.
13. Arslan, A. M., Agatz, N., Kroon, L., & Zuidwijk, R. (2018). Crowdsourced delivery—A dynamic pickup and delivery problem with ad hoc drivers. Transportation Science, 53(1), 222-235.
14. Ismail, S. N., Ku-Mahamud, K. R., & Abdul-Rahman, S. (2017). A Review on delivery routing problem and its approaches. Journal of Theoretical & Applied Information Technology, 95(2).
15. Kohl, N., Desrosiers, J., Madsen, O. B., Solomon, M. M., & Soumis, F. (1999). 2-path cuts for the vehicle routing problem with time windows. Transportation Science, 33(1), 101-116.
16. Rochat, Y., & Taillard, É. D. (1995). Probabilistic diversification and intensification in local search for vehicle routing. Journal of heuristics, 1(1), 147-167.
17. Homberger, J., & Gehring, H. (1999). Two evolutionary metaheuristics for the vehicle routing problem with time windows. INFOR: Information Systems and Operational Research, 37(3), 297-318.
18. Cordeau, J. F., Laporte, G., & Mercier, A. (2001). A unified tabu search heuristic for vehicle routing problems with time windows. Journal of the Operational research society, 52(8), 928-936.
19. Soonpracha, K., Mungwattana, A., & Manisri, T. (2015). A re-constructed meta-heuristic algorithm for robust fleet size and mix vehicle routing problem with time windows under uncertain demands. In Proceedings of the 18th Asia Pacific Symposium on Intelligent and Evolutionary Systems-Volume 2, 347-361. Springer, Cham.
20. Calvet, L., Ferrer, A., Gomes, M. I., Juan, A. A., & Masip, D. (2016). Combining statistical learning with metaheuristics for the multi-depot vehicle routing problem with market segmentation. Computers & Industrial Engineering, 94, 93-104.
21. Cordeau, J-F. The VRP with time windows, Montréal: Groupe d'études et de recherche en analyse des décisions, 2000.
22. Lamere, P and Green, S , "Project aura : Recommendation for the rest of us", 2008. En ligne : http://www.oracle.com/technetwork/systems/ts-5841-159144.pdf
23. Erdougan, G. An open source spreadsheet solver for vehicle routing problems, Computers & Operations Research 84 (2017) 62-72.

I L S 2020
INTERNATIONAL CONFERENCE ON INFORMATION SYSTEMS, LOGISTICS & SUPPLY CHAIN
Austin, Texas April 22-24, 2020

Towards Hybrid Machine Learning Models in Decision Support Systems for predicting the Spare Parts Reverse Flow in a Complex Supply Chain

Hamza EL GARRAB[1,3], Bruno CASTANIER[1], David LEMOINE[2], Adnane LAZRAK[3], Robert HEIDSIECK[3]

[1] Université d'Angers, LARIS, Angers, France
[2] IMT Atlantique, LS2N, Nantes, France
[3] General Electric Healthcare, Buc, France
{hamza.elgarrab@ge.com, bruno.castanier@univ-angers.fr, david.lemoine@imt-atlantique.fr, adnane.lazrak@ge.com, robert.heidsieck@med.ge.com}

Abstract. A key goal of after-sale services is to develop customer satisfaction through high-quality service after the purchase. In this context, repairable spare parts play a considerable role in the service level vs inventory balance considering the relative cost of these parts. The objective of this paper is to elaborate a methodology to improve the repair spare parts supply chain. We present an approach for predicting the reverse repair flow using Hybrid Machine Learning models and Simulation. Numerical experiments are conducted on real field data from General Electric Healthcare.

Keywords: Hybrid Machine Learning, Simulation, Forecasting, Spare Parts Supply Chain, Repair.

1. Introduction

In today's business environment, the importance of after-sales service is high, lost revenues due to disservice are significant [1] and after-sale services are often perceived as a necessary evil [2]. Despite the aftermarket's obvious benefits, most organizations squander its potential. After-sales support is notoriously difficult to manage, and only companies with efficient operations can make a margin from them [2]. One of the most important post-sale services is equipment maintenance, which consists of reducing downtime on customer's systems by predictive or corrective repairs.

Spare parts availability is a crucial component of this service to ensure proper service level. However, in asset-intensive fields, where high system availability is required, spare parts fulfillment is often a critical issue [4]. To increase the availability of spare parts and reduce costs, many companies recognize the benefits of closed-loop supply chains that integrate product returns into business operations [9]. In a closed-loop spare parts supply chain, failed parts, the so-called Line Replaceable Units or LRUs [3], are recovered from the field at system failure, upgrade or removal thanks to a reverse logistics to be repaired or refurbished rather than scrapped [3]. Due to the high cost of spare parts, efforts are made to reduce the inventory of new parts as it can immobilize a significant amount of capital.

At General Electric Healthcare (GEHC), the medical branch of conglomerate General Electric, one of the global leaders in sales and services of medical systems, usage of refurbished and repaired parts enables a significant improvement of the service level vs inventory trade-off. Works regarding spare parts demand forecasting have been done in this context [38]. However, repairing spare parts has additional challenges. Firstly, it is difficult to predict the repaired spare parts demand due to the sporadic nature of the installed base evolution, system failures, and customer upgrades. Secondly, the complexity of the reverse supply chains makes the return forecast even more challenging. Thirdly, demand spikes may occur without notice.

This drives the need to find new algorithms to adapt to business/supply chain evolution faster than classical models. The Machine Learning (ML) approaches brings value by adapting to changes without explicit formulation. Machine learning algorithms are successfully utilized to describe the behavior of the dataset and forecast output features based on historical records [33].
An important amount of works regarding spare parts demand forecasting is available, using a wide variety of models from classical statistical approaches [34] to more modern machine learning methods. However, only a limited number of works repair supply chain are present in literature [36, 37]. And none of them used a machine learning approach.
In this paper, we describe a forecasting method for the repair spare parts demand using ML models trained on historical data. This method shows an improved performance thanks to a Hybrid Machine Learning model. We also describe the test and comparison with classical models and independent ML models in terms of accuracy and capacity to detect future demand spikes.
The main contributions of this paper can be listed as follows:

- Spare Parts repair demand forecast, in a closed-loop SC using ML and Simulation
- Spare Parts repair demand spikes detection, using ML models
- Three Individual ML models were tested and compared to predict spare parts repair demand
- A Hybrid Machine Learning model is build combining multiple Classification and Regression models along with Simulation

2. LITERATURE REVIEW

The combination of Simulations and Machine Learning model have been successfully applied in several industrial-oriented applications. In their work, Laszlo *et al.* [6] presented different architectures and use cases in manufacturing processes to optimize the production processes and process chains. Carbonneau *et al.* [7] studied the performance of non-linear machine learning techniques in forecasting the distorted demand signals in an extended supply chain, showing an improved accuracy. Sobie *et al.* [8] have used simulation-driven machine learning models to predict physical failures of rotating systems such as wind turbines and industrial machinery, the usage of simulation compensates lack of data to train the models. In the paper [10] simulation and machine learning models predict the stability of milling processes showing the interest of instant feedback and predicting more than 22,900 observations with an averaged error measure lower than 10%. In their work, Wang *et al.* [11] presented a study around manufacturing process optimization using a global simulation data mining framework in order to discover the interrelations between key design parameters and global performance parameters. The results of the models show that the predicted and actual real simulations are almost identical. The paper [12] is studying the prediction of the boiling and critical points of polycyclic aromatic hydrocarbons via a hybrid model that uses Monte Carlo Wang Landau (HMC-WL) generating training data to train a Neural Network. The paper [13] presents a study on molecular dynamics simulations and how can machine learning models be used in order to improve the throughput and reduce the latency of molecular dynamics simulation models.
In their article, Nutkiewicz *et al.* [14] also did a study on urban buildings energy simulations and the integration of machine learning models to improve the accuracy of the simulation related to the energy consumption of a given urban area. Li *et al.* [15] also studied large scale distributed learning systems showing that most large-scale machine learning applications are running on distributed systems like Hadoop, Spark or Hazelcast and suggests the integration of organic relationships between the cluster nodes. Rohit *et al.* [16] proposed a Hybrid Machine Learning System, combining a Support Vector Machines (SVM) model with a Genetic Algorithm (GA) for stock Market Forecasting. Kim et al [17] proposed a Hybrid Model of Genetic Algorithms and Neural Networks - the recurrent neural network (RNN) - for detecting temporal patterns in stock markets with improved performance vs standard neural network (NN). Tsaih *et al.* [18] presented a hybrid AI approach to the implementation of trading strategies in the S&P 500 stock index market, results show that the proposed model outperformed the classical NN model. Shon *et al.* [19] presented a hybrid machine learning approach to network anomaly detection more effective compared to non-hybrid ones. Choudhry *et al.* [16] also proposed a hybrid machine learning system for stock market forecasting.
As a conclusion while the combination of simulation and machine learning and the hybrid approaches proved their success in multiple areas, it was never applied to the closed loop supply chain and particularly to the LRU supply chain. The complexity of such supply chain with multiple criterions to consider in the

models shows the potential of such approaches as an alternative to the classical ad-hoc methods, this is the goal of the following sections.

3. Preliminaries and problem definition

In this section, the spare parts repair demand forecasting problem is defined, the used machine learning algorithms are introduced, and the performance metrics of forecasting are presented.

3.1. Problem Definition

At GEHC, and other companies, spare parts replenishment can be done by either repairing defective parts or buying new ones. The decision between the two solutions is based on multiple criterions such as the lead time to get the part and the price difference. The decision process can be either made manually, by a management system or by a combination of both. In our case, suggestions are made by a management support system, implementing a DRP (Distribution Requirement Planning), then processed by a team of planners to approve, modify or decline the propositions. In general, the distribution network of parts takes the form of a tree (Figure 1). This tree often has more than two echelons, the intermediate nodes are warehouses, the leaves are storage points [30]. A DRP takes in consideration the demand in order to suggest how the goods should be distributed to meet this demand in an optimal way.

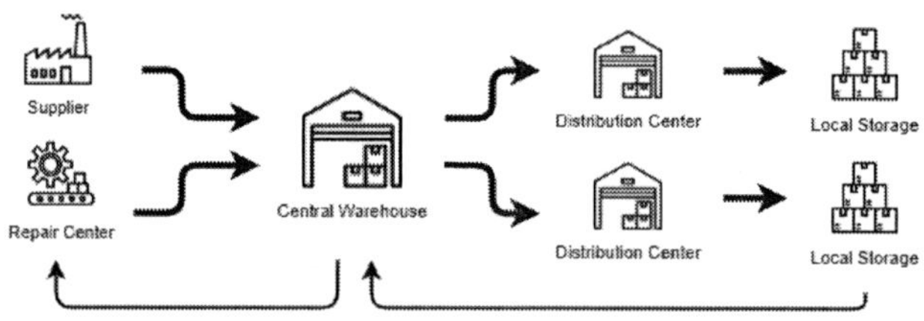

Figure 1: Simplified Spare Parts Distribution Network and Reverse Repair Flow

Due to the high complexity of the supply chain, many variables in the inventory control process of this distribution network may be fuzzy and some components of the setup may be unknown [31]. In addition to this, numerous real-world constraints cannot be integrated into an automatic decision process, such as the real-time supplier's performance or installed base evolution. For this reason, the DRP system is mainly used for recommendation and real decisions are made by a planning team based on experience and supply chain data. The main priority for the planning team is to ensure high availability of spare parts for customers, options are among others: (i) buying additional spare parts, (ii) reducing transportation times or (iii) reducing repair shop throughput times [3].

This work will focus on reducing repair shop throughput times by improving forecast at the repair shop level. The performance of repair centers depends on three factors: labor, materials and space/layout. Repair centers managers adjust these three variables based on the estimated future repair demand, which can be a challenging task [3]. Another challenge for the repair centers is repair demand spikes that occur due to multiple reasons such as an installed base increase, quality issues, equipment's end of life... In these cases, repair centers should be extremely performant and prepared in terms of materials to maintain a low repair cycle time. Many attempts to tackle the challenges have been done, however, existing models such as MA (Moving Average), SES (Simple Exponential Smoothing), Seasonal Model... lack the ability to adapt to demand changes and to detect repair demand spikes.

3.2. Machine Learning

Machine learning (ML) is a field of computer science that tries to provide learning capabilities to software without being explicitly operated [33]. ML models are designed to learn from experience then predict based on new inputs. ML algorithms are utilized to describe the behavior of the datasets [33].

The use of Machine Learning was chosen due to the poor performance of classical models when applied to complex systems, especially when demand spikes are present. In addition to this, implementing a system with all the inventory management algorithms, decision trees and logistics is highly complex and continuous maintenance is required to adapt it to new changes [43]. Machine Learning algorithms have the capability to handle complex systems and perform well when the relationship between inputs and output is not clear or there is no mathematical of it. ML algorithms can detect environmental changes and adapt to the new environment. Table 1 shows a short description of the ML models used in this paper.

Table 1: Short description of used ML models

Category	Model	Short description	Study
Classification	kNN	ML algorithm that Classifies an input by using its neighbors in a like polling process.	[22]
	Decision Trees	ML technique that builds the classification in the form of a tree with decision branches class leaves	[26]
	SVM	The approach uses the principle of optimal separation, the idea that a good classifier finds the largest gap possible between data points of different classes	[24]
	Random Forests	Collection of classification and regression trees, using binary splits on predictor variables	[35]
Regression	Polynomial Regression	Describes the relationship between the inputs and outputs as an nth degree polynomial in x	[41]
	Ridge Regression	The model has an objective to minimize the loss function.	[40]
	LASSO	Model applying an L_1norm to linear models to encourage both shrinkage and automatic variable selection	[39]

4. The Dynamic Hybrid Machine Learning System

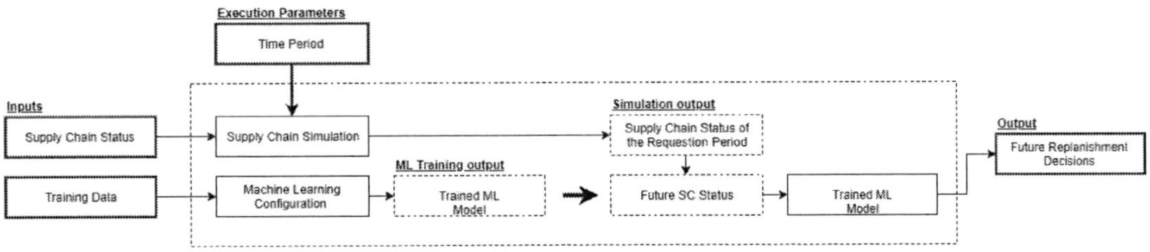

Figure 2: High-level Hybid Machine Learning model design

Figure 2 shows a high-level view of the model design. The model has two inputs, one parameter and one output. The inputs are: (i) The current status of the supply chain (inventory levels, in route parts...) (ii) Past data (used for training). The parameter of the model is the requested time period (the fiscal week in our case) for which we are looking to predict the repair demand. The output is the repair demand for the requested period. The model is made from three principal bricks, a simulation model and a hybrid machine learning training system that trains and chooses the best performing machine leaning models.

4.1. The Simulation Model

The main purpose of the simulation system is to generate the evolution of the supply chain, in order to provide the required inputs to Machine Learning models.

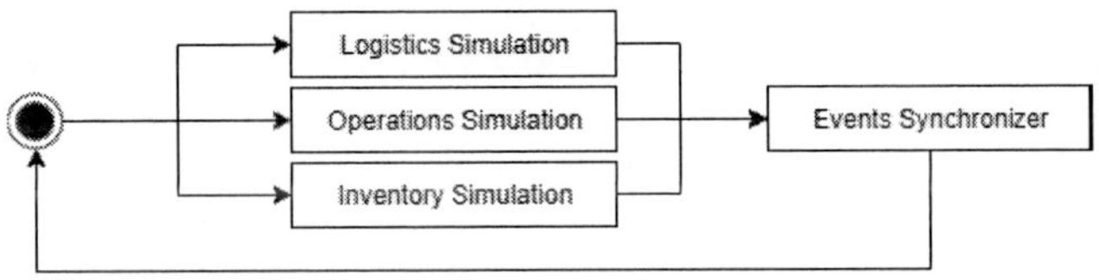

Figure 3: Simulation model Parallel Processes

The simulation is applied simultaneously to events and the decisions of three main processes of the supply chain: logistics (transport time, warehousing…), operations (time to repair, repair success rate, repair center capacity…) and inventory (stock level, safety stock level…). Figure 3 shows the Events Synchronizer that merges the results of the 3 simulation processes together and prepares it for the next iteration.

4.2. The Hybrid Machine Learning Model

In this part of the model, we propose a new approach where we take advantage of a knowledge base to transform the original problem (Repair demand prediction) into a set of multiple sub-problems.

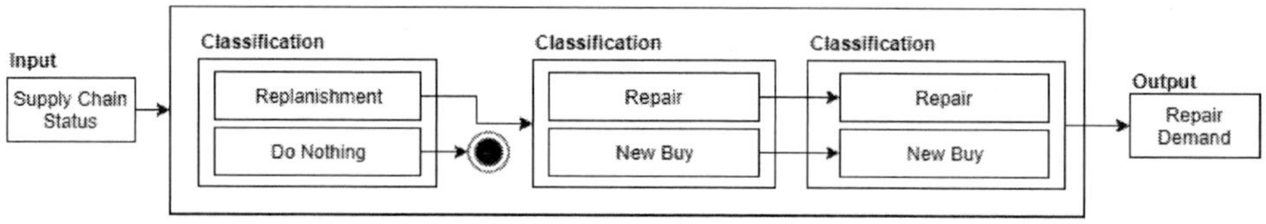

Figure 4: Simulation Parallel Processes.

The decision process can be divided into 3 separate steps: (i) replenishment decision (ii) replenishment solution choice (iii) replenishment volume estimation. The approach we are proposing is solving the general problem of estimating the repair demand by predicting every sub-decisions in the process. This kind of approaches can be found in literature, Rowida et al [21] for example proposed an approach for Opinion Mining; the knowledgebase-Machine Learning approach improve the classification accuracy considerably.

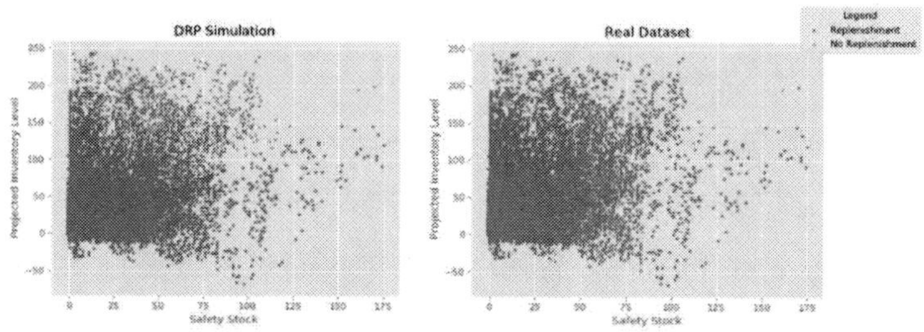

Figure 5: DRP Simulation vs Real decisions

For each step of the decision process, different criterions are considered to decide if we do replenishment or not. Figure 5 shows the suggestions made by a DRP and real decisions of the planning team. The classical DRP model will predict, an order placement every time the projected stock is lower than the safety stock. The figure to the right shows what real decisions. Even though the two classes look mixed, the planning team's decisions are not random, they are integrating more criterions than we can implement or plot on two dimensions. To predict the different sub-parts of our decision process (Figure 4), we implemented a Hybrid Machine Learning Model, the proposed model will combine a set of classifiers along with a set of regressors (Table 1). The model will automatically try all the possible combinations of the models and parameters in our context and choose the best one for the requested time period, which simplifies the process of implementing, testing and evaluating the performance of Machine Learning models.

4.3. The link between Machine Learning and Simulation

The model is made of multiple sub-systems: Repair and new buy Suppliers, Planning, Inventory Management and Logistics. Each sub-system has inputs and outputs. For example, the repair center module has an input of how much it receives, then it outputs how much it repairs and ships per day. The input of each module is provided by the previous component and an output that is injected into the next component.

We applied ML specifically to the Planning component due to its complexity and the high number of indicators considered to take planning decisions. The accuracy gains by applying ML to the other components of the chain doesn't justify the use of such models, which is why we used classical simulation.

5. Implementation and Results

5.1. Dataset Description

Our application case is General Electric Healthcare, we possess data representing the activity of twelve Repair Centers (Owner of the repair of the returned parts) and three Central Distribution Centers (owner of stocking and logistics from and to the repair centers). Data ranges from **2017** to **2019**. The dataset contains data for each fiscal week and each part, which is presented by 46 features and 12 million records.

5.2. Results

We created a Data Warehouse containing organized and timestamped data. HDFS (Hadoop File System) was used for storage. We used Python to implement all the models and for data processing we used libraries such as: Pandas, Numpy and Scickit-learn. We performed a data cleaning consisting of identifying and replacing incomplete, inaccurate records. The presence of incorrect data may impact the performance of Machine Learning models.
After running the model and generating all Hybrid combinations, every combination is trained then evaluated during both the training and test phases. The model selects the best performing combination and applies it to predict the final output. Table 2 shows the different combinations, each with its respective training, test and final score. We are using the coefficient of determination as our performance metric. The best possible score is 1 (in case $\sum_0^n(y_i - \hat{y}_i)^2 = 0$) and it can be negative.

$$R^2 = 1 - \frac{SS_{res}}{SS_{tot}} = 1 - \frac{\sum_0^n(y_i - \hat{y}_i)^2}{\sum_0^n(y_i - \bar{y})^2} \tag{1}$$

Table 2: The set of the Hybrid model combinations, each with its respective training, test and final score

Hybrid Combination			Training Performance			Test Performance			Score	Hybrid Combination			Training Performance			Test Performance			Score
C1	C2	R	P1	P2	P3	P1	P2	P3	P123	C1	C2	R	P1	P2	P3	P1	P2	P3	P123
kNN	kNN	RR	0.513	0.804	0.317	0.405	0.775	0.208	0.119	DT	kNN	RR	0.483	0.804	0.317	0.303	0.775	0.208	0.381
kNN	kNN	PR	0.513	0.804	0.613	0.405	0.775	0.581	0.452	DT	kNN	PR	0.483	0.804	0.613	0.303	0.775	0.581	0.477
kNN	kNN	Lasso	0.513	0.804	0.401	0.405	0.775	0.332	0.291	DT	kNN	Lasso	0.483	0.804	0.401	0.303	0.775	0.332	0.291
kNN	SVM	RR	0.513	0.833	0.317	0.405	0.744	0.208	0.180	DT	SVM	RR	0.483	0.833	0.317	0.303	0.744	0.208	0.412
kNN	SVM	PR	0.513	0.833	0.513	0.405	0.744	0.581	0.391	DT	SVM	PR	0.483	0.833	0.513	0.303	0.744	0.581	0.571
kNN	SVM	Lasso	0.513	0.833	0.401	0.405	0.744	0.332	0.103	DT	SVM	Lasso	0.483	0.833	0.401	0.303	0.744	0.332	0.221
kNN	DT	RR	0.513	0.602	0.317	0.405	0.594	0.208	0.082	DT	DT	RR	0.483	0.602	0.317	0.303	0.594	0.208	0.359
kNN	DT	PR	0.513	0.602	0.513	0.405	0.594	0.581	0.311	DT	DT	PR	0.483	0.602	0.513	0.303	0.594	0.581	0.410
kNN	DT	Lasso	0.513	0.602	0.401	0.405	0.594	0.332	0.172	DT	DT	Lasso	0.483	0.602	0.401	0.303	0.594	0.332	0.204
kNN	RF	RR	0.513	0.782	0.317	0.405	0.610	0.208	0.140	DT	RF	RR	0.483	0.782	0.317	0.303	0.610	0.208	0.418
kNN	RF	PR	0.513	0.782	0.513	0.405	0.610	0.581	0.332	DT	RF	PR	0.483	0.782	0.513	0.303	0.610	0.581	0.533
kNN	RF	Lasso	0.513	0.782	0.401	0.405	0.610	0.332	0.461	DT	RF	Lasso	0.483	0.782	0.401	0.303	0.610	0.332	0.401
SVM	kNN	RR	0.903	0.804	0.317	0.849	0.775	0.208	0.303	RF	kNN	RR	0.719	0.804	0.317	0.681	0.775	0.208	0.538
SVM	kNN	PR	0.903	0.804	0.613	0.849	0.775	0.581	0.704	RF	kNN	PR	0.719	0.804	0.613	0.681	0.775	0.581	0.602
SVM	kNN	Lasso	0.903	0.804	0.401	0.849	0.775	0.332	0.461	RF	kNN	Lasso	0.719	0.804	0.401	0.681	0.775	0.332	0.421
SVM	SVM	RR	0.903	0.833	0.317	0.849	0.744	0.208	0.271	RF	SVM	RR	0.719	0.833	0.317	0.681	0.744	0.208	0.388
SVM	SVM	PR	0.903	0.833	0.513	0.849	0.744	0.581	0.304	RF	SVM	PR	0.719	0.833	0.513	0.681	0.744	0.581	0.590
SVM	SVM	Lasso	0.903	0.833	0.401	0.849	0.744	0.332	0.293	RF	SVM	Lasso	0.719	0.833	0.401	0.681	0.744	0.332	0.484
SVM	DT	RR	0.903	0.602	0.317	0.849	0.594	0.208	0.102	RF	DT	RR	0.719	0.602	0.317	0.681	0.594	0.208	0.300
SVM	DT	PR	0.903	0.602	0.513	0.849	0.594	0.581	0.171	RF	DT	PR	0.719	0.602	0.513	0.681	0.594	0.581	0.476
SVM	DT	Lasso	0.903	0.602	0.401	0.849	0.594	0.332	0.044	RF	DT	Lasso	0.719	0.602	0.401	0.681	0.594	0.332	0.379
SVM	RF	RR	0.903	0.782	0.317	0.849	0.610	0.208	0.241	RF	RF	RR	0.719	0.782	0.317	0.681	0.610	0.208	0.303
SVM	RF	PR	0.903	0.782	0.513	0.849	0.610	0.581	0.376	RF	RF	PR	0.719	0.782	0.513	0.681	0.610	0.581	0.491
SVM	RF	Lasso	0.903	0.782	0.401	0.849	0.610	0.332	0.228	RF	RF	Lasso	0.719	0.782	0.401	0.681	0.610	0.332	0.399

Table 3: Accuracy comparison of: The Hybrid Machine Learning Model, Single Machine Learning models and Classical approaches on the top 400 consumed parts.

Category	Model	Best for x parts		Avg Score
Classical Approaches	SMA	19	4.75%	0.2336912
	SES	10	2.50%	0.0945333
Single Machine Learning Models	Polynomial Regression	61	15.25%	0.5413877
	Ridge Regression	28	7.00%	0.1833402
	Lasso	22	5.50%	0.1071830
Hybrid Machine Learning Model	Dynamically Combined [classifier, classifier, regressor]	261	65.25%	0.7690038

Table 3 summarizes the results of the application of the different models on our dataset. The system we put together automatically applies the 6 models on all the parts, then tags the model with the highest accuracy for each part, by testing it on the past. After that, we calculate the number of times each model was tagged, which we present in the second column (and in the third in a percentage format). For our dataset, the Dynamic Hybrid model gave the highest score (61.75%) and was chosen the best for 247 parts out of 400. The average score of the model is 0.80 which is the best average performance. We can also notice that the simple Polynomial Regression was the best for 14.75% of cases (59 parts), which is interesting taking in consideration that we applied the model directly on data without any prior problem transformation.

6. Conclusion

This paper presents a Hybrid Machine Learning forecasting model for the repair demand in a spare-parts closed loop supply chain, based on two ML classifiers to predict planification decisions and one ML regression model to forecast the volume in case the first classifiers predict a replenishment decision. When we compare the Hybrid model to its individual base models in terms of performance, the proposed hybrid model appears to be the best-performing option in terms of test accuracy score. The hybrid model achieved the highest accuracy (0.769). Moreover, the model was capable to learn seasonal patterns in the repair demand as well as demand spikes patterns, which was one of the main motivations of this work. Additional research could be performed to apply the proposed forecasting model for the optimization of internal repair centers materials and labor planification and evaluate the potential savings related to that. Other opportunities to improve and further this research could include the inclusion of Deep Learning models such as Neural Networks in Hybrid model as well as the comparison.

7. References

1. Van Houtum, Geert-Jan, and Bram Kranenburg. Spare parts inventory control under system availability constraints. Vol. 227. Springer, 2015.
2. Cohen, Morris A., Narendra Agrawal, and Vipul Agrawal. "Winning in the aftermarket." Harvard business review 84.5 (2006): 129.
3. van der Heijden, Matthijs C., E. M. Alvarez, and Johannes MJ Schutten. "Inventory reduction in spare part networks by selective throughput time reduction." International journal of production economics 143.2 (2013): 509-517.
4. Pascual, Rodrigo, *et al.* "Optimal repairable spare-parts procurement policy under total business volume discount environment." Reliability Engineering & System Safety 159 (2017): 276-282.
5. Basten, Robertus Johannes Ida, and Geert-Jan van Houtum. "System-oriented inventory models for spare parts." Surveys in operations research and management science 19.1 (2014): 34-55.
6. Monostori, László, *et al.* "Combined Use of Simulation and AI/Machine Learning Techniques In Designing and Manufacturing Processes and Systems." Journal for Manufacturing Science and Production 3.2-4 (2000): 111-118.
7. Carbonneau, Real, Kevin Laframboise, and Rustam Vahidov. "Application of machine learning techniques for supply chain demand forecasting." European Journal of Operational Research 184.3 (2008): 1140-1154.
8. Syntetos, Aris A., *et al.* "Supply chain forecasting: Theory, practice, their gap and the future." European Journal of Operational Research 252.1 (2016): 1-26.
9. Fleischmann, Moritz, Jo AEE Van Nunen, and Ben Gräve. "Integrating closed-loop supply chains and spare-parts management at IBM." Interfaces 33.6 (2003): 44-56.
10. Saadallah, Amal, *et al.* "Stability prediction in milling processes using a simulation-based Machine Learning approach." Procedia CIRP 72 (2018): 1493-1498.

11. Shao, Yanli, *et al.* "A machine learning based global simulation data mining approach for efficient design changes." Advances in Engineering Software 124 (2018): 22-41.
12. Groven, Steven D., C. Desgranges, and J. Delhommelle. "Prediction of the boiling and critical points of polycyclic aromatic hydrocarbons via Wang-Landau simulations and machine learning." Fluid Phase Equilibria 484 (2019): 225-231.
13. Pérez, Adrià, Gerard Martínez-Rosell, and Gianni De Fabritiis. "Simulations meet machine learning in structural biology." Current opinion in structural biology 49 (2018): 139-144.
14. Nutkiewicz, Alex, Zheng Yang, and Rishee K. Jain. "Data-driven Urban Energy Simulation (DUE-S): A framework for integrating engineering simulation and machine learning methods in a multi-scale urban energy modeling workflow." Applied energy 225 (2018): 1176-1189.
15. Li, Tie, *et al.* "Study on Multi-Agent Based Simulation of Team Machine Learning." Procedia Computer Science 91 (2016): 847-854.
16. Choudhry, Rohit, and Kumkum Garg. "A hybrid machine learning system for stock market forecasting." World Academy of Science, Engineering and Technology 39.3 (2008): 315-318.
17. A hybrid approach based on neural networks and genetic algorithms for detecting temporal patterns in stock mar kets
18. Tsaih, Ray, Yenshan Hsu, and Charles C. Lai. "Forecasting S&P 500 stock index futures with a hybrid AI system." Decision Support Systems 23.2 (1998): 161-174.
19. Shon, Taeshik, and Jongsub Moon. "A hybrid machine learning approach to network anomaly detection." Information Sciences 177.18 (2007): 3799-3821.
20. Vieira, Antonio AC, *et al.* "Supply chain hybrid simulation: From Big Data to distributions and approaches comparison." Simulation Modelling Practice and Theory 97 (2019): 101956.
21. Alfrjani, Rowida, Taha Osman, and Georgina Cosma. "A Hybrid Semantic Knowledgebase-Machine Learning Approach for Opinion Mining." Data & Knowledge Engineering 121 (2019): 88-108.
22. Ferreira, João Elias Vidueira, *et al.* "The use of the k nearest neighbor method to classify the representative elements." Educación Química 26.3 (2015): 195-201.
23. Rodrigues, Érick O. "Combining Minkowski and Cheyshev: New distance proposal and survey of distance metrics using k-nearest neighbours classifier." Pattern Recognition Letters 110 (2018): 66-71.
24. Cortes, Corinna, and Vladimir Vapnik. "Support-vector networks." Machine learning 20.3 (1995): 273-297.
25. Tanveer, Muhammad, *et al.* "Sparse pinball twin support vector machines." Applied Soft Computing 78 (2019): 164-175.
26. Trabelsi, Asma, Zied Elouedi, and Eric Lefevre. "Decision tree classifiers for evidential attribute values and class labels." Fuzzy Sets and Systems 366 (2019): 46-62.
27. Elouedi, Zied, Khaled Mellouli, and Philippe Smets. "Classification with belief decision trees." International Conference on Artificial Intelligence: Methodology, Systems, and Applications. Springer, Berlin, Heidelberg, 2000.
28. Coelho, Francisco, and João Pedro Neto. "A method for regularization of evolutionary polynomial regression." Applied Soft Computing 59 (2017): 223-228.
29. Hoerl, Arthur E., and Robert W. Kennard. "Ridge regression: Biased estimation for nonorthogonal problems." Technometrics 12.1 (1970): 55-67.
30. Moreno-Salinas, David, *et al.* "Modelling of a surface marine vehicle with kernel ridge regression confidence machine." Applied Soft Computing 76 (2019): 237-250.
31. Vollmann, Thomas E. Manufacturing planning and control for supply chain management. 2005.
32. Gen, Mitsuo, Yasuhiro Tsujimura, and Dazhong Zheng. "An application of fuzzy set theory to inventory control models." Computers & Industrial Engineering 33.3-4 (1997): 553-556.
33. Alpaydin, Ethem. Introduction to machine learning. MIT press, 2009.
34. Van der Auweraer, Sarah, Robert N. Boute, and Aris A. Syntetos. "Forecasting spare part demand with installed base information: A review." International Journal of Forecasting (2018).
35. Breiman, Leo. "Random forests." Machine learning 45.1 (2001): 5-32.
36. Pascual, Rodrigo, *et al.* "Optimal repairable spare-parts procurement policy under total business volume discount environment." Reliability Engineering & System Safety 159 (2017): 276-282.
37. Wong, Hartanto, Dirk Cattrysse, and Dirk Van Oudheusden. "Stocking decisions for repairable spare parts pooling in a multi-hub system." International journal of production economics 93 (2005): 309-317.
38. Lazrak, Adnane. "Amélioration des processus de prévision et de gestion des stocks dans le cas d'une chaîne logistique des pièces de rechange". PhD Thesis. Nantes, Ecole des Mines, 2015.
39. Tibshirani, Robert. "Regression shrinkage and selection via the lasso." Journal of the Royal Statistical Society: Series B (Methodological) 58.1 (1996): 267-288.
40. Hoerl, Arthur E., and Robert W. Kennard. "Ridge regression: Biased estimation for nonorthogonal problems." Technometrics 12.1 (1970): 55-67.
41. Edwards, Jeffrey R., and Mark E. Parry. "On the use of polynomial regression equations as an alternative to difference scores in organizational research." Academy of Management journal 36.6 (1993): 1577-1613.
42. Lee, Keon Myung, et al. "Autonomic machine learning platform." International Journal of Information Management 49 (2019): 491-501.

I L S 2020
INTERNATIONAL CONFERENCE ON INFORMATION
SYSTEMS, LOGISTICS & SUPPLY CHAIN
Austin, Texas April 22-24, 2020

On the Interest of Reconsidering a Real-Life Car Sequencing Model

Adèle LOUIS [1,2], Gülgün ALPAN [1], Bernard PENZ [1], Alain BENICHOU [2]

[1] Univ. Grenoble Alpes, CNRS, G-SCOP, F-38000 Grenoble, France
[2] RENAULT – Alliance Supply Chain Process Engineering, F-78140 Vélizy-Villacoublay, France
{adele.louis@renault.com, gulgun.alpan@grenoble-inp.fr, bernard.penz@grenoble-inp.fr, alain.benichou@renault.com}

Abstract. One of the most strategic processes in the automotive industry is to generate the car sequence to produce per day. The sequencing objective is to position high and low workload vehicles in the sequence to produce, such that the work overloads for the operators or emergency situations are avoided. To do so, most of the car manufacturers adopted an approach based on the Car Sequencing (CS) model, at the expense of other models like the Mixed-Model Sequencing (MMS) or the Level Scheduling (LS). The CS model has the advantage of simply addressing the industrial environment's constraints via sequencing rules, that are easy to understand and interpret for decision makers. Nevertheless, this CS model is hardly facing new challenges and presents some computing weaknesses. We discuss in this paper our motivations in reconsidering the Car Sequencing model of a French manufacturer, RENAULT, in its challenging and fast-changing industrial context.

Keywords: Car Sequencing, Mixed-Model Sequencing, automotive industry, spacing constraints

1. Introduction

Sequencing vehicles is part of the daily routine of a car assembly plant. Its goal is to determine the order (the sequence) in which the vehicles will be manufactured during the production day. It is a strategic process for those plants, at both technical and economic levels. Indeed, the occurrence of high workload vehicles must be balanced with lower ones so that workers can handle the delay that is induced by intensive tasks. If the accumulated delay is too long, then the workers may not be able to catch up on time to handle the following vehicles. Then, there are only two solutions to manage this kind of situation: the line is either stopped to allow the workers to finish their tasks (an original Toyota Production System's method) or a utility worker is called for help. Even if both solutions can be used to manage work overloads, the help of a utility worker is to be preferred because it only costs an additional workforce, while the line stoppage should be used as little as possible because of its high induced costs. In a nutshell, work overload situations must be minimized in the sequencing process to avoid overspending. Do to so, car manufacturers can adopt several sequencing strategies. Yet since the 1990s, most of them adopted an approach based on the Car Sequencing (CS) model.
To better understand the different sequencing strategies that can be used by car manufacturers, this article introduces a state-of-the-art of the main sequencing models in Section 2. Even if most car manufacturers chose a strategy based on the CS model, some recent contextual challenges are disturbing the sequencing process. Therefore Section 3 is dedicated to contextual motivations in reconsidering an actual CS model, based on the case study of a French car manufacturer, RENAULT. Section 4 focuses on a numerical example that illustrates the weaknesses of a sequencing approach based on the CS model. And, finally, Section 5 presents some concluding remarks and perspectives.

2. State-of-the-Art of Sequencing Models for Mixed-Model Assembly Lines

Sequencing vehicles at a mixed-model assembly line is truly a strategic process for automotive factories. The sequencing strategy can help smoothing the production of high workload vehicles, by distributing them evenly over the production horizon, or it could also rely on Just-In-Time requirements, with the objective of balancing part consumption over the production period to avoid demand peaks. Ultimately, two objectives emerge when it comes to sequencing vehicles in a mixed model assembly line: minimizing work overload situations and smoothing part consumption. From those two objectives, the scientific literature discusses three different models: Car Sequencing (CS), Mixed-Model Sequencing (MMS) and Level Scheduling (LS).

2.1. Sequencing Cars by Minimizing Work Overloads

Work overload or emergency situations occur when a succession of intensive work vehicles causes an unrecoverable delay for operators. In practice, it happens when operators work on high workload vehicles (i.e. vehicles with an assembly duration higher than the cycle time) and cannot achieve all tasks in a single cycle time. Consequently, they accumulate some delay. This delay can be recovered by the following vehicles, if their assembly duration is sufficiently shorter than the cycle time. If not, the delay must be compensated either by an additional utility worker or worse, by a line stoppage. These two compensations being very expensive (for a European automotive manufacturer, a line stoppage can represent a shortfall in income of several thousands of euros per minute), the sequencing strategy might aim to minimize work overload situations by balancing high workload models with low ones. For this purpose, the scientific literature discusses two sequencing strategies: Car Sequencing and Mixed-Model Sequencing models.
The Car Sequencing (CS) model was first introduced in 1986 [1]. Since then, a lot of researchers have been taking interest on this study field. As illustrated by a recent survey on sequencing mixed-model assembly lines, more than 20 major scientific contributions have been published in the 20 years that followed [2]. Furthermore, the ROADEF Challenge in 2005 has greatly increased the research interest on this topic thanks to the publication of real-life instances on sequencing [3]. Succinctly, this model takes into consideration a set of cars to sequence in a given production window, defined by their features and options, and a set of sequencing rules that indirectly avoids work overloads. As they reflect production capacities, those rules define a feature's maximum occurrence in a subsequence of determined length. In the literature, those rules are called spacing constraints or ratio constraints of type N/P where only N cars can bear the constrained feature out of P successive cars [4]. Thanks to these spacing constraints, high work intensive models and options, such as sunroofs or right-hand drives, can be evenly spread among lower workload options in sub-sequences of vehicles. For example, **Figure 1** illustrates a spacing constraint of 1/3 on electric vehicles (EVs). The very first subsequence of three cars respects this constraint with a ratio of exactly 1/3 while the second subsequence of three is composed of two EVs: in case of non-respect, the constraint is qualified as breached or violated. In the following sub-sequences, no other violations occur. The CS objective for minimizing work overload situations is expressed as the minimization of the number of violated sequencing constraints.

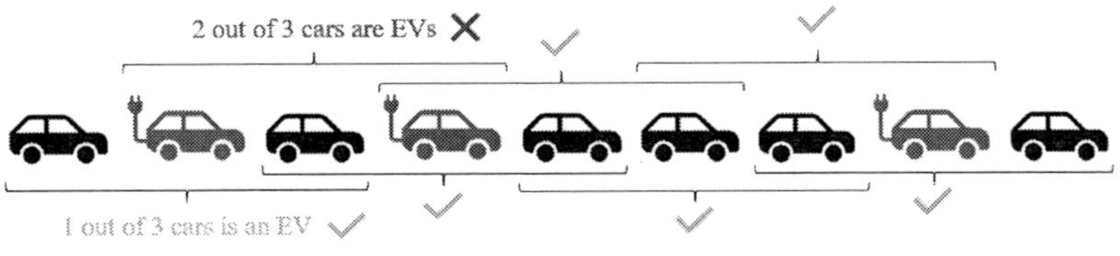

Figure 1: Illustrative car sequence with a 1/3 ratio constraint on electric vehicles (EVs)

The Mixed-Model Sequencing (MMS) model. Another way to minimize work overloads is to take explicitly into account operational times, lines features and tasks repartition over the assembly line. The MMS model intends indeed to determine a sequence of products that maximizes productivity. The literature displays different objectives: maximizing the completed work, minimizing idle times, minimizing the cumulated delays or even maintaining the production rate as constant as possible [5]. Work overloads occur when operators cannot complete their work within their workspace. As an illustration of the MMS principle, **Figure 2** shows two movement diagrams of an operator in a workstation. In time metrics (minutes for example), the length of the workstation equals the cycle time *Tcycle* but the overall workspace is delimited by two boundaries: the lower limit *Min* and the upper limit *Max* ($Min \leq 0$ and $Tcycle \leq Max$). The operator follows the vehicle while performing the assembly tasks and then goes back upstream to handle the next vehicle. In general, and as with vehicle #01 in both situations, if the workers finish before reaching *Tcycle*, then they can start their tasks on the following vehicle before it enters the workstation limits (case of vehicle #02). Even if they can work beyond their workstation limits, they must not trespass the upper boundary *Max* as it is the case with vehicles #05 and #06 for the movement diagram A. In fact, due to the proximity of two high workload vehicles, two situations of work overload occur. In this case, there is only three possibilities to finish the delayed tasks: the line is stopped so that the operators can finish their tasks; utility workers can either finish the task when the vehicle crosses the *Max* boundary or treat the complete intensive task by themselves from the beginning [6]. In comparison, the quality of the second sequence is way better: it generates no work overloads. Interested readers can refer to further industrial case studies that examine a motor assembly plant [7] or a truck assembly line [8] for example.

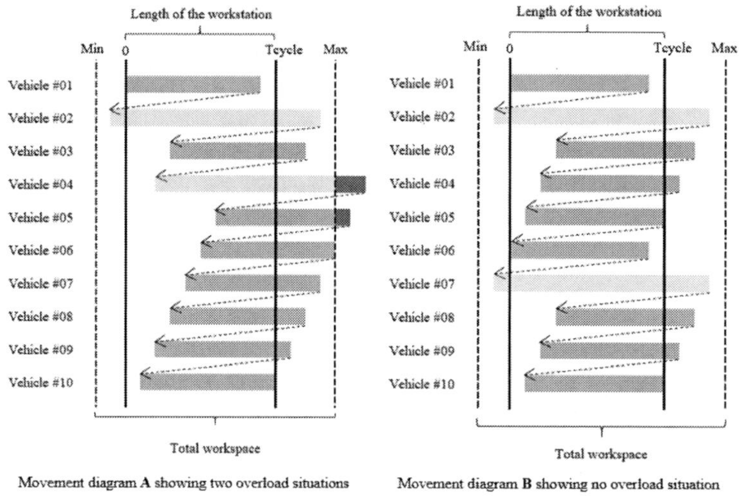

Figure 2: Movement diagrams of an operator at his workstation

2.2. Sequencing Cars by Smoothing Part Consumption in a Just-In-Time Environment

When it comes to sequencing vehicles, another approach is also mentioned in the scientific literature and aims to fulfill Just-In-Time requirements: the **Level Scheduling** (LS) model. By smoothing part consumption, this model helps balancing part consumption over the production period to avoid demand peaks and enlarged safety stocks. As an integral part of the Toyota Production System, LS model is also known as just-in-time scheduling or production smoothing. Its goal to level the part consumption variation is achieved in two stages [9]:

- Firstly, define an ideal part consumption rate and then evenly smooth the total material demand over the given production period. This ideal schedule is said to be a level target schedule.
- Secondly, sequence the actual set of vehicles to produce through a minimization of the differences between the actual and the theoretical part demands per production period.

In other words, the main objective of LS is to minimize the deviation between actual and theoretical part consumption rates over the production period. By this mean, LS attempts to ease just-in-time material supply and to minimize safety stocks, space requirements and operational costs.

Figure 3 illustrates the deviations between an ideal and an actual sequence of products having two features: one colour (red, blue or green) and one possible option. Six different product combinations are then feasible. The ideal sequence is determined by decision makers to smooth the assembly of products that have the considered option and to group same coloured ones. Nevertheless, the actual sequence is quite distant from the theoretical one: the final sequence generates a total of seven deviations.

		Sequence										
		1	2	3	4	5	6	7	8	9	10	
Ideal	Color	R	R	R	B	B	B	B	G	G	G	
	Option?	No	Yes	No	Yes	No	Yes	No	Yes	No	Yes	
Actual	Color	R	R	B	B	B	B	G	G	B	B	
	Option?	No	No	No	Yes	No	Yes	No	No	Yes	Yes	
Deviations		0	1	1	0	0	0	1	1	2	1	Total: 7

Figure 3: Example of the deviations between ideal and actual sequence

Nonetheless, in a very diversified products context such as automotive industry, the part-oriented LS approach has been shown as barely solvable to optimality [2]: this explains why many car manufacturers do not give a preference to this model.
Although "minimizing work overloads" and "minimizing deviations between an ideal and an actual part consumption" both seem relevant objectives, they give rise to divergent sequencing models. In practice and to our best knowledge, most of the car manufacturers chose a sequencing model based on the original Car Sequencing model. The advantages of the CS model over the other two models lie in the ease of definition and interpretation of sequencing rules for decision makers. The CS model also requires less data collection efforts than MMS or LS models, and by extension, it has a better running time. Still, Section 3 will illustrate our interests in reconsidering a real-life Car Sequencing model, in its challenging and fast-changing industrial context.

3. Motivations in reconsidering a real-life Car Sequencing model

Like many car manufacturers, French company RENAULT chose a sequencing strategy based on the original Car Sequencing model. Since 2000s, a hybrid CS model allows RENAULT to compute the daily production sequence (section 3.1). Very innovative in its early days, it inspired many scientific publications following the ROADEF challenge in 2005 [3]. Nevertheless, it now shows some limits and weaknesses in a challenging and fast-changing industrial context (section 3.2). That's why some arguments in favor of a change in the sequencing strategy are exposed in section 3.3.

3.1. Vehicle Sequencing at RENAULT: a Car Sequencing-Inspired Model

The vehicle sequencing process at RENAULT differs from the original Car Sequencing Problem as defined in the previous section. In fact, RENAULT's vehicle sequencing model includes a color-batching objective, in addition to the objective of respecting different types of ratio constraints.
The color-batching objective is an originality that aims to fulfill an economic painting shop requirement. The main point is to minimize the production costs due to color changeovers and to save unused ink, as well as solvent employed to clean color booths [10]. The objective of minimizing color changeovers results in a certain number of consecutive vehicles of the same color in the sequence, within a given limit. This limit is an upper value of the color batch length used to insure periodic and mandatory cleanings, as well as a good paint quality [11]. Furthermore, RENAULT's vehicle sequencing model varies from the original CS model by the characterization of its spacing constraints: they are defined as priority or non-priority. These two categories allow RENAULT plants to distinguish critical assembly shop operations from softer operations (mainly used to smooth workloads).
Consequently, RENAULT's sequencing model is far more complex than the original CS model. By trying to optimize the requirements of both paint and trim shops, the model has to compute a multi-objective model with the following intentions: minimizing the number of color changes (#CC); minimizing the number of violated priority ratio constraints (#PRC) and non-priority ratio constraints (#NPRC). Final car assembly factories arbitrate those three objectives in consideration with labor costs, workforce availability, impossible sequencing configurations, and performance goals (i.e. color batches). Considering that non-priority constraints have a lower importance than priority constraints, three objective rankings must be considered: 1° Minimize #PRC, then #CC, then #NPRC; 2° Minimize #PRC, then #NPRC, then #CC; 3° Minimize #CC, then #PRC, then #NPRC. To evaluate the cost of a sequence, the first objective is assigned with a penalty of 10^6, the second one with 10^3 and the third one with 1.

RENAULT's actual car sequencer is running since 2000s and has known a lot of improvements, especially thanks to the ROADEF challenge in 2005. However, it now seems to struggle facing the new challenges of the automotive industry.

3.2. New Challenges Faced by the Automotive Industry

The automotive industry is challenged by three topics that are related to the sequencing strategy: manufacturing efficiently a high level of car diversity (especially true for the European industry), performing through innovative or disruptive production systems and handling more and more vehicles with specific plant routing requirements.

Steady level of high customization: The automotive industry is characterized by a high level of car diversity, given by a huge number of models, features and options combinations. This high level of customization describes well, especially the European car constructors' strategy, which goes hand in hand with their make-to-order model. Nevertheless, this large amount of customization represents a big challenge for final assembly plants because it increases the complexity of parts' procurement, scheduling, sequencing and manufacturing [12]. For example, the increase of the color palette has a direct and negative impact on color batches and hardens the vehicle sequencing process [10].

Emergence of new plant configurations and alternative production systems: In the age of Industry 4.0, RENAULT plants are being deeply transformed with new types of organization, new information systems (IS) and new tools helping operators to achieve their tasks. New plants incorporate innovative line configurations: plants are getting more and more unique compared to each other. However, it has become a big challenge for RENAULT's vehicle sequencer to adjust to new plant configurations. For example, the original sequencer was made to meet the expectations of configuration A in **Figure 4**. The three other configurations present two issues for which the actual sequencer is inaccurate: vehicles merging in paint shop (configurations B, C and D) and vehicles splitting after it (configuration C).

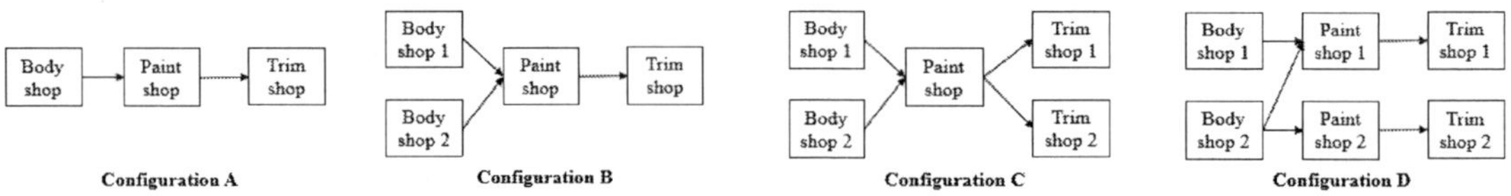

Figure 4: Simplified plant configurations

Moreover, the emergence of studies on reconfigurable lines or alternative production systems have shown up in the last decade and let us glimpse the future of automotive production. For example, let's cite two European auto-makers that already have experienced the future of plants 4.0:

- PSA, a French car manufacturer has recently launched its "*usine excellente*" (excellent plant). Its production facility is centered on a principal regular assembly line, but the car diversity is handled in the end by small derivate lines.
- AUDI, a German auto-maker, is already experimenting its project "Small Factory 2035" in one of its plant in Hungary. Instead of a traditional interlinked conveyor system, the company prefers introducing numerous production stations that act like independent ones. Thanks to the concept of modular assembly, each vehicle has its own route through different production stations.

Finally, future automotive production facilities tend to present new configurations of regular conveyor belts at least, and totally revolutionary disruptive production systems at most. The management of various car routing represents a big challenge for future sequencing models.

Management of vehicles with extended lead times: Another challenge faced by various auto constructors is to deal with vehicles that have extended lead times (ELT). For example, RENAULT faces this kind of challenge with plants that produce the bi-tone vehicles. A bi-tone (or 2TON) vehicle is a car that has two different colors: one primary for the body and one secondary for the roof. Depending on the painting technology, it can take up to two additional hours for a 2TON vehicle to be painted compared with a regular 1TON vehicle. Since 2TON vehicles can represent more than 50% of the production volume for a given plant, sequencing 2TON and 1TON vehicles has become a big challenge for RENAULT's vehicle sequencer. In fact, color batches are more complicated to optimize than previously. Thus, primary color batches have reached a drastically low value and so, consequently, the paint shop operational costs are way higher than expected.

In a nutshell, RENAULT's vehicle sequencer is well suited to meet the expectation of a linear plant defined by a classic conveyor belt going from body shop to trim shop, but it has trouble handling a high and never decreasing level of diversity, adapting to new or even disruptive plant configurations and handling more and more specific vehicle routings. Reconsidering the sequencing strategy now seems required and our expectations rely on the opportunities of an MMS approach.

3.3. Expectations in reconsidering the Car Sequencing with a Mixed-Model Sequencing Approach

The automotive industry is facing numerous challenges that involve its Car Sequencing performance. That's why this section presents our several prospects in challenging the current sequencing model with a different approach based on the Mixed-Model Sequencing concepts.

Firstly, spacing constraints are an easy way to address production constraints for decision makers but could be used too approximately. Sometimes defined intuitively or by the rule of thumb, they may fail to avoid emergency situations [4]. By removing these spacing constraints and substituting them by accurate operational times and an MMS approach, we aim at reaching a greater number of feasible vehicle sequences than with a CS model in terms of work overloads minimization [13].

Secondly and as for the alternative and disruptive production systems, MMS seems more compatible than CS, especially regarding vehicle routing between shops or independent work-stations. The introduction of Industry 4.0 with concepts such as disruptive plant configuration and small derivate lines cannot be achieved without a powerful tool to map the whole workshop. A routing system is required to define the path and the operations sequence for each vehicle. To manufacture the maximum number of cars at the right cost, time and quality, the routing system needs to embed specific MMS data like detailed operations and tasks, work-stations configuration, as well as set up, operational and takt times. This makes MMS a more suitable model to sequence and route vehicles than CS.

Thirdly, specific vehicles with ELT could also be handled more accurately by MMS because of its direct consideration of operational times, work-stations and line configuration. This way, car assembly plants could avoid tremendous investments in manufacturing facilities such as delay lines or secondary paint shops (to deal with the 2TON vehicles issue) and intermediary stocks that reorder vehicles between shops.

Thus, MMS offers many opportunities to address the current automotive industry's issues, but to our best knowledge, very few scientific contributions are considering the real performances of this model over CS with real industrial data. To illustrate this opportunities, section 4 presents an example to numerically illustrate the limits of CS and the opportunities presented by an approach that is more focused on actual field and production data.

4. Example in our industrial case study

This last section is dedicated to a numerical example to illustrate some weaknesses of the Car Sequencing model and the importance of considering a sequencing strategy based on the explicit consideration of operational times and production features. Focused on a single work-station, Section 4.1 describes the scientific calculation of a ratio for a constrained workspace while section 4.2 illustrates the lack of flexibility in the generation of eligible sequences by a CS approach.

4.1. Scientific Calculation of a Ratio for a Constrained Work-Station

In practice, N/P spacing constraints are mostly defined intuitively or by the rule of thumbs, by considering the number of vehicles having a considered feature over the total number of vehicles to produce. Nevertheless, the scientific literature describes a method to calculate the ratio of a spacing constraint using operational times [4][6][14]. It considers some production features (all expressed in time metric, i.e. minutes for example) such as the cycle time (T_{cycle}) and the highest/lowest duration of assembly tasks (T_{sup} & T_{inf}). It also defines the following ones: the reduction delay obtained by assigning a vehicle with a low workload to the sequence (R_{inf}); the supplementary delay that a high workload vehicle adds up to the operator (R_{sup}); the maximum delay that can be accumulated by an operator (R_{max}). R_{inf}, R_{sup} and R_{max} are represented in **Figure 5** and calculated as follow by **Equation (1)**, where Max and Min are the upper and lower boundaries of the operator's workspace, as defined in section 2.1 ($Min \leq 0$ and $T_{cycle} \leq Max$).

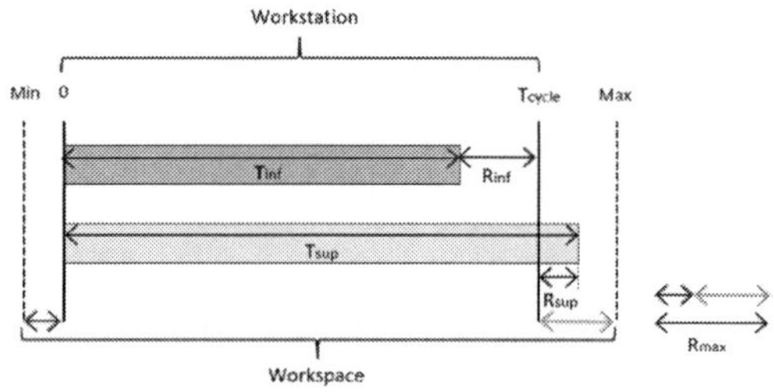

Figure 5: Illustration of production features used for the scientific calculation of an N/P ratio

$$R_{inf} = T_{cycle} - T_{inf}$$
$$R_{sup} = T_{sup} - T_{cycle} \quad (1)$$
$$R_{max} = (Max - Min) - T_{cycle}$$

For a single workstation, the calculation of the ratio N/P is given by **Equation 2.**

$$N = \left\lfloor \frac{R_{max}}{R_{sup}} \right\rfloor \text{ and } P = N + \left\lceil \frac{N * R_{sup}}{R_{inf}} \right\rceil \quad (2)$$

The following section presents a numerical example of this calculation as well as some remarks on the sequence flexibility generated by such an approach.

4.2. Example on the Flexibility of a Sequence Generation for a Constrained Work-Station

This last part focuses on the lack of flexibility in the sequence generation by the Car Sequencing model. As an example, we consider a single workstation on which two different vehicles are assembled: a top-of-the-range model and an entry-level one. Their assembly durations (expressed in minutes) are respectively T_{sup} = 1.30 and T_{inf} = 1.10, for a cycle time of T_{cycle} = 1.20. The upper and lower boundaries of the workspace are *Max* = 1.40 and *Min* = - 0.10. The scientific calculation given above gives us N = 3 and P = 6 so a ratio of 3/6 for the spacing constraint. Nevertheless, setting the ratio to 3/6 deprives us of many other sequence configurations, as shown in **Figure 6.** It illustrates a sequence having a ratio of 3/6 on yellow vehicles (A) and two other sequences (B & C) that neither respect this constraint nor generate work overload for the operator. In configuration A, the spacing constraint of 3/6 is perfectly respected, and no work overloads occur. Configuration B does not respect the 3/6 constraint, as illustrated in the sub-sequence going from vehicle #02 to #07 with 4 high workload (yellow) vehicles in a sequence of 6. Even so, it does not generate work overloads. The observation is the same for configuration C but in this case, an additional high workload vehicle is introduced in the sequence of 12 without causing disruption to the worker. Thus, those three configurations are eligible because they do not put the operator in an emergency. Nevertheless, both sequences B & C are not considered by CS because they do not respect the 3/6 constraint. In a nutshell, the definition of a spacing constraint is critical and impacts sensibly the sequencing possibilities. Even scientific calculations can ban eligible sequences.

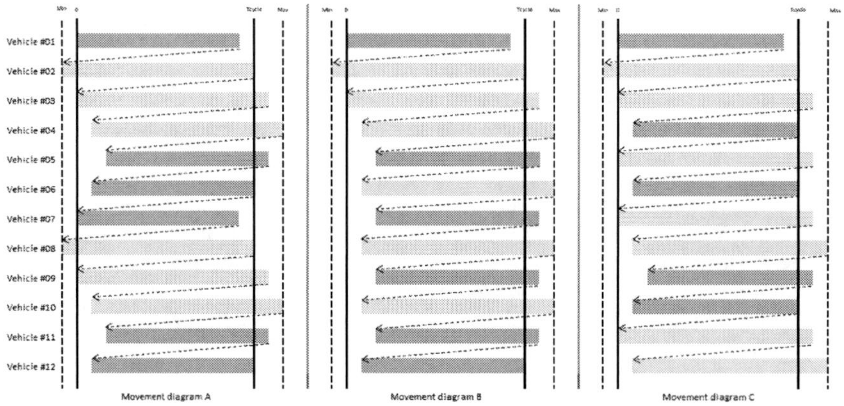

Figure 6: Movement diagrams of three different sequence configurations

In the end, a sequencing approach based on the principles of the Car Sequencing model shows some limits. First, a sequencing strategy based on spacing constraints quickly leads to approximations and impacts downwards production volumes of constrained features. Secondly, the CS model is likely to generate fewer realizable sequences than the MMS model.

5. Conclusion and Perspectives

This conference paper focuses on one of the most strategic processes in the automotive industry, which is the construction of the daily vehicle production sequences. Thereon, three main models are discussed in the scientific literature: the Car Sequencing (CS), the Mixed-Model Sequencing (MMS) and the Level Scheduling (LS). While the LS model focuses on Just-In-Time requirements by seeking for smoothing the part consumption, the two others target the minimization of work overloads. Since 1990s, car manufacturers opted for the CS strategy. This preference is due to CS advantage in simply addressing the industrial environment's constraints via sequencing rules, that are easy to understand and interpret for decision makers. Moreover, since the ROADEF challenge in 2005 and the publication of RENAULT's industrial data, this model has experienced a renewed interest from the scientific community. Nevertheless, the actual RENAULT Car Sequencing model is facing some difficulties regarding new challenges of the automotive industry: a steady high level of customization, some peculiar or disruptive plant configurations, extended lead time vehicles and routing… Our numerical example shows also some limits, due to approximations in the definition of spacing constraints. That's why, in this challenging and fast-changing industrial context, we encourage new industrial case studies to consider whether CS is still the best sequencing strategy.
As a perspective, we aim at conducting a study comparing the performances of RENAULT's Car Sequencer with an MMS approach and real-life data on operational times and production features. As MMS requires a high quantity of data and running time, we are already considering some strategic cuts on the problem data, such as reducing the number of workstations by identifying the critical set of workstations and the number of variants per workstation.

6. References

1. Parello, B., Kabat, W., Wos, L.: Job-shop scheduling using automated reasoning: A case study of the car sequencing problem. Journal of Automated Reasoning 2, 1--42 (1986)
2. Boysen, N., Fliedner, M., Scholl A.: Sequencing mixed-model assembly lines: Survey, classification and model critique. European Journal of Operational Research 192, 349--373 (2009)
3. Solnon C., Cung V.D., Nguyen A., Artigues C.: The car sequencing problem: Overview of state-of-the-art methods and industrial case-study of the ROADEF'2005 challenge problem. European Journal of Operational Research 191, 912--927 (2008)
4. Lesert, A., Alpan, G., Frein, Y., Noiré, S.: Definition of spacing constraints for the car sequencing problem. International Journal of Production Research, 49:4, 963--994 (2011)
5. Bautista, J., Alfaro, R., Batalla, C.: Modeling and solving the mixed-model sequencing problem to improve productivity. Int. J. Production Economics 161, 83-95 (2015)
6. Giard, V., Jeunet, J.: Modélisation du problème général d'ordonnancement de véhicules sur une ligne de production et d'assemblage. Journal Européen des Systèmes Automatisés, 40 (4/5), 463-496 (2006).
7. Bautista, J., Cano, A., Alfaro, R.: Models for MMSP-W considering workstation dependencies: A case study of Nissan's Barcelona plant. European Journal of Operational Research 223, 669-679 (2012)
8. Aroui, K., Alpan, G., Frein, Y.: Minimizing work overload in mixed-model assembly lines with different types of operators: a case study from the truck industry. International Journal of Production Research 55 (21), 1-22 (2017)
9. Yavuz, M., Ergin, H.: Advanced constraint propagation for the combined car sequencing and level scheduling problem. Computers and Operation Research 110, 128-138 (2018)
10. Bysko S., Krystek J., Bysko S.: Automotive Paint Shop 4.0. Computers & Industrial Engineering (2018)
11. Krystek J., Alszer S.: Contemporary aspects of car sequencing problem in a paint shop. Mechanik NR 7/2017
12. Staeblein, T., Aoki K.: Planning and scheduling in the automotive industry: a comparison of industrial practice at German and Japanese makers. Int. J. Production Economics 162, 252--272 (2015)
13. Golle, U., Rothlauf, F., Boysen, N.: Car sequencing versus mixed-model sequencing: a computational study. European Journal of European Research 237, 50--61 (2014)
14. Bolat, A., Yano, C.: Scheduling algorithms to minimize utility work at a single station on a paced assembly line. Production Planning & Control, 3 (4), 393-405 (1992)

I L S 2020
INTERNATIONAL CONFERENCE ON INFORMATION SYSTEMS, LOGISTICS & SUPPLY CHAIN
Austin, Texas April 22-24, 2020

A DDMRP implementation user feedbacks and stakes analysis

Guillaume Dessevre [1], Jacques Lamothe [2], Vincent Pomponne [3], Pierre Baptiste [1], Matthieu Lauras [2], Robert Pellerin [1]

[1] Polytechnique Montreal, Montreal, Canada
[2] IMT Mines Albi, Albi, France
[3] Pierre Fabre Dermo-Cosmétique, Lavaur, France
{firstname.lastname@polymtl.ca, firstname.lastname@mines-albi.fr, firstname.lastname@pierre-fabre.com}

Abstract. Since its appearance, Demand Driven Material Requirements Planning (DDMRP) is under the spotlights in both scientific field and industrial deployment. Although some companies are now sharing their results after their DDMRP implementations, none or very few have collaborated with scholars to scientifically study the important issues and stakes of the method within their specific environment. This paper presents a methodology to answer the real industrial questions raised on deploying DDMRP. A case study from a dermo-cosmetic industry illustrates the method. The main issues that must be answered first are developed. They should be the start of different research subjects in order to unite the industrial problems with the scientific approaches and tools.

Keywords: DDMRP, feedback, stakes, analysis, industrial case.

1. Introduction

Demand Driven Material Requirements Planning (DDMRP) is a material management method introduced by C. Ptak and C. Smith in 2011 [1] and 2016 [2]. Crossover between push flow and pull flow methods, the DDMRP logic is based on strategic buffer positioning and replenishment. Studied more and more lately, DDMRP seems to give good theorical and practical results. However, the method is not deployed in many companies and suffers from a few industrial feedbacks to guide research.

In order to focus research on real industrial issues, this paper presents a methodology to find and solve real-life problems in collaboration with an industry. As an application, a case study from a dermo-cosmetic company willing to deploy DDMRP along its supply chain is developed. This application is currently in progress so only the first steps of the methodology are presented, including the main industrial issues that the company must solve before deploying DDMRP.

These issues concern a lot of industries, not only the dermo-cosmetic ones, and should be the start of different research subjects focused on industrial problems. Three manufacturing departments are targeted: supply, production and distribution. In each department, the three most important questions to answer are raised.

The paper is organized as follows:

- section 2 presents the main points of the method DDMRP and a brief literature review;
- section 3 is the presentation of the methodology used to answer the problematic;
- section 4 presents the current results in a real case study according to the different steps of the methodology; and
- section 5 is the conclusion and opening.

2. Literature review about DDMRP theory and feedbacks

The DDMRP is composed of 5 steps [2]. The first one, "Strategic Inventory Positioning", consists in determining the strategic points in the Bill Of Material (BOM), for each product, where a buffer will be set up to create an independence. The points are called decoupled points and they introduce a new parameter called the Decoupled Lead Time (DLT). The DLT is the longest unprotected (by buffers) lead time in the BOM. The DDMRP recommends three types of buffer: the stock buffer, the time buffer and the capacity buffer. The stock one will lead to physical pieces whereas the time and the capacity ones are just control buffers: for example, a time buffer will indicate if pieces might arrive late, leading to shortage in raw materials or resulting from manufacturing issue, so decision have to be taken to ensure production (it is not used for pieces to arrive early, otherwise it would be quite similar to a stock buffer).
The second step, "Buffer Profiles and Levels", is where the buffers are sized. Each buffer is composed of 3 main zones: the green zone (representing the minimum order quantity to produce or supply), the yellow zone (the heart of the demand coverage, representing the average stock consumed during replenishment) and the red zone (behaving as a safety part). Using parameters such as the Average Daily Usage (ADU), the Minimum Order Quantity (MOQ), the Lead Time Factor (LTF) and the Variability Factor (VF), the zones of a stock buffer are sized as follows:

$$\text{Yellow zone} = \text{ADU} * \text{DLT} \tag{1}$$

$$\text{Red zone} = \text{Yellow zone} * \text{LTF} * (1 + \text{VF}) \tag{2}$$

$$\text{Green zone} = \text{MAX}(\text{MOQ}, \text{Yellow zone} * \text{LTF}, \text{ADU} * \text{desired order cycle}) \tag{3}$$

The sum of the red zone (2) and the yellow one (1) is called the Tof Of Yellow (TOY), and the sum of the TOY and the green zone (3) is the Top Of Green (TOG).
The LTF and VF have no mathematical definition. To choose the LTF, the DDMRP's authors recommend defining three categories (short, medium and long), and affecting one of these categories to each product regarding the DLT of the product among the others (a product considered with a short lead time will have a LTF between 20% and 40%, according to the authors' recommendations). Likewise, The VF is chosen by defining three categories (low, medium and high) according to the variability of the product (known by experience and rules for example).
The third step, "Dynamic Adjustment", is the size adjustment of each buffer regarding the demand changes. With seasonality effect, the buffer sizes might change. This step consists of using a Planned Adjustment Factor (PAF) to consider seasonality, ramp-up or ramp-down (ADU' = ADU * PAF).
The fourth step, "Demand Driven Planning", is the generation of supply order to replenish the buffers using the Net Flow Equation (NFE). The NFE is defined as follows:

$$\text{NFE} = \text{On-hand} + \text{on order} - \text{qualified sales order demand} \tag{4}$$

Where the qualified demand is the sum of the current demand (of the day) and the future demand considered as a spike. To determine if a demand order is a spike or not, two parameters have to be defined: the order spike threshold (below this threshold, a future order is not considered as a spike so it will not be count today) and the order spike horizon (after the horizon, the spike is not considered today). Each time the NFE falls into the yellow zone (or red zone), a supply or production order is generated. The quantity to supply is equal to the TOG minus the NFE (so the buffer will be replenished up to its top).
The fifth and last step, "Visible and Collaborative Execution", is the use of alerts to manage the system from an execution point of view. For the independent points (regarding to the BOM), there are two buffer status alerts: the current on-hand alert and the projected on-hand alert. For the dependent points, the two synchronization alerts are the material synchronization alert and the lead time alert (more details in the authors' book [2]).

Since the introduction of DDMRP in Orlicky's Material Requirements Planning – Third Edition [1], DDMRP has been a rising research subject. Publications on DDMRP (and Demand Driven Adaptive Enterprise [3]) focus on comparisons with other methods ([4], [5], [6]) or with previous system ([7]), on improving the method or adding tools ([8], [9], [10]) or on highlighting some opportunities ([11], [12]). While several companies divulge their results to the glory of DDMRP (Shell, Coasa, Biomérieux, Michelin, British Telecom, etc.), particularly on the Demand Driven Institute website [13], just a few has collaborated with academic researchers to arise fundamental questions and drive science forward.

Although the parameters choice seems fuzzy and subjective, only a few scientific approaches seems to have been done to find the best way to choose them ([10] lately, for example), but some questions remain: how to place the strategic buffers? How to choose between a time buffer, a capacity buffer or a stock buffer? How to decide when the dynamic adjustment of the parameters must be done? Etc.
Moreover, these questions are theory-oriented whereas the DDMRP is a material management method designed to be deployed in the industry. That is why the research problematic of this paper is:
What are the industrial problems linked to DDMRP and how to solve them?
Answering this question will allow scholars to understand the real industrial issues and focus the research on these problems.

3. Methods

To answer the problematic, the following steps have been identified:

1) *Define the current issues and the stakes of deploying the DDMRP*
   This step consists to understand the problems highlighted by managers into a company willing to deploy the DDMRP. It will give an overall view of the problems, and the reasons to choose the DDMRP instead of something else.
2) *Collect different opinions about the subject and the way of thinking/working in the company*
   By interviewing the stakeholders, managers and users, researchers will identify and categorize the problems: is it a common problem? Does is appear often? In which department? Who is in charge of…? Etc.
3) *Gather all the problems and prioritize them*
   After bringing the issues together, a root-cause analysis might be done to some of them to identify the origin of the problem. Using criticality and likelihood of occurrence for example, the problems can be prioritized, in order to focus the research on significant issues.
4) *Identify a mean to solve the problems*
   Now that the important issues and questions have been raised, researches (and stakeholders) must find the best way to answer them (using simulation, for example).
5) *Find solutions*
   A methodology might be defined to find solutions. In the case of using discrete event simulation for example, the sub-steps have been identified:
   a. Create a model of the chosen perimeter
   b. Determine the inputs and outputs
   c. Collect data to feed the model
   d. Define a design of experiments
   e. Simulate each scenario
   f. Analyse and conclude (or start again at a previous step)
6) *Discuss the found solutions with the stakeholders*
   The academic work might be done here, handing the reins to the industrial managers to apply the found solutions, or these solutions might be discussed in order to deploy them into the company.
7) *Deploy the solution(s)*
   According to the company philosophy, the personnel management, the technology involved, etc., the deployment of the solution(s) must be considered and maybe studied too.
8) *Conclude, document and share* (and move on to another issue)
   According to the results and the stakes, the solution deployment must be evaluated. Some corrections might appear. The results, if not subjected to a confidentiality agreement, must be shared among the academic field in order to drive science forward.

To illustrate this method, a dermo-cosmetic industry willing to deploy the DDMRP is presented. The next section gathers and develops the three first steps of this application. Due to space issue, all the problems are not presented in this paper. Therefore, the next section is composed of an overall view of the problems, a DDMRP feedback from the company, and finally the main questions that must be answered before deploying widely the method.

4. Results

4.1. Define the current issues and the stakes of deploying the DDMRP in the company

The company suffers from both a complex market and a complex production environment. The dermo-cosmetic market is characterized by a strong competition, a high product range replacement (about 30% per year), a global distribution with different regulation contingencies and an economic crisis.
In production, the company's managers must deal with large minimum production order quantity, capacity management (particularly with the operator's competences and outsourcing capacity), technology constraints, formula fragilities and crossed flows between plants.
Suffering from bad forecasts, lack of agility, visibility and trust between actors, weakness to absorb variability, use of a complex information system, no stock flow and securing policies, etc., a pure push-flow method within the supply chain did not seem to be efficient. That is why the deployment of DDMRP appears to be a solution.
However, it raised a lot of questions about coupling DDMRP with the dermo-cosmetic company's constraints that must be studied and answered before deploying the method. The questions concern the three following industrial departments: supply, production and distribution.
Moreover, DDMRP is already tested in the company's supply chain (for the buyers in the supply department and in two distribution subsidiaries). This pre-deployment raised other questionings and way of thinking to enlarge the method within the whole supply chain.

4.2. Collect different opinions about the subject and the way of thinking/working in the company

To accomplish this step, the research team (a student and his supervisor) met the stakeholders (project managers, production managers, buyers, users, etc.) of the company during a week. Some interviews have been done to understand the current issues in the company and to collect DDMRP users' feedback where the method has been already deployed.
DDMRP was initially deployed in the supply department, with the raw materials buyers. Due to a complicated start where stocks were increasing then stagnant at a higher level than expected, it has been decided to change some parameters. As there is no automated system within the DDMRP method to adjust the parameters except the ADU ([8]), these empirical adjustments took time. It was difficult but efficient, leading to an expansion of the deployment perimeter.
Nowadays, DDMRP is deployed for all materials (manufacturing components and conditioning components) and deployed and tested in distribution between the central stock and two subsidiaries. With this complicated start, the company's managers understood:

- The difficulties to instantiate DDMRP when the impact of a parameter change is not known;
- The fact that DDMRP buffer stocks might not be the solution for every products or components;
- The parametrization has to be done and studied for each product or family; and
- The setting up of the method arises a lot of questions that must be studied.

Regarding the difficulty to standardize the DDMRP within each sector, it has been decided that each department will deal with it by its own. As a result, DDMRP is set up differently in each sector.

In the supply sector, they use 12 buffer profiles and each product is attached to one of them according:

- The lead time category (short, medium, long); and
- The variability calculated as the ratio between the Minimum Order Quantity (MOQ) and the cover of the yellow part. Hence, they defined four types of variability (from very high if the yellow part is covered by less than half of the MOQ (then the variability factor is 1) to low when the yellow part represents more than twenty MOQs (variability factor is 0.25)).

The Average Daily Usage (ADU) is calculated each week, using historical and/or forecasted data (depending on the lead time of the product and if it is the beginning of the end of the product). The horizons used to calculate the mean demand are between 40 and 120 days of historical and/or forecasted data. The profile affectation of each product is revised each week with the routine previously introduced: when a new affectation is the same during 3 straight days, the buyer should change the buffer profile. The other parameters (DLT, LTF, VF) are not revised periodically.

In the French distribution centre, each supply order is categorized (A, B, C) according to reference rotation. Then, according to the stock location (there are two warehouses), buffer profiles are different. Finally, in one of the two warehouses, the buffer profiles are divided in two categories according to the product type (final product or promotional article). This leads to 9 different buffer profiles. The profile affection is revised each morning: if a product buffer has to change of profile, it is done immediately.
The buffers parameters are rarely changed, especially because there is no stock objective (except the warehouse size) in this subsidiary. In case of shortage, an analysis is done, possibly leading to an increase of the VR for example.

As a test, DDMRP has been deployed in the Spanish subsidiary for only two brands representing about 20% of references. 7 buffer profiles have been identified to respond to different needs (campaign launch, kitting and regular profile) with different parameters: two LTF and two VF.
The ADU is calculated with forecast based on 14 weeks and the order spike horizon is set to three times the DLT. Except for the ADU, none of the DDMRP parameters were dynamic. Due to workload-capacity issues, some DLT has been increased in order to avoid shortages. This was mainly because the central distribution centre was not prepared to send small but regular lots to the Spanish subsidiary (in accordance with the DDMRP logic). The lack of information about parameters change effect constraints to make empirical changes without real knowledge of the impacts.

4.3. Gather all the problems and prioritize them

Within each sector, the main issues of the case study's company are presented and developed here. A summary is given in Table 1. Each issue is specified as a specific problem to the dermo-cosmetic industry or a generic one (potentially shared with other industry) from the author's estimation.

4.3.1. Supply problems

The three main problems raised in the supply department are the "market supply", the double sourcing and the large MOQ with erratic demand.

Market supply (quite specific to the case study): Market supply is a type of supply where the company's suppliers produce the raw materials using large lot sizes in order to gain production efficiency (less set-up times lost). The company gives to its suppliers a forecast for the raw materials, suppliers will group the forecasts into one big production order, and then the company's buyers can pick some materials up from the stock made.
The question here is to couple DDMRP with this kind of supply (if it is relevant).
A solution to study could be a two-stage system where the supplier launches big production order according to the company's forecast and the company picks up little quantity according to DDMRP's recommendations.

Double sourcing (general issue): For many components, the company has to deal with double sourcing: the supplies come from different suppliers. Each supplier has its own lead times, its own minimum order quantity and of course its own variability. How could the buffers be sized in this case? What are the parameters to choose facing double sourcing?
Nowadays, there is no research on DDMRP and double sourcing issue. However, it is a common problem that many compagnies must deal with, so it could be an interesting research subject to investigate.

Large MOQ and erratic demand (quite general issue): The company and its suppliers reached an agreement, several years ago, on the MOQ to order. These MOQs are quite large, in contradiction with DDMRP's politics. The MOQs are so big that they represent about 80-90% of the buffer sizes. This means that the yellow and the red zones are so little that they cannot absorb any demand variation, leading them to be quite useless. This is mainly a problem with raw material used in products suffering from erratic demand (for example two big demand orders a year).
Because of the DDMRP's logic of replenishment, these raw materials are supplied directly when they are used, instead of waiting for a real demand (and so they wait in stock during several months).
DDMRP's stock buffers do not seem to be efficient everywhere: nowadays, do the previous MOQs mean something regarding the company's needs? Does the company have to renegotiate the MOQs with the

suppliers to reach DDMRP's logic? Is the DDMRP's stock or time buffers appropriate for these situations? How could the company decide if a raw material has to be supplied using DDMRP or not?

4.3.2. Production obstacles

In production, the main obstacles are the amalgams management, the workload smoothing and capacity management and the phase-in/phase-out and end-of-life management.

Amalgams (specific to the case study): The main problem the company has to deal with today in its workshop is the notion of amalgam: because of productivity worries and technical constraints, the production lots are bigger than necessary and dispatch into different packaging (types of packaging (bottle, tube, etc.) and capacity (100 ml, 200 ml, etc.)). Moreover, the company is suffering from a quite bad Overall Equipment Efficiency (OEE), leading the production managers to launch big packaging order every time it is possible. Launching a small production order is not even considerable because it would decrease the OEE, whereas the main objective given to them is to have a good OEE.
How must the company do to configure the buffers with these production policies?
Up to now, two solutions have raised lately:

1) When the NFE of a product falls into the yellow part of its buffer, a production order is launched (bigger than just the product's need) and the dispatch is made up using the NFE of each product made of the same recipe than the one that must be produced.
2) The second option is to create a virtual buffer for some products using the same recipe. When the NFE of this virtual product falls into the yellow part, this means that the "sum" of a combination of each product using the recipe has to be refilled. In order to avoid stockout, a strategic decision has to be made to group several products into the same virtual one that will represent them (according to the type of packaging or the container's capacity for example).

The first solution could lead to more stock than expected for some references, but the second one can lead to shortages. These two solutions must be studied, using simulation for example, in order to choose the best one. Some other solutions may appear too.

Workload smoothing and capacity management (generic issue): Due to demand and production variabilities (breakdowns, operators' absences, etc.), production managers have a key role to smooth workload, considering: reactor availability, raw material availability, operators' competences, expected production lead times and production parameters (recipe available for a type of reactor for example).
Moreover, DDMRP works in infinite capacity ([2], [9]). To smooth the workload, the Planned Adjustment Factor can be used, if we know the trend in advance.
The company faces sporadic demand on some products, causing bullwhip effect in the supply chain. The quick descent of need that DDMRP will bring worries the production department, facing more or less long set-up times (between each semi-finished product and between different format). The DDMRP aims to reduce bullwhip effect with its agility but the company's production managers might not be as agile as it would require regarding the production constraints (large production lot, low OEE).
Considering the complexity of the company, the capacity management has a key role in the deployment of the DDMRP and needs to be studied before.

Phase-in/phase-out and end-of-life management (generic issue): These kinds of problem might be dealt in part with the virtual buffer (presented previously) if a new product entering on market is a new version of an old one using the same recipe. For the others, several questions are rising on DDMRP parameters choices and production management (priority management for example), that must be discussed at each level of the decision-making process (strategical, tactical and operational). This subject must be more studied in the literature, because it is a common problem in the industrial world.

4.3.3. Distribution issues

In distribution, the company has to couple DDMRP and allowance constraints, to manage capacity when spikes appear and to deal with phase-in/phase-out and end-of-life management with far-off countries.

Allowances (quite generic issue): The company set up a process for its distribution part based on forecast, orders and stock levels to send products from the central stock to the subsidiaries and distributors. For

each reference, the stock sent each week is called an allowance (this is the stock allowed by the execution team to the subsidiary/distributor). This allowance is calculated each week-end, where an algorithm scatters the released stock between the subsidiaries/distributors, considering a promise (which is a promise of a stock made by the execution team based on forecast and capacity), the local stock (for the subsidiaries only because local stock level is known) and the real demand orders. To summarize, a calculation is made each week to send products from the central stock to the subsidiaries and distributors.
Considering now the DDMRP mechanism, where a supply order can be generated whenever in the week. If the subsidiary/distributor has the allowance for a reference, there is no problem (a supply order will be generated and the execution team will allow it, unless otherwise specified). Now considering there was no allowance for that reference because its stock was not released before allowances calculation: if the stock is released on Monday, knowing that allowances are not updated during the week, if a subsidiary needs stock for that reference on Tuesday or after, the order will be canceled because of the allowance limit.
Even if the execution team authorizes the needy subsidiary to take the stock when it is released, a needier one could need it tomorrow and could have priority. Even though production priority can be dynamic, agile and quick, it seems more difficult in distribution.
Should the company blindly trust the DDMRP logic or should it couple its current model with it?

Capacity and spikes management (generic issue): Like in production, the workload smoothing is an important question within DDMRP method. Some events can be predictable (the start of a new campaign for example) but others are not, particularly the spikes. According to the DDMRP methods, the spikes are managed with two parameters: the order spike threshold (which will determine whether an order is a spike or not, using a percentage of the red zone (typically 50%)) and the order spike horizon (which will determine whether the spike has to be consider now or later, set to a realistic reaction time (at least equal to the DLT)) [1]. However, the company suffers from unpredictable events considered as spikes but without an efficient reaction time to deal with: What should be the recommendations of DDMRP parameters in a such case? Will the DDMRP be able to respond to the unpredictable demand or not?
The DDMRP aims to work efficiently within its "comfort zone" where demand is variable but known in a dedicated horizon, but how should it be configured in order to consider a more volatile demand: larger DLT? Larger variability factor? Larger order spike threshold? Larger order spike horizon (as in the Spain subsidiary where it is equal to three times the DLT)?...

Phase-in/phase-out and end-of-life management and far-off countries (generic issue): As in the production department, the phase-in/phase-out and end-of-life management is a key question of the distribution department because of the complexity of the dermo-cosmetic market (where 30% of the products are changed each year). Even though there is no large lot sizing issue in distribution (contrary to production), the way of managing the end of a product within the DDMRP arises in questioning: how to synchronise the products? How to choose the start/end date and the parameters to slow down an activity/a product?
Moreover, the company has several far-off countries, adding complexity in the wanted agility to deal with phase-in/phase-out and end-of-life management. The company wants to send the right product at the right time in the right country. Following a replenishment logic such as DDMRP might send stock too early, resulting in moving or destroyed stock due to mistakes or expiry dates.
Furthermore, it is the execution team that manages these expiry dates today. Before sending stock in a country, the execution team takes care of the expiry dates (known in the central stock only) in order to send viable products. As the deliveries are made on Monday with the current system today, this work is easily done. With DDMRP generating orders whenever, this represents a bigger workload for the execution team, and they fear to fail to deal with expiry date and far-off countries.

The previous questions are summarized in the following table:

Table 1: Table of the main questions raised according to the department concerned.

Department concerned	Main questions raised
Supply (4.3.1)	How to couple DDMRP mechanism with a "market supply"? How to consider double sourcing in DDMRP parameters? How to deal with large MOQ and erratic demand with DDMRP?
Production (4.3.2)	How to deal with amalgams in DDRMP? How to manage capacity and workload smoothing with DDMRP? How to handle phase-in/phase-out and end-of-life management in production

	with DDMRP?
Distribution (4.3.3)	How to couple distribution allowances and DDMRP? How do deal with DDMRP spike management in a volatile market? How to handle phase-in/phase-out and end-of-life management in distribution with far-off countries and expiry dates in DDMRP?

These are the important questions that must to be answered by the researchers in collaboration with the industrial stakeholders, in order to deploy DDMRP efficiently.

5. Conclusions and opening

With the aim of deploying the DDMRP efficiently in the industrial world, it is important to answer the real questions. In order to do that, this paper presents a methodology to raise the industrial issues and to solve them.

Using a real case study, the main problems in the dermo-cosmetic industry are presented. These questions are not limited to this kind of industry and some of them are addressed to a wide group of company.

In the supply department, the questions are about coupling DDMRP and: supply market, double sourcing, and large MOQ with erratic demand.

In production, the obstacles are about dealing with DDMRP and: amalgams, workload smoothing, and phase-in/phase-out and end-of-life management.

In distribution, the issues are about DDMRP and: distribution allowances, spike management in a volatile market, and phase-in/phase-out and end-of-life management with far-off countries.

These questionings should feed the scholars with industrial research subjects.

6. References

[1] C. Ptak and C. Smith, *Orlicky's Material Requirements Planning 3/E*. McGraw Hill Professional, 2011.

[2] C. Ptak and C. Smith, *Demand Driven Material Requirements Planning (DDMRP)*. Industrial Press, Incorporated, 2016.

[3] C. Smith, C. Ptak, and D. Ling, "The Demand Driven Adaptive Enterprise Model: The Case for a New System of Enterprise Management," *Demand Driven Institute,* 2017.

[4] M. Ihme and R. Stratton, "Evaluating demand driven MRP: a case based simulated study," 2015.

[5] R. Miclo, F. Fontanili, M. Lauras, J. Lamothe, and B. Milian, "An empirical comparison of MRPII and Demand-Driven MRP," *IFAC-PapersOnLine,* vol. 49, no. 12, pp. 1725-1730, 2016.

[6] M. J. Shofa and W. O. Widyarto, "Effective production control in an automotive industry: MRP vs. demand-driven MRP," in *AIP Conference Proceedings*, 2017, vol. 1855, no. 1, p. 020004: AIP Publishing.

[7] A. Kortabarria, U. Apaolaza, A. Lizarralde, and I. Amorrortu, "Material management without forecasting: From MRP to demand driven MRP," *Journal of Industrial Engineering and Management,* vol. 11, no. 4, pp. 632-650, 2018.

[8] G. Martin, P. Baptiste, J. Lamothe, R. Miclo, and M. Lauras, "A process map for the demand driven adaptive enterprise model: Towards an explicit cartography," in *7th International Conference on Information Systems, Logistics and Supply Chain, ILS 2018, July 8, 2018 - July 11, 2018*, Lyon, France, 2018, pp. 664-672: INSA Lyon.

[9] G. Dessevre, G. Martin, P. Baptiste, J. Lamothe, R. Pellerin, and M. Lauras, "Decoupled Lead Time in finite capacity flowshop: a feedback loop approach," in *IESM 19-8th International Conference on Industrial Engineering and Systems Management*, 2019, pp. p. 142-148.

[10] C.-J. Lee and S.-C. Rim, "A Mathematical Safety Stock Model for DDMRP Inventory Replenishment," *Mathematical Problems in Engineering,* vol. 2019, 2019.

[11] P. Baptiste, "DDMRP: Scheduling opportunities in case of complex BOMs," in *7th International Conference on Information Systems, Logistics and Supply Chain, ILS 2018, July 8, 2018 - July 11, 2018*, Lyon, France, 2018, pp. 317-325: INSA Lyon.

[12] B. Bahu, L. Bironneau, and V. Hovelaque, "Compréhension du DDMRP et de son adoption: premiers éléments empiriques," *Logistique & Management,* vol. 27, no. 1, pp. 20-32, 2019.

[13] D. D. Institute. Available (January 2020): https://www.demanddriveninstitute.com/case-studies

I L S 2020
INTERNATIONAL CONFERENCE ON INFORMATION SYSTEMS, LOGISTICS & SUPPLY CHAIN
Austin, Texas April 22-24, 2020

Make-to-Order Production Planning with Uncertain Quality

Dincer Konur [1], Tahir Ekin [1]

[1] Department of Computer Information Systems and Quantitative Methods, McCoy Gollege of Business Administration, Texas State University, San Marcos TX, United States
{d_k141@txstate.edu, tahirekin@txstate.edu}

Abstract. In this study, we investigate a manufacturer's production planning problem for a customer's order under uncertain quality. Particularly, the manufacturer operates under a make-to-order production strategy and needs to determine the production size for a customer order. Due to the manufacturing process, the quality of the units produced vary and we consider that there is an arbitrary number of quality classes. Knowing manufacturer's process, the customer imposes restrictions on the average quality received in addition to the order fulfillment requirement. We formulate a two-stage stochastic optimization model for this problem and present an augmented probability simulation-based optimization solution approach.

Keywords: Make-to-order, Uncertain quality, multiple quality classes, production planning.

1. Introduction and Literature Review

Production planning is a paramount part of the manufacturing processes and has long helped balance supply and demand. Therefore, production planning models are of interest to practitioners and have been extensively studied in literature. This paper presents a manufacturer's production planning problem for a customer's order under quality uncertainty. In particular, the manufacturer works with a make-to-order production strategy. The production size given a customer order needs to be determined under uncertain manufacturing quality with varying levels. Hence, our focus is on production planning problems under quality uncertainty with heterogeneity. Reader is referred to Mundi et al. [1] for a recent relevant review.

Such production planning problems are seen in a wide range of domains. For instance, crude oil selection and procurement is paramount in the oil refining process since it impacts the profit margin of the refinery. However, the manufactured crude oil has an uncertain quality. Yang and Barton [2] have presented a two-stage stochastic optimization model that incorporates such uncertainty in the oil supply availability. Teunter and Flapper [3] considers the uncertainty of core quality levels in determining optimal acquisition decisions by considering multiple quality classes and a multinomial quality distribution for an acquired lot. In the case of deterministic demand, they derive a closed-form expression for the total expected cost. For uncertain demand, they present optimal newsvendor-type solutions for the optimal remanufacture-up-to levels and an approximate expression for the total expected cost given the number of acquired cores. Another example could be diamond cutting. When the expert works on raw diamond, there would be different levels of cuts, which would determine the price. This list could be extended to include solar panel and marble production.

The randomness in supply allocation are major sources of uncertainty in production planning. Li et al. [4] present a generalized supply chain model for both deterministic and random demand subject to supply uncertainty after the supplier chooses the production input level. Chen and Xiao [5] assume the uncertainties in the production disruption risk and capacity allocation and develop supply chain game models for production and outsourcing. Anupindi and Akella. [6] examine the operational issues of quantity allocation between two uncertain suppliers and its effects on the inventory policies of the buyer. Ciarallo et al. [7] discuss the aggregate planning problem for a single product with random demand and random capacity while considering the uncertainty in unplanned machine maintenance, varying production yields and rework.

Lastly, uncertainty of production quality is extensively studied. Galbreth and Blackburn [8] explore the optimal acquisition quantities in remanufacturing with condition uncertainty. This was extended by the investigation of acquisition and sorting policies in the presence of used product condition variability for a remanufacturer facing both deterministic and uncertain demand [9]. Galbreth and Blackburn [10] consider the acquisition and production decisions of a remanufacturer who acquires used products of variable condition and allocates remanufacturing activity to domestic and offshore facilities. Most of the literature on production quality defines yield as the percentage of working products, for instance see the review of Yano and Lee [11].

The simplest yield model assumes that each produced unit follows a Bernoulli distribution resulting with a working or a defective product with a pre-specified probability. On the other hand, stochastically proportional yield models can explicitly model the parameters of the yield rate, independently from the production size. For instance, truncated Normal [12] and Beta distributions [13] are utilized to model the mean and variance of the yield. All these aforementioned approaches for modeling yield uncertainty assume that randomness in yield are independent from previous decisions. A variety of models relax that assumption by considering the dependence of yield on previous production [14-16] and maintenance [17] or both [18].

This paper differs from the previous studies in several ways. First, we assume endogenous yield, i.e., production size, as the manufacturer's decision variable, impacts the yield uncertainty of multiple quality levels for the product. Particularly, we extend the simple Bernoulli yield model to multiple quality levels and use multinomial distribution. Multinomial distribution is utilized to model the quality of the used product returns to determine the fraction of each quality level of returned products when there are more than two quality levels [19]. Second, in planning production size for a customer's order, we explicitly consider the quality restrictions imposed by the customer. As a result, this make-to-order production planning problem for a single-product with multiple quality classes corresponds to a two-stage stochastic optimization model. In the first stage, the manufacturer decides on the production size, which specifies the parameter of the multinomial distribution for the number of resulting end-products within each quality class. In the second stage, given the quality level of each end-product is observed, the manufacturer decides on how many products from each specific quality class are to be used towards satisfying the customer's order with quality restrictions.

Typically, decomposition and Monte Carlo simulation-based methods are used for two-stage stochastic optimization models in the literature. Nevertheless, such methods can be inefficient for the problem under investigation due to endogenous uncertainty. Therefore, we propose an augmented probability simulation (APS) based optimization method to solve the two-stage stochastic optimization model. APS based methods are efficient for searching in the joint decision and random variable space, which enable handling models with endogenous uncertainty.

To the best of our knowledge, a production planning problem under uncertain heterogenous yield quality and with quality restrictions on the customer order has not been analyzed in the literature. Our contributions include realistic modeling for this practical problem in make-to-order environments and developing a methodology to solve the resulting two-stage stochastic optimization problem. The rest of the paper is organized as follows. Next section describes the problem formulation in detail. Section 3 introduces the proposed solution approach and presents its formulation to solve for the described optimization model. The paper concludes with an overview, limitations, and directions for future research.

2. Problem Formulation

Consider a manufacturer, who operates under a make-to-order production strategy. That is, the manufacturer first receives an order from a customer, and then manufactures the customer's order. We consider that the products manufactured might have varying qualities even if they are manufactured through the same processes. That is, we consider a single-product multiple quality classes. In particular, after each product is manufactured, it is tested and inspected for its quality level. Suppose that a finished product can be classified into one of the n quality classes and let these quality classes be indexed by i such that $i \in I = \{1,2,\ldots,n\}$. Furthermore, let q_i denote the quality level of a product in quality class i and, without loss of generality, we assume that $q_1 > q_2 > \cdots > q_n$, i.e., the first class has the highest quality and the last class has the lowest quality. Note that, even if the finished products can have different quality levels, they incur the same unit manufacturing cost as they go through the same processes and use the same materials. Therefore, we assume that unit manufacturing cost is homogeneous and let c denote the unit manufacturing cost.

As noted above, due to uncertainty in production, the quality class of a product is not known until it is tested and inspected after its production. Let p_i denote the probability of a product being in quality class i and $\boldsymbol{p} = [p_1, p_2, \ldots, p_n]$ be the vector of these probabilities. It then follows that, given X products are to be manufactured, the number of resulting products in each quality class will be a random variable. Particularly, let $y_i(X)$ denote the number of products being classified as type i when X products are manufactured and let $\boldsymbol{y}(X) = [y_1(X), y_2(X), \ldots, y_n(X)]$ be the vector of $y_i(X)$ values such that $\sum_{i=1}^{n} y_i(X) = X$. Notice that $\boldsymbol{y}(X)$ has a multinomial distribution with probability mass function $f(\boldsymbol{y}(X))$, where

$$f(\boldsymbol{y}(X)) = X! \prod_{i=1}^{n} \left(\frac{p_i^{y_i(X)}}{y_i(X)!} \right). \tag{1}$$

In this study, we focus on the manufacturer's production planning for a given customer. Suppose that a customer arrives with an order of D units. Knowing that the manufacturer's processes might have uncertain quality yield, the customer imposes a limit on the average quality of the received order as well as the products received from individual quality classes. Specifically, let q^L denote the minimum average quality level required for the customer's order. In addition, the customer might restrict delivery of products that are below a certain quality level. Let $I' \subseteq I$ denote the set of quality classes that the customer accepts.

Even though the finished products have the same manufacturing cost, the manufacturer charges different prices depending on the quality class of the product. Let r_i denote the manufacturer's unit selling price for quality i products. We assume that $r_1 > r_2 > \cdots > r_n$ because a higher quality price has a higher value. In the case the manufacturer is unable to satisfy the customer's order, we consider that the manufacturer will outsource the product from another manufacturer acceptable to the customer. To this end, let q_0 and R_0 denote the quality of the outsourced product and the manufacturer's profit from delivering this product to the customer. Note that one can define $R_0 = 0$ in the case the manufacturer does not incur penalty costs or $R_0 < 0$ in the case the manufacturer is subject to unit penalty cost for being short. Furthermore, it is reasonable to assume that $q_0 > q^L$ because the outsourced product is acceptable for the customer. On the other hand, if the manufacturer is left with finished products that are not used towards the customer's order, we assume that those products can be sold to other customers later but will result in a lower unit revenue, denoted by h_i per unit for a product with quality i. We assume that $h_i < r_i$ considering that products that are not delivered to customer will be subject to inventory holding cost.

The manufacturer's problem is to determine the production batch size, denoted by X, in response to the customer's order for D units. Note that, once X units are produced and the numbers of products within each quality class are revealed, the manufacturer also needs to decide on the allocation of the products towards the customer's order. Let x_i for $i \in I$ denote the number of products from quality class i allocated for the customer's order and x_0 denote the number of products outsourced to be allocated towards the customer's order. Furthermore, let $\boldsymbol{x} = [x_0, x_1, x_2, \ldots, x_n]$ be the $n+1$ vector of x_i values. Figure 1 depicts the sequence of actions.

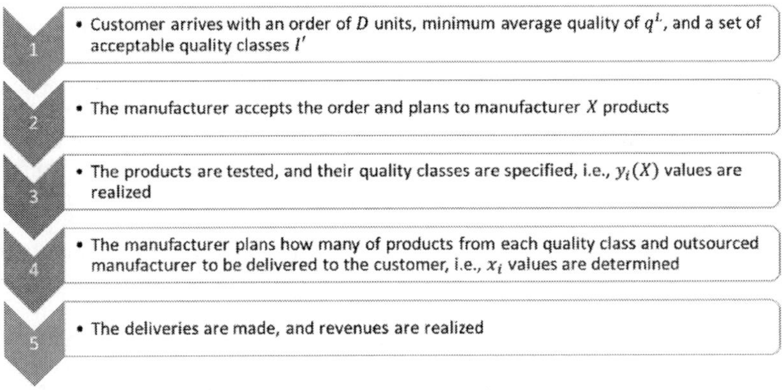

Figure 1: The sequence of events.

The manufacturer's profit from the manufactured batch for the customer will depend on X as well as the allocations made after the quality of the products are realized. Particularly, given X and $\mathbf{y}(X)$, one can note that $x_i \leq y_i(X)\ \forall i \in I$. Also, recall that the customer's set of acceptable quality classes is I', therefore, $x_i = 0\ \forall i \in I \backslash I'$. The manufacturer's revenue from sales of her own products to the customer amounts to $\sum_{i \in I} r_i x_i$ and her revenue from products that are not delivered to the customer amounts to $\sum_{i \in I} h_i (y_i(X) - x_i)$. Finally, her outsourcing related revenue (or cost) is $R_0 x_0$. It then follows that, given X and $\mathbf{y}(X)$, the manufacturer's profit from allocation of the products, denoted by $\Pi(X)$, reads as

$$\Pi(X) = \sum_{i \in I} r_i x_i + \sum_{i \in I} h_i (y_i(X) - x_i) + R_0 x_0. \tag{2}$$

In Equation (2), the first term is the revenues received from the manufactured products delivered to the customer, the second term is the revenues that will be generated from selling the products that are not delivered to the customer, and the last term is the revenue received from the outsourced products delivered to the customer. Note that, when $R_0 < 0$, the last term represents the penalty for under supplying the customer's order.

The manufacturer will determine the optimal values of $x_i\ \forall i \in I \cup \{0\}$ in order to maximize $\Pi(X)$ once $\mathbf{y}(X)$ is realized. This represents the manufacturer's second stage problem. The manufacturer's first stage problem is to determine the optimal production size for the customer's order, i.e., the optimal X value. In doing so, we consider that the manufacturer will maximize the expected net profit, which amounts to $E[\Pi(X)] - cX$, where $E[\Pi(X)]$ denotes the expected profit from allocation of the manufactured products to the customer and cX represents the total manufacturing cost. We consider that the manufacturer has a production capacity of U units, i.e., $X \leq U$. It then follows that the manufacturer's two-stage stochastic optimization problem is:

$$\max_{X} \quad \mathrm{E}[\Pi(X)] - cX \tag{3}$$

$$s.t. \quad X \in \{0,1,2, \dots, U\} \tag{4}$$

$$\Pi(X) = \max_{x} \quad \sum_{i \in I} r_i x_i + \sum_{i \in I} h_i (y_i(X) - x_i) + R_0 x_0 \tag{5}$$

$$s.t. \quad \sum_{i \in I \cup \{0\}} x_i = D \tag{6}$$

$$\sum_{i \in I \cup \{0\}} q_i x_i \geq q^L D \tag{7}$$

$$x_i \leq y_i(X) \qquad \forall i \in I \tag{8}$$

$$x_i = 0 \qquad \forall i \in I \backslash I' \tag{9}$$

$$x_i \in \{0,1,2, \dots\} \qquad \forall i \in I \cup \{0\} \tag{10}$$

The objective function in (3) is the manufacturer's expected net profit. Constraint in (4) assures that the production size is a nonnegative integer and does not exceed the manufacturing capacity. (5) defines the second-stage objective, i.e., the profit from allocation decisions, which is to be maximized. Constraint (6) guarantees that the customer's order is delivered. Constraint (7) assures that the average quality of the deliveries made to the customer is greater than or equal to the minimum average quality acceptable to the customer. Constraints in (8) guarantee that the number of products delivered to the customer from a specific quality class does not exceed the number of products available from that quality class. On the other hand, constraints in (9) assure that no product is delivered to the customer from quality classes that are not accepted by the customer. Finally, constraints in (10) are nonnegativity and integer definition of the deliveries made to the customer.

A special case of the second stage optimization problem defined by (5)-(10) is a bounded integer knapsack problem, which is known to be an NP-hard problem. This, along with the uncertainty being endogenous, makes the problem a challenging one to solve. Particularly, one needs to efficiently search over the joint decision and variable spaces for finding the optimum solution. Widely used decomposition and Monte Carlo simulation methods may not be capable of efficiently searching over this joint space. In the next section, we discuss augmented probability simulation-based optimization approach for the manufacturer's two-stage batch sizing and order allocation problem.

3. Solution Approach

Our solution approach is based on augmented probability simulation. In what follows, we first present an overview and the related literature to the proposed method. Then, we present the solution approach for our formulation in detail.

3.1. Augmented Probability Simulation based Optimization

Simulation based methods are widely used to find approximate solutions for optimization problems with many scenarios and/or analytically unavailable objective functions. Among these, variants of Monte Carlo sampling are extensively utilized given their ease of use and well-established convergence guarantees; see [20] for an overview. Our proposed model has an expectation function based objective function with many scenarios. Therefore, even if Monte Carlo simulation is used for estimation, it still needs to be solved by a deterministic optimization method. There are further challenges of using traditional Monte Carlo based methods. In stochastic optimization problems, most of the models assume exogenous uncertainty, where the random variables are independent from the earlier stage decisions. In our formulation, the multinomial distribution of the quality has the first stage decision of the total production quantity as a parameter. The solution of such models results in additional computational complexity [21] because second-stage optimization problem must be solved over the potential scenario trees for all first-stage decision alternatives. Such need of conducting the optimal decision search within the joint decision and random variable space results in existing decomposition and Monte Carlo simulation-based methods to be inefficient.

We propose an augmented probability simulation (APS) based optimization method to address the above-mentioned computational challenges. APS overcomes the need for sequential estimation and optimization by constructing an artificial augmented probability model in the joint space of decision and random variables. In doing so, APS treats the first-stage decision variable as a random variable. The augmented probability model is proportional to the objective function of interest and the distributions of decision and random variables. Simulating from this artificial augmented probability distribution is sufficient to search for the optimum first-stage decision. The mode of the marginal distribution of the decision variable would be equivalent to the optimal decision.

APS was first introduced to literature by Bielza et al. [22] in the realm of decision analysis. It transforms the decision problem into a simulation problem, in which the mode of the draws from the augmented probability distribution provides the optimal decision. Such augmented search in the joint decision and random variable space deals with decision dependence of the random variable naturally making APS an efficient alternative for decision models with endogenous uncertainty.

Ekin et al. [23] was the first work to extend the use of APS to constrained optimization problems, particularly stochastic programs with recourse. Then, APS was utilized to solve a one stage stochastic call center staffing problem in [24]. Other applications include an integrated maintenance and production model [18] and a cyber-security problem [25]. The main challenge of APS is to simulate from the augmented distribution, since it does not have a known distributional form. Most of the literature has used Markov Chain Monte Carlo (MCMC) simulation, with the exception [26] that uses nested sampling.

Next, we describe the details of the proposed approach that is modified for the solution of our optimization formulation.

3.2. Proposed Solution Approach

In this subsection, we present the use of APS to solve for our optimization model. We construct the augmented probability model on the state space of the first stage decision variable and the random variables. Here, we assume that, given the pair of the first stage decision and the random variables, we have the means of solving the resulting second-stage problem, which is an integer linear programming model. Later, we discuss the details of the second-stage problem.

Using the notation of the optimal second stage decision as $\boldsymbol{x}^*(X, y(X))$, the first stage optimization model can be written as

$$\max_{X} \quad \mathrm{E}[\Pi(X, x^*)] - cX \tag{11}$$

$$s.t. \quad X \in \{0,1,2,\dots,U\} \tag{12}$$

$$\text{where} \quad \Pi(X, x^*) = \sum_{i\in I} r_i {x^*}_i + \sum_{i\in I} h_i\left(y_i(X) - {x^*}_i\right) + R_0 x_0^* . \tag{13}$$

The augmented distribution is written as:

$$p(X, y) \;\alpha\; (\Pi(X, x^*) - cX)p(X)p(y|X). \tag{14}$$

It is shown that the mode of the marginal draws from the distribution of the decision variable, $\boldsymbol{p(X)}$, is equal to the optimal decision [22, 27]. We should note that the decision variable is treated as a random variable for computational purposes, and its distribution $\boldsymbol{p(X)}$ is generally assumed to be a Uniform distribution in the range of the feasible decision space. The random variable distribution is already presented to be a multinomial distribution in Equation (2) with parameters dependent on the first stage decision, hence decision dependent (endogenous) randomness exists.

The remaining challenge is how to sample from the distribution written in Equation (14). One option is to use a Gibbs sampling-based Markov chain Monte Carlo simulation [28] to draw from this distribution. The sequential draws from the following full conditional distributions would provide draws from the joint distribution:

$$p(X|y) \;\alpha\; (\Pi(X, x^*) - cX)p(X), \tag{15}$$

$$p(y|X) \;\alpha\; (\Pi(X, x^*) - cX)p(y|X). \tag{16}$$

4. Conclusion

This paper models a manufacturer's production planning problem in a make-to-order environment under uncertain quality with multiple quality levels. The decision problem includes the first stage decision of production quantity (batch size) given the uncertainty in production yield. Production yield is modelled with an endogenous multinomial distribution. In the second stage, given the production quantity and the random variable realizations, the decision maker should determine the allocations of the products towards customer's order in order to maximize profit while satisfying the customer's quality restrictions for the delivery. We formulate this two-stage stochastic optimization model and present an augmented probability simulation-based optimization solution approach.

This model, when solved efficiently, will help the manufacturer efficiently manage her production and order allocation decisions. Specifically, the model is capable of balancing the trade-offs between batch sizing considering the yield uncertainty and the allocation of the resulting production to the customer's order considering the customer's quality specific restrictions. The model explicitly captures the endogenous uncertainty, varying profit implications of different quality classes, and the cost/profit impact of not being able to satisfy the customer's restrictions.

The next phase is to conduct numerical analyses using various problem sizes to document the effectiveness of the solution methods proposed. This is currently being carried out by the authors. The analyses of this numerical investigation will reveal insights towards the optimum solution as well as provide managerial insights. Furthermore, considering that the second stage is an integer linear programming model, efficient heuristic methods to solve the second-stage model should be developed. The authors are planning to develop such heuristic methods.

Future work includes the following. First, using the insights generated from the numerical investigation, one can explore generating optimum solutions via reducing the two-stage problem to a one-stage approximation newsvendor-type model. Also, we plan to extend the manufacturer's production planning for multiple customers, who simultaneously give orders with their individual quality restrictions. Extension to multiple customer scenario will further complicate the second-stage problem. Nevertheless, the solution methodology proposed in this study can be readily extended to solve for that case. Finally, one can study the single-customer case with random customer demand.

5. References

1. Mundi, I., Alemany, M. M. E., Poler, R., & Fuertes-Miquel, V. S.: Review of mathematical models for production planning under uncertainty due to lack of homogeneity: proposal of a conceptual model. *International Journal of Production Research*, 1-45. (2019)
2. Yang, Y., & Barton, P. I. Integrated crude selection and refinery optimization under uncertainty. *AICHE Journal*, *62*(4), 1038-1053. (2016).
3. Teunter, R. H., & Flapper, S. D. P. Optimal core acquisition and remanufacturing policies under uncertain core quality fractions. *European Journal of Operational Research*, *210*(2), 241-248. (2011),
4. Li, X., Li, Y., & Cai, X. Double marginalization and coordination in the supply chain with uncertain supply. *European Journal of Operational Research*, *226*(2), 228-236. (2013).
5. Chen, K., & Xiao, T. Outsourcing strategy and production disruption of supply chain with demand and capacity allocation uncertainties. *International Journal of Production Economics*, *170*, 243-257. (2015).
6. Anupindi, R., & Akella, R. Diversification under supply uncertainty. *Management Science*, *39*(8), 944-963. (1993).
7. Ciarallo, F. W., Akella, R., & Morton, T. E. A periodic review, production planning model with uncertain capacity and uncertain demand - optimality of extended myopic policies. *Management Science*, *40*(3), 320-332. (1994).
8. Galbreth, M. R., & Blackburn, J. D. Optimal acquisition and sorting policies for remanufacturing. *Production and Operations Management*, *15*(3), 384-392. (2006).
9. Galbreth, M. R., & Blackburn, J. D. Optimal acquisition quantities in remanufacturing with condition uncertainty. *Production and Operations Management*, *19*(1), 61-69. (2010).
10. Galbreth, M. R., & Blackburn, J. D. Offshore remanufacturing with variable used product condition. *Decision Sciences*, *41*(1), 5-20. (2010).
11. Yano, C. A., & Lee, H. L. Lot sizing with random yields: A review. *Operations Research*, *43*(2), 311-334. (1995).
12. Kalirajan, K. An econometric analysis of yield variability in paddy production. *Canadian Journal of Agricultural Economics/Revue canadienne d'agroeconomie*, *29*(3), 283-294. (1981)

13. Sloan, T. Simultaneous determination of production and maintenance schedules using in-line equipment condition and yield information. *Naval Research Logistics (NRL)*, *55*(2), 116-129. (2008)
14. Khouja, M., & Mehrez, A. Economic production lot size model with variable production rate and imperfect quality. *Journal of the Operational Research Society*, *45*(12), 1405-1417. (1994)
15. Iravani, S. M., & Duenyas, I. Integrated maintenance and production control of a deteriorating production system. *IIE Transactions*, *34*(5), 423-435. (2002).
16. Sana, S. S. An economic production lot size model in an imperfect production system. *European Journal of Operational Research*, *201*(1), 158-170. (2010).
17. Wang, H. A survey of maintenance policies of deteriorating systems. *European Journal of Operational Research*, *139*(3), 469-489. (2002).
18. Ekin, T. Integrated maintenance and production planning with endogenous uncertain yield. *Reliability Engineering & System Safety*, *179*, 52-61. (2018).
19. Aydin, R., Kwong, C. K., Geda, M. W., & Kremer, G. O. Determining the optimal quantity and quality levels of used product returns for remanufacturing under multi-period and uncertain quality of returns. *The International Journal of Advanced Manufacturing Technology*, *94*(9-12), 4401-4414. (2018).
20. Homem-de-Mello, T., & Bayraksan, G. Monte Carlo sampling-based methods for stochastic optimization. *Surveys in Operations Research and Management Science*, *19*(1), 56-85. (2014).
21. Dyer, M., & Stougie, L. Computational complexity of stochastic programming problems. *Mathematical Programming*, *106*(3), 423-432. (2006).
22. Bielza, C., Müller, P., & Insua, D. R. Decision analysis by augmented probability simulation. *Management Science*, *45*(7), 995-1007. (1999).
23. Ekin, T., Polson, N. G., & Soyer, R. Augmented Markov chain Monte Carlo simulation for two-stage stochastic programs with recourse. *Decision Analysis*, *11*(4), 250-264. (2014)
24. Aktekin, T., & Ekin, T. Stochastic call center staffing with uncertain arrival, service and abandonment rates: A Bayesian perspective. *Naval Research Logistics (NRL)*, *63*(6), 460-478. (2016).
25. Ekin, T., Naveiro, R., Torres-Barrán, A., & Ríos-Insua, D. Augmented Probability Simulation Methods for Non-cooperative Games. arXiv preprint arXiv:1910.04574. (2019).
26. Ekin, T., Polson, N. G., & Soyer, R. Augmented nested sampling for stochastic programs with recourse and endogenous uncertainty. *Naval Research Logistics (NRL)*, *64*(8), 613-627. (2017).
27. Müller, P., Sansó, B., & De Iorio, M. Optimal Bayesian design by inhomogeneous Markov chain simulation. *Journal of the American Statistical Association*, *99*(467), 788-798. (2004).
28. Gelfand, A. E., Smith, A. F., & Lee, T. M. Bayesian analysis of constrained parameter and truncated data problems using Gibbs sampling. *Journal of the American Statistical Association*, *87*(418), 523-532. (1992).

I L S 2020
INTERNATIONAL CONFERENCE ON INFORMATION SYSTEMS, LOGISTICS & SUPPLY CHAIN
Austin, Texas April 22-24, 2020

Closed loop supply chain optimization for Circular Manufacturing using Industry 4.0 technologies

Delpla Victor, Hof Lucas A., Kenné Jean-Pierre

Ecole de Technologie Supérieure, Montréal, Canada
{victor.delpla.1@ens.etsmtl.ca.com, lucas.hof@etsmtl.ca, jean-pierre.kenne@etsmtl.ca}

Abstract. Closed-Loop Supply Chains (CLSC) fit into the logic of the circular economy aiming to limit the unsustainable use of non-renewable resources. Circular manufacturing refers to the circular economy applied to manufacturing industry. Industry 4.0 introduces new tools such as the Internet of Things (IoT) to optimize CLSC's performance in this circular manufacturing context. This study proposes a CLSC model that meets the sales and collection center (S&C) demands and maximizes total profit by indicating processing to be applied to the End-of-Life (EOL) products collected. This processing is chosen according to the product or component condition which is estimated by data collected during the product's life cycle using sensors and RFID. To solve the proposed CLSC model, linear physical programming is used.

Keywords: "Close Loop Supply Chain", "Internet of Things", "Remanufacturing", "RFID", "Industry 4.0"

1. Introduction

Industry 4.0 is characterized by the intelligent automation and digitization of production, management and decision-making systems in manufacturing companies. Its objective is to improve the productivity and flexibility of the manufacturing sector. In view of increased economic competition in the world and the growing importance of environmental issues, recycling and remanufacturing are becoming essential activities for industry to develop. Circular manufacturing is a model where limited resources are used sustainably, and products are designed to reduce losses [1]. The main objective of supply chains is to provide products to customers in time and in the condition expected. It is therefore necessary to have complete visibility of the products during their manufacture, use and recovery. The processing of EOL products in a CLSC can be determine with integrated sensors [2]. Recycling, as the recovery of raw material, and disposal were the main processing for EOL products, but with technological advances such as additive manufacturing or high-precision machining, remanufacturing is now a possible processing option. Estimating the remanufacturability of a product at the end of its life is crucial to determine its processing after recovery. Its ecological impact and the profit generated by remanufacturing can be examined. [3]. For instance, it is thus more profitable, under certain conditions, to repair a turbine blade by additive manufacturing than to manufacture a new one [4]. If a product or component is in too unsatisfactory a condition to be repaired, recycling is an economically and ecologically viable solution. For example, the way a product is disassembled before being recycled changes the amount of raw materials recovered [5]. In the context of the circular economy, it is important to develop CLSC that consider reuse, remanufacturing and recycling. IoT can be implemented on products with sensors and RFID tags to determine the remaining service life of the products. Optimizing the planning of remanufacturing, disassembly, recycling and disposal of these products is then perfected [6]. Linear physical programming models take up this planning optimization by maximizing total profit and quality. The conception of a product is essential to satisfy the demands for products, components and raw materials [7]. CLSC models consider the remanufacturing and elimination of a single modular product and its components. The processing followed by the recovered products and components depends on their conditions which are evaluated by a number. This number is determined by sensors collecting data, like various usage parameters, and stored on an RFID tag on the product. This installation is called Device of Internet of Things (DIOT). The synthetic number is also called DIOT. An example of current CLSC models using DIOT is shown in Figure 1 [8]. The objective of this study is to: 1) improve the current DIOT based CLSC model (Figure 1) to better approach industrial reality, in particular, raw materials and stocks will be considered in the supply chain, and 2) to determine the processing choice of a product and its components to optimize the total profit of the manufacturer by using the IoT and the information collected on the components during their manufacture and use. This information enables an effective evaluation of the product and components condition, including their remanufacturability. We first set the objectives of the model and the assumptions chosen. We then identify the parameters and variables of the model, its objective function and its constraints. Finally, we test the model with a digital example with a modular smartphone range.

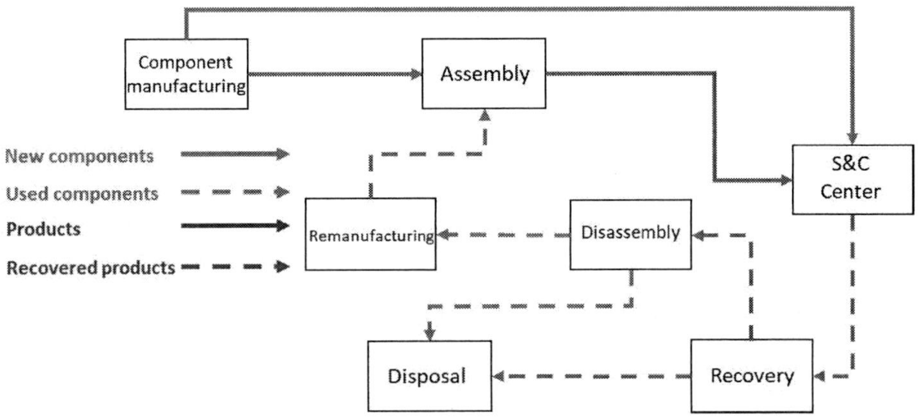

Figure 1: CLSC model already existing in the literature.

2. Problem statement

This study focuses on a product and component manufacturer who wants to satisfy the demands of a sales and collection center (S&C center). The manufacturer produces a range of N different products composed of J separate components. An amount of K raw materials is used for all components. The components of a product have a weight importance of 0 to 1 and their sum is equal to 1. It recovers during each of the T periods up to I units of the products. The manufacturer is supplied with raw material from an external supplier and can also sell unprocessed raw material. The CLSC on which the problem is based is presented in Figure 2. This model, with stocks and raw materials, more accurately reflects the industrial reality. This manufacturer includes several stocks and workshops framed in Figure 2. This model also considers multiple products and not a single product as in the existing models. EOL products collected by the S&C center are purchased at a price corresponding to their value level. In this study, there are three recovery options for products: disassembly, recycling and disposal. In the disassembly option, components can undergo four processing: reuse, remanufacturing, recycling or disposal. Products, components and raw materials are sold or stored to meet the S&C demands.

The model aims to answer the following questions:

1) What recovery options should be selected for returned products (disassembled, recycled or eliminated) and components (reused, remanufactured, recycled or disposed of) for each period?
2) What products, components or raw materials should be sold to meet the demands for each period?
3) How many raw materials should be obtained from external suppliers for each period?

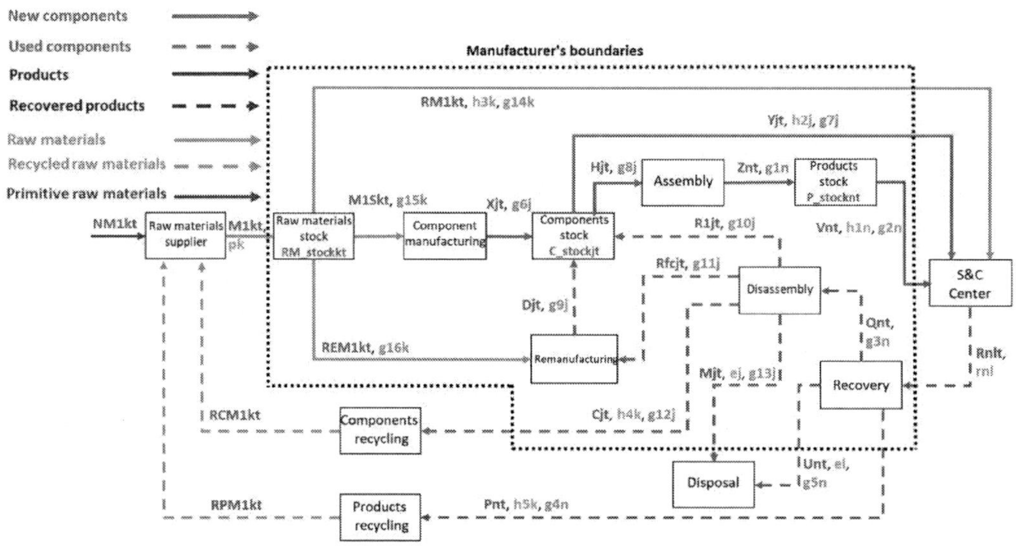

Figure 2: CLSC model developed in the study.

The assumptions of the problem are:

- A component can be used for different products.
- There is no difference between a product composed of new or used components.
- Primitive raw materials and recycled raw materials are considered to be identical.
- Production capacity is sufficient.
- All information on sales, transport and storage costs and prices is known.
- The demand of the S&C center is given and satisfied for each period.

3. Mathematical model

The model calculates the flows of several totally modular products, components and raw materials to maximize total profit and meet demands. The running number indices, parameters and decision variables are given in Table 1, 2 and 3.

Table 1: Running numbers.

t	Time periods	$(t = 1, \ldots, T)$
n	Fully modular products	$(n = 1, \ldots; N)$
i	Returned products	$(i = 1, \ldots, I)$
j	Components usable for each product	$(j = 1, \ldots, J)$
k	Raw materials	$(k = 1, \ldots, K)$

Table 2: Parameters

Parameters	Description	Parameters	Description
el_n	Disposal cost of a product n	$h2_j$	Sales price of a new component j
$rc_{n,j}$	Number of components j in a product n	$dmc_{j,t}$	Components j demand of the S&C center in period t
$weight_j$	Component j importance weight	$g6_j$ ... $g13_j$	Transportation cost of new component j
$r_{n,l}$	Purchasing cost of a l-level product n from the S&C center	sc_j	Composant j storage cost
$R_{n,l,t}$	Number of used product n in the l-level are purchased from the S&C center in period t	$C\_stockin_j$	Initial component j stock
$h1_n$	Sales price of a product n	$C\_stockmax_j$	Maximal component j stock
$dm_{n,t}$	Product n demand of the S&C center in period t	$diot_{n,i,j,t}$	DIOT of component j recovered in period t
$g1_n$ ... $g5_n$	Transportation cost of product n	n_{j1} , n_{j2} , n_{j3}	Threshold value of *diot n.i.j.t*
sc_n	Product n storage cost	rp_k	Recovered part of raw material k on product n
$P\_stockin_n$	Initial product n stock	$rc_{j,k}$	Recovered part of raw material k on component j
$P\_stockmax_n$	Maximal product n stock	p_k	Purchasing cost of raw material k from the raw matrials supplier
$diot_{n,i,t}$	DIOT of the i product n recovered in period t	$h3_k$	Sales price of raw material k for the S&C center
n_{i1}, n_{i2}	Threshold value of *diot n.i.t*	$h4_k$	Sales price of raw material k recylced from components
a_j	Assembly cost of component j	$h5_k$	Sales price of raw material k recylced from products
d_j	Disassembly cost of component j	$dm_{k,t}$	Raw material k demand of the S&C center in period t
e_j	Elimination cost of component j	$g14_k$ ... $g16_k$	Transportation cost of raw material k between the stock and the S&C center
f_j	Repair cost of component j	sc_k	Raw material k storage cost
m_j	Manufacturing cost of component j	$RM\_stockin_k$	Initial raw material k stock
$n_{j,k}$	Number of raw materials k in a component j	$RM\_stockmax_k$	Maximal raw material k stock
$rn_{j,k}$	Number of raw materials k to remanufacture a component j		

Table 3: Decisions variables.

Decisions variables	Description	Decisions variables	Description
$Z_{n,t}$	Number of products n sent to the stock in period t	$Rfc_{j,t}$	Number of components j remanufactured in period t
$V_{n,t}$	Number of products n sold to the S&C center in period t	$R1_{j,t}$	Number of components j reused in period t
$Q_{n,t}$	Number of products n dissassembled in period t	$M_{j,t}$	Number of components j eliminated in period t
$U_{n,t}$	Number of products n eliminated in period t	$C\_stock_{j,t}$	Number of components n in stock in period t
$P_{n,t}$	Number of products n recycled in period t	$NM1_{k,t}$	Number of primitive raw material k entering in the supply chain in the period t
$P\_stock_{n,t}$	Number of products n in stock in period t	$M1_{k,t}$	Number of raw material k purchased in the period t
$X_{j,t}$	Number of components j manufactured in period t	$RCM1_{k,t}$	Number of raw material k recycled from components in period t
$Y_{j,t}$	Number of components j sold to S&C center in period t	$RPM1_{k,t}$	Number of raw material k recycled from products in period t
$H_{j,t}$	Number of new components j sent to assembly in period t	$RM1_{k,t}$	Number of raw material k sold to S&C center in period t
$D_{j,t}$	Number of components j sent to the stock in period t	$REM1_{k,t}$	Number of raw material k sent to remanufacturing in period t
$C_{j,t}$	Number of components j recycled in period t	$RM\_stock_{k,t}$	Number of raw materials n in stock in period t

The DIOT concept is used to determine the component value level. Threshold values are defined for components to decide on the value level and the processing used. In this study, the component DIOT is defined in Figure 3.

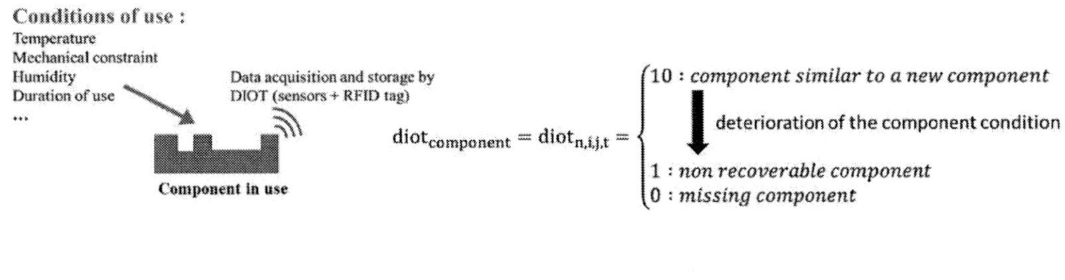

Figure 3: Component DIOT definition

Condition of a recovered product is defined by a product DIOT which is calculated according to the $diot_{component}$ of each of its components and the importance of each component. We define $diot_{product}$ as follows:

$$diot_{product} = diot_{n,i,t} = \sum_j weight_j \cdot diot_{n,i,j,t}. \quad (1)$$

Binary variables are defined to indicate the chosen processing for products.

$$was_{n,i,t} = \begin{cases} 1 \text{ if } 0 < diot_{n,i,t} < n_{i1} \ (eliminated) \\ 0 \text{ otherwise} \end{cases}. \quad (2)$$

$$rec_{n,i,t} = \begin{cases} 1 \text{ if } n_{i1} \leq diot_{n,i,t} < n_{i2} \ (recycled) \\ 0 \text{ otherwise} \end{cases}. \quad (3)$$

$$dis_{n,i,t} = \begin{cases} 1 \text{ if } n_{i2} \leq diot_{n,i,t} \ (disassembly) \\ 0 \text{ otherwise} \end{cases}. \quad (4)$$

Similarly, binary variables are defined to indicate the chosen processing for components.

$$was_{n,i,j,t} = \begin{cases} 1 \text{ if } 1 \leq diot_{n,i,j,t} < n_{j1} (eliminated) \\ 0 \text{ otherwise} \end{cases}. \quad (5)$$

$$rec_{n,i,j,t} = \begin{cases} 1 \text{ if } n_{j1} \leq diot_{n,i,j,t} < n_{j2} \ (recycled) \\ 0 \text{ otherwise} \end{cases}. \quad (6)$$

$$rem_{n,i,j,t} = \begin{cases} 1 \text{ if } n_{j2} \leq diot_{n,i,j,t} < n_{j3} \ (remanufactured) \\ 0 \text{ otherwise} \end{cases}. \quad (7)$$

$$reu_{n,i,j,t} = \begin{cases} 1 \text{ if } n_{j3} \leq diot_{n,i,j,t} \ (reused) \\ 0 \text{ otherwise} \end{cases}. \quad (8)$$

3.1. Objective function

The economic aspect is the only aspect that is considered. The objective function is to maximize the total profit of the manufacturer. Total profit (TP) is calculated by the difference between total revenue (TR) and total cost (TC):

$$TP = TR - TC. \quad (9)$$

Total revenue (TR) of the manufacturer is earned from the sales of products, components and raw materials and equal:

$$TR = \sum_t \Big[\sum_n h1_n \cdot V_{n,t} + \sum_j h2_j \cdot Y_{j,t} + \sum_k h3_k \cdot RM1_{k,t} + \sum_j \sum_k (C_{j,t} \cdot h4_k \cdot n_{j,k} \cdot rc_{j,k} + P_t \cdot rc_{n,j} \cdot h5_k \cdot n_{j,k} \cdot rp_k)\Big]. \quad (10)$$

The manufacturer purchases raw materials and products recovered by the S&C center. The total purchase cost (TPC) is calculated as follows:

$$TPC = \sum_t \Big[\sum_k p_k \cdot M1_{k,t} + \sum_n \sum_l r_{n,l} \cdot R_{n,l,t}\Big]. \quad (11)$$

Different operations on products and components have costs, this is the total manufacturing cost (TMC). The manufacturer produces new components, assembles products, disassembles end-of-life products and remanufactures used components. TMC is equal to:

$$TMC = \sum_t \sum_j \Big[m_j \cdot X_{j,t} + d_j \cdot \big(R1_{j,t} + Rfc_{j,t} + C_{j,t} + M_{j,t}\big) + f_j \cdot Rfc_{j,t} + a_j \cdot H_{j,t}\Big]. \quad (12)$$

The manufacturer also eliminates products and components. The total disposal cost (TDC) is:

$$\mathrm{TDC} = \textstyle\sum_t \left[\sum_n el_n \,.\, U_{n,t} + \sum_j e_j \,.\, M_{j,t}\right]. \quad \textbf{(13)}$$

The total cost of transport (TTC) and the total cost of storage (TSC) of products, components and raw materials can be calculated with the different parameters and variables.

The total cost (TC) of the manufacturer can then be calculated:

$$\mathrm{TC} = \mathrm{TPC} + \mathrm{TMC} + \mathrm{TDC} + \mathrm{TTC} + \mathrm{TSC}. \quad \textbf{(14)}$$

3.2. Constraints

The amount in stocks (products, new components, used components, raw materials) in period t are equal to the amount in stocks in the previous period, plus entering flows, minus outgoing flows:

$$\mathrm{stock}_t = \mathrm{stock}_{t-1} + \text{entering flows} - \text{outgoing flows}, \forall t. \quad \textbf{(15)}$$

For any period t, the amount of components j disassembled and then disposed of, recycled, repaired or reused must be equal to the number of components present in the products sent for disassembly:

$$Rfc_{j,t} + M_{j,t} + C_{j,t} + R1_{j,t} = \textstyle\sum_n Q_{n,t} \,.\, rc_{n,j}, \forall(t,n). \quad \textbf{(16)}$$

For any period t, the amount of components j present in the assembled products must be equal to the amount that arrives at the assembly:

$$H_{j,t} = \textstyle\sum_n Z_{n,t} \,.\, rc_{n,j}, \forall(t,n). \quad \textbf{(17)}$$

For any period t, the amount of raw material k recovered from components and products recycling is respectively calculated as follows:

$$RCM1_{k,t} = \textstyle\sum_j C_{j,t} \,.\, rc_{j,k} \,.\, n_{j,k}, \forall(t,k). \quad \textbf{(18)}$$

$$RPM1_{k,t} = rp_k \,.\, \textstyle\sum_n P_{n,t} \,.\, \sum_j rc_{n,j} \,.\, n_{j,k}, \forall(t,k). \quad \textbf{(19)}$$

For any period t, the amount of raw material k required to manufacture the components that will be sent to the stock of new components is calculated as follows:

$$M1S_{k,t} = \textstyle\sum_j X_{j,t} \,.\, n_{j,k}, \forall(t,k). \quad \textbf{(20)}$$

For any period t, the amount of raw material k required for the repair the recovered components is calculated as follows:

$$REM1_{k,t} = \textstyle\sum_j Rfc_{j,t} \,.\, rn_{j,k}, \forall(t,k). \quad \textbf{(21)}$$

4. Numerical example

We consider the recovery of two smartphone models (N=2) over two periods (T=2). During each period, 8 smartphones are retrieved from each model (I=8). Components and raw materials compositions are given in Figure 4 (J=6, K=7). All variables and parameters in Table 2 are known in the example. This mathematical model was solved using LINGO 16.0.

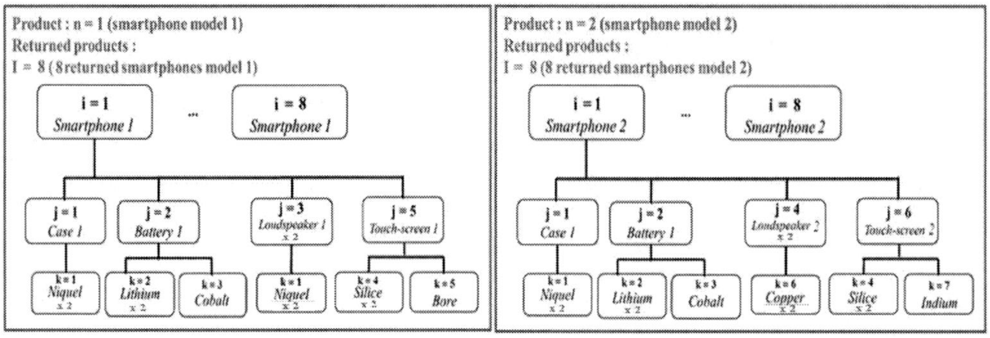

Figure 4: Smartphones studied in the example.

In this example, the maximum total profit over the 2 periods is 191.998: the total revenue is 4345.62 and the total cost is 4153.622. The summary of costs and revenue is given in Table 4.

Table 4: The optimal objective function value.

Objective Function	Value
TR	**4345.62**
TPC	2538.55
TMC	1175.4
TDC	24.2
TTC	414.12
TSC	1.352
TC	**4153.622**
TP	**191.998**

In the first period, the flows of products, components and raw materials to maximize total profit are given in Figure 5. We can note the conservation of all the material.

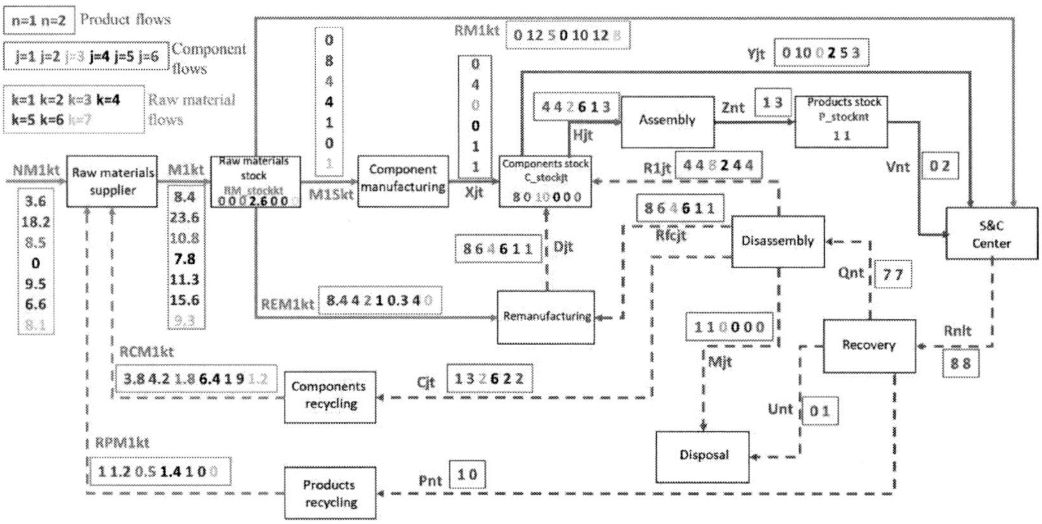

Figure 5: The optimal distribution networks belonging to the first period.

The details of the processing applied to the products recovered during the first period depend on the DIOT values and the threshold values given in Figure 6.

	Smartphone n = 1					Smartphone n = 2				
	$diot_{n,i,j,t}$					$diot_{n,i,j,t}$				
	j=1	j=2	j=3	j=4	$diot_{n,i,t}$	j=1	j=2	j=5	j=6	$diot_{n,i,t}$
i=1	4	7	1	1	3.7	8	6	6	8	7.2
i=2	7	3	8	9	6.5	5	10	7	2	5.8
i=3	7	5	6	6	6	7	3	8	8	6.2
i=4	6	4	6	2	4.2	1	6	4	7	4.6
i=5	9	8	8	9	8.6	3	10	3	8	6.6
i=6	7	1	9	10	6.3	4	3	3	10	5.4
i=7	5	4	3	8	5.4	9	9	2	2	6.2
i=8	9	5	10	3	6.1	1	2	3	1	1.5
weightj	*0.3*	*0.3*	*0.1*	*0.3*	*weightj*	*0.3*	*0.3*	*0.1*	*0.3*	

Component

$n_{j1} = 2$
$n_{j2} = 4$
$n_{j3} = 8$

- Reused
- Remanufactured
- Recycled
- Eliminated

Product

$n_{i1} = 2$
$n_{i2} = 4$

- Disassembled
- Recycled
- Eliminated

Figure 6: Processing details in the first period

In this example, all recovered smartphones are disassembled as shown in Figure 6; except the smartphone (n=1, i=1) which is recycled before disassembly and the smartphone (n=2, i=8) which is eliminated. The model meets the objectives as formulated in section 2 (problem statement). Recovery processing of products and components is selected according to their recovery state for each period in order to maximize profit. The flows of products, components and raw materials in the CLSC are precisely known. These flows meet the S&C center's demands for each period. Finally, the model estimates the impact on natural resources by indicating the quantity of raw materials that enter the supply chain.

5. Conclusion

Manufacturers aim to improve their supply chain to increase their profits while being more respectful of the environment. It becomes necessary to design CLSCs, but these networks are difficult to set up because there are many uncertainties in the recovery of products and the optimal process to follow. IoT reduces this uncertainty by providing information collected during the product life cycle. In this study, connected products provide better traceability to choose the recovery process and optimize flows in the CLSC. Thus, with the example developed in section 4, the flows to optimize profit were determined and the processing of each recovered smartphone and their components were identified. The proposed model is more in accordance with the industrial reality with stocks, raw materials and several different products than the current models. Future research to complement this study will focus on determining how to measure DIOTs for examples of products and we will examine the sensitivity of the model to variation of some parameters.

6. References

1. Van den Berg, M.R., Bakker, C.A.: A product design framework for a circular economy. In: PLATE conference, pp365—379. Nottingham Trent University, Nottingham (2015)
2. Ondemir, O., et al.: Optimal End-of-Life Management in Closed-Loop Supply Chains Using RFID and Sensors. IEEE Transactions on Industrial Informatics 8, 719--728 (2012)
3. Yang, S. S., et al.: EOL strategy planning for components of returned products. The International Journal of Advanced Manufacturing Technology 77, 991--1003 (2014)
4. Wilson, J. M., et al.: Remanufacturing of turbine blades by laser direct deposition with its energy and environmental impact analysis. Journal of Cleaner Production 80, 170--178 (2014)
5. Reuter, M.A., et al.: Limits of the Circular Economy: Fairphone Modular Design Pushing the Limits. World of Mettalurgy – ERZMETALL 71, 68--79 (2018)
6. Ondemir, O., Gupta, S. M.: Quality management in product recovery using the Internet of Things: An optimization approach. Computers in Industry 65, 491--504 (2014)
7. Joshi, A. D., Gupta, S. M.: Evaluation of design alternatives of End-Of-Life products using internet of things. International Journal of Production Economics 208, 281--293 (2019)
8. Paksoy, T., Karaoğlan, I., Gökçen, H., Pardalos, P.M., Torğul, B.: An experimental Research on Closed Loop Supply Chain Management with Internet of Things. Journal of Economics Bibliography 3, 1--20 (2016)

I L S 2020
INTERNATIONAL CONFERENCE ON INFORMATION SYSTEMS, LOGISTICS & SUPPLY CHAIN
Austin, Texas April 22-24, 2020

Measurement of the Business/IT Alignment of Information Systems

Hamza Darii [1], Jannik Laval [1], Valérie Botta-Genoulaz [2], Virginie Goepp [3]

[1] Univ Lyon, University Lumière Lyon 2, DISP lab EA 4570, 69500 Bron, France
[2] Univ Lyon, INSA Lyon, DISP lab EA 4570, 69621 Villeurbanne cedex, France
[3] INSA Strasbourg, ICube lab UMR (7357), Strasbourg, France
{jannik.laval@univ-lyon2.fr, valerie.botta@insa-lyon.fr, virginie.goepp@insa-strasbourg.fr}

Abstract. Nowadays, the performance of organizations is directly related to the efficiency of Information system (IS). It is crucial to quantify this efficiency and evaluate the alignment of the IS with the business. In this context, this work aims to propose a set of metrics to measure the alignment of IS to business requirements based on the constructs of an exhaustive framework. This multi-level and multi-aspect framework considers Information Technology (IT) and Business domains, as well as strategic and operational levels of the enterprise. A total of twenty-five metrics is proposed, within sixteen new ones, to evaluate functional integration at both levels, as well as strategic fit in each domain.

Keywords: Information systems, Alignment, Alignment levels, Metrics.

1. Introduction

In the context of agile and flexible factories of the future, Information System (IS) should be able to answer the new requests of business. In literature, it is generally accepted that business performances are highly related to IS performances [1, 2, 3, 4]. This stake is generally tackled in the alignment domain. In this context, there is a need for real-time alignment processes between IT and business domains [2]. This requires an evaluation of the initial and the final situations of alignment either using indirect or direct measures (metrics) that are based on separate assessment of business and IT constructs [5]. For that, the evaluation of alignment represents a top concern issue [1]. In literature, most of the authors who consider alignment evaluation, usually use qualitative methods owing to the sensitivity of alignment to the quantitative measurements [6]. And those who propose metrics, consider only the assessment of the operational level, and ignore the strategic level which is the most important according to Charoensuk et al. [7]. Therefore, our work aims to propose an exhaustive evaluation of alignment.

The sensitivity aspect of alignment to quantitative measurements comes mainly from the fact that alignment was always very hard to define. To overcome this problem, we propose to exploit the Strategic Alignment Model (SAM) of Henderson and Venkatraman [8]. According to Gerow et al. [6], Tarafdar and Qrunfleh [7], Benbeya and McKelvey [9], Goepp and Avila [10], Avila and Goepp [11], it is the most appropriate and widespread framework that aims to describe the alignment according to the external and internal levels of IT and Business domains. According to the SAM, there are four types of alignment: (1) Alignment in the strategic level (or functional integration in external level), (2) Alignment in the internal level (or functional integration in internal level), (3) Strategic fit in the IT domain, (4) Strategic fit in the business domain.

Our research aims to define a set of metrics enabling to evaluate the degree of alignment for each alignment types as defined in the SAM. To solve this problem, we present in Section 2, a literature review of the existing alignment evaluation methods. In Section 3, we exploit Archimate 3.0 as a mean to work out a meta-model detailing the modelling constructs involved in the assessment of the four types of alignment defined in the SAM. Section 4 presents a classification of the existing metrics in the light of the meta-model set up in section 3 and proposes a set of new metrics enabling to evaluate the remaining types of alignment. In the last section, we present our conclusion and possible perspectives.

2. Literature review

2.1. Alignment definition

The notion of alignment has no formal definition and there are lots of definitions in literature. Among them, we choose the one of Benbeya and Mckelvey [9]: "The degree of congruence of an organization's IT strategy and IT infrastructure with the organization's strategic business objectives and infrastructure" because it highlights the main features of alignment. In this view, the alignment is a process and not an end-state and has two levels also named strategic and operational in [2]. Alignment in the operational level is the one required for ensuring that information system is successfully implemented, maintained and used, and in turn delivers the targeted business benefits, according to Tarafdar and Qrunfleh [2]. Alignment in the strategic level is the degree to which the IT mission, objectives, and plans support and are supported by the business mission, objectives and plans, according to Benbeya and Mckelvey [9].
Another way to consider these levels is to analyse them in the light of the SAM (Strategic Alignment Model) detailed in [8]. It consists of four areas of strategic choices defined by (see Fig. 1):

- *Domains*: Business and Information Technologies (IT);
- *Levels*: (that split domains): external (strategy) and internal (operation),
- *Components* (that characterize and compose each level): scope, competencies and governance in the external level; infrastructure, skills and processes in the internal level.

These areas are linked together through four types of alignment: functional integration in the strategic and operational levels; strategic fit in the business and IT domains (see Fig. 1).

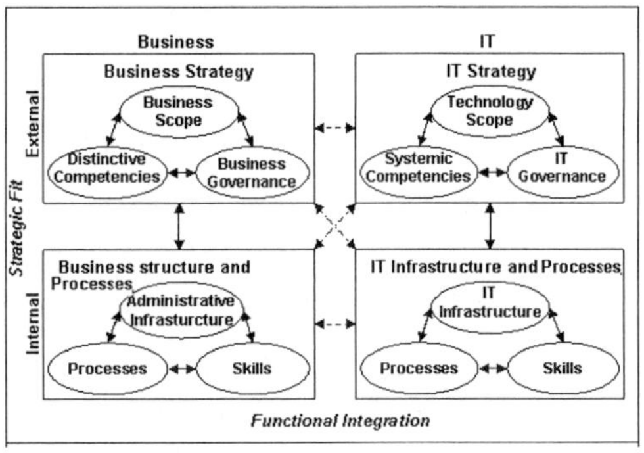

Fig. 1. Alignment types of SAM according to Henderson [8]

In addition to the alignment in the strategic level (functional integration in external level) and the operational level (functional integration in the internal level), Henderson and Venkatraman [8] introduces the strategic fit in the business and IT domains. According to Gerow et al. [6], strategic fit in the IT domain refers to the alignment in the IT domain and is the degree to which the higher level, externally focused IT strategies are aligned with the lower level, internally focused IT infrastructure and processes. Strategic fit in the business domain refers to the alignment in the business domain and is the degree to which the higher level, externally focused business strategies are aligned with the lower level, internally focused business infrastructure and processes.
According to the SAM, both functional integration and strategic fit are required to ensure a proper alignment. In other words, evaluation of alignment, in which we are interested, must enable the evaluation of the four types of alignment described in the SAM. Next section describes the main works related to alignment evaluation.

2.2. Alignment evaluation approaches

Alignment evaluation approaches can be divided into alignment maturity evaluation and alignment degree evaluation.
In order to evaluate the alignment maturity, Luftman and Kempaiah [12] propose a classification of the alignment systems in five maturity levels, based on six criteria (communication, value, governance, partnership, scope and architecture, and skills) by scoring each criterion from one to five. Also, Botta-Genoulaz and Millet [13] propose a qualitative method to classify companies regarding ERP use, based on two criteria (software maturity and strategy deployment). In order to assess the risk of non-alignment, the authors propose a set of alerts to characterize each situation. In addition, they propose a set of corrective actions in order to optimize the use of ERP, i.e. the alignment.

The alignment degree evaluation is either qualitative or quantitative. When the evaluation is qualitative, like in the ATIS approach of Avila and Goepp [14], the business analyst should assess on his own the alignment degree between different instantiated model elements.
The quantitative approaches are generally model-based as the evaluation of the alignment degree is made thanks to metrics based on a meta-model. For example, Pepin [15] divides the elements of his meta-model (processing and data) into: (1) off-line elements and (2) elements to align. Then he divides the elements to align into two subsets (alignable elements, and non-alignable elements). Finally, he divides the alignable elements into: (1) aligned elements, and (2) non-aligned elements. Etien [16] proposes metrics to evaluate the alignment, at the internal level of SAM, based on the correspondence of concepts between two meta-models the Business one (BPRAM) and the System one (SRAM). Otherwise, in Mamoghli [17], the evaluation of alignment is based on the confrontation between the modelling constructs of the Might-Be and As-Wished models, that correspond to each other in case of alignment. This approach is dedicated to the alignment of ERP systems, which is a specific case of alignment. Finally, in Aversano et al.'s approaches [1, 18] the assessment of the alignment is performed through the definition of a measurement framework based on the Goal Question Metrics paradigm. He defines seven metrics related to technological coverage and technological adequacy of the business processes.
Each quantitative approach is based on a specific meta-model that is not related to the type of alignment to be evaluated. To conclude, as the purpose of our work is to propose quantitative metrics to assess alignment, we need to define a common meta-model that enables to analyse the metrics proposed in Aversano et al. [1, 18] and Etien [16] in the light of the type of alignment they intend to evaluate. According to Goepp and Avila [10], Avila and Goepp [11, 19] and Gerow et al. [6], the SAM is the most widespread model proposed in literature that describes alignment. However, its components have a too high-granularity level to be suitable to represent the elements to be considered in alignment evaluation. Therefore, we propose to detail them through lower-granularity level modelling constructs stemming from Archimate 3.0.

3. Meta-model of Alignment Evaluation

The objective of this part is to enrich the components of the SAM with lower-granularity level constructs. For that, we decided to exploit the constructs of Archimate 3.0, the enterprise architecture modelling language from OMG, described in [20]. We choose it because it is a research and practitioner consensus and seems complete enough to consider all alignment types whereas others work [21] such as the meta-models of Etien [16], Pepin [15] or Aversano et al. [1, 18] consider only the functional integration at the operational level. The remaining of this section presents the Archimate language structure and the layer we consider for the mapping with the SAM components.

3.1. Archimate 3.0 modelling language structure

Archimate 3.0 is a visual enterprise architecture modelling language structured around aspects (behavioural, active and passive) and layers.
According our scope, the layers we are interested in are the business and the application layers. The business layer describes products and services realized in the organization by business processes to external partners. The application layer supports the business layer with application services that are realized by software and/or applications.
For the mapping between the SAM components and Archimate 3.0 constructs, we will also keep the Archimate 3.0 constructs belonging to the strategy and the motivation layers required to represent the SAM external level. The motivation layer contains the constructs used to model the motivations, or the reasons that guide the architecture of an enterprise. The strategy layer is composed of three constructs that describe the strategic level of an enterprise.

3.2. Mapping between Archimate 3.0 constructs and SAM components

Petit and Goepp [21] proposed a mapping between the SAM and the business and application layers of Archimate 3.0, we complete this work by mapping the SAM components with the strategic and motivation layers from Archimate:

- *Business scope and IT scope components* correspond to course of action as a strategic element and stakeholder, driver, assessment, goal, outcome, principle, and requirement from the motivation layer.
- *Business distinctive competencies and IT systemic competencies components* correspond to resource and capability from the strategy layer, principle, and constraint from the motivation layer.

- *Business and IT governance components* correspond to resource and capability from strategy layer, and stakeholder from the motivational layer.
- *IT governance components* also correspond to constructs from application layer.
- *Administrative infrastructure and Business processes components* correspond to the business resource from the strategy layer.
- *IT architecture and IT processes components* correspond to IT resource from the business layer.
- *Business and IT Skills* correspond to business role from the business layer.

On this base, we can reinterpret the metrics from literature in the light of the alignment types defined by the SAM. In addition, we can propose new metrics based on these constructs and affect them to their appropriate type.

4. Metrics to evaluate the alignment

In this section, first, we reinterpret existing metrics using Archimate 3.0 constructs and we classify them in the appropriate alignment type according to the SAM. Secondly, we propose new metrics in order to cover all the alignment types of the SAM.

4.1. Equivalence of the existing metrics and classification

4.1.1. Alignment evaluation meta-model mapping with Archimate 3.0

The main works that propose metrics to evaluate alignment are Aversano et al. [1, 18] and Etien [16] and any other work that propose metrics are included in [1, 16, 18]. In order to establish the equivalence between these propositions, we map the meta-models proposed with Archimate 3.0. Tables 1 and 2 detail the mapping between Archimate 3.0 and each construct from Etien and Aversano meta-models.

Table 1. Mapping between Etien [16] and Archimate 3.0 constructs

Etien	*Archimate 3.0*
System event	Application event
Business activity	Business process
Business goal	Business goal
System state	-
System object	Data object
Business resource	Business resources
Business actor	Business role
Business object	Business object
Business state	-
Business Path	Business process
Business transformation	-
System transformation	-

Table 2. Mapping between Aversano et al. [1, 18] and Archimate 3.0 constructs

Aversano et al.	*Archimate 3.0*
Business Activity	Business process
Business actor	Business role
Business artefact	Business object
System class (system artefact)	Data object
Transition	Business event

4.1.2. Equivalence of existing metrics with Archimate 3.0

Based on the mapping presented in Table 1 and Table 2, we propose, in Table 3, the equivalent metrics to the propositions of Aversano et al. and Etien using the Archimate 3.0 constructs. Thanks to the mapping between the SAM components and Archimate 3.0, we can conclude that these metrics only treat the functional integration in the operational level.

So, the remaining of the section proposes additional metrics that we work out by exploiting the relevant parts of the Archimate 3.0 meta-model in [20]. This meta-model formalizes the alignment links between constructs and layers and, in this way, enables a systematic definition of metrics or each alignment type.

Table 3. Equivalence of existing metrics using Archimate 3.0 constructs

Metrics formula	Equivalent metric in literature	Metrics definition
Business process support rate = $\frac{\#\text{Business process served by application services}}{\#\text{ Business process}}$	"Rate of supported activities" of Etien and "Activities coverage" of Aversano et al.	It allows to define the supporting rate of activities by Information system.
Business role support rate = $\frac{\#\text{Business role served by an application interface or application service}}{\#\text{Business role}}$	"Rate of actors existed in the system" of Etien and "Actors coverage" of Aversano et al.	It allows to define the supporting rate of business actors by Information system.
Business object correspondence rate $= \frac{\#\text{Business object realized by data object}}{\#\text{Business object}}$	"Artefact coverage" of Aversano et al.	It allows to define the supporting rate of business objects by Information system.
Resources correspondence rate = $\frac{\#\text{Resources realized by data object}}{\#\text{Resources}}$	"Rate of resources existed in the system" of Etien.	It aims to measure the supporting rate of resources by Information system.
Business event support rate $= \frac{\#\text{Business event served by application service}}{\#\text{Business event}}$	"Transitions coverage" of Aversano et al.	It aims to measure the supporting rate of business events by system.
Completness of information = $\frac{\#\text{Business object accessed by business process and realized by data object}}{\#\text{business object accessed by business process or function}}$	"Completeness of information" and "completeness of activities" of Etien.	It aims to measure the completeness of business processes and activities support.
Business Object Adequacy = $\frac{\sum\text{Business Object Adequacy (i)}}{\#\text{business object}}$, with i belongs to business objects. And, business Object Adequacy (i) = $\frac{\#\text{Business process that accesses to i business and served by application services}}{\#\text{Business process that accesses to i business object}}$	"Artefact adequacy" of Aversano et al.	It aims to measure the support adequacy of business object by the system.
Business Process Adequacy = $\frac{\sum\text{Business Process Adequacy (i)}}{\#\text{Business process}}$, with i belongs to business process. And Business Process Adequacy(i) $= \frac{\sum\text{ Business Object Adequacy (i)(j)}}{\#\text{Business object accessed by business process i}}$ with j belongs to the set of business objects accessed by business process i.	"Activity adequacy" of Aversano et al.	It aims to measure the support adequacy of business process by the system.
Role Adequacy $= \frac{\sum\text{ Role Adequacy (i)}}{\#\text{Business role}}$, with i belongs to business role. And Role Adequacy (i) = $\frac{\sum\text{Business Process Adequacy (i)(j)}}{\#\text{Business process assigned from the business role i'}}$ with j belongs to the set of business process assigned to the business role i.	"Actor adequacy" of Aversano et al.	It aims to measure the support adequacy of business role by the system.

4.2. Evaluation of functional integration in internal level

Besides the existing metrics from literature and based on the alignment links between the Archimate 3.0 constructs defined in [20], we propose two additional metrics that aim to evaluate the support of business function and business interaction (collaboration between two or more business roles) by informatics system.

Table 4. Definition of metrics aiming to assess functional integration in internal level

Metrics formula	Metrics definition
Business function automation rate $= \frac{\#\text{Business function assigned to an application component}}{\#\text{Business function}}$	This metric presents the percentage of business functions supported by an application component of system software. It aims to measure the support of business functions by the system.
Business interaction support rate $= \frac{\#\text{Business interaction served by an application service}}{\#\text{Business interaction}}$	This metric presents the percentage of supporting rate of business interaction by the application services. It aims to measure the support of business interactions by the system.

4.3. Evaluation of functional integration in the strategic level

In order to evaluate functional integration in the strategic level, we present, in Table 5, a set of new metrics. They stem from the analysis of the Archimate 3.0 meta-model [20] alignment links related to the strategic and motivation layers.

Table 5. Definition of metrics aiming to assess functional integration in the strategic level

Metrics formula	Metrics definition
Business actor support $= \frac{\#\text{Business actor that serves an application service}}{\#\text{Business actor}}$	This metric expresses the rate of support of business actor (services department, customer, partners…) which constitutes an important element of the business governance of an organization by informatics systems.
Business service correspondence rate $= \frac{\#\text{ Business service realized by an application service}}{\#\text{business service}}$	This metric expresses the supporting rate of business services, which is a representative element of business scope and business distinctive competences by the system.
Capability automation rate $= \frac{\#\text{Business capabilities assigned to IT resources}}{\#\text{Business capabilities}}$	This metric expresses the rate of support of the business capabilities, which is a representative element of distinctive competences by informatics systems.
Requirements correspondence rate $= \frac{\#\text{Requirement realized by IT resources}}{\#\text{Requirements}}$	This metric expresses the supporting rate of requirements, which constitutes a representative parameter of business scope by informatics systems.
Outcomes correspondence rate $= \frac{\#\text{Outcome for which the correspondent Requirements are realized by IT resources}}{\#\text{Outcome}}$	This metric expresses the business outcomes (which is a representative parameter of business scope) supported by informatics systems, through measuring the support rate of outcomes requirements.
Rate of goals correspondence $= \frac{\#\text{Goals for wchich the correspondent outcomes for which the correspondent requirements are realized by IT resources}}{\#\text{Goals}}$	This metric expresses the business goals (main representative element of business scope) supported by informatics systems, through measuring the support rate of its outcomes requirements.

4.4. Evaluation of the strategic fit in the business domain

In the same way as Table 5, Table 6 details a set of metrics aiming to evaluate the strategic fit in the business domain based on the analysis of the alignment links of the Archimate 3.0 meta-model [20] related to the business layer.

Table 6. Definition of metrics aiming to assess strategic fit in business domain

Metrics formula	Metrics definition
Business service correspondence rate internally $= \frac{\#\text{Business service realized by business process or function}}{\#\text{Business service}}$	This metric presents the rate of support business processes or function to business services.
Requirements correspondence rate internally $= \frac{\#\text{Requirement realized by business processes, business events or business functions}}{\#\text{Requirement}}$	This metric presents the rate of requirements treated by business behavioural elements.
Business resource correspondence rate internally $= \frac{\#\text{Business resource realized by business role, business actor or collaboration}}{\#\text{Business resource}}$	This metric presents the rate of business resources that correspond to the business structure active elements.
Business capabilities correspondence rate internally $= \frac{\#\text{Business capability realized by business processes, and business functions}}{\#\text{Business capability}}$	This metric presents the rate of correspondence of business capabilities to business behavioural elements.

4.5. Evaluation of alignment in IT domain

Finally, the metrics defined in Table 7 aims to evaluate the strategic fit in the IT domain based on the analysis of the alignment links of the Archimate 3.0 meta-model [20] related to the application layer.

Table 7. Definition of metrics aiming to assess strategic fit in IT domain

Metrics formula	Metrics definition
Application service automation rate internally $= \frac{\#\text{Application service assigned from application interfaces}}{\#\text{Application service}}$	This metric aims to calculate the automation rate of application services (representative element of IT scope) by applications interface.
Application service correspondence rate internally $= \frac{\#\text{Application service realized by Application functions}}{\#\text{Application service}}$	The purpose of this metric is to calculate the correspondence rate of application services (representative element of IT scope) to application functions.
IT resources correspondence rate internally $= \frac{\#\text{IT resource realized by application components}}{\#\text{IT resource}}$	This metric aims to present the rate of IT resources support by application components.
IT capabilities correspondence rate internally $= \frac{\#\text{IT capabilities realized by application services or application function}}{\#\text{IT capabilities}}$	This metric presents the rate of correspondence of IT capabilities to IT behavioural elements.

5. Conclusion and perspectives

IS Alignment being nowadays a crucial issue for all companies around the world. It became clear that IS have a great impact on the global performance of organizations. So, making it evolves at the same pace as business strategy is a very important stake for companies. Many researchers deal with the alignment problem. However, its evaluation remains less discussed. Existing evaluation approaches are either qualitative or quantitative. The quantitative one are based on different meta-model and do not address the functional integration at the strategic level, nor the strategic fits in the business and IT domains whereas these alignment types are, according to the SAM [8], the most important model to describe and define alignment types, also required to ensure a proper alignment. To tackle this research gap, we first propose a general meta-model based on the components of the SAM. To obtain a lower-granularity level meta-model that is necessary for alignment evaluation, we map the SAM components with Archimate 3.0 constructs [20]. On this base, we reinterpret existing metrics in the light of this meta-model and the related alignment type. We also complete these metrics with a set of new metrics that aim to evaluate all the alignment types.

The working out of these metrics is systematic and complete because we exploit the alignment links of the Archimate 3.0 meta-model.
All these twenty-five metrics are a first step to evaluate IS alignment in a complete way. However, these metrics are only partial because we did not include constructs linked to business or system states, and business or system transformations. Those constructs could help us to measure the alignment degree of the dynamic behaviour between IT and business. In parallel, an implementation and validation of these metrics should take place, by applying it to a real case study.

6. References

1. Aversano, L., Grasso, C., & Tortorella, M. (2016). Managing the alignment between business processes and software systems. Information and software Technology, 72, 171-188.
2. Tarafdar, M., & Qrunfleh, S. (2009). IT-business alignment: A two-level analysis. Information Systems Management, 26(4), 338-349.
3. Laval, J., Cherifi, C., & Cheutet, V. (2018). Towards the measurement of Enterprise Information Systems agility to support EIS improving projects.
4. Thevenet, L. H. (2008, October). Modeling strategic alignment using INSTAL. In International Conference on Conceptual Modeling (pp. 261-271). Springer, Berlin, Heidelberg.
5. Coltman, T., Tallon, P., Sharma, R. et al. Strategic IT alignment: twenty-five years on. J Inf Technol 30, 91–100 (2015) doi:10.1057/jit.2014.35
6. Gerow, J. E., Thatcher, J. B., & Grover, V. (2015). Six types of IT-business strategic alignment: an investigation of the constructs and their measurement. European Journal of Information Systems, 24(5), 465-491.
7. Charoensuk, S., Wongsurawat, W., & Khang, D. B. (2014). Business-IT Alignment: A practical research approach. The Journal of High Technology Management Research, 25(2), 132-147.
8. Henderson, J. C., & Venkatraman, H. (1999). Strategic alignment: Leveraging information technology for transforming organizations. IBM systems journal, 38(2.3), 472-484.
9. Benbya, H., & McKelvey, B. (2006). Using coevolutionary and complexity theories to improve IS alignment: a multi-level approach. Journal of Information technology, 21(4), 284-298.
10. Goepp, V., & Avila, O. (2015). An Extended-Strategic Alignment Model for technical information system alignment. International Journal of Computer Integrated Manufacturing, 28(12), 1275-1290.
11. Avila, O., & Goepp, V. (2015, July). Meta-modelling the strategic alignment model for aligning Information Systems support to specific application domains. In 2015 12th International Joint Conference on e-Business and Telecommunications (ICETE) (Vol. 2, pp. 94-99). IEEE.
12. Luftman, J., & Kempaiah, R. (2007). An Update on Business-IT Alignment:" A Line" Has Been Drawn. MIS Quarterly Executive. 2007, Vol. 6 Issue 3, p165-177.
13. Botta-Genoulaz, V., & Millet, P. A. (2005). A classification for better use of ERP systems. Computers in Industry, 56(6), 573-587.
14. Avila, O., Goepp, V., & Kiefer, F. (2011). ATIS: A method for the complete alignment of technical information systems. International Journal of Computer Integrated Manufacturing, 24(11), 993-1009.
15. Pepin, J. Enterprise Architecture: Business-IT alignment. PhD Thesis. Université de Nantes (Unam) (2016)
16. Etien, A. (2006). L'ingénierie de l'alignement: Concepts, Modèles et Processus. La méthode ACEM pour la correction et l'évolution d'un système d'information aux processus d'entreprise (Doctoral dissertation).
17. Mamoghli, S., Goepp, V., & Botta-Genoulaz, V. (2017). Aligning ERP systems with companies' real needs: an 'Operational Model Based'method. Enterprise Information Systems, 11(2), 185-222.
18. Aversano, L., Grasso, C., & Tortorella, M. (2010, March). Measuring the alignment between business processes and software systems: a case study. In Proceedings of the 2010 ACM Symposium on Applied Computing (pp. 2330-2336). ACM.
19. Avila, O., Goepp, V., & Kiefer, F. (2018). Addressing alignment concerns into the design of domain-specific information systems. Journal of Manufacturing Technology Management, 29(5), 726-745.
20. ArchiMate® 3.0.1 Specification, http://pubs.opengroup.org/architecture/archimate3-doc/toc.html
21. Petit, M. & Goepp V. (2015). An Evaluation of Archimate as an Architecture Framework for Business-IT Alignment, In proceedings of CIE45 International Conference on Computers & Industrial Engineering, Metz, France.

I L S 2020
INTERNATIONAL CONFERENCE ON INFORMATION SYSTEMS, LOGISTICS & SUPPLY CHAIN
Austin, Texas April 22-24, 2020

Retailing Competition for Substitutable Products in Greenness- and Price-Dependent Market

Erfan Asgari [1], Ramzi Hammami [2], Yannick Frien [1]

[1] Univ. Grenoble Alpes, CNRS, Grenoble INP*, G-SCOP, 38000 Grenoble, France
* Institute of Engineering Univ. Grenoble Alpes
[2] Rennes School of Business, 35065 Rennes, France
{erfan.asgari@grenoble-inp.fr, hammami.ramzi@gmail.com, yannick.frein@grenoble-inp.fr}

Abstract. We consider two retailers that offer two substitutable products and compete in greenness- and price-sensitive market. One retailer offers a product that is produced abroad and the other one offers a product that is produced locally. The local product is greener (releases less carbon emission) than abroad product. The demand function is decreasing in price and carbon emission's level of product. Since the products are substitutable, the price and carbon emission level of each product affect the other product's demand. The first retailer decides its product's price and stock level. The second retailer decides its product's greenness level, price and stock level. An analytical approach is used in order to solve the model. By using the Nash equilibrium, we find the best strategy for both retailers. We show how the market's structures affect the strategy of each retailer.

Keywords: Supply chain management, Greenness, Competition.

1. Introduction

In this paper, we consider two competing retailers that offer two substitutable products in a market that is sensitive to the price and the greenness level of the product. More precisely, we consider a situation where a first retailer sells a product produced by an abroad company. This product has a given level of carbon emission that is relatively high especially due to transport. It is referred to by "Standard" product. A second retailer intends to propose a greener substitutable product, referred to by "Green" product, and consequently competes with the first retailer. This second retailer can offer a greener product as it can be provided from a local supplier that can use a green production process. The two products are equivalent in terms of usage, function, and performance, but they differ in terms of carbon emission level. The demand for each product is a decreasing linear function of its own carbon emission level and price (Endogenous demand) and increasing in other product's price and carbon emission level. The second retailer decides its carbon emission level, price and inventory level. The first one decides the price and the inventory level. Bestseller, one of the leading fashion retailers in Denmark, is a good example of a retailer acting as a gatekeeper. Bestseller, besides developing eco-friendly logistics center and organic product collection, tries to give its customers an opportunity to buy a wide range of environment-friendly products. We consider a dynamic game where each retailer maximizes its profit under other retailer's decisions. Our work closes the gap by studying the dynamic competition from a carbon emission perspective. We address these main research questions: (i) How greenness-driven competition affects the retailers' best strategies? (ii) Do different market structures affect retailers' best strategies?

2. Literature Review

Liu et al. [1], proposed a nonlinear deterministic model for a two-stage supply chain. A linear demand function that is sensitive to price and eco-friendly level of the product is used in order to maximize the profit. Three different cases are considered that the manufacturer decides the wholesale price and eco-friendly level first and after that retailer determines the selling price. Except for the first case, in the rest cases, retailers offer two substitutable products. In addition, competition between retailers is considered too. The main point of the study is to show the connection between CEA and the intensity of the competition and their effects on the supply chain. Results extract some insight as CEA has a direct influence on the manufacturer (with the better eco-friendly level product) and retailer(s) profit. In addition, competition intensity has a direct effect on retailers and reverse effect on a manufacturer with less eco-friendly level.

Qin [2] presented a nonlinear stochastic model. The demand function is sensitive to price and carbon emission reduction. Qin studied a MTO supply chain system composed of a manufacturer and a retailer. The main point of this study is combining various demand forecasting and supply chain strategy (e.g. price and carbon emission reduction). In all scenarios, which are Without Information Sharing, Full Information Sharing and Retailer-only Forecasting, the manufacturer is the leader, which determines the wholesale price and carbon emission reduction level, and the retailer is the follower, which determines selling price. The results show that in the high uncertainty market, both manufacturer and retailer tend to choose the third forecasting scenario (retailer-only Forecasting) and in a low uncertainty market, the manufacturer tends to choose the second scenario, while the retailer tends to choose the first scenario.

Basiri and Heydari [3], worked on a two-stage supply chain. The supply chain offers two substitutable products that are traditional and green. The demand function is sensitive to the price, green quality and also sales efforts. The manufacturer decides the product's green quality, while the retailer decides sales price and sales efforts. Three scenarios are considered and compared: 1- Decentralized model, which both parties try to maximize their own profit 2- Integrated model, which one decision-maker exists and 3- Collaborative model, which offers a win-win situation. All of the scenarios are deterministic. The models are solved by the analytical approach and numerical example results show that the manufacturer's profit in collaboration setting is higher than the two other situations.

Zhou et al. [4] investigated the carbon tax policy's effect on a two-stage supply chain with the MTO system. The model is deterministic and the demand is a linear function of price and carbon emission. Demand is decreasing in price and carbon emission. The system is composed of three players, the government which determines the carbon tax rate for a manufacturer, the manufacturer that determines the wholesale price and carbon emission and the retailer who determines the selling price. Two cases are considered based on this configuration: Bilateral monopoly scenario (as a benchmark) and Scenario with multiple competing retailers (which offer N substitutable products). A three backward step is used in order to find optimum solutions. They declared that retailer and wholesale prices are increasing in the carbon tax rate. In addition, in a competitive market (retailers' competition), the government has to impose a carbon tax policy in order to decrease social welfare losses.

Hong and Guo [5], studied a supply chain composed of one manufacturer and one retailer under different cooperation contracts (Price-only contract, Green-marketing cost-sharing contract, Full channel coordination). The system follows a MTO production with a sensitive demand to the price and product's greenness. The demand function is increasing in the product's greenness and decreasing in price. A stochastic model is presented in order to maximize the profit (manufacturer and retailer). Manufacturer's decisions (wholesale price and greenness of product) and retailer's decisions (selling price and exerted effort for green marketing) are obtained by following the Stackelberg game. The retailer decides after the manufacturer's decisions. As a conclusion, they declared that cooperation is needed to make the supply chain's environmental efficiency better.

In Section 3, we present the problem description, assumptions, and mathematical model. The solutions and proofs are provided in this section. We highlight some insights that are deduced from the optimal solutions, in Section 4. In Section 5, we finally conclude and give future work directions.

3. Problem Description

In this study, two supply chains are considered that offer two products, Standard and Green, to the customers through different retailers. The green product that is produced by the local manufacturer is better than the standard product, which is produced abroad, in term of greenness (i.e. releases less carbon emission). Both products are equivalent in terms of usage, function, and performance. Retailers are close to the market and hold the product as inventory and sell it as soon as a customer arrives (subsequently, the inventory level drops one unit). Figure 1 shows the inventory and refilling policy.

The refilling time of all the retailers' warehouses follows an exponential distribution with mean rate μ. A service level constraint ensures that the probability of customers who face to the empty stock, ψ_{0i} (see [6] for more details), is less than a predetermined level (r).

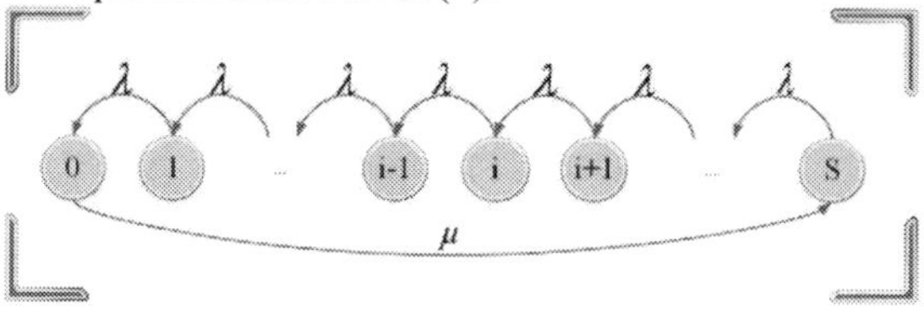

Figure 1: Inventory refilling policy

Since the model is stochastic, there is always a probability that customers find an empty stock. For this reason, a safety stock serves the customers when the stock is empty. Therefore, there is no backorder or lost sale. Furthermore, its filling is not our concern.

As Figure 2 shows, the standard products, produced by the abroad manufacturer, are sent to a local distributor. The distributor sends the products as soon as an order is received from retailer 1. To avoid stock-out, we assume that the distributor's stock is always available. In the second supply chain, the local manufacturer sends directly the green products as soon as the order is received from retailer 2.

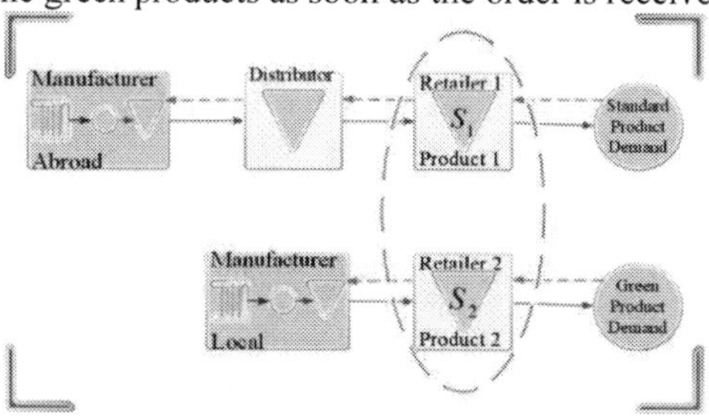

Figure 2: Competition supply chain structure

The customer's arrival follows Poisson distributions with rate λ. λ depends on carbon emission and price. Demand is linearly decreasing in price and carbon emission. Similar to Liu et al. [1] and Xiong et al. [7], the demands functions are presented as follows:

$$\lambda_1 = A - \alpha_p p_1 + \alpha_s(p_2 - p_1) - \beta_e(x_1 + e_1) + \beta_s((x_2 + e_2) - (x_1 + e_1)), \quad (1)$$

$$\lambda_2 = A - \alpha_p p_2 + \alpha_s(p_1 - p_2) - \beta_e(x_2 + e_2) + \beta_s((x_1 + e_1) - (x_2 + e_2)). \quad (2)$$

where A is the potential market size for the product, α_p and β_x are price and carbon emission sensitivity, respectively, and α_s and β_s are the sensitivity of switchover toward price difference and carbon emission difference, respectively. Standard and green products' prices and carbon emission levels are p_1, p_2, x_1 and x_2, respectively. Obviously, $\lambda_1 + \lambda_2 = 2A - \alpha_p(p_1 + p_2) - \beta_e(x_1 + x_2 + e_1 + e_2)$ which implies that total demand is sensitive to prices and carbon emissions; switchovers (price and carbon emission) don't affect the total demand. Retailers can get more customers by decreasing their own product's price (at the rate $\alpha_p + \alpha_s$) or by decreasing their own product's carbon emission (at rate $\beta_e + \beta_s$). When a retailer increases the price (or carbon emission), not only it decreases its own demand but also increases the other retailer's demand.

3.1. Parameters, Variables and Model Assumptions

The following assumptions are used in this paper: (i) The potential market size (A) is big enough. (ii) The green product's regular cost is equal to or greater than the standard product's regular cost ($c_2 \geq c_1$). Considering that the local manufacturer has a more advanced machine to produce a greener product that abroad manufacturer, it is normal to assume that the regular production cost can be equal to or greater than standard products. (iii) The local manufacturer is closer to the retailer than the abroad distributor. Then refilling time of green products' stock is less than standard products' stock ($\mu_1 \geq \mu_2$). (iv) Since the local manufacturer is near to the retailer, the green products' transportation emission is negligible compared to standard products' transportation emission and can be considered to be equal to zero (without loss of generality). (v) The relevant report on the product's carbon emission analysis reveals that approximately 70 percent of the total carbon emissions produced in the product's life cycle (AACE 2015) [8] are related to the production process. Thus, in this paper, we assume that the transportation carbon emission of the standard products is approximately 30 percent of the production carbon emission [9]. (vi) Each retailer follows the MTS policy in both supply chain structures. (vii) Both retailers have equal power and there is no dominating strategy. Thus, retailers decide about their own decision variables under other retailer's actions.

The goal of retailers is to maximize their profits. Attracting more customers can help to achieve the goal, which leads the manufacturer to produce either better (greener) product or offers a lower price. However, decreasing carbon emission has an extra cost. It is well known in the literature that decreasing carbon emission at lower levels will cost more. (viii) Accordingly, $b(x_1 - x_2)^2$ is considered as cost function of carbon emission reduction, where b is the carbon emission reduction cost factor, x_1 is the carbon emission reference (standard product carbon emission) and x_2 is the carbon emission of the green product. The quadratic cost function illustrates that decreasing more carbon emission will have a higher cost. (ix) The fractional stock levels can be rounded up without significant loss of optimality.

By taking assumption (iv) into account, the demand functions (Equations 1 and 2) can be simplified as:

$$\lambda_1 = A_1 - \alpha p_1 + \alpha_s p_2 + \beta_s x_2, \tag{3}$$

$$\lambda_2 = A_2 - \alpha p_2 + \alpha_s p_1 - \beta x_2. \tag{4}$$

where $A_1 = A - \beta(x_1 + e_1)$, $A_2 = A + \beta_s(x_1 + e_1)$, $\beta = \beta_e + \beta_s$ and $\alpha = \alpha_p + \alpha_s$. Note that $\beta > \beta_s$ and $\alpha > \alpha_s$.

3.2. Competitive Scenario

As we discussed earlier, a local manufacturer produces a new substitutable product. The retailer who offers a green product to the customers decides green product's carbon emission level (x_2), its price (p_2) and inventory level (S_2). Meanwhile, the abroad manufacturer keeps standard product's carbon emission level (x_1), but the retailer who offers standard product decides standard product's price (p_1) and inventory level (S_1). This is a dynamic competition and both decision makers (retailers) seek the best strategy under other decision maker's strategy. We formulate the mathematical model of the problem as:

$$\max_{S_1, p_1} \pi_1 = (p_1 - c_1)\lambda_1 - hS_1, \tag{5}$$

$$\max_{x_2, S_2, p_2} \pi_2 = \left(p_2 - (c_2 + b(x_1 - x_2)^2)\right)\lambda_2 - hS_2 \tag{6}$$

$$Subject\ to: \tag{7}$$

$$\psi_{01} = \frac{\lambda_1}{\lambda_1 + \mu_1 S_1} \leq r,$$

$$Subject\ to: \tag{8}$$

$$\psi_{02} = \frac{\lambda_2}{\lambda_2 + \mu_2 S_2} \leq r,$$

$$\lambda_1 = A_1 - \alpha p_1 + \alpha_s p_2 + \beta_s x_2, \tag{9}$$

$$\lambda_2 = A_2 - \alpha p_2 + \alpha_s p_1 - \beta x_2, \tag{10}$$

$$S_1, p_1 \geq 0,\ \lambda_1 \geq 0. \tag{11}$$

$$x_2, S_2, p_2 \geq 0,\ x_2 \leq x_1,\ \ \lambda_2 \geq 0. \tag{12}$$

The objective functions of retailers (equations 5 and 6) are to maximize their total profit (i.e. net profit of selling product – total inventory cost) under the opponent player's decisions. Since the model is stochastic, the expected value of the stock is equal to $\sum_{i=1}^{S_j} i\psi_{ij}$ (where ψ_{ij} represents the probability retailer j of having i items in stock when a random customer arrives). The expected value is too complex; therefore, we consider a close approximation. The inventory cost is proportional to S and we consider it as hS_j. There are two service level constraints (equations 7 and 8) that ensure that the probability that customers face to empty stock is less than or equal r. Equations 9 and 10 show the demand for each retailer. Other constraints are related to the demand, price and carbon emission positivity. The following of this section aims to determine the optimal solutions.

In the first step, we consider that retailer 2's decisions are known and we optimize the retailer 1's decisions. Then we consider that retailer 1's decisions are known and optimize the retailer 2 decisions. After that, under dynamic game consideration and using the Nash equilibrium, the optimal solution of the competition will be deduced.

Lemma 1. The regular product's service level constraint is binding at optimality and the optimal value of the stock is equal to $S_1^*(p_1^*, p_2^*, x_2^*) = \frac{1-r}{r\mu_1}\lambda_1^*$.

Proof. Since the objective function is linearly decreasing in S_1, the smallest possible S_1 is the optimal stock. According to the service level constraint, $S_1 \geq \frac{1-r}{r\mu_1}\lambda_1$, therefore, the optimal value is $S_1^* = \frac{1-r}{r\mu_1}\lambda_1^*$, which implies that service level constraint is binding in optimality. ■

Lemma 2. The optimal standard product's price under green product's price and green product's carbon emission is $p_1^*(p_2, x_2) = \frac{A_1+\alpha_s p_2+\beta_s x_2+\alpha\left(c_1+\frac{h\gamma}{\mu_1}\right)}{2\alpha}$.

Proof. The second derivative of objective function with respect to p_1, $\frac{d^2\pi_1}{dp_1^2} = -2\alpha < 0$, is negative. Then:

$$\frac{d\pi_1}{dp_1} = 0 \leftrightarrow p_1^{max}(p_2, x_2) = \frac{A_1 + \alpha_s p_2 + \beta_s x_2 + \alpha\left(c_1 + \frac{h\gamma}{\mu_1}\right)}{2\alpha}$$

If $p_1^{max} > 0$ and $\lambda_1(p_1^{max}) \geq 0$, then it can be considered as the optimal price.

$$p_1^{max} = \frac{A_1 + \alpha_s p_2 + \beta_s x_2 + \alpha\left(c_1 + \frac{h\gamma}{\mu_1}\right)}{2\alpha} > 0 \leftrightarrow A_1 + \alpha_s p_2 + \beta_s x_2 + \alpha\left(c_1 + \frac{h\gamma}{\mu_1}\right) > 0$$

Recall that A_1 is positive and since all other expressions are positive then we conclude that $p_1^{max} > 0$. We also need to verify that $\lambda_1(p_1^{max}) \geq 0$.

$$\lambda_1 \geq 0 \leftrightarrow A_1 - \alpha\left(\frac{A_1 + \alpha_s p_2 + \beta_s x_2 + \alpha\left(c_1 + \frac{h\gamma}{\mu_1}\right)}{2\alpha}\right) + \alpha_s p_2 + \beta_s x_2 \geq 0$$

$$\leftrightarrow \frac{A_1 + \alpha_s p_2 + \beta_s x_2 - \alpha\left(c_1 + \frac{h\gamma}{\mu_1}\right)}{2} \geq 0 \leftrightarrow \alpha_s p_2 + \beta_s x_2 \geq -A_1 + \alpha\left(c_1 + \frac{h\gamma}{\mu_1}\right)$$

Under $A_1 \geq \alpha\left(c_1 + \frac{h\gamma}{\mu_1}\right)$, the right side of the inequality is negative. Since the left side of inequality always positive $(p_2, x_2 > 0)$ the condition is always true. Thus $p_1^*(p_2, x_2) = p_1^{max}$. ■

The price of retailer 1's product is increasing in retailer 2's price and carbon emission. Increasing one unit of retailer 2's price increases $\frac{\alpha_s}{2\alpha}$ unit of retailer 1's price.

So far, we solve the retailer 1's problem for given retailer 2's decisions. In the following, we solve retailer 2's problem for given retailer 1's decisions.

Lemma 3. The local service level constraint is binding at optimality and the optimal value of the stock is equal to $S_2^*(p_1^*, p_2^*, x_2^*) = \frac{1-r}{r\mu_2}\lambda_2^*$.

Proof. Similar to Lemma 1, the objective function is linearly decreasing in S_2, and the smallest possible S_2 is the optimal solution.

Lemma 4. The optimal green product's price under regular product's price and green product's carbon emission is $p_2^*(p_1, x_2) = \frac{\alpha b x_2^2-(\beta+2\alpha b x_1)x_2+A_2+\alpha_s p_1+\alpha\left(c_2+b x_1^2+\frac{h\gamma}{\mu_2}\right)}{2\alpha}$.

Proof. The second derivative of objectives function with respect to p_2, $\frac{d^2\pi_2}{d(p_2)^2} = -2\alpha < 0$, is negative and demonstrates that objective function is concave with respect to p_2. Therefore the root of the first derivative (called p_2^{max}) maximize the objective function.

$$\frac{d\pi_2}{dp_2} = 0 \leftrightarrow p_2^{max}(p_1, x_2) = \frac{\alpha b x_2^2 - (\beta + 2\alpha b x_1)x_2 + A_2 + \alpha_s p_1 + \alpha\left(c_2 + b x_1^2 + \frac{h\gamma}{\mu_2}\right)}{2\alpha}$$

p_2^{max} can be considered as the optimal price when satisfies $p_2^{max} > 0$ and $\lambda_2(p_2^{max}) \geq 0$.

$$p_2^{max} = \frac{\alpha b x_2^2 - (\beta + 2\alpha b x_1)x_2 + A_2 + \alpha_s p_1 + \alpha\left(c_2 + b x_1^2 + \frac{h\gamma}{\mu_2}\right)}{2\alpha} > 0$$

$$\leftrightarrow \alpha b x_2^2 - (\beta + 2\alpha b x_1)x_2 + A_2 + \alpha_s p_1 + \alpha\left(c_2 + b x_1^2 + \frac{h\gamma}{\mu_2}\right) > 0$$

The discriminant of the above equation is $\Delta_1 = -4\alpha b\left(A_2 - \beta x_1 + \alpha_s p_1 + \alpha\left(c_2 + \frac{h\gamma}{\mu_2}\right) - \frac{\beta^2}{4\alpha b}\right)$. Recall assumption (i) and assume $A_2 > \beta x_1 - \alpha_s p_1 - \alpha\left(c_2 + \frac{h\gamma}{\mu_2}\right) + \frac{\beta^2}{4\alpha b}$, then, Δ_1 is negative and consequently, p_2^{max} is always positive.

As of last condition, the p_2^{max} is the optimal solution if $\lambda_2(p_2^{max}) \geq 0$.

$$\lambda_2 \geq 0 \leftrightarrow \frac{-\alpha b x_2^2 - (\beta - 2\alpha b x_1)x_2 + A_2 + \alpha_s p_1 - \alpha\left(c_2 + b x_1^2 + \frac{h\gamma}{\mu_2}\right)}{2} \geq 0$$

$$\leftrightarrow -\alpha b x_2^2 - (\beta - 2\alpha b x_1)x_2 + A_2 + \alpha_s p_1 - \alpha\left(c_2 + b x_1^2 + \frac{h\gamma}{\mu_2}\right) \geq 0$$

The discriminant of the above equation is equal to $\Delta_2 = 4\alpha b\left(A_2 - \beta x_1 + \alpha_s p_1 - \alpha\left(c_2 + \frac{h\gamma}{\mu_2}\right) + \frac{\beta^2}{4\alpha b}\right)$. The $\Delta_2 = -\Delta_1$ and earlier we mentioned that $\Delta_1 < 0$, therefore, $\Delta_2 > 0$ and the above equation has two roots (called R_1 and R_2). λ_2 is positive between these two roots and negative outside them,

$R_1 = \frac{(\beta - 2\alpha b x_1) - \sqrt{\Delta_2}}{-2\alpha b} = x_1 + \frac{-\beta + \sqrt{\Delta_2}}{2\alpha_p b}$ and $R_2 = \frac{(\beta - 2\alpha b x_1) + \sqrt{\Delta_2}}{-2\alpha b} = x_1 - \frac{\beta + \sqrt{\Delta_2}}{2\alpha_p b}$.

We have $R_1 > x_1$ and $R_2 < 0$. Therefore, demand is positive in the feasible region ($[0, x_1]$). Since two conditions are validated, thus $p_2^*(p_1, x_2) = p_2^{max}$. ■

Proposition 1. The optimal emission intensity of the green product is $x_2^* = \max\{0, x_1 - \frac{\beta}{2\alpha b}\}$.

Proof. After substituting S_2^* and p_2^*, the objective function is equal to $\frac{\lambda_2^2}{\alpha}$. Since $\lambda_2 \geq 0$, maximizing λ_2 is equivalent to maximizing $\frac{\lambda_2^2}{\alpha}$. The second derivative of demand with respect to x_2, $\frac{d^2\lambda_2}{dx_2^2} = -\alpha b < 0$, is negative and the root of the first derivative is the x_2^{max} that maximize the demand (equivalently, objective function).

$$\frac{d\lambda_2}{dx_2} = 0 \leftrightarrow \frac{-2\alpha b x_2 + (2\alpha b x_1 - \beta)}{2} = 0 \leftrightarrow -2\alpha b x_2 + (2\alpha b x_1 - \beta) = 0 \leftrightarrow x_2^{max} = x_1 - \frac{\beta}{2\alpha b}$$

It is obvious that $x_2^{max} < x_1$. As long as the x_2^{max} is in the feasible region, the optimal solution is x_2^{max}, otherwise, if $x_2^{max} \leq 0$ then the optimal solution is equal to zero. So $x_2^* = \max\{0, x_1 - \frac{\beta}{2\alpha b}\}$. ■

Now, we try to find the Nash equilibrium in order to reach the optimal solution. Based on Nash equilibrium no retailer is motivated to change his/her chosen strategy after considering other retailer's choices.

Proposition 2. The optimum value of standard and green products' prices are $p_1^* = \frac{2\alpha(2\alpha z_1 + \alpha_s z_2)}{4\alpha^2 - \alpha_s^2}$ and $p_2^* = \frac{2\alpha(\alpha_s z_1 + 2\alpha z_2)}{4\alpha^2 - \alpha_s^2}$, where $z_1 = \frac{A_1 + \beta_s x_2 + \alpha\left(c_1 + \frac{h\gamma}{\mu_1}\right)}{2\alpha}$ and $z_2 = \frac{\alpha b x_2^2 - (\beta + 2\alpha b x_1)x_2 + A_2 + \alpha\left(c_2 + b x_1^2 + \frac{h\gamma}{\mu_2}\right)}{2\alpha}$.

Proof. After substituting x_2^*, the retailers' best strategies become:

$p_1(p_2) = \frac{A_1 + \alpha_s p_2 + \beta_s x_2 + \alpha\left(c_1 + \frac{h\gamma}{\mu_1}\right)}{2\alpha}$ and $p_2(p_1) = \frac{\alpha b x_2^2 - (\beta + 2\alpha b x_1)x_2 + A_2 + \alpha_s p_1 + \alpha\left(c_2 + b x_1^2 + \frac{h\gamma}{\mu_2}\right)}{2\alpha}$

As you can see, the reaction equations are linear in the function of opponent decisions. According to **Nash equilibrium**, the intersection point of these equations is the best strategy. There is no better strategy, which improves retailers' profit under the opponent's decision.

$p_1^* = \frac{2\alpha(2\alpha z_1 + \alpha_s z_2)}{4\alpha^2 - \alpha_s^2}$ and $p_2^* = \frac{2\alpha(\alpha_s z_1 + 2\alpha z_2)}{4\alpha^2 - \alpha_s^2}$,

where $z_1 = \frac{A_1 + \beta_s x_2 + \alpha\left(c_1 + \frac{h\gamma}{\mu_1}\right)}{2\alpha}$ and $z_2 = \frac{\alpha b x_2^2 - (\beta + 2\alpha b x_1)x_2 + A_2 + \alpha\left(c_2 + b x_1^2 + \frac{h\gamma}{\mu_2}\right)}{2\alpha}$.

The optimal inventory levels, S_1^* and S_2^*, are obtained from substituting x_2^*, p_1^* and p_2^*. ■

4. Discussion

Similar to Boyaci and Ray [10], which distinguished three market structures based on lead time and price sensitivity parameters, we distinguish three market structures that impact our analysis. Price and Carbon emission Difference sensitive (PCD) market (i.e., $\alpha_p\beta_s > \beta_e\alpha_s$), where the market is more sensitive to price, but switchovers are more governed by the difference in greenness. Carbon emission and Price Difference sensitive (CPD) market (i.e., $\alpha_p\beta_s < \beta_e\alpha_s$), where the market is more sensitive to carbon

emission, but switchovers are more governed by the price difference. Neutral market where the customers equally care about price and carbon emission (i.e., $\alpha_p\beta_s = \beta_e\alpha_s$).
Proposition 3. The green products are always offered at a higher price than standard products.
Proof and more details are provided in Appendix A. It is an intuitive result. We expected that the price of the green product would be higher than the standard product. Consider that both manufacturers have the same situations ($c_1 = c_2$, $\mu_1 = \mu_2$ and $e_1 = 0$). We have two substitutable products with different carbon emission level. It is logical that the better (greener) product has a higher price than the standard product.
Proposition 4. Decreasing abroad supplier's transportation emission (i.e., selecting a less distant supplier) leads to decreasing the price differentiation ($p_2^* - p_1^*$).
See Appendix A, the price differentiation is $\frac{\beta(3\beta+2\beta_s)}{4\alpha^2} + (\beta+\beta_s)e_1 - \mathrm{b}\left(c_1 - c_2 + h\gamma\left(\frac{1}{\mu_1} - \frac{1}{\mu_2}\right)\right)$.
Decreasing one unit of standard product's transportation carbon emission leads to decreasing products' price differentiation at rate $\beta + \beta_s$. The implication of Proposition 4 is that the price differentiation of the green and standard products is critically linked to the transportation carbon emission of standard product.
Proposition 5. A decrease in the optimal carbon emission of green product results in:
(i) A nonlinear increase in optimal green product's price. (ii) A nonlinear decrease in optimal standard product's price if $\alpha_p\beta_s > \beta_e\alpha_s$ and a nonlinear increase if $\alpha_p\beta_s < \beta_e\alpha_s$.
Proof in Appendix B. The first part of the proposition is intuitive because providing the green product with lower carbon emission, by a local manufacturer, increases the total cost. The second part implies the impact of market characteristics on the optimal pricing strategy.
The market separation, that we mentioned earlier, makes the second result quite intuitive. For a PCD market where customers are more sensitive to price and the differentiation is led by carbon emission, when x_2 decreases, there are few new customers, which more of them buy a green product. By decreasing the standard product's price, the first retailer, who offers standard product, attract more customers, since in this market price has more influence than carbon emission. This strategy helps the first retailer to increase further the profit. For a CPD market, when x_2 decreases, there are significant new customers. Because the switchovers are more sensitive to the price differential, the first retailer increases the standard product's price as the second retailer increases the green product's price, without considerably decreasing new demand.

5. Conclusion

In this study, a stochastic dynamic competition is considered between two retailers who offer two substitutable products to the customers, in a price and carbon emission sensitive market. There are many real example in this context like automobiles industries, clothes industries and etc. Both retailers follow the MTS policy. Since the products are substitutable, the products' demand not only depends on their own price and carbon emission but also, depends on other product's price and carbon emission. We formulate the problem and solve it through an analytical approach. The Nash equilibrium is used to find the best strategy for each player against the other one. Finally, we distinguished different markets' categories to extract important insights into our results. The results showed the impact of market characteristics and competition on retailers' strategy. In future work, we would like to consider a collaboration scenario and compare the results to the competitive scenario.

6. References

[1] Z. L. Liu, T. D. Anderson, and J. M. Cruz, "Consumer environmental awareness and competition in two-stage supply chains," *Eur. J. Oper. Res.*, vol. 218, no. 3, pp. 602–613, 2012.
[2] J. Qin, L. Ren, and L. Xia, "Carbon emission reduction and pricing strategies of supply chain under various demand forecasting scenarios," *Asia-Pacific J. Oper. Res.*, vol. 34, no. 01, p. 1740005, 2017.
[3] Z. Basiri and J. Heydari, "A mathematical model for green supply chain coordination with substitutable products," *J. Clean. Prod.*, vol. 145, pp. 232–249, 2017.
[4] Y. Zhou, F. Hu, and Z. Zhou, "Pricing decisions and social welfare in a supply chain with multiple competing retailers and carbon tax policy," *J. Clean. Prod.*, vol. 190, pp. 752–777, 2018.

[5] Z. Hong and X. Guo, "Green product supply chain contracts considering environmental responsibilities," *Omega*, vol. 83, pp. 155–166, 2019.
[6] E. Asgari, Y. Frein, and R. Hammami, "Lead Time Quotation Under MTO and MTS Delivery Modes with Endogenous Demand," in *2018 IEEE International Conference on Industrial Engineering and Engineering Management (IEEM)*, 2018, pp. 22–26.
[7] Z. K. Xiong, P. Zhang, and N. Guo, "Impact of carbon tax and consumers' environmental awareness on carbon emissions in supply chains," *Syst. Eng. Pract.*, vol. 34, no. 9, pp. 2245–2252, 2014.
[8] China's carbon trading website, "Analysis of Apple's Carbon Emissions(AACE)." [Online]. Available: http://www.tanpaifang.com/jienenjianpai/2015/0306/42879.html. [Accessed: 19-Sep-2019].
[9] United States Environmental Protection Agency, "Overview of greenhouse gases," *Epa*, 2013. [Online]. Available: https://www.epa.gov/ghgemissions/overview-greenhouse-gases. [Accessed: 19-Sep-2019].
[10] T. Boyaci and S. Ray, "Product differentiation and capacity cost interaction in time and price sensitive markets," *Manuf. Serv. Oper. Manag.*, vol. 5, no. 1, pp. 18–36, 2003.

Appendix A.

We use proof by Contradiction. We assume ${p_2}^* > {p_1}^*$, then:

$${p_2}^* > {p_1}^* \leftrightarrow \frac{2\alpha(\alpha_s z_1 + 2\alpha z_2)}{4\alpha^2 - {\alpha_s}^2} > \frac{2\alpha(2\alpha z_1 + \alpha_s z_2)}{4\alpha^2 - {\alpha_s}^2}$$

$$\leftrightarrow \alpha_s z_1 + 2\alpha z_2 > 2\alpha z_1 + \alpha_s z_2 \leftrightarrow (2\alpha - \alpha_s) z_2 > (2\alpha - \alpha_s) z_1 \leftrightarrow z_2 > z_1$$

$$\leftrightarrow \alpha b {x_2}^2 - (\beta + 2\alpha b x_1) x_2 + \alpha b {x_1}^2 + A_2 - A_1 - \beta_s x_2 > \alpha\left(c_1 - c_2 + h\gamma\left(\frac{1}{\mu_1} - \frac{1}{\mu_2}\right)\right)$$

By substituting $A_2 - A_1 = (\beta + \beta_s)(x_1 + e_1)$ and $x_2 = x_1 - \frac{\beta}{2\alpha b}$, above inequality turns to:

$$\leftrightarrow \alpha b\left({x_1}^2 - \frac{\beta x_1}{\alpha b} + \frac{\beta^2}{4\alpha^2 b^2}\right) - 2\alpha b\left({x_1}^2 - \frac{\beta^2}{4\alpha^2 b^2}\right) + \alpha b {x_1}^2 + (\beta + \beta_s)(x_1 + e_1) - \beta_s\left(x_1 - \frac{\beta}{2\alpha b}\right)$$
$$> \alpha\left(c_1 - c_2 + h\gamma\left(\frac{1}{\mu_1} - \frac{1}{\mu_2}\right)\right)$$

$$\leftrightarrow \frac{\beta(3\beta + 2\beta_s)}{4\alpha^2} + (\beta + \beta_s) e_1 > b\left(c_1 - c_2 + h\gamma\left(\frac{1}{\mu_1} - \frac{1}{\mu_2}\right)\right)$$

According to the assumption (ii) and (iii), the right side is negative (or zero) and the left side positive. Therefore the initial assumption, which is ${p_2}^* > {p_1}^*$, is true.

Appendix B.

Recall Proposition 2, the first and second derivative of the green product's price with respect to x_2, are presented in the following.

$$\frac{d{p_2}^*}{dx_2} = \frac{1}{4\alpha^2 - {\alpha_s}^2}\left((\alpha_s\beta_s - 2\alpha\beta) + 4\alpha^2 b(x_2 - x_1)\right)$$

$$\frac{d^2{p_2}^*}{d{x_2}^2} = \frac{4\alpha^2 b}{4\alpha^2 - {\alpha_s}^2} > 0$$

Since the second derivative is positive, the optimal price is strictly convex with respect to x_2. Since the first derivative is negative, therefore the optimal price of green products is decreasing in x_2. Therefore, as x_2 decreases, green products have a higher price. In other word, the price nonlinearly decreasing in x_2.

The first and second derivative of the optimal price of the standard product are presented in the following:

$$\frac{d{p_1}^*}{dx_2} = \frac{1}{4\alpha^2 - {\alpha_s}^2}\left((2\alpha\beta_s - \alpha_s\beta) + 2\alpha_s\alpha b(x_2 - x_1)\right)$$

$$\frac{d^2{p_1}^*}{d{x_2}^2} = \frac{4\alpha^2 b}{4\alpha^2 - {\alpha_s}^2} > 0$$

Since the second derivative is positive, the optimal price is strictly convex with respect to x_2. The first derivative can be negative or positive. In the optimal carbon emission, we have $\frac{d{p_1}^*}{dx_2}\left(x_2 = x_1 - \frac{\beta}{2\alpha b}\right) = \frac{2(\alpha\beta_s - 2\alpha_s\beta)}{4\alpha^2 - {\alpha_s}^2}$. Therefore, the optimal price of the standard product is increasing in x_2 when $\alpha_p\beta_s > \beta_e\alpha_s$ (equivalent to $\alpha\beta_s > \alpha_s\beta$) and it is decreasing when $\alpha_p\beta_s < \beta_e\alpha_s$ (equivalent to $\alpha\beta_s < \alpha_s\beta$).

I L S 2020
INTERNATIONAL CONFERENCE ON INFORMATION SYSTEMS, LOGISTICS & SUPPLY CHAIN
Austin, Texas April 22-24, 2020

An efficient heuristic for the multi-product straight pipeline scheduling problem

Meryem BAMOUMEN [1,2], Selwa ELFIRDOUSSI [1], Libo REN [2], Nikolay TCHERNEV [1,2]

[1] EMINES School of Industrial Management, University Mohammed VI Polytechnic
LOT 660 Hay Moulay Rachid, 43150 Benguerir, MAROC

[2] LIMOS, UMR CNRS 6158, University of Clermont Auvergne
1 rue de Chebarde, 63178 Aubière, France

{Meryem.Bamoumen, Selwa.Elfirdoussi}@emines.um6p.ma
{Libo.Ren, Nikolay.Tchernev}@uca.fr

Abstract. This paper deals with the multi-product straight pipeline scheduling problem. In this problem, a straight pipeline is used for the transport of different products from the pumping station to the distribution center. The objective is to find a sequence of batches that ensures all daily product demand with a minimum total cost, while respecting the different constraints. An efficient heuristic is developed to tackle this problem. The proposed approach incorporates a randomized greedy algorithm for generating an initial solution and an improvement procedure with volume optimization operators. Our approach is evaluated on an instance from an operational pipeline on a one-month time horizon. The computational results show that it gives very competitive results.

Keywords: Scheduling, Multi-product pipeline, Heuristic, Phosphate

1. Introduction

1.1. Research context

OCP Group is a Moroccan firm that produces and exports phosphate and its derivatives around the world. The group established a new project called "Slurry pipeline" to increase the production capacity and reduce the logistics costs. The pipeline is a transportation mode for liquid and gaseous material, and is mainly exploited in petroleum industries to transport petroleum and derived products. The transportation of phosphate via pipeline is achieved by adding water to phosphate grains to obtain "phosphate slurry". The slurry operates like a homogenous liquid material and it can be transferred through the pipeline. The implemented pipeline, which transports phosphate products from the mine site to the distribution center, is a main straight pipeline with a length of 187 km and a diameter of 90 cm.

Phosphate slurries can be perceived as different qualities, in reliance on their Bone Phosphate of Lime (BPL) composition. Each quality of phosphate corresponds to a product, which has its demand and storage capacity. Consequently, the pipeline is used for the transportation of multi-products, which consists of pumping a sequence of batches consecutively from the upstream of pipeline to the distribution center. Only one product is allocated to each batch, and its volume is comprised between an upper and a lower bound. In addition, a constant volume of water is injected between two batches as a separation tag in order to be able to identify the batch during the discharging period at the distribution center.

In this work, our focus is on the multi-product pipeline scheduling problem in the context of mining. The objective is to arrange the sequence of batches to be transported via pipeline on a predefined time horizon, by considering the downstream inventories to ensure demand satisfaction, while minimizing some associated costs. A heuristic incorporates a randomized greedy algorithm for generating an initial solution and an improvement procedure with volume optimization operators is proposed to tackle this problem.

1.2. Problem definition

The problem we are focusing on involves of a straight multi-product pipeline that links the upstream (pumping station) to a unique distribution center. The following information must be given:

- The number of products to be transferred via pipeline;
- The time horizon (in days);
- The initial pipeline state (the type of products and their volumes);
- The pipeline specifications (diameter, length and pumping flow rate);
- The inventory properties (initial inventory and storage capacity of each product);
- The product properties (minimum and maximum size of batch)
- The customer demand during the scheduling time horizon;
- The matrix of forbidden product sequence between two consecutive batches;
- The volume of water separating two batches.

The following assumptions have been made:

- The phosphate slurry is viewed as a homogenous fluid;
- The flow pumping rate is stable and the slurry flow is always turbulent;
- All daily demand in the scheduling time horizon is given.

The objective is to schedule a sequence of batches to ensure all daily product demand with a minimum total cost, while respecting the following constraints:

- At any time, the pipeline must be entirely full;
- Product inventory at any time should respect its storage capacity, and should not be negative;
- Flow conservation constraint: the entire input volume must be equal to the output volume;
- The compatibility of two successive batches;
- Each batch contains only one product;
- Upper and lower bounds on the volume of batch.

1.3. Organization of the paper

The rest of the paper is organized as follows: Section 2 presents a literature review. Section 3 describes the proposed approach. Section 4 gives the computational experiments before the conclusion.

2. Literature review

In the literature, the multi-product pipeline scheduling problem has drawn the attention of many researchers over the last few years. However, most of the existing work on pipeline scheduling concerns the petroleum industry. The multi-product pipeline scheduling problems can be classified by the pipeline structure: straight line (linear), tree, etc. In this paper, we focus mainly on the work related to the problems with a straight pipeline. The linear pipeline scheduling problems can be divided into two following categories according to the pipeline configuration: One-to-One: pipeline with one source (upstream) and one destination (downstream); One-to-Many: pipeline with one source and several consecutively arranged destinations. In this paper, we are interested particularly in work related to One-to-One straight pipeline scheduling problems.

2.1. One-to-One pipeline scheduling problem

In the literature, several approaches were developed for the one-to-one scheduling problem. Shah et al. (1996) [14] and Sasikumar et al. (1997) [13] are considered among the first works to tackle the scheduling of petroleum products with a One-to-One linear pipeline. Shah et al. (1996) [14] developed a mathematical programming approach that divides the linear model into two sub models, which are solved successively. Sasikumar et al. (1997) [13] proposed a heuristic which gives the sequence of batches to be inserted in the pipeline, while considering a set of constraints including the demand and the inventory management.

Relvas et al. (2006) [11] proposed a mixed integer linear program (MILP) that considered the inventory management and the settling period after receipt of each new lot at the distribution center. The model has been evaluated on a real-world case study form the petroleum industry. In addition, Relvas et al. (2009) [9] developed a heuristic to improve the efficiency of the linear program. The approach provides an adequate identification of feasible products sequences.

Cafaro et al. proposed (2008) [2] a mixed integer linear program with a continuous time formulation. The model provides better results within a shorter computational time compared to Relvas et al. (2006).

Relvas et al. (2013) [10] developed a new MILP model for a generic oil transportation system with a multiproduct pipeline that connects a single refinery to a distribution center. The objective is to ensure demand satisfaction and minimize the average flow rate at the same time. Consequently, two approaches were proposed: the first one considers fixed batch size and the second one uses variable batch size.

MirHassani el al. (2013) [5] proposed a heuristic with two steps: the construction step inserts interactively batches to build an initial solution, in which backorders can be accepted. The improvement step uses two following methods: the first one is based on batch-size modification and the second works with a population of the K best solutions. Crossover operations between solutions are performed to renew the population. The local improvement procedure ends if the maximum number of iteration is reached or if there is no improvement after a fixed number of iterations.

Moradi and MirHassani (2015) [6] proposed a MILP model based on the work presented in Relvas et al. (2013) [10]. The objective is to optimize the batch sequence and the unloading time of each batch at the distribution center. The constraints such as discrete or continuous flow rate, electricity consumption peak periods were taken into account. Later, Moradi and MirHassani (2016) [7] developed a robust method in which the deterministic linear model in Moradi and MirHassani (2015) is enlarged to a robust formulation.

Kirschstein (2018) [4] considered the multi-product pipeline scheduling problem as an Economic Lot Scheduling Problem (ELSP) with additional constraints. The author developed an adaptation of the heuristic initially proposed by Dobson (1992) [3] to study this problem.

Recently, Bamoumen et al. (2019) [1] proposed a hybrid approach for the multi-product straight pipeline scheduling problem. The proposed approach is composed of a construction heuristic and a MILP model as a post-optimization procedure to adjust the volume of batches. It was evaluated on an instance from an operational pipeline on a one-month time horizon.

3. Proposed approach

The proposed approach is composed of a construction method (section 3.1), an evaluation function (section 3.2) and an improvement procedure (section 3.3). The proposed construction method generates a solution in which all customers demand is satisfied. The evaluation function verifies all constrains and calculates the associated costs. The improvement procedure attempts to reduce the cost using volume optimization operators.

3.1. Construction method

The construction method generates an initial solution iteratively: a new batch is inserted at each iteration. The evaluation function checks the feasibility of the current solution. In case of infeasibility, a repair process is applied to reassign several newly inserted batches to other products.

The proposed construction method is composed of two parts: a greedy algorithm and a repair process. The detail of the construction method is given on Figure 1.

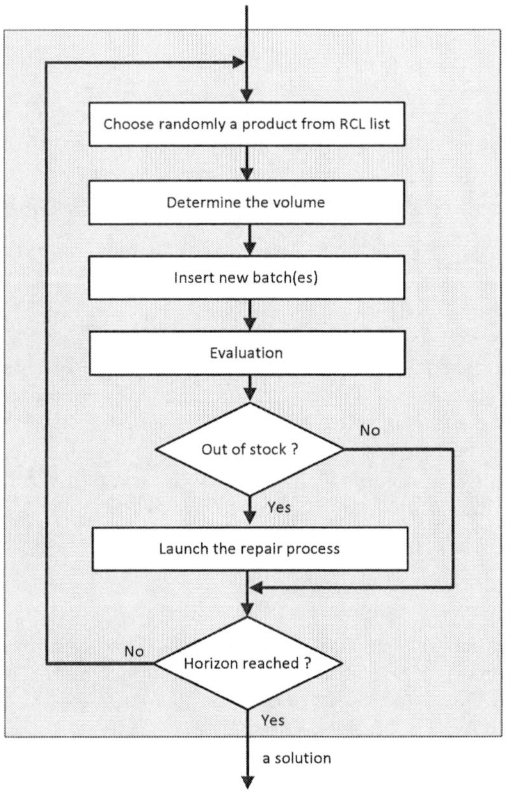

(a) greedy algorithm

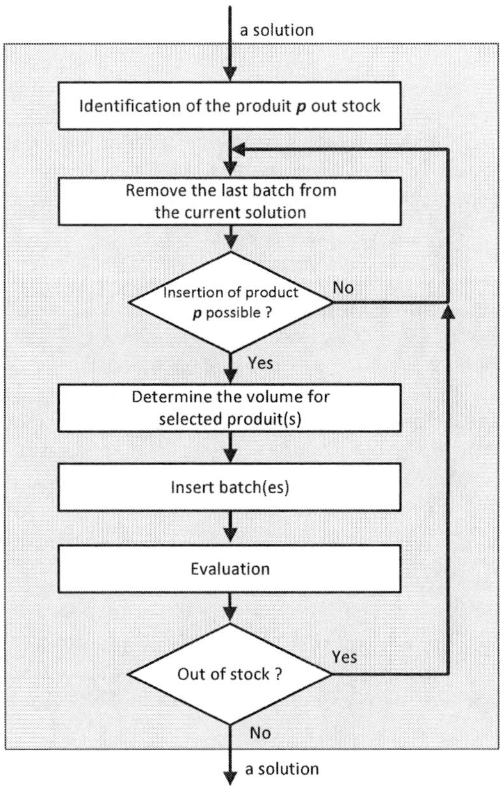

(b) Repair process

Figure 1: Construction method

3.3.1 The greedy algorithm

The greedy algorithm (Figure 1 - a) consists of several steps as follows:

- Step 1: selection of a product for the new batch

In this step, the product selection considers the autonomy of products. The autonomy of a product is measured from its inventory level. In order to increase the probability to get a feasible solution, we create a restricted candidate list (RCL) that contains several products with the smallest autonomy. The selection of a product in the RCL list is done in a random way.

- Step 2: Determine the volume of the new batch(es)

For each selected product, we create a new batch with the largest possible volume by considering the storage capacity and the maximum batch size.

The compatibility of products imposed by the matrix of forbidden product sequences is examined before insertion of the new batch. If the selected product is not compatible to the previous one, we use a tree structure to search a path between two products, and create a new batch for each product met on the path.

- Step 3: Insert new batch(es) into solution

All new batches are inserted iteratively in the current solution.

- Step 4: Evaluation

The daily demand satisfaction is examined and the total charging duration of batches is evaluated. The evaluation of the total charging duration takes into account of the pipeline stoppages duration when the inventory level of a product being unloaded reaches its storage capacity. In case of out of stock, the repair process will be applied. The algorithm reiterates until the time horizon is reached.

3.3.2 The repair process

As illustrated on Figure 1 (b), the repair process works with a remove-and-reinsert operator that extracts newly injected batches from the solution and tests another alternative path on the tree structure. If all alternative paths form the last batch are explored, then the last batch will be removed from the current solution and we restart the search of alternative paths. We repeat the same operations until a feasible path is found.

3.2. Evaluation function

The evaluation of a batch sequence consists of determining the charging and discharging time of each batch, of updating inventory levels and calculating the related costs. The evaluation function is composed of two steps: the first step determines the charging and discharging time of batches as soon as possible, and updates the inventory levels. The solution obtained is called a "forward solution"; the second step uses the solution obtained at the previous step. It pushes the discharging of batches at the end of horizon, while considering inventory levels and demand. The solution of this step is called a "backward solution".

3.3. Improvement procedure

The improvement procedure takes an initial solution generated by the construction method and improves it by adjusting the volume of batches. As stressed on Figure 2, it is composed of three groups of operators. Each group of operator is applied successively.

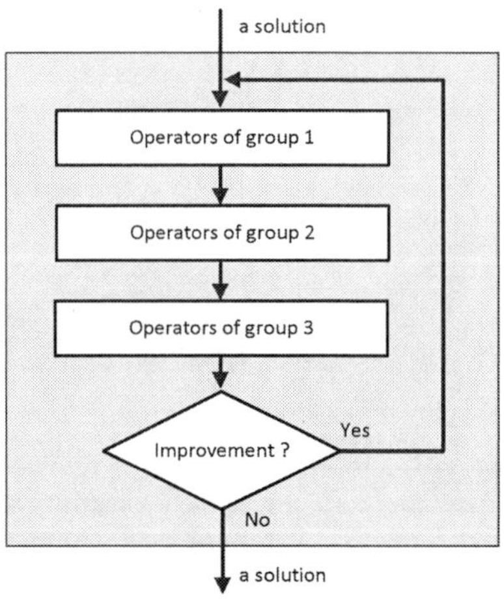

Figure 2: Improvement procedure

The operators of the first group consist of reducing the batch size to avoid the stoppage of pipeline caused by the excess of capacity and to reduce the storage cost. The second group increases the volume of batches in order to reduce the pipeline stoppage duration. The two first groups of operators use the same algorithm structure (algorithm 1). In the algorithm 1, the **estimate_residual_volume** function determines the residual volume of a batch i (line 5). The residual volume is a negative value for an operator of first group and a positive value for second group. The **Adjust_batch_size** function will reduce or increase the volume of batch (line 7) before the re-evaluation (line 8).

```
Algorithm 1: reduce/increase the volume of batches
1.  Data set
2.    { Batches, Var} : an evaluated solution
3.  Begin
4.    For i = | Batches | to 1 Do
5.       VR <- Estimate_residual_volume(Var,Batches,i)
6.       If VR ≠ 0 then
7.          Adjust_batch_size(Batches,i,VR)
8.          Var <- evaluation_function(Batches)
9.       End If
10.   End For
11.   Return {Batches, Var}
12. End
```

The last group of operators aims to transfer the volume between a pair of batches with same product. For a given pair, the residual volume to be transferred is determined by considering the remaining volume of the destination batch, the daily demand of the corresponding product and the last daily discharging volume of the origin batch. For a given origin batch, it may has several possible destination batches and the first-accept selection policy is applied.

4. Computational experiments

The proposed heuristic is implemented in Java and all tests are performed on a PC with an Intel Xeon E7-8890 (2.5 GHz) under Linux (CentOS 7.4 646bit). The number of used cores is set to 1. The computational experiments are based on the instance presented in MirHassani et al. (2013) [5], which is from a real-world case study from oil industry. In this instance, we consider a unidirectional One-to-One linear pipeline that transports six different products. The pipeline has a length of 147 km, a capacity of 18000 m^3, and an average transfer rate of 519.4 m^3/h.

Table 1: dataset related to products

Product Number	Volume max. (m^3)	Volume min. (m^3)	Monthly demand (m^3)	Storage capacity (m^3)	Initial inventory (m^3)
1	18000	17300	198043	81500	52397
2	16000	800	64800	32000	17565
3	16000	800	14642	24000	18569
4	16000	3800	68244	27800	19888
5	3440	860	10934	10320	10027
6	8200	4920	16955	13120	7309

The Table 1 illustrates the following data related to each product: the minimum/maximum volumes of a batch, the monthly demand, the storage capacity and the initial inventory. The planning time horizon is fixed to 30 days. Since the daily demands are not presented in the dataset, we consider that the daily demands are distributed uniformly over the time horizon. Moreover, it is assumed that the pipeline is initially filled with one product (usually the most requested product). The initial state of the pipeline therefore gives the first batch (batch number 1) to be unloaded. The settling time is set to 24 hours.

The matrix of compatibility for the succession of the two products is given in Table 2. The sequence of two successive products is authorized with a value of 1, otherwise 0. Note that the matrix is symmetric: for example, the product 1 can only be preceded or followed by the products 2, 3 or 4.

Table 2: Matrix of compatibility

		Product					
		1	2	3	4	5	6
Product	1	0	1	1	1	0	0
	2	1	0	0	0	0	0
	3	1	0	0	1	1	0
	4	1	0	1	0	1	0
	5	0	0	1	1	0	1
	6	0	0	0	0	1	0

The Table 3 gives the performance of improvement procedure with volume optimization operators. For this study, 10 solutions are generated using the construction method. For each initial solution, the volume of batches is optimized, without changing the sequence of product, using the MILP model (solved by Gurobi 8.1) presented in Bamoumen et al. (2019) [1]. We compared the result of the proposed improvement procedure to the result of the MILP. We can note that the proposed improvement procedure reaches the best optimal value for 8 solutions out of 10, and the average gap is 0.03%. In term of CPU time, the proposed improvement procedure is more efficient than the MILP model.

Table 3: Performance of improvement procedure

	Total cost			CPU Times (second)	
Solution	improvement procedure	MILP	GAP	improvement procedure	MILP
1	2 291 284	2 291 227	0.003%	0.171	105.97
2	1 965 257	1 965 257	**0.00%**	0.141	161.30
3	1 914 724	1 914 724	**0.00%**	0.062	125.32
4	1 864 525	1 864 525	**0.00%**	0.078	309.25
5	2 031 632	2 031 632	**0.00%**	0.078	374.74
6	2 256 208	2 256 208	**0.00%**	0.016	113.53
7	2 047 347	2 047 347	**0.00%**	0.031	158.76
8	1 894 927	1 894 927	**0.00%**	0.031	143.57
9	2 350 207	2 343 038	0.31%	0.016	391.71
10	1 877 224	1 877 224	**0.00%**	0.047	863.67
		Average :	0.03%	**0.0671**	274.78

Figure 3 illustrates the Pareto front between the total cost and the number of iterations of the proposed heuristic. Each point on the graph represents an improvement. The total number of iterations is fixed to 500 and it takes about 11 seconds. A strong convergence can be observed on the first iterations and it slows down significantly after about 15 first iterations.

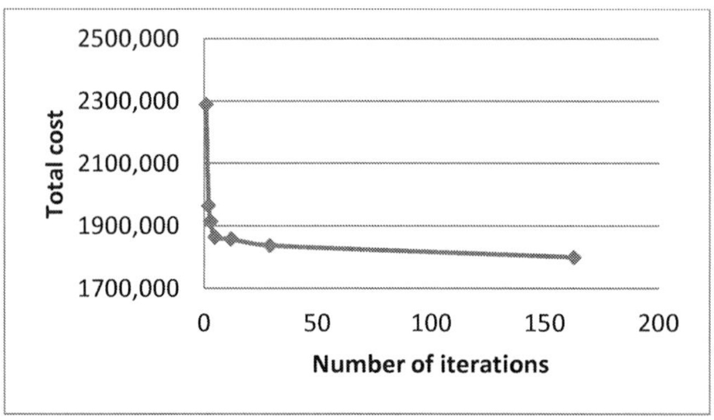

Figure 3: convergence of the proposed approach

5. Conclusion

In this paper, we propose an efficient heuristic for the multi-product straight pipeline scheduling problem. The heuristic is composed of a construction method and an improvement procedure. The construction method is a randomized greedy algorithm that choses randomly a product from a restricted candidate list (RCL) for a new batch. A repair process is proposed to favour the obtention of feasible solutions. The improvement procedure with volume optimization operators shows. The computational results show that it gives very competitive results.

Concerning the future work, we are interested in the creation of others improvement operators based on the sequence optimization firstly. Several techniques may be envisaged: for example, the use of a vector for sequence coding combined with permutation or crossover operators to implement a genetic algorithm. Other local search strategies (such as Path-relinking) can also be considered in the improvement step to intensify the exploration of solution space.

6. References

1. Bamoumen, M., Belil, S., Elfirdoussi, S., Ren, L., Tchernev, N.: A hybrid heuristic for the multi-product straight pipeline scheduling problem, 9th IFAC Triannual Conference on Manufacturing Modeling, Management and Control - MIM 2019, Berlin, 28-30 August (2019).
2. Cafaro, D.C., Cerdá, J.: Efficient tool for the scheduling of multiproduct pipelines and terminal operations, *Industrial & Engineering Chemistry Research*, vol. 47, n° 24, p. 9941–9956, (2008).
3. Dobson, G.: The cyclic lot scheduling problem with sequence-dependent setups, *Operations Research*, vol. 40, n° 4, p. 736–749, (1992).
4. Kirschstein, T.: Planning of multi-product pipelines by economic lot scheduling models, *European Journal of Operational Research*, vol. 264, n° 1, p. 327–339, (2018).
5. MirHassani, S.A., BeheshtiAsl, N.: A heuristic batch sequencing for multiproduct pipelines, *Computers & Chemical Engineering*, vol. 56, p. 58–67, (2013).
6. Moradi, S., MirHassani, S.A.: Transportation planning for petroleum products and integrated inventory management, *Applied Mathematical Modelling*, vol. 39, n° 23-24, p. 7630–7642, (2015).
7. Moradi, S., MirHassani, S.A.: Robust scheduling for multi-product pipelines under demand uncertainty, *The International Journal of Advanced Manufacturing Technology*, vol. 87, n° 9-12, p. 2541–2549, (2016).
8. Rejowski, R., Pinto, J.M.: A novel continuous time representation for the scheduling of pipeline systems with pumping yield rate constraints, *Computers & Chemical Engineering*, vol. 32, n° 4-5, p. 1042–1066, (2008).
9. Relvas, S., Barbosa-Póvoa, A.P.F., Matos, H.A.: Heuristic batch sequencing on a multiproduct oil distribution system, *Computers & Chemical Engineering*, vol. 33, n° 3, p. 712–730, (2009).
10. Relvas, S., Magatão, S.N.B., Barbosa-Póvoa, A.P.F.D., Neves, F.: Integrated scheduling and inventory management of an oil products distribution system, *Omega*, vol. 41, n° 6, p. 955–968, (2013).
11. Relvas, S., Matos, H.A., Barbosa-Póvoa, A.P.F., Fialho, J., Pinheiro, A.S.,: Pipeline scheduling and inventory management of a multiproduct distribution oil system, *Industrial & Engineering Chemistry Research*, vol. 45, n° 23, p. 7841–7855, (2006).
12. Sahebi, H., Nickel, S., Ashayeri, J.: Strategic and tactical mathematical programming models within the crude oil supply chain context—A review, *Computers & Chemical Engineering*, vol. 68, p. 56–77, (2014).
13. Sasikumar, M., Prakash, P.R., Patil, S.M., Ramani, S.: PIPES: A heuristic search model for pipeline schedule generation1, *Knowledge-Based Systems*, vol. 10, n° 3, p. 169–175, (1997).
14. Shah, N.: Mathematical programming techniques for crude oil scheduling, *Computers & Chemical Engineering*, vol. 20, p. S1227–S1232, (1996).

I L S 2020
INTERNATIONAL CONFERENCE ON INFORMATION SYSTEMS, LOGISTICS & SUPPLY CHAIN
Austin, Texas April 22-24, 2020

Biofuel Supply Chain Design Using Coffee Crop Residues: The Effect of a Dynamic Capacity Strategy on Sustainable Performance

Marcela María Morales-Chavez [1], William Sarache [2], Yasel Costa [3,4]

[1] Universidad Libre, Pereira, Colombia
[2] Universidad Nacional de Colombia, Manizales, Colombia
[3] MIT-Zaragoza Logistics Center, Zaragoza, Spain
[4] Universidad de Manizales, Manizales, Colombia

{marcelam.moralesc@unilibre.edu.co, wasarachec@unal.edu.co, ycosta@zlc.edu.es}

Abstract. Supply Chain Network Design (SCND) is a strategic decision aimed to establish network structure. Decisions such as facility locations, route selection, material flows, transportation mode selection, and inventory levels form part of SCND problems. However, optimization models that simultaneously consider capacity levels and facility locations as decision variables (dynamic strategy) are almost nonexistent. In particular, capacity allocation is a variable that significantly affects network structures and their sustainable performance. Therefore, the aim of this paper is to present an optimization model to support a biofuel SCND, using coffee residues from the Colombian context. The model addresses a dynamic capacity strategy (facility expansion or closure). When compared to fixed capacity strategies, dynamic capacity strategies present superior performance in both economic (net present value) and environmental dimensions. However, negative effects were observed in the social dimension. The proposed model is a useful tool for the establishment of long-term investment portfolios.

Keywords: supply chain network design, dynamic capacity, biofuel, sustainability, coffee residue.

1. Introduction

Supply chains may be defined as a group of arrangements that generate products and services, and which involve a number of players, from raw material producers to final consumers. Throughout the supply chain, material, money, and information flows are identified. These interact to generate value for clients and other stakeholders [1, 2]. Supply Chain Network Design (SCND), then, is a strategic decision which aims to establish network structure. Decisions such as facility locations, route selection, material flows, transportation mode selection, and inventory levels form part of SCND problems [3,4]. SCND demands the simultaneous evaluation between facility (capacity-location), transport, and inventory decisions [5,6].

Traditionally, economic efficiency has reigned as a performance measurement in supply chain design and management. However, from the so-called sustainability approach, environmental and social impacts have risen to greater prominence in recent years [7,8,9]. From said perspective, proper SCND requires the identification of the best configuration to balance economic (cost minimization), environmental goals (minimization of environmental impacts, such as the generation of greenhouse gases, energy and water consumption, pollution, etc.) and social goals (maximization of positive social impacts such as job creation, producer income, etc.) [10,11]. Said condition not only complicates decision making, but also implies the search for strategic design decision combinations to achieve a balance between economic, environmental, and social goals [12].

On the other hand, given global concerns regarding the generation of greenhouse gases caused by fossil fuel consumption, one global trend has focused on supply chain design for biofuel production [13]. According to [14], biofuel is a viable alternative for energy generation that also reduces environmental impacts. Specifically, the use of agricultural residue for bioethanol production has been identified as a promising energy alternative [15]. However, the biofuel-SCND problem, using crop residue, poses major mathematical challenges from a sustainability approach [16].

From the mathematical modelling perspective, typically, location and capacity decisions have been made from a static perspective. It is assumed that a given facility (e.g. a factory) is designed with a fixed capacity and located in a certain area (city or region), such that said decisions cannot change over project lifetimes (see Figure 1a). Said assumption is unrealistic, insofar as the fact that a facility may require capacity changes over time, owing to long-term market fluctuations (demand increases or decreases) and/or supply restrictions (especially when the raw material is an agricultural residue). As such, facility capacities may be either expanded or reduced, or plants may even be closed if their operation is no longer viable. Capacity may also expand at the same or a different location (see Figure 1b). Thus, SCND, considering dynamic facility strategies, permits the establishment of a structure and more realistic investment plan.

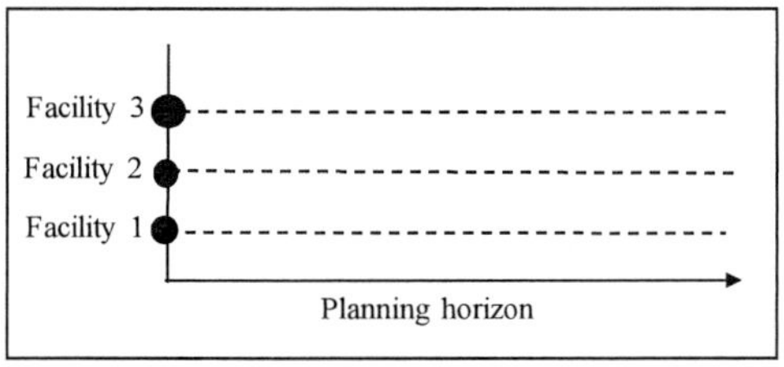

Figure 1a. Fixed capacity strategy

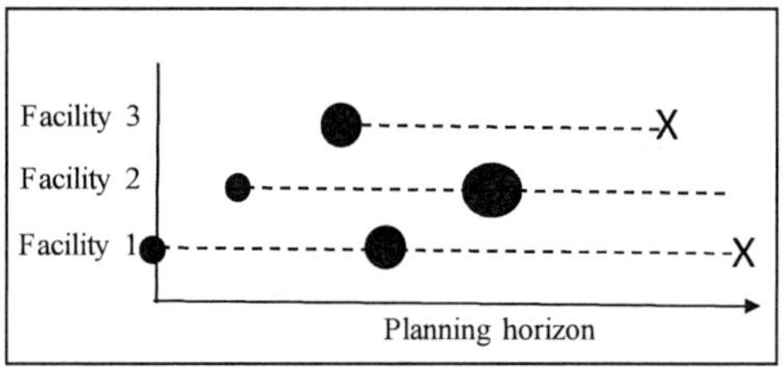

Figure 1b. Dynamic capacity strategy

According to [17], "*Capacity strategy includes a number of interrelated decisions, which include defining the overall scale of the operation, the number and size of the sites between which capacity is distributed, the specific activities allocated to each site, when capacity levels should be changed, how big each step change should be, and the location of each site*". This concept clearly implies the need to consider facility strategy (capacity-location) from a dynamic perspective. Additionally, said strategic decision "*...usually involves deciding when capacity levels should be changed (up or down), how big each change step should be and overall how fast capacity levels should change*" [17].

However, the literature review conducted in the present investigation revealed that the generation of models considering dynamic facility strategies is practically nonexistent. In [7], [9], [15], [18], [19], and [20], relevant biofuel-SCND models may be found. However, none of these have addressed dynamic capacity strategies (expansion or closure). The majority of the articles analyzed consider facility opening with fixed capacities in the t = 0 period, and lack analysis of the effects of inventory or transport decisions. They further fail to analyze the effects of a fixed capacity strategy in the chain's sustainable performance. Only in [21] was the possibility of facility opening and expansion considered, while the possibility of closure was not.

Thus, the objective of the present document is to analyze, on one hand, the effect of dynamic facility strategy on inventory and transport decisions, and on the other, the effect thereof on supply chain performance, in economic, environmental, and social terms. To achieve said goal, a Multiple Objective Mixed Integer Linear Programming model (MOMILP) was developed for the design of a sustainable supply chain for bioethanol production, considering multiple raw materials (agricultural residue), in order to analyze strategic decisions in the long term (multi-period SCND). The model contemplates a four-echelons supply chain, which includes raw material providers, gathering centers, production plants, and blending centers.

By applying the model to a case study in the Colombian coffee region, using coffee residue, it was possible to establish a dynamic supply chain structure which permitted capacity changes (opening, expansion, or closing) in different locations, throughout time. Thus, a more realistic investment portfolio could be provided to decision makers. When compared to a fixed capacity strategy, the dynamic capacity strategy performed better in the economic (net present value) and environmental dimensions. However, negative effects were observed in the social dimension (job creation).

This document has been structured as follows: Section 2 presents the fundamental aspects of the optimization model. Section 3 shows the results obtained from model application to a Colombian case study. Finally, Section 4 reveals the most relevant conclusions and proposes some lines of investigation.

2. Model description

Due the the complexity of the mathematical model, in this section we provide a general description of its main components. Supply chain configuration requires a complex combinatorial problem which seeks to establish the appropriate mixture of facility, transport, and inventory decisions that would lead to a proper balance between economic, environmental, and social goals. For said purpose, a Multiple Objective Mixed Integer Linear Programming model (MOMILP) was proposed to structure a bioethanol production supply chain with three coffee residues (stems, pulp, and mucilage). As observed in Figure 2, the supply chain consisted of four echelons: providers (farms which produce the agricultural residue; *Fi*), gathering centers (receipt, pre-treatment, and storage; *Gj*), biorefineries (bioethanol production; *Bk*), and blending facilities (mixing bioethanol with gasoline, in accordance with national regulations; *Mm*).

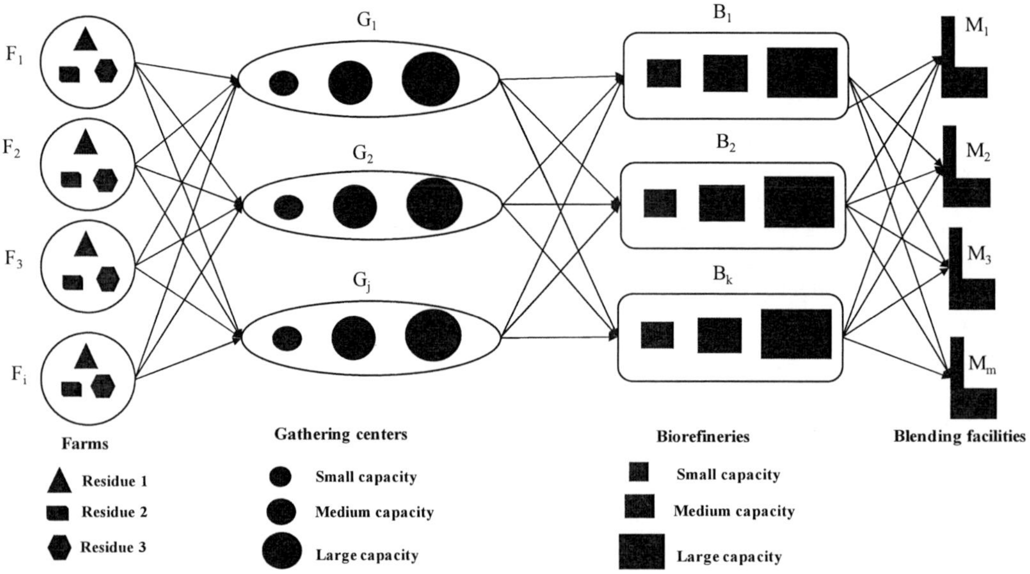

Figure 2. Supply chain configuration

The objective of the model was to determine the material flows, capacity, and location of facilities (using a dynamic strategy) and the inventory levels that would achieve an acceptable balance between the economic, environmental, and social goals. For gathering centers and biorefineries, the model considered three capacity alternatives for each of these: small, medium, and large. The model's assumptions were the following: 1) four echelons (*Fi, Gj, Bk, and Mm*); 2) three raw material types; 3) known main residue characteristics (raw materials) (e.g. degradation rate, seasonality, and yield); and 4) multiperiod. Given the model's complexity, a brief explanation is provided as follows:

Considering a multi-objective approach, three objective functions conform the model in line with the sustainability approach (F_1, F_2 and F_3). The objective function F_1 sought maximization of the supply chain's net present value (income-costs). Incomes include bioethanol sales and the salvage value when facilities are closed (gathering centers and biorefineries); in turn, costs are represented by raw material purchasing, opening and closing of facilities, capacity expansion, variable cost, inventory, and transportation. The objective function F_2 was oriented toward the minimization of negative environmental impacts (water and air contamination caused by farmers, facilities and transport). The objective function F_3 worked toward the maximization of positive social impacts in terms of job creation and contribution to food security.

The model contemplated four groups of constraints related to facilities, capacity, inventory, and transport. Regarding facilities, a dynamic capacity strategy is proposed. In this way, gathering centers and biorefineries can be opened, expanded or closed throughout the planning horizon. If any facility is closed after having expanded its capacity, that expansion must cease in the remaining planning horizon. This condition provides a more realistic analysis of the supply chain performance in terms of economic, environmental and social impacts. Also, facilities can be supplied by multiple providers. Due to speedy rate of decomposition, pulp and mucilage are directly sent to the gathering centers; therefore, inventory constraints only consider the required levels of stems in these facilities. Also, in order to avoid exceeding the facilities capacity, and also, the normal operations in the supply chain, material flow was restricted.

3. Case study and results

The model described above was applied to a real case in Colombia. In this country, all bioethanol is produced from sugar cane, which affects the internal price of said raw material. The objective was to study the structure of a supply chain using coffee residue (stems, mucilage, and pulp), as an alternative biomass for bioethanol obtention. Owing to its geographical and climatological characteristics, Colombia is the third largest global producer of coffee [22]. Here, the main coffee harvest occurs between September and December, and there is a secondary harvest between April and June. Mucilage and pulp are generated, then, from these two harvests. However, stem production occurs differently, as they are generated as a result of crop renovation. It is estimated that 25% of farms renew their coffee trees on a yearly basis [23]. The application of the model, in this case study, was based upon two principal motivations derived from literature review: 1) the need to explore new, second-generation biomass (agricultural waste) for bioethanol production [15], and 2) the research challenge, owing to the complexity of those supply chains that employ agricultural residue [24].

In order to apply the mathematical model, coffee farmers were grouped into five zones (F_1....F_5). Four location alternatives for gathering centers (G_1...G_4) and three possible regions for biorefinery locations (B1...B3) were considered. Finally, zones of demand were grouped into three regions: north (M_1), central (M_2), and south (M_3). Parameters were obtained from governmental (Colombian Ministry of Mines and Energy, Colombian Ministry of Transportation) and non-governmental (National Coffee Growers Federation of Colombia) information sources, as well as previous studies carried out by [25] and [26]. The planning horizon was set at 20 years, divided into 240 months. The model was solved using the ε-restriction method, and was implemented using GAMS 23.5.1 computational tool. A model with 96,363 variables and 56,992 constraints was obtained. This result permitted the identification of 12 non-dominated solutions on the Pareto front. Given that the objective of the present article was to analyze the effect of the dynamic capacity strategy on supply chain structure and performance, non-dominated solution four was selected to illustrate the most relevant results. The model provided a dynamic structure, establishing the moments of facilities opening, with the possibility of expansion or closing throughout the planning horizon (see Figure 3).

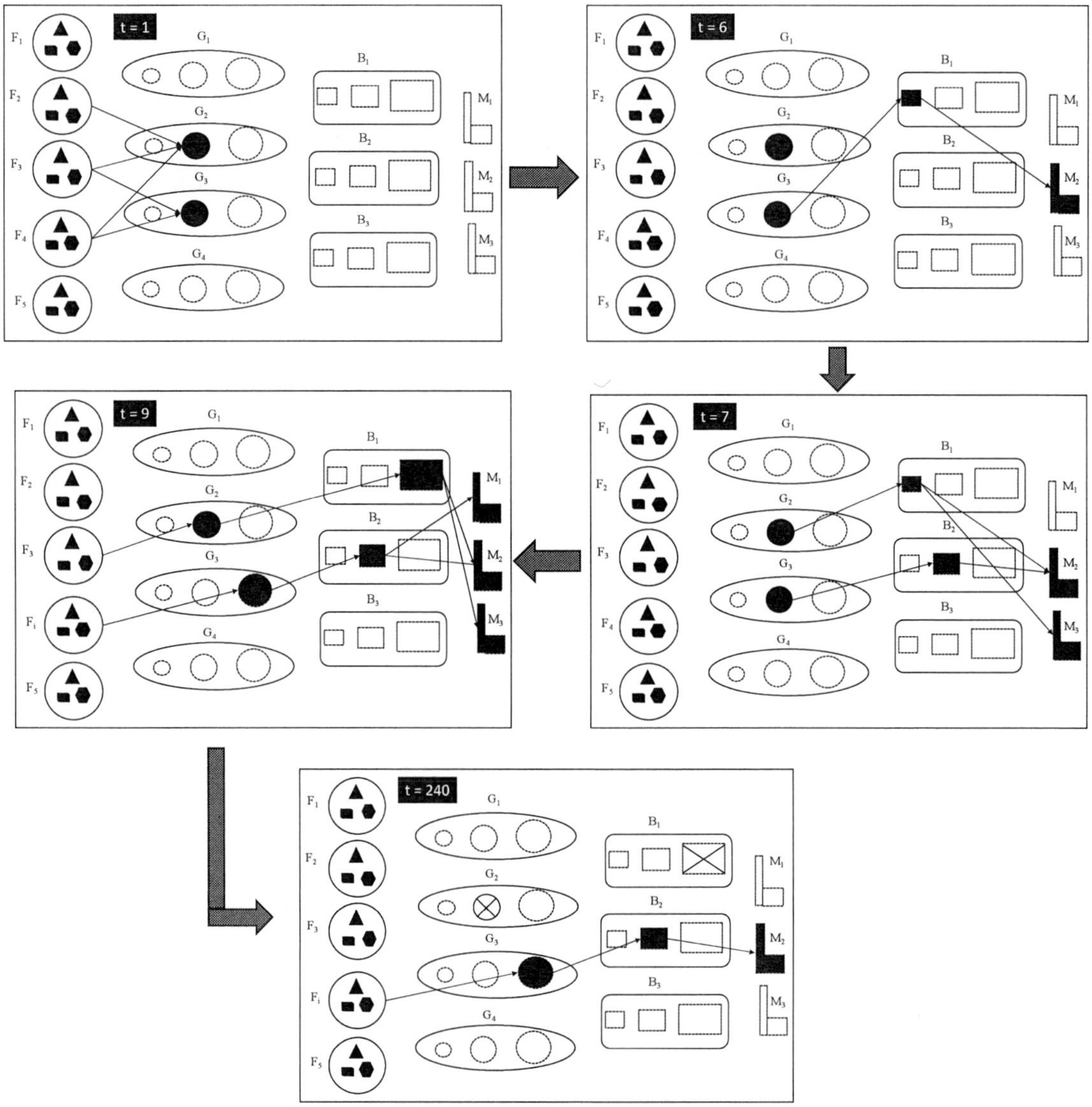

Figure 3. Biofuel supply chain dynamic configuration using coffee crop residue

As observed in Figure 3, in the period t = 1, two medium-sized gathering centers were opened at the G_1 and G_3 locations. The G_1 center was supplied by the farms located at F_2, F_3, and F_5, while the G_3 center was supplied by farms at F_4 and F_5. In the period t = 6, a small biorefinery was opened at B_1, which was supplied by G_2, and provided bioethanol to the blending facility located at M_2. During the 7, 9, and 240 periods, the supply chain saw structural changes which permitted the establishment of times for capacity expansion or contraction. For example, at t = 240, the supply chain was comprised of a medium-sized gathering center located at G_3, which was supplied by farms at F_4, and provided for a medium-sized biorefinery located at B_2. This biorefinery supplied the blending facility located at M_2. Further, during this period, facilities located at G_2 and B_1 were closed. Thus, more realistic information may be provided to support the investment decisions making.

3.1 Dynamic capacity strategy vs. fixed capacity strategy: effect on supply chain performance

A comparative analysis between fixed (traditionally used in the literature) and dynamic capacity strategies was performed. The results proved the benefits of a dynamic capacity strategy, in terms of supply chain costs. For the case analyzed, the total unitary bioethanol cost was $US 0.39/liter with a dynamic capacity strategy, while with a fixed strategy, it increased to $US 0.43/liter. Figure 4 presents the comparison of the costs involved in each strategy, in terms of facilities (fixed and variable costs), transport, and inventory. Although the transport and inventory cost differences are relatively small, the greatest advantages of a dynamic capacity strategy are observed in facility costs.

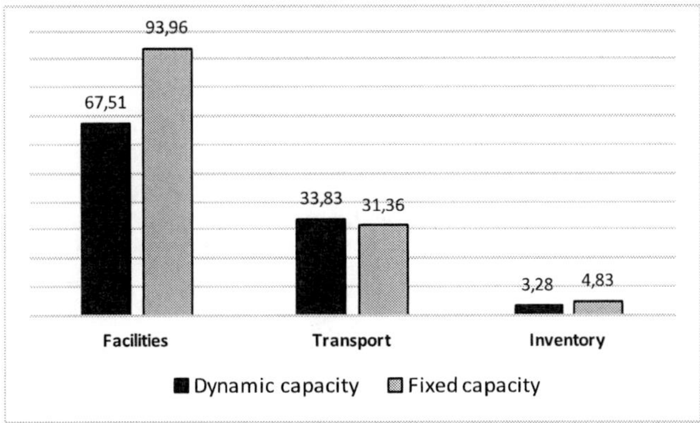

Figure 4. The effect of capacity strategy on supply chain costs (USD$ millions)

On the other hand, on analysis of the effect of each capacity strategy on sustainable supply chain performance, notable differences were encountered between the economic, environmental, and social dimensions. As observed in Figure 5, a dynamic capacity strategy presents NPV (Net Present Value) and environmental impact advantages. In this case, an adequate facility investment plan, adjusted to a dynamic strategy, would permit capacity growth, together with long-term market fluctuations. Thus, cost overruns would be avoided for underutilized facilities. In terms of environmental performance, a dynamic capacity strategy would generate fewer environmental effects, given that water consumption and gas emissions would only grow if the system required production increases and additional material transport. A fixed capacity strategy, conversely, would generate greater benefits from the social point of view, as one of the performance dimensions is job generation. Undoubtedly, a dynamic capacity strategy, in which gradual capacity growth and the ability to close facilities is considered would most heavily affect the social dimension.

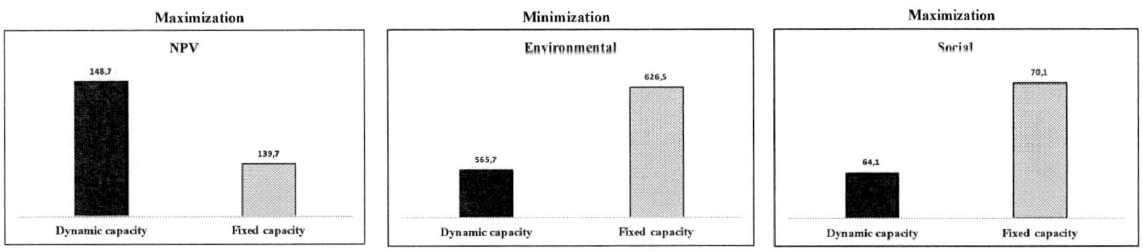

Figure 5. The effect of capacity strategy on supply chain performance

4. Conclusions

Since the literature review revealed that models considering dynamic facility strategies are practically nonexistent, the proposed model contributes in the field of SCND and, in particular, in the context of SCND from agricultural residues. The proposed dynamic capacity strategy (facility aperture and closure) provides a flexible and realistic investment plan to support long-term decision making. Although the model was designed for a biofuel production chain from agricultural waste, this strategy may be applicable in other supply chains. Results indicate that a dynamic capacity strategy outperforms other strategies, in terms of supply chain cost. In particular, relevant differences were found regarding facility costs. Dynamic capacity strategy exhibits superior performance in terms of NPV and environmental impact. However, for job creation purposes (social impact), a fixed strategy seems to be more attractive. Future lines of research might include the incorporation of new aspects, in order to improve this model's practical contribution. For instance, due to the characteristics of crop residues, their collection from farms requires the inclusion of a vehicle routing problem. SCND that considers stochastic analysis is a research topic that requires further investigation, in the context of agricultural residue. Regarding sustainability, aspects related to positive environmental impacts generated by residue use, as well as the incorporation of new social variables, pose challenges of note, from the mathematical perspective. Finally, the effect of a dynamic capacity strategy on supply chain performance can be studied in other contexts.

Acknowledgments

The authors thank Colciencias (Fondo Nacional de Financiamiento para la Ciencia, la Tecnología y la Innovación "Francisco José de Caldas") for its financial support (Project 111971551628). We also acknowledge the institutional support provided by Universidad Nacional de Colombia and Universidad Libre.

5. References

1. Council of Supply Chain Management Professionals. CSCMP Supply Chain Management Definitions and Glossary, https://cscmp.org
2. Oliveira, J. B., Lima, R. S., Montevechi, J. A. B.: Perspectives and relationships in Supply Chain Simulation: A systematic literature review. Simulation Modelling Practice and Theory, 62, 166--191 (2016).
3. Khatami, M., Mahootchi, M., Farahani, R.Z..: Benders' decomposition for concurrent redesign of forward and closed-loop supply chain network with demand and return uncertainties. Transp. Res. Part E: Logistics Transp. Rev. 79, 1--21 (2015).
4. Morales-Chavez, M.M., Sarache, W., Costa-Salas, Y.: Towards a comprehensive model of a biofuel supply chain optimization from coffee crop residues. Transp. Res. Part E: Logistics Transp. Rev. 116, 136--162 (2018).
5. Ballou, R.: Business Logistic and Supply Chain Management: planning, organizing, and controlling the supply chain. Prenctice Hall, N.J. (2004).
6. Baghalian, A., Rezapour, S., Farahani, R. Z.: Robust supply chain network design with service level against disruptions and demand uncertainties: A real-life case. European Journal of Operational Research, 227(1), 199--215 (2013).
7. Bairamzadeh, S., Pishvaee, M.S., Saidi-Mehrabad, M. Multiobjective robust possibilistic programming approach to sustainable bioethanol supply chain design under multiple uncertainties. Ind. Eng. Chem. 55 (1), 237--256 (2016)
8. Pishvaee, M.S., Razmi, J., Torabi, S.A.: An accelerated Benders decomposition algorithm for sustainable supply chain network design under uncertainty: A case study of medical needle and syringe supply chain. Transp. Res. Part E: Logistics Transp. Rev, 67, 14--38 (2014).
9. You, F., Tao, L., Graziano, D.J., Snyder, S.W.: Optimal design of sustainable cellulosic biofuel supply chains: Multiobjective optimization coupled with life cycle assessment and input-output analysis. AIChE J., 58 (4), 1157--1180 (2012).
10. Giannakis, M.,Papadopoulos, T. (2016). Supply chain sustainability: A risk management approach. International Journal of Production Economics, 171, 455--470 (2016).
11. Barbosa-Póvoa, A. P., da Silva, C., Carvalho, A.: Opportunities and Challenges in Sustainable Supply Chain: An Operations Research Perspective. European Journal of Operational Research, 268(2), 399—431 (2017).
12. Eskandarpour, M., Dejax, P., Miemczyk, J., Péton, O.: Sustainable supply chain network design: An optimization-oriented review. Omega, 54, 11--32 (2015).
13. Fattahi, M., Govindan, K.: A multi-stage stochastic program for the sustainable design of biofuel supply chain networks under biomass supply uncertainty and disruption risk: A real-life case study. Transportation Research Part E: Logistics Transp. Rev, 118, 534--567 (2018).
14. Azadeh, A., Vafa Arani, H.: Biodiesel supply chain optimization via a hybrid system dynamics-mathematical programming approach. Renewable Energy 93, 383--403 (2016).
15. Ng, R.T.L., Maravelias, C.T.: Design of cellulosic ethanol supply chains with regional depots. Ind. Eng. Chem. Res. 55 (12), 3420--3432 (2016).
16. Costa, Y., Duarte, A., Sarache, W.: A decisional simulation-optimization framework for sustainable facility location of a biodiesel plant in Colombia. J. Cleaner Prod. 167, 174--191(2017).
17. Slack, N., Lewis, M.: Operations Strategy (Third edit). Pearson Education, U.K. (2011).
18. Ghaderi, H., Moini, A., Pishvaee, M.S.: A multi-objective robust possibilistic programming approach to sustainable switchgrass-based bioethanol supply chain network design. J. Cleaner Prod. 179, 368--406 (2018).
19. Lin, T., Rodríguez, L.F., Shastri, Y.N., Hansen, A.C., Ting, K.C.: Integrated strategic and tactical biomass-biofuel supply chain optimization. Bioresour. Technol.156, 256–266 (2014).

20. Ekşioğlu, S.D., Acharya, A., Leightley, L.E., Arora, S.: Analyzing the design and management of biomass-to-biorefinery supply chain. Comput. Ind. Eng. 57 (4), 1342–1352 (2009).
21. Moradi Nasab, N., Amin-Naseri, M.R.: Designing an integrated model for a multi-period, multi-echelon and multi-product petroleum supply chain. Energy 114, 708--733 (2016).
22. International Coffe Organization.Total exports by all exporting countries, www.ico.org
23. Federación Nacional de Cafeteros de Colombia, www.federaciondecafeteros.org/
24. Tsolakis, N.K., Keramydas, C.A., Toka, A.K., Aidonis, D.A., Iakovou, E.T.: Agrifood supply chain management: A comprehensive hierarchical decision-making framework and a critical taxonomy. Biosystems Engineering, 120, 47--64 (2014).
25. Duarte, A.E.: Análisis técnico y económico para el diseño preliminar de tres plantas de producción de biocombustibles a partir de residuos de café. Informe de Investigación. Universidad Nacional de Colombia (2017).
26. Trujillo, M.: Análisis técnico y económico para el diseño preliminar de 3 centros de acopio para el almacenamiento de los residuos de café. Informe de Investigación. Universidad Nacional de Colombia (2018).

I L S 2020
INTERNATIONAL CONFERENCE ON INFORMATION SYSTEMS, LOGISTICS & SUPPLY CHAIN
Austin, Texas April 22-24, 2020

Collaborative Supply Chain Distribution Planning under uncertainty

Sanaa Tiss[1], Jacques Lamothe [2], Caroline Thierry [3]

[1] Universite de Toulouse, Centre Génie Industriel, IMT Mines Albi, Albi, France
[2] Universite de Toulouse, Centre Génie Industriel, IMT Mines Albi, Albi, France
[3] Universite de Toulouse, IRIT, Université Toulouse Jean Jaurès,Toulouse, France
{sanaa.tiss@mines-albi.fr, jacques.lamothe@mines-albi.fr, caroline.thierry@univ-tlse2.fr}

Abstract. The need for agility in a collaborative supply chain leads to rescheduling decisions in order to align the plans of the various SC partners throughout the planning rolling horizon. However, these decisions affect the nervousness of the system and do not necessarily change much in terms of network performance, hence the need to improve planning decision-making processes. In this work, we propose a decision support interface that will provide the decision-maker with a dual perspective for evaluating his/her planning decisions. On the one hand, the impact of rescheduling decisions on the nervousness and instability of the planning system and, on the other hand, the impact of these changes on the system's performance and risk assessment considering the uncertainties of the planning parameters. This will help the decision-maker in finding the right compromise between these two levels of assessment.

Keywords: Decision Support Interface, Collaborative SC Planning, Planning Assessment.

1. Introduction

In a collaborative supply chain network consisting of manufacturing units (plants) and distribution units (CDC and subsidiaries) (see Figure 1), planners at the different nodes of the supply chain are collaborative partners in a planning process. Their objectives are to align their different plans and avoid stock shortages and overstocks at the ends of the supply chain. As a result, they achieve a high service level and low overall costs throughout the network.

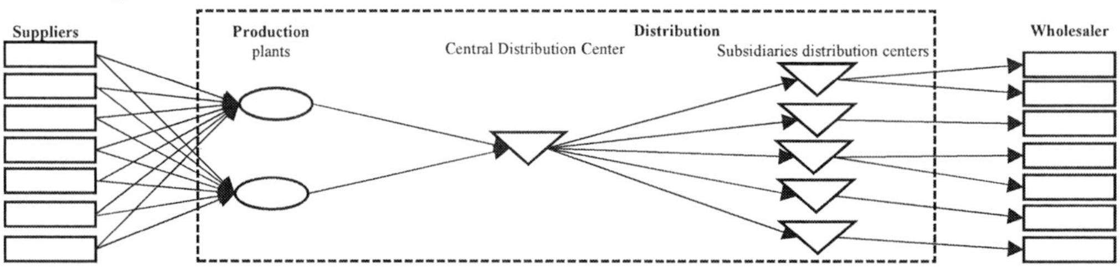

Figure 1: Supply Chain Distribution system

In this article our focus will be on the distribution system (i.e [1]). In this system, the Central Distribution Center has the richest view of the entire supply chain in the SC planning system.

SC collaboration has been widely discussed in literature and different types of collaboration in supply chain network were identified. In our study, the various planners collaborate in a tactical SC planning process (see Figure 2), but each partner organizes his activities and retains responsibility for his decisions. This type of collaboration was called in [2] "Information Exchange" and the main characteristics were that *"retailer and supplier still order independently, yet exchange demand information and action plans in order to align their forecasts for capacity and long-term planning.* ". In [3], a typology of SC's collaborative approaches was also identified. But this typology was linked to the level of the decisions involved in a collaboration. The tactical level refers to the type called "Collaborative event management" which is mainly characterized by the fact that *"activities tend to be more oriented toward problem prevention, identification and resolution than collaborative transaction management.* ".

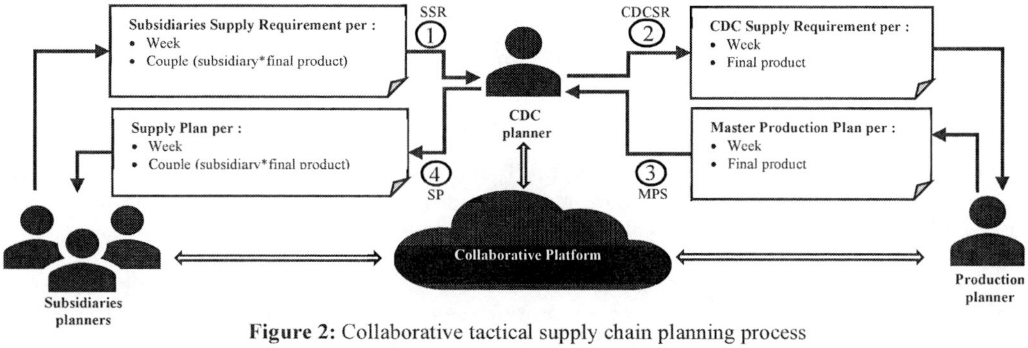

Figure 2: Collaborative tactical supply chain planning process

In the collaborative SC planning process above, Subsidiaries planners send out desired supply plans (SSR) based on sales forecasts and market information at the beginning of each month. According to his internal needs planning and replenishment strategies at the plant, the CDC supply planner sends the desired receipts (CDCSR) to the plant. According to his load/capacity adequacy, the production planners send his Master Production schedule (MPS) in return. Based on this response and the CDC's resources, the supply planner decides on the supply plans (SP) for each subsidiary.
However, the exchanged plans on which the decision makers are based to plan their activities are uncertain and may change over time. Therefore, for the sake of agility, these plans are reviewed weekly in order to reflect unplanned events.

The decision to reschedule or accept an exceptional request from another partner in the supply chain becomes more difficult when a change in forecasts could affect the stability of all the supply chain and increase the nervousness of the system. As a result, the need for anticipation increases to avoid the repetitive insignificant changes and to have more robust plans against uncertainties.
In literature several strategies dealing with nervousness exist such as: Freezing the Schedule Within the Planning Horizon, Lot-for-Lot Policy, Safety Stocks and Change Cost Procedure [4] [5]. These strategies are already being used in these collaborative networks, but do not seem sufficient. Other works like [6] assess the impact of the operating environment on MRP system nervousness based on that propose several dampening strategies to deal with this nervousness. More recent works deals with nervousness differently by considering uncertainties in demand. [7] and [8] consider uncertainties in demand (stochastic) and propose a model that aims to mitigate nervousness without excessive costs. These models have not been integrated with others to optimize decision-making.

In our case, we assess the nervousness of the system as well as the instability of the master plans at each rescheduling cycle. Furthermore, we consider uncertainties in demand also in receipts in order to assess SC risks .We use an interval representation approach to model the uncertainty of these parameters [9].
We consider two dimensions of the nervousness assessment: the occurrence of planning changes (setups)[7] and disruption planned quantities[7]. Those two dimensions are respectively called "setup-oriented planning instability" and "quantity-oriented planning instability" in [10]. However, instability in our work quantify the variations in the programmed quantities around the average programmed quantity per period related to a plan. This measure is used to assess the stability of a plan following smoothing decisions. In a decision support interface, these indicators will be integrated with other system performance evaluation indicators to help the decision-maker decide on relevant changes and effectively manage resources.

For the remainder of this article, the focus will be on **Decision 4 (SP)** of the collaborative planning process in Figure 2 of the **CDC supply planner** decision-making process. The rest of the paper is organized as follows. In the next section, we present the structure of the proposed support decision platform and its different modules. In section 3, we take a user perspective to describe an experience using this platform. Finally, in Section 4, conclusions and future research directions are discussed.

2. Decision support for distribution planning under uncertainty

2.1. General presentation of the tool structure

The idea in this paper is to provide the decision maker a decision support platform. The objective of this platform is not to find the optimal decision (Supply Plan) or to give the possible solutions or paths. The platform will generate different indicators by confronting the decision to the possible scenarios of deviations of the received plans in order to help the decision maker to evaluate his plans and his rescheduling decisions.
The supply planner receives the planning from the other decision-makers in the supply chain (prod planner and subsidiaries planners). The received plans (MPS) and Subsidiary Supply Requirements (SSR) are deterministic plans. By applying an uncertainty model to these plans, a set of scenarios can be generated to be used in the supply planner decisions support.

Two main modules are identified in the backend program of the decision support platform architecture (see Figure 3). The first module called scenario generator which generates from the nominal values of a received plan at least two scenarios (min and max) while having knowledge about the uncertainty related to these data previously developed and ready to be integrated as an input to this module. Those scenarios are used in the second module called the decision evaluator to assess the decisions (Supply Plans) and generate different indicators. These modules are used indirectly for front-end services.

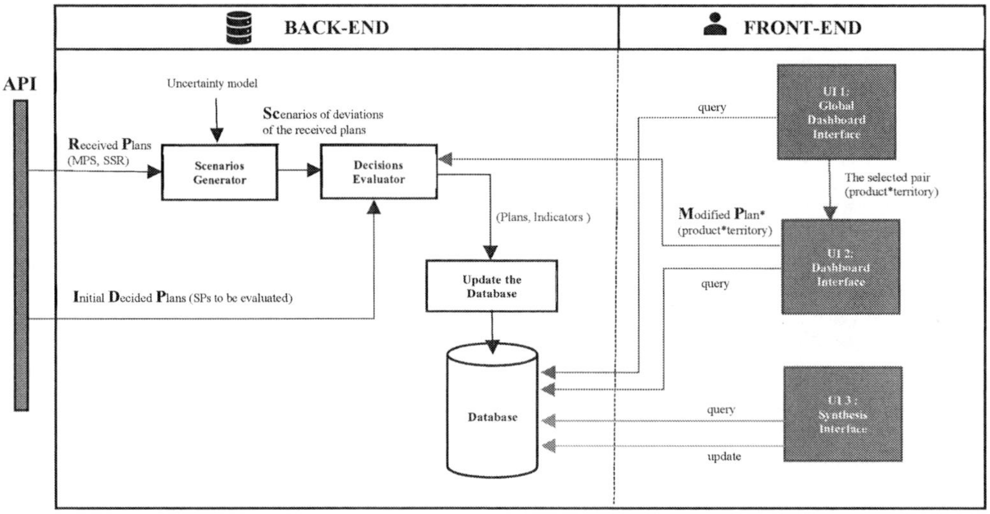

Figure 3: Support decision making interface architecture

Users interact directly with the front-end application. Three main **U**ser **I**nterfaces/services are identified. **UI 1** provides an overview of the evaluation of decisions made for the current rescheduling cycle and allows the decision-maker to choose the focus scale of the evaluation. This choice will be the entry of user **UI 2** which will allow the user to modify his decision via a modification sub-interface and re-evaluate it again with the support of a detailed assessment view. All tests and modifications are saved, and a summary of all tests is always available with the main indicators generated during the evaluation in the **UI 3** which facilitate comparison between decisions. Re-accessing the details of the evaluations is also possible for a final validation of the chosen decision. The interface is a graphical interface that will be connected to the ERP collaborative interface for initialization of the decision support system.

From a user point of view, the main features of this interface are the simplicity of use and the readability of information. In addition, the user will be able to understand and interpret the information without the need for advanced statistical knowledge. In addition, the indicator-chart link helps the decision-maker to easily identify the default location where action should be taken to improve the relevance of planning decisions.

2.2. Uncertainty modeling and planning decision assessment

Table 1: Notation

	Definition
Index	
c	Rescheduling cycle
t	Period
j	Product
i	Subsidiary
$IJ_{i,j}$	The set of subsidiaries consuming the product j
Parameters	
n	Planning horizon length
$d_{ij,c,t}$	Supply requirements of the subsidiary i of the product j for the period t in the cycle c at the date of exit from the CDC to i
$m_{j,c,t}$	Master production schedule of the period t at c to date of availability at the CDC
$w_{j,c,t}$	Production delivery in progress of the period t at c to date of availability at the CDC
$o_{j,c,t}$	Objective stock of the product j for the period t at c
$x_{ij,c,t}$	Supply plan for the subsidiary i of the period t at c
$ps_{j,c,t}$	Projected stock of product j for the period t at c

2.2.1. Uncertainty modeling

We consider the Supply Requirement of Subsidiaries (SSR) and the Master Production Schedule (MPS) as subject of uncertainty. The supply plans (SP) are the decisions to be evaluated.

Regarding uncertainty modeling, we consider the simplest approach for representing uncertainty which is intervals representation: $d_{ij,c,t}(S) \in [\underline{d_{ij,c,t}}, \overline{d_{ij,c,t}}]$; $m_{j,c,t}(S) \in [\underline{m_{j,c,t}}, \overline{m_{j,c,t}}]$.
We define SSR(S) and MPS(S) as possible plans related to scenario S, such as: SSR(S) = $((d_{ij,c,t}(S))_{t\in[T]=\{c,\dots,t+n-1\}})$ and MPS(S) = $((m_{j,c,t}(S))_{t\in[T]})$
In the interval, we consider the extreme scenarios S (minimum and maximum) in addition to the nominal value actually programmed. The combinations of scenarios C1=$((\overline{m_{j,c,t}})_{t\in[T]} ; (\underline{\sum_{i\in IJ_{i,j}} d_{ij,c,t}})_{t\in[T]})$ and C2=$((\underline{m_{j,c,t}})_{t\in[T]}; (\overline{\sum_{i\in IJ_{i,j}} d_{ij,c,t}})_{t\in[T]})$ are identified as the worst-case scenarios, respectively, the first linked to a high risk of overstock and the second linked to a high risk of shortage at CDC level.

$D_{IJ,c,t} = \sum_{k=c}^{t} \sum_{i\in IJ_{i,j}} d_{ij,c,k}$ *and* $M_{j,c,t} = \sum_{k=c}^{t} m_{j,c,k}$. $D_{IJ,p,t}$ and $M_{j,p,t}$ are respectively the cumulative total supply requirements of the product j up to the period t at c and the cumulative master production schedule up to the period t at c.

2.2.2. Decision assessment under uncertainty

For planning the distribution activities, we consider a classic DRP planning model that is not the subject of this article. From initial plans proposed by the planning system, the decision-maker decides on supply plans for each subsidiary. Based on the generated scenarios of the received plans from other SC partners, we evaluate these decisions on different levels.

$$\text{System nervousness 1} = \frac{\sum_{t=c}^{c+n-1} number\ of\ set\ ups}{n \times number\ of\ rescheduling\ cycle} \quad \textbf{(1)}$$

$$\text{System nervousness 2} = \sum_{\forall c>1} \frac{\sum_{t=c}^{c+n-2} |x_{ij,c,t} - x_{ij,c-1,t}|}{\sum_{t=c}^{c+n-1} x_{ij,c,t}} \quad \textbf{(2)}$$

$$\text{Plan instability} = \frac{\sum_{t=c}^{c+n-1} |x_{ij,c,t} - A_{ij,c,t}|}{\sum_{t=c}^{c+n-1} x_{ij,c,t}};\ A_{ij,c,t} = \frac{\sum_{t=c}^{c+n-1} x_{ij,c,t}}{n} \quad (3)$$

$$\text{Subsidiary satisfaction} = \frac{\sum_{t=c}^{c+n-1} x_{ij,c,t}}{\sum_{t=c}^{c+n-1} d_{ij,c,t}} \quad (4)$$

$$\text{Bullwhip effect} = \frac{instability\ of\ SSR}{instability\ of\ SP} = \frac{\sum_{t=c}^{c+n-1} |d_{ij,c,t} - R_{ij,c,t}|}{\sum_{t=c}^{c+n-1} |x_{ij,c,t} - A_{ij,c,t}|};\ R_{ij,c,t} = \frac{\sum_{t=c}^{c+n-1} d_{ij,c,t}}{n} \quad (5)$$

$\forall s \in S$:

$$ps_{j,c,t}(s) = ps_{j,c,t-1}(s) + m_{j,c,t}(s) + w_{j,c,t} - \sum_{i \in IJ_{i,j}} x_{ij,c,t} \quad (6)$$

$$\text{Unavailability risk} = \sum_{s \in S} \frac{\sum_{t \in [c,c+n[; x_{ij,c,t} < d_{ij,c,t}(s)} |d_{ij,c,t}(s) - x_{ij,c,t}|}{\sum_{t=c}^{c+n-1} d_{ij,c,t}(s)} \quad (7)$$

$$\text{Shortage risk} = \sum_{s \in S} \frac{\sum_{t \in [c,c+n[; ps_{j,c,t}(s) < 0} |ps_{j,c,t}|(s)}{\sum_{t=c}^{c+n-1} O_{j,c,t}} \quad (8)$$

$$\text{Consumption of safety stock risk} = \sum_{s \in S} \frac{\sum_{t \in [c,c+n[; ps_{j,c,t} < O_{j,c,t}} |O_{j,c,t} - ps_{j,c,t}|(s)}{\sum_{t=c}^{c+n-1} O_{j,c,t}} \quad (9)$$

Each change in the plan from one rescheduling cycle to another increases the nervousness of the system, but the magnitude of these changes is also important to value. Equations (1) and (2) present the two dimensions of the system's nervousness calculation. (1) is the nervousness in terms of occurrence of plan changes (set ups) from one rescheduling cycle to the other. The (2) is the nervousness of the system in terms of the amount of these changes. This calculation is based on the rescheduling history throughout the planning rolling horizon.
In equation (3), we calculate the instability of a plan as the differences between the planned quantities per period and the average value $A_{ij,c,t}$ scheduled per period throughout the planning horizon for the same rescheduling cycle.
In equation (4) and (5), the nominal values of the received plans from the other partners (MPS, SSR) are used to calculate the satisfaction rate of subsidiary requests (4) and the bullwhip effect (5). The subsidiary satisfaction indicator is the ratio between the subsidiaries' requests (the desired supply plan) and the decided supply plan. The bullwhip effect is the ratio between the instability of the SSR expressed by a subsidiary and the supply plan for that subsidiary.
In equations (7), (8) and (9), we use the possible scenarios of deviations from the received plans to assess the risks of unavailability, shortage, and consumption of the safety stock, respectively. In (7), we assess the capacity of the decided supply plan to meet the demand of a subsidiary despite possible variations in this demand (SSR) during the next rescheduling cycles.
In (6), we recalculate the projected CDC stock of each period for each possible receipt scenario (MPS(S)). This calculation is used to assess the shortage risk ($ps_{j,c,t} < 0$) (8) and consumption of the safety stock risk ($ps_{j,c,t} < O_{j,c,t}$) (9).

3. Case study : User experience

In this part we present a user experience with the decision-support platform on a small scale: 4 subsidiaries, 5 products (P1, P2,P3,P4,P5) and a planning with a short horizon length of 5 weeks. Each product is consumed by one or more subsidiaries.

First, the decision-maker elaborates his/her Supply Plans for each subsidiary according to the current collaborative planning process. Then he uses the decision support platform, before validating his planning choices face to uncertainties. The first overview **(UI1)** of the supply plan assessment is shown in the following figure:

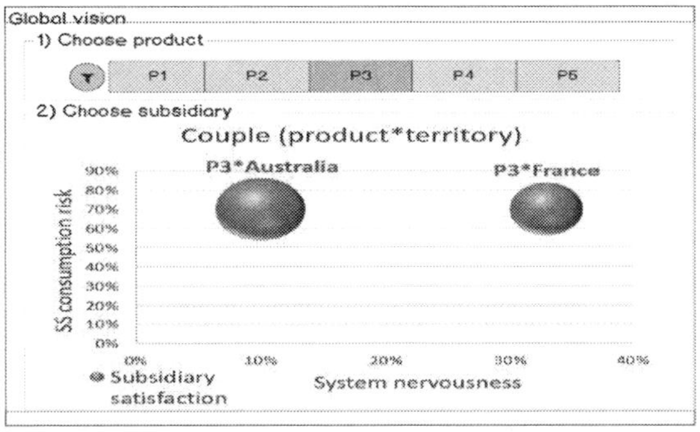

Figure 4: Overview of the supply plans evaluation (UI1)

In this tab, the decision-maker selects first a product and the chart is updated to display an overall evaluation of all Supply Plans per subsidiary of the selected product.

According to this global vision, the decision maker specifies the scope of the evaluation that interests him. We assume that the decision-maker chooses the SP of the couple (France, P3) because, as shown in the graph in Figure 4, it belongs to the critical risk zone.

By clicking the bubble (P3*France), the system moves to more detailed evaluation level of this decision. More rich view **(UI2)** with detailed indicators and graphical visualization (see Figure 5 and Figure 6).

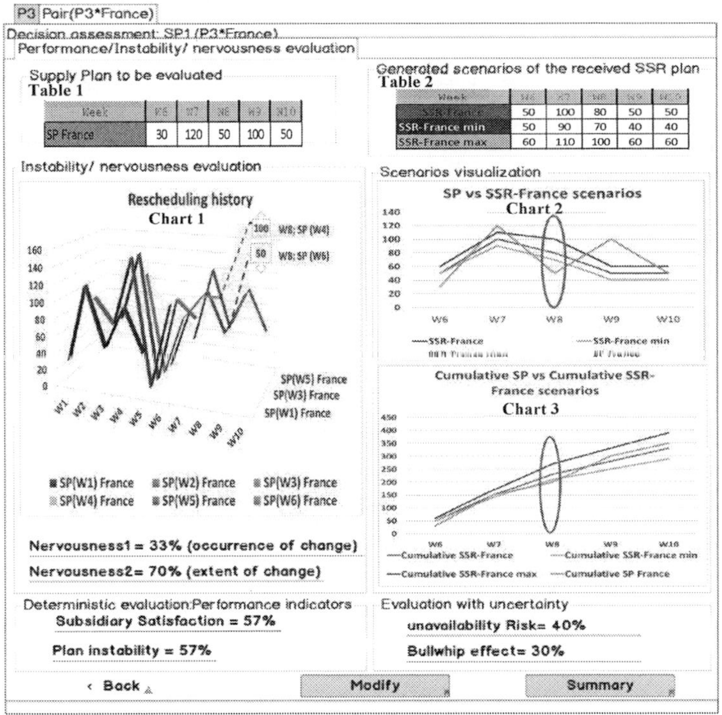

Figure 6: SP (product*subsidiary) assessment (UI2)

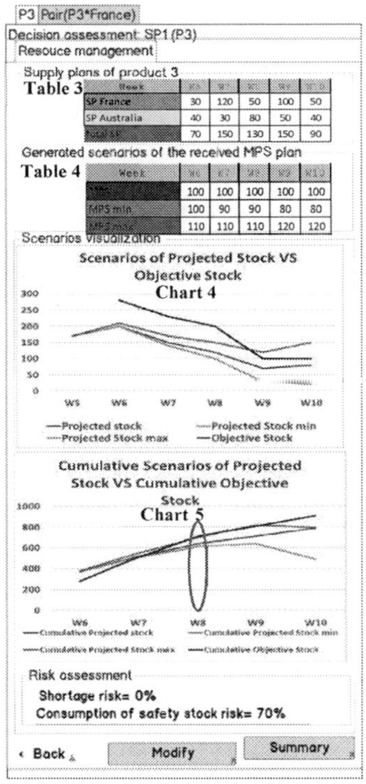

Figure 5: Resource-oriented assessment (UI2)

In the two tabs (Figure 5 and Figure 6), the system proposes different levels of evaluation to help the decision-maker decide on appropriate changes.

Product 3 is consumed by two subsidiaries, French and Australian subsidiaries. The current planning period is week 6.

The tab in **Figure 5** presents an evaluation specific to the Supply Plan related to the couple (P3, France). Based on the SSR scenarios (Table 2) of the selected French subsidiary and the rescheduling planning history (Chart 1) of the Supply Plan, indicators assessing the two dimension of nervousness, subsidiary satisfaction, plan instability, unavailability risk and bullwhip effect are calculated.
Although the choice of the scope of assessment was linked to the couple (France, P3), the tab in **Figure 6** is necessary to be able to decide on the modifications linked to the selected couple. Here the CDC planner has a vision on its stocks (Chart 4) as well as the total SP (France SP+ Australia SP) (Table 3). This vision allows the decision maker to review the dispatching of the stock of product 3 between the two subsidiaries while having a vision on the different possible reception scenarios (MPS(S))(Table 4). Cumulative projected stock (Chart 5) is also displayed to assist the decision-maker in allocating quantities over time.

We consider the user's point of view to analyze the results of this example and study the possible planning decisions using this interface. In Figure 5, Chart2, the user notices that on week 8 he cannot satisfy the demand of the subsidiary even the minimum demand scenario. Moreover, even the cumulative SP (Chart 3) will not satisfy the lowest demand. So, it seems necessary to increase the supply plan for week 8. In Chart 1, he realizes that in fact he has recently produced a very low supply plan for week 8 whereas he had much higher version in the rescheduling cycle of week 4 for the same week.
So, the decision-maker would like to increase the supply plan for week 8. He switches to the tab of figure 6, Chart 5 to notice that the cumulative stock is above the objective stock in this week. In conclusion, he could increase the supply plan for week 8 without any risk of shortage or significant increase in the risk of consumption of the safety stock. In addition, it is possible to make up for the additional planned quantity of week 8 by reducing the planned quantity of week 7. The tool will allow the decision-maker to re-measure the impacts of these decisions.

The decision to increase quantities for week 8 will reduce the risk of unavailability and increase subsidiary satisfaction, as it will approach the nominal value of subsidiary demand. On the other hand, the nervousness of the system will increase since it is a change at week 7 and week 8 of the previous Supply Plan (PS(w5)), however the instability of the plan will decrease because the plan will be smoothed more. From a resource point of view, this decision will not increase the risk of consumption of the safety stock or the risk of shortage given the compensation that exists between the two changes. The results of the new evaluation will be available in the synthesis interface (UI3) below.
The decision maker may modify his Supply Plan at any time and as much as he wishes by clicking on the "Modify" button. The various test and modification sessions are saved, and the user has access to the

History	Deterministic evaluation	Evaluation with uncertainty	Instability /Nervousness	Decision
Plan 1 (P3, France)	Subsidiary satisfaction=57% Unavailability Risk= 40%	SS consumption risk=70% Shortage Risk= 0%	Nervousness 1= 33% Nervousness 2= 57% Plan Instability= 57%	Validate
Plan 2 (P3, France)	Subsidiary satisfaction= 65% Unavailability Risk= 30%	SS consumption risk=70% Shortage Risk= 0%	Nervousness 1=37% Nervousness 2= 59% Plan Instability= 52%	Validate

Figure 7: Assessment tests history (UI3)

summary of the evaluations performed from the "Summary" button. This tab allows the decision-maker to have a view of all tests. Moreover, he can always change in the saved tests or choose and validate the decision that suits him (see **Figure 7**).
By applying the changes studied above (Plan 2 (P3, France)), the decision-maker was able to increase the satisfaction of the French subsidiary without affecting the consumption of its resources or significantly increasing the nervousness of its system. Then it is up to the decision-maker to choose either to continue the tests or to validate the plan of the second test and move on to another decision.

The different levels of decision assessment will allow the decision-maker to have an overall view of the main areas for improvement that constitute the contradictory objectives of the objective function: increasing the service rate, maintaining the objective stock level and reducing the nervousness of the planning system.

4. Conclusion and future works

In this paper we have proposed a decision support to assist the central distribution center planner in making planning decisions and managing the supply of different subsidiary distribution centers during rescheduling cycles.
In a traditional DRP planning process, decision-makers exchange deterministic plans. Considering the uncertainties in the demands of distribution centers as well as in the scheduled receipts from plants, extreme scenarios of deviations from these plans will be generated and integrated for the evaluation of performance, nervousness and risks. This exhaustive assessment will allow the decision-maker to validate decisions that respect the right compromise between these different levels. A user experience was also presented, which confirmed the complementarity between these different levels of evaluation. In addition, the decision-maker will not need advanced statistical knowledge to be able to interpret the results of the interface.

However, in our current conception of this decision support system, we have not integrated at any time the advantage of visibility of the subsidiaries' inventories as well as the actual production outstandings that the CDC supply planner has. This information must also be integrated into decision support, more specifically for the management of CDC supply priorities. For example, there are subsidiaries that tend to demand increasingly knowing that they have enough stock to cover their sales forecasts. They adopt this behaviour for safety reasons regarding CDC decisions on the allocation of products between other distribution centers consuming the same products which makes decision making more difficult for the CDC planner.

An actual data collection from a company's planning system is in progress. In our research work, the next step will be to analyze these data using data analysis tools to model uncertainties. Then, develop the different modules of the interface architecture which will necessarily evolve according to the progress of the research. Finally, study the integration of this interface with the company's ERP system and manage the real size of the data circulating in this system. But before being able to model the planning process and simulate the decision-making process in order to study human behavior with the interface is necessary for proof of concept needs.

5. References

[1] J. Hegeman, D. Peidro, M. del Mar Alemany, et M. Díaz-Madroñero, « A Decentralized Production and Distribution Planning Model in an Uncertain Environment », in *Supply Chain Management Under Fuzziness: Recent Developments and Techniques*, C. Kahraman et B. Öztayşi, Éd. Berlin, Heidelberg: Springer Berlin Heidelberg, 2014, p. 317-353.
[2] M. Holweg, S. Disney, J. Holmström, et J. Småros, « Supply Chain Collaboration »:, *European Management Journal*, vol. 23, n° 2, p. 170-181, avr. 2005.
[3] J. M. Whipple et D. Russell, « Building supply chain collaboration: a typology of collaborative approaches », *The International Journal of Logistics Management*, vol. 18, n° 2, p. 174-196, août 2007.
[4] J. D. Blackburn, D. H. Kropp, et R. A. Millen, « A Comparison of Strategies to Dampen Nervousness in MRP Systems », *Management Science*, vol. 32, n° 4, p. 413-429, avr. 1986.
[5] S. N. Kadipasaoglu et V. Sridharan, « Alternative approaches for reducing schedule instability in multistage manufacturing under demand uncertainty », *Journal of Operations Management*, vol. 13, n° 3, p. 193-211, oct. 1995, doi: 10.1016/0272-6963(95)00023-L.
[6] C.-J. Ho, « Evaluating the impact of operating environments on MRP system nervousness », *International Journal of Production Research*, vol. 27, n° 7, p. 1115-1135, juill. 1989.
[7] C. Herrera et A. Thomas, « Un modèle pour limiter la nervosité et l'instabilité du Programme Directeur de Production », p. 8.
[8] E. Koca, H. Yaman, et M. S. Aktürk, « Stochastic lot sizing problem with nervousness considerations », *Computers & Operations Research*, vol. 94, p. 23-37, juin 2018.
[9] R. Guillaume, C. Thierry, et P. Zieliński, « Robust material requirement planning with cumulative demand under uncertainty », *International Journal of Production Research*, vol. 55, n° 22, p. 6824-6845, nov. 2017.
[10] K. van Donselaar, J. van den Nieuwenhof, et J. Visschers, « The impact of material coordination concepts on planning stability in supply chains », *International Journal of Production Economics*, vol. 68, n° 2, p. 169-176, nov. 2000.

I L S 2020
INTERNATIONAL CONFERENCE ON INFORMATION SYSTEMS, LOGISTICS & SUPPLY CHAIN
Austin, Texas April 22-24, 2020

Disjunctive Scheduling with Setup Times: Optimizing a Food Factory

Nicolas Blais [1], Alexis Remartini [1], Claude-Guy Quimper [1], Nadia Lehoux [1], Jonathan Gaudreault [1]

[1] Université Laval, Québec, Canada
{nicolas.blais.7@ulaval.ca, alexis.remartini.1@ulaval.ca, claude-guy.quimper@ift.ulaval.ca, nadia.lehoux@gmc.ulaval.ca, jonathan.gaudreault@ift.ulaval.ca}

Abstract. We propose a new approach to solve scheduling problems applied to a food factory. The goal is to schedule the recipes in a way that minimizes the total setup time. Our model allows splitting a recipe in two batches if necessary. It also considers other specific constraints like avoiding too long setup on a day shift, having a maximum of tasks done during days shift, etc. A good heuristic based on the idea of scheduling the most difficult tasks as soon as possible is presented.

Keywords: Scheduling, Constraint Programming, Minimizing Setup Times.

1. Introduction

The food industry is an environment with many standards to respect that can quickly become complex if multiple products are made on the same production line. In some factories, planners must manage the availability of the ingredients and of the production line in addition to the allergens of each product. They have to take into account the setup time between all the products which depends largely on the allergens of the products. The setup time, that includes the cleaning efforts, typically takes much longer between a recipe that contains allergens and a recipe that does not because workers must conduct an allergen clean-up for the entire production line which can involve many hours. This clean-up does not occur when passing from an allergen-free product to a product with allergens.
The aim of this work is to schedule a set of tasks for a planning horizon over the weeks 5 to 8 with the objective of minimizing the setup times. The first 4 weeks are not considered (frozen horizon) because changes at this time generate conflicts for the schedule and the procurement of raw materials. The schedule is recomputed weekly. The tasks are sequentially performed, i.e. we schedule on a single machine.
The following methodology was followed. First, an analysis of the problem was carried out to clearly identify the problem. Then, the collaboration with the company made it possible to obtain data and constitute a benchmark. We designed a model and improve the search strategy of a constraint solver to obtain the best possible results on the instances. The solutions were presented to the company (validation of the model) and modifications were made to satisfy the set of constraints that must be taken into account by the planners. We reduce by 26%, in average, the setup time compared to what the human planners did.
In the literature, there are a few papers that use constraint programming applied to the food industry. Our model contributes to the field by creating a set of constraints adapted to the branching strategy we propose. This paper is organized as follows. Section 2 states the problem. Section 3 presents the literature surrounding our problem. The model and the branching strategy are presented in Section 4. The experimental results are presented in Section 5. Section 6 concludes the paper.

2. Problem Description

The problem was observed in a world recognized granola bar and cookie factory that offers a wide range of products, some of them being allergen-free. To help the planners manage such a complex product portfolio, we develop an application which takes their production system's dynamics into account.
In our notation, we use capital letters to denote decision variables and sets and small letters for parameters or constants. We consider a set of tasks T^* that correspond to cookie recipes. Each task $i \in T^*$ has a due date lct_i called Latest Completion Times, release date est_i called Earliest Starting Time which is computed according to the availability and the preservability of the ingredients, and a processing time p_i that is proportional to the number of cookies to produce. A task i has a starting time S_i which is unknown and needs to be computed. The transition time (or setup time) between a task i to a task j is given by $t_{i,j}$. This time takes into account the cleaning time and the machine reconfiguration. All production lines are stopped on the weekend and some are idle during the nights. These downtimes can be used to conduct a setup, but the production itself is stopped. Let J be set of days in the scheduling horizon. For each day d $\in J$, the working shift starts at time $shiftBegin_d$ and ends at time $shiftEnd_d$. There is only one shift per day.
There are two types of tasks: *production orders* and *planned orders*. The *production orders* are already scheduled and cannot be moved. We therefore have $est_i + p_i = lct_i$ which leaves no freedom on the time the task is scheduled: $S_i = est_i$. The *planned orders* need to be scheduled so the time window in which the task must be scheduled is not tight: $est_i + p_i < lct_i$. Moreover, planned orders can be executed in two segments in order to have a better use of the production line i.e. avoiding having unused time before the end of the shift. For instance, a task i can start on Monday, be stopped during the night and be resumed on Friday. At the end of its execution on Friday, the task must be completed, i.e., the time spent on Monday and Friday must sum up to the processing time p_i. Nothing forces the two tasks to be adjacent in the schedule i.e., there may be other tasks running between them. When a task is executed in two parts, the duration of each of its part must be greater or equal to a threshold *minDuration*. Tasks cannot be separated into more than two parts, because starting a new production can decline the productivity. Indeed, the first minutes of production are often unstable. So, separating a task into too many parts increases the chances of not getting the right amount of product in the allotted time.
There is a limit of *maxTaskShift* tasks that can be achieved during a workday (or shift) to avoid too many setups during a day. Only setups with duration below a threshold *maxSetup* are permitted during a working day in order to avoid idle workers and to maximize the use of daytime. A subset of tasks $T_M \subset T^*$ requires setups that can only be done on the weekend. Tasks in T_M can be scheduled on Mondays ($J_M \subset J$) or right after another task in T_M. All parameters and sets are summarized in Tables 1 and 2.

Table 1: List of Sets.

Sets	Definition
T^*	Set of all fictive tasks
T_M	Set of tasks that must be done on a Monday
J	Set of working days
J_M	Set of working days that are Mondays
T	Set of task parts
T_1	Set of the first parts of the tasks
T_2	Set of the second parts of the tasks

Table 2: List of Parameters.

Parameters	Definition
$t_{i,j}$	Transition time from a task i to a task j
est_i	Earliest starting time of the task i
lct_i	Latest completion time of the task i
p_i	Processing time needed for the task i
$shiftBegin_d$	Starting time of the working day d
$shiftEnd_d$	Ending time of the working day d
minDuration	Minimum duration of separated task
maxTaskShift	Number maximum of tasks during a shift
maxSetup	Maximum setup time allowed during day

3. Literature Review

Scheduling problems are numerous and varied. *Allahverdi* [12] presents a survey of scheduling problems with setup times. The notation used ($\alpha|\beta|\gamma$) classifies our problem in the category $1|ST_{sd}|TST$: 1 because there is a single machine, ST_{sd} for sequence-dependent setups and TST for minimizing the sum of the setup times. Few papers explore this problem [12].
The core of the studied problem has the same form as the Traveling Salesman Problem with Time Windows (TSPTW) which was proved to be NP-Hard [8]. Indeed, tasks can be represented as cities and setup times between tasks as distances between cities. The shortest Hamiltonian path provides an ordering of the tasks

that minimizes the sum of the setup times. Several methods have been developed to solve this problem. *Ángel-Bello et al.* [6] used Mixed Integer Programming MIP. *Abdallah et al.* [7] used a heuristic approach (Family Splitting Algorithm) to find quality solutions. *Fagerholt et al.* [5] use dynamic programming. *Claassen et al.* [3] uses a relax-and-fix heuristic. *Hebrard and Grimes* [4] use Constraint Programming (CP) to solve job shop problems with setup times. Given the range of possible solving methods, it becomes difficult to know which one is the best. *Ku and Beck* [1] compare MIP and CP methods. The results showed that CP outperforms MIP on larger instances. As a result, using CP for our case becomes a natural choice. Constraint programming is a technology originating from artificial intelligence that solves combinatorial and optimization problems. It offers a large collection of constraints to model the problems: from simple constraints such as linear constraints to more complex ones that entirely model the usage of a resource in a scheduling problem. A *constraint satisfaction problem* is defined by a set of variables. Each variable X_i has a domain denoted dom(X_i). Each constraint is posted on a subset of variables and restricts their possible assignments. A solution is an assignment where each variable is given a value from its domain and each constraint is satisfied. In a *constraint optimization problem*, one also aims at minimizing/maximizing an objective function. Constraint solvers usually explore a search tree and perform a branch and bound to solve optimization problems under constraints. At each node of the tree, filtering algorithms associated with each constraint of the problem prune the branches that cannot lead to a solution.
Some constraints can be simple. For example, the ELEMENT constraint ensures that a variable X takes the value at index I in an array of variables Y, i.e. X = Y[I]. However, what makes constraint programming so efficient is the use of global constraints posted on many variables whose filtering algorithms significantly prune the search space. For example, the DISJUNCTIVE([S_1, …, S_n], [p_1, …, p_n]) constraint introduced in [9] prevents any pair of tasks *i* and *j* with starting time variables S_i and S_j and processing times p_i and p_j from executing simultaneously: $S_i + p_i \leq S_j \vee S_j + p_j \leq S_i$. This constraint uses filtering rules (e.g. time-tabling) to remove inconsistent values from the domain of the starting time variables. *Dejemeppe et al.* [2] created a variation of DISJUNCTIVE that takes into account setup times. The global constraint WEIGHTEDCIRCUIT([N_1, …, N_n], W) [15] accepts assignments that encodes a Hamiltonian cycle in a graph with a total weight smaller than or equal to W. The nodes are labeled with integers from 1 to *n*. The node next to node *i* in the cycle is N_i. The Global Cardinality Constraint [10] GLOBALCARDINALITY([X_1, …, X_n], [l_1, …, l_m], [u_1, …, u_m]) ensures that the value *v* occurs between l_v and u_v times in the vector $\vec{X}$. Finally, meta constraints allow enforcing relations between constraints. For instance, in the constraints $C_1 \Rightarrow C_2$ and IFTHENELSE(C_1, C_2, C_3), constraint C_2 is satisfied whenever constraint C_1 is satisfied and constraint C_3 is satisfied whenever constraint C_1 is violated.

4. Methods and model

4.1. Variables

We present a model that encodes our problem. The main decision variables are the starting time of a task $\in T$ denoted S_i and the task that follows a task *i* in the schedule denoted N_i. All other variables are auxiliary, which means their values are function of S_i and N_i. Table 3 summarizes the variables and their domains.

Table 3: List of variables.

Variable	Domain	Definition
W	$[0, \infty)$	Sum of all transition times
N_i	$T \setminus \{i\}$	Task next to task i
PR_i	$T \setminus \{i\}$	Task preceding task i
S_i	$[est_i, lct_i]$	Starting time of the second part of task i
P_{i1}	$[minDuration, p_i]$	Processing time of the first part of task i
P_{i2}	$[0, p_i - minDuration]$	Processing time of the second part of task i
$\tilde{P}_i$	$[0, p_i + \max_{j \in T^*} t_{i,j}]$	Processing time, including the transition to task next to *i*
D_i	J	Working day of the task i
D_i'	$J \cup \{-1\}$	Working day of the task i if $\tilde{p}_i > 0$ and -1 otherwise
TND_i	*shiftBegin*	Starting time of the upcoming morning of the task i
POS_i	[1, maxTaskShift]	Position of the task i in the shift

M_i	*shiftBegin* ∪ {0}	Starting time of the morning following task *i* if the maximum number of tasks is reached and 0 otherwise.

Since the tasks are preemptive and can be executed in two parts, we declare a set of tasks *T* that contains two tasks i_1 and i_2 for each task *i* in T*. These tasks represent the first part and the second part of task *i*. We also have in *T* two virtual tasks, *sentinel-begin* and *sentinel-end,* that mark the beginning and the end of the schedule. Each task i_1, i_2 in *T* has starting time variables S_{i1} and S_{i2} with domain dom(S_{i1}) = dom(S_{i2}) = [est_i, lct_i]. They also have processing time variables $P_{i_1}$and $P_{i_2}$with domains dom(P_{i_1}) = [*minDuration*, p_i] and dom(P_{i_2}) = [0, p_i – *minDuration*]. When P_{i_2} = 0, the task entirely executes in the first part. The *next* variable N_i indicates which task follows task *i* and has for domain dom(N_i) = $T \setminus \{i\}$. The variable PR_i represents the task that precedes task *i* and has the same domain as N_i. The variable $\tilde{P}_i$, for *i* in *T*, is duration of the task part *i* plus the setup time that follows the task. The *working day* variable D_i tells the day which a task part is done with *J* as domain. D_i' is used to represent the working day of task *i* if $P_i > 0$ and -1 otherwise. The value -1 occurs when *i* is the second part of a task that is entirely executed in its first part. The starting time of the upcoming morning of a task *i* TND_i can take any value in *shiftBegin*. The position of a task *i* in a shift is denoted with POS_i and has for domain dom(POS_i) = [1, *maxTaskShift*]. Finally, the variable M_i takes the value of the next morning of task *i* if the maximum number of tasks is reached and 0 otherwise. So, its domain is dom(M_i) = *shiftBegin* ∪ {0}.

4.2. Main Constraints

We present the constraints of the model that is summarized below. The objective function (1) minimizes the total setup time (*W*) i.e. the transition time t_{i,N_i} of a task *i* with its successor N_i for all task *i*.

$$\text{Minimize } W = \sum_{i\in T} t_{i,N_i}. \qquad (1)$$

$$P_{i_1} + P_{i_2} = p_i. \qquad \forall i \in T^* \qquad (2)$$

$$S_{i_1} + P_{i_1} \leq S_{i_2}. \qquad \forall i \in T^* \qquad (3)$$

$$N_{i_2} \neq i_1. \qquad \forall i \in T^* \qquad (4)$$

$$P_{i_1} = p_i \Rightarrow N_{i_1} = i_2 \land D_{i_1} = D_{i_2}. \qquad \forall i \in T^* \qquad (5)$$

$$P_{i_1} = \min\left(p_i, \text{shiftEnd}_{D_{i_1}} - S_{i_1}\right). \qquad \forall i \in T^* \qquad (6)$$

$$S_{i_1} + p_i > \text{shiftEnd}_{D_{i_1}} \Rightarrow S_{i_1} + p_i > \text{shiftEnd}_{D_{i_1}} + \text{minDuration}. \qquad \forall i \in T_1 \qquad (7)$$

$$\tilde{P}_i = P_i + t_{i,N_i}. \qquad \forall i \in T \qquad (8)$$

$$\text{DISJUNCTIVE}(S, \tilde{P}). \qquad (9)$$

$$\text{WEIGHTEDCIRCUIT}(N, t, W). \qquad (10)$$

$$N_{\text{sentinel-end}} = \text{sentinel-begin}. \qquad \forall i \in T \qquad (11)$$

$$D_i \geq d \Rightarrow S_i \geq \text{shiftBegin}_d. \qquad \forall i \in T, \forall d \in J \qquad (12)$$

$$D_i \leq d \Rightarrow S_i \leq \text{shiftEnd}_d. \qquad \forall i \in T, \forall d \in J \qquad (13)$$

$$\text{IFTHENELSE}(P_i > 0, D_i' = D_i, D_i' = -1). \qquad \forall i \in T \qquad (14)$$

$$\text{GLOBALCARDINALITY}(D', \text{maxTaskShift}). \qquad (15)$$

$$t_{i,j} > \text{maxSetup} \land D_i = D_j \Rightarrow N_i \neq j. \qquad \forall i, j \in T \qquad (16)$$

$$t_{i,j} > (\text{maxTaskShift} - 1)\text{maxSetup} \land t_{j,i} > (\text{maxTaskShift} - 1)\text{maxSetup} \Rightarrow D_i \neq D_j. \qquad \forall i, j \in T \qquad (17)$$

$$i = N_{PR_i} \qquad \forall i \in T \qquad (18)$$

$$D_i \notin J_M \Rightarrow PR_i \in T_M. \qquad \forall i \in T_M \qquad (19)$$

$$TND_i = \text{ShiftBegin}_{D_i + 1} \qquad \forall i \in T \qquad (20)$$

$$D_{N_i} = D_i \land P_{N_i} \neq 0 \Rightarrow POS_{N_i} = POS_i + 1. \qquad \forall i \in T \qquad (21)$$

$$D_{N_i} = D_i \land P_{N_i} = 0 \Rightarrow POS_{N_i} = POS_i. \qquad \forall i \in T \qquad (22)$$

$$D_{N_i} \neq D_i \Rightarrow POS_{N_i} = 1. \qquad \forall i \in T \qquad (23)$$

$$\text{IfThenElse}(POS_i = \text{maxTaskShift} \land p_{N_i} \neq 0, M_i = TND_i, M_i = 0). \qquad \forall i \in T \qquad (24)$$

$$N_i \in \{T_1\} \land [(p_{N_i} \geq 2\,\text{minDuration} \land \text{shiftEnd}_{D_i} - S_i - P_i \geq \text{minDuration}) \lor (p_{N_i} < 2\text{minDuration} \land \text{shiftEnd}_{D_i} - S_i - P_i \geq p_{N_i})] \Rightarrow S_{N_i} = \max(S_i + \tilde{P}_i, M_i, est_{N_i}). \qquad \forall i \in T \qquad (25)$$

$$N_i \in \{T_1\} \wedge [(p_{N_i} \geq 2minDuration \wedge shiftEnd_{D_i} - S_i - P_i < minDuration) \vee (p_{N_i} < 2minDuration \wedge shiftEnd_{D_i} - S_i - P_i < p_{N_i})] \Rightarrow S_{N_i} = \max(TND_i, est_{N_i}). \quad \forall i \in T \quad \textbf{(26)}$$

$$N_i \in \{T_2\} \wedge [(p_{N_i} = 0) \vee (p_{N_i} \geq minDuration \wedge shiftEnd_{D_i} - S_i - P_i \geq p_{N_i})] \Rightarrow S_{N_i} = \max(S_i + \tilde{P}_i, M_i). \quad \forall i \in T \quad \textbf{(27)}$$

$$N_i \in \{T_2\} \wedge (p_{N_i} \geq minDuration \wedge shiftEnd_{D_i} - S_i - P_i < p_{N_i}) \Rightarrow S_{N_i} = TND_i. \quad \forall i \in T \quad \textbf{(28)}$$

A task i in T^* can be executed in two parts that are represented by two tasks i_1 and i_2 in T. Constraint (2) makes sure that the sum of the durations of the parts in T is equal to the duration of the original task in T^*. Constraint (3) forces the first part to execute before the second. Constraint (4) is redundant and prevents the first part to follow the second. In the situation where a task is executed in one part, the duration of the first part is the duration of the original task: $P_i = p_i$. In this case, we force the second part, with a null duration, to succeed to the first part (5). If a task executes in two parts, (6) forces the first part to complete at the end of the shift. In other words, only the end of a shift can justify not to fully execute a task. Constraint (7) ensures that the time left to execute in the second part is longer than minDuration.
The variable $\tilde{P}_i$ gets the duration to execute a task part $i \in T$ and to complete the setup after the task (8). These durations are passed to the DISJUNCTIVE constraint (9) to ensure that starting time variables S_i are set in a way that no two tasks nor setups overlap. The constraint WEIGHTEDCIRCUIT (10) takes as input the next variables N_i and the setup time matrix t and maps them to the variable, the sum of the transition times. In order for the next variables to form a cycle, we force the sentinel task *sentinel-begin* to follow the task *sentinel-end* (11). Constraints (12) and (13) force the execution of a task during a work shift. This encoding with two constraints allows a stronger filtering between the variables S_i and D_i.
A specificity of the production lines limits the number of tasks during a day (*maxTaskShift*). Tasks with a null processing time are not included in the total number of tasks. Constraint (14) sets the variable D_i' to the working day if the processing time of a task i is greater than 0 and -1 otherwise. Constraint (15) prevents any day (except -1) to occur more than *maxTaskShift* times in vector D'.
Setups longer than the parameter *maxSetup* during a working day are not permitted. Constraint (16) ensures that a transition beyond that threshold leads to a task that is performed another day. Exploiting the triangle inequality, Constraint (17) states the condition in which the transition time is simply too large to allow two tasks executing on the same day, even if these two tasks execute first and last on that day.
Tasks in T_M are either executed on a Monday or preceded by a task in T_M. The variable PR_i is the tasks that precedes i. Constraint (18) maps the predecessor variables to the next variables. Using the predecessor variable, Constraint (19) enforces that a task in T_M is either done a Monday or after a task in T_M.

4.3. Additional Constraints

The constraints that we presented so far fully encode the problem. However, constraint programming takes its efficiency from its filtering algorithm and it is sometimes necessary to add additional constraints in order to speed up the search process. These constraints are presented in this section. Note that these constraints might eliminate some solutions that are known to be suboptimal.
The solver constructs a solution by choosing variables and assigning them a value. We add to the model constraints whose filtering algorithm sets the value of the starting time variable S_{N_i} whenever the next variable N_i is affected to a value. Before explaining these constraints, we declare two variables. The variable TND_i (time of next day) is the time at which the upcoming shift starts. It is set by Constraint (20). The variable POS_i is the position of a task i in its shift.
The position of a task is determined by three cases. The first case occurs when a task i and its next task are executed on the same day and the next task has a non-null processing time. In this situation, the Constraint (21) is applied and the positions of the tasks are one apart. The second case occurs when a task i and its next task are executed on the same day, but the next task has a null processing time. In such a case, Constraint (22) makes both tasks have the same position. The third case occurs when a task and its next task occurs on different days. In that case, Constraint (23) resets the position of the next task to one. When the variable POS_i is given the value *maxTaskShift*, the following tasks must be executed on the next day. If this happens, Constraint (24) sets the variable M_i to the value of the next morning and 0 otherwise.

Now we have all what is needed in order to be able to set the starting time variable S_{N_i} when the next variable N_i is set. There are four possible cases. Constraint (25) handles the first case when the task is a first part. This constraint checks whether a task can be immediately executed after another task before the end of the day shift. If so, the task starts after the preceding task, the next morning if the day is full, or at its earliest starting time (whichever comes first). For a task with a processing time greater than or equal to twice *minDuration*, we need to have a minimum of *minDuration* time before the night to start it. For the task with duration less than twice *minDuration*, we need to have enough time to execute the task entirely to be in this condition.
The second case is applied only for the first part of a task and is handled by (26). This constraint manages the case when the next task must start on the upcoming morning (TND_i) or at its earliest starting time. Except for the fact that it is only applied to the first part of the task, this constraint manages the opposite case of the Constraint (25). If there is not enough time before the end of the day shift, the task must be done in the upcoming morning. If the processing time of the next task (p_{N_i}) is greater than twice the *minDuration* and there is less than *minDuration* time before the night, or if a task has less than twice *minDuration* and there is less than the processing time p_{N_i} before the end of the working day, this case is applied.
The third case is only applied to the second part of a task and is handled by (27). This constraint manages the case when a second part of a task must start directly after the previous task or start the next day if the current day is full. It happens when the first part executes completely, and the second part has a null processing time. The task must start directly after the first part. It should be noted that in that case, M_i will always be zero. It also happens there is enough time before the end of the working day to finish the task.
Finally, the last case is also applied to the second part of the task and is modelled with Constraint (28). It manages the case when there is not enough time to complete the task before the end of the working day. The task must therefore start in the beginning of the upcoming morning TND_i.

4.4. Search Strategy

Constraint Programming is an exact method that guarantees an optimal solution, given sufficient time. A branching heuristic can help speeding up the search process. We design search heuristic called *opportunity cost heuristic* that analyses the domains of the next variables N, the starting time variables S, and the transition matrix t, and that branches on the next variables N. We recall that filtering algorithms keep removing values from the domains during the search process and that the heuristic makes a choice according to the current domains rather than the initial domains stated in Table 3. The heuristic's principle relies on the preference to schedule now the tasks that will be harder to schedule later. Branching on the variables N is a strategic choice. If branching on $N_i = v_1$ leads to a failure, the solver branches on $N_i = v_2$ which is a significantly different solution. If the heuristic was branching on the starting time variables, say $S_i = 1$, upon a failure, the solver would try another value such as $S_i = 2$. However, starting the task i one minute later is not significantly different. Let i be the current task (initially the task *sentinel-begin)*. The heuristic finds which task v should be assigned to N_i. After the branching $N_i = v$ is performed, v becomes the new current task. The heuristic chooses the task v with the smallest value in the domain of its starting time S and breaks ties by selecting the task that is more difficult to schedule later. This is conducted based on these rules:

1. Choose v that contains the smallest value in dom(S_v). If v is unique, choose v, else go to Step 2.
2. For each task v computed in Step 1, calculate the sum of the transition times of a task not yet scheduled toward v. Go to Step 3.
3. Randomly choose the next task with probability proportional to the sums computed in Step 2.

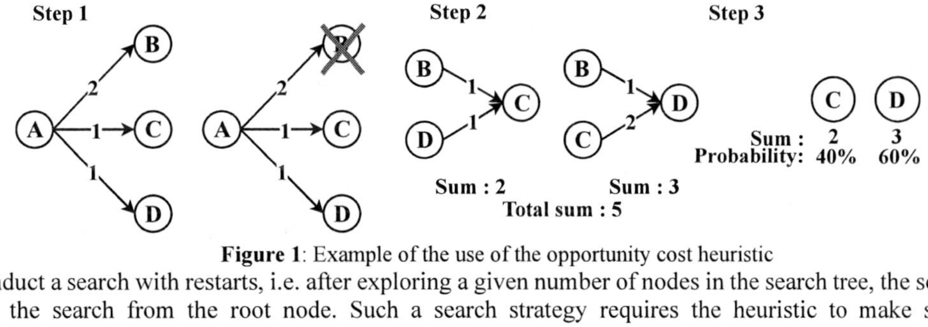

Figure 1: Example of the use of the opportunity cost heuristic

We conduct a search with restarts, i.e. after exploring a given number of nodes in the search tree, the solver restarts the search from the root node. Such a search strategy requires the heuristic to make some randomized decisions in order not to re-explore the same portion of the search, hence the randomization of Step 3. Figure 1 shows an example of the use of the heuristic. In the first step, task A is already scheduled, and we want to know what task should be executed afterwards. B is automatically eliminated because it can start one unit of time after the others. In step 2, the setup of tasks not yet scheduled towards tasks C and D is calculated. This result is useful in step 3 in order to make task D more likely to be chosen. Task D is therefore more difficult to schedule because it has a chance to end up after task C causing a setup of 2 units.

5. Experimentation

The experiments were carried out in collaboration with a cookie factory. During the development of the model, the company sent data that was used by their planners. Instances of the problem were solved with the model and the solutions were returned to the planners. They analysed them and gave feedback to improve the model. This has been repeated until the results were of good quality. For some of these instances, we had the actual schedules used by the planners which allowed us to make a comparison between the schedules made manually and those automatically generated by our model.
Branching heuristics: Prior to designing the *opportunity cost heuristic* described in Section 4.4, we tried standard branching heuristics available in most constraint solvers. We used *Smallest,* a heuristic that selects the starting time variable S_i with the smallest value in its domain and assign it to its smallest value. *Smallest* can be used in conjunction with two meta branching heuristics: Last Conflict [12] and Conflict Ordering [13]. These meta branching heuristics apply the *Smallest* branching heuristic, but as the search explores the search tree, the meta heuristics learn which variables are conflictual and start altering the original *Smallest* heuristics in order to give more importance to these variables. These meta branching heuristics were specially designed for scheduling problems. All these heuristics are already implemented in the solver Choco 4.0.6. We also implemented and integrated the *opportunity cost heuristic* to that solver.
Search strategy: When the exploration of the search reaches a dead end, i.e. when the choices made so far by the branching heuristics cannot lead to any solution, the search needs to reconsider the choices that were made. Generally, a solver reconsiders the last choice that was made until all choices are exhausted. It then reconsiders the previous last choice, and so on. This search strategy is called Depth First Search (DFS). Another search strategy called Limited Discrepancy Search (LDS) has been effective in many industrial cases [14]. This strategy explores the solution with zero reconsidered choice, then all solutions with exactly one reconsidered choice, then all solutions with exactly two reconsidered choices, and so on. LDS requires the branching heuristics to be deterministic, for that purpose, we replace Step 3 of the opportunity cost heuristic with a deterministic choice: we select the task with the largest sum computed at Step 2.

Table 1: Comparison between the planners and computed schedule

Instances	Human Planners	Smallest time	Last conflict	Conflict ordering	Opportunity cost heuristic	Opportunity cost heuristic with LDS
1	1665	1135	1175	1145	**1070**	**1070**
2	2965	2160	2160	2185	2085	**2045**
3	1645	1390	-	-	**1305**	-
4	1225	1260	1260	1290	**1110**	-
5	1655	1470	-	1555	1185	**1105**

The experiments were done on a MacBook Pro with a 2.6 GHz Intel Core i7 processor. We solve 5 industrial instances counting from 45 to 65 tasks. Table 1 reports the best objective value (cumulative setup time in minutes) obtained for each solving technique after a 15-minute cut-off as well as the objective value obtained by the human planners. Our solutions have shorter setup times than what the human planners obtained. The Last Conflict and Conflict Ordering fail to always return a solution within 15 minutes. With that respect, the opportunity cost heuristic is a better solution than Smallest, Last Conflict, and Conflict Ordering. Breaking the ties with the sum of the entering setups gives better results on the studied instances and a solution is found for each instance. LDS sometimes gives better results than any branching heuristics used with DFS. However, sometimes, it does not find a single solution which makes this heuristic unusable for the case study. The reason for this performance is that the number of side constraints can regularly leads to failures. Depth First Search (DFS) can quickly correct this error by making another branching, but LDS tries to explore all solutions with fewer reconsidered choices rather than quickly fixing the solution.

Overall, our model with the opportunity cost branching heuristic and a DFS search strategy offers the best performances. It makes it possible to find better solutions than the planners with a reduction of setup time of 26%. Only the use of LDS allows better solutions, but it could not solve all instances. The difference in the objective values between opportunity cost heuristic with DFS and with LDS was not significant.

6. Conclusion

In the food industry, setup times can affect the efficiency of a production line since it is not a value-added activity. In addition, planners must take into account several constraints such as the availability of ingredients and the production line. The goal of this work is to schedule a set of tasks on a single machine for the weeks 5 to 8 of the upcoming horizon. This one is done weekly using constraint programming. The model has been developed iteratively with the company.
The scientific contribution of this work is to use constraint programming to solve an industrial problem in scheduling that minimizes setup times. Indeed, there is very few papers that use this method to solve applied cases. Also, the model's originality is to have created a set of constraints that aim to help the heuristic in its branching. For the industrial contribution, we managed to solve complex cases by obtaining good results. We obtain an improvement of 26% on average compared to what was done with the planners.

7. Acknowledgement

We thank Vincent Gingras who laid the basis of the model in the early stage of this project.

8. References

1. Ku, W.Y., Christopher Beck, J.: Mixed Integer Programming Models for Job Shop Scheduling: A Computational Analysis. In : Computers & Operations 73, pp. 165--173 (2016)
2. Dejemeppe, C., Van Cauwelaert, S., Schaus, P.: The Unary Resource with Transition Times. In : Principles and Practice of Constraint Programming, pp. 89--104 (2015)
3. Claassen, G.D.H., Gerdessen, J.C., Hendrix, E.M. and van der Vorst, J.G.: On production planning and scheduling in food processing industry: Modelling non-triangular setups and product decay. In : Computers & Operations 76, pp. 147--154 (2016)
4. Grimes, D., Hebrard, E.: Job shop scheduling with setup times and maximal time-lags: A simple constraint programming approach. International Conference on Integration of Artificial Intelligence (AI) and Operations Research (OR) Techniques in Constraint Programming, pp. 147--161 (2010)
5. Fagerholt K, Christiansen M.: A travelling salesman problem with allocation, time window and precedence constraints - an application to ship scheduling. In: Int. Transactions in Operational Research, pp. 231-244 (2000)
6. Ángel-Bello F, Álvarez A, Pacheco J, Martínez I.: A single machine scheduling problem with availability constraints and sequence-dependent setup costs. In: Applied Mathematical Modelling 35, pp. 2041--2050 (2011)
7. Abdallah KS, Jang J.: Scheduling a single machine with job family setup times to minimize total tardiness. In: 2017 International Conference on Engineering, Technology and Innovation (ICE/ITMC), pp. 665--672 (2017)
8. Carlier J.: The one-machine sequencing problem. In: European Journal of Operational Research, pp. 42--47 (1982)
9. Benchimol P, Van Hoeve WJ, Régin JC, Rousseau LM, Rueher M. Improved filtering for weighted circuit constraints. In: Constraints 17, no. 3, pp. 205--233 (2012)
10. Oplobedu A, Marcovitch J, Tourbier Y.: CHARME: Un langage industriel de programmation par contraintes, illustré par une application chez Renault. In: Ninth International Workshop on Expert Systems and their Applications: General Conference, pp. 55--70 (1989)
11. Allahverdi A.: The third comprehensive survey on scheduling problems with setup times/costs. In: European Journal of Operational Research, pp. 345--378 (2015)
12. Lecoutre C, Saïs L, Tabary S, Vidal V.: Reasoning from last conflict(s) in constraint programming.In: Artificial Intelligence, pp. 1592--1614 (2009)
13. Gay S, Hartert R, Lecoutre C, Schaus P.: Conflict ordering search for scheduling problems. In: International conference on principles and practice of constraint programming, pp. 140--148 (2015)
14. Harvey WD, Ginsberg ML.: Limited discrepancy search. In: International Joint Conferences on Artificial Intelligence, pp. 607--615 (1995)
15. Focacci F, Lodi A, Milano M.: Cost-based domain filtering. In: International conference on principles and practice of constraint programming, pp. 189--203 (1999)

I L S 2020
INTERNATIONAL CONFERENCE ON INFORMATION
SYSTEMS, LOGISTICS & SUPPLY CHAIN
Austin, Texas April 22-24, 2020

Toward Assessing Physical Internet Potential Benefits for Humanitarian Supply Chains

Manon Grest[1], Benoit Montreuil[2], Matthieu Lauras[1]

[1] IMT Mines Albi, Albi, France
[2] Georgia Tech University, Atlanta, U.S.A.
{manon.grest@mines-albi.fr, matthieu.lauras@mines-albi.fr, benoit.montreuil@isye.gatech.edu}

Abstract. In the view of the issues faced by humanitarian organizations to deliver beneficiaries in an effective, efficient and sustainable manner, the Physical Internet (PI) approach offers potential as an appropriate solution. Indeed, its high resilience, adaptability, efficiency and sustainability capabilities are attractive yet need to be proved as relevant and suitable for the humanitarian sector. Based on this consideration, it is judicious to assess the potential benefits of introducing Physical Internet concepts to humanitarian organizations and demonstrate the impact on performance. In this perspective, this paper proposes a methodology to organize such an investigation as well as some first experimental illustrations to present the approach and to highlight early positive insights.

Keywords: Physical Internet, Humanitarian, Supply Chain, Hyperconnectivity, Performance assessment methodology, Experiment

1. Introduction

Humanitarian organizations in their daily activities are concerned with alleviating human suffering through relief emergencies or development programs. Since logistics account for 80% of activities performed [1], it is crucial to be effective and efficient as they deal with lives. However, those objectives are not straightforward to meet considering the difficult context and constantly evolving environment. Besides, the growing number of humanitarian organizations generate a competition climate while the part of funding allocated for each crisis is decreasing. Also, donors and media put pressure on humanitarian organizations to better monitor and provide evidences of the relief quality and quantity provided. Finally, new growing concerns regarding the environment would be at some point to integrate in organizations' operating modes. Those first trends highlight the need for some changes in the logistics and potentially as a whole. A recent concept, named Physical Internet [2], intends to overcome similar difficulties faced by the business sector. The main idea is to turn from private and dedicated logistics networks to a single and shared one. Based on this idea and the hyperconnection concept, it proposes a better way for the product to be moved, handled, produced and used. Similarly, it presents attractive elements for the humanitarian logistics and this is the starting point of this study. Indeed, before considering assessing the stakes for humanitarian organizations to become more hyperconnected, the following study proposes a performance assessment methodology to follow, to reach this objective. The paper starts with a literature review about the main humanitarian supply chain characteristics and a Physical Internet presentation. It is then, followed by the presentation of the different stages of the proposed methodology. After that, through an illustrative case study inspired from the Indonesian Red Cross organization, the paper intends to highlight some first interests of integrating Physical Internet approach to the humanitarian sector.

2. Background

2.1. Humanitarian Supply Chain

The Humanitarian Supply Chain (HSC), also referred to 'humanitarian logistics', encompasses all the operations required for Humanitarian Organisations (HO) to achieve the goals of alleviating human suffering [3] and minimising casualties [4]. This concern induces daily engagement over the long run as since disasters regularly occur across the globe and show an upward trend [5]. For a long time, HOs did not recognise logistics as a crucial activity affecting their performance. However, studies have demonstrated that logistics encompasses 80% of efforts performed in a relief operations and directly impacts its success [1]. Thus, especially since HOs are dealing with lives, it is mandatory for HSCs to be effective and efficient as each minute matter. Although easy to affirm, these targets are not straightforward to meet. Indeed, the HOs evolve in a specific context with characteristics that vary from their counterpart in the business sector. To discuss this point, the next sections discuss HSC structure and management in relation to the humanitarian operating context.

2.1.1. Typical HSC Network

Basically, whatever the type of supply chain, the network is composed of nodes that in the logistics context can be actors or facilities, edges to connect the nodes and three main types of flows circulating through its components. In HSCs, the actors are numerous and show various roles, objectives and approaches which often lead to coordination issues [1]. Some stakeholders may be belonging to the same HO institution but distributed at national, regional and local levels [6]. Others include suppliers, international or national HOs offering additional aid support, host government(s) or political partners, supporting or coordinating military forces, logistics providers, and donors from the public or private sector [3]. As for the affected people, also called beneficiaries, they are not always considered as part of the supply chain even if they represent the end nodes of the supply chain. As for facilities, they are centres where the physical flow may transit through before reaching its destination. These can be permanent or temporary facilities that may vary in size. Their main role is to receive, handle, store, produce or distribute the stocks [7]. Similarly, as in the business sector, there are three types of flows in HSCs. First, the physical flow includes materials (relief items, equipment, etc.) and human (volunteers, experts, etc.) [8]. Secondly, the information flow carries situation reports, tracking data and other decisional information needed for the fluidity of the physical flow [1]. Lastly, the financial flow mainly initiates from donors to support HOs action. However, recent trends show that funding is expected to be more distributed by HOs as an aid mean and thus would add new connections to manage [9]. Finally, edges connect HSCs, for example there are transportation edges connecting the logistical nodes, and communication edges connecting the various stakeholder nodes.

2.1.2. Typical HSC Management

As any supply chains, HSCs aim at delivering the right products at the right place, quantity, quality and time. However, each disaster represents a new operating context for HOs to deal with. Indeed, each humanitarian operation phase heads toward a different resource and supply mobilization: e.g. (i) the preparation phase – to limit potential negative effects, (ii) the immediate response phase after the strike, and (iii) the reconstruction phase to reach toward a stable acceptable situation [3]. In fact, each new crisis is the occasion of a new HSC development since numerous logistics nodes and linkages come in addition to the existing structure, inducing many coordination issues [1]. Besides, since most of the disasters occur too suddenly to allow precise anticipation, humanitarians face many uncertainties regarding the disaster itself (occurrence and impacts) and the resources they are to rely on. Indeed, funding takes time to be gathered and liquidity is limited, volunteers are restricted due to a high turnover and finally, the infrastructure may be damaged or under-equipped [10]. Consequently, HOs struggle making plans [8] and generally apply a firefighting approach [10]. Regarding logistics, this represents a challenge because HOs must be ready to deploy at any moment even with some blur regarding the future needs and the damages. Therefore, to be able to deliver the products to beneficiaries, the HSC management encompasses a range of operations related to material, information and financial flows [11]. However, unlike the business sector, it currently does not integrate any production operation. Consequently, the core functions remain the supply and distribution. Regarding the supply operations, relief items are directly purchased from suppliers, gathered from pre-positioned stocks or provided by donors both either across borders or locally [12]. Supplies arrive in the country via airport, seaport or land border points, and before entering the country they usually need to go through a relatively long custom clearance process. Then, the distribution is proceeded in a cascading effect according to a hierarchical tree structure. For example, once items cross the border of the affected country, they may be sent to a primary hub, then to secondary warehouses, to finish at local level depots for fulfilling the needs of beneficiaries [13], [12], [14].

2.2. Physical Internet

The 'Physical Internet' (PI, π) is an innovative concept that completely remodels the logistics foundations, aiming to enable improving by an order of magnitude the economic, environmental and societal sustainability of the way physical objects are moved, handled, stored, realised, supplied, designed and used through the world [2]. Unsustainability symptoms abound. As an illustration, global demand for freight transportation is expected to triple by 2050, while induced CO2 emissions are also projected to significantly increase and compromise Paris agreement targets [15]. Alongside with these, studies show that transportation assets are underused, with 25% empty truck travel and 10% carrying space efficiency [16]. In view of these observations, the Physical Internet proposes a restructuring of the current logistics system with new components and management principles.

2.2.1. PI Main Components

PI is inspired from the Digital Internet (DI) but instead of dealing with data it is dealing with physical objects. In fact, while the Digital Internet is defined as 'the network of computer networks', similarly the Physical Internet is 'the network of logistics networks' [17]. A rapid explanation about the DI operating mode can help better understand the parallel. Indeed, within the DI, when an email must be sent, it is broken down into standardised data packets. Then, these transit to the recipient through different information networks connected between each other with routers. The role of routers is to orient data packets toward the next node toward reaching their destination [17]. Similarly, within the Physical Internet, senders are mainly suppliers and receivers are mainly clients. The networks are logistics networks, the routers become logistics hubs, while the physical packets are standardised packaging, handling and transport containers (π-containers) [17]. PI is based on the following building blocks: (1) unified set of standard modular containers; (2) containerized logistics equipment and technology; (3) standard logistics protocols; (4) certified open logistics facilities and ways; (5) global logistics monitoring systems; (6) open logistics decisional and transactional platforms; (7) smart data-driven analytics, optimization, simulation and artificial intelligence; and (8) certified open logistics service providers and users (adapted from [18]).

2.2.2. PI Management Principles

Nowadays, supply chains mostly operate independently with dedicated assets (warehouses, equipment, trucks, etc.), sharing only the transportation infrastructure. Besides, they are not well connected due to interoperability issues [17]. Knowing this, PI tempts to overturn this structuration as "a hyperconnected global logistics system enabling seamless open asset sharing and flow consolidation through standardized encapsulation, modularization, protocols and interfaces to improve the efficiency and sustainability of fulfilling humanity's demand for physical object services [18]. PI is global as it spans the world at all scales, from within buildings and cities to crossing continents and the globe. It is hyperconnected as its components and actors are intensely interconnected on multiple layers, ultimately anytime, anywhere. Interconnectivity layers include digital, physical, operational, business, legal and personal layers [18], collectively easing PI nodes to exchange physical objects and information and to coordinate [18]. It shifts towards interconnecting once private networks into an open logistics web accessible to and shared by any certified user and operated by many distinct parties. As a concept illustration, assume a client wants to order some products via the PI from different suppliers. Once they get the information, the items would be packed into adapted π-containers. Then, they would transit node to node through the different logistics networks. The order's progress would be notified to both the suppliers and the client since the containers are digitally connected. Each time a π-hub receives some π-containers, similar as a digital router would do, those are sorted and reorganised with other π-containers going to the same destination [17]. Based on criteria like the targeted arrival date and destination as well as an assigned budget, the π-containers are routed accordingly in the perspective to meet these objectives [18].

Based on these characteristics, PI enables offering a more resilient, efficient, sustainable and adaptable logistics web service to its users [18]. Indeed, by connecting nodes and creating a larger and open network, PI offers more routing opportunities and storage allocation availability [16]. Consequently, unforeseen events like the temporary loss of one or multiple nodes would be easier to manage by rerouting or using other available facilities [16]. Secondly, service levels would be improved by the gain in efficiency in the transport and warehousing domains. By mutualising containers going to the same destination, transportation would be optimised using the appropriate combination of modes and parties, with a higher loading ratio and less empty travel [16]. Besides, fewer vehicles would be required and thus, would lead to traffic disgorgement, costs reduction and less green gas emissions [16]. Additionally, the global design of all PI elements enables smoothing and speeding up the physical flow which would be noticeable in the delivery lead time capacity [16]. Regarding warehousing, the possibility to share and use storage areas that most of the time are unsaturated [2], would allow optimising the facilities and amortising the logistics costs, while enabling to deploy stocks across numerous distributed facilities near demand across wide geomarkets [16]. Finally, by the use of standardised protocols and contracts, PI allows a high degree of open cooperation between the different types of actors [18].

2.3. Hyperconnected Humanitarian Supply Chain

Regarding the state of the art related to hyperconnected humanitarian supply chains, it appears that this domain has benefited from meagre attention. Indeed, using the combination of key words such as 'Physical Internet' or 'Hyperconnected' and 'Humanitarian' has ensued in few results. A possible explanation relies on the Physical Internet is a recent concept and since it is increasing its visibility in the commercial sector, it appears plausible few applications in other domains have been investigated. Nonetheless, the two papers found [19];[20] are in accordance with this one as they are at all of them the point of conceptualizing what being hyperconnected would mean in the humanitarian sector and highlighting the early positive insights.

3. Research Question and Methodology

In the view of the issues faced by HOs to fulfil the relief needs of beneficiaries in a more effective, efficient and sustainable manner, the PI approach seems an appropriate solution to overcome these problematics. Indeed, its capabilities enhanced resilience, adaptability, efficiency and sustainability capabilities, demonstrated for commercial supply chains, are attractive but need to be proved as relevant and suitable for the humanitarian sector. In this perspective, this paper proposes a performance assessment methodology for organizing and realizing such an investigation and provide preliminary experimental illustrations to present the premises of the approach. The introduced methodology consists of seven stages namely, system definition, system grasp, system modelling, experiment design, experiment testing, results & analysis, and reporting findings.

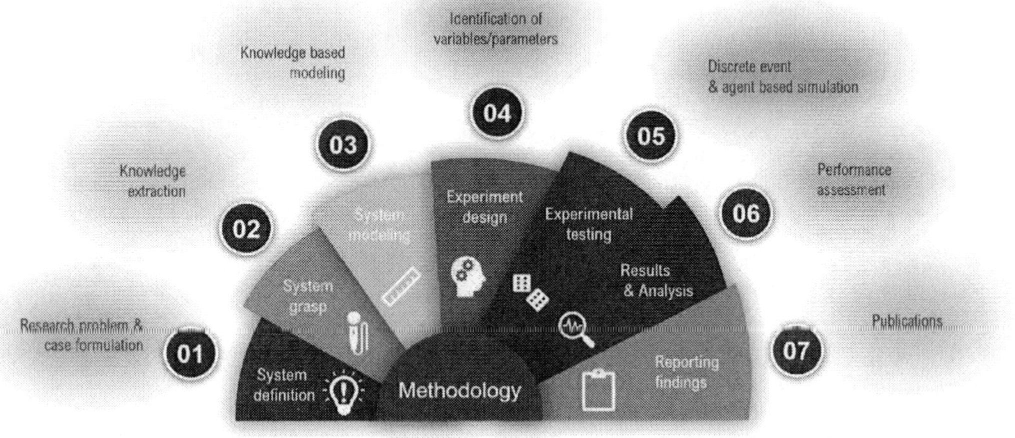

Figure 1 - The research methodology in 7 stages and associated tools

Starting with the system definition, since the study intends to check the possibility of PI internet applied to the humanitarian domain, a small-scale study needs to be developed to explore and test the PI approach [21]. In that sense, we are planning to focus on a region where populations are distributed and upon which, HOs are engaged in the perspective to deliver relief items to victims in case of a disaster. The second phase, the system grasp, is about extracting knowledge from experts through data collection, field observations, interviews and literature review to get a better understanding about the defined system. Such survey has not only the objective to get a picture of HOs objectives, strategies and available resources but also requires investigating the territory characteristics and its vulnerabilities that are directly directing the relief demand in the event of a disaster. Additionally, to give more authenticity to the case, we would require past disasters information to replay a period that HOs had to face and respond to. Then, the modelling phase consists in building a representation of the defined system to observe and learn lessons from its behaviour. It includes the creation of a territory model with its typology and administrative division, a demand model based on population distribution and the impacts of past disasters as well as, a HOs model which, for each HO would associate their management rules (decision rules, objectives, specifications…) and logistics networks. At that progress, an expert validation will be required before any further action can be taken. After that, the experiment design comes about. It is a question of first, determining the scope of the experiment e.g. which of the supply chain functions we seek to observe (procurement, warehousing…). Secondly, it is about defining which variables or parameters we intend to modulate. Indeed, since we are considering applying PI to HOs, the territory and demand models created are regarded as a fixed baseline. However, some PI oriented change can take place at the level of two major components within HOs which the management principles and the logistics network organisation are. From those two, a multitude of subcomponents is possible to vary and combine to create scenarios such as for instance, the transport and stock-level strategies for the management principles or even the assets location for the network organisation. At last, since we plan to make an assessment through the HOs performance, we need to select some metrics as key performance indicators (KPIs) to draw conclusions. Then, the fifth step is about testing the proposed experiment design. To do so, we intend to use a discrete event and agent-based simulation to free from costs and risks associated to a concrete implementation. With the simulation, we would be able to play different response scenarios based on the same environment and disaster context. From those, we would be in position to analyse the performance results and make comparisons. In the end, the conclusions would be shared through publication to suggest if further investigations need to be undertaken or not in such domain of PI applied to the humanitarian aid.

4. Experiment and Discussion

To get a better insight of the methodology proposed, we suggest an overview of its implementation through a rapid case study built for the occasion and serving as a support to highlight first perspectives of the PI for the humanitarian sector.

4.1. System Definition, System Grasp and Modelling

As previously mentioned in the system definition phase of the methodology, we focus on a region where populations are distributed and upon which, HOs are engaged in the perspective of delivering relief items to victims in case of a disaster. The following case is inspired by the current Indonesian Red Cross organization following a 10-day field survey made in July 2019. It has been worked to become as generic as possible and applicable to diverse regions of the world where HOs would be positioned.
The system modelling has started with the region conception. Indeed, as any territory, the model is divided administratively into several layers. For simplification purposes of the case, as displayed in Figure 2, the region encompasses 3 provinces differentiated by red lines, each of them contains about 16 districts highlighted by black lines. Finally, each district is supervising 25 subdistricts or villages appearing as coloured squares. Then, since humanitarian organisations are closely linked to people, population density has been integrated in the model. Concretely, through a dedicated Python code, we generated a population density mapping based on statistics and distribution rules defined at the region and district levels. The generated population distribution is depicted in Figure 2 by colouring the subdistricts in light, medium or dark blue according to the assigned population density. Also, from the survey about relief logistics practices in Indonesia [22], we identified different types of humanitarian organizations (governmental, NGOs…) and associated roles (coordinator, ministries, local or international…) that may co-exist within the same territory.
For the case, we have considered 5 different HOs represented by geometric shapes (star, circle, triangle, pentagon and octagon), and managing 2 or 3 of the 5 relief items defined for the case: Products 1 & 2 (P1, P2) and Kits 1,2 & 3 (K1, K2 and K3) (See Table 1). The logistics network of each HO depicted in Figure 2 is based on criteria outlined in [22] and field observations in terms of location of the permanent relief logistics facilities. At last, the response behavior and preparation strategy from HOs are inspired from interviews.

Table 1 - HOs' relief items catalogue

	HO1	HO2	HO3	HO4	HO5
Product 1 *(P1)*	X			X	
Product 2 *(P2)*			X	X	
Kit 1 *(K1)*	X	X			X
Kit 2 *(K2)*		X	X		X
Kit 3 *(K3)*	X		X		

4.2. Experiment Design and Testing

As a reminder, the experiment intends to assess the advantages of introducing PI approach in the humanitarian domain and to show the impacts on response performance. Since this represents a large spectrum, the scope has been restricted to two core functions of the downstream part of the chain, namely the warehousing and delivery activities. Using the case study, we investigate how different transport and storage strategies, relocations, as well as the addition of the interconnection concept, are prone to affect some major metrics such as the coverage level, the transportation cost and the assets use. Regarding the experimental testing, since the case is fictional, we decided to lead the investigations through several experimental illustrations.

4.3. Results and Analysis

So far, each HOs is accustomed to position facilities autonomously, and tends to base its decisions on administrative, transport access and human resources criteria. This is illustrated in Figure 2 that shows the distribution of the different logistics networks associated with each HO through HO-specific maps, and then their overlapping on an integrated map. It stands out that the coverage over HOs is heterogeneous. Indeed, facilities are mostly concentrated in areas with clusters in high-level population density areas, while four districts have no facilities from any HO.

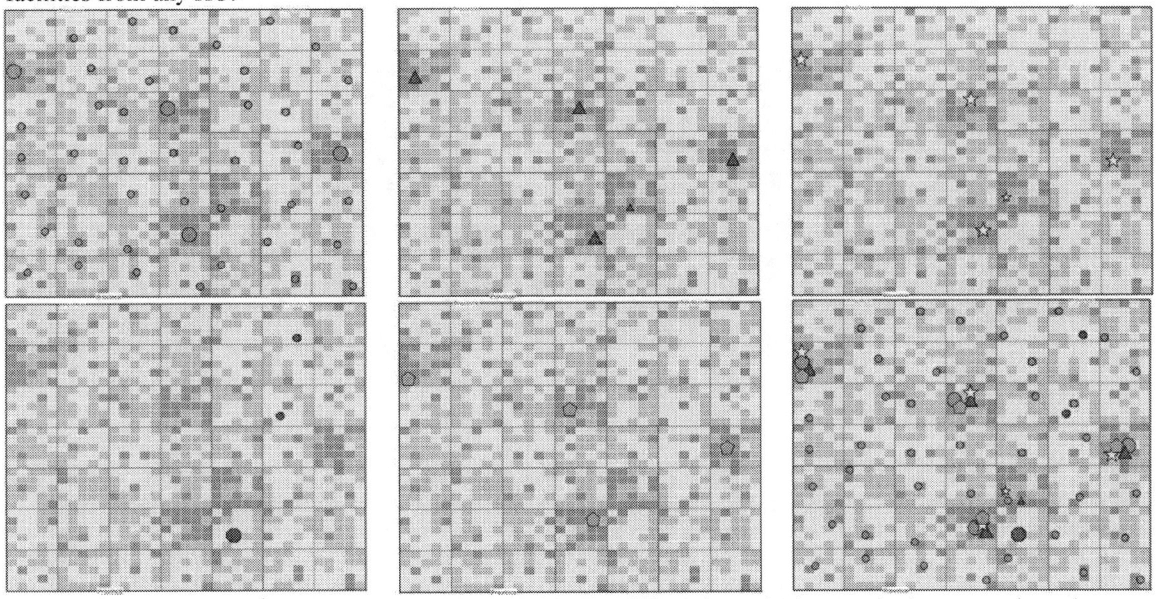

Figure 2 – (From 1st to 5th map) Logistics distribution of the five different humanitarian organizations across the region. (6th lower right map) The aggregation of the different network nodes displayed on the same territory.

In the event of a disaster, the first few hours are decisive for the number of victims. That is why, aid agencies must be prepared to provide first aid at any moment and this, as fast as possible. In that sense, investigation of the response time to supply relief items across the territory, i.e. the coverage, we can see variances between the different relief products. Indeed, if we consider the green circle as the reachable zones in 24 hours, the 24-hour coverage has been assessed for P1, P2, K1, K2 and K3 respectively as 28, 88, 24, 83 and 83% (See Figure 3).

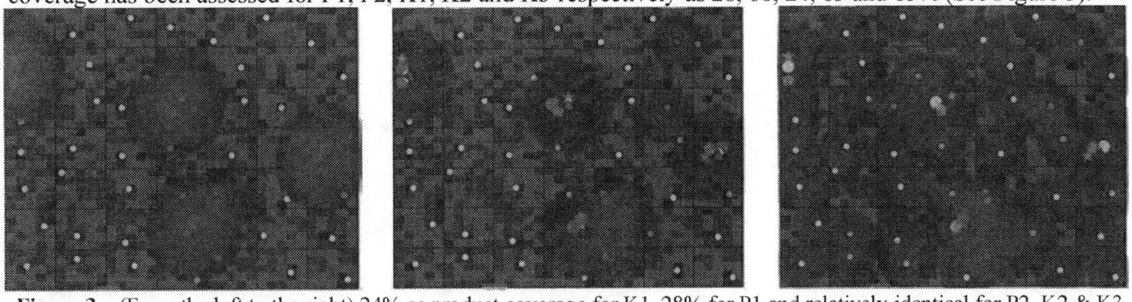

Figure 3 – (From the left to the right) 24% as product coverage for K1, 28% for P1 and relatively identical for P2, K2 & K3 with a range from 83 to 88%

By merging and sharing facilities, as PI suggests it, any HO would have access to additional storage areas and get the opportunity to fulfil remaining spaces with their products. Consequently, the delivery lead time for products K1 and P2 would significantly decrease while the asset use and global service level would increase (See Figure 4). Additionally, we can expect to optimise assets and coverage. First, by reducing the number of facilities in some too much covered areas and by relocating them smartly, it is possible to increase the coverage with the same number of assets. Besides, it is not even necessary to relocate them all. For the same coverage level, the total amount of relief facilities can be reduced, and money saved could serve other purposes. However, reducing this amount would probably induce to resize some facilities according to the demand. As an illustration, by evaluating the number of subdistricts uncovered, the coverage level reaches 88% with 61 assets while in the second scenario, it is possible to get 96% as coverage with only 47 positions (See Figure 4).

Now considering delivery both within the same organisation and between the agencies, some adjustments are possible. Currently, within the same institution the supply and delivery between the different warehouses are generally organised according to a hierarchical tree. In other words, regional warehouses oversee supplying district facilities and so on from district to subdistrict. Such organisation has been set for strategy reasons such as better control and minimal safety stock, yet it increases delivery lead time and transportation costs, notably when the target supplier node does not have the stock required. One opportunity suggested by the PI approach is adding an

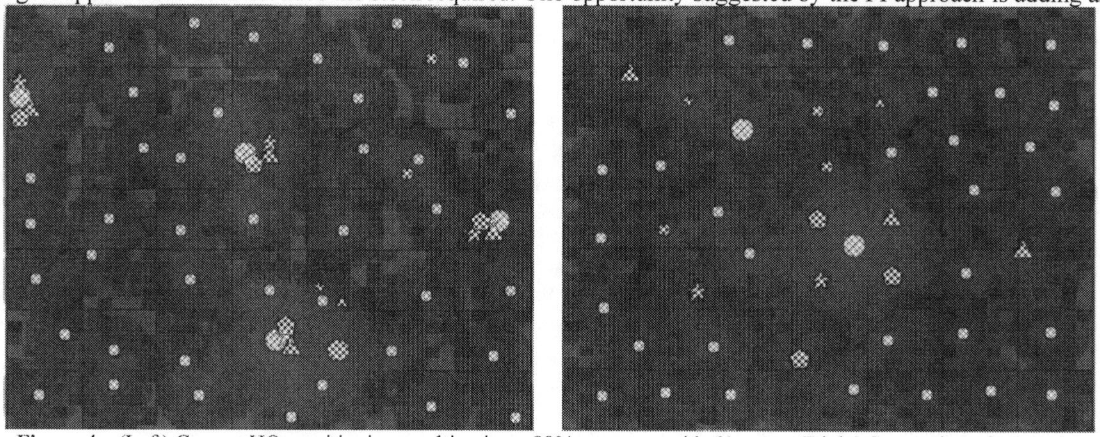

Figure 4 – (Left) Current HOs positioning resulting in an 88% coverage with 61 assets (Right) Suggestion of relocation leading to a 96% of coverage with 47 facilities.

horizontal flow capability to the up to now hierarchical vertical distribution. The different facilities could supply based on need and availability (See Figure 5). Consequently, we can expect to increase stock agility, enabling to move inventory based on disaster-prone seasonality. Besides, the delivery lead time between nodes would be reduced as well as the transportation costs. HOs are accustomed to use dedicated delivery networks. This approach is simpler to manage, offers fewer interferences and guarantees a higher control and availability of the assets. However, as a result, we note a duplication of transport means targeting the destinations and so, a duplication of costs and trucks less than fully filled (See Figure 5, on the left). To overcome this issue, PI puts consolidating transport forward e.g. grouping deliveries having the same destination. Consolidating deliveries shows promises in increasing truck loading rate, reducing transport costs and transport induced gas emissions. Indeed, as an illustration, Figure 5 presents on the left the current approach where each institution is sending a vehicle and where most of them are lowly filled. Alternatively, in the right part of Figure 5, horizontal and transport consolidation has been employed, leading at an organisation level to transportation cost reduction of 42% for yellow organisation, 59% for orange, 41% for red and 24% for purple, based on the routes taken and shared. Additionally, the improved coordination leads to optimized delivery with less trucks, less mileage, and less greenhouse gas emissions.

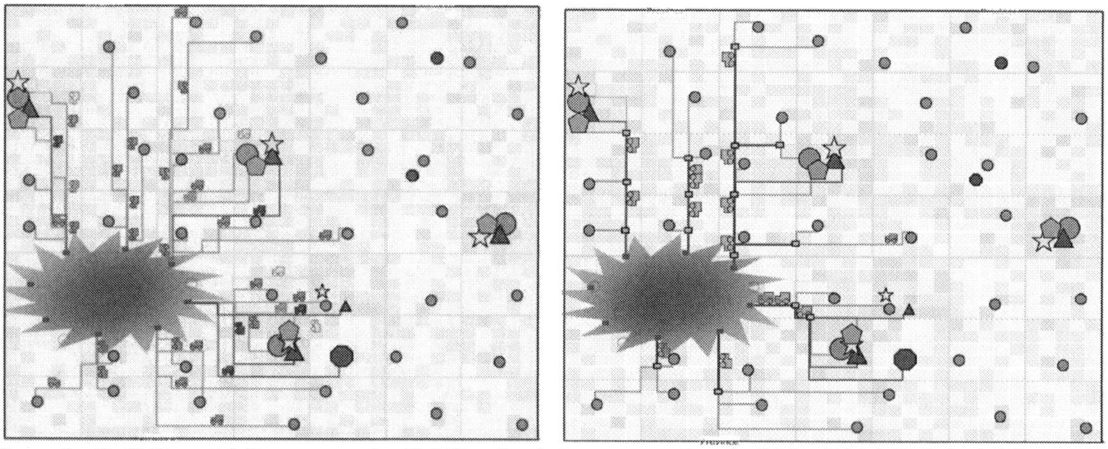

Figure 5 – (Left) Current delivery approach with HOs using their own network and vehicles (Right) Optimized delivery with the introduction of the transport consolidation and interconnection of the HOs.

5. Further Research

At the core of this article is to assess whether Physical Internet properties unlock keys for the success of tomorrow's humanitarian organizations. Becoming more hyperconnected requires some significant changes that have to be evaluated before any implementation. In that sense, the study presented a 7-step methodology to organise such investigation. Using a modelling and simulation approach enables to make this assessment free from any risk and engagement. However, in such a complex domain, it would be hasty jumping to conclusions from the few experiment illustrations presented previously. Indeed, those were destined to highlight some first advantages of the Physical Internet in the humanitarian sector. Consequently, to gain in authenticity and legitimacy, and to uncover relevant and valuable insights, we plan to build and investigate through the proposed approach a more realistic and complex case based on a real system, with the validation of humanitarian actors. Besides, we intend playing scenarios based on a large period to certify as stable the observed behaviours and performance. Additionally, we intend to complexify the experiment design with additional supply chain functions and widening the scope as well as the variables to modulate and the choice of KPIs.

6. References

1. Van Wassenhove, L.N.: Humanitarian aid logistics: supply chain management in high gear. Journal of the Operational Research Society. 57, 475–489 (2006). https://doi.org/10.1057/palgrave.jors.2602125
2. Montreuil, B.: Toward a Physical Internet: meeting the global logistics sustainability grand challenge. Logistics Research. 3, 71–87 (2011). https://doi.org/10.1007/s12159-011-0045-x
3. Kovacs, G., Spens, K.M.: Humanitarian logistics in disaster relief operations. International Journal of Physical Distribution & Logistics Management. 37, 99–114 (2007). https://doi.org/10.1108/09600030710734820
4. Thomas, A.: Humanitarian Logistics: Enabling Disaster Response. Fritz Institute (2008)
5. Cozzolino, A.: Humanitarian Logistics: Cross-Sector Cooperation in Disaster Relief Management. Springer-Verlag, Berlin Heidelberg (2012)
6. Altay, N., Heaslip, G., Kovács, G., Spens, K., Tatham, P., Vaillancourt, A.: Innovation in Humanitarian Supply Chains: A Systematic Review. 27 (2018)
7. Pishvaee, M.S., Jolai, F., Razmi, J.: A stochastic optimization model for integrated forward/reverse logistics network design. Journal of Manufacturing Systems. 28, 107–114 (2009). https://doi.org/10.1016/j.jmsy.2010.05.001
8. Charles, A., Lauras, M.: An enterprise modelling approach for better optimisation modelling: application to the humanitarian relief chain coordination problem. OR Spectrum. 33, 815–841 (2011). https://doi.org/10.1007/s00291-011-0255-2
9. Kopczak, L.R., Matthews, G.: Measuring Markets That Supply Cash-Based Humanitarian Interventions. In: Zobel, C.W., Altay, N., and Haselkorn, M.P. (eds.) Advances in Managing Humanitarian Operations. pp. 79–109. Springer International Publishing, Cham (2016)
10. Tomasini, R., Wassenhove, L.V.: Humanitarian Logistics. Springer (2009)
11. Kovacs, G., Spens, K.M. eds: Relief supply chain management for disasters: humanitarian aid and emergency logistics. Information Science Reference, Hershey, PA (2012)
12. Balcik, B., Beamon, B.M., Krejci, C.C., Muramatsu, K.M., Ramirez, M.: Coordination in humanitarian relief chains: Practices, challenges and opportunities. International Journal of Production Economics. 126, 22–34 (2010). https://doi.org/10.1016/j.ijpe.2009.09.008
13. Beamon, B.M., Balcik, B.: Performance measurement in humanitarian relief chains. International Journal of Public Sector Management. 21, 4–25 (2008). https://doi.org/10.1108/09513550810846087
14. Laguna Salvadó, L., Lauras, M., Comes, T., Bénaben, F.: Structuring humanitarian supply chain knowledge through a meta-modeling approach. (2018)
15. ITF: ITF Transport Outlook 2019. OECD Publishing, Paris (2019)
16. Ballot, É.: L'Internet physique: le réseau des réseaux des prestations logistiques. la Documentation française, Paris (2014)
17. Sarraj, R., Ballot, E., Pan, S., Montreuil, B.: Analogies between Internet network and logistics service networks: challenges involved in the interconnection. J Intell Manuf. 25, 1207–1219 (2014). https://doi.org/10.1007/s10845-012-0697-7
18. Montreuil, B., Meller, R.D., Ballot, E.: Physical Internet Foundations. In: Borangiu, T., Thomas, A., and Trentesaux, D. (eds.) Service Orientation in Holonic and Multi Agent Manufacturing and Robotics. pp. 151–166. Springer Berlin Heidelberg, Berlin, Heidelberg (2013)
19. Abdoulkadre, A., Intissar, B.O., Marian, M., Benoit, M.: Towards Physical Internet Enabled Interconnected Humanitarian Logistics. 30 (2014)
20. Grest, M., Lauras, M., Montreuil, B.: Toward Humanitarian Supply Chains Enhancement by using Physical Internet Principles. 8th International Conference on Industrial Engineering and Systems Management. (2019)
21. Bairagi, V., munot, mousami: Research Methodology: A Practical and Scientific Approach. (2019)
22. Kusumastuti, R.D., Insanita, R., Wibowo, S.S.: Relief Logistics Practices in Indonesia: A Survey. Social Science Research Network, Rochester, NY (2010)

I L S 2020
INTERNATIONAL CONFERENCE ON INFORMATION SYSTEMS, LOGISTICS & SUPPLY CHAIN
Austin, Texas April 22-24, 2020

Best Practices for Implementing Building Information Modeling in the Prefabrication Sector

Basma Ben Mahmoud [1], Nadia Lehoux [2], Pierre Blanchet [3]

[1,2] Laval University, CIRCERB, Department of mechanical engineering, Quebec, Canada
[3] Laval University, CIRCERB, Department of wood science and forestry, Quebec, Canada
{basma.ben-mahmoud.1@ulaval.ca, Nadia.Lehoux@gmc.ulaval.ca, Pierre.Blanchet@sbf.ulaval.ca}

Abstract. Nowadays, Building information modeling (BIM) seems to be an asset to face the gap that may occur in the presence of several tools, various disciplines and different experience levels in the construction industry. In fact, this approach helps stakeholders speak a common language by working on the same 3D model. Nevertheless, implementing BIM raises interesting challenges linked to many aspects, especially the human resource factor. Thus, this paper aims to reveal the best strategies to implement BIM in SMEs and to highlight the best practices that help face the main barriers during this phase. On the basis of a literature review and semi-structured interviews, the most notable findings are the impact of human barriers which are significant, the importance of starting the implementation phase by analyzing the company's current business processes so as to maximize BIM benefits, as well as, setting a strategic plan to outline the main steps and the different factors of this digital shift in order to better lead and support the whole staff.

Keywords: BIM, Prefabrication, Implementation, Best practices, Semi-structured interview, SMEs

1. Introduction

During the post First World War period, off-site construction appeared as the best technique to provide numerous temporary and emergency prefabricated buildings such as houses and schools [1]. Due to its potential benefits such as saving time, improving labor productivity and enhancing project quality [2], this industry has been widely spread all over the world, particularly in Canada. Likewise, Quebec remains the leading province in this field as it provides 29.7% of Canadian manufactories in 2015 [3]. Nonetheless, construction projects have been known for their fragmentation, complexity, and challenges [4] due to the involvement of different stakeholders from various fields (architectural, structural, electrical, mechanical, etc.) and other factors such as deadlines, budgets, human resources, etc. Thus, an approach such as Building Information Modeling (BIM) seems to be an efficient way to face these challenges and to better achieve prefabrication benefits. In fact, it aims to facilitate communication and coordination between stakeholders along different phases of a construction project using a shared 3D model containing relevant information about the building. However, transition from a traditional method to BIM requires investments in terms of budget, time and skills. These requirements may seem risky for small and medium enterprises (SMEs) that represent the largest proportion of the construction industry in Canada (99.8% in 2017 [5]). Even though BIM has captured academics' and practitioners' attention over the years, finding a specific methodology to implement and manage the approach, especially in SMEs, remains an open question.

Hence, this study aims to reveal the best strategies for BIM deployment in SMEs as well as to highlight the best practices to support the firm's progress while avoiding issues. To do so, a series of semi-structured interviews were conducted with several BIM experts.

This paper will be divided into three main sections. The first one proceeds with a review of relevant literature that highlights the baselines of BIM. The second section outlines the methodology used to better conduct the interviews, and the third presents the results of the study. Finally, a conclusion summarizes the main achievements and perspectives.

2. Literature review

In order to outline the baselines of BIM and its potential in the prefabricated sector, the first part of this project was dedicated to a literature review. Thus, several key words, such as BIM, Building Information Modeling, implementation, deployment, prefabricated construction, prefabricated building, prefabrication, off-site construction, best practices, medium and small firms, etc., were used to formulate the search criteria used in different databases, such as Compendex, Inspec, Proquest and Web of Science.

2.1. BIM definition and process

As a broad approach, many definitions have been associated to BIM (Building Information Modeling) over time. Some researchers and professionals see it as a 3D modeling software, others consider it as a new technology, while some define it as a new process that aims to facilitate communication and coordination between the stakeholders as well as management of a building project [3], [6]–[10]. Another relevant definition, cited in the BIM Handbook [11], introduces BIM as a modeling technology and associated set of processes to produce, communicate, and analyze building models. To avoid confusion, many authors use three key concepts to clarify the BIM process: Model, Modeling and Management [12], [13], [14]. To sum up, Building Information Modeling can be defined as a new way of working on a building project, based on a strong collaboration between stakeholders using a 3D model created via the advanced software. Used properly, it provides an efficient way to share information along the project lifecycle, leading to several benefits such as better project management and monitoring.
In order to describe the BIM process, we will first define the main levels of this process that are presented in figure 1: level of maturity, level of capability and level of development.

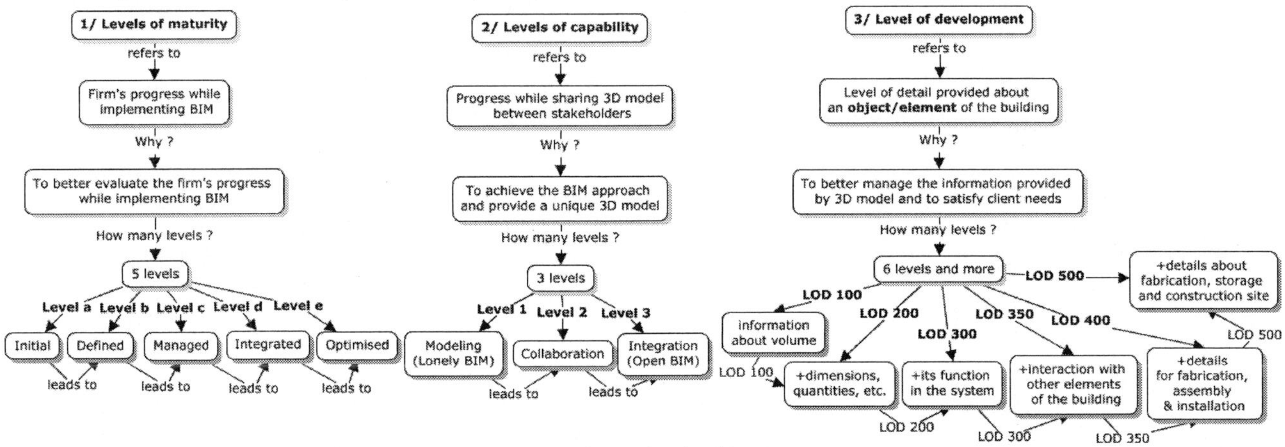

Figure 1: The relevant levels of BIM.

The maturity level refers to the performance improvement milestones that organizations, teams and the whole market aspire to achieve while implementing BIM. There are five levels according to Succar BIMMI (BIM Maturity Index)[15] [16]: the first level is called "Initial" as it is the first step of BIM deployment. BIM tools are installed but there is a shortage of defined processes, responsibilities, goals, etc. as when working with traditional method while using BIM software. The second one, called "Defined", is characterized by well-defined baselines of this approach. The third level "Managed level" refers to a better management of the whole process. This level is known for an efficient communication and a better understanding of the BIM process but productivity is not yet predictable. The fourth one, called "Integrated level", is characterized by better quality management and performance improvement through performance benchmarks. The productivity is consistent and predictable compared to the previous level. The last level "Optimized level" leads to review and updating of different factors related to the BIM approach (strategies, processes, tools, contractual models, etc.) in order to align it with the company's target. The capability level refers to the expertise of the company while using BIM and sharing the 3D model [17]. In fact, there are three levels of capability: the first level is called "modeling/Lonely BIM" as each actor will be interested in his/her own model, the second one is called "collaboration" so all stakeholders will exchange their models for a better communication. The third level known as "Integration/Open BIM" requires an

integration of different models (architectural, structural, MEP, etc.) in order to make one shared 3D model that will be used in the following phases of the construction project [18]. The level of development (LOD), refers to the information provided to introduce an element of the building in the 3D model. From one level to another, more details will be provided (dimensions, materials, connection details, etc.).
Based on the previous concepts, the BIM process starts with an intradisciplinary modeling, after a planning phase, in which every actor (architect, structural/MEP engineer) creates his/her own model. Once a quality control, a revision and an approval are made by a BIM expert of each department, models will be shared between those actors in order to ensure a better coordination and communication. The last step leads to the creation of a unique 3D model that will be shared and used by stakeholders to detect any conflict or error before the construction phase. This 3D model is called a federated model [19].

2.2. BIM benefits and limits

During the last decade, the construction industry faced a notable transition towards the BIM approach given the advantages offered by this new process. Many authors studied these benefits with interest in order to quantify their effect on a firm's progress [6], [20], [21]. The most commonly reported benefits are enhancing communication and coordination between the stakeholders through centralized information, reducing the total cost and duration of the project, enhancing the quality of the building and increasing the productivity and safety of the employees [13]. Moreover, many advantages could be deducted through the different BIM applications such as clash detection that allows to avoid a lot of errors and rework during the construction phase, a better visualization via the shared 3D model, better scheduling offered via BIM 4D, cost estimation through BIM 5D and so on [3], [18], as shown in Table 1.

Table 1 : BIM benefits based on BIM dimesions and applications.

BIM 3D Modeling	**BIM 4D Scheduling**	**BIM 5D Cost estimation**	**BIM 6D Sustainability**	**BIM 7D Facility management**
Better visualization; More details; Better coordination/ communication; Clash detection.	Project phasing simulation; Sequencing of activities on site; Avoiding delays; Better monitoring of the project.	Quantity extraction to support cost estimate; Risk management; Order checks through fabrication models.	Energy analysis; Performance analysis; Sustainable tracking; Better quality.	Better facility management; Better operation of the building during its lifecycle; Maintenance plans and technical support.

Although it has numerous potential benefits, BIM raises interesting challenges and barriers that may be faced during the implementation phase. These barriers are related to resistance to change from the staff, several tools and software, the confidence level between stakeholders, lack of data integration and intellectual property of 3D model, etc.[22]. In fact, the deployment and efficient operation of BIM in a company require a systematic effort from various teams and multiple disciplines with problem solving interactions throughout the project lifecycle [23]. Moreover, many other issues may occur such as lack of sufficient knowledge of BIM, need of well-trained staff, lack of well-defined objectives, misunderstanding of the client's needs, interoperability problems and low rate of return in investment (ROI) that requires a longer time to profit from BIM, etc.[24][25].

2.3. BIM in prefabrication

Prefabrication is a vast concept that refers to any element of a building (truss, floor, module, etc.) that has been fabricated in a location other than its final location (workshop, factories, etc.) to be transported, installed and assembled on site [1]. Compared with traditional methods of construction, the global demand for prefabricated buildings is increasing due to its energy and time savings, environmental considerations, as well as quality and safety improvement. In fact, producing most of the elements in a factory improves working conditions and speeds up the project progress [26] [2]. According to a recent survey, the typical process used by most manufacturers in Quebec is based on three main axes: design, fabrication and installation [18]. The design phase includes project definition, task identification and preparation of relevant documents (plans, contract, etc.) that take place in the offices. The fabrication stage takes place in the

factory and consists of construction and assembly of prefabricated elements. The last step includes transportation, installation, on-site assembly and finishing of the modules to deliver the final building.
Despite its numerous advantages, prefabrication faces the same problems and issues that may affect any construction project such as lack of coordination and communication between stakeholders especially during the design phase, shortage of details and information sharing that leads to interference problems during the construction stage and on-site storage problems. Thus, BIM helps resolve these problems and achieve better prefabrication benefits due to its capacity to promote effective information exchange while also automating several steps in the design, estimation, and planning phases [27].
Applying BIM in the prefabrication sector will be detailed based on the three main axes of this process. At the planning and design stage, BIM brings several applications including: information sharing, visualization, modeling, code reviews, site planning and analysis, fabrication drawings, communication, cost estimating, construction sequences, and collision detection [28]. Moreover, accurate building information not only provides support to the estimation department but also enables an increased level of detail for production scheduling and for simulation that is frequently used in this field for production line performance assessment [27]. During the manufacturing phase, several advantages could be noticed such as better quality control using accurate information of the 3D model and better management, monitoring and optimization of the production line using the efficient simulation offered by BIM tools [29]. Regarding the last phase which is the installation of prefabricated components on site, the use of BIM 4D allows to simulate different processes (transport, storage, lifting, etc.) which optimizes component inventory and site management. Thus, combining prefabrication with BIM can significantly lead to time/cost/energy savings, emission reduction and green environmental protection, which plays a great role in bolstering the transformation and upgrade of Canada's construction industry.

3. Methodology: Main steps to conduct the interviews

The second part of this project consists of conducting a series of interviews with BIM experts in order to collect relevant information from the industry as to the state of BIM adoption in Canada. From these interviews, a set of best strategies and practices will be developed to help SMEs make this digital shift.
In particular, a list of open-ended questions was first developed so as to get a better picture of the BIM approach and its deployment process. Fifteen questions was prepared, covering various aspects such as: experience of each participant and her/his background in BIM, BIM benefits, challenges and barriers faced while implementing this approach, the most suitable projects for BIM, strategies and steps taken to implement BIM, the best practices to progress via BIM, tips to maintain better communication and coordination between stakeholders, the role of each actor, the group hierarchy to better conduct this approach, the best software for the prefabrication sector, the most reluctant actors and the reasons leading to this behavior, etc. After that, a list of nine interviewees was established based on experts' experiences with BIM. The experts had different backgrounds and various positions (researchers, architects, engineers, BIM managers, BIM directors, etc.) and came from different organizations (government company, private consulting company, nonprofit organization, universities, etc.). They are known as the leaders of BIM in Quebec and their experience in this field ranges from two to twelve years with an average of eight years. Then, a series of meetings with the experts were planned. Different types of meetings (via Skype, phone or face-to-face) were proposed to facilitate this task. During the meetings, permission to record the interviews was obtained. The voice recordings were then transcribed into word files and imported into QDA Miner software for a qualitative analysis leading to a framework for the best strategies and practices to implement and conduct the BIM process. The main results are detailed in the next section.

4. Analysis and results

As explained previously, the use of QDA Miner allows for a better analysis of the massive amount of information collected during the interviews. Only the most important findings will be discussed in this section such as barriers for BIM deployment and best strategies and practices to implement the approach.

4.1. Main barriers for BIM implementation

The interview analysis lead to five main barriers to BIM deployment: human, technological, financial, organizational and contractual. Figure 2 shows the importance of each barrier in terms of percentage.

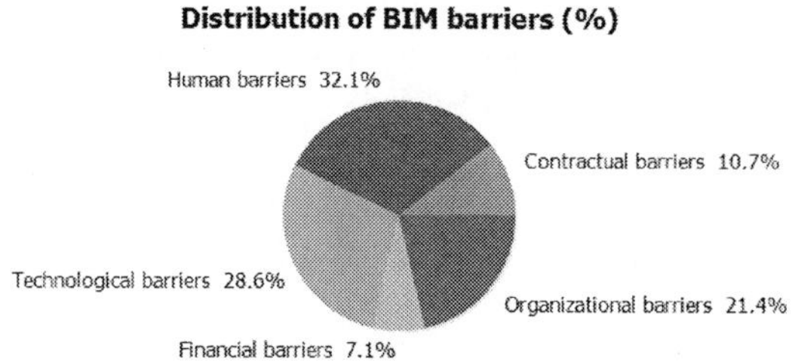

Figure 2: Distribution of BIM barriers according to the interview analysis.

Technological barriers arise in the form of various tools that may be used without planning or proficiency, as well as, information reliability and interoperability problems when goals are undefined. Organizational issues refer to management problems such as the absence of a management plan, lack of coordination between technical and BIM staff and information overload that must be well managed and used. Regarding financial barriers, it is mainly based on the cost and time investment required for BIM implementation. Most of this investment is spent on purchasing software, personal training, and recruiting specialized staff so the main challenge is to justify and explain these costs to project stakeholders [30]. Contractual barriers are highly linked to classic contract forms and the intellectual property of the 3D model. According to the interview results, 77.8% of experts think that the 3D model is not yet a contractual document but should be shared while 22.2% think it is a contractual one, whereas all of them think that, sooner or later, it will be a contractual document. Hence, some conflicts may occur between stakeholders and prevent them from having a clear view of their responsibilities and rights. Furthermore, the BIM approach is based on information sharing, liability and collaboration between stakeholders that require a new form of contract to outline the role of each actor and emphasize sharing responsibilities and risks. As claimed by most of the interviewees, the new contract must be seen as a management plan that aims to highlight the goals of the project and of using BIM, to organize the relations between actors, to clarify responsibilities and risks, to put the light on information sharing and to set the standards that will be used along the project. Regarding human barriers, this category seems to be the riskiest one as mentioned previously, so it will be interesting to reveal its different forms as well as the best practices to manage them. The most prominent ones arise in the form of resistance to change, lack of communication, skills shortage, lack of information sharing, weak sense of responsibility, misunderstanding of the BIM approach, bad habit of working at the last minute unlike the BIM process that requires a great effort at the early stage, etc. In order to face these barriers, rigorous planning, continuous training and team support must be taken as serious actions, see Figure 3.

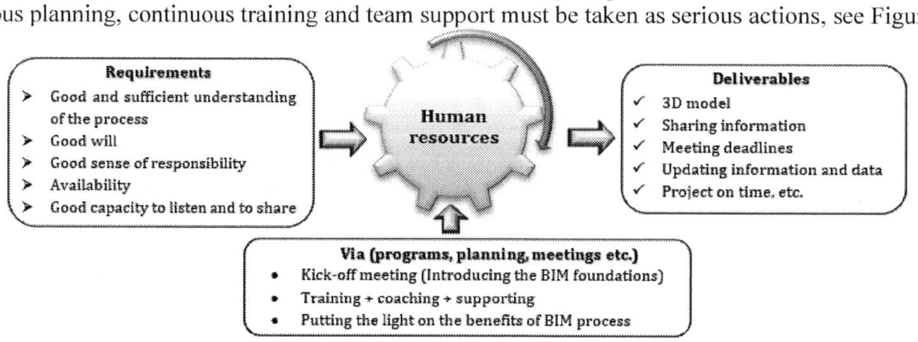

Figure 3: Human resources as a driver of the BIM process.

4.2. Best strategies to implement BIM in SMEs

Based on the interview outcomes, we were able to establish a BIM deployment framework in order to facilitate this phase, especially for SMEs, as shown in Figure 4. According to the experts, the BIM deployment process can be divided into three main axes: analysis, planning & conducting and piloting & monitoring [25][4]. The first axis is based on two main steps. In fact, all of the experts claimed that deploying BIM is innovating and improves the firm's existing situation, so it must start by analyzing this situation. Thus, the first step will be dedicated to examining the current situation of the company using process mapping, surveys or SWOT (Strength, Weaknesses, Opportunities and Threatens) analysis. This step aims to reveal the company's current means (processes, human resources, financial state, IT tools, standards, etc.). Moreover, the company must pay attention to the maturity and capability levels that have been introduced in the literature review, so as to better monitor its evolution while implementing BIM. Then, based on this analysis, the company should be able to detect the issues and areas of improvement in the current business model and identify the most profitable BIM application to implement first in order to enhance the existing situation. Once identified, a roadmap or strategic plan must be set up as a reference for BIM deployment. This plan includes answers and details about the main questions [31]: Why implement BIM (to increase productivity, to save time and cost, to be more competitive, to increase market share, etc.)? Who are the main actors of this process (BIM director, BIM manager, BIM coordinator, etc.)? Their roles and responsibilities? Their benefits? BIM applications to use in the first stage and how to make this transition? Different steps and tools used to do so? How to share information? What are the deliverables? Then, senior management has to establish the committee that will be responsible for this process deployment (assign members, their roles, required skills, availability, etc.). Once this plan is set, a kick off meeting must be planned in order to better introduce the BIM approach to all members. During this meeting, everyone will obtain a clear view of the responsibilities of each one, as well as, the deliverables that must be provided and the deadlines. Hence, this meeting aims to highlight the main steps, concepts and rules to better conduct BIM deployment. The tools required by the main committee, such as software and hardware, must also be set up at this point. Furthermore, all respondents agreed that an important step in the planning phase consists of aligning BIM processes with the current ones. Once tools are installed, staff is ready and all the concepts are clear, the next step will be dedicated to applying BIM in a pilot project in order to test it and to evaluate the firm's progress using this new approach. It is important to choose an appropriate pilot project as it is the first project realized using BIM. In this case, it is better to avoid critical projects limited by a short duration and/or an important budget. Finally, during the interviews, most of interviewees pointed out the need to set key success factors for BIM deployment assessment. These key factors may refer to time and cost saving, productivity increase, quality improvement, etc. Finally, meeting, reviewing and updating must be done after each step.

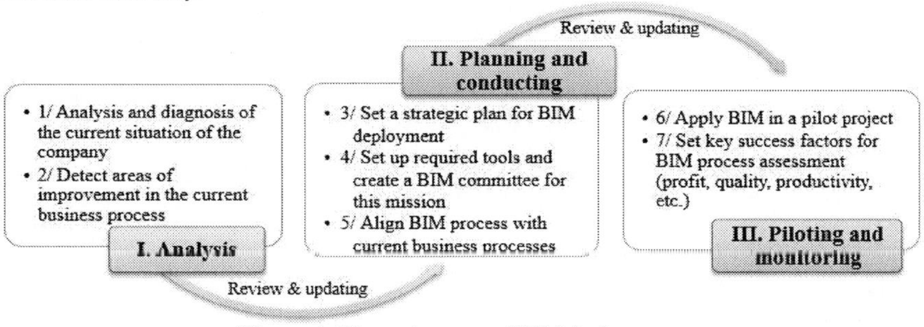

Figure 4: The main steps of BIM deployment.

4.3. Best practices for BIM adoption

Based on barrier classification, best practices will be related to each barrier class. Thus, there are five classes of best practices, linked to human resources, technologies, organization, financial and legal aspects. In the first class, one of the best practices is to better understand the different positions and responsibilities of each actor in order to ensure good functioning of the BIM process. According to most of the interviewees, the roles to occupy in a BIM approach are classified into three main functions, as shown in figure 5: management, coordination and modeling. The management function is given to a BIM manager/director who has the strategic vision and conducts the deployment phase. According to most of the interviewees, the BIM process can function without a BIM manager or director, but needs someone who has this vision to establish training plans, standards at the office level, to set best practices, to coach and support the group and to gather resources on the project, whatever its status. The coordination function is covered by the BIM coordinator or creator who has to ensure that the models respect the requirements, that they are well integrated and functioning, and to monitor the model evolution and project progress. The modeling function is delegated to the BIM modeler who should create and manage the 3D model based on the client needs so he/she must be well-skilled in using the basic modeling software.

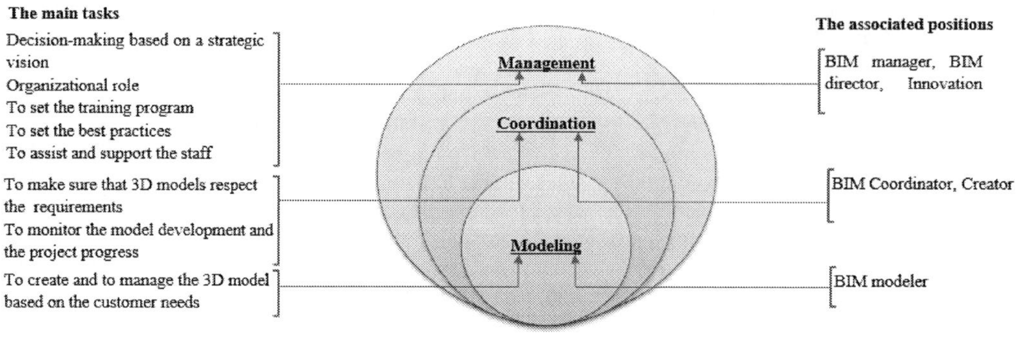

Figure 5: Three main functions in the BIM process.

The previous main classes of responsibilities must be present in each company in order to help stakeholders to better integrate the BIM approach and to achieve its benefits. Due to the importance of human resources in the BIM process, all respondents pointed out the need to support and coach BIM staff, to keep them motivated by sharing successful experiences and relevant knowledge, as well as, the main information about the company's progress. Furthermore, one of the main elements revealed in the interviews concerning this factor was to initially limit the number of members on the BIM committee and to ensure that they are given the time and resources to master this task. Then, they can become facilitators for the company. Another relevant practice is to invest considerable effort in the early stages of the project (planning and design phase) as it affects the following phases. It is also important to start the BIM transition with people who support this approach in order to create a favorable first BIM experience that will be shared among the group. Regarding the technological field, the committee must choose the right IT tools for the company's needs that will bring benefits and fit with group skills as well as the software that allows file exchange without interoperability problems. For the organizational factor, it seems better to start working with BIM 3D and to avoid working on all BIM dimensions at an early stage of the implementation. In fact, one of the most common mistakes made by some companies is aiming to reach all BIM applications from the first stage of BIM deployment without checking on the company maturity and capability levels. This mistake requires enormous effort and raises high risks. Another tip proposes to simplify and to facilitate the BIM process by avoiding the use of various tools and software so that standardization of practices (conventions, file extensions, data forms, etc.) helps offer better team support and process operation. Finally, it is extremely important to provide reference manuals and handbooks and to keep detailed records documenting each step. As for the legal aspect, it seems relevant to look for a new kind of contract that encourages the collaborative process, information sharing and outlines professional responsibilities. In fact, one of the new forms, mentioned during the interview, that may fit with the BIM approach, is CCDC 30 which is a new form of contract called Integrated Project Delivery Contract specific to IPD projects including scope allocation, payments, changes, conflict management, termination, insurance and contract security, and liability allocation [32]. In addition, intellectual property of the 3D model must be clarified at the beginning of the project to avoid conflicts throughout the execution. Finally, regarding the financial aspect, it is important to estimate a return on investment (ROI) and to use it as a reference for BIM profit assessment. According to the experts, showing financial benefits to headmasters will be valuable to maintain their support.

5. Conclusion

This paper aimed to reveal, at first, fundamental concepts of BIM through a literature review to ensure a better understanding of this approach and then to analyze the findings of semi-structured interviews that were conducted in order to detect the state of BIM adoption in the province of Quebec, in Canada, and to highlight the strategies and tips that facilitate implementation and use of the BIM process by SMEs. One of the most relevant outcomes of this study was the classification of barriers to BIM deployment. Hence, the most critical barriers were highly linked to human resources: resistance to change, lack of communication and coordination, habit of working at last minute, weak sense of liability, etc. So that, more interest must be given to how to lead, support, motivate and manage human resources. Also, most of the respondents agreed on the crucial need for a new form of contract that fits with BIM as a collaborative approach. Regarding the best strategies to implement BIM in SMEs, analysis and diagnosis of the current business model and processes of the company seems to be a mandatory step to start this transition. Furthermore, to ensure better communication and coordination between stakeholders, meetings, revisions and updates must be frequent in the committees that are involved in this process. As stated by one of the experts, a BIM model is not a gold mine! It brings benefits only if it holds accurate and relevant information which depends on the stakeholder's responsibilities. The next step of this project will be dedicated to investigating real case studies so as to update the current results and help SMEs make this digital shift.

6. References

1. C. Newton *et al.*, "Plug n Play : Future Prefab for Smart Green Schools," 2018.
2. G. Zhanglin, G. Si, and L. Jun-e, "Application of BIM technology in prefabricated building," *IOP Conf. Ser. Earth Environ. Sci.*, vol. 100, no. 1, 2017.
3. D. Forgues, L. Rivest, and P. Collot, "Étude d'opportunité du BIM pour la préfabrication des bâtiments résidentiels," 2016.
4. C. Egbu and P. Coates, "Building Information Modeling (BIM) implementation and remote construction projects : issues, challenges and critiques," vol. 17, no. May, pp. 75–92, 2012.
5. "5. http://www.ic.gc.ca/eic/site/061.nsf/fra/accueil." .
6. K. Barlish and K. Sullivan, "Automation in Construction How to measure the bene fi ts of BIM — A case study approach," vol. 24, pp. 149–159, 2012.
7. R. Miettinen and S. Paavola, *Beyond the BIM utopia: Approaches to the development and implementation of building information modeling*, vol. 43. Elsevier B.V., 2014.
8. C. M. Herr and T. Fischer, "BIM adoption across the Chinese AEC industries : An extended BIM adoption model," *J. Comput. Des. Eng.*, vol. 6, no. 2, pp. 173–178, 2019.
9. B. Succar, *The Five Components of BIM Performance Measurement 1 . Building Information Modelling : a brief introduction*. 2009.
10. M. F. Antwi-afari, H. Li, and D. J. Edwards, "Critical success factors for implementing building information modeling (BIM) : a longitudinal review," *Autom. Constr.*, no. July, 2018.
11. C. Eastman, K. Liston, R. Sacks, and K. Liston, *BIM Handbook Paul Teicholz Rafael Sacks*. 2008.
12. S. Azhar, M. Hein, and B. Sketo, *Building Information Modeling (BIM): Benefits , Risks and Challenges*, vol. 18, no. 9. 2007.
13. E. A. Poirier, "L'Initiative québécoise pour la construction 4.0 : soutenir le virage BIM au Québec," 2018.
14. S. Staub-french *et al.*, "An investigation of 'Best practices' through Case studies at Regional, National and International levels," 2011.
15. https://www.bimthinkspace.com/2009/12/index.html.
16. A. Dakhil, J. Underwood, and M. Al Shawi, "Critical success competencies for the BIM implementation process : UK construction clients," vol. 24, no. November 2018, pp. 80–94, 2019.
17. B. Succar, "BIM framework : Essentials BIM Maturity," 2009.
18. J.-F. Lapointe and F. Murat, "Diagnostic et stratégie d'implantation du BIM," 2017.
19. S. Tremblay *et al.*, *Guide D ' Application Du Bim à la société québécoise des infrastructures*, Version 1. 2016.
20. S. Kalinichuk, *Building Information Modeling Comprehensive Overview.*, vol. 6, no. 3. 2015.
21. M. Gray, J. Gray, M. Teo, S. Chi, and F. Cheung, "Building Information Modeling : An International survey."
22. M. Ben Hassine, P. Collot, J.-P. Dionne, S. Frenette, and S. Raphaël, *Le BIM : Planifier pour mieux collaborer Discussion sur la planification des projets en mode BIM: Synthèse et recommandations*. 2014.
23. A. P. C. Chan *et al.*, "Achieving leanness with BIM-based integrated data management in a built environment project," 2018.
24. D. Holzer, *Best practice BIM*. John Wiley & Sons Ltd, The Atrium, Southern Gate, Chichester, West Sussex, PO19 8SQ, United Kingdom, 2015.
25. A. M. Kouch, K. Illikainen, and S. Perälä, "Key Factors of an Initial BIM Implementation Framework for Small and Key Factors of an Initial BIM Implementation Framework for Small and Medium-sized Enterprises (SMEs)," 2018, no. August.
26. J. Cribbs, *Workflow Management Using Building Information Modeling (BIM) for Prefabrication in a Construction Retrofit Environment*, no. April. 2016.
27. B. Barkokebas, Y. Zhang, and C. Ritter, "Building Information Modeling and Simulation integration for modular construction manufacturing performance improvement," no. c, pp. 409–415, 2017.
28. N. Lu and T. Korman, "Implementation of Building Information Modeling (BIM) in Modular Construction : Benefits and Challenges," *Constr. Res. Congr.*, pp. 1136–1145, 2010.
29. M. Luo and D. Chen, "Application of BIM technology in prefabricated building," pp. 263–270, 2018.
30. J. M. Sardroud, M. Mehdizadehtavasani, and A. Khorramabadi, "Barriers Analysis to Effective Implementation of BIM in the Construction Barriers Analysis to Effective Implementation of BIM in the Construction Industry," no. July, 2018.
31. U.S. General Services Administration, *GSA Building Information Modeling Guide Series 01 – Overview*. 2007.
32. https://www.ccdc.org/document/ccdc30/.

I L S 2020
INTERNATIONAL CONFERENCE ON INFORMATION SYSTEMS, LOGISTICS & SUPPLY CHAIN
Austin, Texas April 22-24, 2020

Automating the avocado Supply Chain with Blockchain and Off-chain

Juan Carlos López-Pimentel[1], Omar Rojas[2], Miguel Alcaraz-Rivera[1], Guillermo Sosa-Gómez[2], Leslie Verteramo-Chiu[3]

[1] Universidad Panamericana. Facultad de Ingeniería. Zapopan, Jalisco, México
[2] Universidad Panamericana. Escuela de Ciencias Económicas y Empresariales. Zapopan, Jalisco, México.
[3] Charles H. Dyson School of Applied Economics and Management, Cornell University, Ithaca, NY, USA
{clopezp@up.edu.mx, orojas@up.edu.mx, malcaraz@up.edu.mx, gsosag@up.edu.mx, ljv9@cornell.edu}

Abstract. Currently, there is a lack of transparency of goods from avocado producers to the final destination: consumers. In this work, we take on the task of using Blockchain technology to strengthen trust among members of an avocado supply chain, providing more transparency across the value chain and creating value for stakeholders. We maintain transparency, integrity, and reliability of the data as a key problem, from a technological perspective. The proposed solution takes advantage of blockchain and classification of geospatial images to properly track the assets.

Keywords: Blockchain, Supply chain management, Agribusiness, Agent-based modeling, Cloud computing, Big Data.

1. Introduction

Avocado is one of the most important agricultural products in Mexico. Its annual production value in the country is about 30,000 million Mexican pesos (about 1,500 million US dollars), being overpassed only by corn and sugar cane production [1]. Mexico is the most important producer and exporter of avocados in the world; it produces around 2 million tons of avocado per year, of which more than half is exported, representing 45% of the value of world exports. The principal export destinations for Mexican avocados are United States, Japan and Canada. It is estimated for 2030 that national production and exports to be above 3 and 2 million tons per year, respectively [1].

Avocado's world production has grown around 5% yearly in the last twenty years. Such a growth responds to the rise in consumption given that avocado is considered as a food with many health benefits, associated to a better diet [2]. Some preliminary studies indicate that avocado consumption contributes to a better cardiovascular health and might aid in weight control and improvement of health in third age people [3]. In order to compete and maintain their leadership as avocado exporters, Mexican producers need to adapt quickly to international consumers demands since there is a growing number of certified products, considering the way they are produced or because they take care of all aspects in the value chain. For example, producers with organic production certification might have access to international markets and receive a premium on their product's market price [4]. However, certification cost might be so high that it creates a barrier for a lot of producers, specially the small ones [5]. On the other hand, as a growing strategy for avocado exports for 2030, SAGARPA (Mexico's Secretariat of Agriculture and Rural Development) recommends increasing the promotion of vegetable sanitary measures, including the maintaining and rising the sanitary status of the production zones recognized by foreign governments. This strategy is important to expand exports to European Union.

Maintaining a certification of organic production, or any other that might be demanded by consumers and the sanitary status recognized by the proper entities of foreign governments requires to watch over all

processes and make sure that all norms are complied with along the avocado value chain, requiring official verification [6]. If the cost of certification and verification is sufficiently low, this might prove attractive to a lot of consumers.
In this study we propose the use of Blockchain and Off-chain technologies as a tool to verify that all processes along the avocado value chain are according to the norms and what the consumers expect, in an efficient and less costly way than traditional ways. By implementing the proposed technology, the information of each lot of product is traced from its origin to the final consumer without being manipulated [7]. Thus, one of the greatest benefits of using Blockchain technology in agribusiness is the increase of transparency in the value chain [4], [8]. For example, illegal products or those not according to consumers expectations and specifications cannot be incorporated to the value chain.
The actual food system, i.e., the way food is incorporated from the farm to the table, has become a complex network of interdependent entities [9]. In the past, there have been events related to the quality of food and agricultural products that have led to sanitary crises in some countries [10], [11]. These events have had a negative effect not only in the health of implied consumers but on the economy as well. When this has happened, the need for a quick, efficient and mistake free way of accessing traceability data of agricultural products has become imminent.
The rest of the paper is organized as follows: Section 2 explains the background, the computer technologies we are proposing to give solution to the problem; Section 3 describes in general our proposal; Section 4 and 5 details our proposal, given a detailed description about the Client-Server Model and the Blockchain and Off-chain interactions. Finally, we state our conclusions.

2. Background

2.1. Blockchain and hash function

Blockchain was first applied in 2008 for the use of Bitcoin in a white paper introduced by Satoshi Nakamoto [12]. Blockchain technology can be seen as a data structure where the information is contained as a series of linked blocks. Every block on the chain contains information about one or more transactions in the system. The following block will be linked to the previous block through a hash of that previous block. The hash will also be contained as part of the new block. As part of the block creation, process can be automatically triggered through programmable conditions.
A hash function is a one way function that can be used to map data of any size to fixed string value. Hash function is widely used in computer security as an integrity tool. It permits to verify integrity network transmission and storing integrity verification. The result of applying a hash function is also know like hashing. Let $r_1=hash(d_1)$ and $r_2=hash(d_2)$ be hashing operations, which $r_1 \neq d_1$ and $r_2 \neq d_2$; it must held that $r_1==r_2$ if and only if $d_1==d_2$; applying the same hashing algorithm the length of the result always will be the same for both r_1 and r_2.

2.2. Smart Contracts

Nick Szabo introduced the concept of Smart Contracts in 1994 in an unpublished manuscript. Szabo suggested the introduction of contract clauses as programming code, so they could be inserted as part of the software [13]. This insertion would minimize the involvement of third parties in the transaction processes and would clear the e-business protocols between complete strangers. Smart contracts can be compared to relational database triggers. When used correctly, Smart contracts can even be a major binding improvement over traditional legal contracts. Smart Contract was firstly implemented in Ethereum cryptocurrency like a scripting language, [14], but it can be applied in other contexts, for example, it will contribute to the development of the full eco-system of Internet of Things and digital data traceability [15].

2.3. Off-chain

An off-chain transaction is the movement of value outside of the blockchain[1]. Blockchain-based applications have been criticized for requiring high computational and storage expenses in the transactions, impacting considerably in the performance and scalability of the already established systems. Some alternatives have worked in off-chain solutions, [16], but continuing with the benefits gained by using Blockchain. In addition, many systems already established were born without the Blockchain part and their transactions are natively developed off the chain. Within the off-chain we can consider Relational and Object Oriented Databases; stored files out of the databases and out of the blockchain.

2.4. Geolocalization

Agricultural and farmland systems benefit greatly from both GPS and satellite images. GPS has been a research study as a way of controlling and monitoring processes like cattle [17], and crops [18]. Satellite also inserts additional information, that can be used for precise monitoring of climate conditions, soil states or crop health [19].

3. Technological proposal

We propose an integration of various emergent technologies to deal with the exposed challenge. A combination of Blockchain, Off-chain, Satellite images, and Geo-localization by GPS. Blockchain is a recent technology that can help to improve the traceability steps of the entire value chain. Blockchain offers these improvements by allowing a reliable and safe way to obtain information on the current status of certain supplies transparently; it also allows to know the origin of a finished product from its raw materials, transformation processes and quality tests that are carried out, with the assurance that the information cannot be altered once it has been validated. This can also be used by end consumers when performing audits or quality controls.

One important part of the Blockchain is the Smart Contracts, being an interface to store information within the Blockchain. Smart contracts are having a big boost because they can be applied to solve several problems: a) traceability; b) automatic task scheduling (e.g. messages to customers about the status of their order, request to the material purchasing area, alerts about critical processes); c) reliability of the data (the data cannot be manipulated maliciously once entered into the system); d) accessibility of real-time data; e) quality assurance and trust. Smart contracts through the Blockchain network, can make an entire value chain in the avocado agricultural production, increasing its value since they can provide more confidence to buyers and sellers about its traceability; and with the confidence that the data is recorded in an immutable distributed network like Blockchain.

One of the common questions to Blockchain technology is its energy consumption when mining data. This problem will be attacked in the proposed model by means of a combination of Off-chain storage and Blockchain verification. This combination allows having light mining of low energy consumption that does not limit taking advantage of all the safety and transparency features offered by these technologies.

In addition to the above, the use of satellite images in the agricultural industry is common in countries with a high degree of technology. It is used, among other things, for geolocated irrigation control, climate alerts and location of possible problems (whether in the chemical composition of the soil, pests, etc.). Useful information can be abstracted from images not only of the visible part of the electromagnetic spectrum but also of infrared and near-infrared images. The combination of GPS geolocation and satellite images can provide valuable information for the agricultural industry in a timely and manageable way. So, we propose to insert into the Blockchain and Off-chain system information like climatic conditions, health and soil conditions of the fields for an additional guarantee of the final quality and the presence or absence of pests, insecticides or other related data in the product. This information will be inserted for full, validated and completely transparent tracking that can be used by all actors of the value chain.

The goal will be achieved by placing an identifier in the product that could be a QR code, bar code, serial number or similar, that can be read by a human or machine to obtain the information. The information can

[1] Off-Chain term obtained via `https://en.bitcoin.it/wiki/Off-Chain_Transactions`

be retrieved by anyone who has physical access to the code. The amount of information will be limited accordingly to the level access of the user, with two main levels: limited or total. This will protect sensitive data, but will still be useful for consulting purposes. Fig. 1 explains this.

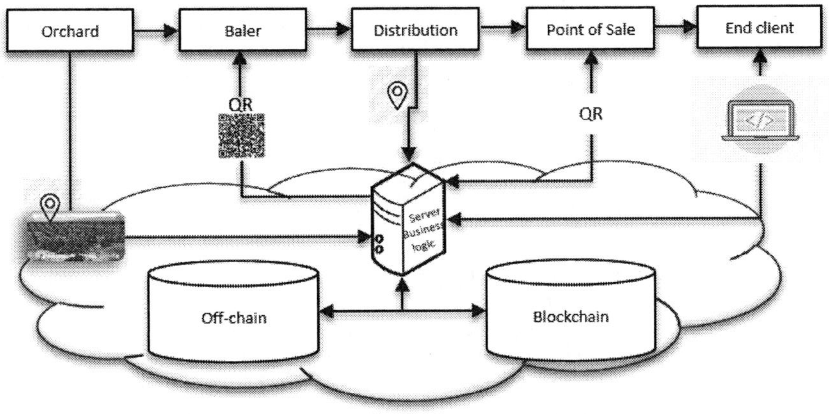

Figure 1: General model including each stage and how they interact with the Blockchain and Off-chain.

The model will interact with the Blockchain as follows: a) Orchard: The orchard's location, the subtracted information from satellite imaging and some other photographs are collected. b) Packing company: The avocados are packed in boxes and a physical label with a printed QR code will be printed and glued on the box. This will allow the traceability of the avocados as a group. c) Distribution: Will collect information from the transportation vehicle GPS to have real-time information on the complete route. It will also ensure that the product arrives at destiny at an optimal time. d) Retail point: The QR code is attached to each avocado individually -or in a package- and will be available to final customers with specific information useful to the users. The retailer will also have assurances about quality, origin, organic features, etc. e) Final client: Will have the option to interact with a webpage with some useful and interesting information about the product: origin, orchard conditions, distribution channels, on-side photos, etc. Everything validated through the Off-Chain model.

4. Client-server model

This section describes mainly three parts: a) how the communication between the different participants is privately carried out; b) how the authentication is implemented; and b) who are the participants in the model, and what type of data they are going to exchange with the server.

4.1. Privacy communication

It is widely known that messages transmitted on the Internet are sensitive to be seen by sniffers, who could be able to manipulate them in order to take advantage of the situation. The common application layer protocol (based on The Internet Protocol) used in this context is HTTP (*Hypertext Transfer Protocol*) that permits the communication on the web. To avoid this problem, the protocol to be used is HTTPS, meaning *HTTP Secure*, this protocol is built using the Transport Layer Security (TLS) protocol and its predecessor, Secure Socket Layer (SSL). Both are *cryptographic protocols* that work over the transport layer of the Internet Protocol (TCP/IP model). This protocol allows a Client to communicate securely with a Server using a Browser. TLS protocol is the standard in e-commerce, although it does not provides authentication to the client, so an additional step is required.

4.2. Authentication

It is important not only to encrypt the sensitive information using TLS protocol but also to implement more security mechanisms (including authentication procedures) to avoid possible attacks.
The authentication process trusts the users' *username* (email) and *password* for each profile of the user. This information will be stored in a database (off-chain) and the hashing of the concatenation of the username and password will be stored within the Blockchain. While in the Off-chain is stored u and $Hash(p)$, in the Blockchain is stored $Hash(u, Hash(p))$. The goal is to store periodic information within the off-chain and auditable information within the Blockchain.

4.3. Participants in the model

Our solution includes an application able to generate and read a QR code. The application must be able to connect with a Server, stated as the Server Business Logic, in order to execute different operations. In particular, the application is denoted as the client *C*. From the application different profile users may be connected, independently of that, the general communication view will be between the Server Business Logic and the Client. The QR code is generated from the Server Business Logic, but to put it in a visible place is part of the Client activity (e.g. print the QR and stick it). The QR code information is only an individual identifier and must be uninterpreted by anyone reading it. The Server Business Logic is the general controller of our model. It is dedicated to interacting with the Client, attending requests, emitting answers and sending the different views to the users. In addition, the Server Business Logic sends data information to the Off-chain and Blockchain, according to the instructions sent by the Users through the Client.

5. Off-chain and Blockchain

Considering that off-chain and the blockchain will be physically distributed in different parts we will explain how they interact. Figure 2 illustrates the logic of storing information and validation procedure of our model. Let D be a set of data to be stored within a relational database system, stated as off-chain in the figure; let d_1, d_2, and d_n be each individual data obtained from the supply chain of the avocado; T be a timestamp, containing current date information (dd/mm/yy hh:mm:ss:ms); and Id be an identifier of the transaction. As can be seen in Figure 2, the information will be stored within the Off-chain system, while only the result of the hash function is stored within the Blockchain. On the other hand, in order to validate the information (maybe for audit issues), we can see another procedure. It consists of getting the Information I from the Off-chain and getting the hashed information previously stored within the Blockchain, $getBC(i)$; both when comparing $Hash(I)$ with $getBC(i)$ should be equals. If it is held, transaction data must be shown to the user, otherwise, an error must be shown.
With the previous proposal we avoid high computational and storage resources within the Blockchain. Thus, a light transaction within the Blockchain is required and only when auditing procedures are required will be used the Blockchain using reading operations. This solution is consistent with many already established systems, which were born without the Blockchain technology but audit procedures are highly necessary to increase their values.

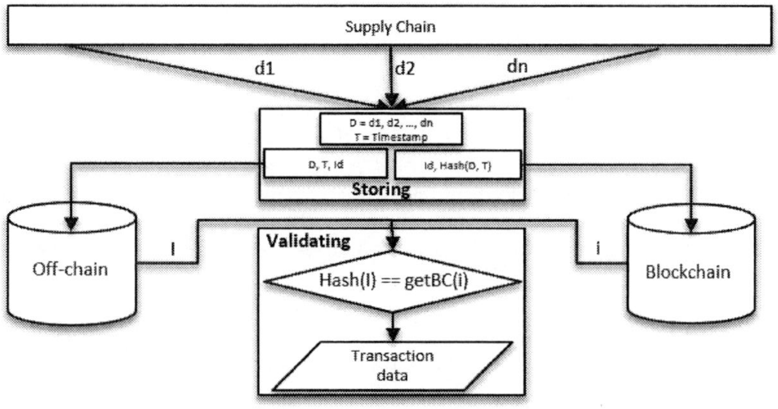

Figure 2: Logic: Storing and validating scheme.

6. Conclusions

We have proposed a distributed model that keeps a record of every pertinent transaction used on an avocado supply chain. The model implements blockchain technology for auditing aspects. Our proposal may contribute to improve the value chain in the avocado farming sector. Our model is focused on improving the avocado farming sector in Mexico. But it can also be applied to other countries around the world who are looking to have a comprehensive automated model with various technological aspects including security, traceability and monitoring throughout the whole supply chain. The model involves the creation of a computationally light part included in the Blockchain, and enforced with an Off-chain side to store the bulkier part of the data.

We have included the description of every party involved in the supply chain and how they interact between them. The interaction is described in terms of messages. The security aspects over the message exchanges uses the TLS protocol. The potential benefit of greater traceability, efficiency and avocado marketing security justifies further research and development towards engineering an integrated Blockchain and geolocation enterprise solution. In addition, our ongoing work is also about verifying our model with a multi-agent system able to simulate different transactions and creating different sceneries of attacks. Our next steps will be application of active tokens in traceability scenarios and the use of digital contracts to manage physical objects.

7. References

[1] SAGARPA, "Planeación Agrícola Nacional 2017-2030," 2017.

[2] V. L. 3rd Fulgoni, M. Dreher, and A. J. Davenport, "Avocado consumption is associated with better diet quality and nutrient intake, and lower metabolic syndrome risk in US adults: results from the National Health and Nutrition Examination Survey (NHANES) 2001-2008.," *Nutr. J.*, vol. 12, p. 1, Jan. 2013, doi: 10.1186/1475-2891-12-1.

[3] M. L. Dreher and A. J. Davenport, "Hass avocado composition and potential health effects.," *Crit. Rev. Food Sci. Nutr.*, vol. 53, no. 7, pp. 738–750, 2013, doi: 10.1080/10408398.2011.556759.

[4] FAO, "E-Agriulture in Action: Blockchain for Agriculture Opportunities and Challenges," 2019.

[5] C. E. Hattam, D. J. Lacombe, and G. J. Holloway, "Organic certification, export market access and the impacts of policy: Bayesian estimation of avocado smallholder 'times-to-organic certification' in Michoacán Mexico," *Agric. Econ.*, vol. 43, no. 4, pp. 441–457, 2012, doi: 10.1111/j.1574-0862.2012.00595.x.

[6] H. M. Kim and M. Laskowski, "Toward an ontology-driven blockchain design for supply-chain provenance," *Intell. Syst. Accounting, Financ. Manag.*, vol. 25, no. 1, pp. 18–27, 2018, doi: 10.1002/isaf.1424.

[7] A. Kamilaris, A. Fonts, and F. X. Prenafeta-Boldú, "The rise of blockchain technology in agriculture and food supply chains," *Trends Food Sci. Technol.*, 2019, doi: 10.1016/j.tifs.2019.07.034.
[8] J. F. Galvez, J. C. Mejuto, and J. Simal-Gandara, "Future challenges on the use of blockchain for food traceability analysis," *TrAC Trends Anal. Chem.*, vol. 107, pp. 222–232, Oct. 2018, doi: 10.1016/J.TRAC.2018.08.011.
[9] F. Yiannas, "A New Era of Food Transparency Powered by Blockchain," *Innov. Technol. Governance, Glob.*, vol. 12, no. 1–2, pp. 46–56, Jul. 2018, doi: 10.1162/inov_a_00266.
[10] E. B. Peterson and D. Orden, "Avocado Pests and Avocado Trade," *Am. J. Agric. Econ.*, vol. 90, no. 2, pp. 321–335, May 2008, doi: 10.1111/j.1467-8276.2007.01121.x.
[11] R. Kamath, "Food Traceability on Blockchain: Walmart's Pork and Mango Pilots with IBM," *J. Br. Blockchain Assoc.*, vol. 1, no. 1, 6AD.
[12] S. Nakamoto, "Bitcoin: A peer-to-peer electronic cash system," 2008.
[13] N. Szabo, "Smart Contracts," 1994. .
[14] G. Wood, "Ethereum: A secure decentralised generalised transaction ledger," *Ethereum Proj. yellow Pap.*, vol. 151, no. 2014, pp. 1–32, 2014.
[15] K. Christidis and M. Devetsikiotis, "Blockchains and Smart Contracts for the Internet of Things," *IEEE Access*, vol. 4, pp. 2292–2303, 2016, doi: 10.1109/ACCESS.2016.2566339.
[16] J. Eberhardt and S. Tai, "On or Off the Blockchain? Insights on Off-Chaining Computation and Data," in *Service-Oriented and Cloud Computing*, 2017, pp. 3–15.
[17] A. Sirotek and J. Hart, "Possibilities of monitoring cattle via GSM and A-GPS," 2019.
[18] N. Dybro, "Agronomy Based Crop Production System," in *2015 ASABE Annual International Meeting*, 2015, p. 1.
[19] C. Yang, "High resolution satellite imaging sensors for precision agriculture," *Front. Agric. Sci. Eng.*, vol. 5, no. 4, pp. 393–405, 2018.

I L S 2020
INTERNATIONAL CONFERENCE ON INFORMATION
SYSTEMS, LOGISTICS & SUPPLY CHAIN
Austin, Texas April 22-24, 2020

Data-Driven Scalable E-commerce Transportation Network Design with Unknown Flow Response

Shuyu Chen[1], Jing-Sheng Song[1], Yehua Wei[1]

[1] Fuqua School of Business, Duke University, Durham, NC 27708
{shuyu.chen@duke.edu, jingsheng.song@duke.edu, yehua.wei@duke.edu}

Abstract. Motived by the experience with a large online marketplace, we study a middle-mile network design problem in e-commerce. One novel feature in our problem is that while we decide the network configuration, the network flow and shortfall are controlled by the fulfillment policy employed by a different decision entity and are unknown. We develop a predictive model for the unknown response using observed shipment data. In particular, we apply the idea of decomposition in developing the predictive model. The predictive model is then embedded in the network design. To solve this problem, we characterize it as a c-supermodular minimization problem and propose two linear time approximation algorithms. In a numerical study, we demonstrate that these two algorithms are scalable and effective.

Keywords: E-commerce Fulfillment, Scalability, Machine Learning, Approximation Algorithm.

1. Introduction

With the rapid growth of online retailing, e-commerce marketplaces has observed increasing pressure on its partner couriers for delivering the packages. For example, Amazon was forced to cancel and refund for customer orders after 2013 Christmas because UPS failed to deliver many of its packages on time [18].
Taking lessons from such incidents, some e-commerce marketplaces started to build their own transportation network to provide a faster and more reliable delivery service. Even such improvement leads to greater customer loyalty, it is costly to directly control the transportation network

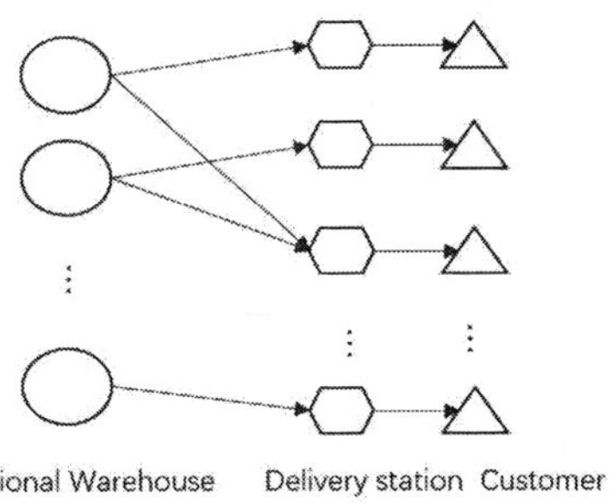

Figure 1: Outbound Transportation Network for E-commerce Marketplace

Our work focuses on optimizing the middle-mile of a transportation network to save cost. Middle-mile refers the first leg of the process in figure 1. It is the process where packages are shipped from regional warehouses to smaller delivery station in urban area. This process is less known than the last-mile (the second leg in figure 1) process because it is invisible to the customers, but its importance cannot be ignored. According to [21], the middle mile process could be the most expensive part of the whole supply chain and the market of middle-mile could reach $1 trillion
There is a unique challenge of unknown flow response in this network design problem for e-commerce marketplace: the middle-mile manager cannot anticipate the volume of package flow in the network when deciding the network configuration. Before going through the details of this challenge, we first explain two

important decisions in the middle-mile network: network configuration and fulfillment decision. Network configuration decides lane connections between regional warehouses and delivery stations in a bipartite graph. Fulfillment decision decides how individual customer order is fulfilled: from which warehouse, using which transportation mode, at what time, etc. It directly decides the number of packages shipped in each lane.

The reason behind unknown flow response is that the fulfillment policy needs to make decision for every incoming customer order and every product type, while network configuration decision is made infrequently and only the total number of packages are important. Naturally these two decisions are decided separately and it is difficult for middle-mile manager to integrate fulfillment decision because the scale of SKUs in the network can be several millions. As a result, the fulfillment policy is treated as a black box in the middle-mile manager's view. In practice, middle-mile manager follows ad-hoc rules to adjust the network configuration and uses simulation to evaluate the changes. However, this method often leads to truck under-utilization and simulation takes several days. It remains an open question that how the network configuration could be better designed.

Omni-channel retailers can have similar problem: they also make fulfillment decisions in a high frequency to guarantee satisfactory delivery service and have much larger product-mix compared to brick-and-mortar store, e.g., a typical Walmart supercenter offers 150,000 SKUs, while Walmart.com offers 9 million SKUs in 2016 [22].

Our main contributions are (1) We formulate a new type of network design problem which features unknown flow response. We adopt a data-driven approach where observational data is used to predict the effects of adding/dropping a lane in the network. (2) We develop three linear-time approximation algorithms: random greedy on primal (RGP) algorithm, random greedy on dual (RGD) algorithm and a hybrid (H) algorithm combining the previous 2 algorithms. The numerical studies show that the actual performance of all three algorithms are both efficient and effective. (3) We provide an upper bound on the gap between the expected network profit achieved by the best network configuration and the one achieved by our approach. This bound offers a theoretical performance guarantee of our approach. (4) In the construction of the predictive model, we find it is sufficient to use information only about packages and lane connectivity instead of information about every single product type and the configuration of the entire network. For approximation algorithms, it is also shown that they performs much better than their theoretical performance guarantee.

2 Literature Review

There are 4 streams of related literature.

E-commerce Fulfillment: Our work concerns e-commerce fulfillment process. Most existing works on fulfillment process assume the fulfillment process is done through third party courier's service. (e.g. [23] [1], [16], [12], [17], [16] , [2]). Our work departs from these studies by focusing on the design of the internal middle-mile transportation network. This problem is new and faced by companies like Amazon, JD.com, etc.

Capacitated Multicommodity Network Design (CMND) Problem: The classic CMND problem arises from the network design problem for traditional retailing and it is shown to be NP-hard. Scholars usually study tabu-search metaheuristic (e.g. [11], [14], [15], [8]). However, these studies consider at most several hundreds of products for brick-and-mortar store, which is not appliance to today's e-commerce marketplaces selling millions of products. Moreover, in our problem, flow response is unknown rather than being endogenously decided, which adds another layer of complexity.

Combining Predictive Model with Optimization: Our work contributes to the literature on two-stage optimization where the second stage is constructing a predictive model using observational data. (e.g. [13], [9], [10], [4], [3] and [19]). In our work, we use random forest to build a predictive model which can predict flow on every lane, then solve the network design problem with these predictions.

Submodular Maximization: We show our problem is a c-submodular maximization problem (c-submodular is first introduced by [3]), which generalizes submodular maximization. The algorithm in [3] is not applicable to ours because our problem does not have a monotone objective function. We focus on fast approximation algorithms, which are partially inspired by [5],[6], [7] and [20].

3 Model Formulation

The middle-mile network configuration decisions for e-commerce marketplace are decided in *cycles*. Each cycle consists of multiple weeks. Within each cycle, the network configuration is decided at the beginning and will remain the same during the rest of the time. This is the consistent with the time required by the e-commerce platform to assign a new truck working in the network and the network is only revised at the beginning of the each cycle. In this paper, we aim to optimize the network configuration for the next cycle given the historical data from previous cycles.

Let $\mathcal{I}, \mathcal{J}$ denote the set of origins and destinations, indexed by i, j with cardinality I, J respectively. We develop a network configuration $\mathcal{Y}$ by selecting lanes from the ground set, $\mathcal{G} = \{(i,j) : i \in \mathcal{I}, j \in \mathcal{J}\}$, which corresponds to all potential lanes in the network and let $|\mathcal{G}| = IJ = G$. Including a lane (i,j) in the network configuration $\mathcal{Y}$ incurs a fixed line-haul cost κ_{ij}. One key feature of our model is that we do not differentiate different packages. There is a unit revenue θ_{ij} of shipping a package from origin i to destination j, bounded above by $\bar{\theta}$. The proposed network configuration $\mathcal{Y}$ contains at most K lanes due to budget constraint. Network flow $\mathbf{x}(\mathcal{Y}) = \{x_{ij}(\mathcal{Y}), \forall i, j\}$ is defined as the expected number of packages (including every product type) shipped on each lane (i,j) in network configuration $\mathcal{Y}$ during one entire cycle. Here, the flow is seen as a response to a network configuration and it is unknown to the e-commerce marketplace. The objective of e-commerce marketplace is to maximize the expected network profit $R(\mathcal{Y}) = -\sum_{i,j:(i,j)\in\mathcal{Y}} \kappa_{ij} + \sum_{(i,j)\in G} \theta_{ij} x_{ij}(\mathcal{Y})$, which is the difference between fixed lane cost and revenue earned from network flow.

Our problem is

$$\begin{aligned} \max_{\mathcal{Y}\subseteq\mathcal{G}} R(\mathcal{Y}) = \quad & -\sum_{(i,j)\in\mathcal{Y}} \kappa_{ij} + \sum_{(i,j)\in\mathcal{G}} \theta_{ij} x_{ij}(\mathcal{Y}) \\ s.t. \quad & |\mathcal{Y}| \leq K \end{aligned} \tag{1}$$

We next consider using flow prediction to replace the unknown flow response. The details of how the predictive model is built will be introduced in section 5.

Denote the flow prediction on lane (i,j) in network configuration $\mathcal{Y}$ for the next cycle as $\hat{x}_{ij}(m_i(\mathcal{Y}), n_j(\mathcal{Y}))$. Then we maximize the network profit based on predicted flow $\hat{R}(\mathcal{Y})$.

$$\begin{aligned} \max_{\mathcal{Y}\subseteq\mathcal{G}} \hat{R}(\mathcal{Y}) \quad = \quad & -\sum_{(i,j)\in\mathcal{Y}} \kappa_{ij} + \sum_{(i,j)\in\mathcal{Y}} \theta_{ij} \hat{x}_{ij}(m_i(\mathcal{Y}), n_j(\mathcal{Y})) \\ s.t. \quad & |\mathcal{Y}| \leq K \end{aligned} \tag{2}$$

Problem (2) is very difficult as no useful structural properties of the prediction function is known. For example, the objective function in problem (2) is not monotone and submodular.

4 Solution Approach

4.1 c-submodularity

We show problem (2) can be treated as a c-submodular maximization problem subject to a cardinality constraint: $\max_{S\subseteq G} f(S)\ s.t.\ |S| \leq K$, where function f is c-submodular. That is for every X, Y with $X \subset Y$, and every element $\phi \notin Y$, we have $f(Y+\phi) - f(Y) \leq f(X+\phi) - f(X) + c$ where $X + \phi \equiv X \cup \{\phi\}$, and $X - \phi \equiv X \backslash \{\phi\}$ for any element ϕ and set X. $f(\cdot)$ is submodular when $c = 0$.

Specifically, we have theorem 1 to show how to characterize our objective function as c-submodular.

Theorem 1. *The objective function of (2) is c-submodular with*

$$c \quad = \quad \bar{\theta}\Big(\delta_{12}\hat{x} + (I-1)\big((\delta_2\hat{x})^+ + (\delta_{-2}\hat{x})^+\big) + (J-1)\big((\delta_1\hat{x})^+ + (\delta_{-1}\hat{x})^+\big)\Big) \tag{3}$$

following the definition of

$\Delta_1\hat{x}_{ij}(m,n) = \hat{x}_{ij}(m+1,n) - \hat{x}_{ij}(m,n)$, $\Delta_2\hat{x}_{ij}(m,n) = \hat{x}_{ij}(m,n+1) - \hat{x}_{ij}(m,n)$

$\Delta_{-1}\hat{x}_{ij}(m,n) = \hat{x}_{ij}(m-1,n) - \hat{x}_{ij}(m,n)$. $\Delta_{-2}\hat{x}_{ij}(m,n) = \hat{x}_{ij}(m,n-1) - \hat{x}_{ij}(m,n)$

$\delta_1\hat{x} = \max_{i,j}\{\Delta_1\hat{x}_{ij}(m,n) : 1 \leq m < J, 1 \leq n \leq I\}$, $\delta_2\hat{x} = \max_{i,j}\{\Delta_2\hat{x}_{ij}(m,n) : 1 \leq m \leq J, 1 \leq n < I\}$

$\delta_{-1}\hat{x} = \max_{i,j}\{\Delta_{-1}\hat{x}_{ij}(m,n) : 1 < m \leq J, 1 \leq n \leq I\}$, $\delta_{-2}\hat{x} = \max_{i,j}\{\Delta_{-2}\hat{x}_{ij}(m,n) : 1 \leq m \leq J, 1 < n \leq I\}$

$\delta_{12}\hat{x} = \max_{i,j}\{\hat{x}_{ij}(m+k_1, n+k_2) - \hat{x}_{ij}(m,n) : 1 \leq m \leq J-k_1, 1 \leq n \leq I-k_2\}$

Next, we present three algorithms to solve the c-submodular maximization problem.

4.2 Random Greedy on Primal (RGP) Algorithm

RGP considers an variant of the random greedy algorithm proposed by [20]. It is named as primal method because the working set can be considered as primal feasible in each iteration.

Algorithm 1: Random Greedy on Primal Algorithm

$S_0 \leftarrow \emptyset$
for $i = 1$ *to* K **do**
  $M_i \leftarrow$ a random subset obtained by sampling s random elements from $\mathcal{G}$
  $\phi_i \leftarrow \text{argmax}_{\phi \in M_i \setminus S_{i-1}} f(S_{i-1} + \phi) - f(S_{i-1})$
  $S_i \leftarrow S_{i-1} + \phi_i$
end
Return S_K

4.3 Random Greedy on Dual (RGD) Algorithm

RGD is called "dual" algorithm because it first selects a set which may not satisfy the primal cardinality constraint, and then keeps removing elements in a greedy fashion until it is feasible.

Algorithm 2: Random Greedy on Dual Algorithm

Step 1: Double Greedy
Adapted from [6]
output is S
Step 2: Revise Candidate Set
if $|S| \leq K$ **then**
  Return S
else
  while $|S| > K$ **do**
    $\phi' \leftarrow \text{argmax}_{\phi \in S} f(S - \phi) - f(S)$
    $S \leftarrow S - \phi'$
  end
  Return S
end

4.4 Hybrid (H) Algorithm

H is a combination of RGP and RGD.

Algorithm 3: Hybrid Algorithm

Step 1: Double Greedy
Same as step 1 in RGD
Step 2: Revise Candidate Set
$\phi_i' \leftarrow i$th element of S
for $i = 1$ *to* K **do**
  if $f(S) - f(S - \phi_i') < 0$ **then**
    $S \leftarrow S - \phi_i'$
  end
end
Step 3: Random Greedy on Primal
Use RGP algorithm by considering S as new ground set

Table 1: **Approximation Guarantee and Complexity of Approximation Algorithms**

Algorithms	Approximation Guarantee	Complexity
DG	$\frac{1}{4}f(S^*)-\frac{3}{4}Kc$	$O(KG)=O(\lambda IJ^2)$
RG	$\frac{1}{e}f(S^*)-2Kc$	$O(KG)=O(\lambda IJ^2)$
RGP	$\frac{1}{4}f(S^*)-2Kc$	$O(G)=O(IJ)$
RGD	$\frac{K}{2G}f(S^*)-3Kc+\frac{2K^2}{G}c$	$O(G)=O(IJ)$
H	$\frac{1}{2}(1-\frac{1}{e}-\varepsilon)f(S^*)-(1-\frac{1}{e}-\varepsilon)Gc$ $-2c(\frac{K}{1-\varepsilon}-(\frac{1}{e}+\varepsilon)(\frac{K}{1-\varepsilon}-1))$	$O((1+\log\frac{1}{\varepsilon})G)=((1+\log\frac{1}{\varepsilon})IJ)$

Table 1 summarizes the performance of these approximation algorithms. Random Greedy (RG) algorithm is developed by [5] and deterministic greedy (DG) algorithm is a classic algorithm. We include RG and DG for comparison. The complexity refers to the number of function evaluations, where an evaluation is the process to use predictive model to predict network profit for a given network configuration. For e-commerce marketplace, J grows much faster than I and we assume on average one destination connects to λ origins, then $K\approx\lambda J$. As a result, our proposed RGP, RGD and H algorithms are much more efficient in theory.

5 Predicting the Flow Response

In section, we discuss how to construct the predictive model $\hat{x}(\cdot,\cdot)$ for problem (2).
First, we describe the historical data we use. We observe a collection of data $S_N=\{(\mathbf{x}^1,\mathcal{Y}^1,\boldsymbol{\alpha}^1),...,(\mathbf{x}^N,\mathcal{Y}^N,\boldsymbol{\alpha}^N)\}$ from N different cycles following an unknown joint distribution of random variables $(\mathscr{X},\mathscr{Y},\mathscr{A})$.

$\mathbf{x}=\{x_{ij},\forall i,j\}$ is data on flow distribution. It includes total flow on each individual lane over a cycle.

$\mathcal{Y}\subseteq\{(i,j):i\in\mathcal{I},j\in\mathcal{J}\}$ is the network configuration, which includes lanes added in the network.

$\boldsymbol{\alpha}=\{s_{ip},d_{jp},\eta_{ij},\ \forall i\in\mathcal{I},j\in\mathcal{J},p\in\mathcal{P}\}$ is auxiliary data to describe the property of the network, where the set of product is denoted by $\mathcal{P}$, indexed by p with cardinality P and

(i) $s_{ip}\in\mathbb{Z}_+$ is the amount of total inventories of each product p at every origin i.

(ii) $d_{jp}\in\mathbb{Z}_+$, where $\sum_{ij}d_{jp}=1$, is the demanded probability distribution of each product p at every destination j, .

(iii) $\eta_{ij}\in\{0,1\}$. 1 indicates whether the origin i is the closest to the selected destination the j.

Due to limited access to real data, we use artificial data generated via simulation to illustrate our approach. To generate input data, we first design a simple fulfillment policy, called *closest first* policy. This policy works as follows in the simulation: in each period, there is one random product demand arriving at a random destination in each period. This policy first checks whether the closest origin has inventory to cover the demand. If not, then it randomly selects another origin with active lane connecting this origin and destination pair. Trucks shipped from these origins departures early for the longer travel distance. As a result, 40% of the packages will be split to third-party courier. If no such origin has inventory, then this demand is shipped by inventory from a backup origin using third-party courier's service.
We have tested 5 different common machine learning methods: ridge regression, LASSO, support vector regression (SVR), decision tree regression and random forest regression using 5-fold nested cross-validation and we choose random forest regression for its highest accuracy for our problem.

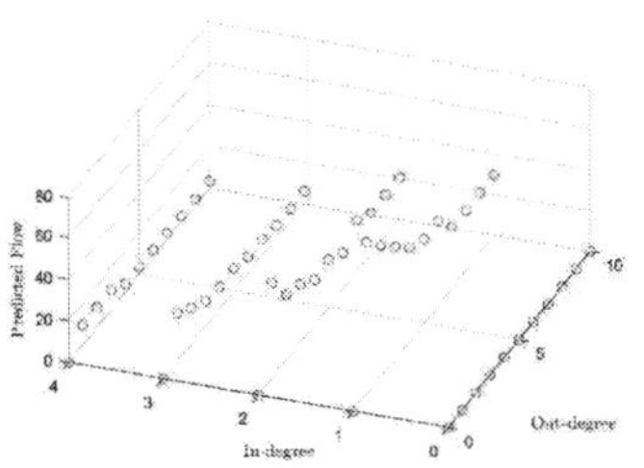

Figure 2: **Illustration of Flow Prediction**

Figure 2 is an example of predicting flow on a selected lane. We fix all features except degree of connectivity (in-degree/out-degree is the number of lanes connected to destination/origin). In general, the flow decreases when in-degree and out-degree increases and there is 0 flow when either in-degree or out-degree is 0. The predicted flow lacks property such as strictly decreasing or convex, which is consistent with actual flow.

6 Performance Evaluation

6.1 Estimation of Error Bound

We first analytically study the performance of our data-driven approach. We use S^{**} to denote the optimal network configuration for problem (1) and S^{*} to denote the optimal network of problem (2). We choose random greedy on primal algorithm for illustration and denote its output as S^{a}. Our target is to find the gap between $R(S^{**})$ and $R(S^{a})$.
We make three important assumptions.

Assumption 1. *(i) The confounding error is bounded by ω_1. (ii) The error caused by missing strong features is bounded by ω_2. (iii) The error caused by missing strong features is bounded by ω_3.*

Theorem 2.

$$R(S^{**}) - R(S^{a}) \quad \leq \quad \frac{3}{4}R(S^{**}) + \frac{5}{4}\bar{\theta}K(\omega_1 + \omega_2 + \omega_3) + 2Kc$$

Theorem 2 evaluates the theatrical error bound of our approach. To summarize, the error bound consists of three terms. The first term $\frac{3}{4}R(S^{**})$ is the loss caused by approximation algorithm; the second term $\frac{5}{4}\bar{\theta}K(\omega_1 + \omega_2 + \omega_3)$ is the loss caused by confounding error in observational data, estimation error in random forest and our omission of using the entire network as feature; the third term $2Kc$ is the loss caused by the flow prediction not being submodular.

6.2 Numerical Study

We conduct a numerical study to compare different approximation algorithms and demonstrate our proposed algorithms are scalable.
For this purpose, we consider a network with 4 origins and 30 product types. There are 4 different scenarios for the number of destinations: 10, 20, 40 and 80. We consider the closest first policy introduced in section 5 is the current policy for the e-commerce marketplace. Each cycle has 2500 periods. For each scenario, we consider 48 cases of the set of parameters to ensure our result is robust. There are three cases for the maximum number of lanes: 15, 20, 25; For fixed cost and unit revenue, we have two cases: (a) high fixed cost: half of the lanes connected to each origin has fixed cost 50 and unit profit 2, and the other half has fixed cost 50 and unit profit 5; (b) low fixed cost: half has fixed cost 20 and unit profit 2, and the other half has fixed cost 20 and unit profit 5; The lane capacity has two cases 100, 150; There are two cases for inventory: (a) balanced inventory: every origin has 20 units inventory for each product; (b) imbalanced inventory: every origin has 10 units inventory for half of the products and 30 units of inventory for the other half; The demand distribution also has two cases: (a) balanced demand: there is equal chance for every product in every destination to be demanded in every period (b) imbalanced demand: the demand can arrive in every destination with equal probability. For each destination the products are divided into two half and products within each half has equal probability to be demanded. The probability of the first half being demanded is two times the chances for the other half. For the second till the last scenario, system parameters including number of periods, inventory at origins and maximum number of lanes is increasing in the same rate as the number of destinations. This is to reflect the fact that the network is more loaded than before.
We test different approximation algorithms, RG, DG, RGP, RGD and H, indexed in sequence by k.
The performance of an approximation algorithm is evaluated by two metrics: relative gap in predicted profit and relative gap in actual profit. Before explaining these two metrics, we need to define the actual profit for a given network configuration. Actual profit R_k^a is the network profit computed by actual flow generated via simulation. Relative gap in predicted profit and in actual flow are then defined as

$$Gap_p\% = \frac{\hat{R}_k - \hat{R}_1}{\hat{R}_1}, \ \forall k = 2,3,4,5, \ Gap_a\% = \frac{R_k^a - R_1^a}{R_1^a}, \ \forall k = 2,3,4,5. \tag{4}$$

Table 2: **Relative Performance and Scalability of Selected Approximation Algorithms**

J	$Gap_p\%$				$Gap_a\%$				Time (sec)				
	DG	RGP	RGD	H	DG	RGP	RGD	H	RG	DG	RGP	RGD	H
10	19.25	12.80	16.76	12.48	7.64	5.25	5.29	0.2	0.43	0.44	0.08	0.26	0.22
20	18.73	11.74	17.84	12.16	6.83	6.32	5.66	3.08	3.52	3.54	0.32	1.38	0.95
40	15.73	9.96	15.50	10.81	1.89	4.4	0.29	0.48	24.12	24.22	1.15	7.50	3.36
80	10.95	5.74	13.20	4.11	4.09	4.53	4.04	0.29	187.78	186.87	4.60	29.99	13.15

Table 2 shows the average gap and time for each algorithm in each scenario. The performances in predicted profit and actual profit are consistent. This implies using predictive model is a good approach in achieving good performance in reality. As for the comparison in relative gap, it is a bit surprising that DG has very good performance. This may be due to the fact that the objective grows almost monotonicity when the set is near the cardinality constraint, and greedy algorithm is known for its superior performance for monotone function. Our proposed RGP, RGD and H have much better performance than RG. As for time, proposed RGP and H are the fastest. DG and RG takes the longest time and will not be practical for large-scale network. These results are consistent with the complexity of the algorithms.
Based on both the theoretical and numerical result, we can give a general guidance on selection of approximation algorithm: (i) if the cardinality constraint has high chance not to be binding, use RGD and H ; (ii) if the objective function is nearly monotone, use DG; (iii) if the computation time is the most important, use RGP or H; (iv) if K is close to G, use RGD.

7 Conclusion

To stay competitive and sustain the growth, e-commerce marketplace and omnichannel retailers constantly seek solution to optimize their network with large-scale of SKUs. Motivated by our experience with a large e-retailer, we have developed a novel approach to solve such network optimization problem: First, we use machine learning methods to build a predictive model from observational data. Our predictive model is non-parametric, and thus makes the network design problem a nonlinear integer programming problem, which is difficult to solve; We then characterize our problem as a c-submodular maximization problem subject to a cardinality constraint. Three linear-time approximation algorithms are developed to solve the c-submodular maximization problem. We provide the theoretical performance bound and also use extensive numerical tests to compare proposed approximation algorithms. In the end, we want to highlight the importance of fast approximation algorithm as the real transportation network can be in large-scale, and the manager need to carefully select an algorithm best fit to his own network.

References

[1] Jason Acimovic and Stephen C Graves. Making better fulfillment decisions on the fly in an online retail environment. *Manufacturing & Service Operations Management*, 17(1):34–51, 2014.

[2] Jason Acimovic and Stephen C Graves. Mitigating spillover in online retailing via replenishment. *Manufacturing & Service Operations Management*, 19(3):419–436, 2017.

[3] Lennart Baardman, Setareh Borjian Boroujeni, Tamar Cohen-Hillel, Kiran Panchamgam, and Georgia Perakis. Detecting customer trends for optimal promotion targeting. *Available at SSRN 3242529*, 2018.

[4] Lennart Baardman, Maxime C Cohen, Kiran Panchamgam, Georgia Perakis, and Danny Segev. Scheduling promotion vehicles to boost profits. *Management Science*, 2018.

[5] Niv Buchbinder, Moran Feldman, Joseph Seffi Naor, and Roy Schwartz. Submodular maximization with cardinality constraints. In *Proceedings of the twenty-fifth annual ACM-SIAM symposium on Discrete algorithms*, pages 1433–1452. Society for Industrial and Applied Mathematics, 2014.

[6] Niv Buchbinder, Moran Feldman, Joseph Seffi, and Roy Schwartz. A tight linear time (1/2)-approximation for unconstrained submodular maximization. *SIAM Journal on Computing*, 44(5): 1384–1402, 2015.

[7] Niv Buchbinder, Moran Feldman, and Roy Schwartz. Comparing apples and oranges: Query trade-off in submodular maximization. *Mathematics of Operations Research*, 42(2):308–329, 2016.

[8] Mervat Chouman and Teodor Crainic. *A MIP-tabu search hybrid framework for multicommodity capacitated fixed-charge network design*. CIRRELT, 2010.

[9] Maxime C Cohen, Ngai-Hang Zachary Leung, Kiran Panchamgam, Georgia Perakis, and Anthony Smith. The impact of linear optimization on promotion planning. *Operations Research*, 65(2):446–468, 2017a.

[10] Maxime C Cohen, Jeremy Kalas, and Georgia Perakis. Optimizing promotions for multiple items in supermarkets. 2017b.

[11] Teodor Gabriel Crainic, Michel Gendreau, and Judith M Farvolden. A simplex-based tabu search method for capacitated network design. *INFORMS journal on Computing*, 12(3):223–236, 2000.

[12] Levi DeValve, Yehua Wei, Di Wu, and Rong Yuan. Understanding the value of fulfillment flexibility in an online retailing environment. *Available at SSRN 3265838*, 2018.

[13] Kris Johnson Ferreira, Bin Hong Alex Lee, and David Simchi-Levi. Analytics for an online retailer: Demand forecasting and price optimization. *Manufacturing & Service Operations Management*, 18 (1):69–88, 2015.

[14] Ilfat Ghamlouche, Teodor Gabriel Crainic, and Michel Gendreau. Cycle-based neighbourhoods for fixed-charge capacitated multicommodity network design. *Operations research*, 51(4):655–667, 2003.

[15] Mike Hewitt, George L Nemhauser, and Martin WP Savelsbergh. Combining exact and heuristic approaches for the capacitated fixed-charge network flow problem. *INFORMS Journal on Computing*, 22(2):314–325, 2010.

[16] Stefanus Jasin and Amitabh Sinha. An lp-based correlated rounding scheme for multi-item ecommerce order fulfillment. *Operations Research*, 63(6):1336–1351, 2015.

[17] Yanzhe Lei, Stefanus Jasin, and Amitabh Sinha. Joint dynamic pricing and order fulfillment for e-commerce retailers. *Manufacturing & Service Operations Management*, 20(2):269–284, 2018.

[18] Josh Levs. Ups backlog means missing christmas gifts; amazon responds, 2013. URL `https://www.cnn.com/2013/12/25/us/ups-delays/index.html`.

[19] Sheng Liu, Long He, and Zuo-Jun Max Shen. Data-driven order assignment for last mile delivery. 2018.

[20] Baharan Mirzasoleiman, Ashwinkumar Badanidiyuru, Amin Karbasi, Jan Vondrák, and Andreas Krause. Lazier than lazy greedy. In *Twenty-Ninth AAAI Conference on Artificial Intelligence*, 2015.

[21] Keith Naughton and Matthew Boyle. Walmart targets automated 'middle-mile' delivery to cut shipping costs, 2019. URL `https://www.ttnews.com/articles/walmart-targets-automated-middle-mile-delivery-cut-shipping-costs`.

[22] Phil Wahba. Walmart's plan to catch amazon? vastly expand its online assortment, 2016. URL `http://fortune.com/2016/04/13/walmart-amazon-channel-advisor/`.

[23] Ping Josephine Xu, Russell Allgor, and Stephen C Graves. Benefits of reevaluating real-time order fulfillment decisions. *Manufacturing & Service Operations Management*, 11(2):340–355, 2009.

I L S 2020
INTERNATIONAL CONFERENCE ON INFORMATION SYSTEMS, LOGISTICS & SUPPLY CHAIN
Austin, Texas April 22-24, 2020

PROPOSAL FOR IMPROVING THE SERVICE PROCESS IN THE MAINTENANCE TO CLIENTS OF A NATURAL GAS DISTRIBUTOR: A VBA AUTOMATION STUDY

José Carlos Jacintho[1,2]
Lucas Ferrer Franco[1]. Athos Claudio Martins da Silva[1]. Marinete Fernandes da Silva[1]. Ridnal João do Nascimento[1,2].

[1]Instituto Federal de Educação, Ciencia e Tecnologia de São Paulo - IFSP
Rua Dr. Pedro Vicente, 625 - São Paulo, SP, Brasil.
[2] Conselho Nacional de Desenvolvimento Científico e Tecnológico – CNPq Grupos de Pesquisa
{jcj5847@yahoo.com.br, lucasff94@hotmail.com, athos_a1hotmail.com, marinetefsilva@gmail.com ridnal@ifsp.edu.br}

Abstract: The company under study is a natural gas distributor in Brazil and has problems in their Customer Service System. This paper aim is to identify the reasons why the company is not being able to achieve their goals of 92% to customer service success rate, as well as to suggest enhancements to their process. The analyzes of the process identified problems of the delays in maintenance solicitations and the solution was the process automation with VBA (Visual Basic for Application) to mitigate the delays. It is estimated that the VBA automation could mitigate almost 77% of the demand problems.

Keywords: Maintenance and service, VBA (Visual Basic for Application), delays, automation.

1. Introduction

The natural gas distribution company, object of this study, presents difficulties in its process of meeting maintenance demands because of the numerous delays that exceed company estimates.
This article aims to mitigate the problem through optimized management data processing and maintenance demands in order to eliminate the delays and remedy the issue of customer service. It was decided to use the quality and process tools to identify key bottlenecks in the process and their causes and, through an action plan, mitigate such bottlenecks. The proposal seeks to organize maintenance process data and information via automation in VBA (Visual Basic for Applications).
The quality tools are useful techniques for diagnosing a sector's commitment to organize, analyze, increase, income, propose solutions and prevent future waste. Therefore, they are used as a management system in the implementation of improvements in services and processes [1].
Using quality tools makes it possible to improve, solve and avoid problems. However, the tools worked should be known and accepted by all employees with the intention of be successful [2].
The current process of the maintenance area of the natural gas distributor receives demands for various types of work, each of which has a standard deadline for pre-stipulated care by the maintenance sector.

2. Status of the Art

2.1. The Maintenance and Services Management Process

In the interest of maintain, repair or even replace a component in a building it should be done through a process and decisions taken by the maintenance management team, taking in on consideration that this decision may affect a building function which means affect the indirect cost of a project through its operational phase, however the maintenance management process can be divided into two parts: Maintenance strategy and Implementation of Strategy [5].
According [5], to define a maintenance strategy is necessary to first identify the objectives to be achieved, which can be obtained directly from the business plan. Consequently, the first actions of maintenance management determine the success and effectiveness with which maintenance is being deployed in the organization, such as plans, schedules, controls and improvements.
Through effectiveness one can assess how the goals and needs of the organization are being addressed in terms of the quality of service provided by customer's opinion and perspective.
After the specification of a maintenance strategy, it is implemented it. The management of the maintenance implementation process requires efficient skills in favor of minimize the waste, expenses and necessary efforts, which impacts in direct factors of maintenance. Thus, an efficient maintenance process is one in which it is better working at the lowest cost. However, according to [6], customer service when worked effectively is a very important variable and provides significant impact on demand creation and customer loyalty. To [7], the customer service has function to provide "utility of time and place" in the transfer of goods and services between the buyer and the seller, it means that the product or service have no value until they are in the customers' hands, featuring a proactive integration. Although there is an empirical understanding of the practice of the services its conceptualization remains a challenge. The classical view considers that the services rely on four specific characteristics - intangibility, heterogeneity, inseparability and perishability (IHIP) - but [8], based on service marketing paradigm argue that service is a resource sharing between actors or a social network, since there is no transfer of ownership from the provider to the customer.

2.2. VBA Automation

The evolution of technology has enabled the emergence of various procedures that facilitate the way of working in specific areas. Among these procedures, there is automation: a technique widely used in industries over time [9]. This technique consists of refining the machines in order to considerably reduce the workload of the workers, conserving the productivity and the quality of the processes.
Automation can be total or partial, it will depend on the steps taken during the execution of the project or process. According [9], in most cases, automation is associated with robotization, but it goes beyond simple mechanization. It needs numerical and electronic tools such as computers, information receivers; power drives and amplifiers; the microprocessors. It also uses industrial computer programs equally indispensable for their improvement.
Visual Basic Application (VBA) was not a language that was created in parallel with early versions of Windows. At that time Microsoft provided only macro commands that were essential to solve some basic problems.
According [10], the VBA language is the improvement of macro recording, allowing to go beyond what the tool itself could follow, interacting with Power Point, Internet Explorer, in short, the whole Office package created by Microsoft and if constitutes in an object oriented language.
Today, VBA has become one of the leading programming languages in the main offices of companies due to its great ease of training and addressing the most varied problems in large companies.

3. Methodology

The paper is based on an exploratory research on the literature about Maintenance and Services Management Process and VBA automation and their correlation. As for nature, it is an applied research quantitative which uses practical approach as research-action.

According to [11], action research is defined as the type of study that uses consolidated research techniques to inform the action that is intended to be taken to improve practice. In other words, it requires action in the research and practical areas, changing the way a given situation is lived and perceived.
On the other hand [12] highlights that action research is a type of empirical investigation, which essentially consists of relating research and action in a process in which actors and researchers are involved, cooperatively participating in the elucidation of reality in which they are inserted. Therefore, proposing ideas and making decisions is an action that allows the researcher to have direct contact with the object of study. This study proposes a solution to a problem in the managing of the current process flow and in the database (big data) of the maintenance of the company.
Databases were downloaded with demands that were within the established deadline and others that were outside the stipulated deadline; the bottlenecks were found of the information flow within the maintenance sector. Among the main problems, it was pointed out that in the short term and the best solution would be the automation of the analyst's tasks.
Thus, it was proposed to create an algorithm added to the company's website with capacity to the navigate it and apply the necessary filters to extract the desired database, update the spreadsheet emitting beeps in case of service deadlines are close to expiring. This process will be repeated every 3 minutes to standardize the data extraction time.

4. Problem Identification

4.1 Natural Gas

In recent years there has been a growing concern about global warming and sustainability. Due to this concern, the role of Natural Gas has been strengthened as a global energy source, being considered the cleanest of fossil fuels, it can be used in homes, offices, businesses, industries and even in automobiles and, consequently, to replace fuels such as cylinder gas, gasoline, diesel and ethanol and still produce electricity [3].
Natural gas is distributed through pipelines, which are managed by natural gas distribution companies. In São Paulo - Brazil, there are 3 concessionaires: Comgás, Brasiliano Gas and Naturgy. These companies, due to their state concession, are audited by the São Paulo State Sanitation and Energy Regulatory Agency (ARSESP), which is responsible for regulating, controlling and supervising them through price control, quality indicators, safety and positioning. obligations to ensure that customers can receive the best service and enjoy the benefits of piped natural gas [4].
The natural gas distribution company that will be addressed in this study presents difficulties in the process of meeting maintenance demands, as it has several delays in meeting maintenance that exceed the estimates projected by the company.

4.2 Current Process Flow

The figure 1 is a macro-flow elaborated for the sake of understand the actions of each agent.

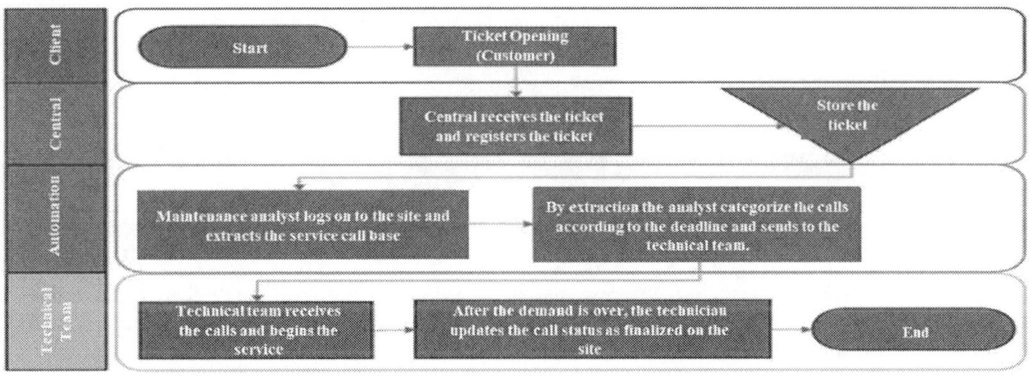

Figure 1: Current Process Flowchart. Source: Authors

From the macro process described above, it is possible to list in detail each step of incident handling:

- The customer, identifying the need to support the services offered by the company, creates a ticket with the central, through the website Ticket Rapido or telephone;
- Upon receiving the ticket from the customer, the center registers the ticket on a company intranet site, sorting according to its importance and starting the countdown of the service time.
- Maintenance analysts access the site, download ticket information and create their database; prioritizing requests with shorter deadlines for service.
- From the analysis of the database, analysts report the calls to the technical team, according to the deadline for the call;
- When service is initiated, the technical team notifies the analysts, who updates the call status on the website to know that the process is in progress;
- At the end of the service, the technical team notifies analysts who in turn finalize the call with the central.

The faults identified in the flow of the process:

- High number of calls answered late;
- Possibility of human error when parameterizing filters in report extraction;
- Possibility of human error in performing report analysis;
- Lack of standardization of the information update period;
- Bottleneck in the process of extracting and analyzing information, and the need to use part of an employee's workload;
- Late receipt of demand by maintenance technicians;
- Customer dissatisfaction due to non-compliance with the agreed deadline.

4.3 Current Service Performance

To better highlight the impacts generated by the failures found in the process, we extracted the report of meeting demands from November 2017 to August 2018, where it is possible to observe the volume of demands met out of time and on time, table 1:

Table 1 – Call Control: November 2017 to August 2018

Open Date	Out of time	Out of time %	On time	On time %	Goal	Total
NOV	122	27%	334	73%	90%	456
DEC	130	30%	297	70%	90%	427
JAN	124	23%	418	77%	92%	542
FEB	216	20%	846	80%	92%	1.062
MAR	248	19%	1.024	81%	92%	1.272
APR	79	21%	291	79%	92%	370
MAY	72	19%	316	81%	92%	388
JUN	142	22%	504	78%	92%	646
JUL	144	21%	528	79%	92%	672
AUG	63	24%	195	76%	92%	258
Total	1.340	22%	4.753	78%	92%	6.093

According to the incidents historical, the responsible area did not reach the goal set by the company in any month. The goal set by the Operational Excellence area was 90% of requests fulfilled on time in 2017 and 92% for 2018. In the opinion of your employees, all delayed incidents with a service time of less than 48h have already arrived at the technical team at the deadline due to the bottleneck in the process of extraction, categorization and distribution of demands. The table below was elaborated, filtering all incidents attended with delay and grouped according to the solution deadline in order to measure such impacts

Table 2 – Volume of calls answered after the deadline categorized according to the deadline.

Open Date	0,5 h	0,83 h	1 h	5 h	24 h	45 h	48 h	270 h	360 h	Total
NOV		3		31		31	11	28	18	122
DEC		2	1	39		31	15	25	17	130
JAN		3		53		35	3	16	14	124
FEB				70	2	56	18	30	40	216
MAR	2	4	2	96	2	98	16	4	24	248
APR	1	4		34	1	23	10	3	3	79
MAY	1	4	1	32	1	16	6	1	10	72
JUN		3		15	1	27	8	2	7	63
JUL	3	7		1		1	1			13
Total	7	30	4	371	7	318	88	109	133	1067
Accumulated Representativity (%)	1%	4%	4%	39%	40%	69%	78%	88%	100%	-

To better highlight the information, the demands with a term of service up to 48 h were grouped, table 3.

Table 3 - Deadline incident analysis.

Open Date	Total out of date	Delay until 48 h	(%)
NOV	122	76	62%
DEC	130	88	68%
JAN	124	94	76%
FEB	216	146	68%
MAR	248	220	89%
APR	79	73	92%
MAY	72	61	85%
JUN	63	54	86%
JUL	13	13	100%
Total	1067	825	77%

It can be seen from the table 3 that the biggest offender is the incidents with a deadline of up to 48 hours.

5. Proposed Solution

It was identified by using the Ishikawa Method, that one of the main causes of the undesirable effect was the slow extraction and prioritization of demands made by the analyst area. Through analysis and in-depth study of the process, it was possible to identify that the excess of activities performed by it and the method used are not efficient.

Consequently, the Brainstorming method was used to bring together the team that experiences the process closely in the company, conducive to explore the team's ideas and identify if any of them would be viable to solve the delays that are occurring with the calls. The entire flow was detailed, and sticky notes was distributed so that everyone described what could be improved in the process to mitigate delays. At the end we presented all the proposals to those present and qualified which were viable and pasting on a blackboard. Among the main ideas it was pointed out that in the short term the best solution would be the automation of the analyst's tasks. The 5W1H tool, table 4, was used to map the process and identify possible improvements.

Table 4 - 5W1H Application

WHAT	**Standardization, Resetting Responsibilities Roles, Standardization of Procedures, Process Information Level Elevation, Speed and Reliability**
WHY	High number of backlogs, Customer Dissatisfaction, Employee Need to Update Information, Delay to report technician calls
WHERE	Maintenance Sector
WHEN	February / 19
WHO	Process Automation Consulting
HOW	Data extraction process automation and demand prioritization

It is understood as necessary to automate the process of data downloading and incident prioritization, eliminating any errors caused by human action, in furtherance of optimize the time spent and provide the whole cycle of real-time information updating, as illustrated in figure 2. In this new process, the analyst will have the function of following this information in real time in the alert panel of near maturity demands.

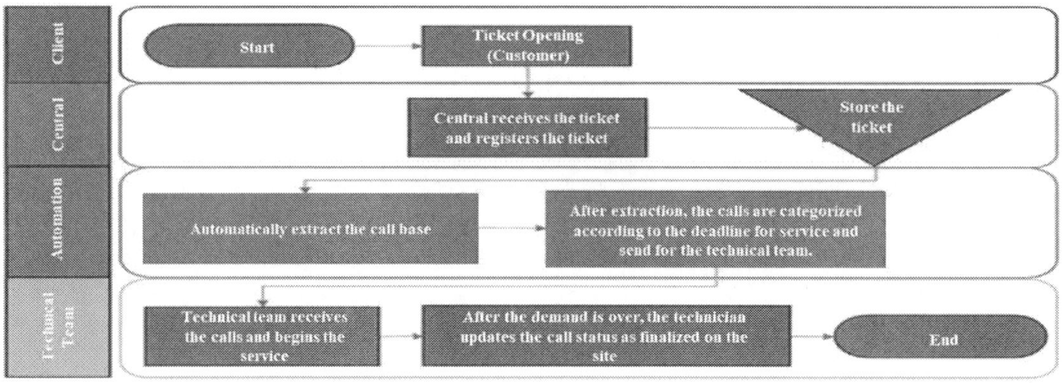

Figure 2: Proposed Process Flowchart. Source: Authors

The failure analysis performed, identified that in step 3 there is a bottleneck in the process, because it is directly linked to the analyst's action. To mitigate such impacts, it is proposed to automate this step by implementing an algorithm in VBA. This schedule will be shown in blocks to elucidate this project, figure 3.

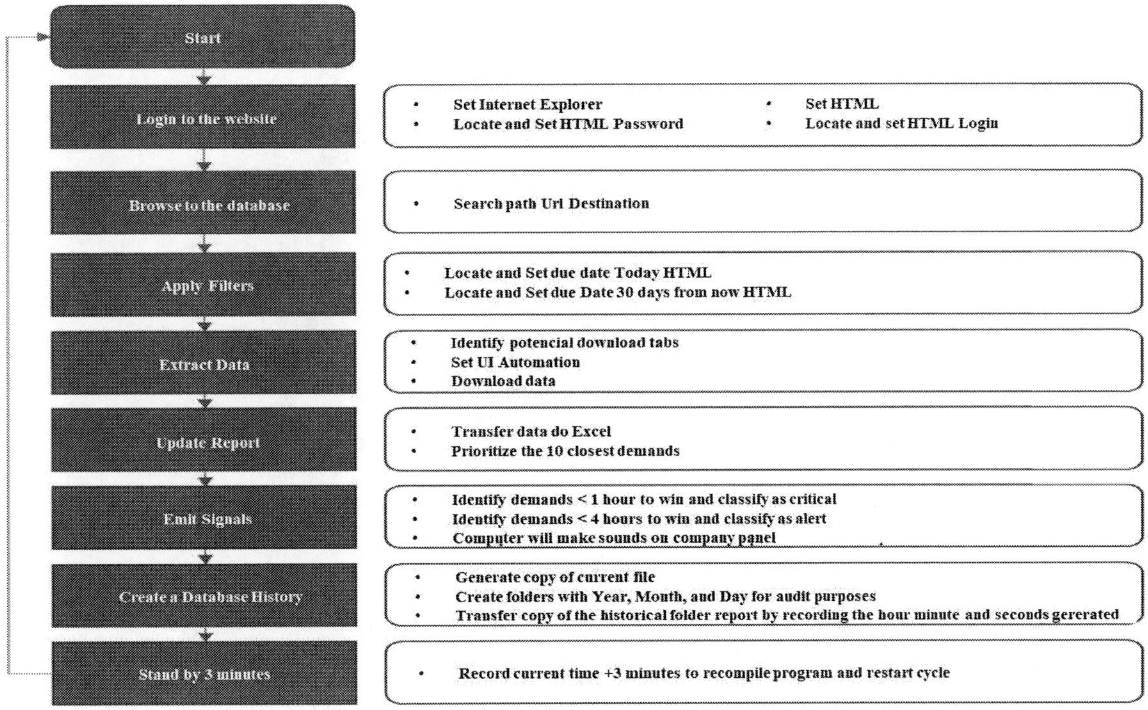

Figure 3 - Proposed Automation Flow. Source: Authors

6. Results

Implementing the proposed automation mitigated the bottleneck process and ensured the speed in receiving the demands. Soon the problem described by the company of receiving claims close to maturity or overdue for a period of up to 48h can be solved.
The table 5 shows the results of a simulation after step 3 automation for demands until 48 hours.

Table 5 - Simulation of meeting demands

Open Date	Total out of time	On time	Total	On time (%)
NOV	46	410	456	90%
DEC	42	385	427	90%
JAN	30	512	542	94%
FEB	70	992	1.062	93%
MAR	28	1.244	1.272	98%
APR	6	364	370	98%
MAY	11	377	388	97%
JUN	9	249	258	97%
JUL	-	67	67	100%
Total	242	4600	4.842	95%

By analyzing the table 5, considering a deadline of up to 48 hours, it was observed that it is possible to achieve the goal required by the company, as illustrated in the figure 4. Therefore, automation becomes effective to meet the company's main quality objective. It can be highlighted that the proposed changes will reduce the time spent by the analyst and generate indicators with updates every 3 minutes.

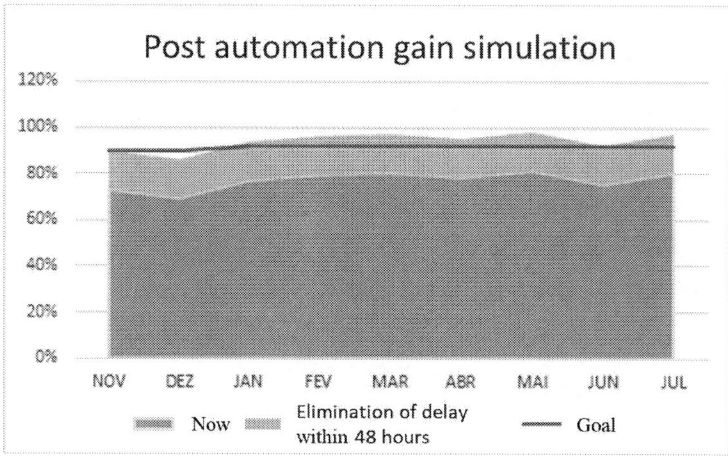

Figure 4 – Post Automation Gain. Source: Authors

7. Conclusion

The present paper presented a feasibility project for the implementation of process automation with the purpose of gain speed, mitigate the problems and increase the quality of the company's maintenance services to clients. In addition, quality tools such as Ishikawa Method, Brainstorming, Flowchart, Histogram as well as 5W1H were used to assist in finding the solution as well as its development. The definitions of the adopted models were based on projects already executed and accepted by the company; such models provided greater efficiency in the development of the work in relation to the time dedicated and effectiveness of automation VBA. The simulation performed, considering the VBA automation, designed to optimize the process step performed by the analyst, would ensure all demands with a deadline of up to 48h, were met within this period. Thus, it is estimated that it is possible catch up the company's target of 92% of the demands met on time. For future studies, it is intended to work with analysis of demands over 48 hours and migration to python applications to keep up with the growth of the database.

8. References

1. Paladini, E. P. Gestão da qualidade: teoria e prática. São Paulo: Atlas, 2004.
2. Oliveira, O. J. (org.) et al. Gestão da Qualidade: tópicos avançados. São Paulo: Cengage Learning, 2012.
3. Aneel – Agência Nacional de Energia Elétrica. **No Renewable Sources**. Available in: <http://www2.aneel.gov.br/arquivos/PDF/atlas_par3_cap6.pdf>. Access in 01/31/2019.
4. Arsesp – Agência Reguladora de Saneamento e Energia do Estado de São Paulo. Piped Gas Surveillance. Available in: <http://www.arsesp.sp.gov.br/SitePages/gas-canalizado/fiscalizacoes-gas-canalizado.aspx>. Access in 01/31/2019
5. Identifying the impact of integrating building information modelingwith maintenance management a literature review. Available in https://www.researchgate.net/publication/333699514. DOI: 10.21608/auej.2019.33343
6. Hompel, M.; Kerner, S. Logistik 4.0: die Vision von Internet der autonomenDinge. Informatik-Spektrum, v. 38, n. 3, p.176-182, 2015
7. Lee, I.; Lee, K. The Internet of things (IoT): applications, investments, and challenges for enterprises. Business Horizons, Blomington, v. 58, n. 4, p. 431-440, 2015
8. Reis, J.G.M., Neto, M.M., Vendrametto, O., Neto, P.L.O.C. Qualidade em Redes de Suprimentos: qualidade aplicada ao supply chain management. São Paulo: Editora Atlas, 2015
9. Conserm - Qu'est-ce que l'automation? Available in: <https://conserm.fr/quest-ce-que-lautomation-2/ > Access in 12/18/2018
10. GONARD, D. Le VBA qu'est ce que c'est?Available at: https://didier-gonard.developpez.com/tutoriels/office/vba-qu-est-que-c-est/#LIII. Access in 12/18/2018
11. Davis, R. Industry 4.0: digitalisation for productivity and growth. Briefing from European Parliamentary Research Service 2015: <http://www.europarl.europa.eu/thinktank/en/document.html?reference=EPRS_BRI(2015)568337>
12. Thiollent, M. Pesquisa-ação nas organizações. São Paulo: Atlas, 1997.

I L S 2020
INTERNATIONAL CONFERENCE ON INFORMATION
SYSTEMS, LOGISTICS & SUPPLY CHAIN
Austin, Texas April 22-24, 2020

An Integrated approach for Analyzing Outlets' Performance for Centralized Retail Chain Using Machine learning and Multicriteria Decision Making Techniques

Hafsa Binte Mohsin [1], Brian Huff [2]

[1] PhD candidate, UTA, Arlington, USA
[2] Associate Professor, UTA,Arlington, USA
{hafsa.mohsin@mavs.uta.com, bhuff@uta.edu.com }

Abstract. For a centralized retail chain where everything is controlled centrally for all the outlets, to monitor the performances of all outlets and identify the problems in product level, is difficult than in a decentralized retail chain. A centralized retail chain having twenty-two outlets and eight thousand six hundred and ninety-three unique products, has been considered for this study. In this paper, we used K-mean clustering as a machine learning tool to cluster the outlets from where we measured each cluster's performance. To further analyze at product level, we used analytical hierarchy process (AHP), as multi criteria decision-making technique, for cluster wise inventory classification. Revenue per square foot and average basket value for each cluster, is the basic performance indicator. From basic performance indicator, decision makers can get an idea about which cluster needs immediate attention. This will lead them to investigate that cluster's class wise inventory situation for performance improvement.

Keywords: Cluster, Performance, Machine learning, Multi criteria decision making.

1. Introduction

To improve overall sales of a retail company, it is required to monitor the sales of all the retail outlets under it. Outlet's performance can be measured using different measurements techniques and considering different factors. In some existing works, delivery cost, order fulfillment time, and customer satisfaction have been considered as performance indicators [1][2]. For this study, we considered return per square feet and average basket value, as performance measure. Dividing total sales or revenue by number of customers purchased, we got average basket value. This performance measurements can be done for every single outlet of a retail company. It can give an idea about how each outlet is performing individually. But to have an idea on overall business for a centralized retail chain, it is necessary to classify the outlets based on some attributes. From that classification or segmentation, it will be easy to know which group of outlets are performing well and which group needs attention. For classification of retail outlets, several methods have been discussed in literatures [3]. Some classify based on types of items sold (food retailers, drink retailers, clothing household, other non-food retailers) and some classify based on shopping trip purpose (convenience and comparison outlets). Classification based on the size of retail outlets has also been studied by researchers (convenience outlets under 200m square, Small supermarket-250 to 1000 m square, large supermarket having area of 1000m square to 2500m square, and, hypermarket which is over 2500 m square). According to the ownership, retail outlets can also be classified as independent and multiple retailers. For independent retail outlet, one or few outlets have same ownership. On the other hand, for multiple retail outlets, ownership is for several outlets. Segmentation of retail outlets which are under one central control, has not been studied enough as far our

knowledge. For taking strategic decision and overall idea about the performance of the retail outlets, it is necessary to segment or classify the outlets. This paper is inspired by this necessity.
Cluster analysis by using machine learning tools is an easy and effective way to segment items based on some attributes [4]. By using clustering, similar type of outlets are grouped together. This similarity is based on selected attributes. Clustering outlets based on the attributes: revenue, number of customers, square footage area, will help to segment outlets in a way that it will be easy for decision maker to identify the performance of the outlets as a group. Here number of customers who purchase is considered as number of customers. For example, if one cluster's return on per square foot is high, the number of average customer basket value is low and the number of customers are low than the other clusters; than the decision makers can check the stock levels of different classes of SKUs at that cluster and decide whether more space is required to have more inventory to attract customers or not. To know which SKUs are important, many classification methods have been developed. Yi-yong et al. [5] used lost profit to classify the inventory, where Hasan et al. [6] used multiple criteria decision-making (MCDM) tool, AHP for inventory classification. In traditional ABC analysis, inventories are classified based on a single criteria-annual revenue. Many modifications of traditional ABC analysis have been developed by the researchers [7-9]. In this study, we used MCDM tool. MCDM can help to achieve the optimal option by evaluating decision makers preferences toward different criteria. In traditional ABC analysis, inventories are classified based on a single criteria-annual revenue. But many other attributes are closely related while deciding the class of inventories. Many researchers select different criteria for the classification [10-11]. Some of the criteria are number of customers purchasing, current stock, and, unit price. We have used here number of customers purchasing a product and current stock of product, along with sales or revenue volume of product, as criteria for products classification. Number of customers purchasing a product is related to the stock of that product. And revenue or sales earned from a product is also dependent on number of customers purchasing it and the products stock level. For these reasons, we choose these three attributes for MCDM analysis. Multiple criteria-based decision making, are not only used for inventory classification, it is also used for supplier selection [12] and for many other sectors [13]. AHP is one technique of MCDM. AHP is a flexible and robust technique of MCDM. Organizations or individuals can place their weights or importance on different attributes which will help to make final decision [14]. Using AHP as a MCDM tools has been studied by the researchers for inventory classification [15-16]. Its large use has inspired us to use it for inventory classification for different clusters' outlets.

In the next sections, we have described about the methodology of this integrated approach, case study, result and discussion, and conclusion.

1.1. Methodology

The purpose of the study is to identify the opportunities for improving outlets' performance; return on per square foot and average basket value of customers. To achieve this purpose, it is required to follow an integrated methodology. This methodology has two main steps. First one is clustering outlets and second one is classifying SKUs of each cluster. Machine learning tools has been used for clustering outlets and multi criteria decision making tool for classifying SKUs. Total process flow has been demonstrated in Figure 1. Revenue, number of customers, and area (square feet) have been considered as attributes for machine learning tool, K-mean cluster analysis.

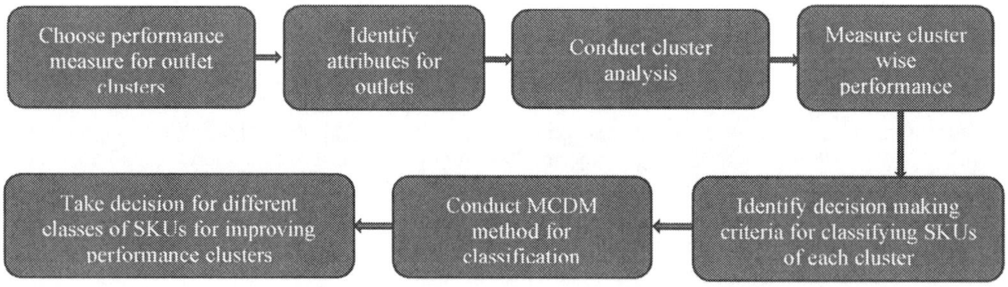

Figure 1: Process flow of proposed methodology

After the completion of clustering, performances of each cluster have been measured. By comparing the cluster performances, decision makers can see which cluster have high performance and which have low. To increase performance of each cluster, it is required to investigate in product level. As it is not possible to check all products one by one, ABC classification needs to be performed. Product classification will help to identify important products. But in our study, we didn't use traditional ABC analysis which depends annual revenue only. We used MCDM tool, AHP for ABC classification. Revenue, number of customer and stock for all the SKUs are used as decision criteria. Different weightage has been given to different criteria based on decision makers judgements. Based on those weightages, ABC analysis has been conducted for classifying SKUs. This classification will help to check how many of each class items have low stocks but have high demand. It will also provide an insight of how many of each class have overstock with low or no demand. This will give an idea to the decision makers to take necessary steps like purchasing inventory for low stock high demand or giving promotion on overstock low demand items, to improve the performances of the outlet clusters. For example, if one cluster has high return on square foot and high basket value and high customer foot fall, maintaining enough stocks for fast moving SKUs at that cluster will keep the performance high.

1.2. Case Study

A Bangladeshi retail company has been considered for this case study. That company has twenty-two retail outlets at different locations and deals with eight hundred and ninety-three unique SKUs. As different outlets are at different location, demand of different types of products, buying capacity of customers, population of those areas, may vary. If any company has many outlets, monitoring outlets revenue, customer footfall, stock levels of different SKUs, are sometimes difficult. If we can cluster the outlets based on some attributes and evaluate their performance, it will be better to take a decision about how to improve the performances of the outlets on that cluster. In Table 1, number of SKUs, areas of outlets, number of customer purchasing, sales value, sales amount and stock amount have been listed.

Table 1: Attributes of the outlets

Outlets	Stock amount	Sales amount	Footfall	Sales Value (TK)	Area (Square Feet)	Number of SKUs
1	55,590	206,842	153,518	15,181,359	7,712	5221
2	57,057	225,705	175,784	14,601,097	8,129	4290
3	46,889	153,020	115,634	10,949,352	6,502	4612
4	42,124	160,020	133,776	10,894,928	5,711	3232
5	51,411	167,714	125,362	13,264,184	6,330	4461
6	52,439	441,047	342,886	30,992,779	8,724	5668
7	158,225	420,410	316,905	28,979,465	8,257	6268
8	45,649	61,784	52,484	4,611,505	8,083	2758
9	29,501	143,326	113,439	7,990,533	8,009	2961
10	50,832	154,713	123,703	8,848,066	8,183	3876
11	39,677	237,735	176,657	15,698,880	8,276	4023
12	35,536	210,344	172,010	12,814,055	8,686	4053
13	31,840	98,498	80,982	6,448,477	5,524	2890
14	45,314	227,572	191,929	14,793,999	8,062	3423
15	47,969	315,588	246,633	20,305,305	6,205	4743
16	83,787	321,651	266,172	23,580,655	9,400	6280
17	61,849	212,853	159,641	13,437,650	9,435	4300
18	32,157	221,550	195,041	14,924,703	9,554	3261
19	68,950	270,988	208,665	17,906,263	9,133	4535
20	48,119	267,173	189,348	17,718,061	9,591	4446
21	111,947	242,072	204,422	15,970,992	8,877	5958
22	26,324	156,316	114,152	9,571,825	5,925	3162

From Table 1, it can be seen that areas of the outlets vary between 9,591 square feet and 5,524 square feet, number of customers varies between 342,886 and 52484, and revenue varies between TK 30,992,779 and TK 4,611,505. The number of SKUs sold in these outlets also varies in a wide range from 6280 and

2758. There were 94421 data points. Cluster analysis using K mean clustering and ABC classification using MCDM, have been performed on this data set.

1.3. Results and Discussion

After doing cluster analysis using K mean clustering, outlets have been segmented in to three groups. Table 2 shows the outlets which are at cluster 1, cluster 2 and cluster 3.

Table 2: Outlets in different clusters.

Cluster	Outlets in cluster
1	6,7
2	3,4,5,8,9,10,13,22
3	1,2,11,12,14,15,16,17,18,19,20,21

Nine percent outlets are in cluster 1, thirty six percent outlets in cluster 2 and 55 percent in cluster 3. As the outlets have been clustered depending on their revenue, number of customers, and area of the outlets, we can compare now the cluster wise performances. Average basket value of customers and revenue per square foot have been considered as performance measure. In Table 3,we can see that total number of customers for cluster 1 and 2 are less than cluster 3.

Table 3: Cluster wise average basket value and revenue per square feet

Cluster	Number of Outlets	Total Footfall	Average of area (Square Feet)	Total Area (Square Feet)	Total Sales Value (TK)	Average basket value	Revenue per square foot (Total)
1	2	659791	8491	16981	59972244	91	3532
2	8	859532	6783	54267	72578870	84	1337
3	12	2339820	8588	103060	196933018	84	1911
Grand Total	22	3859143	7923	174308	329484133		1890

Between cluster 1 and cluster 2, cluster 2 outlets' total number of customers and revenue are not significantly higher than cluster 1 although the number of outlets is four times higher than cluster 1. Average area of cluster 1 is higher than cluster 2. When comparing average basket value and revenue per square feet, it is clear that cluster 1 with the lowest number of outlets is the high performing cluster. So, decision makers should give enough importance to have stocks of the highly demanded SKUs at the outlets of cluster 1. In addition to that, as the average basket value of customers are higher in cluster 1 than the other 2 clusters, there is an opportunity to sell more SKUs. This is because of high buying capacity of the customers of cluster 1. On the other hand, for revenue per square feet, cluster 1 has the highest performance. It can indicate that the outlet space is well utilized for cluster 1 than the other two clusters. For cluster 2 and cluster 3, average basket value is same but revenue return per square feet is higher for cluster 3 than cluster 2. Here, decision makers also need to check the inventory levels for highly demanded products and also check whether any slow-moving products are overstocked in the outlets of these two clusters .By identifying low stock high moving products, decision makers can take steps to have enough stock and for slow moving overstocked products, they can give promotions.

Products have been classified for all three outlet clusters based on AHP. Revenue, number of customers and stock amount, these attributes have been compared using a decision matrix (Table 4). Importance weight of these attributes have been provided by the decision makers. By using geometric mean, the weight for the attributes have been calculated. Consistency ratio for the decision matrix has been calculated as 2.13% which is less than the threshold value of 10%. It proves the importance the decision makers gave, was valid.

Table 4: Decision matrix for AHP

	Sales Value	Stock	footfall	Weight
Sales Value	1	7	5	0.7379705
Stock	0.1428571	1	0.5	0.0944354
footfall	0.2	2	1	0.1675941

For all the SKUs of a cluster, total weight of each SKU has been calculated by adding the attribute weight*attribute value for all the attributes. SKUs are then sorted in a descending order based on the weight points. After that top 20% was classified as A class,50% as class B and 30% as C class.

Table 5: ABC classification of Cluster 1 outlets' SKUs

Class	Number of SKUs	Number of SKUs without Stock	Total Footfall	Total Sales Value	Percent of total SKUs not having stock
A	2387	350	572518	50578253	15%
B	5968	2467	75671	8291509	41%
C	3581	2825	11602	1102482	79%
Grand Total	11936	5642	659791	59972244	47%

From Table 5, we can see that for class A SKUs, 350 SKUs don't have stocks. To investigate deeply, from Table 6, we can see that for SKUs not having stock for class A has minimum sales history of TK 1860 and maximum sales as TK88,182.Average number of customers purchased these 350 SKUs is 69. These values are greater than class B and class C stock out SKUs. As cluster 1 is the highest performing outlet cluster, to increase its performance, decision makers can think of maintaining at least those 350 SKUs inventory.

Table 6: Statistics of stocked out SKUs of different category for cluster 1

Class	Min of Sales Value	Max of Sales Value	Average of Sales Value	Sum of Sales Value	Average number of customers	Sum of Footfall
A	1,860	88,182	7,849	2,747,206	69	24,075
B	220	4,140	1,524	3,759,590	12	30,611
C	10	750	308	869,029	3	9,216
Grand Total	10	88,182	1,307	7,375,824	11	63,902

For cluster 2, total number of SKUs is 27,952 among which 13,134 SKUs do not have stocks. Based on average basket value and return on per square foot area, cluster 2 has lower performance than cluster 1. From table 7, we can see that for class B, from 13976 skus,2598 SKUs have over stock. In this study, if a SKU has stock level fore than 2 months demand, it is considered as an overstock item. On the other hand, for class A, it has 1193 overstocked SKUs. As, Class A contributes more to the total sales, decision makers can think of keeping those overstocked SKUs. Otherwise based on supplier agreement, they can keep their SKUs at suppliers' warehouse. But for class B and C, items with overstock can be set for promotion.

Table 7: ABC classification of Cluster 2 outlets' SKUs

Class	Number of SKUs	Number of SKUs without Stock	Number of SKUs with Over Stock	Total Number of Customers	Total Sales Value	Percent of total SKUs not having stock
A	5,590	568	1193	716,543	58,208,216	10%
B	13,976	5,319	2598	120,965	12,574,686	38%
C	8,386	7,247	380	22,024	1,795,969	86%
Total	27952	13134	4171	859532	72578871	47%

On the other hand, for the SKUs that do not have stock, for class A items, decision makers can think of getting stocks for those 568 products and observe the cluster performance. From Table 8, we can see that the minimum and maximum value for class C stockout SKUs are very low than class A. While considering overstock SKUs of class C, it is better to flush out those SKUs by promotion or return to vendor if vendor agrees.

Table 8: Statistics of stocked out SKUs of different category for cluster 2

Row Labels	Min of Sales Value	Max of Sales Value	Average of Sales Value	Sum of Sales Value	Average of Footfall	Sum of Footfall
A	530	52,325	5,817	3,303,891	49	28,077
B	56	3,320	1,110	5,904,917	10	51,058
C	4	580	219	1,586,648	3	19,732

Cluster 3 nearly has the same performance (Table 3) like Cluster 2. Number of SKUs with over stock is very small (Table 9), 19. However average sale value for Class A stock out items are higher than class B and class C (Table 10). Total number of SKUs without stock is the highest among all the clusters. In class A, 1397 SKUs do not have stock. Decision makers can think of getting stocks of these class A stock out items for increasing the performance of cluster 3. For class B, they also think of including high selling SKUs step by step to avoid overstock. It also required to observe the performance of cluster 2.

Table 9: ABC classification of Cluster3 outlets' SKUs

Row Labels	Number of SKUs	Number of SKUs without Stock	Number of SKUs with overstock	Total Footfall	Total Sales Value	Percent of total SKUs not having stock
A	10,906	1,397	9	1,999,726	162,818,006	13%
B	27,267	11,055	11	288,314	29,897,198	41%
C	16,360	13,692	0	51,780	4,217,814	84%
Grand Total	54,533	26,144	19	2,339,820	196,933,018	48%

Table 10: Statistics of stocked out SKUs of different category for cluster 3

Row Label s	Min of Sales Value	Max of Sales Value	Average of Sales Value	Sum of Sales Value	Average number of customer	Sum of Footfall
A	1,548	2,441,184	8,835	12,342,391	106	148,216
B	100	3,520	1,279	14,143,649	11	121,557
C	2	650	262	3,589,153	3	44,278
Grand Total	2	2,441,184	1,150	30,075,193	12	314,051

All the results from clustering and classification, decision makers can get an idea about in which sectors like inventory purchasing, marketing promotion, they need to focus to achieve the desired performance.

2. Conclusion

For a centralized retail chain where all the decisions regarding product purchasing and distributing to all the outlets are monitored and controlled from a single point, it is sometimes difficult to check the performances of all the outlets. This performance measure may be different depending on the organization or company's criteria. Profit, cost, customer satisfaction, are some of the performance measures those are practiced in current industries. Here we used average basket value and return on per square foot area of outlet. These two are related to profit and cost. By using cluster analysis to segment the outlets based on their revenue, number of customers, and area, we had three groups of outlets. From our analysis, cluster 1 performed the best in both respect, revenue on per square feet and average basket value. Without only using ABC analysis based on revenue, AHP has been used where the decision criteria were number of customers, revenue and stock. SKUs were classified in a way that it was easy for the decision makers to take decision not only based on the revenue but also number of customers and stock. This process of segmenting or clustering outlets will make it easy for the decision makers to identify the problems and think of the appropriate solution. This study has some limitations. More attributes like number of days a product was delivered to outlet, number of days after last delivery, can be used for SKU classifications. Though the outlet cluster give an idea about overall performance of the outlets of that cluster, sometimes when the performance is very bad, it is required to do the analysis for all the outlets separately in a cluster. More research in outlet segmentation and SKU classification can help to provide the ways of identifying problems of poor performances of the outlets.

3. References

1. Chou, Chih-Fen. "Development of a comprehensive supply chain performance measurement system: A case study in the grocery retail industry." PhD diss., Massachusetts Institute of Technology, 2004.
2. Gomez, Miguel I., Edward W. McLaughlin, and Dick R. Wittink. "Customer satisfaction and retail sales performance: an empirical investigation." Journal of retailing 80, no. 4 (2004): 265-278.
3. Guy, Clifford M. "Classifications of retail stores and shopping centres: some methodological issues." GeoJournal 45, no. 4 (1998): 255-264.
4. Sousa, Ines., and Wallace, David.: Product classification to support approximate life-cycle assessment of design concepts. Technological Forecasting and Social Change 73, no. 3, 228-249 (2006).
5. Xiao, Yi-yong., Zhang, Ren-qian., and Kaku, Ikou. A new approach of inventory classification based on loss profit. Expert Systems with Applications 38, no. 8, 9382-9391 (2011).
6. Kartal, Hasan., Oztekin, Asil., Gunasekaran, Angappa., and Cebi, Ferhan.: An integrated decision analytic framework of machine learning with multi-criteria decision making for multi-attribute inventory classification. Computers & Industrial Engineering 101, 599-613 (2016).
7. Ramanathan, Ramakrishnan. "ABC inventory classification with multiple-criteria using weighted linear optimization." Computers & Operations Research 33, no. 3 (2006): 695-700.
8. Liu, Fan, and Ning Ma. "Multicriteria ABC Inventory Classification Using the Social Choice Theory." Sustainability 12, no. 1 (2020): 182.
9. Teunter, Ruud H., Babai,M. Zied., and Syntetos, Aris A.: ABC classification: service levels and inventory costs. Production and Operations Management 19, no. 3, 343-352 (2010).
10. Flores, Benito E., and Whybark, D. Clay.: Multiple criteria ABC analysis. International Journal of Operations & Production Management 6, no. 3, 38-46 (1986).
11. Keshavarz, Ghorabaee., Mehdi., Zavadskas, Edmundas Kazimieras., Olfat, Laya., and Turskis, Zenonas.: Multi-criteria inventory classification using a new method of evaluation based on distance from average solution (EDAS). Informatica 26, no. 3, 435-451 (2015).
12. Ho, William., Xu, Xiaowei., and Dey, Prasanta K.: Multi-criteria decision making approaches for supplier evaluation and selection: A literature review. European Journal of operational research 202, no. 1 (2010): 16-24.
13. Zeleny, Milan, ed.: Multiple criteria decision-making Kyoto 1975. Vol. 123. Springer Science & Business Media (2012).

14. Ossadnik, Wolfgang, and Oliver Lange. "AHP-based evaluation of AHP-Software." European journal of operational research 118, no. 3 (1999): 578-588.
15. Flores, Benito E., David L. Olson, and V. K. Dorai. "Management of multicriteria inventory classification." Mathematical and Computer modelling 16, no. 12 (1992): 71-82.
16. Partovi, Fariborz Y., and Jonathan Burton. "Using the analytic hierarchy process for ABC analysis." International Journal of Operations & Production Management (1993).

I L S 2020
INTERNATIONAL CONFERENCE ON INFORMATION SYSTEMS, LOGISTICS & SUPPLY CHAIN
Austin, Texas April 22-24, 2020

A Case Study of the Reliability of Time-Sensitive Drone Deliveries

Travis B Glick [1], Miguel Figliozzi [2], Avinash Unnikrishnan [3]

[1] PhD Candidate in Civil Engineering, Portland, OR, USA
[2] Professor of Civil & Environmental Engineering, Portland State University, Portland, OR, USA
[3] Associate Professor of Civil and Environmental Engineering, Portland State University, Portland, OR, USA
(tglick@pdx.edu, mafiglio@pdx.edu, uavinash@pdx.edu)

Abstract. The use of drones for the delivery of time-sensitive supplies is an open area of research. Drones arrive quickly by taking more direct paths and avoiding ground-based obstructions. However, drones are not completely reliable and may also experience failures and delays. For consumer products, delivery delays are an inconvenience, but for some medical supplies, delays may be fatal. This research focuses on the drone reliability of one special type of supply and event: automatic defibrillators for out-of-hospital cardiac arrests (OHCA). Tradeoffs among drone reliability, fleet size, population size, and meteorological conditions (wind and temperature) are modeled utilizing stochastic approach.

Keywords: Drone Deliveries, Reliability, Stochastic Modeling, Time-sensitive, Case Study

1. Introduction and Motivation

Drone deliveries are being tested across the globe to meet not only parcel delivery demands but also to open new service models and opportunities where traditional ground delivery methods are relatively slow and unreliable. The delivery of medical supplies is an area that has sparked high interest because such supplies are often subject to strict temporal constraints. For example, drones have already been employed for the delivery of medical supplies in Rwanda, a country that experiences heavy rains that often lead to road impassibility [1]. Hospital supply chains in Rwanda now utilize drones for the delivery of blood from central storage facilities [2] [3]. While blood deliveries are time sensitive, some medical supplies are subject to even more stringent time considerations.

Cardiac defibrillation [4] needs to be administered minutes after diagnosis to avoid patient death, but a majority (63%) of cardiac arrest cases occurs outside of hospitals where defibrillators are not readily available. The survival rate for out-of-hospital cardiac arrest (OHCA) in 2016 was 12%; almost half that of the in-hospital rate (25%) [5]. Currently, automatic external defibrillators (AED) are 1.1 kg (2.4 lb), take just 1.77 L (108 in^3) of space, and come with instructions to guide non-medical persons through the machine's use [6]. This makes AEDs an ideal candidate for drone delivery. However, the seriousness of cardiac arrest puts tight constraints on adequate arrival times. Even in hospitals, defibrillation survival rates after 3 minutes are reduced from 39% to 22% and each additional minute reduces the chance of survival by approximately 4% [7]. Currently, the average ground-based (ambulance) emergency response time in the United States is much longer than three minutes with a mean of 7.0, 7.7, and 14.5 minutes for urban, suburban, and rural areas, respectively [8]. As drones are not subject to the typical ground road infrastructure restrictions, they may have a higher probability of timely response.

Pilots for medical supply deliveries using drones have begun in the United States [9] and recent research into drone deliveries of AEDs has attempted to quantify delivery times, estimate mortality rates, and optimize delivery networks through theoretical models [10] [11] [12]. These studies have provided useful tools for AED delivery, but have ignored key factors, such as weather. Such exclusions and the lack real-world data means the viability of drone deliveries for time-sensitive supplies remains an open question.

This research focuses on drone deliveries of AEDs for OHCA and fills a gap in recent research by using real-world data to model and assess the impact of weather on drone delivery reliability and to quantify the impact of fleet size and population on failure rates. Determining the number of drones required to service an area is a difficult challenge as the rate of cardiac events for an area is dependent on population size and time of day [4]. Section 2. models demand as a function of fleet size, population, and failure rate for two types of operations: battery recharging and battery swapping. Section 3. models the impact of wind and temperature on range and drone delivery failure. Section 4. discusses the results and Section 5. concludes this research with key takeaways and recommendations for future studies.

2. Modeling Demand, Fleet Size and Failure Rate

The American Heart Association (AHA) provides means and confidence intervals for the number of OHCA events in a year as a rate per 100,000 people [5]. Modeling the number occurrences in a given time interval is a common application of the Poisson distribution [13]. As such, random OHCA events may be simulated using a Poisson distribution with rate parameter, λ_n, defined by AHA data.

OHCA events are time-dependent with high day-of-week and time-of-day variability. Incidence rate ratios (IRR) with 95% confidence intervals are used for simulation, where the highest increases are seen on Mondays [1.18, 1.38] and during the 8 to 9 morning hour [1.96, 2.59] [14]. Combined, Monday mornings have an average rate increase of 2.91 over the yearly average OHCA rate. Normal distributions are assumed for each IRR, based on the Central Limit Theorem of probability [13], and the time between consecutive OHCA events may be simulated utilizing a Poisson process of rate λ_n. Figure 1 shows the asymmetry of the distribution around the mean time between events as a function of population size.

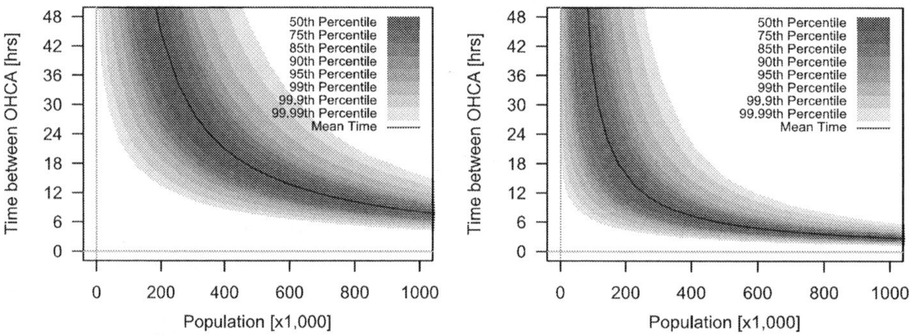

Figure 1: Time between consecutive OHCA events versus population. US average rate (left) and Monday 8 to 9 am (right)

2.1. Fleet Size, Drone Reposition and Battery Swapping Times

The number of required drones is based on the time between events, but also on the time it takes to serve a patient and reposition a drone. Two options are considered: in-drone battery recharging and battery swapping. For this study, we assume that a high performance multicopter MD4-3000 drone is utilized [15].

Table 1: MD4-3000 Drone characteristics

Specification	MD4-3000
Take off / Gross weight m	11.1 kg (24.5 lb)
Tare / Curb Weight m_t	10.0 kg (22.1 lb)
Payload m_l	1.1 kg (2.4 lb)
Empty weight factor c_m	0.90
Battery/Fuel Storage Capacity*	777 wh
Loaded Flight Time ($m_l = 1.1$ kg)	42 minutes
Range ($m_l = 1.1$ kg)	50 km (31 mi)

The optimal range is assumed to be 50 km (31 mi), which assumes ideal weather conditions and a cruise speed of 20 m/s (44.7 mph). With a 1.1 kg (2.4 lb) payload, the flight time will be approximately 42 minutes. The battery capacity of drones used in this study has a 21,000mAh [16]. The LiPo battery has a recommended recharge rate of 2A at greater than 90% charge efficiency [17]. Therefore, the charge time following a complete drain of the battery for one of these drones is between 10 hours 30 minutes and 11 hours 40 minutes. However, batteries will not experience a full drain each time they are used and there will be variability in the charge times based on distance traveled.
Given the random distribution of OHCA events and the combination of service and charge time of batteries, M/M/C queuing theory may be employed to determine the number of needed drones. For service times, it is assumed that a drone must stay with a patient until paramedics arrive (an average of 8 minutes) [8], stabilize patient (averaging 2 minutes), have the automatic defibrillator repackaged for the return trip (averaging 5 minutes), and return to base (averaging 5 minutes of flight and landing time). In addition to these 20 minutes, where drones are unavailable to service new patients, they must also have their batteries recharged. In case one, the drone is additionally unavailable during the time it takes to recharge the battery; in case two, the drone is unavailable for the time it takes to swap to a fully charged battery.
In case one, given an average of 10 minutes of active flight time to and from a patient, and the available flight time of 42 minutes, the average recharge time will be about 2 hours 40 minutes for average usage time of 3 hours. This corresponds to an average of 8 services per day. Using an M/M/C queueing model, a failure was defined as the probability that there will be one or more people people in the queue (i.e. a person is waiting to be served due to drone unavailability).

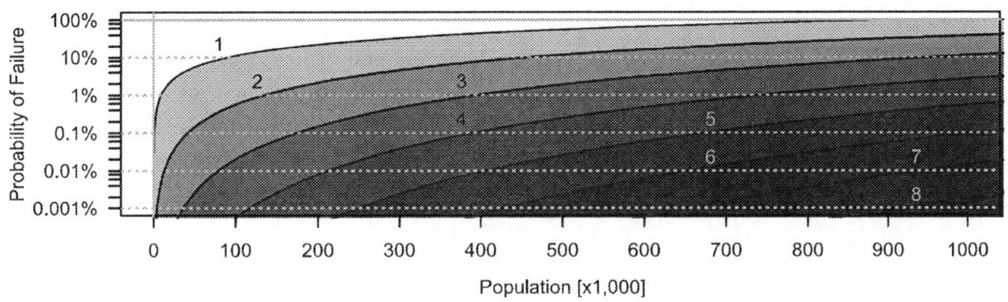

Figure 2: Case 1: Probability of failure versus population and number of drones for 8-9 am demand rate

In case two, each drone is unavailable for an additional 10 minutes (30 minutes total) to allow for the battery to be swapped with a fully charged battery. By swapping batteries, the number of potential services per day increases from 8 (in case one, battery recharging) to 48 (in case two, battery swapping).

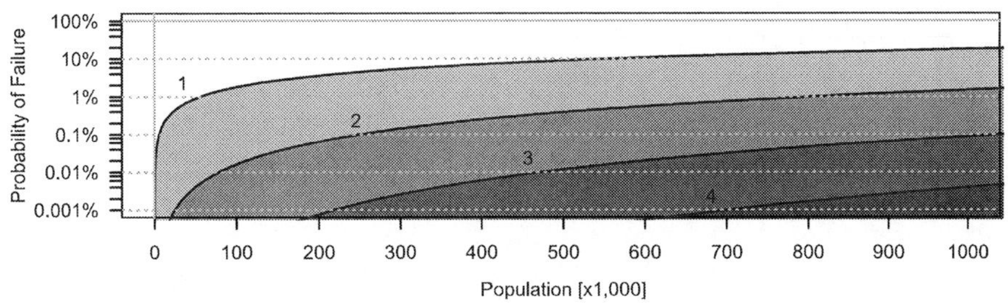

Figure 3: Case 2: Probability of failure versus population and number of drones for 8-9 am demand rate

For 100,000 people, a single drone would fail to provide service 10.9% of the time in case one versus just 1.8% of the time in case two. Picking an acceptable failure rate for vital medical supplies of <0.1%, three drones are required in case one, and two drones are required in case two. For 300,000 people and <0.01% failure, five drones are required in case one and three drones are required in case two. This difference corresponds to notable cost savings. As each drone can cost between $50,000 to $100,000 [18], but batteries can be less than $300 to $600 [17], fewer drones is ideal. A theoretical requirement for ten spare batteries instead of a spare drone would still result in 90%+ of cost savings.

3. Range and Weather Modelling

The range of a drone is determined by its weight, flying efficiency, and battery capacity. For applications with a central hub, this range is half of the distance a drone can travel, as a return trip must be accommodated. The following gives the energy necessary for level flight [15]:

$$p_l\, t = \frac{(m_t + m_b + m_l)g}{\vartheta(s)\eta_p}\, d \tag{1}$$

where:

p_l = power required for level flight [watts]
t = travel time [seconds] = d/s
m_b = drone battery mass [kg]
m_l = drone load (defibrillator) mass [kg]
m_t = drone mass tare, i.e. without battery and load [kg]
d = travel distance [m]
$\vartheta(s)$ = lift-to-drag ratio or L/D [unit-less]
s = travel speed [m]
η_p = total drone power transfer efficiency [unit-less] < 1.

From (1) it is possible to observe that energy consumption is directly proportional to drone mass and travel time and distance. The range estimations of this research consider the defibrillator 1.1 kg (2.4 lb) payload.

3.1. Modeling the Impact of Temperature

Temperature can have a significant impact on drone performance because drone lithium-ion batteries show optimal performance at approximately 20°C (68°F) but perform significantly worse at lower temperatures (see Figure 4). For lithium batteries, the output voltage is dependent on its operating temperature [19]. In this study, battery available energy or capacity is assumed to decrease following a parabolic curve. The maximum (100%) will be at 20°C (68°F) and the minimum (50%) at -20°C (-4°F). At higher temperatures, the capacity decreases linearly from 100% to 95% from 20°C (68°F) to 55°C (131°F). Battery makers recommend no operation outside this temperature range [17].

$$capacity = \begin{cases} -0.0003125t^2 + 0.0125t + 0.875 & -20 < t < 20 \\ 1 - .05\left(\frac{t-20}{55-20}\right) & 20 \le t < 55 \\ 0 & otherwise \end{cases} \tag{2}$$

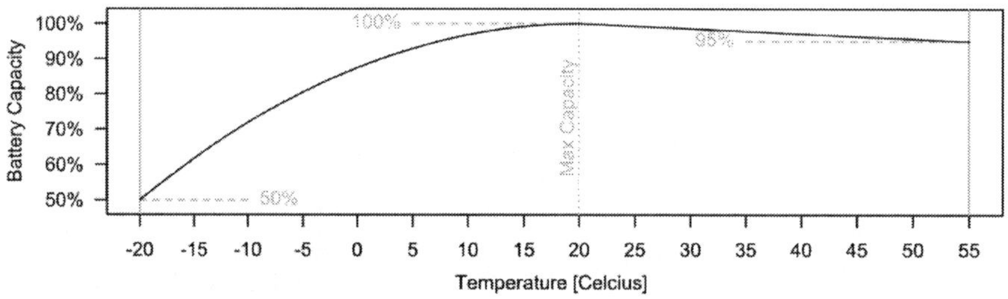

Figure 4: Battery capacity versus temperature

In addition, battery capacity degrades linearly with the number of cycles up to a point. Often, the degradation accelerates when a battery reaches 80% of optimal capacity. At this point, the battery is considered unreliable and no longer used. Prior to this point, the battery will have above 80% optimal capacity, but the exact amount will be unknown for any specific trip. As such, a random uniform distribution from 0.8 to 1.0 may be used in association with temperature for simulation to define the initial condition of the battery with an assumption that faulty or unreliable batteries will not be used.
OHCA events are more frequent between 8-9 am, typically the coldest hour of the day in winter. As such, only the distribution of low temperatures is needed in this study. Given the histograms of the temperatures, low temperatures are assumed to follow a normal distribution. Figure 5 shows the distribution of daily average temperatures in January.

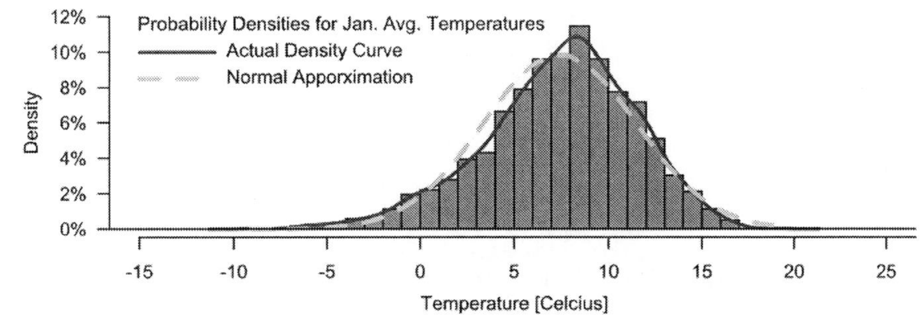

Figure 5: Histogram, density, and normal approximation of historical January daily average temperatures

Figure 4 shows the probability of failure as a function of total distance traveled, assuming an ideal 42-minute flight time. Ideal weather conditions from a reliability perspective assume no wind and a 20°C temperature. The potential range of a drone will be half of the total available flight distance, as return trips must be accommodated. The probability of failure is the percent of simulated trips that failed to reach a given range. High and low temperatures give the range of potential failure probabilities.

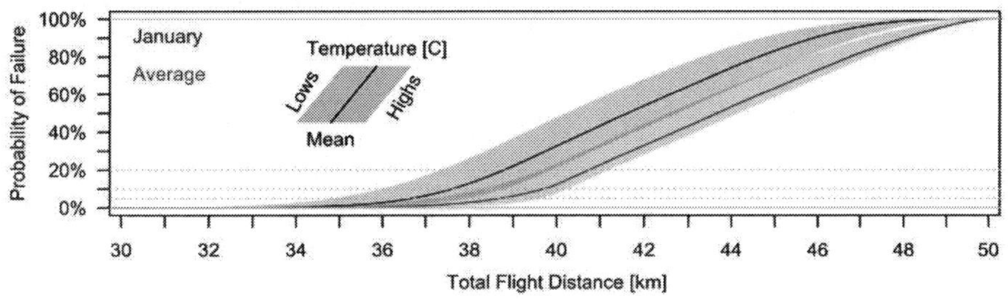

Figure 6: Probability of failure due to temperature and available battery charge versus flight distance

Winter will have worst-case flight ranges as compared to the yearly averages. Yet, the range in the worst case is still larger than the maximum allowable due to time constraints for urgent medical deliveries. Even allowing for 14.5 minutes of flight time, the average ambulance arrival time in rural areas, more than 95% of drones will have enough battery for the 35 km (22 mi) trip, 17.5 kms or 11 miles in each direction.
In addition, the available range corresponds to a large service area. The 3-minute delivery area covers 40 km^2 (15.7 mi^2), while 7 minutes (the urban ambulance average response time) allow for an area of 222 km^2 (86 mi^2). This is functionally the size of many cities. Based on Portland weather conditions, large cities would require just a few drone hubs for full coverage.

3.2. Modeling the Impact of Wind

Drones are highly susceptible to wind speed and direction due to their limited power and weight. The distribution of wind speeds may be modeled using a variety of known probability distributions with the Weibull ranking among the best [20]. As such, the choice of a probability distribution should be based on what can provide a reasonable approximation based on available data [21].
There are long time series for Portland wind data, including historical average speeds, maximum gusts, percent calm, and direction. In our weather data, the actual variances of wind speed were not included. Simulation was employed to find parameters that provided reasonable approximations of wind variance. In Portland, different times of year have different distributions of wind, which will directly influence failure odds. The distribution of wind speeds is as follows:

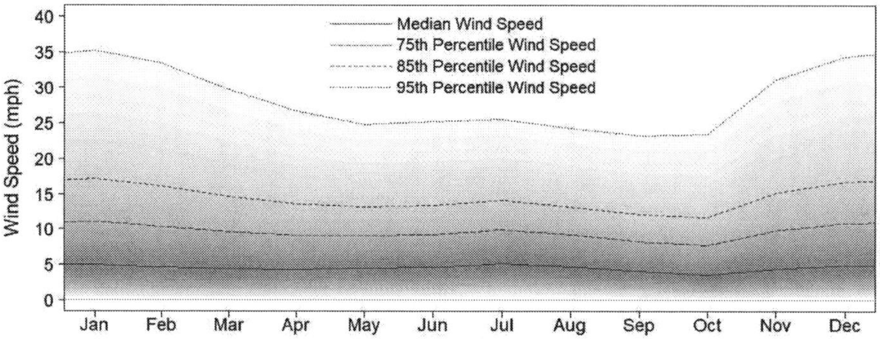

Figure 7: Mean and confidence interval of wind speed in Portland, OR

For headwind and tailwind simulations, flight times are held constant for arbitrarily selected two-minute and ten-minute cases. For each trial, distance traveled, within the time-limit, is recorded. The probability of delivery failures due to wind was calculated based on the percent of trips that fail to reach a given distance within the allowable time. The shaded region of the following graphics shows a range of failure probabilities between a simulated headwind versus simulated tailwind and the result using a random bearing as the central line. As the flight time increases, the probability of failure also increases.

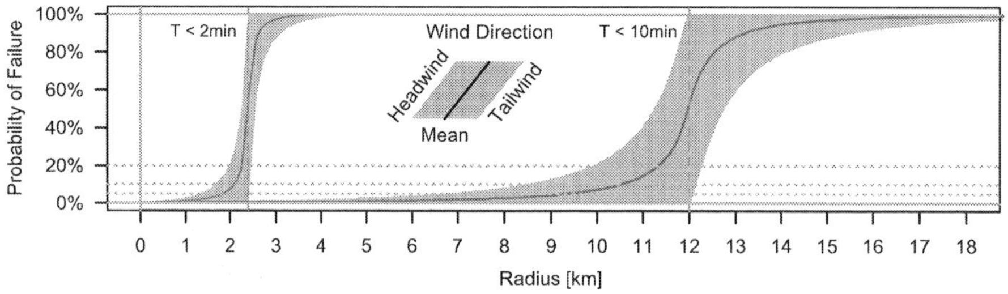

Figure 8: Probability of failure versus radius due to wind with linear y-axis

At a 20% acceptable fail rate for 2-minute deliveries, the worst case for range has decreased from 2.4 km (1.5 mi) to about 2 km (1.2 mi); a reduction of 16%. At a 5% acceptable failure rate, the range is further reduced to about 1.3 km (0.8 mi). While the theoretical range of drones is large (see Figure 6), the practical range for timely deliveries is a limiting factor. In figure 9, the y-axis of Figure 8 is transformed from linear to logarithmic.

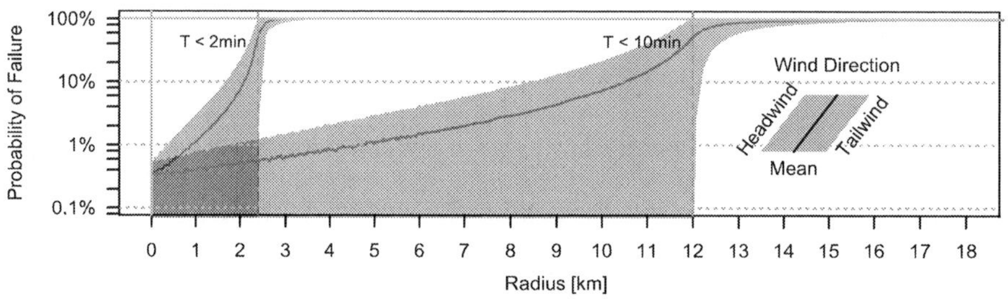

Figure 9: Probability of failure versus radius due to wind with logarithmic y-axis

Figure 9 shows the average potential failure from wind is above 0.1% for a 2 minute or a 10-minute trip. Wind plays a key role in determining acceptable failure rates and for determining a potential range for drone deliveries. Notably, having multiple hubs will reduce failure rates from the wind as different hubs may be employed depending on wind direction. Headwinds and potential failure from one direction may be tailwinds and success from another.

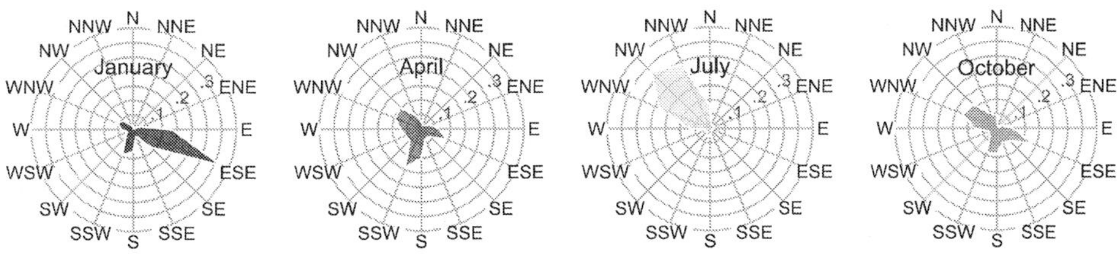

Figure 10: Probability of wind direction for each month in Portland, OR

In Portland, winds mostly blow in the ESE direction during winter months and the NW direction during the summer months (see Figure 10). This factor is important for determining a drone's range at different times of the year. In January, areas to the NW of a depot will be restricted by a headwind, while the opposite is true in July.

4. Discussion

Wind is a key factor; even average winds of Portland in January will cause failures more than 1% of the time. The direction of winds also changes depending on the time of year. The placement of drone hubs should consider ranges defined both by temporal constraints given by OHCA events survival rates as well as probabilistic failure odds caused by winds.
Temperature in Portland is not a key factor. The large potential delivery range of high-quality drones combined with strict delivery time limits reduce the negative effects of temperature and charge cycles. Hence, temperature may be ignored for these types of deliveries since the potential for failure remains low. For example, a 14 km (8.7 mi) trip (28 km or 17.4 mi both ways), would have less than 0.001% failure odds due to temperature and charge decay in the worst case.
The number of drones needed is highly dependent on charge times, the use of battery swapping, and the population in the service area. Given the average rate increase of 2.91 in the morning on Mondays for OHCA, the number of required drones increases as well. This worst-case scenario should likely be used to define the required equipment for a service area.

5. Conclusions and Limitations

For the delivery of time sensitive supplies, drones may provide the means to bypass many obstacles experienced by ground transportation. However, drones are subject to their own set of constraints that limit the likelihood of successful deliveries. While a typical package from an online retailer can be delayed by hours or days without substantial ill effect, even short delays, in the context of medical supplies, can be fatal. This paper examined several of the mechanical and meteorological impacts on drone deliveries to examine which factors are most important and to define limits. Results indicate that successful drone deliveries of AEDs are highly influenced by wind speeds and wind direction; however, the ambient temperature may be ignored for short and strict delivery times limits. Additionally, battery swapping may be highly effective at reducing equipment requirements given worst-case demand.
Given adequate historical data about weather and demand, drone delivery operators should be able to plan efficiently to meet peak demand periods without unacceptable failure rates or excessive costs. Winds will remain an obstacle in some parts of the year unless drone speeds can be improved. While drones may provide fast delivery times for the vast majority of cases, some failures will be difficult to avoid. Ideally, service areas should remain small enough that travel times are not limited by distance and overlap of service hubs will provide alternative delivery routes when wind direction is not ideal.

5.1. Future Research Opportunities

Future research should examine the likelihood that the delivery of automatic defibrillators will be able to be operated given that only one-third of OHCA events are witnessed by another person. If someone can

call emergency services, drone deliveries may be valid, but cannot be employed when another person is not present for operations. This paper assumes 100% reporting for OHCA events; as such, the rates and time between events is an over-estimate as not all events will be reported. The presented methodology can be still used after demand rates are adjusted considering reporting and operator presence.
Other weather events that may impact drone operations are rain and snow. Water resistance is a key marketing factor for many drone manufactures, but most advise against operation in adverse weather, such as heavy rain. The increased drag in rain and its adverse effect on flight speed and ranges could be considered in future studies as could the effects of freezing rain and snow on drone operations. Finally, there is an access and equity question associated with a drone's ability to deliver to some areas. For example, airports are often restricted flight zones that do not allow drone operations. Such areas often contain higher proportions of lower income communities. Future research should examine where a delivery system could be employed and what ground delivery systems are required locally to adjust for access differences.

6. References

1. Ministry of Infrastructure, (2012). "Public Transport Policy and Strategy for Rwanda." Republic of Rwanda.
2. Chen, J. (2017). "Rwanda has Shown That Healthcare Innovation in the Developing World Means More than Investing in Technology," Thomas Reuters Foundation News, 22 August. [Online]. Available: https://news.trust.org/item/20170821144058-29rg6/ (Accessed Aug. 2019).
3. Denby, S., (2019). "The Super-Fast Logistics of Delivering Blood By Drone," Wendover Productions. [Online]. Available at: https://www.youtube.com/watch?v=bnoUBfLxZz0 (Accessed Aug. 2019).
4. Brooks, S. C., Schmicker, R. H., Rea, T. D., et al. (2010). "Out-of-Hospital Cardiac Arrest Frequency and Survival: Evidence for Temporal Variability," *Resuscitation: Official Journal of the European Resuscitation Council*, vol. 81, no. 2, pp. 175-181.
5. American Heart Association (2018). "Heart Disease and Stroke Statistics - 2018 Update: A Report From the American Heart Association," *Circulation*, vol. 137, no. 12.
6. Foremost (2019). "HeartSine Samaritan PAD 450P AED" [Online]. Available at: https://www.foremostequipment.com/heartsine-samaritan-pad-450p-aed-new/ (Accessed Oct. 2019).
7. Chan, P.S., Krumholz, H.M., Nichol, G., & Nallamothu, B.K. (2008). "Delayed Time to Defibrillation after In-Hospital Cardiac Arrest," *The New England Journal of Medicine*, vol. 358, no. 1, pp. 9-17.
8. Mell, H.K., Mumma, S.N., Heistand, B., et al. (2017). "Emergency Medical Services Response Times in Rural, Suburban, and Urban Areas," *JAMA surgery*, vol. 152, no. 10, pp. 983-984.
9. Glover, M. & Colton, T. (2019). "Workhorse Partners with USOG to Launch Pilot Programs for Drone Delivery of Medical Supplies," BioSpace. [Online]. Available at: https://www.biospace.com/ article/releases/workhorse-partners-with-usog-to-launch-pilot-programs-for-drone-delivery-of-medical-supplies/ (Accessed Oct. 2019).
10. Claesson, A., Bäckman, A., Ringh, M., et al. (2017). "Time to Delivery of an Automated External Defibrillator Using a Drone for Simulated Out-of-Hospital Cardiac Arrests vs Emergency Medical Services." *JAMA*. vol. 317, no. 22, pp. 2332–2334
11. Pulver, A., Wei, R., (2018). "Optimizing the spatial location of medical drones," *Applied Geography*. vol. 90, pp. 9-16.
12. Boutilier, J. J., Brooks, S. C., Janmohamed, A., et al. (2017) "Optimizing a Drone Network to Deliver Automated External Defibrillators," *Circulation*. vol. 135, no. 25, pp. 2454-2465.
13. Casella, B., & Berger, R. L., (2002), Statistical Inference: Second Edition. Duxbury. Pacific Grove, CA.
14. Nordenskjöld, A. M., Eggers, K. M., Jernberg, T., et al. (2019). "Circadian Onset and Prognosis of Myocardial Infarction with Non-Obstructive Coronary Arteries," *PLOS ONE*, vol. 4, p. 14.
15. Figliozzi, M. (2017). "Lifecycle Modeling and Assessment of Unmanned Aerial Vehicles (Drones) CO2e emissions," *Transportation Research Part D*, vol. 57, pp. 251-261.
16. Microdrones (2019). "The Heavy-Lifting Drone md4-3000." [Online]. Available at: https://www.microdrones.com/en/drones/md4-3000/ (Accessed Aug. 2019).
17. Alibaba (2019). "36v 10ah lipo battery for e-bike battery pack" [Online]. Available at: https://www.alibaba.com/product-detail/36v-10ah-lipo-battery-for-e_60444386060.html (Accessed Aug. 2019).
18. Aniwaa (2019). "MD4-3000 Microdrones," Aniwaa Pte Ltd. [Online]. Available at: https://www.aniwaa.com/product/drones/microdrones-md4-3000/ (Accessed Au. 2019).
19. Samadani, E. (2015). "Modeling of Lithium-ion Battery Performance and Thermal Behavior in Electrified Vehicles," University of Waterloo, Waterloo, Ontario, Canada.
20. Qin, Z., Li W., & Xionga, X. (2011). "Estimating Wind Speed Probability Distribution Using Kernel Density Method," Electric Power Systems Research, vol. 81, no. 12, pp. 2139-2146.
21. NOAA, "Climate Data Online" [Online]. Available at: https://www.ncdc.noaa.gov/cdo-web/ (Accessed July 2017).

I L S 2020
INTERNATIONAL CONFERENCE ON INFORMATION SYSTEMS, LOGISTICS & SUPPLY CHAIN
Austin, Texas April 22-24, 2020

A Study of the Competitiveness of Autonomous Delivery Vehicles in Urban Areas

Miguel Figliozzi [1], Dylan Jennings [2]

[1] Professor of Civil & Environmental Engineering, Portland State University, Portland, OR, USA
[2] Research Assistant, Portland State University, OR, USA
{figliozzi@pdx.edu, dwj@pdx.edu}

Abstract. The rapid growth of e-commerce and package deliveries across the globe is demanding new solutions to meet customers' desire for more and faster deliveries. This research focuses on the cost competitiveness of autonomous air and ground delivery vehicles. Three types of autonomous vehicle are analyzed: drones, sidewalk autonomous delivery robots (SADRs), and road autonomous delivery robots (RADRs). Autonomous vehicles are compared against a typical delivery van. The impact of capacity, range and time constraints are analyzed. Results show that each type of autonomous delivery vehicle is suitable in different scenarios and can therefore complement each other to reduce costs or on-road distance traveled.

Keywords: Last mile, delivery, drone, robot, cost, time

1. Motivation and Literature Review

Autonomous delivery robots (ADRs) that travel on sidewalks and roads are being tested in several US cities by startups. Even large delivery companies like FedEx are also testing this technology [1]. Online retailers like Amazon are also testing a drone prototype that can deliver packages under five pounds to customers in less than 30 minutes; this is noteworthy because 75% to 90% of Amazon deliveries weigh less than five pounds [2].

The potential of autonomous vehicles for passenger transportation has been studied extensively. In comparison, significantly less work focuses on the potential of autonomous vehicles in the logistics and parcel delivery sector. Some researchers have studied the implications of autonomous vehicles for long-haul freight. For example, Short and Murray [3] discuss the impact of long-haul autonomous trucks on hours-of-service, safety, driver shortage and driver retention, truck parking, driver health and wellness, and the economy. The work of Slowik and Sharpe [4] focuses on the potential of autonomous technology to reduce fuel use and emissions for heavy-duty freight vehicles.

There are even less studies focusing on urban deliveries or short-haul freight trips. Jennings and Figliozzi [5] recently studied the potential of sidewalk autonomous delivery robots (SADRs). Given the relatively short range of SADRs, these small robots are usually complemented by a "mothership" van that can transport SADRs near the delivery zone or service area. The work of Jennings and Figliozzi (2019) analyzed current SADR regulation in the US, their characteristics, and their potential to reduce delivery times or costs. Jennings and Figliozzi (2020) analyzed the competitiveness of road autonomous delivery robots (RADR) when compared to conventional vans [6]. Results show that RADRs can provide substantial cost savings in many scenarios but in all cases, at the expense of substantially higher vehicle miles per customer served. The novel contribution of this research is to evaluate both air and ground (SADR and RADR) autonomous vehicles potential to reduce delivery times and costs in urban areas. To the best of our knowledge there is no publication comparing the costs of both air and both types of ground autonomous vehicles.

2. Vehicle Characteristics

A conventional van is defined as a delivery van in the traditional sense, with rear storage for parcels and a human driver and delivery person. A mothership for the purposes of our analysis is defined as a van which has been outfitted to transport SADRs, with a human driver who drops off or picks up SADRs. Finally, RADRs are defined as vehicles which operate autonomously to deliver parcels. See Figure 1 to find an illustration of the mothership-SADR and RADR vehicles analyzed in this research.

Figure 1: Mothership Van with Starship SADRs (left) and NURO (right)

A Starship Technologies' SADR in conjunction with a Daimler SADR Van, or "mothership", is utilized in the numerical analysis. Each Starship SADR weighs 40 lbs (18.1 kgs), has a speed of 4 mph (6.4 kph), and a range of 4 miles (6.4 kms). As discussed in [5] it is assumed that a Starship can deliver to up to six customers. A uDelv RADR is utilized in the numerical analysis. The uDelv is a modified Ford Transit Connect that has 32 individual compartments to store delivery items [6]. The Ford Transit Connect can travel at up to 60 mph, with a range of 60 miles before recharging, and a carrying capacity of 1,300 pounds [6]. The uDelv has individual compartments that can be opened one at a time, which would prevent theft of other delivery parcels. The drone analyzed is a cargo multicopter MD4-3000 that was already utilized to analyzed the comparative advantages of drones regarding CO_2 emissions against a Dodge RAM conventional van [7]. Key vehicle characteristics are provided in Table 1.

Table 1: Key Vehicle Characteristics

Vehicle	Tare (kg)	Max. Speed (kph)	Max. Payload (kg)	Range (km)
Starship	18.1	6.4	18.1	3.2
Nuro	680	56	110	16.1
uDelv	1890	97	590	97
MD4-3000	10.2	72	5.0	36
Dodge RAM	2170	180	1890	695

2.1. Vehicle Costs

While autonomous vehicles are beginning to be tested across the United States, the costs associated with manufacturing autonomous vehicle are still significantly higher than the manufacturing cost of conventional vehicles. A 2015 estimate indicates that the additional cost of just the Light Detection and Ranging (LIDAR) sensors to allow a vehicle to be fully autonomous (level 4+) is $30,000 to $85,000 per vehicle, and over $100,000 per vehicle for LIDAR and other sensors and software [6]. Autonomous vehicles could eventually cost $25,000 to $50,000 more than typical vehicles with mass production, over time, not less than 10 years, reaching prices of around $10,000 per vehicle. Price of automation implementation 20 to 22

years after introduction is expected to be $3,000 per vehicle, eventually reaching a low of $1,000 to $1,500 per vehicle [8].
The mothership and conventional van require a human driver. We assume a cost of $40 USD per hour for motherships and $35 USD per hour for conventional vans. The mothership is a more expensive vehicle since it is larger and requires a specialized configuration. We assume a value of $30 USD per hour for RADR vans after removing driver costs and adding higher autonomous vehicle costs and accounting for an operator monitoring several vehicles. We assume a relatively conservative cost of $1.5 USD per delivery for SADRs [5].
The cost of drone deliveries is estimated utilizing figures provided by Wright et al. [9] and Jenkins et al. [10]. The former reference indicates a cost of $0.41 per kg-km or $0.18 per lb-km for a multicopter; assuming 2.5 lbs per delivery results in $0.47 per km. The latter reference indicates that drone costs range between $0.10 and $0.60 per mile or $0.06 to $0.37 per km. Another report [11] provides a cost of delivery assuming different levels of regulation and labor participation. A low and high cost of $15.98 and $67.64 per hour are estimated. Assuming a 20 m/s operating speed the costs are estimated from $0.22 to $0.94 per km. The differences in drone costs are mainly due to different assumptions regarding the number of staff necessary to operate a drone delivery system. In this research a compromise value of $0.5 per kilometer is assumed which translates into $36 per hour. The drones also incur a fix setup time between flights of 10 minutes; this setup time is necessary to load the drone and swap the battery if necessary.

3. Methodology

The methodology used for comparing travel, time and cost of the studied vehicles is based on continuous approximations. As indicated by Daganzo et al. [12] this type of analytical approximation is appropriate to address big picture questions because they are parsimonious, tractable, and yet realistic when the main tradeoffs and constraints are included. This type of modeling approach has been successfully used in the past by many authors to model urban deliveries and logistic problems [13,14]. A circular area of service is assumed and capacity, range and tour duration constraints are considered. The range of a drone is determined by its weight, flying efficiency, and battery capacity. Drone range calculations are estimated as in [7] assuming a 5 pound delivery weight. According to Amazon 75 to 90% of its parcel deliveries are less than 5 pounds. The following notation is used throughout the paper.

n = Total number of customers served
k_l = Routing constraint (constant value), representing non-Euclidean travel on sidewalks and roads
a = Area (units length squared) of the service area, where n customers reside
$\delta = n/a$, customer density
d = Distance between the depot and the geometric center of the service area
T = Maximum duration of shift or tour (same for all vehicle types)
$l_i(n)$ = Average distance a vehicle travels to serve n customers for vehicle type i
m_i = Minimum number of vans for vehicle type i
R_i = Range of a vehicle for vehicle type i
Q_i = Capacity (number of parcels for vans or number of SADRs for motherships) for vehicle type i
τ_i = Total van time necessary to make n deliveries for vehicle type i
ϕ_i = Stop percentage (percent of the time a vehicle is stopped due to traffic control)
s_i' Average speed of the vehicle on urban streets, not including ϕ
$s_{i,h}'$ = Average speed of the vehicle while on a highway, not including ϕ
$s_i = s_i'\phi_i$ = Average speed of the vehicle on urban streets
$s_{i,h} = s_{i,h}'\phi_i$ = Average speed of the vehicle while on a highway
t_0 = Time it takes to wait for the customer to pick up their order from the vehicle or delivery person
t_u = Time it takes the vehicle and/or driver to unload the delivery
$t = t_0 + t_u$ = Total time vehicle is idle (i.e., not traveling) during a delivery
$c_{h,i}$ = Cost per hour of operating vehicle type i, including cost of a driver if applicable
$c_{d,i}$ = Cost per delivery for vehicle type i

The average distance $l(n)$ to serve n customers can be estimated as a function of customer density, number of vehicles, network characteristics and route constraint coefficients, and the distance between the depot and the delivery area [15]. In this paper, the equation used to calculate the distance traveled to visit n customers by a ground vehicle is:

$$l_i(n) = 2dm_i + k_l\sqrt{an/m_i} \quad (1)$$

In equation (1), d represents the average distance from the depot or distribution center (DC) to the customer(s). The parameter d is multiplied by two, the number of times the vehicle goes to and from the service or delivery area (SA). The parameter k_l is a constant value representing network characteristics and routing constraints in the SA [15]. The average area of the SA where customers are located is represented by a. The number of parcels or stops is represented by n. The following formula is used to calculate the route duration constraint of a ground vehicle accounting not only for driving time but also waiting for the customer and unloading the parcels:

$$\frac{2d}{s_{h,i}} + \frac{k_l\sqrt{an}}{s_i\sqrt{m_i}} + (t_0 + t_u)\frac{n}{m_i} < T \quad (2)$$

3.1. Baseline

In equation (2), the first term represents the driving time and the second term represents the time it takes to park, wait for or go to the customer and unload the parcels. To determine the maximum number of deliveries that can be made by the conventional van within a shift of duration T, equation (2) is solved for n when the available time is T (to ease notation the sub index for conventional van i is dropped). The resulting equation for the maximum number of customers that one conventional van can deliver is:

$$n = \left\lfloor \frac{k_l^2 a + 2s^2Tt - \frac{4ds^2t}{s_h} - k_l^2\sqrt{\left(\frac{4ds^2t}{k_l^2 s_h} - \frac{2s^2Tt}{k_l^2} - a\right)^2 - \frac{4t^2s^2}{k_l^2}\left(\frac{s^2T^2}{k_l^2} + \frac{4d^2s^2}{k_l^2 s_h^2} - \frac{4s^2Td}{k_l^2 s_h}\right)}}{2s^2t^2} \right\rfloor \quad (3)$$

The floor function is used in equation (3) to avoid a fractional number of customers. In this research, a conventional van is utilized as a baseline and equation (3) provides the maximum number of customers that can be served with one vehicle. Vans route duration constraints is given by (2) and capacity and range constraints are as follows (4):

$$m_i \geq \left\lceil \frac{n}{Q_i} \right\rceil \quad (4)$$

$$\frac{k_l\sqrt{an}}{\sqrt{m_i}} + 2d < R_i$$

For the conventional van constraints (2) and (4) are always satisfied in the scenarios analyzed, given the high value of R (range) and the large capacity of conventional vans when compared to SADRs and RADRs. Formulas and constraints for drones are simpler since there is one costumer per delivery [7]. For SADRs the range, time, and capacity constraints presented in [5] are utilized.

3.2. Scenarios

Table 2 shows a summary of the key scenario parameters by delivery vehicle type. These parameters are set to meet vehicle characteristics or reasonable operational values in urban areas. As area size a changes, following equation (3), the maximum number of customers that can be served by one conventional delivery van also changes. Hence, one conventional delivery van is the baseline utilized to create different scenarios that are labeled from A to I as the area size a increases from 10 to 130 square miles or 26 to 337 square kilometers (see Table 3). In all cases it is assumed that the delivery time per customer is $t = 3$ minutes and that the depot-SA distance is $d = 10$ miles or approximately 16.1 kilometers.
Fleet size and utilization for the other vehicles (uDelvs, motherships, SADRs and drones) also changes to meet the respective time, range, and capacity constraints as shown in Table 3. More customers can be served when the delivery area is smallest (scenario A) than largest (scenario I). Hence the customer delivery

density is reduced as the area increases. There are tradeoffs among number of customers served, area size, and fleet size; fleet size varies to satisfy range, capacity, and time constraints per vehicle type.

Table 2: Default values for variables used in calculations

Variable	Description of variable	Units	uDelv	SADR	Mother.*	Conv. Van	Drone
T	shift time (max)	hours	10	10	10	10	10
R_i	range of vehicle (max)	Miles (km)	60	4 (6.4)	400	400	22.4 (36)
Q_i	capacity (max)	unitless	32	6	8**	200	1
$c_{h,i}$	cost per hour of operation	USD	30	n/a	40	32	36
$c_{d,i}$	cost per delivery	USD	n/a	1.5	n/a	n/a	
s_i'	full unlimited vehicle speed in residential	mph (kph)	30 (48.3)	4 (6.4)	30 (48.3)	30 (48.3)	44.8 (72)
$s_{i,h}'$	full unlimited vehicle speed on highway	mph (kph)	60 (96.6)	n/a	60 (96.6)	60 (96.6)	44.8 (72)
s_i	vehicle speed in residential	mph (kph)	21 (33.8)	2.8 (4.5)	21 (33.8)	21 (33.8)	44.8 (72)
$s_{i,h}$	vehicle speed on highway	mph (kph)	42 (67.6)	n/a	42 (67.6)	42 (67.6)	44.8 (72)
k_i	routing constraints	unitless	0.7	0.7	0.7	0.7	n/a
ϕ	stopping factor	unitless	0.3	0.3	0.3	0.3	n/a

* Motherships can make multiple tours and ** capacity is number of SADRs per mothership instead of parcels

Table 3: Scenario Characteristics

Measure	Scenarios A	B	C	D	E	F	G	H	I
Time per customer [min]	3.0	3.0	3.0	3.0	3.0	3.0	3.0	3.0	3.0
Number of customers	163	149	140	133	127	122	118	114	110
Delivery area [mi^2]	10	25	40	55	70	85	100	115	130
Delivery area [km^2]	26	65	104	142	181	220	259	298	337
Cust. density [cust./ km^2]	6.3	2.3	1.4	0.9	0.7	0.6	0.5	0.4	0.3
Number of uDelvs	6	5	5	5	4	4	4	4	4
Number of motherships	1	1	1	1	1	1	1	1	1
Rounds per mothership	4	4	3	3	3	3	3	3	3
Number of SADRs	28	25	24	23	22	21	20	19	19
Number of drones	5	5	5	5	5	5	5	5	5

4. Results

In this section results obtained for scenarios A to I are analyzed. Table 4 shows the delivery distance per customer as a function of vehicle type and delivery scenario. In the case of the drones the distance per customer increases considerably as the service area increases. However, for the other vehicles the change is less marked as there is a tradeoff between the efficiency of the vehicle fleet size, the number of customers served, and the size of the delivery area. In the case of the conventional van with constant fleet size, it is possible to observe a clear trend with an increase in the delivery distance per customer as the customer density decreases from scenario A to I. RADRs can bring about more congestion in scenarios A to I as their on the road travel (per customer served) is substantially higher distance.

Table 4: Delivery distance per customer [km.] by vehicle type

Vehicle Type	Scenario								
	A	B	C	D	E	F	G	H	I
uDelv Van	1.5	1.5	1.8	1.9	1.9	2.0	2.1	2.3	2.4
Mothership	1.5	1.7	1.3	1.4	1.5	1.6	1.7	1.8	1.9
SADR	0.3	0.5	0.6	0.7	0.8	0.9	1.0	1.1	1.2
Conv. Van	0.5	0.7	0.8	1.0	1.1	1.2	1.3	1.4	1.5
Drone	3.8	6.1	7.7	9.0	10.1	11.2	12.1	13.0	13.8

Table 5 shows total time spent per customer by vehicle type in each of the different scenarios. Although drones are fast and can reach a given customer in a short time, their overall efficiency is heavily penalized by two factors: the battery swap time and the numerous trips to the depot since their capacity is just one package per delivery. The average drone time per customer increases substantially as the delivery area increases. However, for the uDelv and vans the changes are less marked as there is a tradeoff between the efficiency of the vehicle fleet size, the number of customers served, and the size of the delivery area. There is a large increase in SADRs time per customer as a consequence of longer travel distances and the slow speed of the SADRs.

Table 5: Total delivery time per customer [min.] by vehicle type

Vehicle Type	Scenario								
	A	B	C	D	E	F	G	H	I
uDelv Van	4.5	4.8	5.1	5.4	5.4	5.6	5.8	6.0	6.2
Mothership	2.4	2.7	2.4	2.5	2.6	2.8	2.9	3.0	3.1
SADRs	6.7	9.1	11.0	12.6	14.1	15.5	16.8	18.1	19.3
Conv. Van	3.7	4.0	4.3	4.5	4.7	4.9	5.1	5.3	5.4
Drone	16.2	18.0	19.4	20.5	21.4	22.3	23.1	23.8	24.5

Regarding costs, Table 6 summarizes the results. Drones are clearly more expensive than the other modes. The drone flight time per customer is reduced substantially as the service area decreases but this reduction is not enough to compensate for the swap times and low efficiency of the drone routes.

Table 6: Cost per customer by vehicle type [$/cust.]

Vehicle Type	Scenario								
	A	B	C	D	E	F	G	H	I
uDelv Van	2.3	2.4	2.6	2.7	2.7	**2.8**	**2.9**	**3.0**	**3.1**
SADR +Moths.	3.1	3.3	3.1	3.2	3.2	3.4	3.4	3.5	3.6
Conv. Van	**2.2**	**2.3**	**2.5**	**2.6**	**2.7**	2.9	3.0	3.1	3.2
Drone	9.7	10.8	11.6	12.3	12.9	13.4	13.9	14.3	14.7

Regarding ground vehicles, the RADR is more competitive than the conventional van when the vehicle capacity is not binding and the fleet size is four or less vehicles (in bold, scenarios F to I). The conventional van is more competitive with higher densities and longer routes that can be served by just one vehicle (scenarios A to E). SADRs are not the most competitive option in any scenario, but they are very competitive if the mothership vehicles is not utilized, i.e. for deliveries near the depot.

5. Discussion and Conclusions

RADRs can be more competitive than conventional vans but they are limited by their relatively short range and limited storage capacity. The short range can be addressed by more and better batteries. Though this would be at the expense of additional vehicle weight and cost, batteries are one of the major barriers to the electrification of freight [16]. SADRs can be more than conventional vans when delivery time per customer is relatively high. They can also be very competitive if they can operate from a depot and without the support of a mothership [5]. However, this type of operation is only feasible in dense delivery areas near a depot and not in the scenarios discussed in this research where the depot-delivery area distance is 10 miles or 16.1 kilometers. Drones have many potential advantages over ground vehicles, for example they can arrive quickly to a customer by taking more direct paths and avoiding ground-based obstructions. However, drones underperform in terms of payload capacity and delivery costs.
The largest uncertainties related to drone, SADRs, and RADRs are perhaps their cost and future regulatory barriers. The rate and speed of adoption of air and ground autonomous delivery vehicles will greatly depend on their operational costs and ease of regulation and entry into the delivery market, as discussed by previous studies focusing on the adoption of autonomous trucks by freight organizations [17,18].

5.1. Non-monetary considerations

Large-scale introduction of autonomous air and ground vehicles can bring about new business and service models that are made possible by 24-hour operations since autonomous vehicles are not subject to limitations like driver fatigue as well as lunch and rest breaks. On the other hand, RADRs can bring about more congestion unless they become more efficient than conventional vans in terms of vehicle-distance traveled per customer. Although most deployments are still at the pilot level, air drones and ground ADRs may soon be able to complement traditional delivery methods to meet the growing delivery demands caused by e-commerce, which is growing at a double-digit annual rate [19].
According to a recent survey, a large majority of people in the US believe that delivery robots will be in use within the next five years [20]. According to this USPS study, customers highly value the ability to receive deliveries when and where recipients choose. Since RADRs deliver freight, they can prioritize safety of pedestrians and other road users over the safety of the freight being carried by the RADR. Hence, RADRs are not faced with potential ethical issues that passenger autonomous vehicles are likely to face regarding tradeoffs between the safety of passengers and other vulnerable road users such as pedestrians and/or cyclists. Because of this advantage, it is likely that RADRs may be widely used before autonomously driven passenger vehicles. On the other hand, urban freight is complex and the tasks associated to parking, unloading, and delivering may be more difficult to automate than is currently expected. High safety standards for RADRs may result in high delivery times per customer, which in turn decreases RADRs economic appeal as shown in the previous section.
From a public policy perspective, the utilization of RADRs may significantly increase the number of vehicle-miles related to package delivery. The scenarios analyzed indicate that RADRs generate more vehicle-miles per delivery than conventional vans (substantially more in many scenarios). As a secondary effect, new delivery/service models (anytime/anywhere) plus a reduction in delivery costs brought about by a large-scale introduction of RADRs may further increase the already high growth of ecommerce. The combination of higher vehicle-miles per delivery plus the growth of ecommerce can compound congestion and high curb utilization problems in many urban areas.

5.2. Limitations and future research opportunities

This research is a first step towards understanding the key tradeoffs between air and ground automated delivery vehicles and conventional vans. A few scenarios have been analyzed but more research is necessary to analyze specific case studies, future vehicle capabilities and cost figures, and how these new technologies can be integrated into efficient supply chains in urban areas and to optimize their joint deployment [21]. Future research can also study the broader impacts of urban freight autonomous vehicles on urban sustainability as well as future distribution networks and land use patterns.

6. References

1. FedEx, 2019. Meet the FedEx SameDay Bot™. The future is knocking, Available at: https://thefuturefedex.com/?search=true&spterm=bot, accessed June 15, 2019
2. Forbes, 2019, Amazon's New Delivery Drone Will Start Shipping Packages 'In A Matter Of Months', Available at: https://www.forbes.com/sites/jilliandonfro/2019/06/05/amazon-new-delivery-drone-remars-warehouse-robots-alexa-prediction/#7ac8ad4b145f (Accessed 25 August, 2019).
3. Short, J. and Murray, D. (2016). Identifying Autonomous Vehicle Technology Impacts on the Trucking Industry. American Transport Research Institute. http://atri-online.org/wp-content/uploads/2016/11/ATRI-Autonomous-Vehicle-Impacts-11-2016.pdf (Accessed 1 July 2019).
4. Slowik, P. and Sharpe, B. (2018). Automation in the Long Haul: Challenges and Opportunities of Autonomous Heavy-Duty Trucking in the United States. The International Council of Clean Transportation, (online) Working Paper 2018–06, pp. 1–30. Available at: https://theicct.org/sites/default/files/publications/Automation_long-haul_WorkingPaper-06_20180328.pdf (Accessed 1 July 2019).
5. Jennings, D., and Figliozzi, M. (2019). A Study of Sidewalk Autonomous Delivery Robots and Their Potential Impacts on Freight Efficiency and Travel, Transportation Research Record 2673(6), 317–326.
6. Jennings, D., and Figliozzi, M. (2020). A Study of Road Autonomous Delivery Robots and Their Potential Impacts on Freight Efficiency and Travel, Forthcoming Transportation Research Record.
7. Figliozzi, M. (2017) Lifecycle modeling and assessment of unmanned aerial vehicles (Drones) CO2e emissions, Transportation Research Part D: 2017, 57, 251-261.
8. Fagnant, D. J., and Kockelman, K. (2015). Preparing a Nation for Autonomous Vehicles: Opportunities, Barriers and Policy Recommendations. Transportation Research Part A: Policy and Practice, Volume 77, pp. 167–181.
9. Wright, C., Rupani, S., Nichols, K. and Chandani, Y., 2018. White Paper What should you deliver by unmanned aerial systems?. JSI Research and Training Institute.
10. Jenkins, D., Vasigh, B., Oster, C. and Larsen, T., 2017. Forecast of the commercial UAS package delivery market. Embry-Riddle Aeronautical University.
11. Figliozzi, M.A., 2018. Modeling the Sustainability of Small Unmanned Aerial Vehicles Technologies. FMRI Report Y1R1-17, December 2018
12. Daganzo, C., Gayah, V. and Gonzales, E. (2012). The Potential of Parsimonious Models for Understanding Large Scale Transportation Systems and Answering Big Picture Questions. EURO Journal on Transportation and Logistics, Volume 1(1-2), pp.47–65.
13. Ansari, S., Başdere, M., Li, X., Ouyang, Y. and Smilowitz, K., (2018). Advancements in Continuous Approximation Models for Logistics and Transportation Systems: 1996–2016. Transportation Research Part B: Methodological, 107, pp.229-252.
14. Franceschetti, A., Jabali, O. and Laporte, G., 2017. Continuous Approximation Models in Freight Distribution Management. Top, 25(3), pp.413-433.
15. Figliozzi, M. (2008). Planning Approximations to the Average Length of Vehicle Routing Problems with Varying Customer Demands and Routing Constraints. Transportation Research Record (2089), 1-8.
16. Feng, W., Figliozzi, M., An Economic and Technological Analysis of the Key Factors Affecting the Competitiveness of Electric Commercial Vehicles, 2012 Transportation Research Part C, Volume 26, pp 135-145, 2013
17. Talebian, A. and Mishra, S. (2018). Predicting the adoption of connected autonomous vehicles: A new approach based on the theory of diffusion of innovations. Transportation Research Part C: Emerging Technologies, Volume 95, pp. 363–380.
18. Simpson, J., Mishra, S., Talebian, A. and Golias, M. (2019). An Estimation of the Future Adoption Rate of Autonomous Trucks by Freight Organizations. Forthcoming Research in Transportation Economics.
19. USCB, 2018. Quarterly E-Commerce Report 1st Quarter 2018. U.S. Census Bureau News, Publication CB18-74. Washington, D.C.: U.S. Department of Commerce, pp. 1–3. Available at: https://www2.census.gov/retail/releases/historical/ecomm/18q1.pdf (Accessed 1 March 2019).
20. USPS, 2018. United States Postal Service Report: Public Perception of Delivery Robots in the United States Report Number RARC-WP-18-005, published April 9, 2018.
21. Boysen, N., S. Schwerdfeger, and F. Weidinger (2018). Scheduling Last-Mile Deliveries with Truck-Based Autonomous Robots. European Journal of Operational Research.

I L S 2020

INTERNATIONAL CONFERENCE ON INFORMATION SYSTEMS, LOGISTICS & SUPPLY CHAIN

Austin, Texas April 22-24, 2020

Improvements in the Brazilian School Feeding Programme Routing: A Spatial Analysis and Discrete Event Simulation Approaches

João Roberto Maiellaro[1,2], João Gilberto Mendes dos Reis[2], Oduvaldo Vendrametto[2], Fernando Juabre Muçouçah[3], Valéria Rufino Maiellaro[1], Sivanilza Teixeira Machado[4]

[1] Fatec Zona Leste, São Paulo, Brazil
[2] RESUP/PPGEP - Paulista University, São Paulo, Brazil
[3] Fatec Ferraz de Vasconcellos, Ferraz de Vasconcellos, Brazil
[4] IFSP Campus Suzano
{joao.maiellaro@fatec.sp.gov.br, betomendes reis@msn.com, oduvaldov@gmail.com}

Abstract. School feeding programmes are present in many countries and the connection of local family farming with these initiatives is a practice that brings gains to the local economy and to school indicators and promotes healthy eating for children and young people. In Brazil, the National School Feeding Programme - PNAE, stimulates the purchase of food from local family farmers. In Mogi das Cruzes city, 58 family producers provide fresh food for school meals for 209 public schools with financial resources of the PNAE. Despite guaranteeing regular purchases, producers complain about the high cost of distribution. This paper studies the current routing scenario of PNAE in Mogi das Cruzes city through spatial analysis and simulation of discrete events approach. The results proposed a new routing scenario, reducing the traveled distances with no relevant changes in transport times

Keywords: Routing, Simulation, School Feeding

1. Introduction

Researchers recognized the importance of studies about Food Supply Chains (FSC), Short Food Supply Chains (SFSCs) and the role played by school feeding programs [1–5] to ensure food security during childhood and youth [6–9].

School-age nutritional deficits bring a strong impact on behavior and intellectual development. Studies about the feeding of children in the school stage have been conducted [10–13].

School feeding programmes are widespread. Countries with low and medium-income economies increasingly understand that Home Grown School Feeding (HGSF) initiatives, that connect the family local food farmers to governmental school feeding programmes, are fundamental opportunities to improve livelihoods for smallholder farmers and local communities and to strengthen the relationship between nutrition, agriculture, and social protection [14, 15].

In Brazil, the Programa Nacional de Alimentação Escolar – PNAE (National School Feeding Programme) transfers resources for purchasing food from family farmers to be destined for school meals. According to Law 11947, at least 30% of the resources should be destined to purchase food from local family farming [16]. Brazil has 5570 municipalities [17]. The PNAE attended in 2016, 5333 municipalities and more than 40 million students were benefited by the PNAE resources [18].

Mogi das Cruzes is one of the main cities of the green belt of São Paulo, with great relevance in food production [19]. The municipality of Mogi das Cruzes buys food from 58 family farmers by using PNAE financial resources to feed students of 209 public schools. Family farmers transport the food to the Associação dos Produtores Rurais de Jundiapeba e Região (APROJUR) headquarters. APROJUR is a family farmers association that is in a rural area, near most of 58 family farmers' properties. In this shed, cooperatives perform a cross-docking operation, separating the loads into 8 routes.

Family farmers complain about the high cost of distribution. The logistics operator argues that because of the high perishability, it is not possible to reduce the number of 8 routes because longer delivery times would deteriorate the food transported in small urban trucks. The staff of the municipality suggests the adoption of a new cross-docking point in the Departamento de Alimentação Escolar (DAE - School Feeding Department), a sector in charge of purchases, reception, storage and distribution of non-perishable foods. The DAE is in an urban area near many schools.

Governments try to ensure that all regions of the country have coverage of school feeding. This increases the political attractiveness of the programme but dilutes the efficiency. There also may be a tendency to prefer covering urban areas to the detriment of rural areas, or schools that already have the infrastructure or are easier to reach than schools which would need additional investment in infrastructure or logistics [20].

In this context, questions can be raised: Is it possible to reduce the number of routes? The clustering of schools can be improved, aiming to reduce travel distances? The routing scenario can be analyzed and improved to reduce the distribution cost without a relevant influence on the distribution times?

This paper evaluates the scenario of the routing of the PNAE in the city of Mogi das Cruzes through spatial analysis in a Geographic Information system (GIS) and proposes an alternative routing scenario through the discrete events simulation, seeking to reduce the cost of the distribution of food purchased from family farming and without affecting transport times. This research adopted the QGIS and Arena tools for the spatial analysis and the simulation experiment respectively.

The results show a new routing scenario where the number of routes declined from 8 to 6 and the travel times were not steadily disturbed. The simulation considered the DAE facilities as a new cross-docking and distribution point.

The paper is organized as follows: In Section 2, a literature review brings information about School Feeding Programmes, the Mogi das Cruzes city and aspects about of the PNAE and Food Supply Chains. The methods are described in Section 3. Section 4 develops the spatial analysis using QGIS and the simulation experiment using Arena and results and discussions are provided. Finally, conclusions are given in Section 5.

2. Literature review

School feeding programmes are widespread. The World Food Programme estimated that in 2013, 368 million children, or one in five, received a school meal at a total cost of US$ 75 billion. The rationales for school feeding investment are abating hunger, improving health and nutrition and improving schooling outcomes [21]. School feeding programmes that operate in a planned number of days per year, with predetermined meals, and provide opportunities for local agriculture, generating stable and predictable demand, are the conceptual basis of the Home Grown School Feeding Programmes [22, 23].

Studies have been conducted addressing food supply chains that connect local producers directly with consumers [24–26]. About 90% of the 570 million of the rural properties in the world are small, and most are in developing countries and are operated by families. Many of these small family farmers have limited access to markets and services [14]. The term used by the literature to define chains in which food is produced near the consumers, establishing a direct relationship of commercialization is Short food Supply Chains [27] and it was cited for the first time by [28].

In Brazil, family farming is extremely important for agricultural production (Berchin et al., 2019). In 2006 there were 5,175,489 agricultural properties in Brazil. Within these properties, 4,367,902 were linked to family farming, representing almost 85% of the total (Froehlich et al., 2018).

Mogi das Cruzes has great relevance in the vegetables, fruits and flowers production in Brazil, besides the important portion of the national market of mushrooms, khaki, medlar, with great presence of farmers with a Japanese origin [19]. Agricultural activity is remarkable. The number of agricultural establishments in the city was 1379 in 2017 [29].

Detailed data on agricultural production in the municipality of Mogi das Cruzes are shown in Table 1, in which the areas are divided by different characteristics [30].

Delivery available for loading and unloading operations is critical to reducing times and costs of logistics operations, as well as for improving city sustainability and livability. Planning with transportation modeling through simulation allows the computation of performance indicators to be used for assessment in studying delivery scenarios [31].

Table 1 – Agricultural data of Mogi das Cruzes ([30])

	Quantity of properties	hectares
Total area	1,616	26,077.20
Perennial farming	574	1,905.30
Temporary farming	933	3,939.80
Pastures	190	2,109.20
Reforestation	358	5,773.80
Natural vegetation	954	7,058.70
Swamp and floodplain vegetation	272	495
Resting	678	2,367.50
Complementary	1,551	2,427.90

Despite the importance of the food industry, the management of food supply chains receives less attention from the literature. The reason can be the complex management of these chains and the specificity of the products and processes [32].

Many small farmers live in remote areas with poor road infrastructure, creating high transaction costs to access markets in the School feeding. In addition, the lack of a diversity of products and inadequate practices post-harvest handling and storage generate difficulties for farmers' compliance with the quality requirements of school feeding programmes [33].

Family farmers need logistical capabilities. It is common that the storage capacity and unitization of loads to be deficient and that knowledge about business models is low [34, 35].

The poor qualification of farmers, a small level of integration between producers, municipalities, logistics services providers and schools, and lack of knowledge of legal aspects of the school feeding program are noted in SFSCs [36]. These issues combined with problems as the poor quality of roads and inadequate vehicles can turn the logistics operation a crucial matter.

Organizations and cooperatives could provide the structure for family farmers to be competitive to provide for school feeding programmes [33], however, they face governance challenges, particularly in developing countries because of limited managerial skills and lack financial resources [37].

QGIS is an open source platform that is widely adopted in different analyses, as software modeling [38].

In distribution systems, there are many uncertainties involved in the operation, such as vehicles and product availability, loading time, unloading time, transport time, and demanded quantities. By generating random observations of the relevant probability distributions, the simulation can readily deal with these types of uncertainties and is used frequently to test various possibilities for project improvement and operation of these systems. A consecrated application of this type was the combination of mixed binary linear programming and simulation that reduced the annual costs with freight on more than US$ 7 million from Reynolds Metal Company [39].

Among different simulation softwares, Arena has been applied by several researchers in various disciplines [40]. Arena has been widely used to simulate traffic modes [31, 41, 42] in different modes of transportation and various general or specialized simulation packages have been employed [40].

The benefits of modeling for decision making are the lower cost in relation to the interference in the real system, the anticipation of needed information, the usefulness of the models when it is impossible to perform tests in reality and the gains of insights and understanding about the investigated problem or object [43].

3. Methods

The methods adopted in this research are based on spatial analysis and discrete event simulation. Both technics were combined. Spatial analysis allowed us to study the eight current routes visually and allowed to propose a new scenario with six routes. Both scenarios were evaluated in a simulation model, considering the variations in the travel times between schools.

We performed the spatial analysis using a Geographic Information System (GIS). The PNAE's family farmers suppliers and the 209 schools of the network were geo-referenced. The spatial analysis allowed us to study the current routes and to elaborate on a new proposal for the routing. It also included the headquarters of APROJUR and DAE in the maps. The headquarters of APROJUR is the current distribution point and the headquarters of the DAE is a distribution alternative proposed by the staff of the Secretariat of Agriculture of the city of Mogi das Cruzes. The QGIS software was used.

The schools, producers, and headquarters of APROJUR and DAE were included in QGIS by using Keyhole Markup Language files, generated in Google Earth Pro software.

A discrete event simulation model was elaborated in the ARENA © software to compare the current distribution operation with a proposed alternative scenario. Simulation approach reduces the deficiencies in the existing pragmatic models.

The elimination of uncertainties related to cost, time and overall project management is possible by simulation models. Arena is an event management software extensively used for project managing purposes. The software includes diverse actions in terms of different modules that can be linked and sequenced [44].

The discrete events simulation was adopted instead of optimization methods as VRP Spreadsheet Solver, because the time of distribution is the most critical variable in the studied system, according to family farmers, schools and the logistics operator. The longest routes show a variation in the transport time because of the unpredictability of the traffic volume and roads paving conditions. The simulation model also allows large flexibility in analyzing an extensive number of new routing scenarios, which would be unfeasible through the use of VRP methods.

Besides the probabilistic behavior of the transport times, there are other reasons that justify the adoption of the discrete event simulation method. The model was elaborated to allow the flexibility of studying different routing scenarios. The animation resources are an important issue because it allows a deeper understanding of the proposed and tested scenarios.

The lack of actual data for the simulation modeling process occurs when the simulated systems do not exist when the cost involved for the data collection is high or technically unfeasible, or when the involved actors do not provide the data by unavailability or confidentiality. The rule in these cases is to adopt intuitive distributions as exponential, to represent the time between successive arrivals, and triangular distribution when an estimation of typical, minimum and maximum values that can occur in the simulated system is known [45]. Delays due to transportation and unloading in schools were collected and modeled. The eight different drivers provided varying times based on empirical skills in the transport operation. The minimum, typical and maximum times of the longest routes were requested. In the simulation model, the route times were represented by triangular distributions. Based on the empirical experience of the eight drivers, we also collected the unloading times in schools.

In order to increase the reliability of the simulation results, it is common to apply a big number of replications of the experiment until the confidence interval decreases, even though this practice can make the study more time-consuming [39]. The number of replications can be defined by the formula [46]:

$$n = n_0 \frac{h_0^2}{h^2} \quad (1)$$

Where n_0 is the number of initial replications, and h_0 is the half width the model got from the n_0. The pre-specified desided for the half width of a choosen metric of the model is h.

Among the various techniques for validation of a simulation model, the face-to-face validation is one in which the analyst who assembled the model makes the conceptual validation and the validation of the results of the model, through the opinion of professionals with extensive experience and empirical knowledge of the simulated system. Other validation techniques are the duplication of models, in which two independent teams develop similar models, comparison with similar models previously developed, and sensitivity analysis, in which the influence of changes in input parameters in the results are pre-determined and tested [45].

4. Results and Discussion

The deliveries of the purchased food from family farmers are carried out by eight urban cargo vehicles. The headquarters of APROJUR is the current cross-docking point. The municipality's team suggested deploying a new cross-docking point in the DAE facilities, where the purchases of all food for school feeding are made and non-perishable foods are stocked. The DAE is in an urban area and cross-docking operations and deliveries to non-perishable food schools are carried out at this location.

Spatial analysis was built aiming at the improvement of the clustering of schools. The different colors represent the eight delivery routes (figure 1) where the points represent the 209 schools in Mogi das Cruzes city. The cross-docking operation is performed at the APROJUR headquarters. A new scenario with 6 routes, where the headquarters of the DAE is a cross-docking point, was elaborated in the QGIS software. Figure 1 shows on the left side, the current routes and on the right side, the proposed routes. The APROJUR's shed is represented by the green symbol and the DAE's headquarter is represented by the orange symbol. The spatial analysis showed that the current routes do not adequately group the schools. The proposed routing scenario allowed to reduce the traveled distances by the small trucks. Because of the variability of route times, a simulation model was elaborated to compare the current scenario with the proposed scenario in the spatial analyses. Due to the high perishability, the aim of the simulation was to reduce the distribution efforts and to decrease the transport time. The family farmers harvest the food a few hours before delivering. Shorter transport times can provide a very healthy and fresh diet for the students.

Figure 1 - Current and proposed routing scenarios by using QGIS (authors)

The schools were numbered from 1 to 209. The spatial analysis redefined the routing to decrease the total traveled distance. The simulation seeks improvements in transport times so that children's feeding is as healthy as possible. We also considered in the simulation model the change of the cross-docking point and distribution of the headquarters of APROJUR to the headquarters of the DAE suggested by the team of the city of Mogi das Cruzes.

The model assumes that the weight capacity of the vehicles is enough to transport the quantities of food historically demanded in the current and the proposed scenarios and that there is no change in the sequence of the visited schools, nor interruption in transport because of accidents or maintenance of the vehicles. We assume constant transport times for the very short routes. For the longer routes times, it was assigned triangular type distributions. The eight drivers and the managers of the logistics operator validated the model which tested and concluded that the output results are similar compared to the actual operation. To observe the stochastic behavior of the simulation model, the results of five replications were performed, incorporating the uncertainties of the routing times. The half-width results of the unloading and transfer times were 0.1 for an average of 4.02 and 3.5 hours respectively in the current routing scenario.

Table 2 shows the distances and travel times of the 8 routes. Route 4 spends much more time than other routes and its distance traveled is higher. Balancing distances and transport times it is essential to ensure the food freshness. The shortest routes such as 6 and 8 spend proportionately shorter times compared to longer routes.

Table 2 - Transport times and distances of the current routing scenario (authors)

Route	Cross-docking and distribution point	Average travel time (minutes)	Distance (km)
1	APROJUR	273.87	103.40
2	APROJUR	152.93	75.20
3	APROJUR	168.83	63.25
4	APROJUR	414.04	202.57
5	APROJUR	212.94	70.50
6	APROJUR	108.32	44.00
7	APROJUR	236.87	92.25
8	APROJUR	113.74	39.28

Table 3 shows the distances and travel times of the 6 routes in the new proposed routing scenario. Only Route 1 maintained the headquarters of APROJUR as a point of cross-docking and distribution. The other routes depart from the DAE. The staff of the municipality states it is possible to transport the quantities of Routes 2 to 6 from APROJUR to the DAE with a local government's truck.

Table 3 - Transport times and distances of the proposed routing scenario (authors)

Route	Cross-docking and distribution point	Average travel time (minutes)	Distance (km)
1	APROJUR	263.04	112.00
2	DAE	184.23	85.95
3	DAE	263.01	118.40
4	DAE	262.76	147.82
5	DAE	295.09	107.35
6	DAE	194.65	78.90

Even with the reduction of the number of routes from 8 to 6, the proposed scenario reduced the total traveled distance. The average transport times per route increased in 0.5 hours, but with a lower standard deviation. The difference between the longest and shortest path times has decreased (Table 4). Transport times are a key factor in maintaining the logistical operation at satisfactory levels of performance.

Table 4 – Current and proposed routing scenarios

	Current scenario	Proposed scenario
Quantity of routes	8	6
Average number of schools per route	25.8	34.5
Total distance (km)	690.45	650.42
Total spent time of distribution operation (h)	28.03	24.38
Average travel time (h/route)	3.5	4.06
Standard deviation of transport times (h/route)	1.68	0.73
Average of unload times in schools (h/route)	4.02	5.36
Average route time (h/route)	7.52	9.42
Faster route time (h)	5.16	7.9
Slower route time (h)	11.1	12.03

5. Conclusion

School feeding programmes are essential actions to promote healthy feeding and better education indicators. In Brazil, the law 11947 guarantees the purchase of local family farming for school meals. The Brazilian National School Feeding Programme – PNAE, is a benchmark in the world.

This study analyzed the food supply chain of the PNAE in the city of Mogi das Cruzes. As cited in the literature, the program suffers from problems and difficulties in logistics operation because of the low qualification of family farmers and school managers in this field.

The research proved to be useful because it proposed a new scenario of routing with a reduction in the number of routes from 8 to 6, still achieving to reduce the total distance traveled and without substantially affecting the transport times, which is a critical variable in the study because of the high perishable items transported, and the government investment in the purchase of food directly from family farming. Other Brazilian cities can gain insights to study analogous situations.

In Mogi das Cruzes, managers can revise the cost of the logistics operation that impacts severely on the viability of the PNAES's Short Food Supply Chain based on the results of the proposed routing scenario. The research raises the study of other routing scenarios based on the simulation model. The modeling allows simulating scenarios with a higher or smaller number of routes and other routes' sequences of visited schools.

Increasing the number of replications of the model did not reduce the half-width results. But we consider the limitations of this research are the impossibility of collecting measurements of transport and unloading times, which could provide higher assertiveness of the results. It is also a limitation of the research the lack of studies of another routing scenario that maintains the 8 original routes and could reduce the transport times, although possibly without significant impacts in reducing the costs of distribution.

We can replicate the method that combined spatial analyses to resize routes with routing scenario studies in a simulation model in places where family farming provides food for school feeding, with social improvements in Brazilian and Latin American cities.

It is suggested for future applications, a study involving other the food supply chain activities, including in the simulation model the receipt of food, the use of resources in the cross-docking activity and the inbound logistics in schools. Current standards of demand can be studied to scale the movement and transport capacity of vehicles. Similarly, new studies can prospect the capacity of transport movement assuming new scenarios with increased demanded quantities or including new items. It is also possible to study scenarios including new family farmers because the city has over 1000 small rural enterprises and only 58 actively take part in the PNAE.

6. References

1. Chauhan, A.: Plates for slates: The impact of a school feeding programme on community representations of schools. International Journal of Educational Development. 41, 292–300 (2015). https://doi.org/10.1016/j.ijedudev.2014.07.013.
2. Sonnino, R., Lozano Torres, C., Schneider, S.: Reflexive governance for food security: The example of school feeding in Brazil. Journal of Rural Studies. 36, 1–12 (2014). https://doi.org/10.1016/j.jrurstud.2014.06.003.
3. Torres, I., Benn, J.: The rural school meal as a site for learning about food. Appetite. 117, 29–39 (2017). https://doi.org/10.1016/j.appet.2017.05.055.
4. Rueda, F., Monsalve-Salamanca, A., Adarme-Jaimes, W.: Methodology for the Design of Traceability System in Food Assistance Supply Chains: Case Bienestarina, Colombia. Presented at the July 8 (2019). https://doi.org/10.4018/978-1-5225-8160-4.
5. Palacios-Argüello, L., Gonzalez-Feliu, J., Gondran, N., Badeig, F.: Assessing the economic and environmental impacts of urban food systems for public school canteens: case study of Great Lyon region. Eur. Transp. Res. Rev. 10, 37 (2018). https://doi.org/10.1186/s12544-018-0306-8.
6. Belik, W., Fornazier, A.: Chapter Three - Public Policy and the Construction of New Markets to Family Farms: Analyzing the Case of School Meals in São Paulo, Brazil. In: Barling, D. (ed.) Advances in Food Security and Sustainability. pp. 69–86. Elsevier (2017). https://doi.org/10.1016/bs.af2s.2017.09.001.
7. Kristjansson, E.A., Gelli, A., Welch, V., Greenhalgh, T., Liberato, S., Francis, D., Espejo, F.: Costs, and cost-outcome of school feeding programmes and feeding programmes for young children. Evidence and recommendations. International Journal of Educational Development. 48, 79–83 (2016). https://doi.org/10.1016/j.ijedudev.2015.11.011.
8. López-Olmedo, N., Jiménez-Aguilar, A., Morales-Ruan, M. del C., Hernández-Ávila, M., Shamah-Levy, T., Rivera-Dommarco, J.A.: Consumption of foods and beverages in elementary schools: Results of the implementation of the general guidelines for foods and beverages sales in elementary schools in Mexico, stages II and III. Evaluation and Program Planning. 66, 1–6 (2018). https://doi.org/10.1016/j.evalprogplan.2017.08.009.

9. Palacios-Arguello, L., Sánchez-Díaz, I., Gonzalez-Feliu, J., Gondran, N.: Towards a logistic organization for organic-local product supply Case of study: School canteen distribution system. In: Proceedings of the 7th International Conference on Information Systems, Logistics and Supply Chain. Springer International Publishing, Lyon, France (2018).
10. Azeredo, C.M., Rezende, L.F.M. de, Canella, D.S., Claro, R.M., Castro, I.R.R. de, Luiz, O. do C., Levy, R.B.: Dietary intake of Brazilian adolescents. Public Health Nutrition. 18, 1215–1224 (2015). https://doi.org/10.1017/S1368980014001463.
11. Cabrera-Vique, C., Briones, M., Muros, J.J., Seiquer, I., Sánchez, J.A., Rodríguez, G., Giménez, R.: A pilot duplicate diet study on manganese, selenium and chromium intakes in institutionalised children and adolescents from Guatemala. British Journal of Nutrition. 114, 1604–1611 (2015). https://doi.org/10.1017/S0007114515003207.
12. Condon, E.M., Crepinsek, M.K., Fox, M.K.: School Meals: Types of Foods Offered to and Consumed by Children at Lunch and Breakfast. Journal of the American Dietetic Association. 109, S67–S78 (2009). https://doi.org/10.1016/j.jada.2008.10.062.
13. Gonzalez-Feliu, J., Osorio-Ramírez, C., Palacios-Arguello, L., Talamantes, C.A.: Local production-based dietary supplement distribution in emerging countries: Bienestarina distribution in Colombia. In: Establishing Food Security and Alternatives to International Trade in Emerging Economies. pp. 297–315 (2017). https://doi.org/10.4018/978-1-5225-2733-6.ch014.
14. FAO: Agricultural Development Economics: Smallholder family farms, http://www.fao.org/economic/esa/esa-activities/smallholders/en/, last accessed 2019/03/23.
15. HGSF: Policy and Governance, http://hgsf-global.org/mali/en/policy/policy-and-governance, last accessed 2019/04/03.
16. Brasil: L11947, http://www.planalto.gov.br/ccivil_03/_Ato2007-2010/2009/Lei/L11947.htm, last accessed 2019/02/11.
17. IBGE: IBGE | Brasil em Síntese | São Paulo | São Paulo | Panorama, https://cidades.ibge.gov.br/brasil/sp/sao-paulo/panorama, last accessed 2017/09/25.
18. FNDE, A. de C.S. do: Dados da Agricultura Familiar - Portal do FNDE, http://www.fnde.gov.br/programas/pnae/pnae-consultas/pnae-dados-da-agricultura-familiar, last accessed 2018/12/23.
19. Santos, V.N., Bello, E.M.: Aspectos gerais da cultura alimentar do município de Mogi das Cruzes - SP. Revista Científica Linkania Master. 1, (2014).
20. WFP: 2013 - State of School Feeding Worldwide | World Food Programme, https://www1.wfp.org/publications/state-school-feeding-worldwide-2013, last accessed 2019/02/11.
21. Chakraborty, T., Jayaraman, R.: School feeding and learning achievement: Evidence from India's midday meal program. Journal of Development Economics. 139, 249–265 (2019). https://doi.org/10.1016/j.jdeveco.2018.10.011.
22. Bundy, D.A.P.: Rethinking School Health: A Key Component of Education for All. World Bank Publications (2011).
23. HGSF: Document Details | Omeals Snap Shot July 2014, http://www.hgsf-global.org/en/bank/downloads/doc_details/433-omeals-snap-shot-july-2014, last accessed 2019/04/02.
24. Aubry, C., Kebir, L.: Shortening food supply chains: A means for maintaining agriculture close to urban areas? The case of the French metropolitan area of Paris. Food Policy. 41, 85–93 (2013). https://doi.org/10.1016/j.foodpol.2013.04.006.
25. Chiffoleau, Y., Prevost, B.: Les circuits courts, des innovations sociales pour une alimentation durable dans les territoires. Norois. Environnement, aménagement, société. 7–20 (2012). https://doi.org/10.4000/norois.4245.
26. Mundler, P., Criner, G.: Food Systems: Food Miles. In: Caballero, B., Finglas, P.M., and Toldrá, F. (eds.) Encyclopedia of Food and Health. pp. 77–82. Academic Press, Oxford (2016). https://doi.org/10.1016/B978-0-12-384947-2.00325-1.
27. Skallerud, K., Wien, A.H.: Preference for local food as a matter of helping behaviour: Insights from Norway. Journal of Rural Studies. 67, 79–88 (2019). https://doi.org/10.1016/j.jrurstud.2019.02.020.
28. Marsden, T., Banks, J., Bristow, G.: Food Supply Chain Approaches: Exploring their Role in Rural Development. Sociologia Ruralis. 40, 424–438 (2000). https://doi.org/10.1111/1467-9523.00158.
29. IBGE: IBGE | Brasil em Síntese | São Paulo | Mogi das Cruzes | Panorama, https://cidades.ibge.gov.br/brasil/sp/mogi-das-cruzes/panorama, last accessed 2019/03/25.
30. SÃO PAULO (Estado): Portal LUPA - Levantamento de Unidades de Produção Agropecuária do Estado de São Paulo, http://www.cati.sp.gov.br/projetolupa/dadosmunicipais.php#m, last accessed 2019/06/02.
31. Comi, A., Schiraldi, M.M., Buttarazzi, B.: Smart urban freight transport: tools for planning and optimising delivery operations. Simulation Modelling Practice and Theory. 88, 48–61 (2018). https://doi.org/10.1016/j.simpat.2018.08.006.
32. Rong, A., Akkerman, R., Grunow, M.: An optimization approach for managing fresh food quality throughout the supply chain. International Journal of Production Economics. 131, 421–429 (2011). https://doi.org/10.1016/j.ijpe.2009.11.026.
33. Maijers, W., Nalla, V.R.: Analysis of Supply Chain Studies for Home Grown School Feeding. Procurement Governance for Home Grown School Feeding Project Learning. 30 (2014).

34. Casey, K., Commandeur, D.: Supplier Development for Inclusive School Feeding Procurement. SNV. 22 (2016).
35. Gelli, A., Kretschmer, A., Molinas, L., de la Mothe, M.R.: Comparison of supply chains for school food: Exploring operational trade-offs. Partnership for Child Development - HGSF working paper 7. 30 (2012).
36. Lopes, S.R.S., Diniz, P.R.: Boas práticas de agricultura familiar para a alimentação escolar / Programa Nacional de Alimentação Escolar. Ministério da Educação/Fundo Nacional para o Desenvolvimento Escolar, Brasilia (2018).
37. Royer, A., Bijman, J., Abebe, G.K.: Cooperatives, partnerships and the challenges of quality upgrading: A case study from Ethiopia. Journal of Co-operative Organization and Management. 5, 48–55 (2017). https://doi.org/10.1016/j.jcom.2017.04.001.
38. Meyer, D., Riechert, M.: Open source QGIS toolkit for the Advanced Research WRF modelling system. Environmental Modelling & Software. 112, 166–178 (2019). https://doi.org/10.1016/j.envsoft.2018.10.018.
39. Hillier, F.S., Lieberman, G.J.: Introdução à Pesquisa Operacional. AMGH (2013).
40. Kamrani, M., Hashemi Esmaeil Abadi, S.M., Rahimpour Golroudbary, S.: Traffic simulation of two adjacent unsignalized T-junctions during rush hours using Arena software. Simulation Modelling Practice and Theory. 49, 167–179 (2014). https://doi.org/10.1016/j.simpat.2014.09.006.
41. Almaz, O.A., Altiok, T.: Simulation modeling of the vessel traffic in Delaware River: Impact of deepening on port performance. Simulation Modelling Practice and Theory. 22, 146–165 (2012). https://doi.org/10.1016/j.simpat.2011.12.004.
42. Sancar Edis, R., Ornek, A.: Simulation analysis of lot streaming in job shops with transportation queue disciplines. Simulation Modelling Practice and Theory. 17, 442–453 (2009). https://doi.org/10.1016/j.simpat.2008.10.002.
43. Ragsdale, C.: Spreadsheet Modeling and Decision Analysis: A Practical Introduction to Business Analytics. Cengage Learning (2014).
44. Frough, O., Khetwal, A., Rostami, J.: Predicting TBM utilization factor using discrete event simulation models. Tunnelling and Underground Space Technology. 87, 91–99 (2019). https://doi.org/10.1016/j.tust.2019.01.017.
45. Chwif, L., Medina, A., Simulate, T.: Modelagem e simulação de eventos discretos, 4a edição: Teoria e aplicações. Elsevier Brasil (2014).
46. Kelton, D.W.: Simulation with Arena. McGraw-Hill Higher Education (2014).

I L S 2020
INTERNATIONAL CONFERENCE ON INFORMATION
SYSTEMS, LOGISTICS & SUPPLY CHAIN
Austin, Texas April 22-24, 2020

Data Supply Chains for Data Science

Hsun-Ming Lee [1], David Angelow [1], Francis A. Méndez Mediavilla [1]

[1] Texas State University, San Marcos, Texas, USA
{sl20@txstate.edu, dal8@txstate.edu, fm16@txstate.edu }

Abstract. This manuscript examines the relevance of information logistics, data supply chain management, information systems analysis and design in support of data science and analytics. Firms find competitive advantage utilizing data science methods and tools in ways that were previously not possible. Data science is enabled by vast data sources, flow and quality of data. The authors see the concept of *managing the data supply chain* as an emergent requirement. This manuscript presents DSC as a new opportunity for organizations to evaluate data as a transformational asset. We propose to use a framework comprised of the following four dimensions: strategy, integration, element of exchange, and tools and methods.

Keywords: data supply chain, data analytics, big data, data science, information logistics.

1. Introduction

This manuscript examines the relevance of information logistics, data supply chain management, information systems analysis and design in support of data science and analytics. The belief that data, analysis and information are needed for decision-making is immemorial. However, data analysis has been occupying headlines within the last eight or nine years. The new discipline called Data Science has emerged.

The fact is that data analysis, as a discipline, has existed for decades. Algorithms for optimization, decision-making, and forecasting are not new. Popular methods that are treated as new, such as "deep learning", have been in existence for decades. Statistics, as a discipline, goes back to the 1660s. Therefore, what is the essence of that which we have been treating as new for the last ten years? It is apparent that the driver is the volume, speed, diversity, and value of the data in play nowadays. This is where data supply chains (DSC) get into play. The authors of this paper believe that DSC are essential for Data Science and Data Analytics to persist.

2. Literature Review

Terms such as "Data Science" and "Data Analytics" are relatively new. Data Science has been defined as a "set of disciplines" with the purpose of solving "big data" problems [1]. Big data has been defined around "challenges" and the information technologies designed to address those challenges [1]. For example, because the explosion of social media usage, a very large amount of user generated data on the internet has created valuable and vast resources for discovering and influencing how people communicate, compute, collaborate, and conduct commerce in the modern age. Data analytics, seemingly a new term for the well-established science of "data analysis" [2] and one of the "disciplines" constituting data science, also portrayed as a necessary function within the entrepreneurial realm. The uses of data science are extensive, from product research and development to directing political campaigns [3].

Data analysis, as a discipline, has been around since the 1960s. It is hard to miss that the methods that are so popular today, have been in existence for decades. For instance, cluster analysis has been around since 1932 [4] and artificial neural networks since 1943 [5]. Some have proposed that data science is the same as the discipline of statistics, which traces its origins back to the 1660s [6].

Why have these, among many other, methods attracted attention in recent times? These methods were available in 1950s and 1960s, when the idea of decision support systems was introduced [7]. These methods were available back when expert systems (today we talk of recommender systems) were introduced in 1959 [8].

Currently data science is treated as a discipline which is novel and relevant [9]. It is undeniable that data analysis has been relevant and introduced, as a science and as a discipline since 1962 [10][11]. Given the long history of data analysis what is really new about *data science, artificial intelligence, machine learning* and *data analytics*?

A survey commissioned by Alegion might point to what is essential and perhaps, what really is new. The survey found that about 80% of the organizations using artificial intelligence (AI) and machine learning (ML) reported projects that have stalled. Of these, 96% reported having data quality, data labelling, and building model confidence problems [12].

Information logistics is a concept that focuses on the idea of providing, the right information, at the right place, in a timely fashion. Today, it relies on the existence of a computer network. It acknowledges the existence of an information demand and an information supply; and that the information supply may be personalized [13][14]. It is a notion introduced as a new information management paradigm. Its goal is to enable effective and efficient delivery of information in the correct format, granularity and quality, at the correct location, at the right time, and to the right people [15].

The idea of having the capability of obtaining data from its numerous, diverse and distributed sources (supply) to the entity that needs or requests the information, in a timely fashion, to use it to make decisions (demand) is, perhaps what is really new. These are precisely the elements that define data supply chain. New supplies of data are available from a large variety of sources, such as sensors, Internet of Things (IoT) devices, unstructured data from user-generated content (UGC) for text, video, voice, location-based data from GPS networks or low-power beacons utilizing blue-tooth capabilities for fine-grained data.

Thuraisingham [16] considers data supply chain management (DSCM) in relation to "regular" supply chain management (SCM), as involving the "design, planning, execution, control and monitoring of data supply chain activities with the objective of creating net value". One of its main functions is "the management of a network of interconnected data centers involved in the ultimate provision of a data product required by end customers". Thuraisingham refers to the types of decisions made in SCM (i.e. location, production, inventory, and transportation) and incorporates a fifth type: "information" [17]; thus, in a way, making SCM dependent on DSCM.

In the DSCM framework, she relates "location" to source of data; production to the decisions about which raw data to produce and from which source. Inventory decision are mapped to the storage of data needed to create the final data product. The transportation decisions determine how the data will flow from one location to the next location.

Therefore, the concept of DSCM is introduced in 2011, by Thuraisingham [16], and is defined as "the network of facilities and distribution options that perform the functions of the production of data, transforming the data into intermediary and finished data products, distributing the data products to customers, and sharing the data products among customers". She also considers three modeling approaches: network design, rough cut, and simulation. The DSC is presented as a network of facilities and distribution options producing, transforming, distributing data and *data products* to customers. Data products are designed based on customers' needs. To design a data product, it is necessary to determine the sources of data and how to pass data from the suppliers to the intermediate processing points, and then, the final demand point. To accomplish this goal, one must consider technologies for: integration of heterogeneous sources, cleaning and transforming data, keeping track of the provenance of data, and data extraction at every stage [16].

Spanaki, et al. [17] defines DSC in a way that emphasizes the value created by the flow of data, as "the upstream and downstream flow of multisource, multiform data artefacts from inbound and outbound activities of the firm, forming innovation opportunities and value outcomes in production/service development as a core business area of the firm". These, *artefacts* or *data-powered products* have become pervasive to companies and integration among functional areas, in the creation of an effective data product, is necessary [18].

The information systems behind these data products should reflect that collaboration in the form of data integration from multiple sources and that data science will only be possible if this collaboration is successful.

In 1996, Connelly, et al., [19] observes managers who operate in environments that are too multidimensionally complex for decisions to be centralized or concentrated at the top. The new business models needed information technology that dispersed measurements quickly and inexpensively. Some of his observations were that quality of information was far more important than quantity. Managers are not necessarily aware that they need to think multidimensionally, since they are attempting to understand interactions between customers, products, salespeople, and other variables (e.g., combinations of color, quality, type or package size that drive customer demand). Delivering information on paper or preprogrammed reports is no longer useful, since managers need to drill-down to significant levels of detail to devise strategy from the bottom-up. This exploration of data can be efficiently achieved by interacting with the data itself. For instance, purchasing managers can only maintain inventory optimum levels if they can monitor if constantly [19]. They can negotiate best prices if they can evaluate suppliers instantly. Simplifying and speeding up activities reduce operating costs. Product and process data is valuable in searching and discovering information from service providers requesting it through a decentralized architecture where the control over data lies in hands of the manager instead of a centralized system [21].

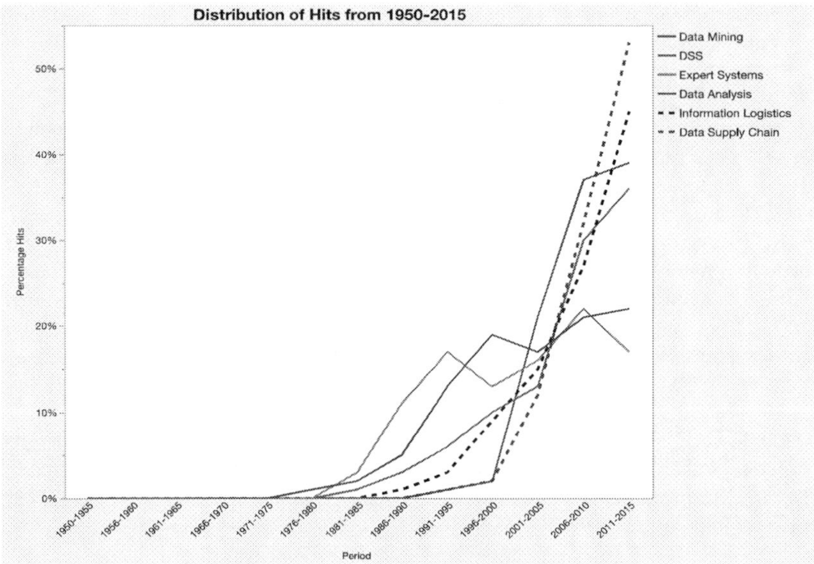

Figure 1: Percentage Topic Hits in Google Scholar Data Mining, Expert Systems and DSS vs DSC

Figure 1 shows the distribution of topic hits from 1950-2015, gathered from a Google Scholar search, for DSC, Information Logistics and the topics of decision support systems (DSS), Expert Systems (ES), Data Mining (DM) and Data Analysis (DA). Publications on Information Logistics, Data Supply Chain together with Data Mining begin growing sometime between 1995 and 2000; which is about the time when Expert Systems and Data Analysis diminish.

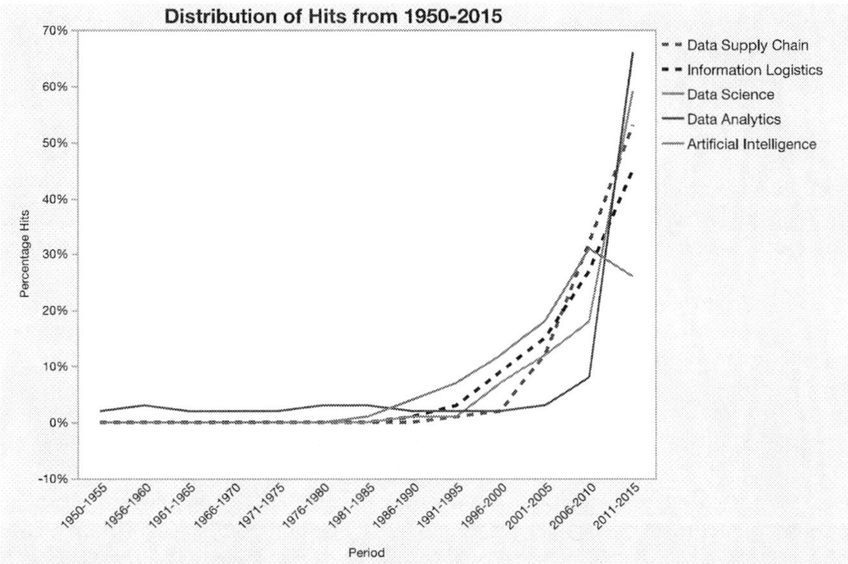

Figure 2: Percentage Topic Hits in Google Scholar, Data Science Topics vs DSC

Figure 2 shows the distribution of topic hits from 1950-2015, gathered from a Google Scholar search, for DSC, Information Logistics and the more recent topics of Data Science (DS), Artificial Intelligence (AI) and Data Analytics (DAcs). Publications on Information Logistics, Data Supply Chain together with Data Science begin growing sometime between 1995 and 2000. The number of occurrences of Data Analytics topics begin their increase in 2001-2005.

The explosive growth in the volume of data available, and the decrease in computing costs to crunch large data sets, result in increased interest in data science. Additionally, because the amount of data and sources systems for data are growing, there is an emerging need to ensure that data is available where needed, when needed.

The global competitive environment requires companies to seek an edge and find competitive advantage. Can firms find competitive advantage utilizing data science methods, techniques and tools in ways that were previously not possible? The authors of this manuscript believe that this is an element of importance; but, perhaps, even more important for data science are data sources, the flow of data and quality of the data. We see the concept of *managing the data supply chain* as an emergent requirement. Talking about data science and data analytics without talking about *data supply chain* is like talking about markets without talking about planned and efficient trade routes.

There is a clear dependency on accurate and timely data, for analysis and decision-making. Certainly, the increase of computational capability to crunch large amounts data is important; but it is also irrelevant if data is not present. Thus, we present this piece with the perspective that data science is only as good as the supply of data enables it to be.

The exploitation of social media is presented as an example of the main dimensions in a data supply chain. Sources of data are disparate, large volumes of unstructured data are uploaded constantly. In many scenarios, the analysis must be performed quickly, if competitive advantage is to be gained. For example, responding near real-time to customers via Twitter messages, or receiving an automated update from an IoT sensor about a production disruption or in a more humanitarian application a such as in suicide prevention [22].

3. System Development Framework

This manuscript presents DSC as a new opportunity for organizations to evaluate data as a transformational asset. We propose to use a framework comprised of the following four dimensions: strategy, integration, element of exchange, and tools and methods [17]. We explore and review recent empirical studies in social computing, where the system development has been driven by empowerment of the individual user using the web and mobile technologies [23].

3.1. Strategy

Strategic decisions for obtaining data and creating a supply chain of data should be aligned with the improvement objectives such as innovation capability, value creation, and competitive advantage of organizations. Just-in-time information distribution are designed in situations in which exactly the information needed is delivered to the user [13]. Institutions develop data-driven strategies to perform real-time analytics [21]. Many corporations use Facebook and Twitter to interact with customers and provide various services; consequently, the monitoring and analysis of the customer-generated content on their own social media sites as well as those on their competitors' social media sites can be used to support decisions in sustaining a positive relationship with customers [24] [21].

From the perspective of social computing, customers and companies can be seen as partners "working together to develop products that are optimally aligned with customer preferences" [23]. Past studies found that product reviews on online forums or online stores play an important role in influencing purchase decisions of other fellow customers. A predictive model can be built to offer significant predictive power to project how sales will be affected by the posted review [25]. The knowledge derived from the analysis of user generated content prove valuable for many industries. For instance, it has been found that customer reviews affect purchasing behavior at book-selling sites: Amazon.com and bn.com [26]. Online reviews analysis helps to identify the impact of online word of mouth on sales in the tourism and hotel industries [27]. Analysis of social media data could provide insights to movie distributors and studios for helping them determining their current and future rollout strategies [28]. Although a decision-making process of venture capitalists is highly complex, it is suggested that the reviews of some kinds of bloggers help ventures in getting higher funding amounts and valuations [29].

In healthcare, researchers are able to apply data science techniques and use data obtained from online communities and Twitter to detect quantifiable signals around suicide attempts and to design an automated system for estimating suicide risk [22]. It is information logistics what allows to provide the correct information, at the right time, and the correct location. Relationship to patients can be improved by providing personalized information before, during and after medical treatment [27].

3.2. Integration

The integration of DSC requires interoperability among tools and maintenance of dependencies among existing data and information. A trend in computational analysis of social media is the utilization of easy-to-use, lightweight, and mostly open-source computing tools, such as JavaScript-Ajax, Python, Perl, Ruby, and MySQL [30]. JavaScript agents can be developed for scraping the web using asynchronous I/O calls, where the obtained data are stored and horizontally scaled in virtual servers. To effectively extract, clean, and organize data from hundreds of thousands of web pages, it is necessary to develop big-data algorithms capable of managing the real-time and data-intensive integration [31]. In a similar fashion, a crawler uses Ruby on Rails to automatically download web pages containing consumer reviews and other business information; subsequently, another Ruby-based system parses data from HTML and XML web pages into a database [27].

People interacts with digital devices through the daily course of their life, including activities via social media and e-commerce systems. The openness of computing technologies facilitates the creation of an automated model integrating multiple social media data sources. When the data from a private online community and public social media (such as Twitter) are combined, advanced algorithms can be utilized to detect patterns of human behaviors [22]. Users want to develop data-driven strategies, perform advanced analytics on real-time data [13].

3.3. Element of exchange

Social media, a group of Internet-based applications that build on the Web, allows the creation and sharing of user generated content [32]. The element of exchange of the DSC is the data generated by Web users. The data available from social media can be of various types, mainly unstructured. For examples, YouTube provides the sharing of video clips and opinions of their viewers, Facebook makes it easy for individuals to share their multimedia contents and build relations with others, and Amazon.com combines their e-commerce platform with online communities to solicit product recommendations and reviews from consumers [23, 30].

3.4. Tools and methods

Researchers have adopted various analytics tools/methods for developing models around the social media data. Text analysis tools, such as TextBlob and Sentistrength, are often used to assess the feeling (sentiment) expressed in the messages of social media [33]. At the market-level analysis, panel data (e.g., the rate, the valence, and the sentiment of messages) extracted from the websites is used to examine the impact of consumer reviews [34]. This line of studies typically applies econometric methods to quantitatively model how user-generated contents influence business success.

Because of the ability to learn the intrinsic nature of patterns from social media data generated by consumers, artificial neural networks are useful in identifying the important predictors of product demands [31]. These prediction models use deep learning for analysis of language achieving high accuracy in equating the relation between input data (social media messages) and output [22].

4. Conclusion

DSCs provide the foundation for the process of organizing and translating data into information for decision-making in industry. With the prevalence of information systems storing and linking data generated from Internet and social networking sites, it is critical to gain more understanding of systems development and underlying infrastructure to support the DSCs. The recent rise of data science/analytics as a now essential business function cannot be seeing in isolation. Data science will only be as effective as the DSC management that supports it. Previous efforts to make data useful for enterprises, such as expert systems and decision support systems and data analysis, did not count with the data infrastructure that exists today. This study focuses on a framework that consider the DSC development as a process of transformation, which requires the specification of distributed data based on the web standardization, the identification of business values that can be produced from the data, use of technologies to support data integration, and developing models around the data by adopting appropriate analytics tools/methods.

In addition, the infrastructure of DSCs is a network of facilities used to distribute data products to customers; therefore, we emphasize that optimization techniques are necessary to make the decisions of location, production, inventory, and transportation for the product. Strategic alignment is fundamental. A company should not have a data science team only because it adds a “magic ingredient”, prestige, or the appearance of being cutting-edge decision-makers. Integration is a key factor of the implementation of the strategy. The elements of exchange should address the needs of the user.

The effectiveness of data science depends on the effective interoperability among tools and maintenance of dependencies among existing data and information. Data integration must facilitate data flow. Management’s tendency to cling to tools that impede the data flow in the company is an issue, and the inefficiency created as a result should not be ignored [35]. Dynamic dashboards are useful for managers; but the value that access to data would provide to managers who are capable of performing data analysis on their own may be greater. DSC needs to be tackled with many aspects of system approaches. Research in data science and related fields in machine learning, operations research, and information systems would help scholars advance DSC models and encourage practitioners to pursue innovative projects.

5. References

1. Song, I. Y., Zhu, Y.: Big data and data science: what should we teach? Expert Systems, *33*(4), 364--373 (2016).
2. Tukey, J. W.: The future of data analysis. The Annals of Mathematical Statistics, *33*(1), 1--67 (1962).
3. Rosenberg, M., Confessore, N., & Cadwalladr, C.: How Trump consultants exploited the Facebook data of millions. The New York Times, 17 (3), 2018.
4. Driver, H.E., Kroeber, A. L.: Quantitative Expression of Cultural Relationships. University of California Publications in American Archaeology and Ethnology. Quantitative Expression of Cultural Relationships. 211--25.
5. McCulloch,W., Pitts, W.: A Logical Calculus of Ideas Immanent in Nervous Activity. Bulletin of Mathematical Biophysics. 5 (4). 115--133 (1943).
6. Wu, C. F. J.: Statistics = Data Science? http://www2.isye.gatech.edu/~jeffwu/presentations/datascience.pdf.
7. Keen, P. G. W.: Decision support systems: an organizational perspective. Reading, Mass., Addison-Wesley Pub. Co. (1978).
8. Ledley, R.S., Lusted, L.B.: Reasoning foundations of medical diagnosis. *Science*. 130 (3366): 9--21 (1959).
9. Davenport, T. H., Patil, D. J.: Data scientist. Harvard Business Review, 90(5), 70--76 (2012).
10. Tukey, J. W.: The future of data analysis. The Annals of Mathematical Statistics, 33(1), 1--67 (1962).
11. Press, G. A.: Very Short History of Data Science, https://www.forbes.com/sites/gilpress/2013/05/28/a-very-short-history-of-data-science/#3f629f0255cf.
12. Violino, B.: Poor data quality causing majority of artificial intelligence projects to stall. Information Management, https://www.information-management.com/news/poor-data-quality-causing-majority-of-artificial-intelligence-projects-to-stall.
13. Heuwinkel, K., Deiters, W.: Information logistics, E-Healthcare and trust. Book Information Logistics, E-Healthcare and Trust, 791--794 (2003).
14. Deiters, W., Löffeler, T., Pfennigschmidt, S.: The information logistics approach toward user demand-driven information supply. In Cross-media service delivery Springer, Boston, MA. 37--48 (2003).
15. Michelberger, B., Andris, R. J., Girit, H., Mutschler, B.: A literature survey on information logistics. In International Conference on Business Information Systems. Springer, Berlin, Heidelberg 138--150. (2013).
16. Thuraisingham, B.: Data supply chain management: supply chain management for incentive and risk-based assured information sharing. Texas University at Arlington Department of Computer Science (2011).
17. Spanaki, K., Gürgüç, Z., Adams, R., Mulligan, C.: Data supply chain (DSC): research synthesis and future directions. International Journal of Production Research, 56(13), 4447--4466 (2018).
18. Hugos, M. H.: Essentials of supply chain management. John Wiley & Sons.
19. Connelly, R.: The Multidimensional Manager 24 Ways to Impact your Bottom Line in 90 Days. National Academies (1996).
20. Glassberg Sands, E.: How to Build Great Data Products. Harvard Business Review, https://hbr.org/2018/10/how-to-build-great-data-products
21. Sherlekar, R., Starly, B., Cohen, P. H.: Provisioned Data Distribution for Intelligent Manufacturing via Fog Computing. Procedia Manufacturing, *34*, 893--902 (2019).
22. Coppersmith, G., Leary, R., Crutchley, P., Fine, A.: Natural language processing of social media as screening for suicide risk. Biomedical Informatics Insights, 10, (2018).
23. Parameswaran, M., Whinston, A. B.: Research issues in social computing. Journal of the Association for Information Systems, 8(6), 22 (2007).
24. He, W., Zha, S., Li, L.: Social media competitive analysis and text mining: A case study in the pizza industry. International Journal of Information Management, 33(3), 464--472 (2013).
25. Ghose, A., Ipeirotis, P. G.: Estimating the helpfulness and economic impact of product reviews: Mining text and reviewer characteristics. IEEE Transactions on Knowledge and Data Engineering, 23(10), 1498--1512 (2011).
26. Chevalier, J.A., Mayzlin, D.: The effect of word of mouth on sales: Online book reviews, Journal of Marketing Research, Vol. 43 No. 3, 345--354 (2003).

27. Ye, Q., Law, R., Gu, B., Chen, W.: The influence of user-generated content on traveler behavior: An empirical investigation on the effects of e-word-of-mouth to hotel online bookings. Computers in Human behavior, *27*(2), 634--639 (2011).
28. Chintagunta, P. K., Gopinath, S., Venkataraman, S.: The effects of online user reviews on movie box office performance: Accounting for sequential rollout and aggregation across local markets. Marketing Science, *29*(5), 944--957 (2010).
29. Aggarwal, R., Gopal, R., Gupta, A., Singh, H.: Putting money where the mouths are: The relation between venture financing and electronic word-of-mouth. Information Systems Research, *23*(3-part-2), 976--992 (2012).
30. Parameswaran, M., & Whinston, A. B.: Social computing: An Overview. Communications of the Association for Information Systems, 19(1), 37 (2007).
31. Chong, A. Y. L., Ch'ng, E., Liu, M. J., Li, B.: Predicting consumer product demands via Big Data: the roles of online promotional marketing and online reviews, International Journal of Production Research, 55:17, 5142--5156 (2017).
32. Kaplan, A. M., Haenlein, M.: Users of the world, unite! The challenges and opportunities of Social Media. Business Horizons, 53(1), 59--68 (2010).
33. Daniel, M., Neves, R. F., Horta, N.: Company event popularity for financial markets using Twitter and sentiment analysis. Expert Systems with Applications, *71*, 111--124 (2017).
34. Cheung, C. M. K., Thadani, D. R.: The impact of electronic word-of-mouth communication : A literature analysis and integrative model. Decision Support Systems, *54*, 461--470 (2012).
35. Shah, J., Mendez, F., Lee, S.: Information Technology for Uncertainty Management in Supply Chain (p. 7). Quebec, Canada: 4th International Conference on Information Systems, Logistics and Supply Chain (2012).

I L S 2020
INTERNATIONAL CONFERENCE ON INFORMATION SYSTEMS, LOGISTICS & SUPPLY CHAIN
Austin, Texas April 22-24, 2020

Technological Trends in Last-mile Contexts: a European Perspective

Anna Corinna Cagliano[1], Giulio Mangano[1], Giovanni Zenezini[1]

[1] Department of Management and Production Engineering, Politecnico di Torino, Torino, Italy
{anna.cagliano@polito.it, giulio.mangano@polito.it, giovanni.zenezini@polito.it}

Abstract. This paper presents an empirical analysis on 65 European cities where different Last Mile technologies have been implemented by both private and public operators, aiming to assess the importance of each technology involved and identify adoption trends. Results show that parcel lockers and low emissions vehicles are the most adopted technologies, while the diffusion of Intelligent Transportation Systems and dynamic routing appears limited. Finally, crowd shipping services are still scattered but show medium level of adoption. Future research will extend the analysis to international projects and include external aspects to refine the understanding of technological adoption patterns.

Keywords: Last Mile Logistics; Empirical Analysis, Europe, Technology, Cities

1. Introduction

Freight delivery in urban areas is one of the most complex processes in current supply chain environments and as such it might become very expensive if not properly managed. In fact, a number of activities accounting for up 40% of the total supply chain cost are usually related to last-mile distribution [1]. Additionally, it has been estimated that up to 20% of vehicle-kilometers travelled on urban roads are due to last mile deliveries [2]. Urban freight distribution is also a major cause for traffic congestion, noise, and pollution which might largely affect both the level of service and the costs in a production-distribution system. Recent studies state that urban logistics activities may account for more than 60% of the total CO2 emissions of distribution organizations [3].
In order to address the negative impacts of urban logistics and ultimately increase its efficiency, in the last few decades both researchers and practitioners have tackled this issue [4]. Thus, the City Logistics (CL) notion has been introduced as a comprehensive set of solutions for "totally optimizing the logistics and transport activities by private companies in urban areas while considering the traffic environment, the traffic congestion and energy consumption"[5].
As a consequence of the increased awareness towards CL themes, both public authorities and private companies have undertaken several initiatives that starting mainly from Europe are now progressively spreading all over the world. Such CL initiatives are usually referred to as CL measures. A lot of attempts to categorize and systematize the existing fragmented CL measures (e.g. low impact vehicle adoption, access regulation to limited traffic zones, urban consolidation center development, dynamic management of vehicle routings and lay-by areas, etc.) have been proposed in literature. Besides the technical papers associated with well-known CL international projects such as BESTUFS I and II, SUGAR, CIVITAS [6–8], there is a number of academic works that are worth to be mentioned. [9] are among the first authors who provided a comprehensive classification of solutions for urban freight transportation. Two different perspectives are taken: the initiative scope (e.g. public infrastructure, land use, access conditions, traffic management, enforcement and promotion) and specific groups of stakeholders (logistics operators, receivers, local authorities). Later on, [10] better detail the previous classification. First, they distinguish infrastructures into material (e.g. use of the urban transportation network) and immaterial (e.g. intelligent transportation systems). Then, they itemize governance measures into several groups such as time window

access, heavy vehicle network, and road pricing management. Finally, they add equipment, including unit loads and transportation means, as a key CL measure category. The various classifications proposed by literature are best summarized and categorized by [11]. They propose six components of CL solutions, namely infrastructure, logistics organization of transport, technologies, communications, funding, and regulations. Based on that, [12] deeply analyses technologies proposing a number of categories including vehicle propulsion systems, material handling equipment, and ICT tools supporting CL initiatives.

Among them, the classifications by [11, 12] are particularly interesting because they take a practical perspective [13]. Moreover, unlike other existing taxonomies, they explicitly take into account the technological aspect, which is a key foundation of most of CL measures.
The present work builds on [11] and [12] classifications and focuses on the technology category. Following the need for sharing best practices and providing guidelines for the effective design and implementation of urban logistics policies, there is so far a large body of literature analyzing single or groups of CL initiatives [14], [15]. Another quite debated topic is assessing the economic, environmental, and social effects of CL measures on the different stakeholders involved [16] as well as the value proposition of new CL services for selected supply chain actors [17]. However, most of the current literature, although recognizing technology as an enabling factor for the success of urban freight transportation services, addresses it just at the degree it is required in order to describe a certain initiative or discuss a given impact. There are few contributions offering comprehensive studies on the state of the art of technological applications to last mile logistics, or identifying the associated trends. Nevertheless, such studies would be beneficial to both policy makers and companies to correctly identify the best technologies to invest in when drafting new CL initiatives.
With the purpose of contributing to bridge such a research gap, this work puts forward an empirical analysis on a dataset of 65 European cities claiming to have applied technological solutions to last mile logistics. First of all, a comprehensive set of reference technologies has been defined according to literature evidence. The analysis of data that have been gathered is aimed to assess the importance of each technology at issue and to identify related several important trends in its level of adoption.
The paper is structured as follows: firstly, main CL technologies are reviewed to ground the work in the relevant literature. Secondly, the research methodology is explained and the dataset is presented. After that, the dataset is analyzed and the results interpreted. Finally, the main implications are discussed and conclusions drawn.

2. Literature review

There is a considerable number of technologies underpinning CL projects, so, as a preliminary step, a comprehensive set of them is selected in order to focus the analysis on. As already discussed in the Introduction, the main inspiring taxonomies for defining the technologies addressed in the present study are [11] and the in-depth technology analysis offered by [12]. In order to make sure to deal with a set of technologies that well represent the main ones adopted by existing CL initiatives, such contributions are leveraged with the outcomes of [18] and [19]. Both these studies investigate real-world CL implementations and classify the associated last mile logistics innovations, where most of them are technological in nature. On the one hand, [18] present three general groups: consolidation of good flows within the urban area, use of novel either low or zero emission vehicles, and regulation with particular attention to limiting activities by time or vehicle type as well as size. On the other hand, [19] distinguish CL innovations in five categories: innovative vehicles, proximity stations (also including crowd-tasking models and parcel lockers), collaborative and cooperative logistics, optimizations of transport management and routing, and innovations in public policies and infrastructures.
By combining all the categories out of these works , the following group of technologies is considered in the present research: i) Intelligent Transportation Systems (ITS) – Electronic control and access; ii) Dynamic routing and lay-by area monitoring and booking; iii) Low emission vehicles; iv) Crowd logistics; and v) Parcel lockers.
ITSs deliver value-added services (e.g. traffic management systems, route planning, etc.) to enable and control transportation operations performed by fleet of vehicles. In the CL context, they can be purposefully applied to support electronic access control, access charges, and road pricing systems by managing the interaction between freight carriers and municipalities and ensuring security and reliability of services [20]. They rely on an integrated IT platform that can be accessed by different stakeholders through both a browser

and mobile devices. ITSs help achieve a more efficient resource usage together with improved physical flows. As far as road pricing is concerned, it is paid for transiting in urban roads and depends on either the access time or the vehicle emission levels, thus discouraging the use of polluting freight transportation vehicles as well as fostering a more rational use of infrastructural resources [21].
Among the provided services, ITSs also offer real-time information about traffic and lay-by availability. The first kind of information is of key relevance to routing planning systems that can dynamically re-route vehicles based on the actual road conditions. This is a technological solution that enhances carrier efficiency and reduce negative impacts of CL activities. A lot of vehicle routing algorithms have been developed for urban freight distribution, many of them taking into account restricted delivery time windows due to either access times to particular city areas or customer needs [22]. Accurate and real time information about the availability of lay-bys is crucial to optimize logistics time and costs as well as improve environmental sustainability [23]. Moreover, it can provide reliable input data to routing planners so that freight transportation vehicles can adjust their routes according to the availability of loading and unloading areas nearby. Finally, the positive effect of lay-by management on urban freight distribution is supported by a proper design of these infrastructures in terms of location and area sizing [24].
As a third technology category, low emission vehicles applied to CL environments include a large variety of types, such as electric, hybrid or fuel cell vans, together with cargo bikes [25]. However, the required initial investment for a large-scale implementation of many low-emission vehicles is very high and sometimes not completely counterbalanced by the related benefits. For this reason, simpler and less expensive transportation means have started being considered for CL purposes. Cargo bikes are an urban distribution solution introduced in recent years to deliver parcels on bike routes, thus contributing to limit traffic congestion, enhance efficiency, and decrease negative CL externalities [26]. Despite public stakeholders increasingly promote the use of electric cargo bikes, logistics providers are still reluctant to their adoption because of a number of operational issues, like the limited parcel size, the short travel distances, and the need for consolidation centers acting as departure points [27].
The fourth technological class addressed in this work, namely crowd logistics, is relatively new and is related to the notion of sharing economy. It has been introduced as a consequence of the more and more widespread diffusion of the online B2C commerce and the need for finding competitive ways of performing last mile and same day deliveries. Big players such as Amazon and Walmart are already adopting such a logistics approach. According to crowd shipping, deliveries are outsourced to private individuals that might be themselves customers of retail business [28]. At least two organizational models exist. According to a first one, individuals might be paid to pick up parcels from dedicated stations and delivery them to final customers, for example during their daily trips to and from work. In a second solution the customers of a logistic service provider are in charge of delivering goods for others for a sum of money [29]. Crowd shipping services usually rely on an electronic platform to connect senders and shippers. Benefits include economic savings due to shipper costs that are less than the average wages of traditional drivers, a reduced need for logistics infrastructures, delivery flexibility to changed time windows, and low environmental impacts since shippers can also sometimes use the public transportation network according to the size of delivered parcels. Moreover, it has been proved that integrating crowd logistics with traditional delivery methods can help containing last mile logistics costs [30]. Crowd shippers might pick up and deliver goods not from/to a private location but a parcel locker [31].
Parcel lockers are sets of unattended lockers located in residential areas, work places or public utility places, such as shopping malls or railways stations. They are opened thorough an electronic code and used by different customers to drop off or pick up goods 24 hours a day, 7 days a week. They can be property of a single B2C company or shared among a group of companies [32]. Similarly to crowd logistics, parcel lockers provide an efficient solution to the fast growth of e-commerce and the associated increase in parcel delivery and return volumes. In particular, they are able to improve the consumer service satisfaction while ensuring a high level of logistics performance as well as competitive advantage to companies [33]. However, one of the relevant efficiency factors for this solution is an appropriate locker site: the area should be considered beneficial for self-collection by potential customers [34]. For this reason, many recent studies are concentrating on the determination of the best location, number, and size of parcel lockers (e.g. [32], [35]).
The performed review reveals that there is quite a large body of literature discussing the various CL technologies. However, most of the contributions on this topic are focused on either a single or a group of implementation projects or study the impacts of one or few technologies. There is a substantial lack of works taking a broader perspective and investigating the current general state of the art of technological measures in CL. Such a comprehensive analysis would provide both researchers and practitioners with

many benefits, including the possibility to trace evolution trends and to offer guidelines for setting effective CL strategies. This is where the present research seeks to contribute to the current state of the art.

3. Methodology

In order to identify the main trends in the use of the innovative technologies able to support logistics activities in urban environments, a sample of 65 European cities where such technologies were implemented is extracted. The cities have been selected, since they have claimed to be involved in the development of CL projects based on most recent technologies. Data on technological implementation are retrieved from project documentation, national and regional reports and scientific literature. The decision of considering only European cities is based on their high demand for technological initiatives and programs aimed at improving urban logistics systems. In this context, the European Commissions' Transport 2050 Strategy proposes a strong reduction of greenhouse emission and sets different modes of transport including CO_2 free logistics in major city centres [8]. Also, more recently the European Digital Agenda has a significant impact of the organization of CL programs [36]. In the sample under study both small (Regensburg, Germany; Vicenza, Italy) and big cities (London, UK; Paris, France) are considered. A value equal to 1 or 0 is related to each technology whether a city reports a CL initiative or not for that specific technology. In other word, the assignment of 1 in a given technology means that a city has at least one project exploiting that technology.

3.1. Sample description

As previously mentioned, the sample is composed by 65 European cities, belonging to 15 countries (Figure 1). The cumulated population of the cities equals roughly 50,1 Mln inhabitants, with an average density of 3'080 inhabitants/km^2. The weighted average GDP per capita of the sample equals 36'276 €, slightly higher than the GPD per capita of the European Union (i.e. 32'672 €).

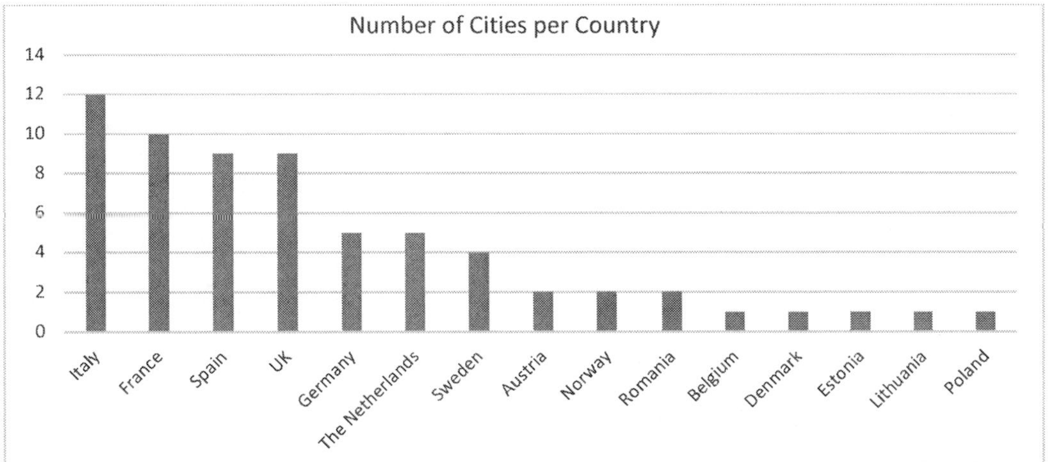

Figure 1: Number of Cities per Country

4. Results

4.1. Coverage of technologies in the sample

Figure 2 shows the number of applications for every technology at issue and for the cities of the sample taken into account, together with the related percentage level. First, almost 100% of the cities are now using parcel lockers in urban logistics processes. This result demonstrates a relevant interest associated with this solution and a certain level of maturity. This phenomenon is related to the broad use of e-commerce that has imposed new challenges in last mile delivery processes [24]. In particular by moving from business to business (B2B) to business to customers (B2C) companies have to deal with an increasing number of smaller parcels [37]. In this context, parcel lockers can play a crucial role, since they can enhance the level of efficiency of urban logistics, by avoiding the missing delivery issue as already stated in the literature review section [33]. Also, in most of the cities the use of environmentally friendly vehicles can be observed. This aspect can be related to the increase awareness of public policy makers about the environmental issue, especially in urban areas. As a matter of fact, low emission vehicles are an effective response for reducing pollutants in city contexts in both terms of emissions and noise levels. In particular, the implementation of cargobikes is proving to be cheaper and more efficient than vans under certain circumstances such as very congested areas or with small parcel delivery [26, 27]. The application of crowd logistics is lower. This might be due to a relative more recent development of such a measure that has been often associated with the adoption of applications based technologies that support the connection along the supply chains [38]. Finally, the implementation of ITS and Dynamic Routing projects is still limited. In particular, only 10% of the cities of the sample are using algorithms for the optimization of the routing and for the management of the lay- by areas. This result might be explained by two main elements. First, a lot of stakeholders are typically involved in the design of these kinds of projects. Since the objectives of every stakeholder are often not perfectly aligned, it could be difficult to set an effective coordination among them. Then, these initiatives require relevant investments in both physical infrastructures and software licenses. Due to the level of uncertain returns, private sponsors are still hesitant in promoting this kind of initiatives, that can only rely on the public support.

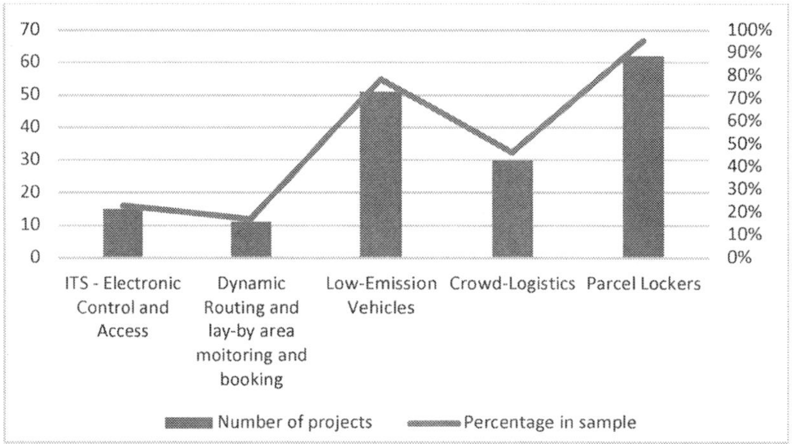

Figure 2: Adoption of technologies

4.2. City Coverage Index

Each city is associated with a coverage index that represents the number of last-mile technology projects implemented in that city. This index is computed as the ratio between the number of technologies used by each city under analysis and the total number of technologies taken into account in the study. It can be considered as an expression of the ability of a city to exploit the new technological solutions that can be used in urban environments for supporting logistics activities. The coverage index takes values from 0.2, meaning that only one project is present, to 0.8, meaning that none of the cities in the sample has adopted all the last-mile technologies at issue. The distribution of cities among the coverage index is quite balanced, with a large majority of cities showing coverage indexes of 0.4 or 0.6. Moreover, a very large share of the cities in the sample cover both Parcel Lockers and Low Emission Vehicles, as shown in Figure 3. The most "technological" cities in the sample are Lyon, Berlin, Rotterdam and London. Such cities are able to combine the efforts by public authorities in managing and controlling urban freight by means of ITS systems or planning algorithms with new delivery solutions used by private companies, such as cargo bikes or crowd shipping. These four cities belong to different countries. This result demonstrates the widespread adoption of last-mile solutions by European cities. Such outcomes also show that large markets are leading the way of technological improvements in last-mile processes, as three out of four cities come from the three largest economies in Europe [39]. Furthermore, Rotterdam implemented a planning tool for delivery trucks due to the large traffic generated by its port[1], which is the largest cargo port by tonnage in Europe [40].

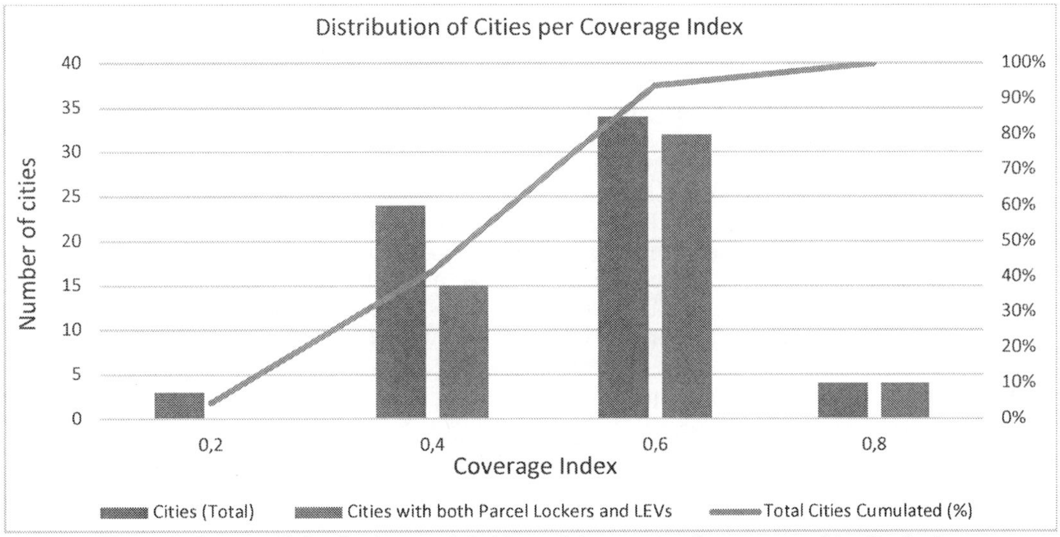

Figure 3: Coverage Index for the sampled cities and the cumulated percentage of the distribution

4.3. Private endeavor or joint private-public effort?

The larger group of cities in the sample (i.e. 34 out of 65) show a coverage index of 0.6. Nevertheless, the cities belonging to this group achieved this result by taking different path towards technological improvements in last-mile contexts. As a matter of fact, we can divide the 34 cities with a coverage index of 0,6 into two subgroups.

The first sub-group, composed by 21 cities, has experienced the adoption of various market solutions, such as cargo bikes or electric vehicles, crowd-shipping platforms and parcel lockers. Hence, in those cities the surge of last-mile technologies can be attributed mostly to last-mile private operators. In particular, we can distinguish three countries that account for 71% of the cities in this sub-group, namely France, The Netherlands and UK. These countries lie at the forefront of last-mile deliveries because they could integrate the efforts brought by small innovative companies with the large-scale adoption by international logistics service providers. For instance, the French courier Le Group La Poste acquired the crowd shipping company Stuart in 2017, which expanded its operations to several cities in France and the UK[2]. Furthermore, in The Netherlands the last-mile delivery with cargo bikes has become widely adopted, as a company such as Fietskoeriers is able to deliver goods in 30 Dutch cities by employing 600 bike messengers [41]. These findings are consistent with previous results by [13], who state that technological implementations do not depend on the specific structure of a city, but rather on the maturity of the technology and on the adoption by private players.

On the other hand, the second sub-group is composed by 13 cities that decided to implement at least one technological project at a urban planning level, either in terms of ITS or freight planning algorithm. Such cities couple an average level of adoption of market solutions, i.e. the most common ones, with a greater interest in urban freight issues by local authorities. Among these cities there is a predominance of Italian ones, which compose 58% of the sub-group (7 cities out of 13). Another geographical area vastly represented in this sub-group is composed by the Baltic and Scandinavian regions, which comprise 4 cities (i.e. Tallinn, Stockholm, Gothenburg and Copenhagen).

5. Discussions and Conclusions

---

[1] https://www.portbase.com/en/services/road-planning/

[2] https://www.ipc.be/en/News-Portal/operations-logistics/2018/05/08/07/38/crowd-sourced-delivery

This paper is intended to propose an analysis on the adoption of innovative technologies in carrying out logistics activities in urban environments. To this end, a set of technologies has been identified, and a sample of European cities that have claimed to adopt such technologies has been created.
The results show that parcel lockers together with low emissions vehicles are the most adopted technologies in the cities under study. This might be due to the fact that big players operating at international levels, such as e-commerce companies and logistics service providers, are involved in these projects. On the contrary, the limited diffusion of ITS, or dynamic routing initiatives, is based on the significant support of public authorities that have also to align the different objectives of the stakeholders that are involved. In addition, it is important to underline that a lot of Italian cities have carried out these services. As a matter of fact, Italian cities, especially in city centers, often suffer from problems of congestion related to their narrow and ancient streets that were not originally designed for the transit of cars, vans etc. Therefore, in these urban areas a structured control of the accesses and a more strictly monitoring of the flow acquire a particular relevance. Finally, crowd shipping services are more diffused in countries such as France, United Kingdom, Norway and Belgium, wherein logistics startups have experienced a more favorable business environment.
The present study gives rise to both theoretical and practical implications. From a theoretical point of view, it can be considered a contribution in the research stream focused on the classification of last mile technological projects. In addition, it might provide a big picture related to the level of adoption of the technologies supporting CL processes at a European level. Finally, this work could be suitable in assessing the level of adoption of the different kinds of services that have been taken into account. From a practical point of view, this paper might give a support to public policy makers to evaluate their technological maturity in their last mile systems and then design coherent future objectives. In such a context, the present research could drive a more thorough assessment of the impact of public investment against the initial goals, in order to evaluate the success of urban freight planning strategies. However, this work suffers from some limitations. In particular, the sample is limited to the European contexts and it is not at a worldwide level. Actually, last mile appears to be a typical European issue and a low number of municipalities are significantly promoting CL initiatives in other international regions. In fact, European cities have been facing all the problems related to traffic congestions and related pollution for a longer period of time compared with cities of other continents. Also, this work does not take into account the effect of factors that might facilitate the introduction of last mile services such as the number of start ups per inhabitants, or the venture capital funding. Future research will be addressed to overcome these limitations, by gathering international city projects for enhancing urban logistics systems and by including external aspects that may more precisely explain technological adoption patterns. In particular, such a research will be a support in the evaluation of the proposed preliminary results through a more quantitative assessment.

6. References

1. Roumboutsos, A., Kapros, S., Vanelslander, T.: Green city logistics: Systems of Innovation to assess the potential of E-vehicles. Res. Transp. Bus. Manag. 11, 43–52 (2014). https://doi.org/10.1016/j.rtbm.2014.06.005.
2. Gonzalez-Feliu, J., Ambrosini, C., Pluvinet, P., Toilier, F., Routhier, J.-L.: A simulation framework for evaluating the impacts of urban goods transport in terms of road occupancy. J. Comput. Sci. 3, 206–215 (2012). https://doi.org/10.1016/j.jocs.2012.04.003.
3. Bohne, S., Ruesch, M.: Best Practice Handbook 1- BESTFACT Deliverable D2.2. (2013).
4. Cagliano, A.C., De Marco, A., Mangano, G., Zenezini, G.: Levers of logistics service providers' efficiency in urban distribution. Oper. Manag. Res. 10, (2017). https://doi.org/10.1007/s12063-017-0125-4.
5. Taniguchi, E., Thompson, R. G., Yamada, T., van Duin, R.: City Logistics. Network Modelling and Intelligent Transport Systems. (2001).
6. Allen, J., Thorne, G., Browne, M.: BESTUFS-Good Practice Guide on Urban Freight Transport. (2007).
7. SUGAR: City Logistics Best Practices: a Handbook for Authorities. (2011).
8. Van Rooijen, T., Quak, H.: City Logistics in the European CIVITAS Initiative. Procedia - Soc. Behav. Sci. 125, 312 – 325 (2014). https://doi.org/10.1016/j.sbspro.2014.01.1476.
9. Muñuzuri, J., Larrañeta, J., Onieva, L., Cortés, P.: Solutions applicable by local administrations for urban logistics improvement. Cities. 22, 15–28 (2005).

https://doi.org/10.1016/j.cities.2004.10.003.
10. Russo, F., Comi, A.: Measures for Sustainable Freight Transportation at Urban Scale: Expected Goals and Tested Results in Europe. J. Urban Plan. Dev. 137, 142–152 (2011). https://doi.org/10.1061/(ASCE)UP.1943-5444.
11. Ville, S., Gonzalez-Feliu, J., Dablanc, L.: The Limits of Public Policy Intervention in Urban Logistics: Lessons from Vicenza (Italy). Eur. Plan. Stud. 21, 1528–1541 (2013). https://doi.org/10.1080/09654313.2012.722954.
12. Gonzalez-Feliu, J.: Sustainable Urban Logistics: Planning and Evaluation. John Wiley & Sons (2018).
13. De Marco, A., Mangano, G., Zenezini, G.: Classification and benchmark of City Logistics measures: an empirical analysis. Int. J. Logist. Res. Appl. 21, 1–19 (2018). https://doi.org/10.1080/13675567.2017.1353068.
14. Cagliano, A.C., Carlin, A., Mangano, G., Rafele, C.: Analyzing the diffusion of eco-friendly vans for urban freight distribution. Int. J. Logist. Manag. 28, (2017). https://doi.org/10.1108/IJLM-05-2016-0123.
15. Schliwa, G., Armitage, R., Aziz, S., Evans, J., Rhoades, J.: Sustainable city logistics - Making cargo cycles viable for urban freight transport. Res. Transp. Bus. Manag. 15, 50–57 (2015). https://doi.org/10.1016/j.rtbm.2015.02.001.
16. Muñuzuri, J., Grosso, R., Cortés, P., Guadix, J.: Estimating the extra costs imposed on delivery vehicles using access time windows in a city. Comput. Environ. Urban Syst. 41, 262–275 (2013). https://doi.org/10.1016/j.compenvurbsys.2012.05.005.
17. Zenezini, G.; Mangano, G.: The Value Proposition of innovative Last-Mile delivery services from the perspective of local retailers. In: 9th Manufacturing Modelling, Management and Control Conference MIM, 2019. , Berlin (Germany) (2019).
18. Patier, D., Browne, M.: A methodology for the evaluation of urban logistics innovations. Procedia-Social Behav. Sci. 2, 6229–6241 (2010). https://doi.org/https://doi.org/10.1016/j.sbspro.2010.04.033.
19. Ranieri, L., Digiesi, S., Silvestri, B., Roccotelli, M.: A review of last mile logistics innovations in an externalities cost reduction vision. Sustain. 10, (2018). https://doi.org/10.3390/su10030782.
20. Castellà-Roca, J., Mut-Puigserver, M., Payeras-Capellà, M.M., Viejo, A., Anglès-Tafalla, C.: Secure and anonymous vehicle access control system to traffic-restricted urban areas. In: 2017 26th International Conference on Computer Communications and Networks, ICCCN 2017 (2017). https://doi.org/10.1109/ICCCN.2017.8038491.
21. Quak, H., Van Duin, J.H.R.: The influence of road pricing on physical distribution in urban areas. In: Procedia - Social and Behavioral Sciences. pp. 6141–6153 (2010). https://doi.org/10.1016/j.sbspro.2010.04.026.
22. Marinelli, M., Colovic, A., Dell'Orco, M.: A novel Dynamic programming approach for Two-Echelon Capacitated Vehicle Routing Problem in City Logistics with Environmental considerations. In: Transportation Research Procedia. pp. 147–156 (2018). https://doi.org/10.1016/j.trpro.2018.09.017.
23. Voegl, J., Fikar, C., Hirsch, P., Gronalt, M.: A simulation study to evaluate economic and environmental effects of different unloading infrastructure in an urban retail street. Comput. Ind. Eng. 137, (2019). https://doi.org/10.1016/j.cie.2019.106032.
24. Pinto, R., Lagorio, A., Golini, R.: The location and sizing of urban freight loading/unloading lay-by areas. Int. J. Prod. Res. 1–17 (2018). https://doi.org/10.1080/00207543.2018.1461269.
25. Muñoz-Villamizar, A., Montoya-Torres, J.R., Faulin, J.: Impact of the use of electric vehicles in collaborative urban transport networks: A case study. Transp. Res. Part D Transp. Environ. 50, 40–54 (2017). https://doi.org/10.1016/j.trd.2016.10.018.
26. Arnold, F., Cardenas, I., Sörensen, K., Dewulf, W.: Simulation of B2C e-commerce distribution in Antwerp using cargo bikes and delivery points. Eur. Transp. Res. Rev. 10, (2018). https://doi.org/10.1007/s12544-017-0272-6.
27. Melo, S., Baptista, P.: Evaluating the impacts of using cargo cycles on urban logistics: integrating traffic, environmental and operational boundaries. Eur. Transp. Res. Rev. 9, (2017). https://doi.org/10.1007/s12544-017-0246-8.
28. Carbone, V., Rouquet, A., Roussat, C.: The Rise of Crowd Logistics: A New Way to Co-Create Logistics Value. J. Bus. Logist. 38, 238–252 (2017). https://doi.org/10.1111/jbl.12164.
29. Akeb, H., Moncef, B., Durand, B.: Building a collaborative solution in dense urban city settings to enhance parcel delivery: An effective crowd model in Paris. Transp. Res. Part E Logist. Transp.

Rev. 119, 223–233 (2018). https://doi.org/10.1016/j.tre.2018.04.007.
30. Guo, X., Lujan Jaramillo, Y.J., Bloemhof-Ruwaard, J., Claassen, G.D.H.: On integrating crowdsourced delivery in last-mile logistics: A simulation study to quantify its feasibility. J. Clean. Prod. 241, (2019). https://doi.org/10.1016/j.jclepro.2019.118365.
31. Gatta, V., Marcucci, E., Nigro, M., Serafini, S.: Sustainable urban freight transport adopting public transport-based crowdshipping for B2C deliveries. Eur. Transp. Res. Rev. 11, (2019). https://doi.org/10.1186/s12544-019-0352-x.
32. Deutsch, Y., Golany, B.: A parcel locker network as a solution to the logistics last mile problem. Int. J. Prod. Res. 56, 251–261 (2018). https://doi.org/10.1080/00207543.2017.1395490.
33. Vakulenko, Y., Hellström, D., Hjort, K.: What's in the parcel locker? Exploring customer value in e-commerce last mile delivery. J. Bus. Res. 88, 421–427 (2018). https://doi.org/10.1016/j.jbusres.2017.11.033.
34. Iwan, S., Kijewska, K., Lemke, J.: Analysis of Parcel Lockers' Efficiency as the Last Mile Delivery Solution - The Results of the Research in Poland. In: Transportation Research Procedia. pp. 644–655 (2016). https://doi.org/10.1016/j.trpro.2016.02.018.
35. Lachapelle, U., Burke, M., Brotherton, A., Leung, A.: Parcel locker systems in a car dominant city: Location, characterisation and potential impacts on city planning and consumer travel access. J. Transp. Geogr. 71, 1–14 (2018). https://doi.org/10.1016/j.jtrangeo.2018.06.022.
36. Szymczyk, K., Kadłubek, M.: Challenges in general cargo distribution strategy in urban logistics - comparative analysis of the biggest logistics operators in EU. In: Transportation Research Procedia. pp. 525–533 (2019). https://doi.org/10.1016/j.trpro.2019.06.054.
37. Heitz, A., Beziat, A.: The Parcel Industry in the Spatial Organization of Logistics Activities in the Paris Region: Inherited Spatial Patterns and Innovations in Urban Logistics Systems. In: Transportation Research Procedia. pp. 812–824 (2016). https://doi.org/10.1016/j.trpro.2016.02.034.
38. Le, T.V., Stathopoulos, A., Van Woensel, T., Ukkusuri, S.V.: Supply, demand, operations, and management of crowd-shipping services: A review and empirical evidence. Transp. Res. Part C Emerg. Technol. 103, 83–103 (2019). https://doi.org/10.1016/j.trc.2019.03.023.
39. International Monetary Fund: World Economic Outlook Database, https://www.imf.org/external/pubs/ft/weo/2018/02/weodata/index.aspx, last accessed 2019/10/17.
40. World Atlas: The Busiest Cargo Ports In Europe, https://www.worldatlas.com/articles/the-busiest-cargo-ports-in-europe.html, last accessed 2019/10/17.
41. Fietskoeriers: We fietsen in alle grote steden, https://www.fietskoeriers.nl, last accessed 2019/10/18.

I L S 2020
INTERNATIONAL CONFERENCE ON INFORMATION
SYSTEMS, LOGISTICS & SUPPLY CHAIN
Austin, Texas April 22-24, 2020

Addressing the water-energy-food nexus through a green supply chain network design strategy

Marco A. Miranda-Ackerman [1], Catherine Azzaro-Pantel [2], Alberto A. Agular Lasserre [3]

[1] Faculty of Chemical Science and Engineering, Universidad Autónoma de Baja California, Tijuana, Mexico
[2] Laboratoire de Génie Chimique, Université de Toulouse, CNRS, Toulouse, France
[3] Tecnológico Nacional de México campus Orizaba, Orizaba, Mexico
{miranda.marco@uabc.edu.mx, catherine.azzaropantel@ensiacet.fr}

Abstract. The importance of water and energy accessibility and use has become more important as new insight into their role for sustainable development goals has become mainstream. The inclusion of water and energy in strategic decision-making is thus key. Supply chain network design (SCND) in the food industry is an interesting case study for the incorporation of water and energy utilization during the design process of global production systems. In the current green SCND research, frequently, single indicators are used such as carbon emissions to measure environmental impact. This paper presents a case study applied to an orange juice supply chain, formulated as a multi-objective optimization model. A single environmental impact indicator optimization approach is paired against one that includes water and energy use explicitly in the objective function set. Mixed conclusions are shown from the results pairing the two strategies side by side.

Keywords: multi-objective optimization, agrofood supply chain, sustainable development, sustainable supply chain, food security.

1. Introduction

Water and energy have become important issues to mitigate and overcome the environmental damage that has stemmed from industrial development. In the quest for a sustainable future, food production is inextricably linked to water and energy given its dependencies during the agricultural and processing stages [1], creating the so-called nexus of water, energy and food. Other important issues of food production are related to logistical and handling activities that are classical of many other globally produced and distributed products.
One pivotal dimension of this problematic is the strategic design of the production systems, including the location and allocation of resources and capacities along the full supply chain. Green supply chain network design (GSCND) formally studies how to incorporate operational, economic and environmental criteria in the supply chain design process. This helps improve performance at a long-term time horizon by minimizing distances, fixing capacities, among other strategic decisions. GSCND has the potential to provide a means to include water and energy consumption within the design process, and measure its economic and environmental impact along the supply chain [2].
Current supply chain design methods take into account a large array of criteria and variable in order to formulate the design decisions related to supply chain performance. Recently GSCND has incorporated some environmental performance indicators sometimes referred to as Key Environmental Performance Indicators [3]. In order to improve on the performance of water and energy use through supply chain design improvement, indirect measurements have been used such as the incorporation of greenhouse gas

emissions as KEPI targets. CO2 emissions have been used previously to reflect the environmental impact of a supply chain network design [4]. Classically, the water and energy challenge has been integrated in the GSCND through its cost and environmental measurements related to water and energy use [5]. In this paper we propose incorporating water and energy consumption as direct indicators within the objective function set of a multi-objective optimization modelling framework.

2. Problem formulation

In order to formulate this supply chain design problem, a case study is developed, that illustrates the approach applied to an orange juice production system. It is made up of four echelons, i.e., supplier, processing, bottling and distribution, as it is shown in Figure 1. In each of the echelons, the main process or operational unit is described by a box with inputs and outputs accordingly.
The globally distributed supply chain component of the production system is taken into account given that the agricultural and initial processing is done in warm and humid climate in Latin America ("Sourcing region"), while the bottling and final costumers are located in western Europe ("Market region"). Indeed each processing and transportation step has energy and water inflows as well as other intakes and their corresponding outflows, mainly intermediate and final product. Not all outputs are included in this figure such as emissions, but indeed are taken into account in the mathematical modelling framework.
This study proposes a multi-objective optimization (MOO) strategy solved through Genetic Algorithms to tackle the problem of GSCND improved to find trade-off solutions through the inclusion of antagonistic objective functions such as Profit vs. Environmental Impact [6]. A Multiple Criteria Decision Making Method (MCDM), i.e., M-TOPSIS (Yoon and Hwang, 1995) is then used to allow the evaluation and ranking of alternatives. This technique provides a means to objectively rank solutions taking all criteria into account based on the decision makers' preferences.

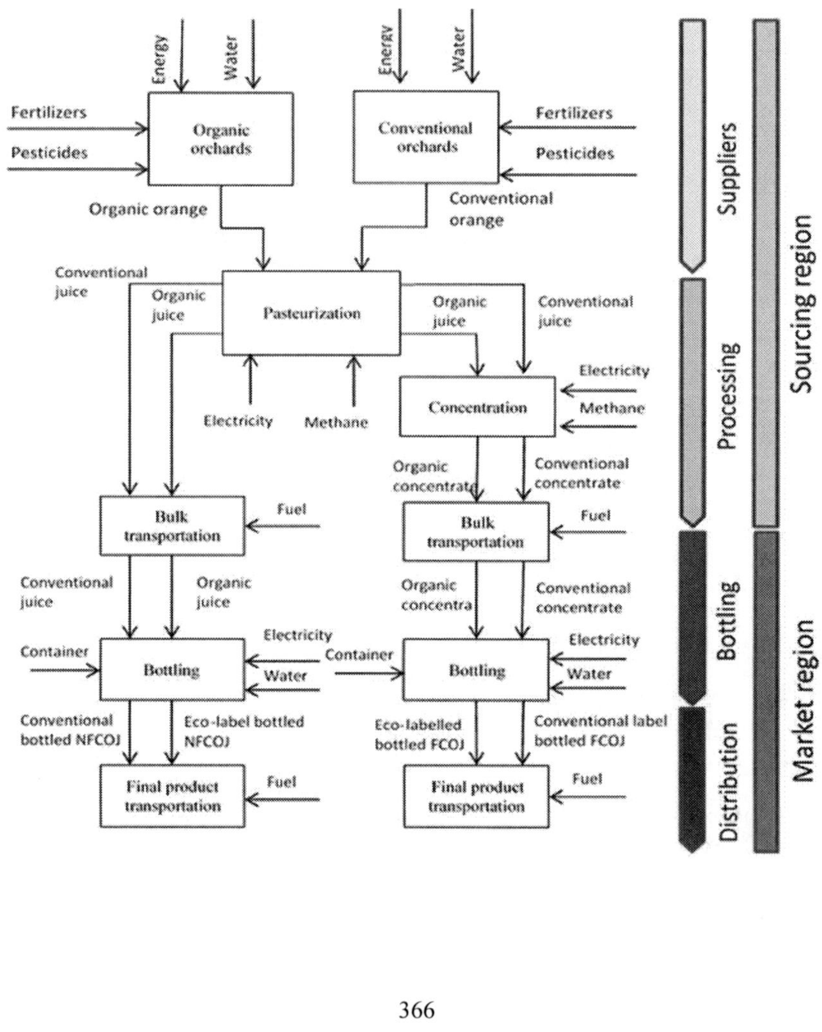

Figure 1. Orange juice supply chain case study production diagram [7]

A mathematical model that describes the supply chain system and the possible design variables is embedded in an external optimization loop. The modelling and optimization strategy is used for the case study. It takes into account a multi-period evaluation of the economic performance through the Net Present Value (NPV), among other economic criteria (e.g. Investment, Operational unit cost, etc.), as well as an environmental assessment through Global Warming Potential (GWP measured in kgCO2-eq) minimization. The modelling strategy considers the most important inputs involved in production (raw materials, intermediate products, and final products), processing and distribution of orange juice.
Water and Energy are some of the most important requirements used throughout the supply chain and that largely contribute to cost and GWP measurements based on Life Cycle Assessment estimations. Indeed according to[8] energy is the most important sustainability indicator category in food supply chains literature. In order to capture its importance in the supply chain design process these measurements are included directly into the objective function set of a multi-objective optimization model. The measurements take into account the use of fuels (e.g. methane, gasoline, diesel ...) and electricity used for transportation, farming, food processing, bottling. The energy and water consumption throughout the supply chain are sensitive to the choices made on the design of the SC and are reflected on the values of the objective functions and the resulting decision variables.

3. Methods and tools

MOO problems can be solved through several techniques. Some of the most commonly used ones are the weighted sum method, utility method, lexicographic, epsilon-constraint [9]. Another solution strategy is to use metaheuristic methods, such as genetic algorithms [10], [11] in order to obtain feasible heuristic solutions, [10], [12]. From a mono-objective point of view a main disadvantage is that when using these techniques there is no guarantee of finding solutions that are near the global optimal, thus basing the quality of the solutions found on the analysis and intuition of the modeler to avoid local optima. Besides, it provides a means to find trade-off solutions when modelling complex problems with multiple criteria such as SCND problems [13] must be taken into account to reflect the multiple objective nature of the issue. Publications in the context of green chain design show a recurrent use of GA [14]–[16]. The solving method used here is based on a variant of a multi-objective genetic algorithm through the Non-dominated Sorting Genetic Algorithm II (NSGA-II) [17]. This algorithm is a population-based stochastic search algorithm that produces Pareto non-dominated solutions. In contrast to other techniques such as weighted sum or lexicographic methods, that are a priori technique (i.e. a weight or order of the objectives as a matter of choice prior to the execution is needed), a multi-objective GA referred as an a posteriori method produces a set of solutions (the so-called Pareto front) to choose from [10], this is to say, without prior judgment or decision making. The NSGA-II is implemented through the so-called MULTIGEN library developed by [18] that allowed to perform evaluations, data analysis and visualization for the case study. The multi-objective strategy is coupled with a MCDM tool TOPSIS that provides a means to select and order the alternative optimal solutions that are obtain through the MOO. It uses distances from the ideal and nadir point to the solution alternatives as a means to measure fitness. The solutions that are nearest to the ideal and farthest from the nadir are ranked higher up than those that fall near in the opposite positions [19].

4. Model framework and case study

For the sake of brevity, we cannot present a full description of the mathematical model. Nevertheless we present a summary of the components of the model and provide a schema of some of the interactions that are mathematically modelled through Figure 2. The supply chain architecture consists of four echelons, i.e. Supplier, Processing, Bottling and Market. Each supply chain echelon has a set of control variables that affect the performance of each component that defines it. The optimization variables are all of integer type.
These control or decision variables are (their number is in parenthesis): (a) Supplier Echelon Decision Variables (81): Raw materials sourcing region location, Supplier selection, Agro practice selection, Land area contracted (Agricultural output capacity); (b) Processing Echelon Decision Variables (2): Processing

technology selection; (c) Bottling Echelon Decision Variables (4): Bottling plant location, Bottling technology selection; (d) Market Echelon Decision Variables (80): Demand coverage (product mix & system wide capacity).

These variables are subject to two main sets of constraints. The first set involves lower and upper bounds of the values that the decision variables can take during the optimization process. These bounds represent the operational capabilities or value limits evaluated during the genetic algorithm run. The second set of constraints represents the feasibility of the network, in other words the interdependencies and operational limitations of the process system under consideration, encompassing mass balances and demand constraints. In addition, the objective functions are constituted by a set of equations describing the system decomposed into three groups: (1) operational and economic functions; (2) environmental impact functions; and (3) transportation functions.

4.1. Mass Balance and Demand Constraints

In terms of materials flow, the network of suppliers, production plants and markets is reflected in a set of constraints insuring that production capacities at each level in the supply chain can meet market demand requirements. It is based on a material flow diagram that follows the raw materials through intermediate and final product outputs. In Figure 2, the initial two echelons are presented for the case study. A set of equations representing the different routes of materials are defined. These are divided in order to represent the different types of final products that can be sent to the different market locations. This figure illustrates only a segment of the full supply chain, and is meant to help the reader understand that the mathematical framework behind the materials flow and balancing is detailed enough to capture the different requirements in resources downstream of the supply chain.

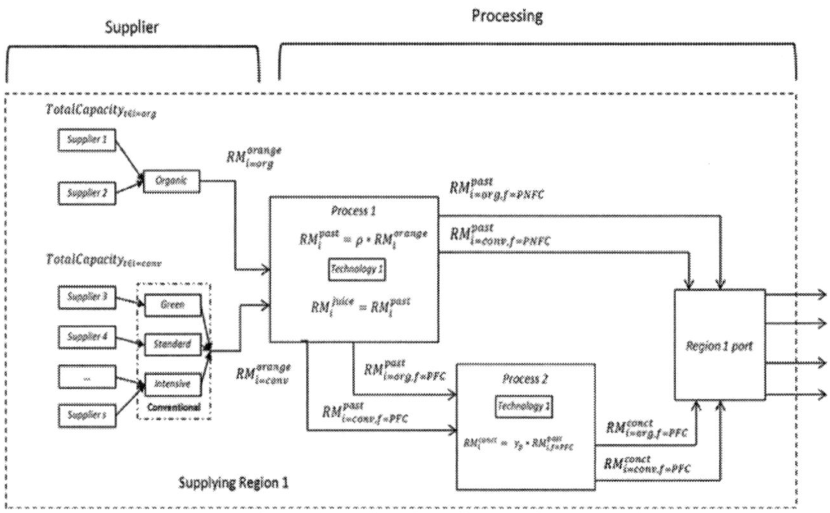

Figure 2: Supplier-Processing echelon interface diagram for case study mass balance [7]

4.2. Operational and Economic Functions

Based on the objectives of the modelling framework laid out previously the economic performance of the production process needs to be reflected in the model. This way, the costs and benefits in economic terms are allocated accordingly based on the different design alternatives being evaluated during the optimization process. In other words, the production cost of each type of product is dependent on the conditions and costs that are relative to each echelon of the network, so that the sales and thus the economic benefits can be measured in a significant criterion via the Net Present Value (NPV).

Each production stage is modelled as interconnected blocks representing stages and decisions that in turn reflect flows. Each block has an "Input", reflecting a different production cost and material flow. Within the block, e.g. "Orchard Production" process, different factors such as land area, and agricultural practices differences in unit cost and land yields are taken into account. The "Output" of this production stage is then raw materials (i.e. intermediate products) that will satisfy the material balance requirements, and will be reflected in economic terms per this modelling structure. This same concept is used throughout the different echelons in the supply chain in order to capture the key economic elements of the system (e.g. capital investment in equipment, transportation costs, etc.). Through this approach, a full picture of the supply chain is integrated into the objective functions set for optimization in the later stage of the methodology.

4.3. Transportation Functions

The transportation activities involved through the supply chain have an economic and environmental cost. For the case study there are four intermediate product types, i.e., pasteurized single strength (NFCOJ) organic and conventional orange juice, and concentrated multiple strength (FCOJ) organic and conventional orange juice that differ from their production cost, related to their operations but share the same transportation cost in terms of (kg.km) per mode of transport. These intermediate products are transported in bulk by different modes and routes; for our case study, transport is limited to sea freight transport from the port of departure of the region r selected, with two arrival port destinations. These ports service two main market regions, mainly France and Germany, the two largest consumers of fruit juice in Europe. Within each market region, a set of markets (10 in the case study) is made up of the most populated cities (10 in the case study). The economic cost from one location to its destination for each echelon connection in the network is expressed in \$/kgkm; while the environmental impact of each transport trajectory is measured in kg of CO2 eq / kg.km. In parallel, the estimation of GWP, Water and Energy consumption is carried out for each component of the supply chain and their respective contribution is cumulated from the whole set of activities.

4.4. Objective functions

The modelling strategy is then formulated as a multi-objective optimization problem as follows:

$$\begin{gathered} \min[-NPV(x,y), GWP(x,y), Water(x,y), Energy(x,y)] \\ s.t.\ g_i(x,y) \le b_i \\ x \in \mathbb{Z}^n, y \in \{0,1\}^m \end{gathered} \quad (1)$$

NPV is the Net Present Value (\$); GWP refers to Global Warming Potential (kgCO2-eq); Water (L); Energy (kWh)

The objective functions are assessed simultaneously, through the NSGA-II algorithm, in order to evaluate the concurrent performances and behaviour of each criterion when evaluating different SC network design configurations, resulting in a Pareto optimal set of solutions.

5. Results

The effect of including water and energy consumption to the set of objective functions can be analysed through the use of the optimization framework. Some differences are observed compared to the case where they have not been explicitly considered. A wider spread of optimized alternatives in Case A (Figure 5a) has been obtained when including water and energy minimization explicitly as objective functions, compared to the detailed frontier formed when excluding them in Case B (Figure 5b). This is due to the non-dominated solutions that are found in the 4-objective Pareto front. A small difference is found at the frontier of the best trade-off solutions located in the range of 2.5 and 3 M\$ of the NPV axes of both cases (Figures 5a and 5b). In this region, high NPVs are found at reasonably low GWP values for both cases using TOPSIS with weights of 0.5 for NPV and GWP respectively. Similar observations can be made when looking at the quantities measured for water and energy use (Figures 5c and 5d). The same type of wider spread is seen for Case A (Figure 5c) that includes four objective functions and a finer

Pareto frontier for the case of the bi-objective Case B (Figure 5d), but with similar consumption rates for both resources.

It must be also highlighted that when water and energy are explicitly taken into account into the optimization criteria, the Pareto front alternatives produce solutions that survive the genetic algorithm discrimination process in the lower NPV values. In contrast, not surprisingly, the solutions of the bi-objective formulation of the problem eliminate solutions under approximately 1.5 M$ for NPV.

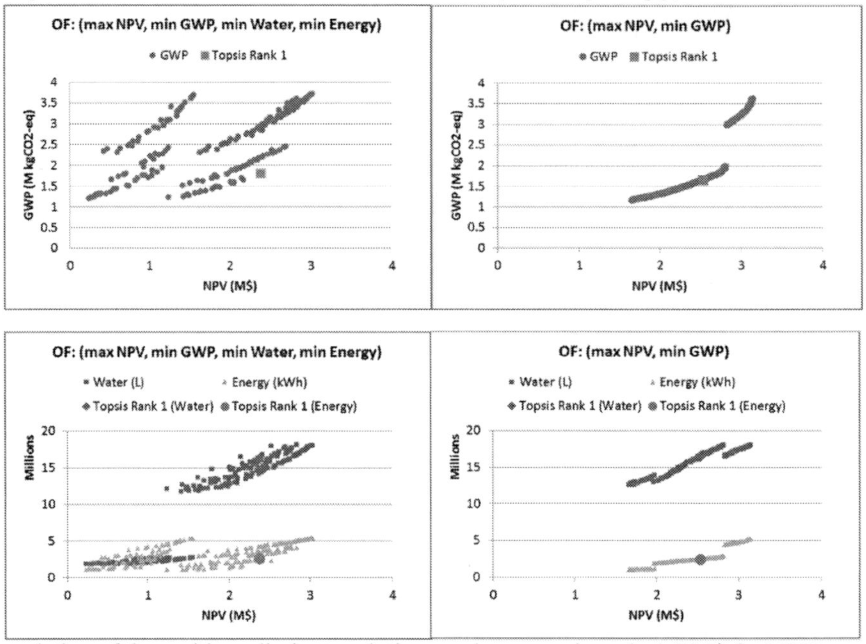

Figure 5 (a)Case A: Pareto front with objective functions (OF) including water and energy; (b)Case B: Pareto front with OF not explicitly including water and energy; (c)Water and energy profiles of Case A; (d)Water and energy profiles of Case B. Note that OF=Objective Functions.

Several weights have been used in the TOPSIS method [19] to rank solutions for the two sets of optimization runs (see Table 1). Indeed there is a large difference for NPV value in favor of the bi-objective approach when using four criteria (e.g. weights), with a poor performance of water usage which is over 4 times higher. If we do not consider water and energy in the MCDM process (e.g. use two criteria; NPV & GWP) the results are very similar. Yet if there is a shift to consider water and energy in the same light as economic and mainstream environmental criteria, different solutions and new alternatives, that would otherwise be eliminated during optimization or taken for granted during the final decision making process, could change the space of feasible and attractive designs going forward.

Table 1: Top ranked solutions via TOPSIS the multi-objective and bi-objective strategies

TOPSIS weights w(NPV, GWP, Water, Energy)	Objective Functions	NPV ($)	GWP (kg CO_2-eq)	Water (L)	Energy (kWh)
(0.25, 0.25, 0.25, 0.25)	(max NPV, min GWP, min Water, min Energy)	910 892	1 769 086	2 621 665	1 533 921
(0.25, 0.25, 0.25, 0.25)	(max NPV, min GWP)	1 976 941	1 312 148	13 990 126	1 109 524
(0.5, 0.5)	(max NPV, min GWP, min Water, min Energy)	2 381 225	1 819 796	16 226 358	2 612 070
(0.5, 0.5)	(max NPV, min GWP)	2 530 056	1 659 620	16 517 445	2 447 303

It must be highlighted that water and energy are captured only within the large blocks but could be modelled in detail in a finer model. For example taking into account agricultural practices with a high irrigation component and cleaning on batch containers represents a large percentage of water use in the

transformation process of many food products; in addition to energy consumption alternatives during transport such as natural gas, ethanol or electric vehicle use in the final mile transportation, the effect of alternative energy sources on food transformation process, such as scenarios with solar, wind, or other decentralized alternative sources of energy could also be incorporated in the design stages of new plants or even when retrofitting is possible.
Water and energy impact is captured only for the direct use of some key elements of the "supra-system" presented but could be extended explicitly through life cycle assessment (estimation of water and energy use for indirect inputs, such as the production of equipment, fertilizers, fuels, etc).

6. Conclusions

The study provides insight on the importance of water and energy evaluation during supply chain network design process in a food production system. Indeed, we are aware that the results concern a specific application, so that it is difficult to generalize the scope of the results. This study also emphasizes that it may be useful for GSCND practitioners to indirectly account for water and energy use along the supply chain by optimizing a correlated benchmark environmental criterion, such as GWP. By doing this practitioners may, at the exploratory stages of supply chain design evaluate performance using fewer objectives functions improving design throughput.
The inclusion of water and energy criteria explicitly in the design process is a key issue for processes especially when these resources are scares, i.e. in regions where energy and water security is a key factor in the feasibility of a supply chain project acceptance. This approach may provide a base framework in order to find interesting alternatives that fulfil local or regional restrictions (e.g. arid regions). Finally, the proposed approach is constructed on well-developed modeling and optimization strategies that can be solved in a straightforward manner. Future models may capitalize on new modeling and optimization strategies and software.

7. References

[1] H. K. Jeswani, R. Burkinshaw, and A. Azapagic, "Environmental sustainability issues in the food–energy–water nexus: Breakfast cereals and snacks," *Sustainable Production and Consumption*, vol. 2, pp. 17–28, Apr. 2015.

[2] P. Beske, A. Land, and S. Seuring, "Sustainable supply chain management practices and dynamic capabilities in the food industry: A critical analysis of the literature," *International Journal of Production Economics*, vol. 152, pp. 131–143, Jun. 2014.

[3] G. Doublet *et al.*, "Key Environmental Performance Indicators for a simplified LCA in food supply chains," in *Proceedings of the 9th International Conference on Life Cycle Assessment in the Agri-Food Sector (LCA Food 2014)*, 2014, pp. 8–10.

[4] Y. Bouzembrak, H. Allaoui, G. Goncalves, and H. Bouchriha, "A multi-objective green supply chain network design," in *2011 4th International Conference on Logistics (LOGISTIQUA)*, 2011, pp. 357–361.

[5] M. A. Miranda-Ackerman, C. Azzaro-Pantel, L. Montastruc, S. Domenech, and A. A. A. Lasserre, "Optimal design of a green supply chain: application to the agro-food industry supplier selection problem," in *Coll. Récents progrès en génie des procédés, n° 104 Les sciences du génie des procédés pour une industrie durable XIVe congrès SFGP 2013 8 au 10 octobre 2013, Lyon*, 2013, vol. 104.

[6] M. A. Miranda-Ackerman, "Optimisation multi-objectif pour la gestion et la conception d'une chaine logistique verte: application au cas de la filière agroalimentaire du jus d'orange," 05-Nov-2015.

[7] M. A. Miranda-Ackerman, C. Azzaro-Pantel, and A. A. Aguilar-Lasserre, "A green supply chain network design framework for the processed food industry: Application to the orange juice agrofood cluster," *Computers & Industrial Engineering*, vol. 109, pp. 369–389, Jul. 2017.

[8] J. M. Bloemhof, J. G. A. J. van der Vorst, M. Bastl, and H. Allaoui, "Sustainability assessment of food chain logistics," *International Journal of Logistics Research and Applications*, vol. 18, no. 2, pp. 101–117, Mar. 2015.

[9] S. De-León Almaraz, C. Azzaro-Pantel, L. Montastruc, L. Pibouleau, and O. B. Senties, "Assessment of mono and multi-objective optimization to design a hydrogen supply chain," *International Journal of Hydrogen Energy*, vol. 38, no. 33, pp. 14121–14145, Nov. 2013.
[10] P. Cortez, *Modern Optimization with R*. Cham: Springer International Publishing, 2014.
[11] X.-S. Yang, *Introduction to Mathematical Optimization: From Linear Programming to Metaheuristics*. Cambridge International Science Publishing, 2008.
[12] Y. Collette and P. Siarry, *Multiobjective optimization: principles and case studies*. Springer Science & Business Media, 2003.
[13] M. A. Miranda-Ackerman, G. Fernández-Lambert, C. Azzaro-Pantel, and A. A. Aguilar-Lasserre, "A Multi-Objective Modelling and Optimization Framework for Operations Management of a Fresh Fruit Supply Chain: A Case Study on a Mexican Lime Company," in *Applications of Metaheuristics in Process Engineering*, J. Valadi and P. Siarry, Eds. Springer International Publishing, 2014, pp. 373–394.
[14] O. Ahumada and J. R. Villalobos, "Application of planning models in the agri-food supply chain: A review," *European Journal of Operational Research*, vol. 196, no. 1, pp. 1–20, 2009.
[15] Y. Arkeman and K. D. Jong, "Development of Multiobjective Genetic Algorithms for Agri-Food Supply Chain Design by Considering Global Climate Change," 2010. [Online]. Available: http://repository.ipb.ac.id/handle/123456789/41683. [Accessed: 01-Oct-2013].
[16] W.-C. Yeh and M.-C. Chuang, "Using multi-objective genetic algorithm for partner selection in green supply chain problems," *Expert Systems with Applications*, vol. 38, no. 4, pp. 4244–4253, Apr. 2011.
[17] K. Deb, A. Pratap, S. Agarwal, and T. Meyarivan, "A fast and elitist multiobjective genetic algorithm: NSGA-II," *IEEE Transactions on Evolutionary Computation*, vol. 6, no. 2, pp. 182–197, Apr. 2002.
[18] A. Gomez, L. Pibouleau, C. Azzaro-Pantel, S. Domenech, C. Latgé, and D. Haubensack, "Multiobjective genetic algorithm strategies for electricity production from generation IV nuclear technology," *Energy Conversion and Management*, vol. 51, no. 4, pp. 859–871, 2010.
[19] K. P. Yoon and C.-L. Hwang, *Multiple Attribute Decision Making: An Introduction*. SAGE Publications, 1995.

I L S 2020
INTERNATIONAL CONFERENCE ON INFORMATION
SYSTEMS, LOGISTICS & SUPPLY CHAIN
Austin, Texas April 22-24, 2020

Cargo Vehicle Combinations: An Economic and Environmental Approach to Soybean Supply Chain in Mato Grosso, Brazil

Rodrigo Carlo Toloi [1,2], Marley Nunes Vituri Toloi [1,2], João Gilberto Mendes dos Reis [2], Antônio Carlos de Oliveira Machado [1], Sivanilza Teixeira Machado [2,3] Audiene Correia dos Santos Rabelo [1] and Silvia Helena Bonilla [2]

[1] Federal Institute of Mato Grosso Campus Rondonópolis, Mato Grosso, Brazil
[2] RESUP - Supply Chain Research Group, Post-graduate Program in Production Engineering, Paulista University, 1212 Dr. Bacelar St., São Paulo, SP
[3] NAPOLE - Advanced Production, Operations, Logistics, and Strategy Center, Federal Institute of São Paulo, 1501 Mogi das Cruzes Avenue, Suzano, SP
{rodrigo.toloi@roo.ifmt.edu.br, marley.toloi@gmail.com, betomendesreis@msn.com, antonio.machado@roo.ifmt.edu.br, sivateixeira@yahoo.com.br, audienerabelo@gmail.com, shbonilla@hotmail.com}

Abstract. There is a growing concern about food production, the rational use of energy, and the impacts caused by anthropogenic greenhouse gas emissions on transport systems. With this concern in mind, the objective of this paper is to discuss the economic and environmental performance of different combinations of cargo vehicles. To do so, we explored the flow of soybean from Mato Grosso state to the ports. The results show that the combination of the stump semi-trailer presented the best economic performance, while the combination of the 'rodotrem' semi-trailer presented the best environmental performance. Moreover, this work points out the importance of the quality of the highways on the economic and environmental performance of soybean transportation.

Keywords: Cargo Vehicle Combinations, Emissions of greenhouse gases, Soybean.

1. Introduction

Food production, the rational use of energy, and the preservation of the environment are considered significant challenges to be overcome in the coming years, given the population growth. According to the UN [1], the world population will reach 8.5 billion in 2030.

In this scenery, Brazil is considered one of the most massive granaries in food scale production [2]. Soybean is one of the most important worldwide commodities, and the country is considered the leading global in its production. The grain has several applications as a strategic protein source for both human and animal consumption. Furthermore, motivated by both the worldwide demand for soybean and the possibility of increased production and productivity, Brazil presents favorable environmental conditions for its production expansion.

Mato Grosso state is one of the leading Brazilian soybean producers, growing 32.30 million tons, equivalent to 27.08% of the national production, in 2017/18 year crop [3]. Around 55% of this production is destined for exportation [4, 5], which is dispatched by Santos/SP (45.34%), Barcarena/PA (20.02%), and Santarém/PA (10.05%) [6].

Furthermore, Mato Grosso production faces enormous challenges, among which stand out the environmental, social, and economic impacts [7–10]. Among them we can cite logistics deficiency such as transportation and storage capacity [11, 12]; great distances between producing areas to export ports, reaching up to 2000 km, and the emission of Greenhouse Gases - GHG, [12–15]. These factors directly affect the competitiveness of Brazilian soybean in the international market, even though the advantage of the low cost of land for production [16, 17] and the high productivity rates [18].

The present study aims to discuss the economic and environmental aspects of the different types of cargo vehicle combinations traveling on good quality, low quality paved and unpaved roads, using as reference the harvest flow of the state of Mato Grosso.

This work is justified due to the importance of the road modal for the soybean supply chain and the national economy where is necessary to carry out thorough studies on the possibilities of economic efficiency gains and reduction of environmental impacts, existing within this modal, by combining different types of cargo vehicles.

The paper is organized as follows: This introduction in Section 1, a brief contextualization of the types, body types used, and Greenhouse Gas (GHG) emissions presented in Section 2, methodology discussed in Section 3, the results in Section 4, and finally final remarks and conclusions in Section 5.

2. Literature Review

2.1. Cargo combinations to transport soybean

The cargo transportation matrix in Brazil is centralized in the roadway transportation modal, which corresponds to 61.1% of the national matrix transportation, moving 485 million tons per useful kilometer, while the railway modal accounted for 20.7%, and the waterway 13.6% of the total cargo handling [19].

Excessive use of road transport presents several obstacles such as low capacity and fleet density, poor condition, high accident rates, and loss of grain in the transport flow [20, 21].

The movement of soybeans between the producing regions of Mato Grosso to export ports, combine different cargo vehicles and body trucks. The most common models are the combinations of a tractor truck and a semi-trailer, such combinations can range from 5 to 9 axles and total gross weight (PBT) range from 41.5 to 74 tons, Figure 1 [22].

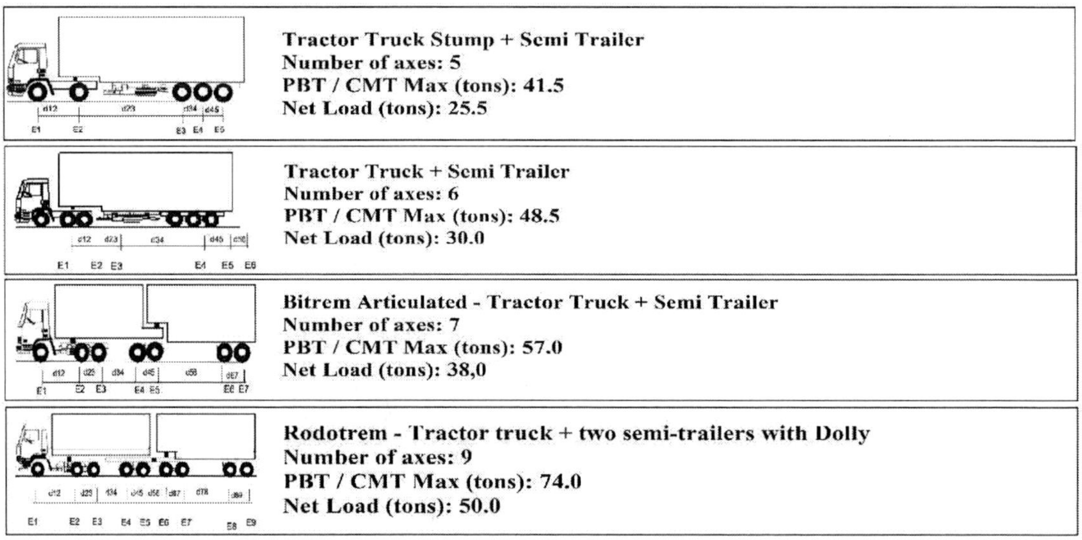

Figure 1: Cargo combinations. Source: Adapted from the National Department of Transport Infrastructure [23].

The semi-trailers shown in figure 1 are: bulk carrier, hopper, or even tipper, respecting the axle and load capacity limits and their load specificities. Roulet [24] suggests that some types of semi-trailers are more flexible as the load handling demand, noting that the hopper semi-trailer can only unload soybean in high-performance hoppers and cannot perform return freight, while the tipper and bulk carrier can transport grain back to the port and back with the fertilizer.

The payload of different combinations have different fuel and tire consumption behaviors, directly impacting both economic and environmental variables [25, 26].

In addition to the economic aspects, it is necessary to consider the environmental aspect, which demands transport modes with lower fossil fuel consumption, as well as a reduction in CO_2 emissions and an increase in the useful life of tires.

According to the Energy Research Company - [25], the Brazilian transportation sector is responsible for consuming 32.2% of the energy matrix among the productive sectors, especially the transportation of cargo with diesel trucks.

Moreover, according to the National Transportation Confederation - [26], Brazil has 1,720,756 km of highways, of which only 211,468 km are paved, 58.2% is poorly maintained. Unpaved roads total 1,509,288 km, which, as well as paved roads, need improvement [26, 27].

2.2. Greenhouse Gas (GHG) Emission in Soybean Production Flow

Soybeans from the State of Mato Grosso are transported by various combinations of transport modes, through the main routes from production to their final destination, of which more than 60% are also carried out by road [28–30]. The main concern revolves around the use of road transport is related to the fact of the modal to be responsible for highest CO_2 emission. That said that in 2020 these emissions will be about 60% more than in 2009, reaching 270 million tons of CO_2 [31–33]. Comparing this forecast with rail and waterway transportation the result is alarming. It represents 62.5 Mt of CO_2, or 92% of the total, against 5% of rail and 3% of waterway [33].

Indeed, Brazil has the potential to mitigate CO_2 emissions in transportation, as it is a matrix of unstructured transport, especially in road mode, and there is a possibility of improving fuel quality using biofuels [32]. Routes using a modal road above 700 km significantly increase greenhouse gas emissions and should be combined with other modes of transport in order to mitigate these emissions, although road transport in Brazil and the state of Mato Grosso is the most important and used in the current scenario [35, 36].

3. Methodology

This work is characterized by exploratory, bibliographic and descriptive research in order to provide greater familiarity to discuss the economic and environmental aspects according to the different combinations of cargo vehicles and the conditions of the road pavements, the flow of soybean production of Mato Grosso/Brazil.

To achieve the proposed objective, the methodology was organized into two stages:

1) **For the analysis of the economic aspects:**

A 420 HP 6x4 tractor truck was used to pull the different types of semi-trailer;

a) The values obtained for Scale Fuel Consumption (km/L), New tire life (Km) and retreaded tire life (Km) were obtained from surveys conducted with independent professional drivers, and values may vary depending on the driver's profile and driving style;
b) The cost of diesel oil (BRL/km) was obtained considering the average price of diesel oil practiced at gas stations in Rondonópolis/MT according to information disclosed on the website of the National Petroleum Agency - [37].
c) The values referring to Cost of new tires (BRL/km) and Cost of retreaded tires (BRL/km) were obtained through the Spread Costs per Km Spreadsheet for the State of Mato Grosso, disclosed by the Association of Transporters Grosso Cargo Station - [38];

2) **Environmental analysis:**

For calculations of greenhouse gas emissions, only one-factor was taken into account, namely the emission factor related to combustion of diesel used [41].

$$Emission\ of\ Diesel: E_{jk} = \sum(FE_i * \frac{Q_{diesel}}{Km} * D_{jk}) \quad (1)$$

Where:

Ejk corresponds to total CO_2eq emission per municipality of origin j and port of destination k; FEi corresponds to the CO_2eq emission factor of diesel, Q_diesel consumed per kilometer, and D is the distance traveled of origin j and port of destination k in km.

a) An outflow route from Rondonópolis/MT to the Port of Santos/SP was established, with an average distance of 1,399 km;
b) The functional unit for this environmental aspect was considered as 1 kg of soybean to allow comparisons with other related studies;

Finally, the data were organized in a table, which will allow us to compare and discuss the economic and environmental aspects of the cargo vehicle combinations used in the production flow.

The variables, considered for analysis, were extracted from the literature consulted show [13, 20, 25, 26, 28, 33, 42] and indicated in the survey responses.

4. Results

The economic and environmental performance of the Combinations was evaluated on three different types of highways. In the first scenario, it was evaluated on a well-paved highway; in the second scenario on a poor-quality highway and finally on an unpaved highway, as can be seen in Table 1.

4.1. Performance of Cargo Vehicle Combinations on Good Paved Road.

In this first scenario, it is observed that despite the net load capacity of the stump semi-trailer is lower than the others, it presented the best economic performance.

When analyzing fuel consumption, this combination compared to the others, had less consumption than 'rodotrem' by 65%, lower than 'bitrem' by 47.14% and lower than the semi-trailer wrecked by 12%.

Another advantage, observed in this combination, refers to the tires, it is necessary to invest BRL 23,274.00 for the 18 tires, while for a 'rodotrem' needs BRL 43,962.00 to replace the 34 new tires.

When considering the cost of retreaded tires, the stump semi-trailer had a lower cost per kilometer, being 53.85% lower than the 'rodotrem', 40% lower than the 'bitrem', and 25% lower when compared to the broken semi-trailer.

The difference in the cost per kilometer of new tires on the stump semi-trailer is 55.56% lower than the 'rodotrem', 33% lower than the 'bitrem', and 20% lower compared to the wrecked semi-trailer.

When considering the environmental performance analysis, the' rodotrem' semi-trailer, traveling on a well-paved highway, had the lowest environmental impact in terms of CO_2eq emissions, as it had up to 50% higher load capacity compared to a stump truck for example, which emitted 0.044 kg CO_2eq/kg of transported soybeans or 44 kg CO_2eq / ton, i.e., 12 to 18.51% lower compared to other body types.

4.2. Performance of Cargo Vehicle Combinations on Low Paved Road.

In the second scenario, it was observed that the performance of different combinations of cargo vehicles was lower compared to good quality highways, such result was expected, as Torres et al. [19] state that road characteristics have a direct impact on transportation performance.

The fuel consumption of the stump semi-trailer, compared to the other combinations, was 52.54% lower than 'rodotrem', 36.72% lower than 'bitrem', and 15.25% lower than the wrecked semi-trailer.

Another advantage of this model over the others is the cost per kilometer of new and retreaded tires. For retreaded tires, it was 56.25% lower than the 'rodotrem', 36.36% lower than the 'bitrem', and 22.22% lower than the wrecked semi-trailer and, for the cost per kilometer of new tires, the stump semi-trailer is 57.14% lower than the 'rodotrem', 35.71% lower than the 'bitrem', and 25% smaller than the broken semi-trailer.

The precariousness of the most paved highways increases transportation costs and increases environmental impacts [19, 40]. In this sense, there is an increase in the CO_2 emission of all semi-trailers analyzed, precisely due to its lower diesel consumption efficiency/km.

It is observed that at low-quality conditions compared to good paving, there was a 20% average increase in CO_2eq emissions for the four body types. The stump semi-trailer had the highest emission of 0.068 kg CO_2eq/kg of transported soybeans, and the lowest emission corresponds to the 'rodotrem' reaching 0.052 kg of CO_2eq/kg of soybeans. The 'rodotrem' emits almost 24% less if compared to the stump, as it has higher load capacity and better fuel efficiency per kilometers driven.

avior of combinations of cargo vehicles in pavement modalities.

Good quality paved highway				Low quality paved highway				
Rodotrem 9 axes 25 meters	**Bitrem Articulate 7 axes (up to 30 meters)**	**Truck**	**Stump**	**Rodotrem 9 axes 25 meters**	**Bitrem Articulate 7 axes (up to 30 meters)**	**Truck**	**Stump**	**Rodotrem 9 axes 25 meters**
74	57	48,5	41,5	74	57	48,5	41,5	74
50	38	30	25	50	38	30	25	50
1.7	1.9	2.5	2.8	1.45	1.62	1.92	2.21	1.23
BRL 2.31	BRL 2.06	BRL 1.57	BRL 1.40	BRL 2.70	BRL 2.42	BRL 2.04	BRL 1.77	BRL 3.19
34	26	22	18	34	26	22	18	34
250,000	280,000	290,000	290,000	212,500	238,000	246,500	246,500	180,625
BRL 0.13	BRL 0.13	BRL 0.13	BRL 0.13	BRL 0.13	BRL 0.13	BRL 0.13	BRL 0.13	BRL 0.13
140,000	150,000	150,000	160,000	119,000	127,500	127,500	136,000	101,150
BRL 0.13	BRL 0.13	BRL 0.13	BRL 0.13	BRL 0.13	BRL 0.13	BRL 0.13	BRL 0.13	BRL 0.13
822.94	703.02	559.6	499.64	964.83	863.58	728.65	633.03	1,137.40
2,205.48	1,884.09	1,499.73	1,339.04	2,585.74	2,314.40	1,952.77	1,696.52	3,048.23
0.044	0.050	0.050	0.054	0.052	0.061	0.065	0.068	0.061

Source: Survey Data

4.3. Performance of Cargo Vehicle Combinations on Unpaved Highway.

Cost efficiency and environmental impacts caused by cargo transport activities depend directly on the quality of the highways. Therefore, Fleury [41] points out that routes with better pavement bring better economic and environmental results and may generate a 7% reduction in GHG emissions into the atmosphere; however, 1,509,288 km of Brazilian highways are still unpaved [26].

The significant quantity of unpaved roads negatively impacts on the economic performance of cargo vehicle combinations, as can be seen in Table 1.

Regarding the fuel consumption of the stump semi-trailer, it has been 52.63% lower than 'rodotrem', 35.88% lower than 'bitrem', and 12.44% lower than semi-trailer.

When considering the cost with retreaded tires, it is observed that the stump semi-trailer costs 50% lower than the 'rodotrem', 30.76% lower than the 'bitrem', and 18.18% lower compared to the broken semi-trailer.

The stump semi-trailer is a more efficient combination of cargo vehicles, when considering the cost of new tires per kilometer, as it is 54.16% lower than the cost per kilometer, 35.29% lower, than the 'bitrem' and, 21.42% smaller with the trailer wrecked.

In the environmental aspect, emissions from the different types of bodies under the unpaved road conditions significantly increased by more than 30% compared to good quality paving roads, confirming what Soliani [40] highlights that unpaved roads and/or inadequate conditions contribute to the increase of diesel oil consumption and consequently an increase in greenhouse gas (GHG) emissions. Trucked and stump body trucks emitted the most in the range of 0.075 and 0.080 kg CO_2eq/kg of soybean respectively, finally the 'rodotrem' truck, although it also increased by 27% compared to the first scenario, it was what had the lowest emission 0.061 kg CO_2eq/kg transported soybean, justified by its carrying capacity.

5. Final Remarks and Conclusions

In the three types of pavements (good and low-quality paved road and unpaved road), when the economic aspect was evaluated, the 420 CV 6x4 tractor trailer stump semi-trailer showed the best economic relations.

The fact that the tractor truck is the same on all types of semi-trailers has justified the economic performance of the stump semi-trailer by the fact that its payload is half the payload capacity of a 'rodotrem' semi-trailer, allowing the tractor truck is driven smoother with progressive accelerations and braking and less torque, significantly reducing fuel consumption.

Another economic aspect to consider is the longer tire life (new and retreaded), which can be observed as a result of the reduced payload carried, is the more significant the mass to be displaced, the higher the rolling resistance, and consequently, the higher will be the tire wear. In this case, the stump semi-trailer has a new advantage, since its payload capacity is half the capacity of a 'rodotrem' semi-trailer.

However, when we consider the need to dispose of 32 million tons of soybeans produced in the state of Mato Grosso, it is observed that 1,280,000 stump semi-trailer combinations, or 1,066,000 wrecked semi-trailer combinations, or 842,105 combinations would be required semi-trailer or 640,000 'rodotrem' semi-trailer to carry the production.

Although the stump semitrailer presented the best economic relations, it is necessary to reflect on the quantity of this combination that would be necessary to drain the Mato Grosso crop, considering that if the harvesting is done by the stump semitrailer combination 50 % more vehicles compared to 'rodotrem' semi-trailer.

Regarding the environmental aspect, it was considered three different scenarios for the quality of the highways, with four combinations of cargo vehicles, and by means of a methodology to calculate the diesel combustion burning emission factor, it was found that the best environmental performance was measured by combining the 'rodotrem' semi-trailer, with the emission of 2,205 kg CO_2eq or 0.044 kg CO_2eq/kg of soybean, for the stretch from Rondonópolis/MT to the port of Santos/SP.

The scenario that obtained the highest emission was the unpaved highway using the stump truck, which had higher emission when compared to CO_2/kg soybean, due to its lower load capacity, lower efficiency and its results in the unpaved road scenario, was 1,994 kg CO_2eq to carry 25,000 kg or 0.0798 kg CO_2eq/kg of soybean.

Eventually, we could conclude that the combination of the stump semi-trailer presented the best economic performance, but obtained the worst environmental result, besides demanding a larger volume of combinations for the harvesting of the produced crop in Mato Grosso state. The best economical, as well as environmental performances, were obtained by the combinations that traveled on good quality paved highways;

The use of the 'rodotrem' semi-trailer combination presented the lowest economic performance when compared to soybean transportation however it was the combination that presented the best environmental performance.

Therefore, the importance of the quality of the highways on the economic and environmental performance of soy transportation is proven. Also, this study made it possible to identify that the Brazilian cargo transportation matrix needs investments, integration between modes, fleet modernization, and the use of technologies to improve both fuel consumption and tire wear performance.

The realization of this study prompted the study using this methodology to calculate the economic and environmental efficiency of the leading soybean outlets used in the state of Mato Grosso.

Acknowledgments

To the Coordination for the Improvement of Higher Education Personnel - CAPES, by the granting of a grant Finance Code 001; to the Federal Institute of Education, Science and Technology of Mato Grosso (IFMT) to support research, and the granting of the training license.

References

1. Organização das Nações Unidas, D. de A.E. e S.: Probabilistic Population Projections based on the World Population Prospects: The 2017 Revision. United Nations, New York (2017)
2. Contini, E., Martha, G.: Brazilian agriculture, its productivity and change. In: Food security and the futures of farms: 2020 and toward 2050. p. 15. THE ROYAL SWEDISH ACADEMY OF AGRICULTURE AND FORESTRY, Falkenberg, Sweden. (2010)
3. CONAB, C.N. de A.: Séries Históricas de Área Plantada, Produtividade e Produção, Relativas às Safras 1976/77 a 2017/18 de Soja, http://www.conab.gov.br/info-agro/safras/serie-historica-das-safras?start=20, (2018)
4. IMEA, I.M.G. de E.A.: Agronegócio no Brasil e em Mato Grosso. IMEA, Cuiabá (2014)
5. MDIC, M. do D., Indústria e Comércio Exterior: Balança comercial brasileira: Unidades da Federação, http://www.mdic.gov.br/index.php/comercio-exterior/estatisticas-de-comercio-exterior/balanca-comercial-brasileira-unidades-da-federacao
6. MDIC, S.A.: Sistema de Análise das Informações de Comércio Exterior Via Internet do Ministério do Desenvolvimento, Indústria e Comércio Exterior. (2016)
7. Zhu, Q., Sarkis, J.: Relationships between operational practices and performance among early adopters of green supply chain management practices in Chinese manufacturing enterprises. Journal of Operations Management. 22, 265–289 (2004). https://doi.org/10.1016/j.jom.2004.01.005
8. Cavalett, O., Ortega, E.: Emergy, nutrients balance, and economic assessment of soybean production and industrialization in Brazil. Journal of Cleaner Production. 17, 762–771 (2009). https://doi.org/10.1016/j.jclepro.2008.11.022
9. Soares, A.F.: Requisitos Ambientais no Mercado de Soja Brasileiro: Descrição e Avaliação de Impacto, (2016)
10. Toloi, R.C., Gunes, A.C.R. da S.L., Toloi, M.N.V., Reis, J.G.M. dos, Bonilla, S.H., Freitas, M.J.: Main variables that are influenced by the anthropic activity resulting from the soybean production in the municipalities of Mato Grosso. Independent Journal of Management & Production. 9, 607–622 (2018). https://doi.org/DOI: 10.14807/ijmp.v9i5.812
11. Lipinski, B., Hanson, C., Lomax, J., Kitinoja, L., Waite, R., Searchinger, T.: Reducing Food Loss and Waste, (2013)
12. Oliveira, F.C. de, Coelho, P.H.M.C., Sousa Neto, M. de S.N., Andre, A.C. de S., Santos, F.L. de S., Oliveira, J.P. de M., Oliveira, B.S. de, Teixeira, I.R.T., Campos, A.J. de C.: Logistics and Storage of Soybean in Brazil. African Journal of Agricultural Research. 11, 3261–3272 (2016). https://doi.org/10.5897/AJAR2016.11198
13. Maia, D.M., Carvalho, R.N. de: ECO2EFICIÊNCIA EM FROTAS DE CARGA. Blucher Engineering Proceedings. 2, 751–761 (2015)
14. Oliveira Neto, M.S. de, Reis, A. da C., Stender, G.H.C., Costa, W.O. da, Souza, C.G.: Avaliação dos Critérios de Seleção de Transportador e Modais para o Escoamento da Safra de Soja Brasileira, (2015)
15. Reis, J.G.M., Vendrametto, O., Naas, I. de A., Costabile, L.T., Machado, S.T.: Avaliação das Estratégias de Comercialização do Milho em MS Aplicando o Analytic Hierarchy Process (AHP), (2016)
16. Goldsmith, P.D., Hirsch, R.: The Brazilian Soybean Complex, https://ideas.repec.org/a/ags/aaeach/94417.html, (2006)
17. Meade, B., Puricelli, E., McBride, W., Valdes, C., Hoffman, L., Foreman, L., Dohlman, E.: Corn and Soybean Production Costs and Export Competitiveness in Argentina, Brazil, and the United States. United States Department of Agriculture, Washington (2016)

18. Todeschini, M.H.: Progresso genético da soja no Brasil quanto à caracteres fisiológicos e agronômicos, http://repositorio.utfpr.edu.br:8080/jspui/handle/1/3061, (2018)
19. Torres, O., Fagundes, M.B.B., Figueiredo, A.M.R., Tredezini, C.A. de O.: Impacto da Implantação do Custo do Pedágio na BR-163 em Relação ao Transporte de Soja do Estado de Mato Grosso. Rev. Econ. Sociol. Rural. 55, 533–550 (2017). https://doi.org/10.1590/1234-56781806-94790550307
20. Kussano, M.R., Batalha, M.O.: Custos logísticos agroindustriais: avaliação do escoamento da soja em grão do Mato Grosso para o mercado externo. Gestão & Produção. 19, 619–632 (2012)
21. Pacheco, E.A., Drohomeretski, E., Cardoso, P.A.: A decisão do modal de transporte através da metodologia AHP na aplicação da logística enxuta: um estudo de caso. In: IV Congresso Nacional de Excelência em Gestão. , Niterói (2008)
22. Calazans, F.M., DUTRA, T.M., BARBOSA, M.V., MONTEIRO, A. de S., COUTINHO, R.E.T.: Gestão de Frotas no Transporte Rodoviário de Carga. In: XI Simpósio de Excelência em Gestão e Tecnologia. p. 1–16. SEGeT, Rio de Janeiro (2014)
23. DNIT, D.N. de I. de T.: Quadro de Fabricantes de Veículos. Departamento Nacional de Infra-estrutura de Transportes, Brasília (2012)
24. Roulet, M.C.: Uma aplicação de análise multicritério para a coordenação vertical no transporte de granéis sólidos agrícolas., (2014)
25. Klvac, R., Kolařík, J., Volná, M., Drápela, K.: Fuel Consumption in Timber Haulage. Croatian Journal of Forest Engineering. 34, 229–240 (2013)
26. Guimarães, P.P.: Consumo de combustível em duas combinações veiculares de carga no transporte rodoviário florestal, (2014)
27. Empresa de Pesquisa Energética: Plano Decenal de Expansão de Energia 2026. Ministério de Minas e Energia, Brasília (2017)
28. CNT, C.N. do T.: Transporte rodoviário: desempenho do setor, infraestrutura e investimentos. Confederação Nacional do Transporte, Brasília (2017)
29. Correa, V.H.C., Ramos, P.: A precariedade do transporte rodoviário brasileiro para o escoamento da produção de soja do Centro-Oeste: situação e perspectivas. Revista de Economia e Sociologia Rural. 48, 447–472 (2010). https://doi.org/dx.doi.org/10.1590/S0103-20032010000200009
30. ANTAQ, A.N. de T.A.: Aumenta participação do Arco Norte no escoamento da soja e do milho para exportação. ANTAQ, Brasília (2019)
31. Danao, M.-G.C., Zandonadi, R.S., Gates, R.S.: Development of a grain monitoring probe to measure temperature, relative humidity, carbon dioxide levels and logistical information during handling and transportation of soybeans. Computers and Electronics in Agriculture. 119, 74–82 (2015). https://doi.org/10.1016/j.compag.2015.10.008
32. Toloi, R.C., Reis, J.G.M., Vendrametto, O., Machado, S.T., Rodrigues, E.F.: How to Improve the Logistics Issues During Crop Soybean in Mato Grosso State Brazil? In: 6th International Conference on Information Systems, Logistics and Supply Chain. KEDGE Business School, Bordeaux (2016)
33. IEA, I.: CO2 Emissions From Fuel Combustion. Highlights 2015. International Energy Agency Paris (2015)
34. PBMC, P.B. de M.C.: Contribuição do Grupo de Trabalho 1 ao Primeiro Relatório de Avaliação Nacional do Painel Brasileiro de Mudanças Climáticas. Painel Brasileiro de Mudanças Climáticas, Rio de Janeiro (2013)
35. Vettorazzi, A.C., João, A.M. (Abner M., Rocha, F.V., CaixetaFilho, J.V.: Emissão de CO2 na Logística de Exportação de Soja do Mato Grosso: O Caso das Exportações pelo Arco Norte. Empreendedorismo, Gestão e Negócios. 6, 226–246 (2017)
36. CNT, C.N. do T.: Anuário CNT do Transporte 2016. Confederação Nacional do Transporte, Brasília (2016)
37. Péra, T.G., Bartholomeu, D.B., Su, C.T., Caixeta Filho, J.V.: Evaluation of green transport corridors of Brazilian soybean exports to China. Brazilian Journal of Operations & Production Management. 16, 398–412 (2019)
38. Toloi, M.N.V., Toloi, R.C., Silva, H.R.O., dos Reis, J.G.M., Bonilla, S.H.: CO2 Gas Emissions of Soybean Production and Transportation in the Different Macro-regions of Mato Grosso State - Brazil. In: Advances in Production Management Systems. Production Management for the Factory of the Future. Springer, Cham (2019)
39. ANP, A.N. do P., Gás Natural e Biocombustíveis: Sistema de levantamento de preços - Óleo Diesel em Mato Grosso. Agência Nacional do Petróleo, Gás Natural e Biocombustíveis - ANP, Rio de Janeiro (2019)
40. ATC, A. dos T. de C. do M.G.: Planilha de Custos por Km Rodado para o Estado de Mato Grosso, (2014)
41. IPCC: Climate Change 2014: Synthesis Report. Contribution of Working Groups I, II and III to the Fifth Assessment Report of the Intergovernmental Panel on Climate Change [Core Writing Team, R.K. Pachauri and L.A. Meyer (eds.)]. Intergovernmental Panel on Climate Change - IPCC, Geneva, Switzerland (2015)
42. Soliani, R.D., Argoud, A.R.T.T., Lopes, L.J.: A Sustentabilidade no Transporte Rodoviário de Cargas no Brasil. In: Simpósio de Engenharia de Produção. , Bauru (2017)
43. Fleury, P.: LOGÍSTICA NO BRASIL: SITUAÇÃO ATUAL E TRANSIÇÃO PARA UMA ECONOMIA VERDE. Fundação Brasileira para o Desenvolvimento Sustentável -, Rio de Janeiro - RJ (2012)

I L S 2020
INTERNATIONAL CONFERENCE ON INFORMATION SYSTEMS, LOGISTICS & SUPPLY CHAIN
Austin, Texas April 22-24, 2020

Humanitarian Response Readiness Metric for More Effective Relief Operations

Mahmut Metin Inan [1], Benoit Montreuil [1], Mohammed Faisal Ahmed[1], Matthieu Lauras[2]

[1] Georgia Institute of Technology, Atlanta, United States of America
[2] IMT Mines Albi, Albi, France
{minan@gatech.edu, benoit.montreuil@isye.gatech.edu, fasialahmed@gatech.edu, matthieu.lauras@mines-albi.fr}

Abstract. Natural disasters are affecting millions of people every year and causing billions of dollars of damage. Humanitarian relief operations aim to alleviate the suffering of the victims after the disaster. Performance of humanitarian relief can be measured with its efficiency and effectiveness. Coverage and speed of humanitarian response are two main components of its effectiveness. In this paper, we are trying to measure the response readiness of a humanitarian supply chain for an immediate disaster, by developing a metric called "humanitarian response readiness". With this metric, we are measuring the coverage and speed capabilities of the humanitarian supply chain together, with a priori measurement approach.

Keywords: Humanitarian Supply Chains, Humanitarian Response Readiness, Humanitarian Logistics

1. Introduction

Natural disasters are one of the biggest challenges humanity is facing today. Over the last 10 years, 3751 natural disasters affected two billion people and caused nearly 1.7 billion dollars of damage (IFRC 2018) [10] and with the effects of climate change, the frequency and intensity of the disasters are expected to increase around the world. After a natural disaster, many different organizations (NGOs, governmental agencies, military) start their relief operations to alleviate the suffering of the victims and prevent further damages and losses. Performance of relief operations depends on preparedness levels of the organizations before the disasters and their operational capabilities after the disaster. Preparedness activities are focused on facility location, prepositioning, resource allocation, transportation planning, and design of partnerships and contracts for relief operations after a disaster occurs [11]. Preparedness activities are directly affecting operational capabilities after the disaster.

Since human lives are at stake in case of a natural disaster, the performance of humanitarian relief operations has crucial importance. Although there are many challenges in defining performance indicators and measuring performance of humanitarian supply chains [12][15][17], it is obvious that with the increased number and intensity of disasters, scare resources, funding competition humanitarian organizations needed to be more and more efficient and effective in their operations [12]. According to Neely *et al.* (1995) [13], effectiveness is the extent to which the customer requirements are met, and efficiency is a measure of how economically the resources are utilized while providing a given level of customer satisfaction. In humanitarian context, it is possible to measure the efficiency by using financial metrics like the cost of relief operations (procurement, transportation, prepositioning, staff), funding, donations and their characteristics over time [12]. For the effectiveness, Beamon and Balcik (2008) [12] suggests using metrics related with response time and number of items supplied and supply availability, since they are measuring the characteristics of the supply chain. In this paper we are using a somehow similar approach and define two capabilities of a humanitarian supply chain 1) response speed capability,

the capability of conducting relief operations in a timely manner and 2) response coverage capability, the capability of satisfying the needs of as many victims as possible.
Current research measures these two capabilities separately by using performance data after the disaster. However, using response speed and coverage together is a better way of measuring effectiveness. For a successful humanitarian response, humanitarian supply chains need a certain level of speed and response coverage capabilities together. Since these two capabilities depend on the preparedness of the organizations, measuring coverage and speed capabilities together before the disaster and provide an idea about the expected performance of humanitarian relief would be very helpful for improving humanitarian response by changing or improving preparedness actions taken. However, due to the complex structure of humanitarian supply chains and uncertainties, it is not an easy task to forecast the expected performance in case of a natural disaster. In this paper we are trying to develop a metric called "*humanitarian response readiness*" that measures the response speed and response coverage capabilities of the humanitarian supply chain together with a certain budget, based on the current preparedness actions taken (i.e. supply-transport contracts, prepositioned inventories, facility locations, fleet, workforce).
In the following section we will provide a literature review, then in the third section continue with the conceptual and mathematical formulation of the humanitarian response readiness. For better understanding, we will provide an illustrative example and finalize the paper with a conclusion about our results and future work.

2. Literature Review

According to Lauras *et al.* (2010) [14], performance measurement can be used either to design/modify a system, or to control an existing system. There are two types of measurement approaches; *a priori* and *a posteriori*. A priori performance measurement helps decision making with the knowledge we have before experience, where a posteriori performance measurement is used to evaluate the quality of the most recent decisions after experience. In our humanitarian response readiness metric, we are trying to measure a priori performance of humanitarian supply chains.
Poister (2003) [15] explains the importance of performance measurement for nonprofit organizations: "Effective performance measurement systems can help nonprofit managers make better decisions, improve performance, and provide accountability". Measuring the performance of humanitarian supply chains is harder than commercial supply chains, in which the performance metrics are relatively clear and easy to measure [16]. In humanitarian supply chains selecting appropriate performance metrics and measuring them is hard due to its complex structure. Kaplan (2001) [17] suggests that success for nonprofit organizations should be measured by how effectively and efficiently they perform under financial considerations. Beamon and Balcik (2008) [12] uses three performance metric types; resource, output, and flexibility, to measure the efficiency, effectiveness, and ability to respond to a changing environment respectively. Cost is taken as the predominant resource metric and cost of supplies, distribution costs, and inventory holding costs are used as the dominant resource metrics of humanitarian supply chains. The outcome metrics are categorized as the ones related with 1) response time and 2) the number of items supplied and supply availability. From here we can see that the paper relates effectiveness with response time and items supplied, similar to our response speed and response coverage definitions. However, the paper uses a posteriori performance measurement approach and measures response time and items supplied separately, while we aim to measure response speed and response coverage together with one metric with a priori performance measurement approach. Santarelli *et al.* (2015) [18] provides five different performance indicators to measure the response time, namely "project duration, average response time, delivery date reliability, goods-to-delivery time and presence of an organization's warehouse in loco". Here we can relate the average response time with our response speed however again the paper uses a posteriori performance measurement approach. Also, the last indicator can be related to response coverage, but it is only denoting the presence of a warehouse with prepositioned inventories within a 200km radius of the disaster area. So, it can only give an idea about the response coverage but cannot be used for measuring it. Although there are some other papers that are using metrics to measure response effectiveness none of them are using a priori performance measurement approach and measure response speed and response coverage together.
To best of our knowledge, there is not a metric that is developed for measuring the response readiness of a humanitarian supply chain. However, the term readiness appears very frequently in the papers about supply chain resilience. Ponomarov and Holcomb (2009) [1] states that to reduce the risk of possible damages,

supply chains must be designed to incorporate event readiness, provide an efficient and effective response, and be capable of recovering to their original state or even better post the disruptive event. This is the essence of supply chain resiliency according to writers. The papers about resilience consider readiness as being prepared for potential interruptions and their effects, and they are not interested in developing a metric that shows coverage and speed capabilities of a supply chain [2][3][4]. So, our definition of humanitarian response readiness is different than the readiness mentioned in resilience literature.
We can relate humanitarian response readiness with preparedness phase activities of a humanitarian organization. In the humanitarian context, disaster management is considered as a process with four sequential stages, mitigation, preparedness, response, and recovery. The mitigation stage aims to minimize the effects of the disaster whereas the preparedness stage aims at decreasing the response time by the advanced procurement and pre-positioning of needed supplies [5]. Papers in that area focus on decisions about facility locations, prepositioned inventory, procurement decisions, etc., however, there is not any metric developed to measure the response readiness of a humanitarian system under the current working scheme [5][6][7][8]. The papers are trying to optimize the response of the humanitarian organizations, not giving them an idea about their readiness in case of an immediate disaster.

3. Humanitarian Response Readiness

In this section, we will introduce our humanitarian response readiness metric, both conceptually and mathematically. After explanations, we will provide an illustrative example based on our experiences and efforts during a project with the Indonesian Red Cross.

3.1. Conceptual Model

In this section, we will first explain the concept of humanitarian response readiness and continue with its mathematical formulation. We mentioned that the humanitarian response readiness metric will be measuring response coverage and response speed capabilities together. Figure-1 shows the relations between humanitarian response readiness and different capabilities of the humanitarian supply chain.

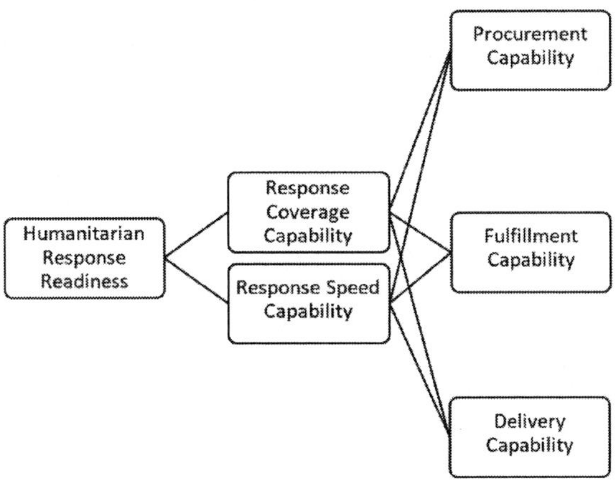

Figure 1: Humanitarian Response Readiness

This figure will constitute the core of this section and we try to explain the relations represented. First, the importance of measuring response speed capability and response coverage capability together with one metric should be discussed. Each humanitarian organization has its target for the percentage of victims to cover through a time frame. For example, an organization may aim to reach the disaster area in the first 6 hours and deliver items for 20, 40, 60 and 100 percent of the victims in the first 12, 24, 30 and 48 hours respectively. This implies that response speed and coverage are not independent performance indicators since they are related to each other. Consider an organization that has enough prepositioned inventory or

procurement capability for covering a hundred percent of the demand, if the organization does not have enough delivery capability it will fail to meet with the target delivery times. Although a hundred percent of the demand will be met at the end, the organization will not be successful. It is the same for the reverse case, if the organization has the capability of delivering items very fast but it is not capable of covering enough demand, humanitarian response is again unsuccessful. We can conclude that response coverage and response speed capabilities are not meaningful performance indicators by themselves and organizations need high response speed and response coverage capabilities together to be successful in humanitarian response.
The effect of these capabilities on humanitarian response can be seen in the following charts. Figure-2 shows the expected value of cumulative demand after the disaster (with black) with cumulative supply scenarios (with red). The shape can change in length and wide based on the disaster and affected region, this figure is adapted from the expected number of arrivals figure in [5]. In the ideal case, the cumulative supply curve should not drop below the cumulative demand curve, which means a shortage. Figure-2 shows some possible scenarios;

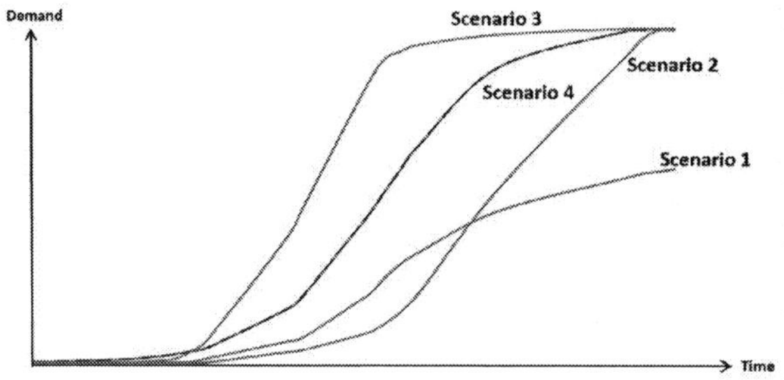

Figure 2: Expected demand with possible supply scenarios

- In scenario-1 organization fails to meet with the demand through time periods, response coverage capacity is not enough for meeting with the expected demand
- In scenario-2 organization meets with demand at the end, however, it faces with shortage until the end. Both capacities might be bounding through time. For example, the organization may have enough coverage capability but may not be able to deliver items on time or vice versa. Moreover, the organization may not have enough response coverage and speed capability at the same time.
- In scenario-3 organization meets with demand and it is capable of meeting with higher demand
- In scenario-4 organization follows the demand exactly

The shape of a given supply curve can be changed in several ways as represented in Figure-3;

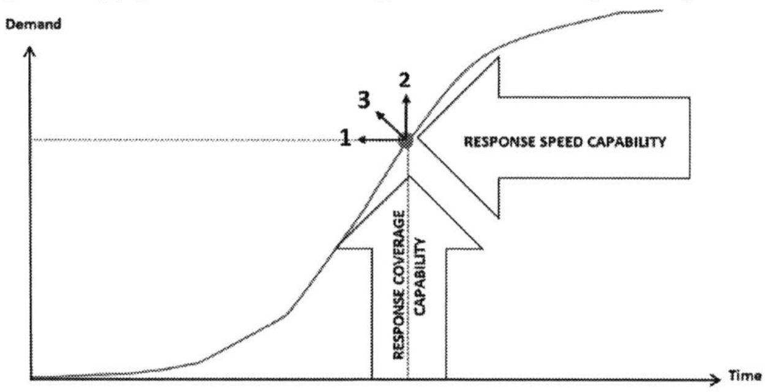

Figure 3: Effects of increasing different capabilities on the supply curve

1. If response coverage capability is enough but response speed capability is bounding, by keeping coverage capability constant and improving speed capability, the supply curve will in direction 1. This means, for delivering the same number of items, we need less time.

2. If response coverage capability was bounding and response speed capability was enough, by keeping speed capability constant and improving coverage capability, the supply curve will move in direction 2. Which means that we can deliver more items for the same time period.
3. If both capabilities are bounding, then both should be improved. Then the curve will move in the direction of 3. Which means that we can deliver more items in less time.

Figure-2 and Figure-3 shows how response speed and response coverage capabilities are affecting humanitarian response, however there are other capabilities of humanitarian supply chain that are affecting these two capabilities. The response speed and response coverage capabilities are directly related to the *procurement, fulfillment* and *delivery capabilities* of the organization. For procurement organizations work with both local and global suppliers around the world. Both options have their own advantages and disadvantages [7]. Choosing local suppliers can provide faster delivery, higher cultural acceptance and stimulate the local economy, however that option cannot guarantee quality, availability and price stability. Choosing global suppliers will increase the availability of high-quality items and organizations can also get some discounts, however, there will be higher transportation cost and longer lead times. The performance of suppliers affects both response speed and response coverage. With higher product availabilities and lower process organizations can increase their response coverage, wherewith lower lead times they can deliver relief items in a shorter time period. We can relate the procurement capability of an organization with the best possible performance of suppliers in terms of number of items procured and delivery time required, with a given budget. Fulfillment capabilities are related to organizations' ability to meet with demand after the disaster from their prepositioned inventory. Location and level of prepositioned inventory and performance of warehouses in dispatching are very important for fulfillment capabilities. If an organization can preposition enough items close to the disaster area and can start dispatching those items quickly after the disaster, it will be able to deliver more items in a shorter time after the disaster. Which implies improved response speed and response coverage capabilities. Delivery capabilities represent the organizations' ability to transport items, equipment, vehicles and humans from or to disaster location in a timely manner. Organizations may have their own fleet (trucks, planes, ships) or rent after the disaster. In any case, the fleet should be able to carry the required items to the disaster area promptly on time. With increased delivery capacities, it is possible to deliver more items in a shorter time. We are trying to measure how ready the humanitarian supply chain to meet with the demand after a disaster, considering these relations and financial constraints.

3.2. Mathematical Model

In this section, the formulation of the humanitarian response readiness metric will be presented with an explanation of the needed parameters.

Sets

$Items, I = \{1,2, \dots . |I|\}$

$Disaster\ scenarios, S = \{1,2, \dots |S|\}$

$Time\ periods\ after\ the\ disaster, T = \{0,1,2, \dots |T|\}$

Parameters

$\boldsymbol{D_{i,s,t}}$: $Expected\ average\ cumulative\ demand\ for\ item\ i\ under\ scenario\ s\ for\ period\ t, i \in I, t \in T, s \in S$

$\boldsymbol{E_i}$: $Weight\ of\ item\ i,\quad \sum_{i \in I} E_i = 1$

$\boldsymbol{Y_{i,s,t}}$: $Maximum\ amount\ of\ item\ i\ that\ can\ be\ delivered\ until\ the\ end\ of\ time\ period\ t\ under\ scenario\ s$

$\boldsymbol{p_s}$: $Probability\ of\ occurance\ of\ scenario\ s$

$\boldsymbol{r_i}$: $response\ readiness\ for\ item\ i\ over\ all\ scenarios$

$$r_i = \sum_{t \in T} \frac{1}{T} \sum_{s \in S} p_s \frac{min\{D_{i,s,t}, Y_{i,s,t}\}}{D_{i,s,t}} .\ for\ \forall i\ such\ that\ D_{i,s,t} \neq 0 \quad (1)$$

$\boldsymbol{R}$: $Response\ readiness\ of\ the\ whole\ system\ over\ all\ items\ and\ scenarios$

$$R = \sum_{i \in I} E_i r_i \quad (2)$$

The idea behind the readiness is very simple, how ready the system is to respond to different disasters with different intensities in different locations. Using scenarios about possible disasters in different locations might be a good way of dealing with the uncertainties. To create scenarios for a region or country, we can use data about disaster history. In each scenario, we need the disaster(s)' type, location, intensity, affected population and can derive expected demand from these parameters. After, by using response coverage and response speed capabilities we are obtaining maximum possible supply ($Y_{i,s,t,l}$) with given budget constraints and derive our response readiness metric by comparing demand and supply. First, we obtain response readiness for each type of relief item, then their weighted sums give the overall response readiness of the whole system over all items and scenarios. It is obvious that $Y_{i,s,t,l}$ depends on the decisions of the organization. It is possible to maximize the $Y_{i,s,t,l}$ with an optimization model, which can be a topic of another paper. Next, we will provide an illustrative example.

3.3. An Illustrative Example

Since we are working with the Indonesian Red Cross Society, we created this illustrative example about Indonesia based on our field experiences and data available at [9]. The values in the example are not real but created in a logical way; since the locations of the warehouses and provinces are real, we were able to create lead times and delivery times based on these locations. During our visit to Indonesia, we collected data and information about the working scheme of the organization. Indonesia has the world's 4th largest population with nearly 268 million people [20]. It has 34 provinces and almost 14 thousand islands, which makes transportation inside the country very complicated. Indonesian Red Cross Society has six regional warehouses to respond to disasters all around the country. In our illustrative example, time periods are 12 hours and we have 9 periods. Also, we assumed that there are six regional warehouses and each of them is serving preassigned provinces in their regions. Figure-4 shows regional warehouses and provinces.

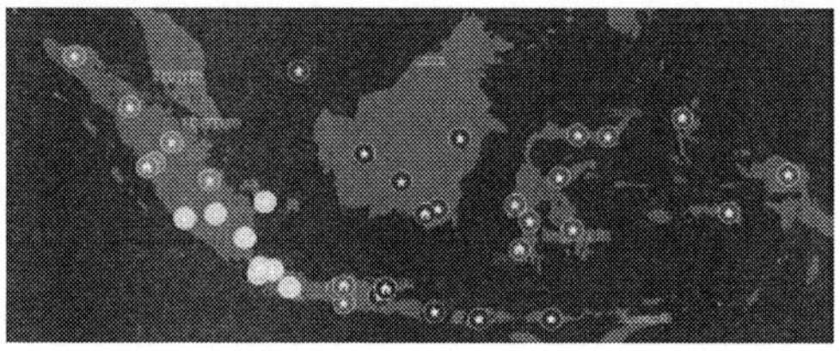

Figure 4: Provinces and regional warehouses

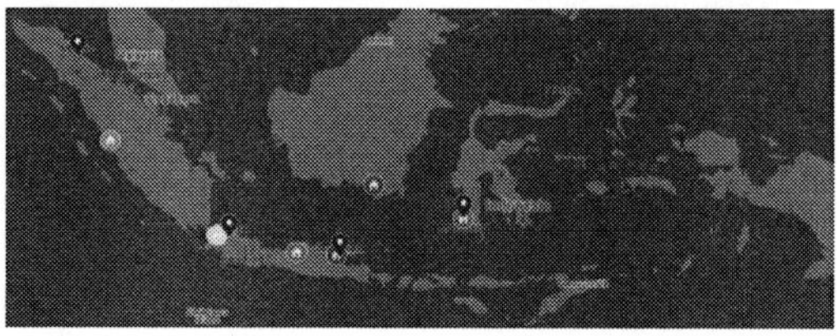

Figure 5: Location of suppliers and regional warehouses

We considered five relief items, representing five main kits Indonesian Red Cross is distributing, with different usage values for the length of time periods. Based on current practices, we assigned some prepositioned inventory for each warehouse, between 2000 and 5000 items. We assume that each item's priority is the same. For cumulative demand, we used the usage values for periods and multiplied them with number of arrivals obtained from the arrival function adapted from [5], which is a logistics function;

$$f(x) = \frac{L}{1 + e^{-k(x-x_0)}} \quad (3)$$

Where x_0 is the sigmoid midpoint, taken as 36 hours [5], L is the curve's maximum value, taken as total affected people in scenario k is the logistic growth rate, taken as 1. For each item, we used five different suppliers (Figure-5) with different capacities, price, and lead time values. Lead times are assumed to be exponentially distributed. We assumed that the items purchased from a supplier directly go to warehouses and delivered from there, without waiting for other suppliers, with some exponentially distributed delivery time. For supplier selection, it is assumed that the organization will always prefer the cheapest suppliers and try to buy as much as possible from the cheapest supplier. Each warehouse has a fleet of 5 identical trucks with a capacity of 10000 for each type of items, for simplicity we assume volumes of items are the same. Also, for simplicity, we assumed that the ships are available at seaports when they are needed. For scenarios, we used the EM-DAT [9] database which contains data of more than 21,000 disasters since 1900. EM-DAT provides information about the type, start-end date, location of the disaster and the number of affected people. EM-DAT disaster data for Indonesia from January 1980 to March 2019 was used in this study. Only earthquakes, floods, and volcanic activities were considered since other disaster types did not have enough available data. Each disaster was categorized as high, medium or low intensity, based on the number of affected people in the disaster. Categorization made by using the percentiles of affected people; the high-intensity disasters belonged to 69 to 100 percentile range, medium intensity disasters belonged to 33 percentile to 69 percentile range and low-intensity disasters belonged to 0 to 33 percentile range of the number of affected people for the corresponding disaster. While creating scenarios we assumed that some disasters may affect the performance of the organization together, if their occurrence time is close to each other. So, we grouped the disasters that happened in the following seven days of an already occurred disaster and assumed they happened at the same time, in other words, the organization needs to face them at the same time. Then, we get the frequencies of different disaster combinations with their intensities. The probability of a scenario is obtained by dividing the corresponding occurrence frequency to total occurrence frequency. Figure 6 shows different types of scenarios, respectively; multiple disasters (earthquake and flood) happened in different locations, single disaster (volcanic activity) affecting single province, and single disaster (flood) affecting multiple provinces.

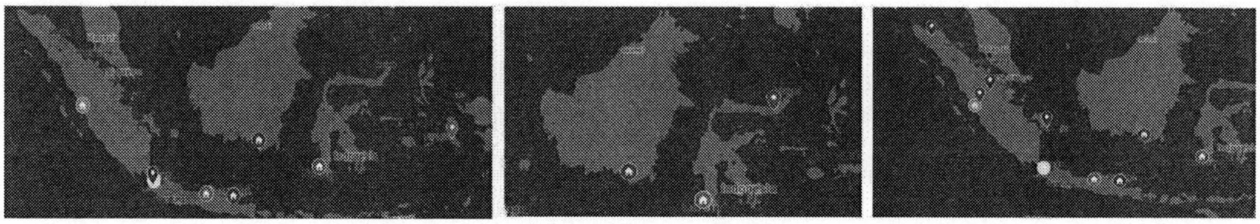

Figure 6: Scenario examples

For each scenario, we selected one representative from the database. After getting all the scenarios, we calculated the humanitarian response readiness with a budget of $100,000 and obtained the readiness value of the humanitarian supply chain. Table-1 shows $\sum_{s\in S} p_s \frac{min\{D_{i,s,t},Y_{i,s,t}\}}{D_{i,s,t}}$ values, which is the expected average fraction of demand met overall scenarios, for each item for each time period. By getting the average of each row, we obtain r_i values for each item. We found r_i values as 0.77, 0.74, 0.81, 0.85 and 0.77 respectively. Since we assume each item has equal importance, our final response readiness value was 79%. This response readiness means that the humanitarian supply chain, with its all components, can meet with overall 79% of expected demand through different time periods in case of a possible set of disaster scenarios. It should be noted that it is possible to get better readiness values under the same conditions with the same budget, by making better decisions. For example, increasing prepositioned inventory levels to 10000 results in an 82% response readiness. As shown here, organizations can use the readiness metric to see the effects of different improvements and changes in their preparedness to their expected performances in case of a disaster and make decisions about how to spend their money accordingly. It is also useful in highlighting the effects of different prepositioned inventory levels or different supplier selections through a single metric. Being able to test the expected results of their actions and decisions before the disaster occurrence is very important, since human lives are at stake in case of a natural disaster.

Table 1: Expected average fraction of demand met over all scenarios for each item and period

Period / Items	1	2	3	4	5	6	7	8	9	Average
1	0.90	0.86	0.80	0.76	0.74	0.72	0.72	0.72	0.72	0.77
2	0.87	0.81	0.77	0.74	0.71	0.68	0.68	0.68	0.68	0.74
3	0.87	0.87	0.84	0.82	0.80	0.78	0.78	0.78	0.78	0.81
4	0.99	0.92	0.89	0.87	0.83	0.80	0.80	0.80	0.80	0.86
5	0.90	0.86	0.80	0.76	0.74	0.72	0.72	0.72	0.72	0.77

4. Conclusion

The complexity of humanitarian supply chains makes it harder to predict the performance of humanitarian response in case of an immediate disaster. If humanitarian organizations can see their expected response performance in case of a disaster, they can better prepare and see the weaknesses of their system. In this paper, we introduce measuring the humanitarian response readiness of a humanitarian supply chain, by using response speed and response coverage capabilities with a priori performance measurement approach.

Having such a metric can help humanitarian organizations to analyze the humanitarian supply chain with a holistic view and see the effects of different improvements and changes on expected response performance after the disaster. Although donations are very important in humanitarian relief, the current assessment of response readiness does not consider them. For different disasters and intensities, we can come up with expected donations for each time period and add it to scenarios as well. At first look, this metric can be seen as a service level indicator, however, we are trying to consider different capabilities (procurement, fulfillment, and delivery) and the relations between different components of the humanitarian supply chain (contracts, agreements, capacities). Building on this exploratory research, we are planning to explore the consequences of low readiness values (i.e. more fatalities and damages, higher costs, etc.) and model how to optimize readiness for the whole humanitarian supply chain.

5. References

1. Ponomarov, Y.S. and Holcomb, M.C. (2009), "Understanding the concept of supply chain resilience", The International Journal of Logistics Management, Vol. 20 No. 1, pp. 124-143.
2. Chowdhury, M. M. H., & Quaddus, M. (2016). Supply chain readiness, response and recovery for resilience. *Supply Chain Management: An International Journal, 21*(6), 709–731. doi: 10.1108/scm-12-2015-0463
3. Hohenstein, N.-O., Feisel, E., Hartmann, E., & Giunipero, L. (2015). Research on the phenomenon of supply chain resilience. *International Journal of Physical Distribution & Logistics Management, 45*(1/2), 90–117. doi: 10.1108/ijpdlm-05-2013-0128
4. N Sheffi, Yossi & Rice, Jr, James. (2005). A Supply Chain View of the Resilient Enterprise. MIT Sloan Management Review. 47.
5. Rawls, C. G., & Turnquist, M. A. (2012). Pre-positioning and dynamic delivery planning for short-term response following a natural disaster. *Socio-Economic Planning Sciences, 46*(1), 46–54. doi: 10.1016/j.seps.2011.10.002
6. Rodríguez-Espíndola, O., Albores, P., & Brewster, C. (2018). Disaster preparedness in humanitarian logistics: A collaborative approach for resource management in floods. *European Journal of Operational Research, 264*(3), 978–993. doi: 10.1016/j.ejor.2017.01.021
7. Duran, S., Gutierrez, M. A., & Keskinocak, P. (2011). Pre-Positioning of Emergency Items for CARE International. *Interfaces, 41*(3), 223–237. doi: 10.1287/inte.1100.0526
8. Rawls, C. G., & Turnquist, M. A. (2006). Pre-positioning of Emergency Supplies for Disaster Response. *2006 IEEE International Symposium on Technology and Society*. doi: 10.1109/istas.2006.4375894
9. The International Disaster Database, https://www.emdat.be/database
10. IFRC (International Federation of Red Cross and Red Crescent Societies), World Disasters Report 2018. Available online at: https://media.ifrc.org/ifrc/world-disaster-report-2018/ (accessed 19 October 2019).
11. Melih Çelik, Özlem Ergun, Ben Johnson, Pınar Keskinocak, Álvaro Lorca, Pelin Pekgün, Julie Swann. Humanitarian Logistics. In INFORMS TutORials in Operations Research. Published online: 14 Oct 2014; 18-49.
12. Beamon, B. and Balcik, B. (2008), "Performance measurement in humanitarian relief chains", International Journal of Public Sector Management, Vol. 21 No. 1, pp. 4-25.
13. Neely, A., Gregory, M. and Platts, K. (1995), "Performance measurement system design", International Journal of Operations & Production Management, Vol. 15 No. 4, pp. 80-116.
14. Matthieu Lauras, Guillaume Marquès, Didier Gourc. Towards a multi-dimensional project Performance Measurement System. Decision Support Systems, Elsevier, 2010, Volume 48 (Issue 2), pp.Pages 342-353. ff10.1016/j.dss.2009.09.002ff. ffemse-00682715f
15. Poister, T.H. (2003), Measuring Performance in Public and Nonprofit Organizations, Jossey-Bass, San Francisco, CA.
16. Sawhill, J. C., & Williamson, D. (2001). Mission Impossible?: Measuring Success in Nonprofit Organizations. Nonprofit Management and Leadership, 11(3), 371–386. doi: 10.1002/nml.11309
17. Kaplan, R.S. (2001), "Strategic performance measurement and management in nonprofit organizations", Nonprofit Management and Leadership, Vol. 11 No. 3, pp. 353-70.
18. Santarelli, G., Abidi, H., Klumpp, M. and Regattieri, A. (2015), "Humanitarian supply chains and performance measurement schemes in practice", International Journal of Productivity and Performance Management, Vol. 64 No. 6, pp. 784-810. https://doi.org/10.1108/IJPPM-11-2013-0185
19. The World Bank, https://data.worldbank.org/indicator/sp.pop.totl?most_recent_value_desc=true

I L S 2020
INTERNATIONAL CONFERENCE ON INFORMATION SYSTEMS, LOGISTICS & SUPPLY CHAIN
Austin, Texas April 22-24, 2020

Logistic requirements considering environmental sensitive demand: evidence from the French food distribution sector

Laura Palacios-Argüello [1], Salomée Ruel [2], Jesus Gonzalez-Feliu [1], Natacha Gondran [1]

[1] Ecole des mines de Saint-Etienne, UMR 5600 EVS, France
[2] CERIIM La Rochelle Business School - Excelia Group, La Rochelle, France & CERAG, Grenoble Alpes University, Grenoble, France
{laura.palacios@emse.fr, salomee.ruel@gmail.com, jesus.gonzalez-feliu@emse.fr, natacha.gondran@emse.fr}

Abstract. As described in the literature, the demand characteristics could influence the food distribution configuration. The aim of this paper is to explain how these demand characteristics can be used to describe the logistic requirements for food distribution configuration. With this aim, the chosen methodological approach integrates a literature review, interviews of stakeholders involved in the distribution system and a survey to the French industrial sector. Results describe the logistic requirements from for food distribution found in the literature review according to the different actors, products and distribution configuration adopted. Furthermore, the logistic requirements extracted from the literature review are compared with the primary data collected to establish the main logistic requirements linked to the conscious demand in the food supply chain for the food distribution configuration. The main logistic requirements defined are linked to facility location, supplier selection and distribution optimization due to the logistic platforms and transportation strategies development. Finally, the results of this research provide information to food supply chain actors when designing the food distribution circuits aiming to answer to conscious demand characteristics that are emerging.

Keywords: Logistic requirements; food distribution system; environmental sensitive demand

1. Introduction

To feed the world, food logistic organization is a crucial factor [1]. The goal of the urban food supply system is to satisfy the food city requirements considering the quality and quantity specifications demanded [2]. Nowadays, there is an increasing need for developing food distribution strategies on a social, economic, and environmental sound basis that have been encouraging a research effort in the fields of food system sustainability. This is reinforced by increased product quality demands [1] and the increasing environmentally consciousness of consumers [3].

Oglethorpe and Heron [3] listed emerging solutions that encourage the reduction of large distribution networks. It involves less processed food, packaging reduction, more organic products and local products consumption making the food distribution process less environmentally damaging. This is one of the reasons why these changes in food quality and consumptions patterns influence changes in how the food is supplied and distributed, and consequently, the way the food distribution circuits are designed. This makes possible to configure different food distribution schemas and a variety of distribution channels by which food is supplied to final consumers [4].

Consequently, the food distribution systems become extremely divers and complex, increasing the complexity of defining and classifying the consequent supply chains []. This complexity can be reflected in the number of food actors involved, the logistic requirements according to the food type and the distribution configuration adopted [4].

With the aim of decreasing this network complexity and of satisfying consumers who demand greater quality and traceability in the food supply chains, alternative forms of consumption in conventional food systems have emerged [1][**Erreur ! Source du renvoi introuvable.**][6]. One of those is the consumption of local products restringing a distribution configuration with a maximum of one (or ideally none) intermediary between the producer and the consumer, reducing externalities caused by conventional long distribution circuits [6].
As described above, the demand characteristics may influence the food distribution configuration. This paper explains how these demand characteristics can be used to describe the logistic requirements for food distribution configuration. With this aim, the paper begins with the definition of the food flows in the distribution system, then explains the food supply and distribution actors, types of products and detail the different configurations of distribution circuits, channels, and networks. Furthermore, it explains the logistic requirements for food distribution according to the different actors, products and distribution circuits adopted. Considering the institutional catering as a sector with a stronger environmental consciousness demand [8], the logistic requirements are identified and compared based on the primary and secondary data collected to establish the main logistic requirements linked to the conscious demand in the food supply chain for the food distribution configuration.

2. Literature review

This subsection explains the main logistic requirements found in the academic literature regarding the actors, the types of products and the distribution schemas adopted. According to Fredriksson and Liljestrand [1], the main stakeholders in the food supply chain can be grouped in 4 categories:

- primary producers: agriculture producers which grow the raw fresh products;
- industrial producers: transformation companies which transform raw products into agro industrial products;
- wholesalers and distribution companies which deal with the distribution processes,
- and retailers which remain the interface with end-consumer.

Moreover, in food retailing and Ho.Re.Ca. (Hotels, Restaurants and Catering), it is important to distinguish between independent retailers, organized/franchised/corporate retailers and grocery stores [9].

The logistic requirements according to the food product types impose constraints such as: perishability, sensitivity to the surrounding environment, seasonality in demand and supply, the dependency on natural conditions for production and the demands on quality and traceability [1]. Moreover, food quality regarding the sensory properties of fresh products (taste, odor, appearance, color, size, and image), and the food traceability regarding the product safety issues are important [1]. For chilled products, demands on the duration and conditions of storage, processing, and transportation, which limit the possibilities of distribution are important. Finally, for frozen products, the warehouse location, either close to the harvest/production or close to the market is important.
Nevertheless, various authors [10][4][11] define as logistic requirements for all types of food products:

- Short lead times and just-in-time deliveries.
- Specific handling procedures.
- Regulatory issues (related to temperature requirements): thermal integrity of the shipments.

Compared with other non-highly perishable food and non-food supply chains, these logistic requirements result in higher consumption of energy, lower levels of consolidation and lower efficiency, leading to additional costs for transport operations [1].

Finally, [1] and [13] describe the main logistic requirements according to the distribution circuit adopted. [16] describes the main logistic requirements according to the distribution circuit and channel adopted. [1], [4] and [10] define the logistic requirements according to the food distribution channels regarding the place of food consumption: logistic requirements for food distribution "at home" consumption and for food distribution "out of home" consumption. Table 1 summarizes this overview.

Table 1: Logistics characteristics and requirements for each stakeholder's category in the food supply chain (authors' elaboration, adapted from [1], [4] and [10].

Stakeholders	Logistics characteristics and requirements
Primary producers	• They need to ensure food traceability and quality during the distribution process. • Collective organization to transport the food.
Industrial producers	• They are interested in delivery speed and geographical location, considering products' perishability and specific distribution solutions, being then cost-sensitive. • They prefer not to postpone production steps to suppliers, because they think logistics service providers have limited knowledge of food quality or lack flexibility. • They need manufacturing flexibility because of their relatively high product and volume variety.
Wholesalers	• They are interested in improving the distribution because for them transport costs are an important issue when source their fresh food products.
Retailers	• They are interested in distribution issues because a substantial part of the operations costs of food retailers are the logistics costs. • They depend on high availability on the store's shelves. • They are looking for well-developed distribution strategies that provide them with a competitive advantage. • They promote vertical integration within retailer's networks, focus on logistics management aiming to improve their logistics systems continuously.
Corporate retailers	• They invest heavily in distribution networks to take control of deliveries and increase overall supply chain efficiency. • They are interested in consolidating supplies upstream of stores at centralized distribution centers. • They are interested in achieving economies of scale through centralized, more consolidated and less frequent deliveries.
Independent retailers and Ho.Re.Ca.[1] sector	• They often do not control deliveries, a shippers are responsible for goods transport. • They usually do not pay for the transportation directly and have no contact with carriers except for the receipt of the delivery. • They are supplied frequently, because they have diverse suppliers, with a predominant use of their own vehicles and low vehicle fill rates.

3. Methodology

The proposed methodology is structured as follows:

1. First, a literature review of logistics requirements and needs was carried out to identify the main logistics requirements related to green food supply chains already shown in the literature. This phase has made the object of previous published works [11][12]. The results of this review allowed identifying a first set factors influencing green products' demand, in agrifood supply chains.
2. Once this first set of factors identified, a set of semi-structured interviews was carried out to affine those factors' set and pre-select a set of requirement categories and prepare a quantitative survey to go in-depth on the question.
3. From that pre-selection of requirements, a quantitative survey is carried out to define the most relevant requirements to green food supply chains. That survey will state on the potential of each requirement category to improve and green the food supply chains (a first part of the survey related to green logistics factors influencing products' demand is presented and analyzed in [11]).
4. With the survey's results, an assessment method is deployed to state on the potential gains (in terms of transport distances and/or times). This part is an ongoing work and will be not presented

[1] Hotels, Restaurants, Catering

here, but it is important to show that the present work aims at feeding a quantitative modelling and assessment approach.

3.1. Semi-structured interviews

The semi-structured interviews are based on open-end questions to stakeholders of the food supply for the school canteens in Saint-Etienne, France. To conduct semi-structured interviews and ensure high-quality research, two documents were created: an interview protocol, and an interview guide. The interview guide was developed following the IDPA model (in French: *Identification, Diagnostic, Prospective, Amélioration*[2]) and the details of the interviews, as well as the guides and protocols, are detailed in [8].

The IDPA model establishes four phases: (1) identification of the situation, (2) diagnosis, (3) foresight and (4) improvement. This guide was used to make the questions as effective and efficient as possible without forgetting any important issue to collect and document all impressions and experiences from each interview.

The sample was designed following the snowball sampling method [13]. In total, six semi-structured interviews were conducted. Such interviews can be seen as a preliminary work to identify variables to consider in the quantitative survey. Therefore, the results of the interviews where then completed with an exchange with a focus group of 6 researchers to ensure that a sufficient number of stakeholders were interviewed, as well as with a set of contextual secondary data read prior to the meetings, to increase trust-worthiness.

3.2. Survey

The survey questionnaire was part of a larger survey about environmental criteria (see [11]), which aim was to examine the influence of environmental quality on product's demand. However, we present here an unpublished part of the survey, the published part dealing with eco-responsible practices that influence products' demand, and this paper being related to the logistics requirements. That survey was completed with a set of 57 questions regarding how those criteria can be declined into logistics requirements, and starting from the list of requirements issued from the literature review and the semi-structure interviews, the importance of each requirement category and the presence of it in current logistics practices was asked. The survey was administrated through a self-completed questionnaire by internet on Limesurvey survey platform. It was conducted from April to August 2018. Firstly, a pilot survey was carried out among few professionals to validate the understanding of the questions.

Regarding the sample, the respondents' database was obtained from 2 different sources: (i) 6600 e-mails of managers of agro-industrial companies from the French Kompass database, and (ii) 850 emails of producers, transformers and distributors from the agro-industrial sector form the Auvergne-Rhône-Alpes Observatory. After e-mails validation, the final size of the population obtained was 5820. The composition of the sample of respondents is shown in Table 2. In total, 555 anonymous questionnaires were received, 307 questionnaires were excluded due to incomplete information, having 248 valid questionnaires (i.e. a response rate of 9.5%, which is high with respect to surveys of that nature, and a rate of valid responses of 4.2%, an average-high value for this type of surveys).

The majority of respondents work in small and medium companies. However, 43% of the total companies surveyed are part of a group. Industry types were grouped according to their main activity based on the NAF typology of the National Institute of Statistics and Economic Studies (INSEE), since it is the French standard used in freight demand modelling and has recently been compared to other classifications, like the NACE or NAICS for quantitative generation of logistics demand [15][16]. Despite some biases due to sampling and clustering of industries, the distribution among the study industries is fairly representative. The profile of the respondents is over 90% of high qualified profiles, including executive officers and engineers. This fact is confirmed by the years of experience that respondents have in that job, the majority have over 6 years of experience in that job, and more than 50% of the respondents have over 10 years of

[2] Identification, Diagnosis, Foresight, Improvement

experience. Finally, each area involved is between 10% and 20% of the total answers, which means that each area is fairly representative in the study.

Table 2: Respondents' demographics

		N	%
Company size (INSEE[3] classification)	Micro: 5 employees or less	13	5,2%
	Small: Between 6 and 50 employees	111	44,8%
	Medium: Between 51 and 250 employees	84	33,9%
	Large: Over 250 employees	40	16,1%
Group	Part of a group	107	43,1%
Industry type (INSEE classification)	Fruit and vegetables industry	19	7,7%
	Meats industry	43	17,3%
	Fish industry	13	5,2%
	Grain industry	16	6,5%
	Dairy industry	29	11,7%
	Beverage industry	10	4,0%
	Pasta and Bakery industry	34	13,7%
	Animal feed industry	17	6,9%
Job position	Executive officer	170	68,5%
	Engineer	55	22,2%
	Technician	20	8,1%
	External consultant	3	1,2%
Experience	Less than 2 years	19	7,7%
	Between 2 and 5 years	41	16,5%
	Between 6 and 10 years	42	16,9%
	Over 10 years	143	57,7%
Area	Corporate Social Responsability - Quality	139	19,8%
	Purchasing - Supplies	104	14,8%
	Production	101	14,4%
	Logistics	72	10,3%
	Marketing - Distribution	100	14,2%
	Communication / Marketing	84	12,0%
	Direction – Human Ressources Management	102	14,5%

4. Results

Based on the feedback from the development of the semi-structured interviews, it was possible to determine that the consumer's consciousness is growing and in consequence, there is a strong demand for sustainable food supply. This enforces the need for adapting the food distribution in order to improve its environmental performance while remaining food supply chains economically competitive.

One of the most common logistic requirements mentioned by all the interviewees was the need for strong involvement of local actors in the food supply. This logistic requirement can be explained as a crucial question of spatial distances; perceived as proximity circuit, a term used to characterize the length in local food approaches [17][18]. which means a short distance between producers and consumers. Another logistic requirement that was raised was the importance of the collaboration between the actors to improve the distribution system activities in the entire supply chain.

This collaboration requirement involves:

- Development of information system to share information about the demand quantities.
- Transportation sharing among the actors involved.
- The food consolidation strategies to be developed between producers to build a robust offer and

[3] National Institute of Statistics and Economic Studies in France

a centralized distribution.

This allows them to take control of deliveries and increase overall upstream distribution efficiency. Regarding the sustainability issues of the distribution system, another logistic requirement evoked was the request of using clean technologies during the food distribution. The retailers and the wholesalers use clean vehicles (gas powered freight vehicles) as a call-tender requirement from the public agent. Finally, another logistic requirement mentioned by all the interviewed was the need for a distribution network flexibility. This flexibility is requested in terms of food conditioning and quantities, but also in terms of delivery time and frequency.

Concerning the survey's results, we observe two main macro-categories of requirements. The first deals with purchasing practices and can be used to describe the logistic requirements for sustainable distribution related with the selection of local suppliers. From those, the most popular measures are the selection of local producers (which is selected by 69% of the as a solid way of increasing the product environmental quality), cooperation with suppliers (indicated by 55% of the respondents) or the establishment of a responsible purchasing policy (48%). Figure 1 shows the selection rate (in percentage) for each practice.

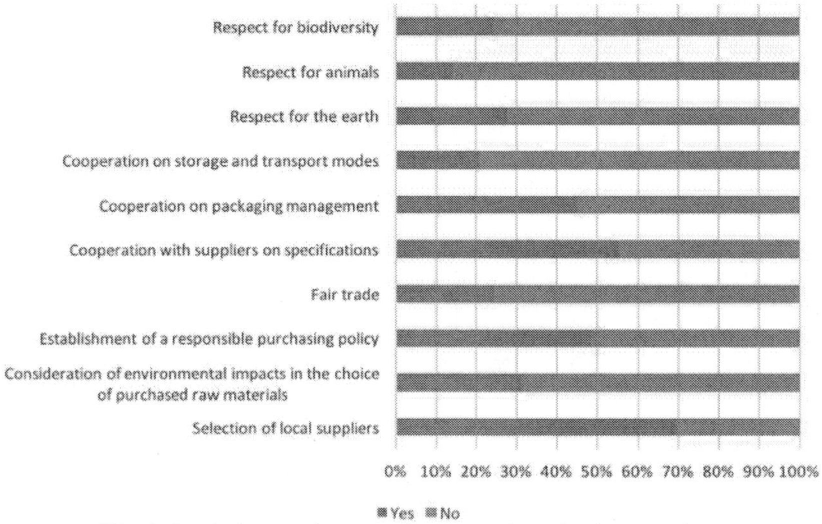

Fig. 1: Logistics requirements in terms of purchasing practices

The second macro-category is related to distribution practices that can be used to describe the logistic requirements for sustainable distribution. The respondents highlighted:

- the optimization of kilometers travelled for transportation and logistics pooling (60,7%)
- internal (warehouse or production) logistics collaboration (53,6%),
- location decisions: near to the market (35,7%) and suppliers (28,6%).

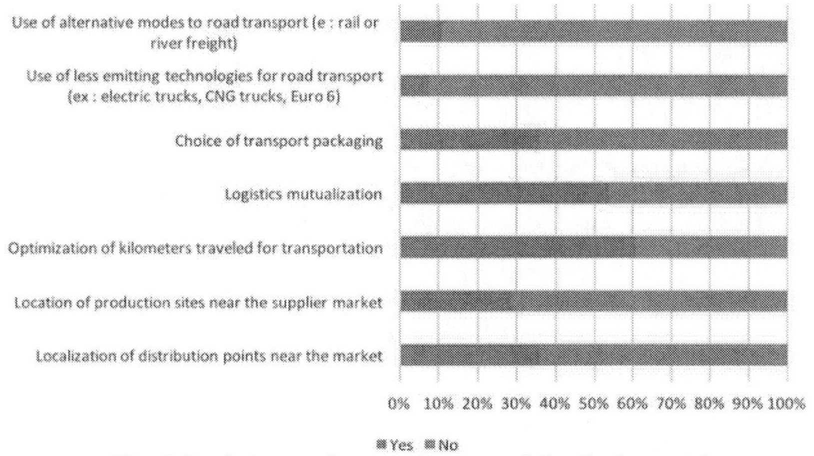

Fig. 2: Logistics requirements in terms of distribution practices

Figure 2 shows the main logistic requirements related to distribution practices. From that, we observe that practices that influence the product demand are related to the geographical proximity with the stakeholders. This impacts the decisions related to the facilities location such as (i) the location of distribution points close to the market and (ii) the location of production facilities close to suppliers.

5. Discussion and conclusion

The actors in the food supply chain are becoming more aware of the need for the food logistic organizations improvement regarding the increasing environmental conscious demand (Palacios-Argüello et al, 2018). Distribution is then a relevant topic of research nowadays with the logistic request of food products going more quickly from primary producers to consumers while they increasingly consider sustainability externalities. However, because of the different logistic requirements, different distribution configurations are needed that reduce the external impacts of food transportation by improving local supply and strengthening the collaboration among the actors of the food supply chain. Therefore, the decision support in distribution scheme configuration is one of the main research directions that will be followed.

Besides, regarding the logistic requirements collected and compared to the literature review, it is possible to affirm, thanks to the semi-directive interviews, that there are three kinds of logistic requirements that actually influence the food distribution configuration: (i) Distribution circuit design regarding the facility location that could be near to the market or near to the suppliers. (ii) Suppliers choice regarding the product characteristics requested and the proximity relationship considering the supplier location. (iii) Distribution optimization considering logistic platforms and transportation strategies (i.e. distance travelled reduction, increasing vehicle's fill rates, decreasing environmental impacts).

In conclusion, the logistic requirement for food distribution configuration collected from the environmental conscious demand characteristics can be: facility location (either near to the market or to the suppliers); the supplier selection (based on product characteristics and supplier location related to a proximity relationship); and the distribution optimization due to the logistic platforms and transportation strategies development (i.e. distance travelled reduction, increasing vehicle's fill rates, decreasing sustainability externalities).

However, the survey being conducted in a national context (France), context and culture factors would have an impact on the nature of responses and transferability issues. Concerning the relationship between cultural factors and the responses, it is difficult to address possible bias and influences with a unique, country-based survey, but two main elements can be stated here. The first is that the agrifood sector, although very heterogeneous, presents a subset of stakeholders having an international, global and standard supply chain orientation. As the surveyed companies were mainly from those supply chains, answers would follow the logic of such global practices, and reduce cultural influences, although they would not be zero. The second is that the methodology is replicable and transferrable, since data collection and processing methods remain standard and follow a scientific path, so they are able to be applied to other contexts. In that sense, replicating the methodology in other countries, if keeping a homogeneity of hypotheses and assumptions,

would allow to produce evidence of this cultural influence (this was not the aim of this research, but would be a possible future development).
Moreover, and to address other research limitations, the logistic requirements for food distribution discussed in this paper are only based on the methodological approach adopted to collect information from the literature review, the interviews of stakeholders involved in the distribution system and the results from a survey to the French industrial sector. However, it is possible that there are some logistic requirements imposed by the final consumers that are not considered. Finally, the results of this research provide information to food supply chain actors when designing the food distribution circuits aiming to answer to conscious demand characteristics that are emerging.

6. Acknowledgements

Part of this work was made in the context of ELUD project (LabEx IMU- Université de Lyon) for the semi-directive interviews and main analysis work and it was also supported by the French National Agency project CONCLUDE in the context of the AAPG 2015 of the ANR.

References

1. Fredriksson, A., Liljestrand, K. (2015). Capturing food logistics: a literature review and research agenda, Int. J. Log. Res. Ap., 18(1), pp. 16–34.
2. Morganti E.: Urban food planning, city logistics and sustainability: the role of the wholesale produce market. the cases of parma and bologna food hubs. Ph.D. dissertation, University of Bologna, Italy (2011)..
3. Oglethorpe D, Heron G.: Sensible operational choices for the climate change agenda," The International Journal of Logistics Management, 21(3), 538–557 (2010).
4. Morganti, E.: Food and urban logistics. In: Urban Logistics: Management, Policy and Innovation in a Rapidly Changing Environment, pp. 196-209 (Browne, M., Behrends, S., Woxenius, J., Giuliano, G., Holguin-Veras, J., eds.). London: Kogan Page (2018).
5. Skilton, P.F., Robinson, J.L. : Traceability and normal accident theory: how does supply network complexity influence the traceability of adverse events? J. Supply Chain Manag. 45(3), 40–53 (2019).
6. Gebresenbet, G., Nordmark, I., Bosona, T., Ljungberg, D.. Potential for optimised food deliveries in and around Uppsala city, Sweden. J. transp. Geogr. 19(6), 1456-1464 (2011).
7. Nsamzinshuti, A., Janjevic, M., Rigo, N., Ndiaye, A.B. Short Supply Chains as a Viable Alternative for the Distribution of Food in Urban Areas? Investigation of the Performance of Several Distribution Schemes. In: *Sustainable Freight Transport*, pp. 99-119 (Zeimpekis, V., Aktas, E., Bourlakis, M., Minis, I., eds.). Springer, Cham (2018).
8. Palacios-Argüello, L.: Characterization and assessment of distribution schemes for food supply and distribution systems considering environmentally sensitive demand. PhD Dissertation. Ecole de Mines de Saint-Etienne (2019).
9. Morganti E, Gonzalez-Feliu J.: City logistics for perishable products. the case of the parma's food hub. Case Stud. Transp. Policy 3(2), 120–128.
10. Blanquart, C. Gonçalves, A., Raton G., Vaillant, L. : Vecteurs et freins d'une logistique plus durable dans les circuits courts: le cas du nord-pas-de-calais. In 52ème colloque de l'Association de Science Régionale de Langue Française (ASRDLF 2015) Montpellier, France, 7-9 July (2015).
11. Palacios Argüello, L., Gondran, N., Nouira, I., Girard, M.A., Gonzalez-Feliu, J.: Which is the relationship between the product's environmental criteria and the product demand? Evidence from the French food sector, J. Clean Prod., in press (2019).
12. Palacios-Argüello, Girard, M. Gondran N, Gonzalez-Feliu, J and Laforest, V.: Product's environmental criteria definition related to supply chain management. In: Proceedings of the 7th International Conference on Information Systems, Logistics and Supply Chain, ILS, pp. 465–474 (2018).
13. Blanquart, C., Gonçalves, A., Vandenbossche, L., Kebir L., Petit, C., Traversac, J.-B.: The logistic leverages of short food supply chains performance in terms of sustainability. In: 12th World Conference on Transport Research, Lisbon, June (2010).
14. Gonçalves, A.: La performance des organisations logistiques des circuits courts de distribution: une analyse des déterminants et leviers d'amélioration. Ph.D. dissertation, Université Lille 1 (2013).
15. Gonzalez-Feliu, J., Sanchez-Diaz, I.: The influence of aggregation level and category construction on estimation quality for freight trip generation models. Transp. Res. E 121, 134-148 (2019).
16. Holguín-Veras, J., Ramírez-Ríos, D.G., González-Feliu, J., Caspersen, E., Rivera-González, C., González-Calderón, C.A., da Silva Lima, R.: Metropolitan Economies and the Generation of Freight and Service Activity: An International Perspective. In: Urban Logistics. Management, Policy and Innovation in a Rapidly Changing

Environment, pp. 19-51 (Browne, M., Behrends, S., Woxenius, J., Giuliano, G., Holguin-Veras, J., eds.). Kogan Page, London (2018).

17. Kebir L., Torre, A.: Geographical proximity and new short supply food chains. In: Creative Industries and Innovation in Europe: Concepts, Measures and Comparative Case Studies (Lazaretti, L., ed.), pp. 194-202. Routledge, vol. 57, (2012).
18. Torre, A., Wallet, F. The role of proximity relations in regional and territorial development processes. In: 54th Congress of the European Regional Science Association: "Regional development & globalisation: Best practices", 26-29 August 2014, St. Petersburg, Russia (2014).

I L S 2020
INTERNATIONAL CONFERENCE ON INFORMATION SYSTEMS, LOGISTICS & SUPPLY CHAIN
Austin, Texas April 22-24, 2020

Improvement of freight consolidation with a data mining technique

Zineb Aboutalib[1,2], Bruno Agard[1,2]

[1] Laboratoire en Intelligence des Données,
Département de Mathématiques et génie industriel,
École Polytechnique de Montréal, 2900 Boulevard Edouard-Montpetit, Montréal, Québec, Canada.
[2] CIRRELT – Interuniversity Research Centre on Entreprise Networks, Logistics and Transportation,
3520-2920 Ch de la Tour, H3T 1J4, Montréal, Québec, Canada.
zineb.aboutalib@polymtl.ca, bruno.agard@polymtl.ca

Abstract. At first glance, freight consolidation may appear simple, but it is supported by many variables and a large diversity of methods and strategies, which make it a complex notion to understand and to apply in many real situations. Freight consolidation consists of grouping different products into a single batch of goods or areas, for different purposes such as maximizing loading space, the quantity delivered in the same vehicle, the quantity delivered to the same destination, or reducing the distribution costs. Through a literature review, it was noticed that operational research is often used to explain the advantages of freight consolidation. The present study improves freight consolidation using the data mining approach. A case study, in a real situation, supports the conclusions. The results show that applying data mining techniques such as association rules provides some insights and helps a manager in the decision-making process.

Keywords: Freight consolidation, data mining, association rules, transportation costs, Logistics 4.0.

1. Introduction

In the area of big data and mass customization, customers are becoming more demanding and versatile. A race toward efficiency is taking place to acquire and retain them. Shorter planning cycles and accelerated deliveries at a lower cost are expected from companies in order to remain competitive. A tradeoff between stocking costs and delivery costs needs to be found. Freight consolidation comes as a plausible solution to the problem.
Even though it is a fairly old concept, freight consolidation is still drawing the interest of many researchers, [1-4] leading to better supply chain management. That's why companies should watch the evolution of technology and techniques that could enhance the efficiency of their processes and allow them to take advantage of the massive amounts of data stored. The choice of literature for solving this tradeoff has mainly used operational research. This paper aims to use data mining techniques as an alternative solution to improve freight consolidation.
The remainder of this paper is organized as follows: section 2 discusses a literature review of freight consolidation and data mining techniques. Section 3 presents a proposed methodology regarding the consolidation using association rules. Section 4 presents a case study using data from our industrial partner, and in section 5 the results will be presented and discussed, followed by the conclusions in section 6.

2. Literature review

This section is an overview of freight consolidation and data mining concepts; each subpart shows the pertinent definitions, objectives and tools that will facilitate an understanding of the case study.

2.1. Freight consolidation

According to [1], "*The consolidation concept has been known for hundreds of years and the practices are widely used in rail, ground, sea, and air transport*". Various definitions of freight consolidation have appeared over the years. This section will present some of them and discuss the objectives and classifications of freight consolidation.

2.1.1. Definition and objectives

Freight consolidation was defined by [1, 5] as the combination of many small shipments so that a larger and more economical load of goods could be grouped together on the same vehicle. Traditionally, the consolidation has been classified as temporal, spatial or product based [11].
The objectives of consolidation are to take advantage of the price reduction associated with larger loading sizes, common to the railways, road haulers and airlines [6, 7]. Consolidation permits managing distribution costs efficiently and effectively [2, 4, 6, 8, 9, 10]. Grouping and combining products at different locations and at different times in a single load or tour can increase earnings and reduce transportation and inventory losses.
To conclude, a compromise between the benefits and the losses of using consolidations should be examined [6]. The literature provides different classifications of freight consolidation that provide solutions to various contexts.

2.1.2. Freight consolidation classification and strategies

Several classifications concerning freight consolidation have been presented in the literature, Brennan's classification [11] considers three principal subdivisions: spatial, temporal and product freight consolidation strategies. In the study that follows, only temporal and spatial strategies will be presented.
a) Temporal consolidation.
Temporal consolidation is the grouping of small orders over time, balancing customer service and inventory costs against delivery costs [6]. It is also called pure consolidation, and can be implemented without the need for coordination [13]. According to [12], temporal consolidation can be applied using the following policies:

- Time-based policies that consist of sending a consolidated shipment every "T" period. These release all pending orders. [13] gave an example of the computer industry, explaining that this policy applies for items with low volume and high value.
- Quantity-based policies that consist of sending a consolidated shipment when an economic shipping quantity is reached. Based on the same example, [13] states that this policy applies for items with high volume and low value.

Another type of temporal consolidation that consists of combining the two policies above to achieve fast delivery and optimized loading is hybrid consolidation [13]. It appears most often in day-to-day operations management associated with accelerated orders [12].
b) Spatial consolidation.
Spatial consolidation is the process of determining the starting and arriving point, the route and the grouping of small orders to be shipped in one large shipment [14]. Spatial consolidation studies focus on determining the minimum cost associated with combining small shipments using a consolidation terminal. [14] considers that spatial consolidation is similar to that of a multi-warehouse vehicle tour problem. [9] on the other hand, explains that a consolidation problem is different from a vehicle routing problem, first because the consolidation can be selective and does not need to combine all products, which can reduce costs and improve service. Second, because vehicles are not necessarily making round-trips, especially if they use for-hire carriers.
Although [14] and [9] have a different perspective, [14] joins [9] in explaining that the spatial consolidation problem includes vehicle touring using a consolidation point rather than a direct tour from deposits to the

customer. To conclude, spatial consolidation takes into account several parameters and its application allows for potentially important gain.

c) Product consolidation

According to [14], product consolidation is the combination of different types of products into a single shipment. When a customer buys different products, consolidation may increase the quantity delivered to each customer by delivery and decrease the delivery costs, resulting in big gains [15]. Product consolidation can also acknowledge that two or more distribution centers can share the same distribution channel and that each customer can request different products in small quantities [11].

Finally, freight consolidation strategies can be classified as upon the repartition given in Table 1 [18]. It should be noted that [6, 11, 16] propose less consolidation classifications than those of [10]. In the state of the art given by [17], redundancy was pointed out in the repartition of [10], who explains it as the likeness between the consolidation of units of the vehicle and by containers. This study will consider Brennan's [11] spatial consolidation and temporal consolidation strategies.

Table 1: Summary of the repartition of various consolidation strategies [18].

Brennan [11]	**Cooper [16]**	**Sheffi [10]**	**Hall [6]**
Spatial consolidation	Customer Consolidation	Vehicle consolidation	Inventory consolidation
Product consolidation	Product consolidation	Container consolidation	Vehicle consolidation
Temporal consolidation	Time unit consolidation	Chanel consolidation	Terminals consolidation
		Network consolidation	
		Time unit consolidation	
		Tour consolidation	

2.2. Data mining

Data mining (DM) is a discipline that emerged with the information revolution and the creation of large amounts of data. Furthermore, using the internet as a channel of distribution in an open market increases the competition between companies in various areas. DM has mainly been used for prediction and description [19] to extract knowledge that will enhance the efficiency and the productivity of companies. Depending on the companies' objectives and the data available, classification, regression, clustering, prediction, association, etc. can be used in decision making [19]. [20] gave an overview and a classification of the existing techniques and their use in an industrial context.

One of the techniques used for descriptions and prediction is the association rules (AR). AR aims to find patterns or co-occurrences in a dataset [21]. It is used in different areas such as: the market basket analysis for commercial planning, the filtering and predicting of anomalies in telecommunication, diagnosis in medical research, etc. To understand how AR works, let us take two item sets U and V, according to [22], an association rule is defined as the rule: if U then V or $\{U\} \rightarrow \{V\}$. Three criteria are used to evaluate the quality of an AR: Support, which can be expressed as the probability that a transaction will contain U and V; Confidence, which is the probability that a transaction will contain V knowing that U is already present, and Lift, which indicates whether the correlation between U and V is higher than the hazard.

3. Methodology

This section presents a methodology that aims to improve freight consolidation with the use of AR. The proposed methodology consists of extracting valuable information and insights to help managers make data-driven, day-to-day decisions regarding freight consolidation. Figure 1 presents the freight consolidation methodology improved with AR. The methodology can be approached in two ways. Either by making a freight consolidation methodology (highlighted in blue) using well established concepts. Or, by including association rules in the process of steps 4 and 5 for enhanced results.

The freight consolidation methodology is depicted in 6 steps: *step 1- Data preparation, step 2 - Grouping and filtering of geocoded data, step 3- Consolidation cycle algorithm,* which is performed in parallel with step 2. Afterward, *step 4 - Spatial consolidation* and *step 5- Temporal consolidation* are also performed in parallel, respectively, following steps 2 and 3. The method ends with *step 6- Spatio-temporal consolidation.*

The AR freight consolidation methodology is depicted by step 4 and 5, which can be conducted using association rules following the steps highlighted in green. Association rules follow 3 steps: *step A- Contingency matrix preparation,* which recaps "*the conditional frequencies of two attributes and shows how these attributes are dependent on each other*" [23]. *Step B- Frequent transaction study,* which consists of exploring frequent transactions; transactions are defined as the orders made frequently at the same time by customers who share geographical units by applying the Apriori algorithm on transaction data. Thus, the rules generated by the algorithm are extracted. S*tep C- Significant rules selection* involves analysing the rules and selecting significant ones according to the AR evaluation criteria.

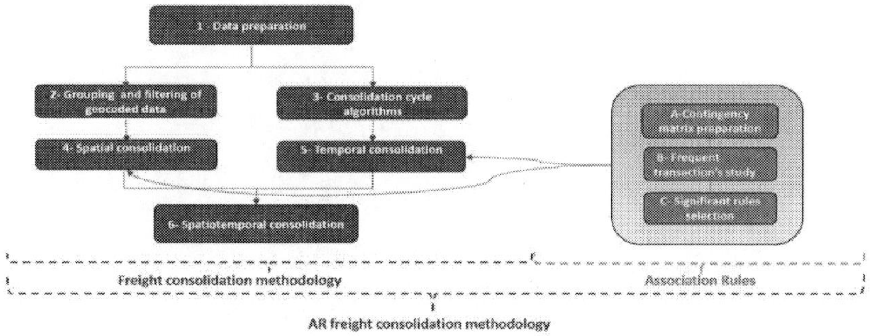

Figure 1: AR freight consolidation methodology.

4. Case Study

This case study will evaluate improvements in freight consolidation strategies using association rules. The data considered are real reception orders from an industrial partner, **Logistik Unicorp**, who supports the uniform program of various Canadian companies both organizational and governmental. Activities of **Logistik Unicorp** are the design, manufacturing, and quality monitoring of those uniforms. The study will focus on governmental clients, using a "clothing online" service, which is similar to e-commerce.
A database that includes several millions of transactions from 2006 to 2018 was provided by **Logistik Unicorp**. Those transactions have been processed and clients' orders were delivered throughout Canada from one unique warehouse. The objective is to evaluate improvements in freight consolidation strategies using real data from our industrial partner.

4.1. Descriptive analysis and data visualization

The reception orders data includes information about the location, entry dates, client code, quantity, and more. Delivery dates are not available in the data; therefore, it is considered to be the day after the entry date.
This subsection starts with the evaluation of tendencies related to the number of orders received from 2012 to 2017. 2018 was excluded from the analysis due to incomplete records.
Figure 2 shows the number of orders as a weekly time series for each of the 6 years. The curves follow a similar trend and seasonality. Two peaks in 2014 near week 20 were identified and linked to a special project that took place in the company during that period.

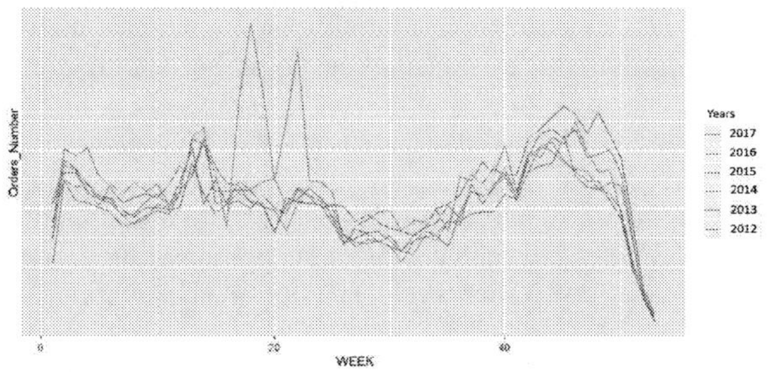

Figure 2: weekly variation in the number of orders (years 2012: 2017).

Curves show a clear trend over the years. Thus, using the last complete year in the development of a consolidation technique should be representative of the current state of orders. For scaling purposes, we also consider using a medium-density city, Winnipeg.

For the city of Winnipeg and the year 2017, the data contains more than 25,000 ordered items, in 2,000 orders, for 1,000 customers.

Figure 3 shows a distribution of customers in the city of Winnipeg. Orange dots represent single customers. Red dots represent set of customers that share the same postal code. The customer distribution map has been modified for confidentiality, but still represents typical behavior.

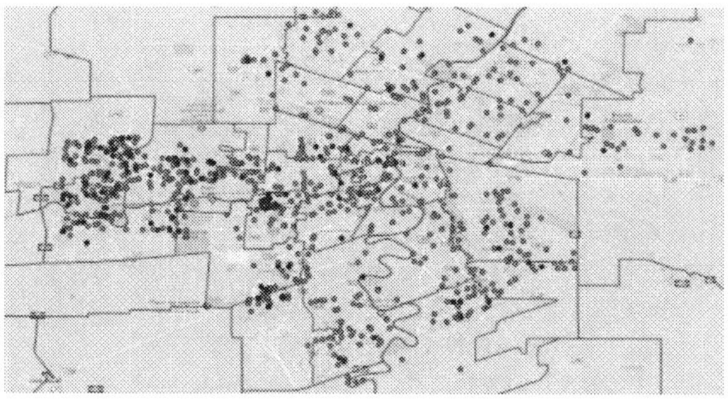

Figure 3: Typical distribution of customers in the city of Winnipeg (an FSA repartition).

4.2. Application of the methodology for consolidation

4.2.1. Freight consolidation methodology

Step 1- Data preparation

The first step in data preparation is formatting and cleaning the data. Location, entry dates, and quantities were formatted into factor, date and numeric structures, respectively. No missing values nor duplicates were recorded during the analysis. The second step of data preparation is data engineering. New variables were created, including forward Sortation Areas (FSA) based on location, year, month, week and day based on entry date and city province, latitude, longitude based on postal code.

The location information initially available for each order were the postal codes, the variable was extracted from it by selecting its first three characters resulting in a new geographical unit. For the consolidation strategy, FSA is the selected aggregation level. It was chosen instead of postal codes because it groups customers sharing the first three characters, which facilitate the logistics by delivering orders to a relay point rather than delivering to each customer.

Step 2- Grouping and filtering of geocoded data: This step groups and filters geocoded data. It leads to setting up the reception order data in step 4.

Step 3- Consolidation cycle algorithm: This step supports four different consolidation cycles (Cc). The "Cc1" scenario groups and delivers orders every 2 days. In the "Cc2" scenario, every 3 days. For the "Cc3" scenario, orders received Monday-Tuesday-Wednesday will be delivered on Thursdays, and those received Thursday-Friday-Saturday-Sunday will be delivered on Mondays. Finally, in the "Cc4" scenario, customers have a 7 day consolidation period. The choice of delivery days in the Cc3 scenario can be arbitrary. In this specific case, it is based on the tendencies noticed in **Logistik Unicorp**'s data. It has been noticed that Cc3 allowed the company to have a balanced number of deliveries for each of the proposed days for delivery. Based on those scenarios, five attributes were added to the database. The first one transforms the entry date into the order day of the week. The remaining four attributes are based on the "consolidated delivery date" for each scenario. Thereby, four consolidated dates are presented for a given order.

Step 4- Spatial Consolidation: This step aggregates small geographical units into a larger one. In this case, postal codes are aggregated into FSA. Concretely, it translates into adding a relay point where customers receive deliveries, instead of delivering to each customer separately at their own address. This results in a reduction in the number of trips performed per week. The optimal relay point will not be discussed in this study.

Step 5- Temporal Consolidation: For each scenario, this step regroups orders that share the same consolidated delivery date. Thus, it enhances the quantity of orders for each delivery.

Step 6- Spatio-temporal consolidation: This step is a combination of steps 4 and 5. Orders are grouped according to the spatial preparation and the consolidated delivery date. The benefit that can be earned from this strategy will be discussed in section 5. In addition, a comparison between this spatio-temporal consolidation strategy and the spatio-temporal strategy using association rules will also be made.

4.2.2. AR freight consolidation methodology

In this section, association rules are explained in the context of freight consolidation. AR are used to discover relationships between orders made by customers in a spatio-temporal setting. Then, patterns that may enhance the performance of freight consolidation strategies are identified. The rules linking FSA to order entry date are evaluated as follows:

Step A- Contingency matrix preparation: This step is required for the pretreatment of data in order to make it into the appropriate form for the association rule package. The package requires a transaction matrix that was built by transforming the orders' reception database into a boolean contingency matrix and converts it to a transaction matrix (See figure 4).

Step B- Frequent transactions study: This step consists of exploring a set of frequent FSAs using the transaction matrix. An apriori algorithm is applied to generate rules. Different supports and confidences are set to explore significant implications.

Step C- Significant rules: In this step, significant rules are selected, based on the aggregation level expected. The operational manager of the company helps to select those rules, depending on the quality of the rules and the degree of tolerance for uncertainties. Thus, it provides the operational manager with good insight for setting when and which geographical units' orders will be consolidated and delivered.

The AR freight consolidation methodology consists of incrementing selected rules of step C into steps 4 and 5. The resulting consolidation rules will provide a starting point to the manager for an initial geographical consolidation strategy.

ENTRY_DATE	R2C	R2G	R2H	R2J	R2K	R2L	R2M	R2N	R2P	R2R	R2V	R2W	R2X	R2Y	R3A	R3B
2017-01-01	0	0	0	0	0	0	0	0	0	0	0	0	0	0	0	0
2017-01-02	0	0	0	0	0	0	0	0	0	1	0	0	0	0	0	0
2017-01-03	0	0	0	0	0	0	0	0	0	0	0	0	0	1	0	0
2017-01-04	0	1	0	0	0	0	0	0	0	0	0	0	0	0	0	0
2017-01-05	0	0	1	0	0	0	1	0	0	0	0	0	0	0	0	0
2017-01-06	0	0	0	0	0	0	0	1	0	0	0	0	0	0	0	0
2017-01-07	0	0	0	0	0	0	0	0	0	0	0	0	0	0	0	0
2017-01-09	1	0	0	0	1	0	0	1	0	0	0	0	0	0	0	0
2017-01-10	0	0	0	0	0	0	0	0	0	0	0	0	0	0	0	1
2017-01-11	0	1	1	0	0	0	0	0	0	0	0	0	0	0	0	0

Figure 2: Sample of contingency matrix.

5. Results

In this study, an analysis of FSAs according to "order number" and "client density" was used in addition to AR selection. The analysis gave an overview of how the rules chosen by the operation manager could impact freight consolidation.

The FSA rules generated by Apriori with a minimum support of 0.1 and a minimum confidence of 0.7, resulted in sets composed by 3 FSA in the form of {U, V} → {W} as presented in figure 5.

rules	support	confidence	lift
{R3J,R3Y} => {R3N}	0.1810345	0.8181818	1.382171
{R3K,R3N} => {R3J}	0.1293103	0.9574468	1.348953
{R3J,R3K} => {R3N}	0.1293103	0.7894737	1.333674
{R2Y,R3N} => {R3J}	0.1982759	0.9324324	1.313710
{R2Y,R3Y} => {R3J}	0.1034483	0.9230769	1.300529

Figure 5: Top 5 rules

An example of one of the top five rules is [R3N, R3K] => R3J.

This can be read as follows: if **Logistik Unicorp** receives customers' orders that live in postal codes grouped into FSA "R3N" and "R3K", it will have 95% certainty that it will receive orders from customers who live in region "R3J" at the same time. In other words, customers from "R3J" always order when customers from "R3N" and "R3K" order as well.

Rules generated by Apriori with parameters set to a minimum support of 0.4 and a minimum confidence of 0.8, resulted in sets composed by 2 FSA in the form of {U} → {V}. It contains 2 rules, implying that 80%

of the customers who order from "R3J" and "R3N" are associated. Therefore, shipping orders for these two regions may be consolidated.

The gain evaluation over implementing AR on different freight consolidation strategies is presented in Table 2. This table represents two results for each scenario: the first one on the left shows the percentage of reduction in the number of deliveries according to a delivery date and/or the area of delivery compared to the current situation. The second result on the right (in bold) highlights the same information after the implementation of the previously described AR. Following the application of the different Cc scenarios on the Clothing Online orders, freight consolidation strategies were compared to a next day delivery policy.

Table 2: Freight consolidation strategies after applying a different consolidation cycle and implementing AR.

Freight consolidation strategies	Consolidation cycle			
	Cc1	Cc2	Cc3	Cc4
Temporal consolidation	41.6 | **41.6**	56.3 | **56.3**	69.8 | **69.8**	84.7 | **84.7**
Spatial consolidation	28.4 | **47.4**	28.4 | **47.4**	28.4 | **47.4**	28.4 | **47.4**
Spatio-temporal consolidation	39.4 | **55.6**	45.9 | **59.7**	48,7 | **62.1**	61.7 | **70.1**

Taking, for example, Cc2, which consists of delivering to customers every 3 days, according to Table 2, temporal consolidation decreases the number of deliveries by 56.3%, for spatial consolidation by 28.4% and for spatio-temporal consolidation by 45.9%. With the consideration of selected AR on freight consolidation, the number of deliveries does not change for temporal consolidation, but it decreases to 47.4% for spatial consolidation and to 59.7% for spatio-temporal consolidation.
We can observe that:

- Temporal consolidation, which does not consider geospatial information, gets no improvement with geospatial association rules.
- Spatial consolidation, which does not consider temporal cycles, remains constant across all scenarios, and improvements from AR stay constant. The reduction in the number of deliveries goes from 28.4% to 47.4%.
- AR improves both spatial consolidation and spatio-temporal consolidation strategies for all scenarios.
- In this case study, temporal consolidations provide better improvement than spatial consolidation because delivery points are not considered.
- Spatio-temporal consolidation is better than spatial consolidation in both cases (whether or not AR is used).
- For Cc1 and Cc2, spatio-temporal consolidation using AR provides better improvement than temporal consolidation.

According to those results, the proposed consolidation technique (using AR) is better than the classical technique for spatial and spatio-temporal strategies. However, the distribution manager can mix both techniques according to the activity and the context of the situation presented to maximize the profit.

6. Conclusion

The objective of this study was to show that data mining techniques, in particular association rules, could improve freight consolidation. The implementation of association rules into the development of consolidation strategies permits the number of deliveries to decrease. A comparison between the freight consolidation methodology and AR freight consolidation methodology proved to reduce the number of deliveries for both spatial and spatio-temporal strategies, but not temporal strategy. This method in turn could also increase the quantity delivered in the same vehicle or delivered to the same destination, thus reducing transportation costs and carbon footprint.
Limits of this method are the level of granularity of the spatial aggregation and the FSA assignation choice. A customer may geographically be located in one FSA, but better improve consolidation in another one. In future studies, those limitations would be taken into account by choosing the optimal dispatch to customer clusters to define a new granularity level. The capacity constraint of the number of consolidated orders that

can be loaded in a truck will be considered. Further improvements could be made to the association rules, such as predicting the Apriori derived rules and employing spatio-temporal AR that take into account longitude and latitude points.

Acknowledgements

The authors express their gratitude to their industrial partner (Logistik Unicorp) for their collaboration in this project and for the supply of data. The authors also thank MITACS (IT 12058) for the financial support. We would also like to express our gratitude to Camelia Dadouchi for sharing her expertise in the preparation of the document.

7. References

1. J. C. Tyan, F.-K. Wang, and T. C. Du: An evaluation of freight consolidation policies in global third party logistics, Omega, 31(1), 55--62 (2003).
2. J. H. Bookbinder and J. K. Higginson: Probabilistic modeling of freight consolidation by private carriage, Transportation Research Part E: Logistics and Transportation Review, 38(5), 305--318 (2002).
3. W. Hu, A. Toriello, and M. Dessouky: Integrated inventory routing and freight consolidation for perishable goods, European Journal of Operational Research, 271(2), 548--560 (2008)
4. A. S. Hanbazazah, L. Abril, M. Erkoc, and N. Shaikh: Freight consolidation with divisible shipments, delivery time windows, and piecewise transportation costs, European Journal of Operational Research, 276(1), 187--201(2019)
5. S. Çetinkaya and C. Y. Lee: Optimal outbound dispatch policies: Modeling inventory and cargo capacity, Naval Research Logistics, 49(6), 531--556 (2002)
6. R. W. Hall: Consolidation strategy: inventory, vehicles and terminals, Journal of business logistics, 8(2), 57 (1987)
7. G. C. Jackson: Evaluating order consolidation strategies using simulation, Journal of Business Logistics, 2(2), 110--138 (1981)
8. Y. P. Gupta and P. K. Bagchi: Inbound Freight Consolidation Under Just-In-Time Procurement, Journal of Business Logistics, 8(2), 74-94 (1987)
9. J. Pooley and A. J. Stenger: Modeling and evaluating shipment consolidation in a logistics system, Journal of Business Logistics, 13(2), 153-174 (1992)
10. Y. Sheffi: Carrier Shipper Interactions in the Transportation Market: An Analytical Framework, Journal of Business Logistics, 7(1), 1-27 (1986)
11. J. J. Brennan: Models and Analysis of Temporal Consolidation, Ph.D.Thesis, University of California at Los Angeles (1981)
12. J. Higginson and J. H. Bookbinder: Policy recommendations for a shipment-consolidation program, Journal of Business Logistics, 15(1), 87--112 (1994)
13. S. Çetinkaya: Coordination of inventory and shipment consolidation decisions: A review of premises, models, and justification, in Applications of supply chain management and e-commerce research: Springer, 92(1),3--51(2005)
14. H. Min: The vehicle routing problem with product/spatial consolidation and backhauling, Ph.D.Thesis .The Ohio State University.
15. M. A. Ulku: Analysis of shipment consolidation in the logistics supply chain, Ph.D.Thesis, University of Waterloo (2009)
16. M. Cooper: Cost and delivery time implications of freight consolidation and warehousing strategies, International Journal of Physical Distribution & Materials Management, 14(6), 47-67 (1984)
17. H. Min and M. Cooper: A comparative review of analytical studies on freight consolidation and backhauling, Logistics and Transportation Review, 26(2), 149--169 (1990)
18. Z. Aboutalib and B. Agard: État de l'art sur la consolidation de marchandise, 13ème Congrès International de Génie Industriel,Montréal (Québec), Canada, 25-28 juin (2019)
19. A. K. Choudhary, J. A. Harding, and M. K. Tiwari: Data mining in manufacturing: a review based on the kind of knowledge, Journal of Intelligent Manufacturing, 20(5), 501--521 (2009)
20. B. Agard and A. Kusiak: Exploration des bases de données industrielles à l'aide du datamining–Perspectives, 9ème colloque national AIP PRIMECA, La Plagne, France, 5-8 avril (2005)
21. R. J. Bayardo Jr: Efficiently mining long patterns from databases, in ACM Sigmod Record, 27(2), 85-93 (1998)
22. R. Agrawal, H. Mannila, R. Srikant, H. Toivonen, and A. I. Verkamo: Fast discovery of association rules, Advances in knowledge discovery and data mining, 12(1), 307--328 (1996)
23. S. Tsumoto.: Statistical independence as linear independence, Electronic Notes in Theoretical Computer Science, 82(4), 274--285 (2003)

I L S 2020
INTERNATIONAL CONFERENCE ON INFORMATION SYSTEMS, LOGISTICS & SUPPLY CHAIN
Austin, Texas April 22-24, 2020

Heuristic for the Continuous and Dynamic Berth Allocation Problem in Dry Bulk terminals with tidal and stock levels constraints

Nicolas Cheimanoff [1], Frédéric Fontane [1,2], Mohamed Nour Kitri [1], Nikolay Tchernev [1,3]

[1] EMINES- Scholl of Industrial management, Mohammed VI Polytechnic University, Ben Guerir, Marocco
[2] Mines ParisTech, PSL Research University, Paris, France
[3] Laboratoire d'Informatique (LIMOS, UMR CNRS 6158), Université Clermont Auvergne, Campus des Cézeaux, 63177 Aubière Cedex, France.

{Nicolas.CHEIMANOFF@emines.um6p.ma, Frederic.FONTANE@emines.um6p.ma, MohamedNour.KITRI@emines.um6p.ma, tchernev@isima.fr}

Abstract. The Berth Allocation Problem (BAP) is one of the main seaside operations planning problems in bulk terminals. The problem consists of allocating space along the quayside to incoming vessels. In this article, the BAP for a continuous quay and dynamic arrivals is considered. The formulation includes both the tidal and stock levels constraints that are common in bulk terminals. A MILP formulation is developed and tested on randomly generated instances using CPLEX. Due to the NP-hard nature of the problem, larger instances are not efficiently solved. Therefore, a heuristic approach is developed to find good quality solutions for these difficult instances. In further experiments, the heuristic solution is used as a starting point for CPLEX. The numerical results show that the scheduling heuristic provides better solutions for larger instances while its use as a starting point for CPLEX improved significantly its performance on solving those instances.

Keywords: berth allocation, dry bulk material, tidal constraints, stock levels constraints, maritime bulk terminal.

1. Introduction

Dry bulk maritime terminals are port terminals specialized in handling and storing dry bulk cargo. They differ from container terminals in that the cargo is loaded continuously. In addition, the tidal cycle has more impact on bulk terminals as the vessels are usually larger than their containers counterparts are, which prevent the vessels from leaving the quay in low tides windows. Dry bulk terminals deal essentially with main commodities such as iron ore, coal and grain. For exporting port terminals, port authorities must ensure the availability of the demanded cargo before berthing any vessel adding more complexity to the process of berthing the incoming vessels.
The annual maritime report of 2018 [9] reports that the global volume of seaborne trades continued its growth with a 4% annual growth in total volume in 2018 after breaking the 100 billion tons in 2016. 30% of which is major dry bulk commodities trades. This growth urges the port authorities to improve the efficiency of their operations to satisfy this increasing demand. One of the main operations in a maritime terminal is the efficient allocation of incoming vessels to berthing areas. This problem is known in the literature as the Berth Allocation Problem (BAP) and was first studied as an optimization problem by [6], the authors explained [7] how the generally adopted rule of First_Come_First_Served results in unused berthing areas and consequently a loss of productivity over the terminal and suggested a better allocation for the incoming vessels.

2. Related Work

Different formulations of the BAP are identified in literature, they can be classified according to four attributes [2] and [3], these are the spatial, the temporal, the handling time and the performance measure attributes. The spatial attribute limits the eligible berthing positions of vessels according to one of 3 predefined quay topologies [8] (*i*) Discrete, the quay is partitioned into a number of segments, in this case a vessel can only berth in one segment and the segments cannot host more than one vessel. (*ii*) Hybrid, as it's the case for the discrete topology the quay is partitioned into a number of segments but this time either the vessel can use many consecutive segments or the segments can host more than one vessel. (*iii*) Continuous, in this case the quay is not partitioned and the vessel can occupy any position as long as it does not moor outside of the quay. The temporal attribute describes the vessels arrival times, distinguish two cases: (*i*) Static, in this case all the vessels are supposedly waiting in the port at beginning of the scheduling horizon and can berth any time. (*ii*) Dynamic, in this case vessels cannot berth before their expected arrival time. The way in which the handling times of the vessels are calculated define the handling attribute, according to [7] it can be: fixed, depend on the quay cranes allocation or the position of the vessel on the quay or could depend on a combination of the previous two cases. Finally, the performance measure attribute describes how the berth plan is evaluated [3], the measure could be time related (lateness, completion time, waiting.) or cost related, furthermore the authors distinguish between objective functions that minimize the sum of the measure for all vessels and the ones that minimize the worst measure.
The literature for the BAP is abundant [3] still few articles dealt with the tidal or stock levels constraints. To our concern, these constraints are only addressed in [1] and [4]. Ernst et al. [4] address the tidal bulk BAP (BAP_TC) for a continuous quay and dynamic arrivals for the objective of minimizing the sum of completion times. In their formulation, the tidal cycle has an effect on the traffic port facility as vessels can only leave the quay in a high tides window. The authors developed two MILPs for the BAP_TC and tested them on real word instances of 16 to 32 vessels. One of their developed models managed an average of 7% gap with the optimal solutions within an hour execution time limit. Barros et al. [1] consider the tidal bulk BAP with stock levels constraints (BAP_TC_S) and seek to minimize the total costs. a discrete quay with dynamic arrivals is considered and a Simulated Annealing (SA) algorithm is developed to solve the problem. Their numerical experiments included instances up to 30 vessels and 3 berth some of which were solved optimally by their SA.
The BAP is an NP-hard problem [5]. Therefore, exact solutions to large-scale instances are difficult to obtain using commercial software. As an alternative metaheuristic approaches are adapted to solve larger instances efficiently. Most of which are genetic/evolutionary algorithms (G/E A) [3]. The rest of these methods are other metaheuristics and problem-specific heuristics.
In this paper, we intend to develop an efficient heuristic to solve the dynamic continuous berth allocation problem with tidal and stock levels constraints. The rest of the paper is organized as follows. In Section 3 the problem is formally introduced and a MILP is formulated for the BAP_TC_S. Section 4 introduces the proposed heuristic algorithm. Section 5 describes the generation of instances for the problem and presents the computational results for the MILP and the developed heuristic approach.

3. Problem Definition and Assumptions

3.1. Overview

In the BAP_TC_S, a continuous quay with a limited length L and a set of vessels $V = \{1, 2, \dots. |V|\}$ are given. Each vessel indexed by $j \in V$, has an arrival time a_j and may have to wait before berthing. Once the vessel berthing S_j, the service can begin. Each vessel will occupy without interruption a length of the berth l_j at a position y_j. The vessel leaves the quay at C_j which is the start time incremented by the pre-computed handling time p_j, the objective is to minimize the total completion time. Each vessel has a quantity to load d_{jp} of a product p from the set of products $P = \{1, 2, \dots. |P|\}$ and may require more than one product. A vessel can only berth if all quantities to load are available in the terminal stocks at S_j and can only leave the quay in a high tides window k from the set of high tides windows $K = \{1, 2, \dots. |K|\}$ where every high tides window $k \in K$ begins at B_k and ends at E_k.

At time 0, initial stocks sr_{0p} of each product p are available and could be used immediately. The stock of each product p is subject to a replenishment sr_{rp} in each period r of the replenishment periods set $R = \{1, ... |R|\}$. Each period r starts at br_r the beginning time of period r and finishes at $br_{r+1}$the date of the next replenishment period, with the last replenishment period ending at $sr_{|R|+1,p} = H$ the planning horizon length. The stock level se_{rp} of product p in period r must never drop to a negative value.

A feasible solution for the BAP is a berth plan in which the berthing times and positions assigned to the vessels satisfy the spatial-temporal constraint of non-overlapping along with the tidal constraints, and where the non-negativity of the stock levels is always ensured. Figure 1 shows a berth plan with 15 vessels and a quay 300m long in a scheduling horizon of hours 200 h. The vertical axis represents time in hours and the horizontal axis the quay. Horizontal bars are used to represent the high tides windows. Each yellow box represents a vessel, the length of the box represents the handling time and the width represent the length of the vessel and the safety margins.

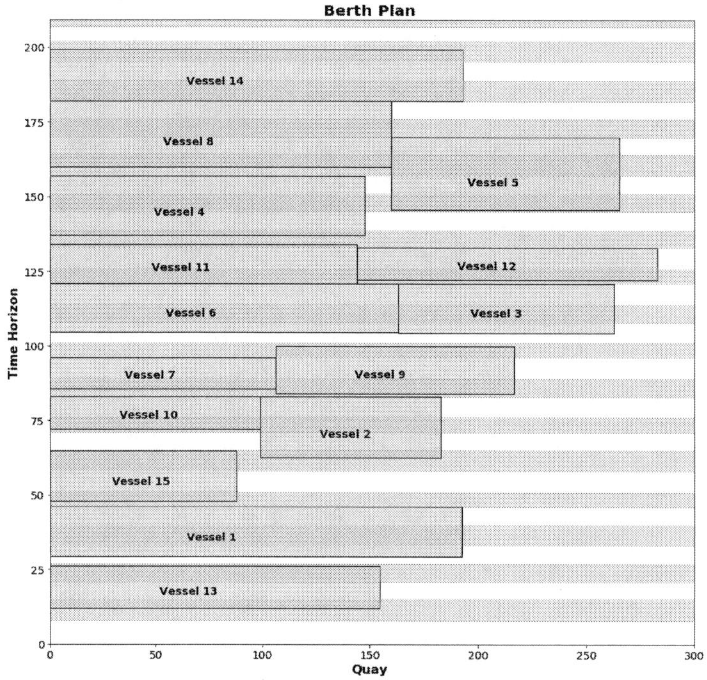

Figure 1: A berth plan with 15 vessels and a quay 300 m long.

3.2. Assumptions

The particular assumptions of this problem are as follows:

- A vessel cannot be moored outside the quay and before its arrival
- A vessel will arrive empty at the port and can be handled during a low tide
- A vessel will require a high tide period to be able to depart from the port
- Once a vessel is moored, its position cannot be changed, nor may its handling be interrupted
- The time for docking and undocking maneuvers is considered to be included in the handling time
- Safety margins are considered to be included in the vessel length
- A vessel might require more than one product type and cannot be moored until all demanded quantities are available
- Loaded quantities are subtracted from the stock levels of the period in which the vessel started berthing
- Stock levels at each period must not drop to a negative below
- The initial stock and the planned replenishment quantities meet the demand of all vessels to schedule
- Cargo loaders deployment during handling is fixed, the number of cargo loaders available in the port facility is considered significantly higher than the number of cargo loaders needed by a vessel.

3.3. Mathematical Model

A mixed integer linear programming model for the continuous with tidal and stock constraints BAP_TC_S is now proposed.

Parameters:

H	Planning horizon length		d_{jp}	Demand for product p of vessel j
L	Quay's length		br_r	Beginning of replenishment period r
V	Set of vessels $V = \{1, \dots . \|V\|\}$		sr_{rp}	Supply of product p in period r
K	Set of high tide windows $K = \{1, \dots, \|K\|\}$		sr_{0p}	Initial stock of product p
P	Set of products $P = \{1, \dots . \|P\|\}$		B_k	Beginning of high tides window k
R	Set of replenishment periods $R = \{ 1, \dots . \|R\|\}$		E_k	End of high tides window k
a_j	Arrival time of vessel j		M	Large number
l_j	Length of vessel j			
p_j	Handling time of vessel j			

Decision variables:

Continuous variables

S_j	Start time for vessel j
C_j	Completion time vessel j
y_j	Position of vessel j in the quay
se_{rp}	Stock level of product p at the end of replenishment period r
se_{0p}	Stock level of product p before the beginning of the first replenishment

Binary variables

x_{ji}	1 if vessel i starts its processing after vessel j departs, 0 otherwise
z_{ji}	1 if vessels j and i are handled at the same time and vessel j to the right of vessel i, 0 otherwise
t_{jk}	1 if vessel j completes its handling in high tides window k, 0 otherwise
sp_{jr}	1 if vessel j is handled in replenishment period r, 0 otherwise

Model

$$Min \sum_{j=1}^{V} C_j \tag{1}$$

$$x_{ji} + x_{ij} + z_{ji} + z_{ij} = 1, \ \forall j, i \in V \ and \ j \neq i \tag{2}$$

$$, \ C_j = S_j + p_j, \ \forall j \in V \tag{3}$$

$$C_j \geq \sum_{k \in K} B_k t_{jk}, \ \forall j \in V \tag{4}$$

$$C_j \leq \sum_{k \in K} E_k t_{jk}, \ \forall j \in V \tag{5}$$

$$\sum_{k \in K} t_{jk} = 1, \ \forall j \in V \tag{6}$$

$$S_i \geq C_j - M(1 - x_{ji}, \ \forall j, i \in V \tag{7}$$

$$y_j \geq l_i z_{ji} + y_i - L(1 - z_{ji}), \ \forall \ j, i \in V, j \neq i \tag{8}$$

$$S_j \geq \sum_{\{0\} \cup R} br_r sp_{jr}, \ \forall j \in V \tag{9}$$

$$S_j \leq \sum_{\{0\} \cup R} br_{r+1} sp_{jr}, \ \forall j \in V \tag{10}$$

$$\sum_{r \in \{0\} \cup R} sp_{jr} = 1, \ \forall j \in V \tag{11}$$

$$se_{0p} = sr_{0p} - \sum_{j=1}^{V} sp_{j0} d_{jp}, \ \forall p \in P \tag{12}$$

$$se_{rp} = sr_{rp} + se_{r-1p} - \sum_{j=1}^{V} sp_{jr} d_{jp}, \ \forall r \in R \ and \ \forall p \in P \tag{13}$$

$$S_j \geq a_j, \forall j \in V \tag{14}$$

$$S_j \geq a_j, \forall j \in V \tag{15}$$

$$0 \leq y_j \leq L - l_j, \forall j \in V \tag{16}$$

$$se_{rp} \geq 0, \forall r \in \{0\} \cup R \ and \ \forall \ p \in P \tag{17}$$

$$x_{ji} \ \in \{0,1\}, \forall j, i \in V \ and \ j \neq i \tag{18}$$

$$z_{ji} \ \in \{0,1\}, \forall j, i \in V \ and \ j \neq i \tag{19}$$

$$t_{jk} \ \in \{0,1\}, \forall j \in V \ and \ \forall k \in K \tag{20}$$

$$sp_{jr} \ \in \{0,1\}, \forall j \in V \ and \ \forall r \in \{0\} \cup R \tag{21}$$

The objective function seeks to minimize the total completion time of the vessels. Constraints set (2) expresses the position of vessel j with respect to vessel i, which can be one of two cases: (*i*) z_{ji} *or* z_{ij} equals to one meaning that the two vessels are handled at the same time with on to the right of the other. (*ii*) x_{ji} *or* x_{ij} equals to one meaning that one of the vessel is handled after the other departs. Constraints set (3) calculates the completion time of a vessel. Constraints set (4), (5) and (6) ensures that the completion time of a vessel lye between the beginning and the end of a high tides window. Constraints set (7) determines the sequence of two vessels along the time horizon. Constraints set (7) and (8) ensures that two vessels will not overlap in time and space. Constraints set (9) to (11) determine the replenishment periods in which the vessel is served, while constraints set (12) and (13) ensure the stock level conservation at each period. Constraints (14) to (21) represent the domain definition of the decision variables. As it could be seen later in the numerical experiences, the MILP fail to solve larger instances efficiently, therefore a heuristic approach is developed thereafter to provide an initial solution for the MILP.

4. Scheduling Heuristic

The developed scheduling heuristic constructs the berth plan systematically. At each iteration, ***Algorithm 1*** examines the current partial berth plan and finds the earliest completion time for each of the unscheduled vessels. The calculated completion times are then compared and the vessel that has the least completion time is scheduled, in case of ties, the vessel with the smallest index is chosen. The next iteration starts with an updated partial berth plan and list of unscheduled vessels and continues until the latter is empty.

Algorithm 1: Scheduling heuristic for the BAP_TC_S

```
SCHEDULING HEURISTIC
Input parameters
     I   :        BAP_TC_S instance
Output parameters
     B   :       A Feasible berth plan for the given instance
Begin
1.   Set λ   ← ∅ //list of indexes of scheduled vessels
2.   Set δ   ← V //list of indexes of unscheduled vessels
3.   While (δ ≠ ∅) Do
4.        For j in δ Do
5.              C'j  ← Find_Earliest_Completion(j,B)
6.        EndFor
7.      j* ← argmin_{j∈δ}(C'j)
8.      Update_Berth(j*,B)
9.      Remove j* from δ and add it to λ
10.  EndDo
End
```

Algorithm 1 starts by initializing the lists of scheduled vessels $\boldsymbol{\lambda}$ and unscheduled vessels $\boldsymbol{\delta}$ (lines 1 and 2). The main loop (lines 3_10) calculates the completion time of each of the unscheduled vessels using the `Find_Earliest_Completion(j,B)` procedure which examines the current partial berth **B** bottom_up and from the right to the left of the quay and returns the earliest completion time for vessel j. ***Figure 2***

shows an example of a partial berth plan $\boldsymbol{B}$ composed of *3* vessels. In this example, we are trying to found the earliest completion time for vessel *4*. If vessel *4* is scheduled as soon as it arrives in position 0 it will overlap with vessel *3*. The next position to test is immediately to the right of vessel *3*. However, vessel *4* cannot berth in this position neither as the available quay space is less than L_4 vessel *4* length. The earliest time in which vessel *4* can berth is C_3 the completion time of vessel 3, vessel 4 can be berthed in position 0 without overlapping with any other vessel. However if vessel 4 starts berthing at C_3 its completion time would not match with a high tides window, the berthing time will therefore be incremented so as the completion time is exactly B_3 which is the beginning of the third high tides window. Finally, vessel *4* is scheduled as sown in ***Figure 3***. It is supposed that the available stocks are sufficient to load the cargo in vessel *4*. If it is not the case, the procedure searches for the earliest date in which enough stocks are available and continue the partial berth evaluation as before. After calculating the earliest completion time for all unscheduled vessels, ***Algorithm 1*** chooses the vessel that has the least completion time j^* (line 7) and then update the partial berth plan (line 8) and removes j^* from $\boldsymbol{\delta}$ to put it in $\boldsymbol{\lambda}$ (line 9). ***Algorithm 1*** terminates if the list $\boldsymbol{\delta}$ is empty.

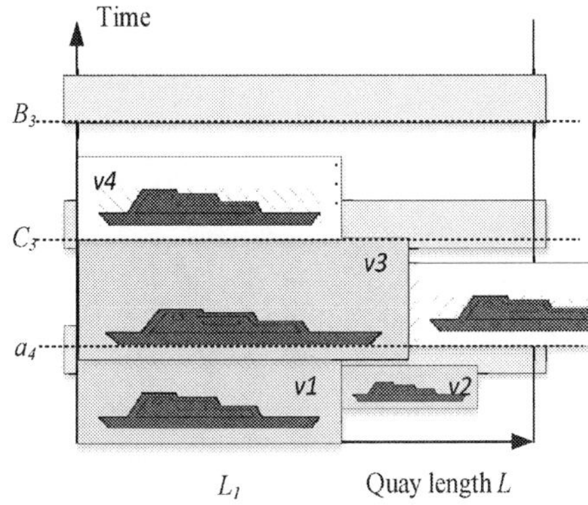

Figure 2: Non-feasible assignments of vessel 4.

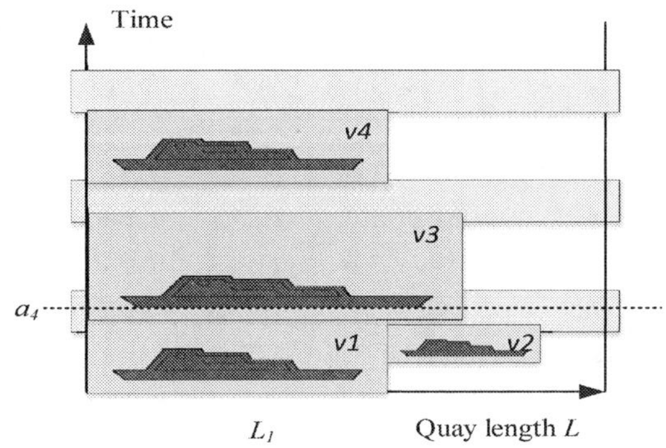

Figure 3: Earliest completion time of vessel 4.

5. Numerical Experiments

In order to test the MILP formulation and the proposed scheduling heuristic, a variety of 32 instances is generated randomly according to the attributes from [4]. The authors define an instance attributes as follows:

V is the number of vessels arriving. For this attribute, 4 cases are considered $|V|$: 20, 40, 80 and 160.

PH is the planning horizon. This attribute depends on *V* the number of vessels with $|PH|$: 1, 2, 4 and 8 respectively for $|V|$: 20, 40, 80 and 160.

VL is the vessels lengths attribute. They are generated from a uniform distribution [0.5, 2].

VA vessel arrival time a_j. Two cases are distinguished: (*i*) the arrival times is generated from a uniform distribution [0, 150]; (*ii*) The arrival times are at 12:00 noon every day, so the above arrival data is rounded to 12:00 noon of their respective day.

VH is the vessels handling times attribute. They are generated from a uniform distribution [10, 25]

The total demand of each vessel is calculated by multiplying the handling time by a fixed parameter, and may randomly cover one or two products. In the latter case, the total demand is divided equivalently between the two products.

In addition to the attributes defined in [4], stock related attributes are added and defined as follows:

P is the number of products. Two cases are considered $|P| = 3$ and 5.

RP is the replenishment planning. Two cases are considered: (*i*) The replenishment is daily, and the total demand is equally distributed over the planning horizon; (*ii*) A replenishment is planned each 3 days.

An instance will be coded as follows *V_VA_P_RP*. 20_Noon_5_3 is therefore an instance with 20 vessels that arrive only at noon; the loaded products in the port facility are 5 and are replenished each 3 days. From each combination of attributes an instance was generated randomly which gives 32 instances.

The conducted numerical experiments were carried on an Intel(R) Core(TM) i7-4600 CPU, 2.90 GHz computer with 16 GB of RAM running under Windows 10. CPLEX 12.7 is used to solve the MILP formulations while the proposed heuristic was coded in Python 3.5. Each instance MILP formulation is solved using CPLEX under 2 hours time limit and using the scheduling heuristic. The solution from the scheduling heuristic is used latter as a starting point for the MILP. Results for the scheduling heuristic and the MILP with (MILP w SH start) and without (MILP w/o SH start) the initialization are depicted in ***Table 1.***

Table 1: MILP formulation and scheduling heuristic results on test instances

V	Instance	**MILP w/o SH start**			**MILP w SH start**			**Scheduling Heuristic**		
		Obj. val.	Gap w LB	Time (s)	Obj. val.	Gap w LB	Time (s)	Obj. val.	Gap w LB	Time (s)
20		**2374,9**	**0,2%**	**1966**	**2374,9**	**0,2%**	**1963**	**2579,0**	**8,1%**	**0,01**
	20_Uniform_3_1	2116,5	0,0%	445	2116,5	0,0%	526	2181,6	3,0%	0,03
	20_Uniform_3_3	2299,2	1,3%	7200	2299,2	1,3%	7200	2510,8	9,6%	0,02
	20_Uniform_5_1	2369,1	0,0%	54	2369,1	0,0%	67	2734,3	13,4%	0
	20_Uniform_5_3	2404,1	0,0%	4778	2404,1	0,0%	4900	2615,2	8,1%	0,02
	20_Noon_3_1	2388,4	0,0%	6	2388,4	0,0%	4	2517,9	5,1%	0
	20_Noon_3_3	2402,8	0,0%	42	2402,8	0,0%	44	2645,3	9,2%	0,02
	20_Noon_5_1	2625,1	0,0%	3170	2625,1	0,0%	2939	2772,7	5,3%	0
	20_Noon_5_3	2394,2	0,0%	30	2394,2	0,0%	26	2654,4	9,8%	0,02
40		**7200,6**	**14,7%**	**7200**	**7123,3**	**13,9%**	**7200**	**7683,7**	**20,1%**	**0,01**
	40_Uniform_3_1	7228,9	7,6%	7200	7129,1	6,5%	7200	7415,6	10,1%	0
	40_Uniform_3_3	7914,7	19,3%	7200	7505,7	15,1%	7200	7775,0	18,1%	0,02
	40_Uniform_5_1	6332,1	13,3%	7200	6365,0	13,8%	7200	7309,3	25,0%	0,02
	40_Uniform_5_3	7267,0	23,4%	7200	7261,3	23,3%	7200	8566,7	35,0%	0,02
	40_Noon_3_1	7300,6	10,6%	7200	7401,0	11,8%	7200	7510,8	13,1%	0,02
	40_Noon_3_3	7247,0	11,5%	7200	7254,0	11,9%	7200	7487,6	14,6%	0
	40_Noon_5_1	6878,1	16,4%	7200	6776,7	14,7%	7200	7579,8	24,2%	0,02
	40_Noon_5_3	7436,6	15,7%	7200	7293,5	13,9%	7200	7825,3	19,9%	0,02
80		**28811,2**	**26,6%**	**7200**	**26125,5**	**19,3%**	**7200**	**26910,7**	**21,5%**	**0,03**
	80_Uniform_3_1	25055,5	10,1%	7200	24744,7	8,9%	7200	24796,2	9,1%	0,03
	80_Uniform_3_3	29930,7	20,6%	7200	27401,0	13,1%	7200	27677,4	14,1%	0,03
	80_Uniform_5_1	31280,8	37,4%	7200	25894,6	24,3%	7200	27010,8	27,5%	0,03
	80_Uniform_5_3	27506,9	32,6%	7200	26386,3	29,9%	7200	27755,4	33,3%	0,03
	80_Noon_3_1	29648,0	20,6%	7200	25680,9	8,3%	7200	25690,3	8,4%	0,03
	80_Noon_3_3	31186,1	24,1%	7200	27444,4	13,9%	7200	27753,0	14,8%	0,03
	80_Noon_5_1	27625,3	35,0%	7200	25094,3	28,4%	7200	26539,0	32,3%	0,03
	80_Noon_5_3	28256,7	32,5%	7200	26357,7	27,8%	7200	28063,4	32,2%	0,03
160		**N/A**	**N/A**	**7200**	**98900,4**	**21,6%**	**7200**	**100851,1**	**23,0%**	**0,12**
	160_Uniform_3_1	N/A	N/A	7200	98465,3	8,9%	7200	98601,4	9,0%	0,14
	160_Uniform_3_3	N/A	N/A	7200	96719,5	9,6%	7200	97073,4	10,0%	0,09
	160_Uniform_5_1	N/A	N/A	7200	101930,3	31,9%	7200	104839,1	33,8%	0,14
	160_Uniform_5_3	N/A	N/A	7200	97573,5	34,8%	7200	101095,4	37,1%	0,08
	160_Noon_3_1	N/A	N/A	7200	101590,8	11,2%	7200	103362,4	12,7%	0,16
	160_Noon_3_3	N/A	N/A	7200	102475,2	12,9%	7200	103491,8	13,8%	0,11
	160_Noon_5_1	N/A	N/A	7200	94977,7	29,7%	7200	98364,5	32,1%	0,14
	160_Noon_5_3	N/A	N/A	7200	97471,0	33,7%	7200	99980,9	35,4%	0,11
Mean		**12795,6**	**13,8%**	**5891**	**33631,0**	**13,7%**	**5891**	**34506,1**	**18,1%**	**0,04**

The results from ***Table 1*** show that 7 of 8 small size instances were solved optimally by CPLEX. As it would be expected, none of the larger instances was solved optimally. Moreover, CPLEX failed to found a feasible solution for all the largest instances. For these instances, the scheduling heuristic was able to provide a feasible berth plan in less than 1 s. The overall performance of SH was good with respect to CPLEX best provided lower bound with an average gap of 18.1%. Using the solution from SH as a starting point for CPLEX improved the results starting from $V = 80$ as the gap with the best LB is reduced by 5 point. CPLEX also improved on the SH solutions for the largest instances. For each number of vessels the hardest instance to solve was the instances with 5 products and 3 days replenishment periodicity meaning that the stock level constraints add to the difficulty of solving the tidal BAP.

6. Conclusion

This paper dealt with the continuous berth allocation problem under tidal and stock level constraints. A MILP formulation of the problem is developed and tested on a randomly generated instances. The MILP provides optimal solutions for the smallest size instances but its performance decreased for larger instances where it sometimes failed to provide a feasible solution. To provide good quality solution for these instances a scheduling heuristic is used. The heuristic schedules the vessel with the least completion time at each of its iterations which minimizes the waiting time for the vessels to schedule later. The heuristic provided good quality solutions in short computation times with a gap of 18% with respect to the best LB provided by CPLEX. In further experiments, the solutions scheduling heuristic were used as a starting point for CPLEX, which improved its performance significantly starting from instances with 80 vessels.
As the MILP did not improve a lot on the given solution for instances with 160 vessels, our next step will be to propose a metaheuristic approach to solve the BAP_TC_S efficiently for these instances.

7. References

1. Barros V. H., Costa T. S., Oliveira A. C. M., Lorena L. A. N.: Model and Heuristic for Berth Allocation in Tidal Bulk Ports with Stock Level Constraints. Comput. Ind. Eng. 60(4), 606--613 (2011)
2. Bierwirth C., Meisel F.: A Survey of Berth Allocation and Quay Crane Scheduling Problems in Container Terminals. Eur. J. Oper. Res. 202(3), 615--627 (2010)
3. Bierwirth C., Meisel F.: A Follow-up Survey of Berth Allocation and Quay Crane Scheduling Problems in Container Terminals. Eur. J. of Oper. Res. 244(3), 675–689 (2015)
4. Ernst A., Oğuz C., Singh G., Taherkhani G.: Mathematical Models for the Berth Allocation Problem in Dry Bulk Terminals. J. Sched. 20(5), 459--473 (2017)
5. Hansen P., Mladenovic´ N.: Variable Neighborhood Search: Principles and Applications. Eur. J. of Oper. Res. 130, 449--467 (2001)
6. Imai A., Nagaiwa K., & Tat C. W.: Efficient Planning of Berth Allocation for Container Terminals in Asia. J. Adv. Tran., 31(1), 75—94 (1997)
7. Imai A., Nishimura E., Papadimitriou S.: The Dynamic Berth Allocation Problem for a Container Port. Tran. Res. B 35, 401--417 (2001)
8. Imai A., Sun X., Nishimura E., Papadimitriou S.: Berth Allocation in a Container Port: Using a Continuous Location Space Approach. Tran. Res. B 39 (3), 199--221 (2005)
9. UNCTAD: Review of Maritime Transport. United Nations Conference on Trade and Development. New York and Geneva (2018).

I L S 2020
INTERNATIONAL CONFERENCE ON INFORMATION SYSTEMS, LOGISTICS & SUPPLY CHAIN
Austin, Texas April 22-24, 2020

The parcel locker location issues: an overview of factors affecting their location

Alexandra Lagorio [1], Roberto Pinto[1]

[1] Department of Management, Information and Production, University of Bergamo, viale Marconi 5, 24044, Dalmine (BG)
{alexandra.lagorio@unibg.it, roberto.pinto@unibg.it}

Abstract. With the spread of e-commerce, there has been an upsurge in the number of B2C deliveries. The limits of home delivery such as the difficulty in finding the exact addresses and the missing deliveries, exhacerbate the negative impacts of last mile logistics (i.e., congestion and pollution) To overcome these problems, solutions such as delivery to supervised or automated points have become more and more widespread. For this reason, there are several case studies aimed at understanding which are the best locations for these type of solutions. The objective of this paper is to identify the main factors affecting parcel lockers.

Keywords: "parcel lockers", "parcel lockers location", "location problems", "e-commerce", "case survey methodology"

1. Introduction

The sudden changes and developments in the last mile delivery segment over the last fifteen years are mainly due to the growth of B2C and e-commerce [1]. Consumers nowadays are less inclined than in the past to wait for goods because of the Amazon effect [2]: they want the opportunity to buy at any time, any day, from anywhere and beyond this they are looking for a service available and accessible 24/7 making delivery operations more complicated from the point of view of the Courier, Express and Parcel (CEP) delivery companies [3]. In the case of missing deliveries , Logistics Service Providers (LSP) have several negative impacts such as idle time and costs. Home delivery has itself some intertwining limits: by delivering the goods door to door it is not possible to optimally consolidate the deliveries as for the B2B deliveries, longer delivery rounds are made, making more stops for loading/unloading, not always using the vehicle at full load. These limitations contribute to all the other negative aspects of urban freight traffic such as congestion, pollution, and an increase in the risk of accidents [4]. Further, home delivery may not represent the best solution anymore due to the modern lifestyles: most people work during the day, so there is a need to find an alternative that can satisfy both the customer and the CEP companies [5]. To overcome these issues, over the last decade the postal operators have decided to invest in offering value-added services, such as delivery to supervised or automated collect points. These new delivery options offer a viable alternative to home delivery, meeting the needs of end consumers.

These alternatives, commonly grouped under the name of Collection-and-Delivery Points (CDP) solutions, can be classified into two main groups: *i*) pick up points, and *ii*) automated locker boxes (also called parcel locker or smart lockers or parcel banks). Pick up points are usually shops and business activities used as a delivery point for the courier where customers could go to retrieve their parcels. Parcel lockers, instead, are

unattended CDP installed in public areas, where parcels are retained for a limited amount of time during which the customer can retrieve them by using the order reference code.
One of the main issues hindering the spread and use by customers of these two forms of alternatives to home delivery lies in the correct location of this type of solution. In particular, the efficient location has to be chosen in order to maximise the customers' satisfaction and willingness to use it, thus, it is necessary to make the use of these type of solutions as "comfortable" as possible. This research focuses on parcel lockers in particular, because their location has some more constraints (i.e., less security and accessibility, interaction with a machine) then an attended pick-up point in a shop or in a supermarket and also more potentiality (i.e., availability 24/7 and not only during the days and hours of opening of a shop). Consequently, the parcel lockers are usually located in such a way that the customers do not have to vary their daily habits. For example, one of the most common solutions is to locate parcel lockers along with the home-work route and near the places where customers usually go when they deviate from this route (e.g., railway stations or subways, parking lots, gas stations, supermarkets). Other alternatives are to place the parcel lockers in places close to the point of departures (homes) or arrivals (work) of the daily trips. For example, there are many applications of parcel lockers located in apartment buildings [6] or large companies [7].
From these reflections, it emerges that choosing where to locate a parcel locker is not a trivial choice since the number of potential customers that can be intercepted depends mainly on it. A wrong location could mean a severe economic loss both in terms of expected investments that have not returned and in terms of missed opportunities for profit. There are many models in the scientific literature regarding the location of facilities that can also be applied in the context of the location of parcel lockers [7][8][9][10], but before apply them it could be useful to understand what are the characteristics of the context and in particular, what are the characteristics that must have the sites intended to host this type of solutions. This paper, therefore, aims to understand which are the factors influencing the parcel locker location to be able to choose in future research the models that can best be adapted to this context.

The paper is structured as follows: in the second section, a deeper parcel lockers context description focusing on the parcel lockers working principles is provided. Then, in the third section, the methodology used for retrieving the location characteristics is described. The fourth section discusses the factors affecting the parcel lockers sites selection, and finally, the fifth section concludes the paper proposing further research directions.

2. Context description

By definition, a parcel locker is a collection point usually accessible 24 hours a day, seven days a week, 365 days a year through which the customer can serve himself in complete autonomy [11]. Parcel lockers can be used as a delivery address or as an alternative delivery location, and used as a service by logistics operators in a customer return strategy (return management). If, for example, the first time a recipient cannot be reached (missing deliveries) during home delivery, delivery can be made via parcel lockers.
They are usually located in easily accessible sites and near places with the high frequency of shipments and high pedestrian traffic such as service stations, shopping centres and squares. According to a survey of users of parcel lockers registered in the InPost database in Poland, the criteria for choosing a locker service for customers were first of all the h24 accessibility, then the service price and the location [12]. The parcel locker system for sending and receiving parcels is quick and convenient. All these features are reflected in the process of purchasing, collecting and returning through the use of a parcel locker.
The entire collection/delivery process can be completed in just seven seconds, but typically takes up to half a minute [12]. This information means that the time required is concise and, among other things, no queues are required.
The interest of CEP companies has only recently shifted towards delivery solutions based on automatic lockers; thus, given its recency, the adoption of this solution can be deemed not yet mature. The necessary investments are still not transparent, and it is not yet possible to thoroughly verify the benefits and returns from the investment in this type of solution. However, the use of lockers allows a reduction in costs and delivery times in the last mile deliveries, without sacrificing proximity to the consumer market.

3. Methodology

In order to analyse the main factors impacting the choice of the location for the parcel lockers, a case survey methodology with secondary data was used.
Initially, a literature review was performed. However, only seven papers in the scientific literature using "parcel lockers location" as research criteria were found, confirming the relative newness of the topic. Then, a careful analysis of these papers were carried out, and main factors impacting parcel lockers location choices were inductively identified. Table 1 summarises the results of this first literature analysis.

Table 1: Factors for parcel locker location retrieved inductively from the scientific literature

Factors	Definition	Reference
Availability	Possibility for delivery and collection of parcels 24/7	[12][11]
Accessibility	Degree of connection with the different infrastructures and modes of transport	[13][14][12][15][16]
Security	The state of being free from danger or threat	[13][15]
Environmental Impact / Land occupation	How parcel lockers impact on the environment in terms of emissions and land occupation	[13][12][15][11]
Costs	Estimate price of the installation and maintance of the parcel lockers	[7][12][15]
Methods of use	Procedures to implement to use the parcel lockers	[14][12][11][16]
Regulations	Official rules issued from different countries in order to regulate parcel lockers activity	[12]

Because of the small numbers of papers found in the scientific literature, the research was extended also to the analysis of real case studies through the use of secondary data. The case survey methodology allows identifying patterns and performing tests across different case studies [17] overcoming the problem of generalising from a single case study, thus providing more in-depth analysis of complex organisational phenomena than questionnaire surveys [18]. Secondary data were used to overcome some limitations of this method (i.e., lack of data, heterogeneity of data, different levels of precision of the data available) [19]. Secondary data can be defined as data collected by others, not specifically for the research question at hand [20]. In the case of this research, the term secondary data mainly refers to data collected by companies (i.e., annual activities report, financial data, official website). Moreover, data from press (i.e., newspapers articles, websites) and grey literature (i.e., not published academic researches, reports, white papers) have been taken into consideration.
According to the case survey methodology proposed by [18], a group of relevant case studies for the analysis of parcel lockers location have been analysed according to the factors impacting location choices that came out inductively from the literature review previously discussed. The analysed cases are summarised in Table 2.

Table 2: Case study analysed form companies implemented parcel lockers in Europe

Company	Country	Type of company	Analysed service	Source*
Australia Post	Australia	Postal operator	MyPost	https://auspost.com.au/
La Poste	France	Postal operator	Pickup Station lockers	https://www.pickup.fr/pudo/pickup-station-en.sls
Bpost	Belgium	Postal operator	Cubee	https://cubee.be/
CTT Portugal post	Portugal	Postal operator	ctt24h	https://www.ctt24h.pt/
HongKong Post	Hong Kong	Postal operator	iPostal Station	https://www.hongkongpost.hk/en/receiving_mail/ipostal/index.html

PostNord	Denmark	Postal operator	PostNord +SwipeBox	https://www.postnord.com/
Posti	Finland	Postal operator	smartpost	https://www.posti.fi/en/private/receiving-of-item/picking-up-from-locker
Poczta Polska	Poland	Postal operator	Poczta Polska + SwipeBox	https://www.posti.fi/en
Swiss Post	Switzerland	Postal operator	MyPost24	https://www.post.ch/en/receiving-mail/receipt-locations/my-post-24
USPS	USA	Postal service provider	Gopost	https://gopost.usps.com/go
InPost	Poland	Postal and parcel lockers service provider	Paczkomaty	https://inpost.pl/
Keba	Austria	Parcel locker Provider	KePol	https://www.keba.com/en/logistics-solutions/products/lockers/lockers
Correos	Spain	CEP company	CityPaq	https://www.correos.es/
DHL	Germany	CEP company	packstations	https://www.dhl.de/en/privatkunden/pakete-empfangen/an-einem-abholort-empfangen/packstation-empfang.html
UPS	USA	CEP company	Access Point	https://www.ups.com/it/en/services/individual-shipper/ups-access-point-deliveries.page
Cainiao Network	China	CEP company	Cainiao Post	https://global.cainiao.com
Amazon	USA	Online shopping platform	Amazon Lockers	https://www.amazon.com/b?ie=UTF8&node=6442600011

* for space constraints, only the main websites referring to the services mentioned are listed. The complete list of secondary data used for research on white papers, reports and newspaper articles is available on request.

The use of the case survey methodology with multiple sources enhanced both the reliability and validity of the study [21], but there are also some limitations. The use of information form different sources and the need to codify the contents the secondary data for extracting homogeneous, unique and well-defined factorsinevitably leads to a simplification of the process.

4. Results and discussion

This section analyses the factors that influence the parcel lockers location according to the performed literature review, and the roles that these factors play in several real case studies of parcel lockers implementation projects.

4.1. Availability

The customer's concern is represented by the delivery time and the risk of non-delivery. According to PostNord [22], most clients use lockers at times when branches are closed or at weekends. Parcel lockers can, therefore, be the solution to these types of problems, because they are one of the most flexible methods and are available 24 hours a day, seven days a week. If located in supermarkets, shopping malls, or post offices, they do not allow a 24/7 coverage: in this case, the hourly flexibility is reduced and depends on the opening hours of the place where the locker is located.
Greater time available for the pickup operations made by customers allows to have a broader range of customers who are available at the parcel reception at very different times. The ability of the buyer to travel to the site once they are finished working or at the weekend avoids having to postpone the time of collection and sacrifice time during the day that would otherwise be engaged in other activities. In other cases, hourly flexibility becomes a factor that favours the courier, guaranteeing the possibility of planning and making deliveries at off-peak times, in the early morning or the evening according with the analysed CEP companies projects (UPS, DHL, Cainiaio, Correos).

In addition, the shorter parcels storage time in the lcokers should be considered: the reduced space dedicated to the storage of the goods and the high turnover (considered as the use of lockers and the need to have free space to position the products) allow in most cases a stay between three and five days. The greater ease and rapidity of access to lockers already allows customers to pick up the ordered goods more comfortably, not requiring a further extension of the parcel storage time.

4.2. Accessibility

The accessibility of a parcel locker depends on its location and the concentration of the market in the served area. It is therefore essential to have a positioning and coverage strategy outlined by couriers and other operators at the design stage. As a result, the number of lockers and their geographical location impact the effort that the customer must make to collect the order. Increasing the number of locations distributed throughout the territory increases the capillarity and proximity of these to the end-user.
The customer will find more easily a comfortable locker, and that requires the least possible deviation from the places that presides so that the locker integrates with the daily journey of the customer. Besides, it can also be challenging to ensure secure locker locations and to ensure the safety of customers and their parcels at potentially dangerous times and places.
In order to maintain a high occupancy rate, the locker must also be efficient. According to InPost, DHL and LaPoste the best locations for this type of measurement, taking into account the concentration density of the population, are also linked to their availability are mainly metro stations, bus stations, industrial areas and high-traffic areas, service stations, shopping centres, supermarket car parks, schools and universities, bank ATMs.

4.3. Security

In order to assess the safety of the delivery models, it is necessary to determine the factors that depend on the delivery process and the volume of products delivered. The first parameter considered for all the projects analysed is "delivery success", which is the real possibility to know if the product has been delivered and then be able to verify the delivery. The second parameter is the use of cameras that record 24 hours a day what happens at the delivery points according with Keba and InPost. Finally, real-time connectivity with a private or local police security system must be considered and this is a common solution for national post operators such as LaPoste, Bpost, Posti and Swiss Post.
In the case of an attended delivery, the courier can have the customer sign a document when he receives the package. In this way, the couries has a document that certifies the success of delivery. It is not possible to guarantee success from the moment the courier deposits the package leaving it at the customer's home without the signature. On the contrary, successful delivery to the parcel lockers takes place when the courier deposits the package in the locker and closes it. For this factor, the locker is a more than safe solution even if the courier must be careful to guard the truck once it loads the packages into the lockers. The solution with locker, is subject to the theft of opportunistic type, despite having security cameras and also real-time connections. There is the possibility of being stolen after picking up the package, outside the surveillance field of the security cameras. In order to guarantee maximum security, they are inserted in the monitored sites (for example, petrol stations, 24-hour car parks, supermarkets). Besides, each machine has usually an anti-intrusion mechanism through cameras for the surveillance of the terminals, which will not record the faces of buyers (for a matter of privacy), active function unless the alarm sounds according with Keba and InPost.

4.4. Environmental Impact / Land Occupation

Consider a simplistic delivery routing route where the courier picks up parcels from the hub, delivers at each node if possible and returns to the sorting centre. The problems that arise with home delivery are determined by the number of customers who are available at home at that time and the capacity of the truck that determines the number of nodes to visit, as well as the distance between them. If customers were not present, the problem of missing delivery is introduced, which leads to the reformulation of a second mission for that package, leaving out another, with a further increase in environmental impacts. If a percentage of the deliveries are destined to the parcel lockers, it means that for the mission there will be fewer points to visit, fewer trucks to use and consequently fewer distances to cover. By adopting this solution consistently with many parcel lockers that allow having a certain capillarity, traffic and environmental impact decrease. The density of lockers does not seem to influence the processes; it has an impact especially on the courier who needs to extend its journey to fill the lockers, thus increasing emissions. However, the possibility of travelling at full load softens the effect of this phenomenon. For this reason, if deliveries are made to a CDP, if it does not have the capacity, the mission will not only visit one node but will also visit many nodes. Parcel lockers can also solve this problem thanks to their modularity: it means that the cabinet can be expanded according to the level of demand during demand peaks periods (i.e., Black Friday, Christmas, Summer Sales) [13].

4.5. Costs

Most customers shop online because it is fast and convenient, but the delivery, in many cases currently is not yet. The main reasons why customers change their logistics operator are lower prices, better convenience, and comfort in receiving parcels. Both the customer and the courier are therefore looking for the option that reduces the overall cost of delivery.
It is difficult to make a direct comparison between the different delivery options because there are many factors involved such as the type of delivery provided by different e-commerce sites, the volume and weight of the package, the distance to travel. All these costs can be mitigated by the possibility of not having to manage undelivered parcels, so there is no need to make another delivery attempt, reducing stock in the warehouse. For this reason, parcel lockers have a lower price for customers. According to postal operators analysed, the reduction in costs using lockers is 42% compared to traditional home deliveries [23] . Moreover, the installation of a parcel locker can also increase traffic to a store (physical or online) by offering an opportunity for commercial space through advertisements printed on the locker, and also allows the customer to manage cross-marketing and cross-selling operations.

4.6. Methods of use

The ease or difficulty of use influences the choice of delivery method or type of delivery adopted by the customer. The difficulty of use takes into account particular obstacles that may arise in economic, psychological, and intellectual form. However, there is an intellectual difficulty that is a minimum knowledge that people must have to make use of the method used for retrieving parcel: they need at least basic knowledge in the use of computers. For example, customers have to know how to use email and the web tools to purchase and choose the nearest locker to pick up the package, customers have to understand how to interact with the screen of the lockers to be able to pick up the package; however, it should not be an activity of high difficulty because these displays are designed to facilitate its use. The inconveniences that could be created can already be overcome by providing a telephone customer service connected to the lockers and the inclusion of voice/commands for people with disabilities. This type of barrier is not of great importance, because since delivery in e-commerce are considered, it is possible to assume that both the customers and the deliveries operators have at least sufficient competences to manage the different technological means.
The goods return could be more difficult than the delivery: to be able to return the product through the locker is essential to use the label (including barcode) that is sent through the online request, and applying it to the outside of the package. To open the locker door and enter the return, the customer has to scan or type on the locker keypad the return code on the label attached to the package. The return through locker is only available for products used for delivery in lockers, whose packaging do not exceeds the size allowed by the locker's boxes. The receipt of the authorisation to return must be included in the package with the item to be returned and usually must be performed within a certain amount of days.

4.7. Regulations

The european legislation actually does not provide for specific provisions on lockers, so the current legislation is referred to for similar cases. The locker could, therefore, be treated as a warehouse. However, because of the lack of specific and uniform rules on the subject, it cannot be excluded that the municipal authorities may also bring lockers back to commercial activity and as such make them subject to the

authorisation system (or authorisation rules) provided for in the case of vending machines. Concerning the building aspects, the installation of lockers in existing buildings does not entail the need to acquire specific building titles.
On the other hand, the building permit, requested in many countries as Italy, is provided in the case of "free-standing" lockers. Also, if the locker is installed in a public place, as is the case, for example, for newsstands, a permit to occupy public land will be required with payment of municipal charges. In this case, however, building permit will change depending on the location and type of structure. The uncertainty of the authorisation and building regime referring to the lockers makes it desirable to intervene in order to qualify the nature and prescribe in terms as similar and univocal as possible the titles and permits required for its installation and use in urban areas. This is one of the main reason why it is not easy to install parcel lockers, and there are very few companies that are able to operate in more than one country, such as Keba and InPost that are parcel lockers providers in the most part of the projects analysed.

5. Conclusions

The purpose of this paper is to find the main characteristics that influence the choice of the positioning of the parcel lockers. Correct positioning of the parcel lockers means being able to reach a more significant number of potential customers and make the delivery service competitive concerning home delivery. Moreover, the spread of the use of parcel lockers and the consequent decrease of home delivery would mitigate the negative aspects of this last (more vehicles used for delivery, more stops and consequently more significant congestion of the roads and emission of pollutants).
Thus, a review of the scientific literature was first made, but it showed the existence of a few articles, mostly conference papers, which dealt with this topic as a demonstration of how the topic is still not mature and still under study. For this reason, it was decided to apply a case-by-case survey methodology with secondary data. The main European and non-European projects concerning the installation and use of parcel lockers carried out by the leading companies operating in the field: postal operators, postal service providers, parcel suppliers, CEP companies and online shopping platforms were then analysed. By analysing the websites, reports, white papers and newspaper articles related to these projects, we confirmed and better understood the importance and role of localisation characteristics deriving from scientific literature. In particular, availability, accessibility, safety, environmental impact, costs, delivery times, usage and regulation emerged as factors to be taken into account when choosing where to locate parcel depots. The paper has some limitations: it is a first exploratory analysis aimed only at identifying and understanding the factors that influence the location of the parcel lockers. Further research is needed to understand how and to what extent these factors affect the choice of location, for example through the analysis of case studies to compare the performance and degree of use of parcel lockers located in different areas with different dominant characteristics. Also, future research should aim to understand how to use these features to build location models to support decisions.

Bibliography

1. Chen, Q., Conway, A.: Commercial Vehicle Parking Availability and Behavior for Residential Delivery in New York City. Transportation Research Board 95th Annual Meeting, Washington DC, United States (2016)
2. Grosman, L.:What the Amazon effect means for retailers. Forbes communicationscouncil (2018) https://www.forbes.com/sites/forbescommunicationscouncil/2018/02/22/what-the-amazon-effect-means-for-retailers/#100aedb22ded. Accessed 20 September 2019.
3. Chiu, C. M., Wang, E. T., Fang, Y. H., & Huang, H. Y.: Understanding customers' repeat purchase intentions in B2C e-commerce: the roles of utilitarian value, hedonic value and perceived risk. Inf. Syst. J., 24(1), 85--114 (2014)
4. Browne, M., Allen, J., Nemoto, T., Patier, D., Visser, J.: Reducing social and environmental impacts of urban freight transport: A review of some major cities. Procedia Soc. Behav. Sci., 39, 19--33 (2012)
5. Emeç, U., Çatay, B., Bozkaya, B.: An Adaptive Large Neighborhood Search for an E-grocery Delivery Routing Problem. Comput. Oper. Res., 69, 109--125 (2016)

6. US9120624B1 - Package Drop-off and Pick-up System - Google Patents. https://patents.google.com/patent/US9120624B1/en. Accessed 20 September 2019.
7. Deutsch, Y., & Golany, B.: A parcel locker network as a solution to the logistics last mile problem. Int. J. Prod. Res., 56(1-2), 251--261 (2018)
8. Lee, H., Chen, M., Pham, H.T., Choo, S.: Development of a Decision Making System for Installing Unmanned Parcel Lockers: Focusing on Residential Complexes in Korea. J. Civ. Eng., 23, 2713--2722 (2019).
9. Gonzalez-Feliu, J., Malhéné, N., Morganti, E., & Morana, J. (2014). The deployment of city and area distribution centers in France and Italy: Comparison of six representative models. Supp. Ch. For. An inter. J., 15(4), 84-99.
10. Wang, Y., Ong, T., Lee, L. H., & Chew, E. P. (2017, August). Capacitated competitive facility location problem of self-collection lockers by using public big data. In 2017 13th IEEE Conference on Automation Science and Engineering (CASE) (pp. 1344-1344). IEEE.
11. Zenezini, G., Lagorio, A., De Marco, A., Golini, R.: The Collection-And-Delivery Points Implementation Process from the Courier, Express and Parcel Operator's Perspective. IFAC-PapersOnLine, 51(11), 594--599 (2018)
12. Lemke, J., Stanisław I.,Korczak, J.: Usability of the Parcel Lockers from the Customer Perspective – The Research in Polish Cities. Transp. Res. Proc., The 2nd International Conference "Green Cities - Green Logistics for Greener Cities", 2-3 March 2016, Szczecin, Poland, 16 (January), 272--87 (2016)
13. Iwan, S., Kijewska, K., Lemke, J.: Analysis of Parcel Lockers' Efficiency as the Last Mile Delivery Solution – The Results of the Research in Poland. Transp. Res. Proc., Tenth International Conference on City Logistics 17-19 June 2015, Tenerife, Spain, 12 (January): 644 --55 (2015).
14. Lachapelle, U., Burke, M., Brotherton, A., Leung, A.: Parcel Locker Systems in a Car Dominant City: Location, Characterisation and Potential Impacts on City Planning and Consumer Travel Access, J. Transp. Geogr, 71, 1--14 (2018)
15. Faugere, L., Montreuil, B.: Hyperconnected Pickup & Delivery Locker Networks, 4th International Physical Internet Conference, 15 (2017)
16. Goethals, F., Leclercq-Vandelannoitte, A., Tütüncü, Y.: French consumers' perceptions of the unattended delivery model for e-grocery retailing. J. Retailing Consum. Serv., 19(1), 133--139 (2012)
17. Lucas, W. A.: The case survey method: Aggregating case experience, R-1515-RC, Santa Monica, CA, Rand Corporation (1974)
18. Larsson, R.: Case survey methodology: Quantitative analysis of patterns across case studies. Acad. Manag. Rev., 36(6), 1515--1546 (1993)
19. Cowton, C. J.: The use of secondary data in business ethics research. J. Bus. Ethics, 17(4), 423--434 (1998)
20. Stewart, D. W.: Secondary Research: Information Sources and Methods (Sage, Beverly Hills) (1984)
21. Frankfort-Nachmias, C., Nachmias D.: Research Methods in the Social Sciences, Fourth Edition (Edward Arnold, London) (1992)
22. PostNord: E-commerce in the Nordics (2019) https://www.postnord.com/contentassets/9e5ef8a408834cb982f30f145a6b2208/en_e-handeln-i-norden_halvar_2019_highres.pdf. Accessed 20 September 2019.
23. DHL: Annual report 2018: Acting Agile (2018). https://www.dpdhl.com/content/dam/dpdhl/en/media-center/investors/documents/annual-reports/DPDHL-2018-Annual-Report.pdf. Accessed on 20 September 2019.

I L S 2020
INTERNATIONAL CONFERENCE ON INFORMATION SYSTEMS, LOGISTICS & SUPPLY CHAIN
Austin, Texas April 22-24, 2020

Preliminaries on Supply Chain Risk & Sustainability

Cecilia Temponi

Texas State University, McCoy College of Business, San Marcos, TX, US.
{c.temponi@txstate.edu}

Abstract. This is preliminary research to increase understanding of a variety of risks in the supply chain. Explore is risk interconnections and implications to supply chain risk management & sustainability of supply chains. A supply chain involves multiple stakeholders including multi-tier suppliers and customers often located in different locations around the world. The business performance (e.g., efficiency, timeliness, stability), environmental and social implications of the supply chain have been increasingly perceived as integral parts of the global supply chain by all the stakeholders. Accountability towards sustainability is demanded from all the stakeholders. Literature review facilitates the classification of existing research streams on these areas and the extrapolation to supply chain risk and sustainability. Findings are the beginning of exciting research in the near future.

Keywords: Supply chain management, Supply chain risk, Sourcing, Sustainable supply chain, Collaboration in supply chain.

1. Introduction

A supply chain involves multiple stakeholders including multi-tier suppliers and customers often located in different locations. The business performance (e.g., efficiency, timeliness, stability), environmental and social implications of the supply chain have been increasingly perceived as integral parts of supply chain performance by stakeholders. Sustainable supply chains demands the supply chain to meet the economic, social, and environmental triple bottom line [1], [2]. As companies become more global in scale and dependent on emerging markets, the associated risks can only escalate [3], [4].

Social, economic, and environmental issues create further vulnerability in the supply chain. For instance, a supply chain disruption attributed to climate change was the unusually prolonged drought in Russia over the summer of 2010 [5], [6]. By early August of that year, over one-fifth of Russia's wheat crop had been destroyed and the government banned all grain exports, contributing to wheat price futures reaching their highest point in nearly 2 years. Consequently, cereal manufacturers were amongst the many food manufacturers facing significant price pressure. As a result, General Mills announced an increases of it cereal line between 4 and 5% in September 2010. These is just an examples of supply disruptions that have severely impacted the global supply chains and have made it critical for supply chain managers to come up with strategies to cope with these unforeseen events that lead to huge monetary losses. The situation of environmental changes, disrupts the supply sources, suppliers resources, strategic sourcing, organizations performance and then reflects on financial and social aspects of society. Sustainable supply chain management demands the supply chain to meet the economic, social, and environmental triple bottom line [1], [2].

Some researchers have explored the qualitative aspects of risk and uncertainty. Other researchers have addressed risk uncertainty through quantitative models. Scenarios have arisen with independent local disruptions and with local and global disruptions that may simultaneously result in all suppliers' disruptions

[7], [8]. Disruptions may arise from equipment break downs, local labor strike, bankruptcy, local natural disasters, etc.

The objectives of this research are: i) a preliminary exploration of the concepts facilitating the development of a framework addressing risk and its interconnections to global organizations and sustainability. ii) a preliminary framework that may assist in identifying risk within the different stakeholders of the supply chain. iii) the future research agenda based on these preliminary findings. A literature review is addressed next to consider the current state of risk, supply chain risk management (SCRM) and the implications to sustainability to both of the topics. The last section addresses conclusions and future research motivated by the findings from the literature review.

2. Literature review

Globalization has brought other significant risks to organizations worldwide and many of these risks evolved due to the nature of worldwide transactions and operations. Risk makes the supply chains vulnerable and consequently impacts the overall organization's performance and that of the partners of the supply chain. [9], [10], [11]. Thus, we will address next, Risk; Sourcing, Sustainability and proposed a framework to be explored in future research. This is a preliminary step and will be followed up with an empirical process in future research.

2.1. Risk related concepts

It is essential to have an understanding of the types of risks associated with supply chains if adequate risk management ought to take place in today's global supply chains. There are several categorizations of risks and several definitions of risk.

[12] indicated that all human endeavors and operations carry some risk and *uncertainty*. Risk is the effect of uncertainty on objectives as per the International Organization of Standards (ISO). Additionally, [13] indicated that "in whatever way people use the term 'risk', there is always a common element, namely, the fact that there is uncertainty about a future outcome." A distinction needs to be made between *uncertainty* due to an unknown event (Uncertainty) and due to a known event (Risk) as per [14]. The degree of uncertainty surrounding the event determines the level of risk. The more uncertain the decision maker is of whether the event will take place and what the outcome will be, the greater the possible deviation of the actual from the expected result. [15] suggested to call the terms "known-unknown" and "unknown-unknown." For instance, suppliers performance and operational risks can fall into the "known-unkown"; however, natural disasters will fall on the "unknown-unknown." In the line spectrum of pure risk to pure uncertainty or known to unknown, different types of risks emerged and can be mitigated up to certain extend, but not eradicated. Thus, risk mitigation has evolved and become more and more important for organizations.

Some researchers [9], [10], [11], [16] have set the basis to categorized supply chain risks into two comprehensive categories: operational and disruption (catastrophic) risks. Operational risks is due to inherent uncertainties in a supply chain such as coordination issues, sudden decrease of supply, sudden rise in cost, technology fallout to name a few. The disruption risks are either man made or caused by natural disaster. Some of them include terrorist attacks, civil unrest, political uncertainty, labor strikes and natural disasters - hurricanes, droughts, earthquakes, and so forth. Catastrophic risks is much more than that of operational risks [17], [18]. Business disruptions due to sustainability issues tend to revolve around global supply chains [19] and with their geographic complexity and pressure for cost and lead time reduction, global supply chains are susceptible [20] Disruptions can lead to various risks, for instance, financial risks due to lost sales and environmental penalties, and reputational risk due to negative publicity [17].

Other researcher categorized risk by Macro and Micro risk factors. Table 1 provides a definition and summary of these risks and sources as well as the classification. Macro elements are classified within the elements of PESTLE analysis proposed by [21]. P = political, E = economic, S = social, T = technological, L = legal and E = environmental elements. It is worth to note that those labeled as "Disruption" are the elements out of the control of organizations or their supply networks. Micro elements are clustered as elements to the organizations and their supply networks. The operational risks, refers to the risks due to inherent uncertainties in a supply chain such as coordination issues, sudden decrease of supply, sudden rise in cost, and so forth.

Table 1: Categorization and types of risks.

*Categories**	*Risk types*	*Factor*	*Description/Example*
Operational or Disruption	**Macro**		
Disruption		Political	Changes in trading policies, internal political instability, regional issues. Unstable country infrastructure,
Disruption		Economic	Global economy issues, elimination of tax benefits to certain organizations, minimum wages, commodity prices, weakness of supply network, exchange rates, interest rates
Disruption		Social	Terrorism, war, national strikes; labor availability; media attention and transparency; Corruption.
Operational		Technological	Unreliable technologies causing disasters.
Disruption or Operational		Legal	Increased regulation toward protection of customers and environment (such as difficulties to obtain environmental certificates of operation or increased product regulations)
Disruption		Environmental	Flood, avalanche, storm, earthquake or other natural disasters
	Micro		
Operational		Demand	Uncertain demand, inaccurate forecast, short lead-times, short lifecycle, cost pressure, high requirements from customers, deficient customer relationships, poor communication of specifications, Bullwhip effect
Operational		Manufacturing	Low capacity/capabilities, accidents, labor strikes, lack of training, poor working conditions, breaks, inventory cost, obsolescence, low manufacturing flexibility and innovation, poor quality controls, maintenance
Operational		Supply	Inability to handle changes, failures to comply with specs, poor service, price, technological issues, poor quality, bankruptcy, small network, lack of tiers visibility, poor relationship with suppliers
Operational		Information	Limited ERP implementation, infrastructure breakdown, information delays, lack of information between areas, IT security, lack of compatibility
Operational		Transportation	Accidents, unnecessary handling, transportation damages, lack of alternatives, pirate attacks, obsolete technology, port strikes, route complexity, deficient port capacity, difficult procedures at customs
Operational		Financial	Financial distress of a company or its suppliers, financial weakness of customers, insurance issues, low profits, market share challenges, poor cash flows management, poor management of accounts receivables–payable

* [9], [10], [11] and [16]
$ Adapted from [22] For an extensive list on risks, refer to [23].

2.2. Defining Supply Chain Risk Management

[24] defined supply chain risk management (SCRM) as 'the practice of managing the risk of any factor or event that can materially disrupt a supply chain, either within a single company or spread across multiple companies.' [19] and [25] indicated that the main objectives of SCRM are i) an assessment of potential risks and ii) the development of an appropriate plane to avoid or mitigate it. The ultimate purpose of SCRM is to enable cost avoidance, to continue customer service levels and to maintain market position [26]. Nonetheless, [27] suggested that SCRM is the identification and evaluation of risks and consequent losses in the global supply chain, and the implementation of appropriate strategies through a coordinated approach

among supply chain members (stakeholders) with the objective of reducing the risks. This definition embraces the supply chain organization and its interactions with the downward and upward components. [27]'s definition acknowledges the complexity inherent in global supply chain. The supply chain not only deals with internal operations but essentially considered external relationships with their partners. Amongst the most commonly referred SCRM definition is the one proposed by [28] "is the identification and management of risks for the supply chain, through a coordinated approach amongst supply chain members, to reduce supply chain vulnerability as a whole." In this definition, it is clear that in additions to the previous points, the element of collaboration is a critical one across the supply chain.

Figure 1, illustrates the risks associated with the supply chain, thus what is involved on SCRM. The elements presented are Global supply chain, Supply chain dynamics, Risks and sustainability. Collaboration is also highlighted through the dotted lines.

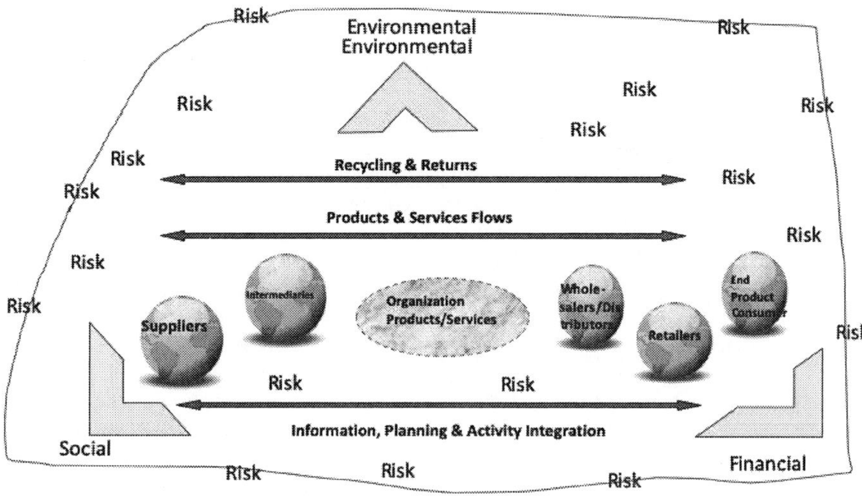

Figure 1. Global Supply Chains within Risk and Sustainability.

[29] and [26] classify supply chain risk into five risks associated with process, control, demand, supply, and environmental. On Fig. 1, it is presented that all five risks impact the organization as well as all of the stakeholders that are located locally and in many places around the world. These stakeholders are also functioning in a sustainable initiatives.

2.3. Sustainability

The term sustainability was originally coined by John Elkington in 1994 in the phrase, "people, planet, and profit" to describe the **triple bottom line** and the goal of sustainability. The phrase has been used since then in a variety of disciplines and contexts. Research has been active to reconcile within other disciplines and areas of science the sustainability concept. Successful sustainability initiatives needed decision models that required proper capital investments. [30] researched the impact of sustainability and external integration. They found that external integration controlled by SCRM impacted manufacturing flexibility and influenced sustainability. Additionally in 2017, [31] converged that communication, commitment, flexibility, synchronous decision-making, and coordination between SC stakeholders was necessary to moderate extreme demand fluctuations. Moreover, sustainability metrics were found to be impacted by organizational flexibility and effective SCM procedures of global organizations [32].

Prior scholars used various research techniques to show thematic and numerical relationships between SCM and organizational sustainability [32], [33], and [34]. Social, environmental, and economic indicators affected global SCM sustainability initiatives to measure performance. [35] specified that environmental and economic dimensions are focal research topics, globally. However, sustainable global SCM has been evaluated from the environmental, economic, and social dimensions; [36] and [37] found that academic research highlighted one or two dimensions, and falsely equated green and sustainability with the social dimension. Therefore, social, environmental, and economic indicators are critical to global SCRM and sustainability initiatives.

It seems clear from previous research that sustainable operations place a particular emphasis on managing economic, environmental, and social sustainability risks (Jaehn 2016). The sustainable management of SC risks is emphasized as an important strategic element. Risk management is then a supporting facet of sustainable supply chain by maintaining the requirements of contingency planning, supply disruptions, and outbound supply chains. Sustainable products are feasible though sustainable operations. Risk management for sustainable supply chains shall improve supply chain performance by reasonable trade-offs and also by a greater number of win–win situations between the sustainability dimensions of the triple bottom line.

3. Conclusions and Future Research

There are numerous definitions for risk sources; the definition that best match with operational definitions includes that risk sources are "any variables which cannot be predicted with certainty and from which disruptions can emerge." [26], [19]. Also of significant importance is that risk sources have become more essentials as supply chain become more complex and modern. The increasing trends of supply chain time compression, responsiveness and agility, and the outsourcing of production to lower labor cost has increased risks to natural and man-made disasters [27], [19]. Business disruptions due to sustainability issues tend to revolve around global supply chains [19], and with their geographic complexity and pressure for cost and lead time reduction, global supply chains are susceptible [36], [37]. Disruptions can lead to various risks, for instance, financial risks due to lost sales and environmental penalties, and reputational risk due to negative publicity. Risk management has become of critical importance due to increased frequency of risks, longer recovery time and the focal firm's responsibility for unethical issues and any actions at any tier in its supply chain. Little is known about the relationship between sustainability and risk issues in supply chains in general [19] and [34]. It is not completely clear what sustainability risk is, how companies in volatile and demand-driven markets should be managing it, how sustainability risk affects operational performance and, finally, what could be an appropriate framework or typology for managing supply chain risk within sustainability. The demand for such investigations is supported by the interrelationships between the components presented in Fig. 1.

The author is currently developing a criteria to be considered for interconnecting sustainability and supply chain risks. Once the framework is developed, some cases studies will be introduced to support the components of such model.

4. References

1. Beske P. Seuring, S. : Sustainable supply chain management practices and dynamic capabilities in the food industry: A critical analysis of the literature. **Supply Chain Management;** 19, 3, 322-333 (2014)
2. Tseng, M.-L., Islam, M.S., karia, N., FAuzi, F.A., Afrin, S.: A literature review on green supply chain management: trends and future challenges. Resour. Conserv. Recycl. 141, 145-162. (2019)
3. O'Rourke, D., The science of sustainable supply chains. Science 344 (6188), 1124-1127 (2014)
4. Nishat Faisal, M.; Banwet, D K; Shankar, R: Mapping supply chains on risk and customer sensitivity dimensions Industrial Management & Data Systems; 106, 6, 878-895 (2006)
5. New York Times. https://www.nytimes.com/2010/08/06/world/europe/06russia.html
6. Reuters news https://www.reuters.com/article/us-russia-heat/drought-ruins-russia-wheat-u-s-says-no-world-crisis-idUSTRE6751T820100812
7. Nouira, I., Temponi, C., Hammami, R., & Frein, Y: Impact of a carbon emissions-sensitive demand on the design of forward supply chains. *International Journal of Production Economics*, *173*, 80–98 (2016).
8. Temponi, C.: Strategic Sourcing and Suppliers' Selection: An Analysis. In 4th Ed. International Conf. on Inf. Logistics & Supply Chain. ILS 2014, Netherlands. (2014).
9. Kilubi, I.: Investigating current paradigms in supply chain risk management—a bibliometric study. Bus Process Manag J 22, 4. 662–692 (2016)

10. Nagurney A, Li D: Equilibria and dynamics of supply chain network competition with information asymmetry in quality and minimum quality standards. Comput Manag Sci 11(3):285–315(2014)
11. Nagurney A, Yu M, Floden J: Supply chain network sustainability under competition and frequencies of activities from production to distribution. Comput Manag Sci 10(4):397–422 (2013)
12. Olson, D. & Dash Wu, D.: A review of enterprise risk management in supply chain, *Kybernetes* 39,5, 694–706 (2010) https://doi.org/10.1108/03684921 011043198
13. Tranchard, S.: *The new ISO 31000 keeps risk management simple*, International Organization for Standardization, (2018) from https://www.iso. org/news/ref2263.html.
14. Kumar, M. & Gregory, M.: An exploration of risk management in global industrial investment', *Risk Management* 15, 4, 272–300 (2013) https://doi.org/10.1057/ rm.2013.8
15. Simchi-Levy, D., Kaminsky, P. & Simchi-Levy, E.: *Designing and managing the supply chain: Concepts, strategies and case studies*, 4th Ed., McGraw-Hill, New York (2009)
16. Berger PD, Gerstenfeld A, Zeng AZ: How many suppliers are best? A decision-analysis approach. Omega Int J. Manag Sci 32(1):9–15 (2004
17. Sawik T Selection of supply portfolio under disruption risks. Omega 39:194–208 (2011)
18. Mehrjoo, M. and Pasek, Z.: Risk assessment for the supply chain of fast fashion apparel industry: a system dynamics framework. International Journal of Production Research, 54, 1, 28-48 (2016)
19. Lee, K. and Vachon, S.: Supply chain sustainability risk, Business Value and Sustainability: An Integrated Supply Network Perspective, Springer, Palgrave Macmillan Publishers, 245-280 (2016)
20. Boström, M. and Micheletti, M.: Introducing the sustainability challenge of textiles and clothing, J. of Consumer Policy, 39, 4, 367-375. (2016).
21. Chanson, G.: Macro-environment's effects on onshore outsourcing: the transaction costs approach, Journal of Global Operations and Strategic Sourcing, 11, 1, 27-38. (2018)
22. Hernandez, D. F. and Haddud, A.: Value creation via supply chain risk management in global fashion organizations outsourcing production to China. Journal of Global Operations and Strategic Sourcing, 11, 2, 250-272 (2018)
23. Ho, W., Zheng, T., Yildiz, H. and Talluri, S.: Supply chain risk management: a literature review, International Journal of Production Research, 53, 16, 5031-5069. (2015)
24. Kessinger, C. & Macmorrow, J.: Supply chain risk management: A perspective from practice, in P. Kouvelis, L. Dong, O. Boyabatli & R. Li (eds.), *Handbook of integrated risk management in global supply chains*, 515–535, Wiley, New YorK (2012)
25. Yaakub, S., & Mustafa, H.K.: Supply Chain Risk Management for the SME's. Academic Journal of Interdisciplinary Studies, 4,1, 151-158. (2015) https://doi.org/10.5901/ajis.2015.v4n1s2p151
26. Kern, D., Moser, R., Hartmann, E. & Moder, M.: Supply risk management: Model development and empirical analyses, *International Journal of Physical Distribution and Logistics Management,* 42, 1, 60–82. (2012)
27. Manuj, I., & Mentzer, J.T.: Global supply chain risk management. Journal of Business Logistics, 29, 1, 133-155 (2008).
28. Jüttner, U.: Supply chain risk management: Understanding the business requirements from a practitioner perspective. The International Journal of Logistics Management, 16, 1, 120-141. (2003)
29. Christopher, M., Peck, H.: Building the resilient supply chain. Int. J. Logist. Manag. 15, 2, 1-14. (2004)
30. Chaudhuri, A., Boer, H., and Taran, Y.: Supply chain integration, risk management and manufacturing flexibility. *International Journal of Operations & Production Management,* 38(3), 690-712. (2018)
31. Almeida, M. M., Marins, F. A., Salgado, A. M., Santos, F. C., and da Silva, S. L.: The importance of trust and collaboration between companies to mitigate the bullwhip effect in supply chain management. *Maringá,* 39(2), 201-210. (2017)
32. Katiyar, R., Meena, P. L., Barua, M. K., Tibrewala, R., and Kumar, G.: Impact of sustainability and manufacturing practices on supply chain performance: Findings from an emerging economy. *International Journal of Production Economics,* 197, 303-316.(2018)
33. Mor, R. S., Singh, S., Bhardwaj, A., and Singh, L.: Technological implications of supply chain practices in agri-food sector: A review. *International Journal of Supply and Operations Management,* 2(2), 720-747. (2015)
34. Ngai, E. W., Law, C. C., Lo, C. W., Poon, J. K., and Peng, S.: Business sustainability and corporate social responsibility: Case studies of three gas operators in China. *International Journal of Production Research,* 56(1), 660-676. (2018)
35. Ekanayake, S., Childerhouse, P., and Sun, P.: The symbiotic existence of interorganizational and interpersonal ties in supply chain collaboration. *The International Journal of Logistics Management,* 28(3), 723-754. (2017)
36. Varsei, M.: Sustainable supply chain management: A brief literature review. *Journal of Developing Areas,* 50(6). 411-419. (2016).
37. Tang, C.S. : Perspectives in supply chain risk management", International Journal of Production Economics, 103, 2, 451-488 (2006)

I L S 2020
INTERNATIONAL CONFERENCE ON INFORMATION SYSTEMS, LOGISTICS & SUPPLY CHAIN
Austin, Texas April 22-24, 2020

Defining and characterizing Urban Logistics Spaces: insights from a port city and generalization issues

Karen Meza-Peralta[1], Jesus González-Feliu[2], Jairo R. Montoya-Torres[1], Laura Palacios-Argüello[3]

[1] Research Group in Logistics Systems, Faculty of Engineering, Universidad de La Sabana, km 7 autopista norte de Bogotá, D.C., Chia (Cundinamarca), Colombia.
[2] Ecole des Mines de Saint-Etienne, EVS UMR 5600, Institut Henri Fayol, 42023 cedex, Saint-Etienne, France.
[3] Laboratoire Ville Mobilité Transport UMR T9403 ENPC UGE, 6-8 Avenue Blaise Pascal, 77455 Marne-la-Vallée cedex 2, France

{karen.meza@gmail.com, jesus.gonzalez-feliu@emse.fr, jairo.montoya@unisabana.edu.co, laura.palacios@emse.fr}

Abstract. This paper presents a preliminary analysis of Urban Logistics Spaces (ULS) in Barranquilla, Colombia, with the aim of defining a typology in port cities in developing countries and examining the relevance of using a specific typology for those cities or having a unique and general typology, for any city in the world. Firstly, the background to the research is presented. Then, the methodology for the characterization of urban facilities and the definition of the typology is presented. A qualitative characterization was carried out through semi-structured interviews, in order to understand the specificities of the ULS located in Barranquilla, and to analyses how the logistic spaces that are not yet in that context could improve the city's logistic system. The data collection was carried out with the participation of nine (9) actors belonging to the logistic system of the city of Barranquilla. The results show that the "standard" typology chosen, typical of the European context, is partially recognized by the professionals of Barranquilla, and therefore the identification of other types of ULS currently operating in the Colombian context was obtained. Consequently, it is necessary to standardize the typology of urban logistic spaces and to deepen the analyses to define a general typology, which would be reduced in relation to the type of city, but which would have a unified general base capable of being later adapted to any city.

Keywords: City logistics, Urban Logistic Spaces (ULS), Typology, Case Study.

1. Introduction

Freight transport in cities is essential to their economic life, while at the same time it is a source of certain nuisances, in particular urban road congestion and pollution. The movement of goods represents approximately 10 to 20% of all journeys in a conurbation[**¡Error! No se encuentra el origen de la referencia.**], so various urban stakeholders deal with proposing solutions to reduce environmental nuisances and cost of urban freight distribution. One strategy is the implementation of ULS, which can be seen as the interface between interurban and urban supply chains, linking producers and urban consumers [2]. ULS are interfaces used to facilitate the relations between dispatches and receptions, between the roads and the point of operation, between the city and its distant surroundings. Their purpose is to reconfigure the flows through the city for the benefit of all or some of the parties affected by economic exchanges. Currently, work on ULS typologies is mainly carried out in Europe (and other developed countries), but its deployment in emerging economies remains less explored [2]. It seems therefore interesting in these contexts to examine the suitability of ULS, mainly in logistics cities such as those related to ports with large industrial and logistics structures. The aim of this paper is to identify existing solutions with respect to ULS in the city of Barranquilla, Colombia and to analyze which logistic spaces (present or not) could improve the city's logistic system. In fact, an important effort has been made in developed countries to evaluate and implement urban logistics solutions for last mile delivery in cities. However, efforts in low- and middle-income countries are not well documented in the scientific literature. Therefore, we also propose a typology of ULS that can be generalized in different contexts and types of cities according to the results obtained of the case study and a review of the existing ULS. The paper is organized as follows. First, background information on the current state of knowledge and practice regarding urban logistics spaces is presented, followed by a description of the research methodology. The results of the study are then discussed and a general typology of ULS was proposed. The paper ends with some conclusions and opportunities for future research.

2. Background

An Urban Logistics Space (ULS) can be defined as an interface used to facilitate the relationship between shipments and receipts, between roads and the point of operation, between the city and its surroundings, with the purpose of reconfiguring the flows through the city for the benefit of all or some of the affected parties (actors) by the economic exchanges [2]. According to [4], in Colombia, logistics facilities are commonly known as logistics centers, with the understanding as strategically located facilities in highly productive regions with the purpose of concentrating and supplying services which are complementary to their main activities and to work in function of the physical integration of the territory and conforming a social factory that propends for the well-being, the strengthening of productive activities and the consolidation of political-administrative bonds to promote territorial competitiveness.

The selection of a specific land use strategy by a private party often depends on the basic operations it will host, the structure and size of the customer orders, the logistics units managed, the material handling costs, the availability of storage space and labor resources, among others, i.e. mainly the technical aspects and the needs of the company. Regarding the conditions for the development of logistics functions in urban areas, and although the most appropriate solution would be to establish large facility complexes in metropolitan areas, large cities tend to have expansion policies not entirely following this logic [6], leading to logistics sprawl phenomena [7]. In this way, the impacts of locating logistics centers in metropolitan centers or peripheral areas have been widely discussed by various researchers [7][8][9]. In relation to immediate port hinterlands, which remain relatively captive, distant hinterlands are highly contested. In cases where road is the dominant mode, transport costs are a function of distance and therefore often the determining factor in the choice of port [9].

The concept of an interface designed to orient flows in direction to urban areas is relatively old. The first approaches date back to about sixty years ago, with the development of the first urban logistics facilities (in the form of urban consolidation platforms), although the systematic proposal of urban consolidation and distribution centers has been deployed in the 90's [10]. In practice, those facilities, initially deployed on an economic viewpoint [11], turned out to be difficult to implement due to the diversity of the application cases encountered, in contrast to the transport of passengers, except for the geography of the movements, which takes forms that are generally similar Those obstacles have certainly prevented the emergence of systems for centralizing consignments. However, the solutions have been refined over time and we have seen the appearance of new and different categories of facilities. Moreover, in cities of emerging countries, and mainly in those with a high logistics activity (like port or intermodal platform cities), this typology merits precision and a more in-depth analysis, to evidence the suitability of that classification and the eventual needs of revising it. For those reasons, we propose below, via a case study, a methodology to adapt and evolve this typology to other contexts. It is important to mention that a general typology of ULS would allow a valuable tool for decision makers on the many aspects that can be useful for the selection, design and/or location of logistics spaces in any type of city or context.

3. Research Methodology

Boudouin et al. [2] present a typology of ULS for the European context, according to their applicable spatial and functional coverage, with slightly different objectives in comparison with the Colombian context. These spaces are classified into two large groups, the Generalist ULS and the Specialist ULS. This typology (see Table 1) was used as the basis for this study. On one side, Generalist Urban Logistics Spaces are considered as high-rotation storage platforms, as points of articulation between urban and interurban areas. Generally, these sites tend to be easily accessible and located near the delivery areas, which makes them very desirable spaces. Among these are the so-called urban logistics areas, distribution centers, and multifunctional buildings. On the other side, the problems of urban deliveries are not of the same type, each city, each context has its own specificities and according to social and economic issues. Therefore, Specialists Urban Logistics Spaces adapt to a wider range of products and clients, and are categorized, spatially and functionally, into three groups.

Table 1: Comparison between Generalist and Specialist urban logistics spaces.

	Types ULS	Summary
GENERALIST	**Urban Logistics Zones (ULZ)**	It allows the actors of Urban Logistics to position themselves close to customers to minimize vehicle movements. Functionality: Transshipment and Operations before final delivery.
GENERALIST	**Urban Distribution Centres (UDC)**	It manages the transport flows in the city to channel it to a site where they are consolidated and sent by a specialized operator. Functionality: Operates dense areas in the most complicated hours.
GENERALIST	**Logistics Hotels: Multi-Functional Buildings**	Multi-purpose building, Ability to integrate various types of activities around logistics and distribution. Large and attractive space increases the economy.
SPECIALIST	**Vehicles Host Point (VHP)**	Vehicle Host Points, due to the negative effects of other users. (Congestion, disorganization and other annoyances.) Appropriate place to park, which allows safe access for delivery drivers to operate their deliveries.
SPECIALIST	**Goods Reception Points (GRP)**	Replacement interfaces of the recipient, to avoid the last meters. The division is both spatial (Point of arrival or departure of the shipment) and temporary (delivery or collection in a period of time according to the interests of both parties.)
SPECIALIST	**Urban Logistics Boxes ULB**	Interfaces between the operator and the client, without any kind of necessary human presence at the place of transshipment. The main advantage of this is the control of time. (The notion of time is very important). The boxes can be fixed or mobile. They are implanted in private or public places.

Source: Adapted for academic purposes in [2].

In Colombia, the development of the logistics sector has been one of the biggest bets in the country in recent years, in a logical attempt to take advantage of land availability and the excellent strategic location of the country's ports, especially in the Caribbean Region[13]. Thus, the city of Barranquilla and its metropolitan area have had in the last years a strong vocation to be a center of logistic, industrial and specialized services, whose main task is to act as a link node of the country and the global economic dynamics. For this reason, the city of Barranquilla is taken as a case study.

Given the exploratory nature of this research, a qualitative study has been carried out to understand the specificities of urban logistics spaces in the city of Barranquilla, Colombia. This research is composed of a set of interviews to address the city's case study. The case study research approach is based on methods and tools used to collect information in the natural and unique context in which the studied phenomenon is developed considering the contextual and temporal aspects [14][15]. The importance and value of this method increases when existing perspectives or previously developed perspectives are not necessarily applied to the study in new contexts [14].Therefore, the above characteristics justify the case study approach as one of the inputs for the diagnosis of the city under study. It should be noted that studies of regulations, standards and other official and technical documents on logistics legislation in Colombia are, at this time, beyond the scope of this study. They will be analysed in future research developments.

The non-concentric characteristics of most Colombian cities, the population size, the growth of the cities, the complexity of mobility, among others, as well as the conditions, characteristics and regulations of the municipalities of the region call for particular and different context that needs to be explored. Information was collected using semi-structured interviews. An interview's guide on a set of selected stakeholders in the city Barranquilla, Colombia, was carried out, to verify how the proposed typology and taxonomy from literature can be changed to deal to the Colombian (and Latin American) realty.

Starting from the European typology of ULS, we identified which of these types of logistics spaces exist in the city of Barranquilla. Nine companies both public and private with different types of logistical participation (one 1PL, one 2PL, one 3PL, four 4PL, one 5PL and one public entity), were selected for the interviews. Logistics Managers, Supply Chain Managers or the equivalent were approached. The guided interview consisted of two main parts. The first was oriented to ask managers if they consider that there are logistics spaces in the city, according to the typology obtained from the literature review. No information on this typology was provided to the interviewee. In a second stage, the respondent was informed about this typology and then asked about his or her knowledge of these types of ULS.

4. Findings

4.1 Types of Urban logistics spaces for Barranquilla city by stakeholders

All cities in the world have particular characteristics in terms of their territorial organization, mobility, regulations and other fundamental aspects for the development of an urban logistics system. In the case of Colombia, the country is very diverse according to the context and needs of each region. The nine (9) actors of the logistic system of the city of Barranquilla who were interviewed, gave us their own definition of the logistic spaces according to the reality they live every day. From the interviews it can be inferred that in the context of Barranquilla an urban logistical space (ULS) is an area, which forms part of the supply chain, in which various essential operations (and services) are developed, allowing the distribution of goods with the objective of satisfying the needs of the clients and final consumers. Subsequently, the interviewees made their own classification (without having the proposal in the background section). Table 2 presents a summary of the ULS mentioned and the frequency.

Table 2: ULS of Urban Logistics System of Barranquilla's city.

STAKEHOLDERS		Types of Urban Logistics Spaces (ULS) Barranquilla																		
		Free trade zone	Industrial Parks	Package Store	Distribution centers	Lots	Ports - Docks	Place of transshipment	Industrial plant	Logistic agencies	Points of sale	Enlistment areas	Logistic centers	Business Centers	Logistics operators.	Customs warehouse	Green zones	Parking lots	Shed	Warehouses
1	1 PL	x	x	x	x	x	x													
2	4 PL	x	x	x	x		x		x	x	x			x						
3	4PL	x	x	x	x	x	x						x		x	x		x		x
4	5 PL	x	x	x	x		x							x	x		x	x	x	x
5	3 PL	x	x	x	x		x						x							
6	2PL	x	x	x	x		x								x			x		x
7	4 PL	x	x	x	x		x								x			x		
8	Public	x	x		x		x								x	x				x
9	4 PL	x	x	x	x		x	x			x				x					x
Total		9	9	8	9	2	9	1	1	1	2	0	2	2	6	2	1	3	1	5

Source: Own preparation based on the results obtained from the study.

According to the definitions of the ULS that are part of the context of the city of Barranquilla, there is a lack of denomination and classification of them. This is evidenced by the fact that most of the ULS that make up the city's logistics system carry out similar or even the same operations. The main reason that makes these logistics spaces easily identifiable by the actors is the volume of goods they handle. However, some of these spaces have more technology than others, which makes them very attractive, especially for users who require a type of integrated logistics service.

Knowing that most of the ULS in Barranquilla are identified by the actors according to the volume and variety of logistic services they offer, in the spaces mentioned by the interviewees, we found that their characteristics allow some of them to be "homologated" according to their functionality and coverage as is the case of the Parcel, Batch and Warehouse; these three spaces can be found in different sizes, and allow the storage of the merchandise before proceeding with its distribution. We also find Distribution Centers and Logistics Centers, both spaces are conceived as relatively large, technified spaces, where various types of basic logistics activities are carried out, to finally distribute goods, generally of all types.

4.2 Types of urban logistics spaces (ULS) in Barranquilla, according to the proposed typology

For the second phase of the study on the typology of urban logistics spaces (ULS), they were made known to the interviewees, the types of ULS that make up the logistics system of Europe and some definitions and characteristics of these spaces. Once the interviewees knew the categorization of the logistics spaces of the European context, they related the spaces of the city of Barranquilla (mentioned above), with the typology provided. Table 3 presents the relationship described by the participants of the study.

Table 3: ULS of Barranquilla's City according to the European typology.

STAKEHOLDERS	Types of Urban Logistics Spaces (ULS) Barranquilla					
	Generalist			Specialist		
	Urban Logistics Zones (ULZ)	**Urban Distribution Centres (UDC)**	**Logistics Hotels: Multi-Functional Buildings**	**Vehicles Reception Point (VHP)**	**Goods Reception Points (GRP)**	**Urban Logistics Boxes ULB**
1	x	x	x	x	x	
2	x	x	x	x	x	
3	x	x	x		x	
4	x	x			x	
5	x	x	x			
6	x	x	x	x	x	
7	x	x	x		x	
8	x	x	x			
9	x	x		x	x	

Source: Own preparation based on [2]

According to the ULS proposed typology, and to the relationship expressed by the interviewees, about the types of logistics spaces, it is denoted that most of the urban logistics spaces (ULS) that make up the logistics system of the city of the case study, they are Generalist spaces; high rotation platforms, where various types of operations are carried out depending on the distribution logistics and generally easy access to participants in the supply chain. Barranquilla is currently venturing into the design, creation and use of modern and more integrated spaces such as the Multi-Functional Buildings. In the opposite case, Barranquilla still does not have many Specialist Urban Logistics Spaces (ULS). In relation to Vehicles Reception Point (VHP), and Goods Reception Points (GRP) can be found today in private companies. While the ULB Urban Logistics Boxes are not part of the city's logistics system.

It should be noted that unlike the European context, in Barranquilla there are no urban logistics spaces that are administered by the government, accessible to any company that requires it. However, there are private companies that have their own points, and logistical spaces for their operation. Nowadays, the collaboration of different stakeholders (public and/or private) is being achieved and they are reaching an agreement for the management and use of this type of space, which is considered an advance for the city's logistics system. Regarding the typology of Generalist ULS, Urban Distribution Centres are present both in Europe and in Colombia, although with some small differences. Unlike the Colombian reality, the typology of European ULS indicates that the Urban Distribution Centres operate in the densest areas and at the most complicated times, while in Colombia, the ULS are generally located in the surroundings of the city (of easy access) and operate at the quietest times, facilitating the dynamism of the city.

4.3 How could the Urban Logistics Boxes (ULB) improve Barranquilla's city logistics system?

As mentioned in the previous section, Barranquilla does not yet have the Urban Logistics Boxes. Once it was identified that this logistical space does not form part of the city's logistical system, the actors involved were asked how they considered that the Urban Logistics Boxes could improve the city's system. All interviewees agreed that an automated and technologically advanced space, such as the Urban Logistics Boxes, could greatly improve the logistics system. They described that it could be a much more agile flow system, more economical in terms of time, transport, human resources and other types of costs that are considered for logistics operations. They considered aspects that affect not only the logistics system, but the pace and dynamism of the city in general. The importance of a space of this type for the reduction of environmental impact was also mentioned, which is part of the main objectives of Colombian Logistics until the year 2022.

5. Generalization issues

Due to its strategic location, Barranquilla´s city, during the last decades has had a strong vocation to be a logistic and industrial centre. Although each city has specific characteristics, it is possible that there are some cities, such as Barranquilla, that have similar logistical spaces, and that their geographical location allows for similar management of these types of spaces. For this reason, this section proposes a classification of ULS, aimed at cities that have specific areas such as ports and docks, especially if they are located in developing countries. The following proposed ULS classification refers to the type of operations carried out and the volume of trade handled (see Table 4). It should be noted that due to its privileged geographical location, Barranquilla has a kind of specialized urban logistics space such as ports, located on the coast or on the banks of a river where ships carry out loading and unloading operations.

Table 4. Preliminary proposed classification of Urban logistics spaces (ULS) for the Barranquilla context

	Generalist			Specialist	
Volume of Goods	**Storage Centers**	**Integral Consolidation Centers**	**Centers for Logistics management**	**International trade handling**	**Specific areas**
	Lots	Point of sale	Logistic agencies	Free trade zone	Enlistment areas
-	Package Store	Logistic centers	Business centers	Customs warehouse	Docks
	Warehouses	Distribution centers	Logistics operators		Transshipment facility
	Shed	Industrial Parks			Green Zones
+	Industrial Plant				Parking lots
					Ports/intermodal structures

Source: Own elaboration based on the results obtained from the study.

Table 4 shows a typology of urban logistics spaces that can be applied to different port cities in the world, given the characteristics of the city of Barranquilla.
When examining it in depth, we observe that most of the types of facilities are found in other contexts:
-Storage centres and integral consolidation centres are located in different cities in both developed and developing countries. However, since these facilities are generally located in areas of activity, the main differences are organizational and location, but not technical and functional, the main characteristics that define these platforms and their organizational issues remain similar in most contexts. In fact, in developed countries, the main industrial and business zones are located in peripheral areas, and in developing countries the mix of space (households, retail and industry/business) is greater, but the difference then arises in the location and socio-economic options, not in the functional aspects of the facilities.
-Logistics management centres are mainly business-related, and then seem to be applicable to different contexts, with cultural and socio-economic issues being on a second level to technical and functional issues.
-The management of international trade and specific areas will not apply to all cities (only those with such activities because they will have customs agencies or specific logistical activities specific to such modes and transport organizations will be able to deploy them), but then, we observe that transhipment/greenfield zones and ports (whether river or sea) and intermodal platforms will be present in a wide variety of cities. The typology seems then a first step into defining a stable, unified categorization but will need further work (for example testing it in other contexts) to state on its robustness and transferability.

Moreover, considering the results obtained, together with an exhaustive analysis of the literature on ULS and the existing ULS typologies, we have been able to propose a general typology of ULS that can be adapted to any type of city (See table 5). It is important to mention that a general typology of SUs according to the design and dimensions of the physical infrastructure, the flows, the types of actors and/or partners interested behind those spaces, and the specific purposes of each type of logistics space would contribute to the relevant location of these, and therefore to the efficiency of the logistics networks, as well as to the improvements in the goods transport sector.

Table 5. General Classification of Urban logistics spaces (ULS).

ULS types		Functionalities
GENERALIST	**Urban Logistics zones (ULZ)**	ULZ are large multipurpose zones that integrate various types of ULS and allow easy access and location near the delivery zones. Reduces the number of vehicles on the roads and improves operations productivity.
	Urban Distribution centers (UDC)	ULS of medium or large dimension designed for the consolidation and shipment of goods, which facilitates flows, especially in dense areas of cities. Improves the urban environment and limits conflicts between users in the public thoroughfare.
	Logistics Consolidation Centers (LCC)	Logistical spaces with large or medium dimensions, where the cargo is shipped at the same time instead of making small separate shipments. To reduce costs, cargo volume rates are paid.
SPECIALIST	**Good Storage Centers (GSC)**	Platforms of various medium and large dimensions, which are responsible for the reception, storage and movement within the same warehouse, as well as processing and securing the information of the data generated in each of the processes of logistics operations.
	Logistics managements centers (LMC)	Interfaces generally of small and medium dimensions, where the design of one or several stages of the supply chain is managed, such as procurement, transport, storage and distribution for customers (companies) who require the service. Better plan and manage logistics operations.
	Vehicle Reception Points (VHP)	Vehicle receiving points, medium and large, is used as an appropriate place to park the transport of cargo, allowing safe access for delivery drivers to operate their deliveries. Reduces time to reach the customer.
	Automated Logistics Centers (ALC)	ULS with operator-client interaction, usually small and medium sized. The main advantage of this is time control. ALCs can be fixed or mobile, in public or private places. They are implanted in public or private places. It allows the delivery or collection of goods in the absence of the customer.

Source: Own elaboration [13].

6. Conclusion

This paper is, to the best of our knowledge, the first that inquiries about the urban logistics spaces of a city in a developing country. The city of Barranquilla, Colombia is taken as a research case study, as it was a city that for many years suffered in its logistical processes, and since eight years ago it has been improving in its logistics system, thanks to the integration between the public and private actors so promoting the development of the city. Without forgetting, of course, its strategic location which makes it the owner of a large urban logistical space such as the city's Port, and the ports of the Caribbean Region, which are not related in the European typology of ULS. Barranquilla's Plan of Territorial Organization has suffered constant changes due to land use regulations. Therefore, new research on these issues, including the ULS, becomes difficult when considering the stability of the political ecosystem. This is a negative impact for the advancement of the city's logistic system. In spite of the fact that the city of Barranquilla is the anchor city of the Colombian Caribbean, where most of the region's goods are received and dispatched, there are not enough logistical nodes for transhipment and last mile operations that could generate high costs, and negative satisfaction for customers. -Based on the findings of the interviews, the functionality of the logistic spaces operating in Barranquilla allows us to propose a new typology of urban logistic spaces (ULS), in addition to the ports of the Region. -The different types of operations are carried out in different ULS in an integrated manner, with the difference in the volume of goods handled in them. According to the definition of the Generalist ULS of the European typology, the spaces that are found in the logistic system of the Colombian context (such as Free Zone and Customs Warehouse) could be part of that qualification. However, due to the special conditions, in terms of tax benefits, and handling of international goods, it is considered that they should be included within the classification of Specialized ULS. -Additionally, the results of this study provide valuable information on the numerous aspects that can be useful for the selection or location of ULS and for decision makers who wish to stimulate the development and economic, social, logistical and even environmental progress of the world's cities through logistical configurations. -It is worth mentioning that it would be relevant to replicate the method of information collection in different cities and countries, we could according to the real information of each context.

References

1. Wang, Q., Hu, J.: Behavioral analysis of decisions in choice of commercial vehicular mode in urban areas. Trans. Res. Rec. 2269, 58-64 (2012).

2. Boudouin, D., Morel, C., & Gardrat, M.: Supply chains and urban logistics: Methods and Information Systems, pp. 1-20 (Gonzalez-Feliu, J., Semet, F., Routhier, J.L., eds.). Springer, Heidelberg (2014).
3. Meza-Peralta, K, Gonzalez-Feliu, J. Montoya-Torres, J.: Urban Logistics Spaces(ULS): A Literature Review. Working paper, submitted to Supply Chain Forum an Int. J. (2019).
4. Varela Villazón, I.M.: Importancia de los Centros Logístico y sus efectos sobre la competitividad territorial Sistemas de Centralidades y equipamientos colectivos. MSc. Thesis, Universitdad Javeriana, Colombia (2010). [Online]. Available: https://www.javeriana.edu.co/biblos/tesis/arquitectura/tesis38.pdf.
5. Kłodawski, M., Lewczuk, K. Jacyna-Gołda, I., Żak, J.: Decision making strategies for warehouse operations. Arch. Transp. 41(1), 43–53 (2017).
6. Cui, J., Dodson, J., Hall, P.V.: Planning for Urban Freight Transport: An Overview. Transp. Rev. 35(5), 583–598 (2015).
7. Dablanc, L., Rakotonarivo, D.: The impacts of logistics sprawl: How does the location of Can, parcel transport terminals affect the energy efficiency of goods' movements in Paris and what we do about it? Procedia - Soc. Behav. Sci. (2010).
8. Woudsma, C., Jensen, J.F., Kanaroglou, P., Maoh, H.: Logistics land use and the city: A spatial–temporal modeling approach. Transp. Res. Part E 44, 277–297 (2008).
9. Heitz, A., Launay, P., Beziat, A.: Rethinking Data Collection on Logistics Facilities. Transp. Res. Rec. 2609, 67–76 (2017).
10. Gonzalez-Feliu, J., Malhéné, N., Morganti, E., Morana, J.: The deployment of city and area distribution centers in France and Italy: Comparison of six representative models. Supply chain forum 15(4), 84-99 (2014).
11. Gonzalez-Feliu, J. (2008). Models and methods for the city logistics: The two-echelon capacitated vehicle routing problem (Doctoral dissertation, Politecnico di Torino).
12. Garcia-Alonso, L. Monios, J., Vallejo-Pinto, J.A.: Port competition through hinterland accessibility: the case of Spain. Marit. Econ. Logist. 21(2), 258–277 (2019).
13. Meza-Peralta, K., Gonzalez-Feliu, J., Palacios-Argüello, L., Montoya-Torres, J.R.: Methodology for examining the sustainability potential of Urban Logistics Space (ULS) networks in a port city: Perspectives from Barranquilla, Colombia. Working paper. Submitted to Sustainability, December 2019.
14. Eisenhardt, K.M. : Building Theories from Case Study Research. Acad. Manag. Rev. 14(4), 532–550 (1989).
15. Yin, R.K.: Case Study Research and Applications: Design and Methods, Sixth edition. SAGE Publications (2017).

I L S 2020
INTERNATIONAL CONFERENCE ON INFORMATION SYSTEMS, LOGISTICS & SUPPLY CHAIN
Austin, Texas April 22-24, 2020

A constraint programming model for a parallel machine scheduling problem under resource constraints

Mohamed Amine Abdeljaouad [1], Zied Bahroun [2], Nour El Houda Saadani [1]

[1] Faculté des Sciences de Tunis, LIP2-LR99ES18, 2092, Université de Tunis El Manar, Tunis, Tunisia
[2] Industrial Engineering, ESM Graduate Program, College of Engineering, American University of Sharjah, P.O. Box 26666, Sharjah, UAE
{amine.abdeljaoued@fst.utm.tn, zbahroun@aus.edu, Houda.Saadani@ensi.rnu.tn}

Abstract. This paper investigates the exact solving of an NP-hard parallel machine scheduling problem where each operation requires the use of a specific type of resource, from a set of resources where each type is available in a single copy. The considered objective is the minimization of the makespan. After a brief literature review on the parallel machine scheduling problems under resource reservation constraints, a constraint programming model is provided. An experimental study is then carried out. The obtained results showed that the proposed model outperforms two linear mathematical models in terms of computational times.

Keywords: scheduling, parallel machines, resources, constraint programming;

1. Introduction

Parallel machine scheduling is among the most studied issues in the literature related to operational research. Early works on the field date back to 1950s [1] and numerous papers have been published since. Multiple areas of application can be found to the parallel machine scheduling, ranging from industrial production and manufacturing to healthcare services, such as operating theatre scheduling [2]. Different configurations of parallel machine scheduling problems have been studied and various constraints have been dealt considered, namely the preemption [3], the setup times [4], the ready and due-dates of the operations [1] [5] or the availability of the resources that may be required in the process [6] and which may refer to workers, mechanic robots or various tools [6] [7] [8].
In this paper, we are interested in the latter configuration and study a scheduling problem where n operations have to be scheduled on a set of m parallel machines $\{M_1, M_2, \dots M_m\}$. To be processed, each operation needs to use a specific type of resource from a set $\{R_1, R_2, \dots R_r\}$ of r resources of different types, which means that two operations requiring the same type of resource cannot be processed at the same time. The considered objective is the minimization of the global completion time of the operations (makespan). The rest of the assumptions are the following: the operations requiring the same resource can be performed in any order (i.e. disjunctive constraints), the operations' preemption is not allowed (i.e. once an operation has started, it cannot be interrupted) but waiting time is authorized between two operations using the same resource.
This problem is formally noted $P|Res.11|C_{max}$ using the three-field notation of Graham et al. [9], with P referring to the parallel machine scheduling issue, $Res.11$ meaning that there is only a single copy of each type of resource and that each operation requires exactly one resource to be processed, and C_{max} referring to the objective function (the makespan minimization). This problem is NP-hard for a number of machines $m \geq 2$ [10]. This complexity can be easily demonstrated as the $P||C_{max}$, which is particular case of the

problem we study (i.e. when each resource is required by only one operation) is already NP-hard for $m \geq 2$ [11].

This paper is structured as follows: In section II, we present a brief literature review of the main works on the parallel machine scheduling problems under constraint reservation constraints. In section III we present a constraint programming model for the exact solving of the $P|Res.11|C_{max}$. In section IV, we lead an experimental study where the performance of the proposed model is compared to two mathematical linear models from the literature. We then end our paper with our conclusion, remarks and perspectives.

2. Literature review

In the literature on the parallel machine scheduling, the studied problems can be classified in three different categories [12]. These classes of problems are based on the nature of the considered machines, which can be identical [13] [5], uniform [14] [15] or unrelated [16] [17]. Identical means that the machines have the same speed of operations' execution; uniform means that the machines have different speeds of execution, while the unrelated machines environment means that the speed of execution of an operation depends on the machine to which it is assigned.

Among the most considered objective functions in the parallel machine scheduling problems, we can mention the makespan minimization, the lateness minimization, the minimization of the number of tardy operations, or the minimization of the sum of the operations' completion times. A literature review on the makespan minimization in a parallel machine environment is provided by Mokotoff [18].

In most of the studied parallel machine scheduling problems, the machines are considered as the only resources necessary for the operations' execution. However, such configurations may sometimes not be representative enough of real production environments, where the operations may require additional resources for their process. Edis et al, [19] present a literature review on the parallel machine scheduling problems under resource reservation constraints, while Blazewicz et al. [10] provide a classification of these problems on the basis of their complexity. From this classification, it appears that the vast majority of the problems is NP-hard, which leads some authors to consider the parallel dedicated machines, where the assignation of the operations to the machines is already fixed, to reduce this complexity.

Kellerer and Strusevich (2008) provide a heuristic method for the $P|Res.11|C_{max}$ with dedicated machines (noted $PD|Res.11|C_{max}$). The algorithm consists in selecting, at every iteration, the machine with the lowest release date, and giving the priority to the operation that can be performed at the earliest, among those that are assigned to it. The authors proved that their heuristic has a performance worst-case ratio $\rho = 2$.

To the best of our knowledge, [20] and [21] are the only papers that have dealt with the $P|Res.11|C_{max}$. In [20], the authors present two linear mathematical formulations of the problems. The first model is based on machine scheduling, while the second one is inspired from strip-packing problems. They also provide a dichotomic algorithm that is based on a lower and upper bound and a feasibility test. They tested two solving strategies: In the first one, the problem instances are directly solved with the algorithm, while in the second, the instance is decomposed into two smaller sub-problems which later will be solved by the dichotomic algorithm. The experimental study showed that strip-packing formulation outperformed the machine scheduling based model, while the solving strategy based on the problem decomposition improved the performance of the dichotomic algorithm. Abdeljaoued et al. [21] are interested in the approximate solving of the $P|Res.11|C_{max}$ and present two heuristic methods and a simulated annealing metaheuristic. The first heuristic is an iterative algorithm that gives the priority to the longest operation requiring the most demanded resource, while the second one uses a lower bound to balance the machines, to which are assigned blocks of operations using the same resource. The authors led an experimental study in which these methods are compared to other adapted heuristics from the literature and the results showed that using the first proposed heuristic and the simulated annealing ensures near optimal solutions.

Another category of problems is the one where the assigned resources determine the speed of execution of the operations. Ruiz-Torres et al. [22] studied such a problem where the resources are assigned to the machines at the beginning of the scheduling, without the ability to switch to another one. The considered objective is the minimization of the number of tardy operations and two versions of the problem are studied: in the first one, the machines are dedicated while in the second, the assignation of the operations to the machines is part of the problem. The authors provide a mathematical model and a set of heuristics to solve the problem. Daniels et al, [23] present a mathematical formulation and an exact algorithm for a problem where the speed of execution of the operations depends on the amount of resources that are assigned to them.

In our literature review, we were also interested in the open-shop problem which share a common characteristic with the $P|Res.11|C_{max}$: the disjunctive constraints. Indeed, in the open-shop problem, the operations of the same job can be performed in any order; the jobs can therefore be considered as resources to be used by the operations. To the best of our knowledge, only Guinet and Saadani [24] considered the parallel machines in an open-shop environment. They provide a set of two-step heuristics to solve the problem. The first step consists in determining an assignation order of the operations for which they tested procedures like LPT (lower processing time), SPT (shortest processing time) and a NEH based heuristic [25]. The second step assigns the operations to the machines and for this phase, the authors propose procedures like FAM (first available machine), LBM (last busy machine) and the heuristics of Bräsel et al. [26] and Herrmann et al. [27]. The comparative study carried out showed that the combination LPT-LBM and NEH-LBM have the best results.

As we can see from this literature review, several of effective heuristic methods have been proposed to solve the $P|Res.11|C_{max}$, while exact methods are limited to linear mathematical formulations. In this work, we attempt to fill in this lack of knowledge and are interested in the exact solving of the $P|Res.11|C_{max}$. We provide a constraint programming model and lead an experimental study to compare its performance to the two mathematical models proposed by Abdeljaoued et al. [20].

3. Constraint programming model

Besides the mathematical formulation of the problems and the models' solving with software like IBM Cplex, we notice that an increasing number of studies dealing with scheduling problems opt now for the constraint programming modeling [28] [29]. Indeed, the CP Optimizer component of Cplex, which is a tool specialized in solving constraint programming problems, can offer more practical techniques for the modeling of scheduling problems, which often leads to better performance in terms of solving times.

Two kinds of problems can be solved with CP Optimizer: constraint satisfaction problems, where the objective is to determine whether a given solution is feasible or not (by checking if all the problem's constraints are respected), and optimization problems, where the objective is to find the solution that optimizes a given objective function. CP Optimizer uses various algorithms to solve the constraint programming models, namely the constraints' propagation and the variables' domain reduction (i.e. the elimination of the non-feasible values for each variable).

3.1. Presentation of the used variables

Among the most important functionalities offered by CP Optimizer are the pre-established variables' and constraints' structures.

The interval type is one of the most useful elements for the efficient modeling of scheduling problems. An *interval* variable x represents a task (operation) to be performed within a time window and has 5 properties. We enumerate them below:

- *startOf(x)*: The starting-time of operation x.
- *endOf(x)*: The ending-time of operation x.
- *sizeOf(x)*: The processing time of operation x.
- *lengthOf(x)*: The time-window within which has been performed the operation x. If x is performed without any preemption, *lengthOf(x)* and *sizeOf(x)* have the same signification.
- *presenceOf(x)*: An *interval* variable can be optional. The presence or absence of such a variable is therefore determined by the property *presenceOf(x)*. In the case where x is absent, the values of all of its properties are considered as *null*.

The precedence constraints between the *interval* variables can be represented in different ways: The *sequence* type is a type of variables used to define the global order of a set of *interval* variables. The constraint type *endBeforeStart* ensures that the ending-time of an *interval* variable is lower than the starting time of another *interval* variable, while the constraint type *noOverlap* ensures that a set of *interval* variables cannot be performed at the same time (i.e. disjunctive constraints).

For the modeling of the $P|Res.11|C_{max}$, we use the following *interval* variables:

- An array M of m optional *interval* variables to represent the activity of the m machines. The use of optional variables is justified by the fact that a machine can be empty, in the case where no operation is assigned to it.

- A two-dimensional matrix A of $n * r$ *interval* variables to represent the processing times of the operations, with r being the total number of resources and n the total number operations. Given that each resource k has to perform a sub-set I_k of operations, with $\sum_{k=1}^{r} |I_k| = n$, the processing time of each operation is given by the property *sizeOf*(A_{ik}), with $i \in I_k$. In the case where the element A_{ik} has an index $i \notin I_k$, *sizeOf*(A_{ik}) is fixed to 0.
- A three-dimensional matrix B of $n * r * m$ optional *interval* variables to represent the assignation of the operations to the machines. *presenceOf*(B_{ik}^{j}) is true only if operation i of resource k is assigned to machine j, and in that case, the value of the property *sizeOf*(B_{ik}^{j}) is equal to the value of *sizeOf*(A_{ik}).

The other needed variables for the modeling of the $P|Res.\,11|C_{max}$ are of a *sequence* type, which allow to fix the order over a set of *interval* variables. It should be noted that the absent *interval* variables will not be taken into account in this order. We present below the *sequence* variables used in our model:

- An array S of m *sequence* variables, defined over the set of *interval* variables B_{ik}^{j} with $i \in I_k$, $k = 1, \dots r, j = 1, \dots m$. The *sequence* variables should indeed be defined over a set of *interval* variables. The *sequence* variable S_j thus represents the order over the set of operations assigned to machine j, with $j = 1, \dots m$.
- An array T of r *sequence* variables, defined over the set of *interval* variables A_{ik} with $i \in I_k$, $k = 1, \dots r$. Each *sequence* variable T_k, with $k = 1, \dots r$, thus represents the order over the set of operations using the resource k.

3.2. Presentation of the model

Below, we give the objective function and the constraints of our constraint programming model:

$$Min\ C_{max} \quad (1)$$

$$alternative(A_{ik}, \{B_{ik}^{1} \dots B_{ik}^{m}\}) \quad \forall i \in I_k, k = 1, \dots r \quad (2)$$

$$span(M_j, B_{ik}^{j}\ \forall i \in I_k, k = 1, \dots r) \quad \forall j = 1, \dots m \quad (3)$$

$$C_{max} \geq endOf(M_j) \quad \forall j = 1, \dots m \quad (4)$$

$$noOverlap(S_j, B_{ik}^{j}\ \forall i \in I_k, k = 1, \dots r) \quad \forall j = 1, \dots m \quad (5)$$

$$noOverlap(T_k, A_{ik}\ \forall i \in I_k) \quad \forall k = 1, \dots r \quad (6)$$

The objective function is given in (1) and consists in the minimization of the makespan (C_{max}). Constraint (2) is of an *alternative* type, which is used for the obligatory selection of an *interval* variable from a set of optional *interval* variables. In our model, this constraint defines the assignation of an operation to one of the m machines, as all the machines are identical. Mathematically, constraint (2) can be substituted by the three following equations (7), (8) and (9):

$$\sum_{j=1}^{m} presenceOf(B_{ik}^{j}) = 1 \quad \forall i \in I_k, k = 1, \dots r \quad (7)$$

$$startOf(A_{ik}) = max_{j=1,\dots m}\left(startOf(B_{ik}^{j})\right) \quad \forall i \in I_k, k = 1, \dots r \quad (8)$$

$$endOf(A_{ik}) = max_{j=1,\dots m}\left(endOf(B_{ik}^{j})\right) \quad \forall i \in I_k, k = 1, \dots r \quad (9)$$

Constraint (3) is a *span* constraint, which is a constraint type used to define a dependence relation between some *interval* variables. In our model, constraint (3) ensures that the duration of work of each machine covers the set of operations that are assigned to it. Mathematically, this constraint can be substituted by the three following equations:

$$n * r * presenceOf(M_j) = \sum_{k=1}^{r} \sum_{i \in I_k} presenceOf(B_{ik}^{j}) \quad \forall j = 1, \dots m \quad (10)$$

$$startOf(M_j) = min_{k=1,\dots r; i \in I_k}\left(startOf(B_{ik}^{j})\right) \quad \forall j = 1, \dots m \quad (11)$$

$$endOf(M_j) = max_{k=1,\dots r; i \in I_k}\left(endOf(B_{ik}^{j})\right) \quad \forall j = 1, \dots m \quad (12)$$

Constraint (4) ensures that the makespan is greater or equal to the work ending-time of each machine. Finally, constraint (5) ensures that the operations assigned to the same machine are not performed at the same time while constraint (6) does the same with the operations using the same resource. For a better understanding of the functioning of constraints (5) and (6), we provide below another way to write those constraints using the mathematical logic and the following propositions:

- u_{ik}^{j}: This proposition is true if $presenceOf(B_{ik}^{j}) = 1$.
- $v_{ikj}^{i'k'}$: This proposition is true if $startOf(B_{ik}^{j}) \leq startOf(B_{i'k'}^{j})$.
- $w_{ikj}^{i'k'}$: This proposition is true if $endOf(B_{ik}^{j}) \leq startOf(B_{i'k'}^{j})$.

Constraint (5) therefore ensures that the following property is true for each couple of operations:

$$v_{ikj}^{i'k'} \wedge u_{ik}^{j} \wedge u_{i'k'}^{j} \rightarrow w_{ikj}^{i'k'}$$

Similarly, constraint (6) can be represented by the following propositions:

- $y_{ik}^{i'k}$: This proposition is true if $startOf(A_{ik}) \leq startOf(A_{i'k})$.
- $z_{ik}^{i'k}$: This proposition is true if $endOf(A_{ik}) \leq startOf(A_{i'k})$.

Hence, constraint (6) ensures that the property below is true for each couple of operations using the same resource:

$$y_{ik}^{i'k} \rightarrow z_{ik}^{i'k}$$

4. Experimental study

We will now assess the computational times of our constraint programming model and determine the limit of the instance sizes that can be solved in a reasonable time with the IBM Cplex solver. The performance of this model will also be compared to those of the two linear mathematical models presented in [1] and that we briefly explain below.

4.1. Comparative linear models

The first model provided by Abdeljaoued et al. [1], named *(F1)*, is based on machine scheduling formulation, where the assignation of the operations to the machines and their processing order are determined with binary variables: the order of the operations using the same resource is thus determined using a binary variable X_i^s which is equal to 1 if the operation i is the sth operation to use its resource and 0 otherwise; and the order of the operations processed on the same machine is decided with a binary variable Y_{ij}^t which is equal to 1 if operation i is the tth operation to be processed on machine j and 0 otherwise.

The second mathematical model of Abdeljaoued et al. [1], named *(F2)*, is inspired by 2-dimensional strip-packing problems, in which a set of rectangular items is to be packed in a strip which total used height has to be minimized. The analogy between this problem and the $P|Res.11|C_{max}$ lays in the correspondence between the items and the operation (i.e. the height of an item represents the duration of the operation), the one between the width of the strip and the machines (the width of every item is equal to 1 to ensure that each operation only occupies a single machine), and the correspondence between the height of the strip and the makespan. To represent the disjunctive constraints between the operations using the same resource, the items are placed in groups and those belonging to the same group cannot be placed at the same height of the strip. Such a model is based on binary variables l_{ij} and b_{ij}, which determine the position of each couple of items in relation to one another.

To improve the performance of models *(F1)* and *(F2)*, we added two inequalities to represent the lower bound of the problem. This technique indeed allows reducing the solving times of the mathematical solvers, since we indicate that when the minimized C_{max} reaches a value that is equal to the lower bound, the solving process can stop. The lower bound of the $P|Res.11|C_{max}$ is given by inequalities (13) and (14), where p_i is the processing time of operation i.

$$C_{max} \geq max_{k=1,\ldots r}\left(\sum_{i \in I_k} p_i\right) \tag{13}$$

$$C_{max} \geq \sum_{k=1}^{r}\sum_{i \in I_k} \frac{p_i}{m} \tag{14}$$

Inequality (13) ensures that the makespan is greater or equal to the total duration of work of the resource with the longest workload, while inequality (14) ensures that the makespan is greater or equal to the total duration of the operations divided by the number of machines.

4.2. Test instances

The instances of our experimental study have been chosen as follows: For every tested number of machines m that we gradually increase, we determine for the number of resources $r = m + 1$, the maximal number of operations that allows reasonable computational times. Then, we gradually increase r and analyze the evolution of the solving times. The operations' durations are generated with a uniform distribution in the interval [1, 99].
Starting each instance size with a number of resources $r = m + 1$ is justified by the fact that for $r \leq m$, the optimal solution of the problem can be intuitively found by assigning all the operations using the same resource to a different machine (i.e. $C_{max} = max_{k=1,\ldots r}\left(\sum_{i \in I_k} p_i\right)$).

4.3. Comparative tests and results

The tests are performed with the IBM Cplex12.5 solver on 4GB RAM computer with an I3 processor. For each instance size, 5 tests are performed. The average solving times of the constraint programming model and models *(F1)* and *(F2)* for each instance size are given in table I, where *min* and *sec* respectively stands for minutes and seconds. Let us note that the solving duration for an instance size can depend on the data generated (i.e. the processing times of the operations) and can therefore slightly vary from a test to another. This variation can go from seconds to minutes as the sizes of the tested instances get larger.

Table 1: Comparing the solving times of the three models

Instance size			**Solving times**		
Machines	*Resources*	*Operations*	*Model (F1)*	*Model (F2)*	*Constraint programming model*
2	3	30	≥ 3 hours	2 min	0.56 sec
		45	≥ 3 hours	26 min	0.78 sec
		60	≥ 3 hours	≥ 3 hours	0.58 sec
	6	30	≥ 3 hours	4 min	0.63 sec
		60	≥ 3 hours	≥ 3 hours	0.73 sec
	10	30	≥ 3 hours	2 min	0.71 sec
		60	≥ 3 hours	≥ 3 hours	0.89 sec
3	4	32	≥ 3 hours	13 min	0.72 sec
		40	≥ 3 hours	≥ 2 hours	0.68 sec
	8	32	≥ 3 hours	40 min	0.72 sec
	10	40	≥ 3 hours	≥ 2 hours	0.95 sec
4	5	25	≥ 3 hours	40 min	0.61 sec
		30	≥ 3 hours	≥ 3 hours	2.03 sec
	10	20	90 min	4 min	0.59 sec
		30	≥ 3 hours	46 min	0.67 sec

From table I, we can see that while the linear model *(F2)*, which uses fewer variables and constraints than model *(F1)* [1], gives respectable outcomes, its computational times are outperformed by far by those of

the constraint programming. Indeed, for all the tested instances the solving times of the constraint programming model barely exceed 1 second while those of models *(F1)* and *(F2)* can go beyond hours. To determine the limit of instance sizes that can be solved in a reasonable time with this model, we therefore enlarged the sizes of the tested instances.
The average computational times obtained with the constraint programming for these bigger instances are indicated in table II. The results show that the solving times of the model starts to become quite long from the (8 machines, 15 resources, 150 operations) instances and reach 1 hour from the (10 machines, 15 resources, 75 operations) instances. These outcomes constitute a significant improvement in comparison with model *(F2)* whose computational times for smaller instances can be much longer.

Table 2: Solving times of the constraint programming model for the bigger sized instances

Instance size			**Solving times of the constraint programming model**
Machines	*Resources*	*Operations*	
5	10	50	1 minute
7	14	70	3 minutes
8	15	150	15 minutes
10	15	75	1 hour

From this experimental study, we can therefore conclude that, dealing with scheduling problems, constraint programming modeling techniques can present a serious advantage in comparison with classical linear formulations, whose solving with mathematical solvers can be based on an ineffective relaxation.

5. Conclusion

In this paper, a parallel machine scheduling problem under resource reservation constraints is studied. This problem consists in a set of operations that have to be scheduled on parallel machines. To be processed, each operation requires the use of a specific type of resource, from a set of resources where each type is available in a single copy. This problem is NP-hard for a number of machines $m \geq 2$ and noted $P|Res.11|C_{max}$ [6].
In this work, we focus on the exact solving of the problem and we provide a constraint programming model. The performances of this model in terms of computational times are compared to those of two linear mathematical formulations from the literature and the obtained results highlight the high performance of the proposed model. Indeed, the computational times obtained with the constraint programming outperformed by far those of the two other models for all the tested instances. The constraint programming model thus allowed solving to optimality and in a reasonable time much bigger instance sizes.
Perspectives of this work consists in investigating whether there is a possibility or not to apply the constraint programming modeling techniques to scheduling problems with more complex constraints. The next step of this work thus includes testing the performance and the limit of constraint programming models when adding new constraints to the $P|Res.11|C_{max}$, such as the setup times or the operations' ready-dates and due-dates.

6. References

[1] McNaughton, R. "Scheduling with deadlines and loss functions". Management Science, 6(1), pp. 1-12, (1959).

[2] Arnaout, J.P.M., & Kulbashian, S. "Maximizing the utilization of operating rooms with stochastic times using simulation". *Proceedings of the 2008 Winter Simulation Conference,* 2008.

[3] Shams, H., & Salmasi, N. "Parallel machine scheduling problem with preemptive jobs and transportation delay". *Computers & Operations Research,* 50, pp. 14-23, (2014).

[4] Lin, Y., & Hsieh, F.. "Unrelated parallel machine scheduling with setup times and ready times". International Journal of Production Research, 52(4), pp. 1200-1214, (2014).

[5] Mensendiek, A., Gupta, J. N. D., & Herrmann, J. "Scheduling identical parallel machines with fixed delivery dates to minimize total tardiness". European Journal of Operational Research, 243(2), pp. 514-522, (2015).

[6] Agnetis, A. Flamini, M. Nicosia, G. & Pacifici, A. "A job-shop problem with one additional resource type". *Journal of Scheduling,* 14(3), pp. 225-237, (2011).

[7] Celano, G., Costa, A., & Fichera, S. "Scheduling of unrelated parallel manufacturing cells with limited human resources". *International Journal of Production Research,* 46(2), pp. 405-427, (2008).

[8] Ventura, J. A., & Kim, D. "Parallel machine scheduling with earliness–tardiness penalties and additional resource constraints". Computers and Operations Research, 30(13) , pp. 1945–1958, (2003).

[9] Graham, R. L., Lawler, E. L., Lenstra, J. K., & Kan, A. H. G. R. "Optimization and approximation in deterministic sequencing and scheduling: a survey". Annals of Discrete Mathematics, 5, pp.287-326, (1979).

[10] Blazewicz, J., Lenstra, J. K., & Kan, A. H. G. R.. "Scheduling subject to resource constraints: classification and complexity". Discrete Applied Mathematics, 5(1), 1983, pp. 11–24.

[11] Lenstra, J. K., Rinnooy Kan, A. H. G., & Brucker, P. "Complexity of machine scheduling problems". Annals of Discrete Mathematics, 1, pp. 343–362, (1977).

[12] Cheng, T.C.E., & Sin, C.C.S. "A State-of-the-Art Review of Parallel-Machine Scheduling Research". European Journal of Operational Research, 47(3), pp. 271-292, (1990).

[13] Blazewicz, J., & Ecker, K. "A linear time algorithm for restricted bin packing and scheduling problems". *Operations Research Letters,* 2(2), pp. 80–83, (1983).

[14] Kovalyov, M.Y., & Shafransky, Y.M.. "Uniform machine scheduling of unit-time jobs subject to resource constraints". *Discrete Applied Mathematics,* 84, pp. 253–257, (1998).

[15] Yeh, W., Chuang, M., & Lee, W. "Uniform parallel machine scheduling with resource consumption constraint". Applied Mathematical Modelling, 39(8), pp. 2131-2138, (2015).

[16] Cappadonna, F. A., Costa, A., & Fichera, S. "Makespan minimization of unrelated parallel machines with limited human resources". *Proceedings of CIRP,* 12, pp. 450-455, (2013).

[17] Pfund, M., Fowler, J.W., & Gupta, J.N.D. "Multi-objective unrelated parallel machine deterministic scheduling problems". Journal of the Chinese Institute of Industrial Engineers, 21(3), pp. 230–241, (2004).

[18] Mokotoff, E. "Parallel machine scheduling problems: a survey". Asia Pacific Journal of Operational Research, 18, pp. 193–242, (2001).

[19] Edis, E. B., Oguz, C., & Ozkarahan, I. "Parallel machine scheduling with additional resources: notation, classification, models and solution methods". European Journal of Operational Research, 230(3) , pp. 449-463 (2013).

[20] Abdeljaoued, M.A., Bahroun Z. et Saadani, N.E.H., "Short term operating room scheduling: a parallel machine under resource constraint problem". *Accepted in June 2018 in International Journal of Operational Research,* 2018a.

[21] Abdeljaoued, M.A., Saadani, N.E.H., et Bahroun Z. "Heuristic and metaheuristic approaches for parallel machine scheduling under resource constraints". *Operational Research an International Journal,* 2018b, *available online June 2018 :* DOI 10.1007/s12351-018-0412-3

[22] Ruiz-Torres, A. J., López, F. J., & Ho, J. C. "Scheduling uniform parallel machines subject to a secondary resource to minimize the number of tardy jobs". European Journal of Operational Research, 179(2), pp. 302–315, (2007).

[23] Daniels, R. L., Hoopes, B. J., & Mazzola, J. B. "Scheduling parallel manufacturing cells with resource flexibility". Management Science, 42(9), pp. 1260–1276, (1996).

[24] Guinet, A., & Saadani, N. E. H. "Nomadisme chirurgical et ordonnancement de blocs opératoires". In *Proceeding of GISEH: Conférence francophone en Gestion et Ingénierie des Systèmes Hospitaliers.* Clermont-Ferrand, France, (2010).

[25] Nawaz, M., Enscore, E. E., & Ham, I. "A heuristic algorithm for the m-machine, n-job flow-shop sequencing problem". Omega, 11(1), 1983, pp. 91–95.

[26] Bräsel, H., Herms, A., Mörig, M., Tautenhahn, T., Tusch, J., & Werner, F. "Heuristic constructive algorithms for open shop scheduling to minimize mean flow time". European Journal of Operational Research, 189(3), pp. 856-870, (2008).

[27] Herrmann, J., Proth, J., & Sauer, N. "Heuristics for unrelated machine scheduling with precedence constraints". European Journal of Operational Research, 102(3), pp. 528-537, (1997).

[28] Wang T., Meskens N., & Duvivier D. "Scheduling operating theatres: Mixed integer programming vs. constraint programming". *European Journal of Operational Research,* 247(2), pp. 401-413, (2015).

[29] Zhao, Z., & Li, X. "Scheduling elective surgeries with sequence-dependent setup times to multiple operating rooms using constraint programming". *Operations Research for Health Care,* 3, pp.160-167, (2014).

Author Index

Keyword Index